WEAVING THE PAST

Weaving the Past

A History of Latin America's Indigenous Women

from the Prehispanic Period to the Present

Susan Kellogg

2/27/07

To John Ross —
With much
admiration,
Sue Kellogg

OXFORD
UNIVERSITY PRESS

2005

OXFORD
UNIVERSITY PRESS

Oxford University Press, Inc., publishes works that further
Oxford University's objective of excellence
in research, scholarship, and education.

Oxford   New York
Auckland   Cape Town   Dar es Salaam   Hong Kong   Karachi
Kuala Lumpur   Madrid   Melbourne   Mexico City   Nairobi
New Delhi   Shanghai   Taipei   Toronto

With offices in
Argentina   Austria   Brazil   Chile   Czech Republic   France   Greece
Guatemala   Hungary   Italy   Japan   Poland   Portugal   Singapore
South Korea   Switzerland   Thailand   Turkey   Ukraine   Vietnam

Copyright © 2005 by Oxford University Press, Inc.

Published by Oxford University Press, Inc.
198 Madison Avenue, New York, New York 10016

www.oup.com

Oxford is a registered trademark of Oxford University Press

Library of Congress Cataloging-in-Publication Data
Kellogg, Susan.
Weaving the past : a history of Latin America's indigenous
women from the prehispanic period to the present / Susan Kellogg.
p. cm.
Includes bibliographical references and index.
ISBN-13: 978-0-19-512381-4; 978-0-19-518328-3 (pbk.)
ISBN-10: 0-19-512381-6; 0-19-518328-2 (pbk.)
1. Indian women—Latin America—History 2. Indian women—
Latin America—Social conditions. 3. Indian women—
Latin America—Politics and government. 4. Latin America—
History. 5. Latin America—Social conditions. I. Title.
E59.W8K45 2005
305.48'898—dc22   2004061716

9 8 7 6 5 4 3 2 1

Printed in the United States of America
on acid-free paper

To my children and my students, past and present,
who are my hope for a better world

ACKNOWLEDGMENTS

There are many people to whom I owe thanks because I received so much support and advice during the course of writing this book, but my deepest appreciation goes to two Oxford editors, one past (Thomas LeBien) who helped me think up the idea for the book and was greatly encouraging, and one present (Susan Ferber) who has been so consistently insightful, patient, and helpful. I am very grateful, as well, to the many people, friends and acquaintances (some I know only through the Internet), who answered questions, gave advice, shared unpublished work, or read parts or all of the manuscript in the most generous ways. These include Thomas Abercrombie, Karen Olsen Bruhns, Elizabeth Brumfiel, David Carey, Susan Deeds, Christine Eber, Karen Graubart, Lynn Guitar, John Hart (who forwarded me so many useful posts from listservs relating to Chiapas and the EZLN), Rebecca Horn, Jean Jackson, Rosemary Joyce, Christine Kovic, Blanca Muratorio, Eileen Mulhare, June Nash, María Rodríguez Shadow, Matthew Restall, Mark Saka, Barry Sell, Barbara Sommers, Kevin Terraciano, and Mary Weismantel. They of course bear no responsibility for the interpretations set forth in the book. One of the most memorable parts of the period of research was a trip to Peru in May 2000, where I had the pleasure of meeting María Emma Mannarelli, who arranged for me to give a talk at the Universidad Nacional Mayor de San Marcos, and, especially, Teresa Vergara and her husband, Francisco Quiroz, who offered help and friendship that made the trip possible and so valuable. A trip in spring 2002 to Guatemala was also memorable, especially a meeting I attended, facilitated by the NGO Madre, where representatives of the group CONAVIGUA (National Coalition of Guatemalan Widows) spoke. While detailing sorrowful events of the past, they emphasized the importance of building democracy for the future with an optimism that, while tempered by reality, remains unforgettable.

Without Sara McNeil's help (of the College of Education at the University of Houston), the illustrations would not have been possible, and others, including Eileen Basso, Karen Olsen Bruhns, Judith Friedlander, Virginia Kerns, Joyce Marcus, Donna McClelland, Ruben Reina, Lynn Stephen, Karen Stothert, Mari Lyn Salvador, and Norman Whitten gave advice about illustrations and permissions. Jerice Barrios (Field Museum), Michael Hironymous (Benson Latin American Collection, University of Texas at Austin), and David Dressing (Latin American Library, Tulane University) provided invaluable help with cover art and illustrations. Research assistants include Katie Harrison, Scott Murray, Victoria Pasley, and Elizabeth Smith. Katie helped heroically as we worked to organize an unwieldy bibliography.

My family and friends were extremely patient as I, at times, struggled to balance writing the book with other obligations. Susan Deeds, Becky Horn, Lorena Lopez, Tom and Diane O'Brien, and Pat Seed have been the best of friends, and my husband, Steve Mintz, along with my children, Seth and Sean, offered computer advice, cheered me up, made me go to movies, and in other ways made this long period an easier time.

CONTENTS

ONE

Introducing the Indigenous Women of Latin America   3

    Some Introductory Remarks   4
    Some Useful Concepts   5
    Some Background on Latin America's Earliest Women   11

TWO

Of Warriors and Working Women: Gender in Later Prehispanic Mesoamerica
and the Andes   18

    Women and Gender among Northern and Central Mexican Peoples: Parallel
        Organizations, Hierarchical Ideologies   19
    The Postclassic Ñudzahui: Elite Gender Complementarity   30
    The Maya of the Classic and Postclassic Periods: The Flexible Patriarchy   35
    The Andes: Women and Supernatural and State Power   41
    Conclusion   51

THREE

Colliding Worlds: Indigenous Women, Conquest, and Colonialism   53

    Gender, Sex, and Violence in the Conquest Era   55
    Laboring Women: Paying Tribute, Losing Authority   63
    Family and Religious Life: The Paradoxes of Purity and Enclosure   71
    A Rebellious Spirit   81
    Conclusion   86

FOUR

With Muted Voices: Mesoamerica's Twentieth- and Twenty-First Century Women 90

Nahua Women: Complementarity within Submissiveness 92
Oaxaca: Land of the "Matriarchs"? 103
Maya Women: Working, Weaving, Changing 112
Conclusion 125

FIVE

Fighting for Survival through Political Action and Cultural Creativity: Indigenous Women in Contemporary South and Central America 127

Women in the Andes: Revolutionizing Tradition in the Highland Cultures of
    Ecuador, Peru, and Bolivia 129
Women in the Tropical Lowlands of South America: Egalitarian Political
    Structures, Female Subordination, and the Fight for Cultural Survival 142
Indigenous Women in Central America: Searching for Empowerment in
    Diverse Circumstances 157
Conclusion 167

SIX

Indigenous Women: Creating Agendas for Change 169

ORGANIZATIONS MENTIONED IN THE TEXT
AND THEIR ACRONYMS 179

GLOSSARY 181

NOTES 185

BIBLIOGRAPHY 239

INDEX 317

Archaeological and Modern Cultures of Mesoamerica. This map of Mesoamerica shows the location of major archaeological sites mentioned in the text and the four major ancient and modern indigenous ethnicities shown in capital letters (located in the countries of Mexico, Guatemala, Belize, Honduras, and El Salvador).

Archaeological and Modern Cultures of Central and South America. This map of Central and South America shows important archaeological sites and ancient and modern ethnicities (the former shown in italic capital letters and latter in regular capital letters) across the countries of Brazil, Venezuela, Colombia, Ecuador, Peru, Bolivia, and Chile.

WEAVING THE PAST

1

Introducing the Indigenous Women of Latin America

This book describes the history of indigenous women in Latin America. It treats them as active agents, instrumental in shaping the region's history. Neither house-bound nor passive, native women have responded to many challenges—demographic, economic, political, and social—over the past millennia. What my research in both primary and secondary sources ranging across the fields of archaeology, ethnohistory, and ethnography repeatedly demonstrates is that indigenous women have a long history of performing productive labor, contributing to familial well-being in a variety of ways, and being politically active. In responding to the forces of change, whether resisting or embracing them or seeking to control the rate and impact of change, women became creators of change and have served as transformative agents.

I began this project thinking it would be interesting to compare Mesoamerican and Andean women across space and time. Along the way the book turned into something bigger—more unwieldy, yet more useful—as I pondered how to tell the stories of women and cultural change across thousands of square miles and years. If every region and group cannot be covered, I nonetheless attempt to include a wide variety of areas and peoples. The book retains some focus on Mesoamerica and Andean South America, in part because these have always been the areas of densest native populations. This focus also reflects the English- and Spanish-language literatures' concentration on these areas, with the depth of these writings helping to shape the selection of peoples. But *Weaving the Past* also discusses women of the Caribbean, Central America, the tropical lowland cultures of Brazil and northern South America, and the northern border area encompassing parts of Mexico and the southwestern United States.

Across these areas, many factors influence the way that cultural transformations influenced women's lives past and present, as well as their activities and responses. Geographic location, extent of integration into trade or market systems, the presence of empires or nation-states, already existing patterns of gender relations, concepts of ethnic and racial identity, and interventions by outsiders (particularly military and religious) all have been important influences on gender patterns. While transformational changes often led to decline in women's authority and status, another theme of *Weaving the Past* is that such decline was and is not inevitable.

To understand the impact of such changes, we must carefully consider region, levels of political and economic integration, ethnicity, and time period. This book offers a synthesis of indigenous women's history, but it is a nuanced synthesis, aiming to provide the bigger picture while at the same time keeping multiple little pictures clearly in focus. It argues that no one single concept or image suffices to describe complex realities. Are indigenous women embodiments of exploitation or of complementarity? Do they serve as agents of acculturation or as guardians of tradition? Have they been history's passive victims or instruments of transformation? While any of these characterizations may be true for a particular time, place, or people, this book argues that observers, scholars, politicians, activists, and even sometimes indigenous men have downplayed indigenous women's agency, in part because until relatively recently, women have not been able to shape or help create a historical record that fully includes them. In order to understand particular configurations of gender patterns, we must look carefully at time, place, power relations, and identity construction while recognizing the existence of hemispheric and global trends in the histories of indigenous peoples and the dynamics of gender relations.

Some Introductory Remarks

In the years I have worked on this project, I have often thought about what drew me to such an undertaking, especially since as a non–Native American, I cannot claim to be telling the story of "my people." My interest in women's studies and women's history is longstanding, dating back to writing a dissertation in the late 1970s on the impact of Spanish law on central Mexico's Nahua peoples. I began to realize—just as the great interest in women's studies and feminist approaches to a variety of academic disciplines was developing—that the historical documentation with which I was working was filled with references to women. I wanted to figure out how I could include them in that story of early colonial change. The publication of Irene Silverblatt's book *Moon, Sun, and Witches* offered a model for understanding women and gender roles, especially how the rise of the state and the impact of European colonial rule might influence these, even if the particulars of the Andean area were somewhat different from those of the Central Mexican region.[1] Through my years of reading and teaching about Latin America's indigenous and other women, I became aware of a constantly expanding literature on women of specific ethnicities, regions, and time periods, yet very little comparative work emerged.[2] What's more, in the torrents of literature on women and modernization in the twentieth century, while Latin American women are often included in discussions of change and development, class rather than ethnicity usually gets highlighted, and thus the particular economic, political, and social situations of indigenous women correspondingly get slighted.[3] More recently, after some years as an anthropologist teaching in a history department, I became interested in reengaging with ethnographic literatures, to use such texts as historical documents to try to understand change not only in the distant past but also for more recent times. My experience as a teacher also influenced the way my scholarly interests developed. I endeavor to have my students understand the richness of indigenous cultures past and present in the Americas and hope they grasp the global implications of the economic and governmental policies of western nations that influence the lives of people everywhere in this increasingly interconnected world.

Weaving the Past is intended as a chronicle of both tradition and change. It focuses on women's work, family lives, and political and social activism and recounts the growing dialogue among indigenous women (and between these women and indigenous rights groups and nonindigenous women's groups) about responding to and managing the increasing impact of globalization. I hope this book will serve as a resource for scholars and students on the immense gender scholarship produced within and beyond Latin America as this literature relates to native women. The chapters also examine the uses to which images of indigenous women are put and accentuate indigenous women's voices wherever possible to counter tendencies in both popular and scholarly literatures to ignore native women's contributions to day-to-day survival and movements for political and social change.[4]

Some Useful Concepts

While the book depends upon a variety of concepts to describe and interpret women's lives, roles, and experiences, there are several that are basic for the themes developed throughout, and they merit discussion here: "woman/women," "agency," "status," "complementarity," "indigenous," and "globalization." Of course the meaning of the terms "woman/women" seem self-evident, but in a postmodern scholarly age in which all terminology is deconstructed and the predictive value of social science theorizing has been undermined, we cannot assume that who women are and how they live their lives is natural, universally patterned, or solely defined biologically. One's sexual or gender identity is both inscribed and performed, societies may have more than two genders (the term preferred here since I see sexuality as part of one's gender identity), yet all the societies described in this book draw distinctions between men and women as individuals and groups.[5] Not only do they see men and women as different but also conversations about the meanings of those differences go on all the time. In other words, both women and men think about and discuss their differences and what those mean in terms of status. And because all societies define gender identities relationally (whether there are two or more), any discussion of female gender identities within communities and cultures or by outside observers necessarily entails reference to male identities as well. Nevertheless, this book highlights *women's* lives and activities, both because I believe such a comparative history is long overdue and because I believe that women's history is not so much a step on the way to gender history as it is a vital component of gendered historical analysis.[6]

Weaving the Past details the long history of such activities, reminding us that women past and present have been active agents; thus agency is a crucial concept underlying the interpretations presented here. In fact, the title of the book emphasizes that women have been creators of history, even if their voices do not survive in the historical record to the same extent as do men's. Readers should not assume, however, that weaving was or is a women's activity everywhere in native Latin America. Male weavers were and are common in some times and places, especially in highland South America.[7] Instead weaving serves here as a metaphor for agency.

The concept of agency has two faces, and both appear in this book. On the one hand, it is, as Sherry Ortner points out, "virtually synonymous with the forms of power people have at their disposal, their ability to act on their own behalf, influence other people and events, and maintain some kind of control in their own lives." On the other hand, there is an "agency of intentions—of projects, purposes, desires," actions that "infuse life with meaning and purpose."[8] Examples of both kinds of agency abound in this book. In many ways, without denying the forms of subjugation indigenous women have often experienced and that are chronicled in succeeding chapters, this book is a history of women's agency, of their political actions and of their purposeful carrying out of the projects necessary for daily life.

Yet both anthropologists and historians continue to find evidence of gender asymmetry, with women usually in the lower status in relation to men, in many of the world's societies past and present.[9] This book assumes neither that such asymmetry is universal nor that a single set of factors (be they biological, economic, ideological, or psychological) underlies this pattern. Nor does the book assume that asymmetry expresses itself the same way throughout Latin America or elsewhere in the world. For ease of communication, I use the term "status" to refer to the ways men and women interpret their respective positions within their societies as individuals and groups, a usage close to Ortner's notion of status as "relative prestige." But while issues of domination, subordination, and access to power shape the possibilities for women to achieve power and prestige, feminist scholarship also generally rejects the idea that women have *a* single status in relation to men in any society. Anthropologist Naomi Quinn argued over twenty-five years ago against assuming that "women's status can be treated as a unitary construction" because age, context, and individual abilities and skills all play some role in how societies define both individual and group statuses.[10] The book shows that women's perceptions of their statuses often play a vital role in influencing them to become active in a variety of political contexts, though these perceptions are not the sole cause of women's political activities.

Another concept that turns up frequently in scholarship about indigenous women is that of "complementarity," sometimes appearing with the term "parallelism." Anthropologist John Monaghan wisely cautions that complementarity carries more than one meaning and these must be disentangled:

> First, there is the sense of two halves "constituting the whole." . . .
> The second sense in which the genders are said to be complementary is that of males and females mutually completing each other to achieve a certain status in society. . . . Finally there is the sense that men and women complement each other in order to produce effects in concert that are different from those produced separately.[11]

While instances of each type can be found in the pages of this book, the third definition, as in the gender division of labor in many parts of Latin America, is a particularly common usage.

The related notion of "parallelism" also appears and overlaps with ideas about complementarity. Referring to the existence of parallel lines of authority and institutionalized positions of leadership held by women and men, parallelism is most appropriate for describing aspects of gender patterns in societies like the Aztec or Inka, with highly developed institutions of trade, diplomacy, and warfare.[12]

These concepts, rather than being ideas that sum up women's status, are better thought of as elements constituting part of male-female relations in particular times and places. Furthermore, several scholars have pointed to the multiple ways that concepts of complementarity and parallelism can mask inequality between the genders and conflict over women's subordination. The downplaying of gendered relations of inequality can occur both within indigenous groups themselves, because a discourse of complementarity may disguise the existence of inequality in everyday life, and within scholarly analysis, through a theoretical discourse that deemphasizes gender hierarchy and male dominance.[13]

Another concept that appears throughout this book is "indigenous." Admittedly I use the term loosely and inclusively to refer to individuals and groups who identify themselves as autochthonous, or original, peoples, as well as groups so identified by archaeologists, historians, and anthropologists. The term as used here thus sits at the intersection of self- and scholarly definition (emic and etic meanings, as anthropologists might term them). These peoples or groups are often more commonly referred to as "Indian," a term of identity that can be used by indigenous or nonindigenous people. I prefer "indigenous" because it points to both the early and persistent presence of native peoples throughout the Americas, as well as their close connections to lands and territories that they once controlled (and sometimes still do) even when they did or do not own them individually in the Euro-American sense. In addition, the term *indio* in Latin America can carry a stigmatizing connotation best avoided.

But because interethnic and interracial mixing, as well as cultural change and synthesis, have been a constant social process from the late fifteenth century on, the interpretations offered here make no assumptions about cultural homogeneity, nor do they assume any essential or persistent basis, biological or cultural, for the definition of identities. While race is not a primary focus, the chapters suggest that constructions of race (or "ethno-race," a term used in places to suggest the amalgamation of ethnic identities that would eventually become racialized in the eighteenth and nineteenth centuries) vary quite significantly in different parts of Latin America. What is "indigenous" in Mexico is not the same as what is indigenous in Guatemala or Honduras, and South America, particularly the Andes, presents yet another variation. There the urban indigenous identity has its own terminology (*chola/o*), and disentangling the ascribed or asserted meanings of *indigenous, chola/o,* and *mestiza/o* (a term used to suggest a "mixed" identity whose primary components are indigenous and Spanish) is no easy task. It is also important to remember that significant class differences can exist within indigenous communities, whether rural or urban.

I therefore treat as indigenous an array of peoples whose biological and cultural identities may be quite mixed, some of who are sometimes seen as nonindigenous within their own nation-states or by scholars. In Central Mexico, for example, the pace of cultural change has been such that in many rural villages language, dress, and ways of making a living all shifted dramatically, especially in the second half of the twentieth century, yet anthropologists find persistent forms of social organization and ritual that suggest that an indigenous identity can and does survive even when its most obvious markers disappear.[14] The black indigenous people of the Circum-Caribbean, such as the Garifuna or Miskito, are also included, in spite of scholarly disagreement about which is the primary component of their identity. This debate may be less interesting than questions about how these people knit together a persistent identity for themselves out of the various cultural and biological strands that became intertwined in the sixteenth and seventeeth centuries, as the indigenous survivors of the European domination of the Caribbean came into close contact with African enslaved populations.[15]

The historical processes of globalizing change that created diverse meanings and ways to be indigenous also led to remarkable amounts of both cultural hybridity and persistence. Many different definitions of globalization exist. On the one hand, it can be seen simply as the "intensification of global interconnectedness."[16] On the other, it may be useful to view globalization more specifically as the continuous processes of economic and cultural change developing primarily out of the expansion of European markets and colonial domination of nonwestern peoples. These processes were rooted in both the economic transformations tied to the rise of capitalism, as described in Wallerstein's "world-system" model, and the cultural changes termed by Norbert Elias the "civilizing process." Such a definition highlights the double-sided nature, both economic and ideological, of transformation in the post-1492 Americas.[17] Yet also clear is that beginning in the second half of the twentieth century, change accelerated, seeped more deeply into remote corners of the world, reorganized divisions of labor, and added or substituted goods and information whose production is organized transnationally rather than nationally or locally.[18] This book shows that globalization has had a strong impact on Latin America's indigenous women, who have responded to the changes associated with it in a variety of ways.

Women everywhere are playing a growing role in the world economy whether or not they work for wages. While more women worldwide perform paid labor than ever before, much of the growth in women's employment, especially factory employment, has occurred in Latin America and Asia.[19] Yet waged employment is only part of the story of economic change for women, especially indigenous women. Even when women do not perform wage labor, they may take on traditionally male tasks because of male outmigration, they may intensify aspects of traditional female productive roles, such as craft production to earn cash in local, regional, national, even transnational markets, often by producing handmade items for tourist markets and foreign demand, or they may themselves migrate. Some of the women cleaning houses and caring for children in what sociologist Arlie Hochschild refers to as "global care chains" in towns or cities in the United States or Europe may well come from indigenous backgrounds and communities.[20]

The increased workload borne by Latin American (and other) women has had a heavy impact on their lives. In addition to the greater time spent working, whatever small increases in autonomy for wage-earning women occur tend to be outweighed by the subordination experienced in workplaces that use gender hierarchy to keep women's wages low and control their potential workplace activism. In addition, male attitudes in homes and communities increasingly define and denigrate work like craft production as housework rather than productive labor. These changes are frequently accompanied by an increasing destabilization of family life in which domestic violence, alcoholism, and single-parent households—usually headed by women—become more common.[21]

This book is about how these long-term processes affected indigenous women in Latin America and how indigenous women experienced and responded to these transformations. My research has drawn upon original documents of various times and places, newspaper and Web resources, and the voluminous writings of archaeologists, historians, and anthropologists on women in indigenous societies, past and present. Each type of source relied upon by various disciplines and scholars presents its own challenges. For archaeologists, the interpretation of gender roles based solely on material remains creates certain difficulties. Reconstructing social patterns and cultural beliefs, not to mention patterns of resistance, on the basis of these remains means relying upon both an incomplete archaeological record (due to processes of decay and human intervention) and forms of inference and interpretation that are speculative. In addition, reconstructing the lives and voices of individual women and men of this long-distant past is a nearly impossible task, yet archaeological remains offer information about changing gender roles, and sometimes these are especially visible in the prehistoric images from which archaeologists draw inferences.

Ethnohistorical evidence offers images, but it also provides vivid descriptions of behavior and ideologies of prehispanic and colonial peoples, although such descriptions often come in the voices of the conquerors, not the conquered. Much ethnohistorical scholarship of the last decades has therefore been devoted to finding other voices, especially those of indigenous people, and I make heavy use of that scholarship here.

Ethnographic descriptions provide a high level of detail but are very specific to time and place, even though past ethnographers often downplayed the impact of colonialism and other forms of change. In addition, issues that capture the atttention of ethnographers of one region may not be of interest to ethnographers elsewhere, making comparison of patterns and processes of change difficult. Nonetheless, ethnographies constitute an incredibly valuable historical source, as long as they are placed carefully into a regional chronological context.

During the most recent past, newspapers in some Latin American countries have paid close attention to indigenous groups and issues, whereas in others these issues receive far less attention. This variation grows out of both the different numbers and density of native populations and is also due to historically rooted conceptions of national and ethnic identities. The number of newspaper articles about native peoples published in Bolivia, Ecuador, Guatemala, Mexico, and Peru attest to the continuing impact of indigenous peoples, demographically and culturally. Their presence influences the self-images and policies of these nation-states even as their governments continue to foster repressive policies toward these populations. In Brazil, Colombia, Venezuela, and many of the nations of Central America, on the other hand, the media pays less attention to indigenous issues, and native women face greater difficulty in organizing to press their agendas within activist indigenous groups or in regional, national, or international governmental or other settings.

Whatever the variation in the extent to which Latin American media cover indigenous and women's issues, the Internet makes sources like newspapers and magazines more widely available than do print editions. It also provides an arena for indigenous activist groups to promote their identities and ideas, especially as these concern an increasingly international agenda of self-determination and human rights.[22] Internet resources proved very useful for an examination of the most recent past and of women's participation in indigenous groups and creation of their own advocacy groups.

Indigenous women's contemporary statuses and activism have deep historical roots, even if this history is neither chronologically linear nor spatially continuous. To explore the depth of those roots, this introductory chapter ends with a discussion of archaeologists' reconstructions of gender relations and roles among the earliest inhabitants of Latin America and considers whether gender hierarchy accompanied the first signs of cultural complexity. The second chapter deals with women and the rise of urban- and state-level societies within prehistoric Latin America, emphasizing highland and lowland Mesoamerica as well as the pre-Inka and Inka Andes. The third chapter covers the impact of conquest and colonial rule, ending with a brief discussion of indigenous women in the nineteenth century as the modern Latin American nation-states began to form. Chapters 4 and 5 look at indigenous women in the twentieth and twenty-first centuries in Mesoamerica, Central America, and South America. These chapters are largely organized by region, ethnicity, and nation-state (a form of territorial and political organization that has had an ever-increasing influence on indigenous groups from the nineteenth century on).

I recognize that there can be no one right way to synthesize the disparate and enormous literatures covered in this book, and writing a synthesis in an age of intellectual uncertainty and skepticism entails some risk. Because there are periods of change that profoundly influence cultural configurations, at times a thematic organization provides the best way to describe what Andre Gunder Frank and Barry Gills refer to as periods of "hegemonic leadership."[23] This introductory chapter and the third and sixth chapters (on the colonial period and the postmodern, globalizing beginning of the twenty-first century, respectively) especially reflect this thematic organization, whereas the organization of the other chapters reflects an emphasis on place and ethnicity. Analysis of this lengthy, complex past shows that change, not continuity, has been the norm for indigenous peoples, and women have been embedded in, responsive to, and creators and shapers of those changes, even in the most distant past.

Some Background on Latin America's Earliest Women

The first people to populate the Americas, known as Paleoindians, were the ancestors of today's Native American peoples. These Asian men and women migrated from Siberia across the Bering Land Bridge at least 15,000 years ago.[24] Scholars have long envisioned this early way of life as revolving around the role of men as hunters. The possible misidentification of Tepexpan Man (perhaps dating to 8000 B.C.E., and who may well have been female) provides only one example of the older tendency in early human studies, Old World or New, to overemphasize male remains and activities at the expense of a more balanced view.[25] More recent archaeological and ethnographic studies of hunting and gathering peoples show that while hunting of large mammals occurred, Paleoindian people probably relied more on the hunting of small game, fishing, collecting shellfish, and gathering plants. Both women and men participated in these activities.

As human settlement spread from north to south and west to east, men, women, and children settled in areas with diverse climates and natural resources, which led to the development of a variety of divisions of labor. Aside from participating in hunting, gathering, and fishing, types of work likely to have been performed by the Paleoindian women of the Americas include food preparation, skin-working, and cloth and basketry making, as well as the production of tools used by both genders in these forms of work. Healing, childcare, and participating in or leading decision-making and rituals constitute other activities carried out by the America's earliest women.[26]

During the Archaic period (about 8000 to 3000 B.C.E.; also known as the Formative in some regions) an important set of changes transformed early American hunting and gathering ways of life. These changes centered on the emergence of horticulture and agriculture, a set of changes in which women probably played a key role, with consequences for the gendered division of labor. While archaeologists find it impossible to trace all the steps involved in the shift from food-procurement strategies centered on collecting and gathering to those based on domestication and production of plant foods, they believe it likely that women played a strong role in this transition across the Americas. Wherever it occurred, the causes were multiple and involved factors including climatic change, experimentation with and spread of new types of plants, and the desire to live in larger, more permanently settled communities and to engage in trade. From this transformation then others flowed, including eventually the appearance in some places of class structures, larger towns and cities, and, in some areas, civilizations.[27] In those places where the diet became particularly dependent on corn (in many parts of Mesoamerica, for example), women's work often grew to be increasingly organized around its cultivation and preparation, with the latter being sometimes quite a time-consuming task. Pueblo women of the U.S. southwest have been noted to spend three or more hours a day grinding the corn needed for feeding their families. Archaeological evidence, especially skeletal, suggests a similar pattern for prehistoric indigenous women in this region.[28]

What may have happened in those areas where maize and other crops, such as squash, beans, peppers, and potatoes, became the basis for daily subsistence is that more overlapping and flexible patterns of work organization gave way to more defined and complementary forms. Within households, male and female work spaces began to develop, with the tools of each gender clustered in identifiable areas. The site of Guilá Naquitz in the eastern Valley of Oaxaca of Mexico shows some of the earliest evidence for such gendered clustering, seen in artifact and food remains from perhaps as early as 7000 B.C.E. Villages from coastal Ecuador (ca. 3000–1500 B.C.E.) also offer evidence for the development of male and female work areas as greater amounts of economic specialization began to develop.[29] The later El Salvadoran Maya site of Ceren shows this clustering too. At its houses, buried under the ash from a volcanic eruption that occurred around C.E. 600, female workplaces with tools for cooking and weaving can be seen, along with evidence of women's production of pottery vessels, used for cooking, eating, drinking, and storage. Payson Sheets, the archaeologist who led the team of researchers who excavated and studied the site, also identified a male meeting space, as well as a building that might have been the home of the village's religious specialist, possibly a woman.[30]

Women of Preclassic Mesoamerica and Central and South America (a period also known as the Formative for some areas, dating from approximately 3000 B.C.E. to C.E. 150, depending on the region) played key roles in ritual and belief systems that often highlighted young women's procreative and other powers. During this period in early Latin America, images of women, often depicted in small clay figurines, were commonly placed in a variety of spatial settings (especially households and burials). Sometimes the depictions emphasize younger women; sometimes they show women across the various stages of the life cycle. While female sexuality and fertility may well have been a theme represented through these figurines (especially in those areas where the depiction of the bodies and genitalia of younger women is dominant), these small clay images probably had a range of meanings and were used in different ways, not just to encourage human, plant, or animal fertility.[31] Archaeologists Joyce Marcus and Kent Flannery think that female figurines from Tierras Largas–phase Oaxaca (1400–1150 B.C.E.) represent female ancestors and were used in a "woman's ritual complex centered in the home" (see fig. 1.1). Such worship could have focused on communicating with or worship of ancestors, divination, life-cycle rituals, or healing.[32]

The female figurines of the Sinú people of the Caribbean lowlands of Colombia (third through tenth centuries C.E.) were more elaborate than the earlier Oaxaca figurines. Often depicted as seated in a position commanding respect, the ceramic women, perhaps produced by women, with their cast-gold adornments reinforce the impression of power and prestige (see fig. 1.2).[33] Across diverse areas, female figurines show us that Preclassic (and early Classic) women carried out a variety of political, religious, productive, and social activities, in addition to horticultural and agricultural labor. As producers of pottery and agents of trade and exchange, women's activities in economic, political, and ceremonial domains of prehistoric life suggest they often played roles complementary to those of men.[34]

This observation leads to the question of what archaeologists can infer about women's status and gender hierarchy in those societies where agriculture, systems of exchange, and power relations within and between groups were becoming more complex. Evidence from late Archaic and Preclassic burials—which can tell us about funerary ritual, beliefs about an afterlife, and social status—provides a means to examine the question of whether the first increases in social complexity and hierarchy indeed meant an intensification of gender hierarchy and subordination for women. While these ideas are often

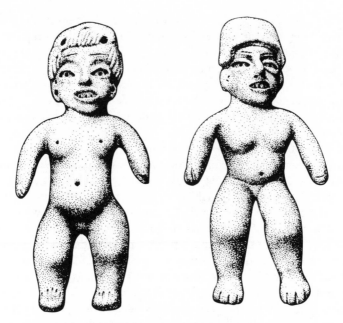

FIGURE 1.1. While most figurines from the period are female (as is the figurine on the left), some are male (figure on the right). (Drawing from Joyce Marcus and Kent V. Flannery, *Zapotec Civilization*, Thames and Hudson, London, 1996, 85. Courtesy of Joyce Marcus.)

linked in feminist scholarship to the origins of gender asymmetry,[35] the evidence from early Latin America does not strongly support such an argument, at least not for the first complex societies of Mesoamerica and Andean South America. The burials from Tlatilco, Mexico (just south of today's Mexico City), show, for example, that both younger men's and women's burials were more elaborate than those of older men and women, and women's burials from Preclassic Tlatilco often contained greater numbers and types and greater numbers of objects than men's. However one male burial—perhaps that of an elder of a kin group or prominent religious specialist—stands out for the number and quality of grave goods associated with it.[36]

The Oaxaca region offers a different pattern, in which Preclassic burials often include paired burials of men and women. Though some male burials are grouped together and contain more grave goods than those of other men or women, the occasional female burial occurs with extensive amounts of grave goods, a different style of cranial deformation (a practice that involves changing the shape of the skull through pressure and was probably intended to convey social rank), or a different burial position from men and other women, all characteristics that may indicate a higher social status for these women.[37] As time went on, the tendency to bury men and women in pairs

FIGURE 1.2. A woman of the Santa Elena peninsula of southwest Ecuador shown using ancient lost wax techniques for metal casting. (Photo by Karen Stothert).

increased, with any tendency toward the single male burials with special grave goods declining. Joyce Marcus and Kent Flannery argue that

> with increasing frequency it seems to have been important to emphasize one's membership in an elite family rather than in a male line descending from Earth or Sky. Most later Mesoamerican elites reckoned descent bilaterally, emphasizing whichever parent had the most noble pedigree. At smaller communities receiving hypogamous brides [brides of higher status than their new husbands], little would be gained by emphasizing a father's relationship to Earth, while ignoring an even more highly ranked mother.

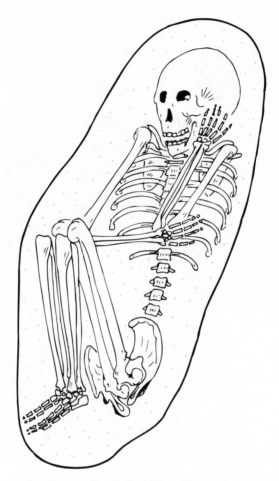

FIGURE 1.3.   Female burial from Paloma. An extensive array of
goods was found with these remains, including textile-producing
tools, beads, a fur skin, and straw wrapping and matting that covered
the body. (Drawing by Bernardino Ojeda E., reprinted from Jeffrey
Quilter, *Life and Death at Paloma*, University of Iowa Press, Iowa City,
1989, 89. Courtesy of University of Iowa Press.)

These ancestors of the later Zapotec civilization developed a form of hierarchy in which male and female elites held power, with female elites from
larger, more important communities frequently marrying leading men from
smaller communities.[38]

Another area where burial sites exist from early periods is coastal Peru.
One of the most extensively studied sites there is Paloma, occupied from
about 5000 to 2500 B.C.E. Many burials were found at the site; the single

most elaborate burial was that of a late adolescent male, placed over a cane grid, with three mats covering the body and numerous funeral goods placed around the grave. While the site's primary excavator, Jeffry Quilter, argues that over time the number of grave goods for women declines, the differences in amounts and quality of goods are slight. The site actually contains more burials of women than men, and several women's burials are quite distinctive, even if they do not contain the same number of grave goods as those of the elaborate male burial (see fig. 1.3).[39] Archaeological data from other coastal Andean areas and sites not only do not show enough consistent differences in male and female burials to support the argument that, while socioeconomic complexity was developing, gender hierarchy was also increasing but also sometimes suggest women's social power and position as heads of kin groups and ritual specialists.[40]

While more evidence of gender hierarchy emerges in the following periods of development, variations in the gendering of political organization, work arrangements, and worship of deities continued. If any factor best predicts those places where older patterns of gender complementarity gave way to more ingrained forms of hierarchy, it is militarism—key to the origin of empire in parts of Mesoamerica and the Andes, a topic that is taken up in the next chapter.

2

Of Warriors and Working Women

Gender in Later Prehispanic Mesoamerica and the Andes

The visual imagery of female deities (such as the decapitated Mexica goddess Coyolxauhqui; see fig. 2.1) is captivating and has drawn much attention from those interested in the later prehistory of indigenous women before the arrival of Europeans. Such complex, often contradictory, images offer scholars rich but often puzzling materials for interpreting and understanding women's lives, their statuses, and gender ideologies in the complex cultures and civilizations of Mesoamerica and the Andes. In many cultures, such as those of the pre-Inka Andes, visual materials constitute some of the few pieces of information available about women in the prehistoric past, and finding voices, reconstructing individual identities, or reading agency from representations and remains presents interpretive challenges. Nevertheless, such images, often dramatic in nature, offer a window onto the gendered worlds of the Latin American prehispanic past, especially those of the Classic and Postclassic periods for Mesoamerica and the Middle Horizon through late Horizon periods for the Andes, when urban, class-based societies developed.

Mesoamerica alone can serve almost as a laboratory for examining women's lives, social patterns, and statuses because the cultures of the Classic (C.E. 150–900) and Postclassic (C.E. 900–1521) offer a surprisingly broad spectrum of gendered arrangements and social valuations of women.[1] They include the gender arrangements of peoples ranging from the hunting, gathering, and cultivating groups of Mesoamerica's far north to the more urban and hierarchically organized Nahuas, to the Ñudzahui people of Oaxaca (also known as the Mixtec), who developed the most seemingly egalitarian gender arrangements of any Mesoamerican cultural group. While the Maya of southern Mesoamerica, a broad and enduring cluster of linguistically and culturally related groups, developed gender patterns characterized by more gender asym-

FIGURE 2.1. Coyolxauhqui image from the Templo Mayor area of Mexico City (photo courtesy of Mexico's Instituto Nacional de Antropología y Historia).

metry than other Mesoamerican peoples, even among them, both the images and realities of women varied. Further south in the Andean region, images of female supernaturals have a particularly ancient history, and later prehispanic groups show significant degrees of gender complementarity, although this pattern would change somewhat with the rise of the Inka empire. Touching lightly on the lowland cultures of South America and the peoples of the Circum-Caribbean, who will be dealt with in later chapters, we begin in the north, where later central Mexican peoples thought their origins lay.

Women and Gender among Northern and Central Mexican Peoples: Parallel Organizations, Hierarchical Ideologies

Numerous late Postclassic central Mexican peoples described themselves as latecomers to this region, arriving after the fall of the city of Tula and its people, the Toltecs, in the mid–twelfth century. After Tula's decline as a dominating power, a series of migrations from the north led to the development of new ethnic identities and cultural traditions, shaped by the cultures of the northern migrants combined with cultural patterns of the center, as these developed from the Preclassic period on.

Because it is not clear exactly from which part of the vast northern region such migrations originated, archaeologists cannot say with any certainty from which northern cultural traditions later central Mexican groups descend. Northern peoples were part of what Linda Cordell has called the "Southwest heartland," encompassing parts of today's borderland region, including the states of Arizona and New Mexico in the United States and Chihuahua and Sonora in Mexico, and they fall into several archaeological, linguistic, and cultural groupings. Many of these groups were characterized by agriculture, permanent settlements, and matrilineal or bilateral kinship structures (with membership in households and kin groups flowing through women or through both parents, respectively).[2] Northern cultural groups seem to have been characterized by a relative degree of gender egalitarianism in work, worship, and household and community decision-making that persisted over a long period of time, a pattern that began in the distant past. While the arrival of the Spanish probably led to the emergence of more asymmetric gender patterns, contemporary Borderlands Native American gender patterns emphasize complementarity, and women have access to roles carrying authority.[3] Other important influences that helped to shape later central Mexican indigenous groups and their gender arrangements included the development of urbanism, market economies, and empire in the central region itself.

While archaeologists have made incredible strides in learning how to analyze the social relations and gender patterns of people from their bones, pots, art, and buildings, challenges remain. This is certainly the case for the huge, significant, yet often puzzling Classic-period site of Teotihuacan. Located north of what is today Mexico City, Teotihuacan anchored the central region, one of the two most populous and culturally dynamic regions of Classic Mesoamerica. Teotihuacan is known for its massive buildings, its clear and distinctive urban planning, and its influential art style, evident in sculpture, murals, and ceramics. What is less well known about Teotihuacan is that one of its most important deities was female.

The murals and large sculptures of Teotihuacan often focus on two main deities, a female deity, referred to by contemporary scholars as either the Great Goddess or the Goddess (see fig. 2.2), and a male deity, usually called Tlaloc, for the later Aztec water deity, but named the Storm God by some scholars. The primary associations of the Goddess were extensive, as she was known as "a goddess of earthly waters, a patroness of warfare who requires sacrifices, mother of the gods, and the fertile mountain from which all things come." She may also have represented the collective well-being of the city of Teotihuacan, a notion that Teotihuacan's rulers and artists often went to great pains to portray. The Storm God's associations were with rain, astrology, the sky, and perhaps science, commerce, foreign relations, even dynastic values. Why did

FIGURE 2.2. Image of Teotihuacan's Goddess. (From "Mural Painting West of Portico of the Patio, Tetitla, Teotihuacan," by Agustín Villagra Caleti, in *Handbook of Middle American Indians*, vol. 10, *Archaeology of Northern Mesoamerica*, pt. 1, edited by Gordon F. Ekholm and Ignacio Bernal, series editor Robert Wauchope, University of Texas Press, Austin, 1971, fig. no. 11. Copyright © 1971, by permission of the University of Texas Press.)

Teotihuacan have a female deity at the heart of its religious imagery? In her reconstruction of the values and beliefs of Teotihuacan, leading art historian Esther Pasztory views the Goddess as Teotihuacan's supreme deity and argues that she probably evolved from an older female cave deity. Her connection to both fertility and the collective values that united Teotihuacanos may help explain the more prominent visual importance and placement of the Goddess over the Storm God.[4]

What might her image communicate about the experience of women living at Teotihuacan during the site's more than 500 years of existence? Certainly, Teotihuacan was no matriarchy. A strong and very centralized government ruled this city of some eight square miles in size and with a population of at least 125,000 at its height. The ruling group expressed its power through both sacred images, images that probably attracted many pilgrims, and warfare, which expanded the city's resource base. While its domain was not huge compared to other ancient empires, the site had significant wealth and power, and a male ruler-priest probably headed its "sacralized polity."[5]

One way in which this governing system displayed its power was through the building of the famous Teotihuacan apartment compounds, many of which were built between C.E. 300 and 400. Most of the city's populace lived in these similar (but never identical) one-story, high-walled, and windowless structures. They served as Teotihuacan's basic social and economic units. Family life, craft production, and religious ritual took place in the compounds, and they probably served as the foundation upon which labor for public works and the military was organized. Skeletal evidence from one apartment compound indicates that biologically related men occupied it, with the compound's women being more genetically diverse. This pattern is consistent with either a patrilineal or cognatic kinship system (systems in which genealogical links are traced and used to form households and larger groups, either through men or men and women, respectively).[6] The labor of women born or married into the compounds—especially in food preparation and craft production—would have been essential for the survival of family and kin groups, especially in periods when male residents left the city on missions of war, diplomacy, or trade. The possibility also exists that priestesses served the Goddess, though images of religious functionaries dressed in female garb in a mural painting from the Tepantitla apartment compound at Teotihuacan could be either women or men dressed in the skirts and women's shift-like shirts known as *huipiles*.[7]

Teotihuacan's burial practices and mortuary goods, relevant for assessing degrees of gender hierarchy, do not show great differences in the overall treatment of deceased women and men. While males more often had more complex grave offerings than did women, these differences were not pronounced, and women's burials were occasionally of greater complexity than men's.[8] This evidence, as well as the Goddess imagery discussed, implies that while Teotihuacanos and their leaders valued the subordination of the individual person and smaller social units to the Teotihuacan collective or united whole, they did not use images of gender subordination to express or reinforce this message.

For the central Mexican region, the post-Teotihuacan legacy of cultural development was centered in and around the Valley of Mexico, first with the rise and fall of Tula and the Toltecs. Later, in the fourteenth through sixteenth centuries, the Mexica, with their allies, came to dominate a broad area known as the Aztec empire. War and military values permeated Mexica culture, and they became what might be called a "martialized polity" (in contrast to the sacralized polity of Teotihuacan). These martial values would shape gender roles, though not determine them completely.

At its height, the Aztec empire claimed to control many parts of central and southern Mesoamerica, but its focal region centered on the Mexica island capital city of Tenochtitlan (underlying today's Mexico City) and the surrounding mainland area. This region included both urban and rural com-

munities, formed the core of the Triple Alliance empire, and was highly influential during the late Postclassic period. It also generated the most historical documentation of all Mesoamerican regions in the early colonial period,
allowing scholars to understand it relatively well.[9]

While Mexica origins remain shrouded in some mystery, their myths tell
of how they migrated from a place known as Aztlan (Place of the Herons),
probably an area to the north of their eventual home, the Valley of Mexico. Arriving first at Chicomoztoc (Seven Caves), the Mexica then left and
travelled in a southeasterly direction, finally settling around C.E. 1325 on a
swampy island in the center of what is today the modern Mexican nation.
This settlement occurred after they saw an eagle perched on a prickly pear
cactus, the sign prophesied by their patron and solar deity, Huitzilopochtli
(Hummingbird on the Left). As he led their journey, Huitzilopochtli was
accompanied by four priests, three male and one female. The woman was
named Chimalma (Shield Lying or Resting), and her presence hints that during this early period of Mexica history, women were active participants in
important religious rituals.[10]

Once the Mexica settled on this island and began to build what became
the city of Tenochtitlan, they created an intricate economic and political
system though diplomacy, warfare, and marital alliances. The martial nature
of Mexica society influenced every aspect of life, including their forms of
gender organization. When a boy was born, his umbilical cord was buried on
a battlefield, and soon after birth, in a naming ceremony, he was given male
clothing and implements for either fighting, if he came from a military family,
or a future occupation, if he did not. The umbilical cord of a daughter was
buried by the household hearth, and she was given female clothing and weaving implements. The Mexica also placed or burned gendered objects with
bodies they buried or cremated at death. The most privileged Mexica afterlife
went to men who died in battle, as well as women who died in childbirth.[11]
Parallel birth and death rituals for males and females represent the ways that
gender identities were defined as different, even opposite, yet at the same
time complementary and thus interdependent. Military organization and the
tlatoani's (supreme leader) skills in conquest and war, nevertheless, were critical parts of the political organization of this expansive society.

Warfare was also deeply intertwined with, indeed sanctified by, religious
beliefs in which Huitzilopochtli and other warrior deities encouraged and
even depended upon Mexica success on the battlefield. This success helped
support their economy by expanding areas for tribute and trade. It also helped
supply captives and human blood that kept the sun in motion and nourished
Huitzilopochtli, thereby sustaining the earth and human life. The Mexica also
worshiped female earth deities, often fierce in nature, symbolic of the fertility
and food production that sustained life.

Most Mexica men participated in warfare at some time during their lives,
having been trained for it in the schools attended by male children. The *telpochcalli*, the schools primarily for the sons of commoners, trained adolescents

for fighting and employed students in public works projects such as constructing or repairing roads, buildings, or bridges. The *calmecac*, attended by sons of the nobility and a smaller number of commoners, prepared them for either the priesthood or military leadership. After their schooling, the young men of Mexica, as well as the other ethnic groups of the central region, could expect to devote some time to armies of either offense or defense as the Aztec empire expanded its domain during the fifteenth and early sixteenth centuries.[12]

Women could and did attend the calmecac and telpochcalli, but their attendance appears to have been largely a familial decision, and was not compulsory.[13] The organized armies of imperial conquest largely excluded women, though there are some examples of women fighting, almost always defensively, in the chronicles detailing the late postconquest era. There is the oft-cited example of the desperate Tlatelolcans using women (and young boys) in 1473 in a last ditch effort to ward off their Tenochcan neighbors. The women attempted to do this by exposing their genitalia and stomachs and squeezing their breasts to produce milk, which they threw on their enemies. But other examples of women fighting in military contexts can be found. Toltec women were said, for example, to have fought alongside men during a civil war (C.E. 1008) and to have even taken captives. Two Tepanec women fought beside Tepanec soldiers as they were defeated by a Tenochcan army in 1428. Fray Diego Durán's historical chronicle also mentions a woman, presumably indigenous, who accompanied Cortés's army to Morelos, where she rode on horseback, helped lead the Spanish to victory over the community of Ocuitulco, and was awarded an *encomienda* grant of the labor and tribute of two communities by Cortés.[14]

While women fought, not only was it somewhat unusual for them to do so but their participation was neither highly structured nor part of the highly organized military organization of the late Postclassic period. Thus women generally lacked access to what both indigenous and Spanish chronicles uniformly depict as the highest prestige activity among the Nahuas. As Mexica society became increasingly warlike and expanded its sphere of influence, gender symbolism increasingly associated maleness with strength and victory, and femaleness with defeat and subjugation.[15] Paradoxically, while Mexica warfare increasingly resulted in the celebration of maleness and masculine values (which has led some scholars to see the Mexica as the paradigm for a male-dominated, patriarchal society), the increasing militarization of Mexica society opened up social space for women to play important, often parallel and complementary, social roles. Mexica ideology, while using a gendered discourse to describe victory as masculine and defeat as feminine, also used a discourse rooted in a notion of the complementarity of maleness and femaleness.[16]

One area where parallel roles are evident is in the world of work. There is no question that women worked hard in Mexica society, whether they came from the noble or commoner stratum. The implements that female newborns were given soon after birth included the tools for spinning and weaving, a central part of *all* women's work. Both girls and boys received training in future work tasks beginning at age five or six. While men were responsible for farming and fighting, as well as hunting, fishing, production of many crafts items, and the long-distance trading of those items, women performed vital household labor, including cooking, cleaning, spinning, and weaving, as well as rearing and socializing the much-prized Mexica infants and children. They also participated in household-based crafts production. Outside the home, commoner women, especially, provided labor in market exchange, worked as midwives, healers, and marriage brokers, and served as teachers and priestesses in temples and song houses (the *cuicacalli*). Rather than being laboring drudges whose productive efforts were socially necessary but not valued, the weight of evidence shows that Mexica women had some control over the conditions and fruits of their labor and that, through work (even when household based), they achieved authority and prestige.[17]

Each Mexica home, or *calli*, contained rooms centered around a patio and hearth area, with three stones "conceptualized as female deities" surrounding the hearth. The calli, often the locus of multifamily households, was the female space par excellence, where labor, often under female control, took place. Mothers, especially the "good mother," as described in the *Florentine Codex*, were thought to be energetic workers, careful and thrifty, who would teach and serve others.[18] This source, consisting of texts written down in the mid–sixteenth century by Nahua scribes and elders in response to questions from the Franciscan friar Bernardino de Sahagún, often depicts what these male elders viewed as ideal social types. For them, good grandmothers and great-grandmothers merited praise and could correct others, and in a discussion of the roles of family and kin group members, the text says that the Mexica valued great-grandmothers as founders of kin groups as well. As Sahagún's Nahua informants themselves said of the role of the great-grandmother: "She is the founder, the beginner [of her lineage]."[19]

Why would women be seen as the founders of kin groups? The notion of women as, ultimately, the originators of kin relations (either by themselves or with their husbands) was rooted in two features of Mexica life, one mythical and historic, the other reflecting the nature of the kinship system. Mexica nobility flowed from female as well as male sources. The first Mexica tlatoani, Acamapichtli, was ennobled through his marriage to Ilancueitl, daughter of a Culhuacan king. More generally, the birthplace and status of a nobleman's mother or wife could enhance or weaken his status in the hierarchy of status among the nobility. In the mythical realm, Chimalma helped lead the Mexica to their eventual settling place, thereby acting as a founding ancestress of the Mexica as a people.[20]

Likewise, in the realm of kinship as conceptualized in everyday life, a child was seen as connected to ancestors by his or her mother's blood and father's semen.[21] This bilateral conceptualization of kinship provided the basis for the Mexica kinship system, one in which household members and members of larger descent units could use ties through mothers or fathers, or other female or male kin, to claim ties or activate rights. Their cognatic kinship structure was neither completely bilateral nor egalitarian in practice, however. Early colonial legal and genealogical evidence shows that men gained greater access to rights over land, and that ties through men were mentioned more often in genealogies. The Mexica also gave more individualizing and varied names to boys than girls, who often bore names referring to birth order. But genealogies frequently included women as links through whom kin connections could be traced and as ancestors, especially as one member of a founding couple, from whom kinship and property flowed.[22]

Women's authority, rooted in both their work and the cognatic kinship system, extended beyond the Mexica household as well. In the marketplace, for example, women were not only buyers but also vendors. They served as marketplace judges or administrators (*tianquizpan tlayacanque*), a position held by both men and women. Women also held supervisory positions within guilds associated with craft production, though whether they oversaw women's guilds within or parallel to those of men is not known. References to a ceremony involving "the most important *joyera*" (female jewelry maker) and "the most important merchant woman," suggest that female crafts workers might have been hierarchically ranked.[23]

In the realm of religion, an arena of immense importance in Mexica life both because of the complexity of their beliefs and the time they devoted to religious activities, women also held positions of religious and political authority. In the song houses that young adolescent girls and boys attended to learn the songs, dances, and moral codes that were part of the Mexica belief system, male officials called *tiachcahuan* and *telpochtlatoque* (older brothers and leaders of youths, respectively) judged young men who misbehaved. Parallel female officials called cihuatetiachcahuan (a term that could be translated literally as female older brothers, with *cihua* coming from the Nahuatl word for "woman," *cihuatl*) judged young women. Like their male counterparts, they could expel those who misbehaved, and the female officials were similarly referred to in hierachical fashion either as cihuatetiachcahuan or as *ichpochtlayacanque* (administrators or directors of young women). In temples (sometimes though not always for female deities) priestesses known as *cihuatlamacazque* (lower level priestesses) and *cihuacuacuiltin* (higher level priestesses) helped care for the buildings, carry out calendrical and other ceremonies, and train other priestesses.[24]

In the neighborhoods and local subdivisions of Tenochtitlan and other cities, women, like men, served as neighborhood leaders who had responsibilities for seeing to daily affairs within these lower level political units. Males holding these positions were referred to as *tepixque* and *tlaxilacaleque* (guards, leaders, and elders of local neighborhoods), and women holding these positions were called either *cihuatepixque* or *cihuatlaxilacaleque*.[25] At higher levels of governance, Nahua women rarely served as rulers, though on occasion they did so briefly, generally when there was no male successor to a rulership. Yet there are also clues that high officials and their wives shared responsibilities. The *tlatocacihuatl* (female supreme ruler) was a "woman ruler, governor, leader—a provider, an administrator." The *cihuatecutli* (high-ranking noblewoman) "governs, leads, provides for one, arranges well, administers peacefully."[26]

Nahua women thus held positions of authority, positions that were hierarchically organized and parallel to those of men and that afforded women prestige on the basis of their own activities and achievements. This shadowy hierarchy, difficult to tease out of early colonial Nahuatl and Spanish sources, is clearly there, yet it does not appear to have been as highly elaborated as the politico-military hierarchies of men. In addition to holding these positions, women gained both respect and access to material goods through their activities in homes, markets, neighborhoods, song houses, and temples. These material items and the property rights attached to or expressed through them, by bequeathal, gifting, or investment, afforded Mexica women a degree of independence.

While there are few statements that clarify how rights of inheritance were passed along in early colonial chronicles, there are several reasons to think that women customarily bequeathed and inherited property. First, the earliest colonial Nahua wills from a variety of communities illustrate women's ownership of houses, land, and a variety of smaller items.[27] Reading such testaments suggests that female control over property reflected prehispanic practice. Second, women's property, gained through dowry and inheritance, was kept separate from men's at marriage, and the Mexica made distinctions between those household goods belonging to women and to men.[28] Furthermore, if women managed their resources skillfully, others saw them as successful. The woman who was not as skillful risked falling into poverty. According to the *Florentine Codex*, a woman merchant, if born under a fortunate day sign, could become "quite rich, she would be a good provider, she would be well-born. She would look to and guard the services and the property of our lord. She would be a guardian and administrator. Much would she gather, collect, save, and justly distribute among her children."[29] But another kind of woman worker, the embroiderer, who did not properly perform her religious obligations would be punished with "complete poverty and misery."[30]

Just as Mexica women could achieve economic well-being and leave property to children and others, so too were they held responsible for their behavior. Mexica women, particularly the daughters of the nobility, were taught to be chaste, circumspect, and dutiful in fulfilling their wifely and maternal obligations. Those women who transgressed social and legal responsibilities could be punished for their misbehavior or crimes. Willful female children, prostitutes, female adulterers, and women who had abortions were subject to strong social sanctions and punishments, including death. Nahuas might punish adulterers and adulteresses, for example, with death by stoning or strangulation, indicating the importance they attached to marriage for both partners.[31]

Male sexuality and expressions of violence were given somewhat freer rein, though such behavior could be seen as socially controlled, since sexuality outside of marriage and violent action most often took place in war or through institutions associated with war. Yet women were also on occasion known to engage in violent, aggressive, or assertive behavior. Marketwomen's fighting, for example, was said to have worsened relations between Tenochtitlan and Tlatelolco prior to the war they fought in 1473.[32] Women who were too aggressive physically or verbally were not admired, such as those born on the day One Eagle, who were fated to be "of evil tongue, vile-mouthed, inhuman in speech" as well as physically aggressive.[33] Women's words, especially taunting and freely spoken words (so very different from the seemingly measured, often highly ritualistic speech of men, especially those holding high governing positions), could mock men and even provoke warfare. But Nahuas also believed that women could speak well, like the women born on the day One Flint Knife, who could be courageous and would have a gift for speaking and leadership, paralleling the men born on this day, who would be brave and successful in war. Not only would such a woman be successful in providing sustenance, becoming wealthy as a result of her own labor, but also she would be "courageous, strong, reckoned as a man, and hardy. She would give honor as a man. And, [among] all her gifts, she would speak well, be eloquent, give good counsel, and arrange her conversation and manner of speaking well in her home."[34]

Women wielded both formal and informal political influence and, while their sexuality was under tighter social control than men's (especially true of the daughters of the nobility), sexuality was associated with pleasure for both sexes and not viewed as inherently sinful. The Mexica thought of heterosexual sex as a natural and healthy part of daily life, though they believed that engaging in too much sex could be harmful and might lead to chaos, a state they feared. Sex carried with it the obligation for men and women to please each other and behave responsibly both toward one another and the children they jointly created.[35]

Thus, in addition to compelling evidence of parallelism in the sociopolitical hierarchy and the mutual enjoyment and responsibilities of sexual relations, both commoner and elite Mexica women held property rights and produced socially valued goods and services. They held positions of authority across a variety of realms of daily life, were liable for their transgressions of rules and laws, and perhaps, as scribes, kept records of matters of concern to women, especially women in positions of authority. Were women, then, under the patriarchal authority of fathers and husbands, as others have argued?[36] Before answering this question, another realm of Mexica life needs to be considered. This is the realm of religion, especially as it is revealed though the iconography of Mexica visual images, particularly those of female deities.

The Mexica pantheon was complex in structure because the deities cannot simply be understood as representing a single (or simple) idea, substance, or social group, nor do they relate neatly to each other through family or kin relations. The gendering of deities also presents a challenge to the decon-struction of their meanings, because many deities have both female and male versions or identities (with the female aspect sometimes labeled as a sister or wife), some are androgynous, and some are either solely male or female. But even those deities who are clearly female have complicated images and asso-ciations that are both life giving and life enhancing yet also are powerfully war-like, with negative images and associations.[37] Sometimes these powerful and war-like female images are also demeaning.

The most important deities of sustenance were all female. The deities associated with maize (Xilonen, Iztac Cinteotl, and Chicomecoatl), maguey (also known as the agave plant, Mayahuel), and salt (Uixtocihuatl) were joined by Chalchiuhtlicue, the water goddess and wife of Tlaloc. Toci (Our Grandmother), Cihuacoatl (Snake Woman), Xochiquetzal (Flowery Feather or Plume), and Tlazolteotl (Deity of Filth) were important earth deities, with both fertility and military associations, whose images and ceremonies were common. These rituals expressed the way that central Mexican peoples prized and conceptually linked agricultural and human fertility.[38] The par-ticularly fierce Cihuacoatl had a lusty appetite for both human hearts and blood. Tlazolteotl was a goddess of sexuality to whom people's sins could be confessed in her guise as Tlaelcuani, or "Eater of foul things."[39] While these earth, fertility, and warrior goddesses were perhaps the most prominent of female deities in this seemingly constantly evolving pantheon, no single female deity stood as supreme (as was also true for male deities). Instead, these goddesses express the multiple complementary oppositions that shaped and formed Nahua worldviews, of which the central ideas and oppositions were male/female, earth/moon, sun/moon, and war (death)/sustenance (life). Such oppositions, with their inherent ambiguities, can be seen even in the famous Coyolxauhqui image, often cited as strong evidence for women's subordina-tion among the Mexica.[40]

Coyolxauhqui (Bells on Cheek or Face) was the sister and adversary of the Mexica patron and war deity, Huitzilopochtli. After she led her brothers in an attempted matricide (against their mother, Coatlicue, Snake Skirt, because she had become pregnant in a shameful way), Huitzilopochtli attacked, defeated, and killed her. Should this myth and Coyolxauhqui's famous bas-relief sculp-ture (at the foot of Huitzilopochtli's temple in Tenochtitlan's ceremonial pre-cinct) be interpreted solely as evidence of the negation of female power and authority, perhaps perceived and portrayed by male leaders as threatening "the power and legitimacy of the state itself"?[41]

Because the control of women can be both a means through which the state controls households and a metaphor for that control, we could readily conclude that Coyolxauhqui's image tells only the story of increasing Mexica male power rooted partly in violence against women. Yet her image haunts the contemporary viewer, not only because she suggests defeat and subordina-tion but also because even in this image of defeat and death, Coyolxauhqui is powerful, sexual, and even faintly maternal, with her pendulous breasts at the

very center of the image.[42] The violence inherent in this stone figure is striking, but the ambiguity of Coyolxauhqui's portrayal speaks to its meaning as
well. The image implies that just as Mexica men could never control women
to the extent they might like (because men needed women for food, clothing,
sex and affection, and child-bearing and rearing, and many men simply were
absent at least some of the time), the Mexica could not control every people
they conquered. Thus her image speaks of fear as well as conquest. The fear
and power articulated by this image expresses and also reinforces a Mexica
worldview that celebrated their hegemony but also acknowledged it as fleeting and impermanent.

Did Mexica men use images of female subordination to bolster a growing state's imperial governing apparatus and ideology? Yes, they did, but Mexica women were not the subordinated, passive, and silent beings dominated
by patriarchal fathers and husbands that have been inferred from stone and
paper portrayals. Their reality was far more varied, and the gender parallelism
of Mexica thought and social institutions formed, expressed, and reinforced
the integration of complementary oppositions. For the Mexica, these oppositions, so often symbolized through gender, constituted that fleeting whole-
ness, the fragile balancing of celestial and human forces, that lay at the root of
their philosophy, their worldview, and the conceptual and social patterns that
constituted basic parts of their everyday life.

The Postclassic Ñudzahui: Elite Gender Complementarity

Just to the south of the Nahua region existed a rather different gender
organization, one in which women were apparently more socially valued
than among the Mexica. Again an image, one that is common across both the
Nahua and Ñudzahui codices, alerts us, as we shift our focus away from the
Nahuas, whose parallel gender structures must be weighed against their belli-
cose warrior ideology and practices, to the fact that gender relations were not
uniform across either space or time. When Nahua women are shown seated
in codices, they kneel with their legs placed under their torsos (see fig. 2.3);

FIGURE 2.3. Opposite top: Nahua woman weaving with legs
tucked under her. (From *Florentine Codex*, General History of the
Things of New Spain, 1950–82, translated by Arthur J. O. Anderson
and Charles E. Dibble, University of Utah Press, Salt Lake City, bk. 10,
image no. 58. Courtesy of University of Utah Press.) Opposite bottom:
The fierce goddess Cihuacoatl is shown with a weaving implement
and also is posed in a submissive fashion. (From *The Book of the Life
of the Ancient Mexicans*, translated by Zelia Nuttall, edited by Elizabeth
Hill Boone, University of California Press, Berkeley, 1983, 45. Courtesy
of University of California Press.)

FIGURE 2.4. A Nudzahui woman shown spinning, with legs placed to the front. (From *Codex Vindobonensis Mexicanus I*, Akademische Druck-u. Verlagsanstalt, Graz, 1974, 9v. Courtesy of the Österreichesche Nationalbibliothek.)

Ñudzahui women are often shown, on the other hand, seated with their legs placed in front of them, with no visible sign of subordination (see fig. 2.4).[43] This simple visual depiction, as well as the prominent attention given to noble women in the Ñudzahui codices, hints that the Ñudzahui of western Oaxaca accorded women a higher status than did Nahuas. An array of evidence supports this conclusion, though much of it pertains to women of the noble and ruling stratum.

Murals of the late Classic or early Postclassic period from the nearby Puebla-Tlaxcala Valley, particularly the Battle Mural from Cacaxtla, contain possible depictions of women as warriors, reminiscent of Teotihuacan's Goddess. The nearby late Classic site of Xochitecatl featured abundant images of goddesses, female rulers, and women at all stages of the female life cycle in sculpture and figurines and may have housed a female-centered cult.[44] Such images suggest that Nahua depictions of fierce women, as well as the shared Nahua and Ñudzahui tradition that marriage to women of ruling groups was ennobling, even when these groups had been defeated, had roots in both the Classic and early Postclassic periods.[45] The Ñudzahui rarely used gendered images to signify subordination in gender, military, or class relations. Instead, such images usually signified gender complementarity. However, Ñudzahui society does not appear to have fostered the gender parallel institutions (which included participation by both elite and commoner women) found among Nahua groups, especially the Mexica.

Evidence of elite women's high status among the Ñudzahui comes from an array of sources and types of data, including chronicles, notarial texts, codices, and material remains.[46] These show that, while elite women were probably not the social equals of men, gender complementarity was culturally valued and that ruling and noble women played important social roles. Examples of complementarity in worldview and social roles can be found across an array of activities and domains of Ñudzahui social life and extend to commoner women as well.

The equivalence and mutuality of the male and female genders can be seen most clearly in the conceptualization of the religious and political realms. Ñudzahui religion focused primarily on using ritual to maintain the balance among natural, human, and supernatural forces. While deities and natural forces could be associated with specific genders, and some had features of both, their complex of deities was not as elaborated or highly structured as that of the Mexica. The Nudzahui believed that the male sky and the female earth gave rise to life through rain, which connected the two. Just as these male and female elements were equally necessary to create and sustain life on earth, so too were they necessary to the conceptualization of leadership and rulership in the Ñudzahui region. The Ñudzahui term for rulership (*yuhuitayu*) combines elements referring to the reed mat (*yuhui*) and the married couple (*tayu*, who are consistently depicted sitting on such mats) and visually and etymologically suggests the equivalence of the male and female partners (see fig. 2.5). The Ñudzahui referred to male rulers as *yya toniñe*

FIGURE 2.5. The ruling couple and mat together symbolize the yuhuitayu; both partners are shown seated with legs to the front. (From *Codex Nuttall: A Picture Manuscript from Ancient Mexico,* edited by Zelia Nuttall, Dover, New York, 1975, 24.)

("lord ruler") and to female rulers as *yya dzehe toniñe* ("lady ruler").[47] Does the consistent imagery tying leadership and rulership to the married ruling couple imply that women as well as men could rule among the Nudzahui kingdoms?

The answer is an unequivocal yes. While some Ñudzahui preference for male succession to rulership can be detected, female succession to positions of rulership was both possible and relatively common.[48] But it would be more correct to emphasize that when a couple from the ruling stratum married, they jointly ruled the polities that were the patrimony of each, and they could live in the capital of either, or sometimes both. After the couple had children, two of them were chosen to succeed to positions and estates of the parents, with the eldest child often succeeding to the rulership of the kingdom of the father, and a younger child succeeding to the rulership of the mother, though variations, often regional, also existed.[49] While sons were preferred, Ñudzahui codices depict daughters succeeding their fathers or mothers as rulers, and examples can be found of early colonial female Ñudzahui rulers seeking to assert, justify, and legally protect their succession and rights to pass on their ruling positions and associated holdings. But because prehispanic rulership was truly joint, Ñudzahui women sovereigns were far more than occasional rulers in place of men or even simply consorts. They represented their communities, participated in these marital alliances, and helped build estates that could be passed on to their children.[50]

Even women of the Ñudzahui nobility (or *yya*) who did not hold ruling positions also played important social roles. These included the exercise of both political and religious responsibilities and authority at lower levels of sociopolitical organization than the yuhuitayu. Priestesses as well as priests are shown in the Ñudzahui codices as active in ceremonies that also depict "women's participation in Mixtec religion as producers of sacred and symbolic food."[51] Both nobles and commoners could serve in the hereditary position of religious practitioner. But their services did not set them apart as a separate group or class within Ñudzahui society, nor did such individuals necessarily serve continuously through their adult lives, because full-time occupational specialization and hierarchies did not exist within this group. In the realm of work, noblewomen supervised the production and exchange of craft goods, reserving the production of the most prized goods—especially high-quality, semi-finished cloth—for themselves.[52] While women of the ruling and noble class played a variety of social roles that afforded them prestige and authority, neither secular nor religious roles were linked to hierarchically organized, parallel structures of institutions or organizations like those of the Nahuas. Nonetheless, the complementarity of Ñudzahui noblemen's and women's political roles is repeated among commoners (or *ñandahi*) in the organization and activities of everyday life.

From personal names and the structuring of labor and work, to the passing on of property and rights to it, the Ñudzahui emphasized gender complementarity, not gender hierachy. For girls and boys, men and women, individual identity was rooted in the divinatory calendar from which one's name came, names that were not gender differentiated, unlike the Nahuas. As with rights of succession among the nobility, noble and commoner men and women owned property separately, inheriting it from their parents and passing it on to their children without pooling it under any male authority figure's control.[53] Labor patterns show more gender differentiation, but here complementarity linked to reciprocity shaped the way work was performed.

The Ñudzahui prehispanic gender division of labor, especially for nonelites, was structured around men planting and tending crops, undertaking communal labor projects, and transporting goods, and women spinning and weaving, preparing food and drink, gathering and preparing wild plants for food and medicines, and caring for young children.[54] While field and home each represented a base for the gendered division of labor, both men and women worked in a variety of settings with little indication of any distinction or ranking of public and private space. Fields and markets were sites of labor and exchange for both men and women. Domestic settings provided the arena for midwifery and healing, which involved women practitioners in cross-household exchanges of goods and services. While Ñudzahui men, especially noblemen, more frequently served as military and ritual leaders, or at least in the public performance of such roles, the Ñudzahui preferred a complementary organization of tasks that depended upon gender-based reciprocity and left less room for gender hierarchy to develop or flourish than among Nahuas.[55] It was not until after Spanish conquest that gender hierachy became more pronounced. But among the Maya, forms of gender hierarchy had deeper prehispanic roots.

The Maya of the Classic and Postclassic Periods:
The Flexible Patriarchy

Visual images of prehispanic Maya women come less from texts drawn or written on paper, such as the codices that Nahua and Ñudzahui scholars rely upon, and more from archaeological evidence. From the prehispanic Maya of the Yucatan and points south, from Guatemala to Honduras, the stone columns, known as stelae, that memorialize the histories of rulers of Maya cities and city-states, bas-relief carvings on buildings, figurines, murals, and painted pottery vessels show scenes of ritual and everyday life. While images of men predominate in Maya art, female images abound in sculpture, murals, painted ceramics, and figurines. These depictions suggest their importance to Maya courtly life.[56] But such depictions also suggest that their roles, while meaningful, were also secondary, even though gendered images sometimes expressed and even emphasized gender complementarity and interdependence rather than male dominance. How does the sumptuous, naturalistic, and highly expressive realm of Maya art portray women?

Much of this art, especially from the Classic period (ca. C.E. 250–900, for the Maya region specifically), treats Maya kings and nobles as the visual representation of Maya society. Such a style creates several interpretive problems for the modern viewer. Do such representations show Maya elites as they were, or do they show them as they wished to be shown? In either case, do these figures shed any light on everyday life and the lives of the vast majority of the Maya—the urban and rural inhabitants of the large, culturally complex, and varied Maya world? Through persistent and painstaking epigraphic study of these elite-centered images, scholars of the Maya have teased out a great deal of information about the prehispanic Maya world, a world of warrior kings, observant astronomers, and productive farmers and craftspeople. To discover what women's lives were like among the Maya, we begin by examining the images of noblewomen depicted on monuments and buildings.

Most human figures depicted in Classic period monumental or public Maya art are men, usually rulers, warriors, ritual leaders, or deities. Women's images are less numerous, appearing most frequently paired with men as mothers or as queen-consorts, with the maternal relationship often the one emphasized. Relatively rare early in the Classic, such images became more common later, after about C.E. 600.[57] But Maya visual designations of gender are relatively muted and shown primarily through clothing, rather than through sexually differentiated bodies, and such images appear more frequently at secondary centers rather than at the largest and most important cities. Noblewomen from cities such as Palenque probably served as a marriage pool from which the kings and high nobles of these more important centers sent wives to create or maintain political alliances with lesser cities or important kin groups. While some women may have ruled in their own right at sites such as Palenque, Yaxchilán, and Copán, images of women are fewer in number and do not depict them as equal partners in leadership.[58]

While the essence of Maya public art, in its gendered aspects, is androcentric, the repetitive use of male-female paired couples communicates a kind of complementarity or interdependence of men and women. Such images imply the necessary interdependence of both production and reproduction for individual, kin group, and community survival.[59] Yet the range of activities shown for women is much narrower than that of men and does not reflect their actual productive contribution. In addition, men often shed blood in this art, seemingly symbolically appropriating women's role in fertility.[60] Perhaps the Maya intended this gendered image to communicate interdependence *and* hierarchy (of both gender and class) at the same time. While the Maya ideological realm used, even emphasized, images conveying both gender complementarity and asymmetry and thus downplayed women's roles, the idea of complementarity appears in a narrower range of contexts, and the parallelism evident in Nahua institutions does not seem to have existed among the Maya. But what of women in everyday life—what kinds of roles of authority did they play? What kinds of work did they do, and how did they function in households and kin groups?

FIGURE 2.6. Pacal, the ruler of Palenque, is helped by his mother at his accession to the throne. Note the position of subordination she assumes. (From Linda Schele and David Friedel, *A Forest of Kings*, Morrow, New York, 1990, 227. Reprinted by permission of HarperCollins Publishers, Inc.)

Though women served as rulers at several Classic-period sites, holding such a position was unusual, probably a function of dynastic weakness, given the Maya preference for both patrilineal succession and primogeniture, especially at the largest and oldest Classic-period cities.[61] For example, when the ruler of Palenque, Pacal, inherited the throne from his mother, he created a dynastic history that his palace artists carved into his sarcophagus and the walls of the Temple of Inscriptions (his funerary building; see fig. 2.6). This self-fashioned dynastic history justified the break with the customary patrilineal succession pattern and at the same time demonstrated how unusual this break with customary practice was. A different pattern may have existed in smaller, more peripheral sites, like Cobá or Naranjo, where in-marrying elite women from major centers like Tikal are shown standing over captives or even carrying "military paraphernalia associated with male warriors or rulers."[62] Yet little other evidence suggests that Maya noblewomen, of either the Classic or Postclassic periods, customarily held offices, whether political, military, or ritual.

As war became an increasingly important part of mid- and late-Classic-period Maya culture, the public art produced typically does not associate women with war, either in the form of warrior goddesses, as did the Mexica, or women warriors, though there are a few exceptions. Two stelae from the sites of Cobá and Calakmul depict women standing on or over captives, and three stelae, two from Calakmul, the other from Usumacinta, show women with a scepter, a shield, or both.[63] At Yaxchilán (ca. 760), a bas-relief carving shows a noblewoman wearing a warrior's headdress, perhaps helping the ruler, Bird Jaguar, to dress for battle, and at Chichén Itzá, a female figure—an "old matriarch"—stands among the carved stone warrior columns of the Temple of the Warriors, which date from the late ninth century. This unusual female figure could represent the matriarch of the leading kin group of the city-state, or she could represent the Maya moon goddess, Ixchel (Lady or Woman Rainbow), patroness of weaving, childbirth, magic, and medicine, and consort of the important deity Itzamná, whose name means Lizard House, inventor of writing and patron of science and learning.[64] Women are never shown taking captives, though the famous late Classic Bonampak murals show them helping to arraign prisoners. Thus Maya sculptors and painters depicted war and politics as almost solely the preserve of Maya men. Yet in-marrying high-elite women, leaving major Maya centers to marry into secondary centers, as earlier described, may have held political offices, even controlling military power on occasion. Likewise, male leaders dominated the religious realm, but occasionally women were included.

Among Maya deities, the Moon Goddess, consort of the sun and sky deities, was the primary representation of women.[65] She is shown in a variety of forms during the Classic and Postclassic periods. Unquestionably, she was the most significant female deity, with archaeologists identifying most goddess images as this deity. During the Classic period, the Moon Goddess on public monuments is often shown seated in a crescent moon holding a rabbit (see fig. 2.7). She can be seen on figurines weaving, appearing either as a shy, youthful weaver or as a more overtly sexual figure, perhaps a courtesan. In the Postclassic period, Ixchel (as she was then known) is also shown in a dualistic style, but age, young versus old, becomes the primary differentiating feature. Apart from her association with weaving, she was identified with fertility, curing, and the earth. The Itzá Maya particularly worshiped Ixchel at her shrine site on Cozumel Island.[66]

In addition to the Moon Goddess, represented as "Woman, first woman, and mother of mankind," other, though lesser, female deities existed.[67] Goddesses associated with Venus and the sun appear on Classic painted ceramic vessels and may be female versions of the Maya ancestral twins, who represent the Sun and Venus and who originated ruling dynasties. While one or more female deities often appear with a male figure in these images, they do not depict a gendered duality underlying creation. Instead the pottery displays female figures with motifs or images that repeat and reinforce masculine solar and Venutian design elements.[68] Other ceramic vessels contain images of primordial earth goddesses associated with death, a possible *pulque* goddess (pulque being a fermented drink made from the maguey plant), and female attendants to the *pauahtuns*, or gods who held up the four corners of

FIGURE 2.7. The Moon Goddess shown inside a moon glyph. (From Linda Schele and David Friedel, *A Forest of Kings*, Morrow, New York, 1990, 412. Reprinted by permission of HarperCollins Publishers, Inc.)

the earth. Shown actively assisting in rituals of purification associated with the pauahtuns, yet clearly the consorts of them, these images imply a female role in religious ritual.[69]

Maya women participated in a variety of rituals, from the self-sacrifice associated with accession to a throne to more mundane birth rituals, but there is little evidence to indicate female religious functionaries, at least in temples. Chronicles from the early colonial period observe that during the late Postclassic period, Maya women helped prepare ritual offerings of food, textiles, and incense. On the rare occasions they entered temples, only older women were permitted to do so, though a woman known as the Ix Mol helped initiate girls into the practice of becoming good workers during the month of Yaxkin. Active participants in household rituals, some focused on fertility and pregnancy, as well as producers of ritual items, the women of Maya Classic and Postclassic societies probably did not participate in a true hierarchy of priestesses as did Mexica women.[70] But greater similarity in women's activities can be found in the realm of everyday life where, like Nahua and Ñudzahui women, Maya women, noble and commoner, actively participated in household and community economies.

Maya women of the Classic period labored at a variety of tasks. Painted ceramics show their primary responsibilities to have been the preparation of food, which included grinding maize and cooking it and other food items, and the production of woven textiles. Men provided many of the necessary raw materials by farming and hunting, and they also labored as ritual specialists and soldiers (with the latter roles perhaps limited to the nobility). The first Spanish observers of the late Postclassic Maya recorded a more extensive list of tasks performed by women, many of which also probably applied to the earlier Classic period. Household lands, for example, were worked in cooperation with other community members, and women may well have participated in such agricultural work. Known to be especially active in working the gardens adjacent to their households, they also raised small animals such as dogs, pigs, bees, fowl, and other birds. Necessary for household survival, such labor also would have provided the food and other goods needed for intra- and intercommunity exchange and tribute payments, and even noblewomen may have produced the textiles used in rituals and elite exchanges of goods.[71]

Women did not perform their labors alone. Instead their work was often carried out in large households that relied upon the labor of wives, daughters, daughters-in-law, servants, and sometimes even orphans or slaves, who wove and spun in large work groups.[72] Kinship structures—which emphasized men over women—probably provided the basis for organizing this household labor. The Classic and Postclassic kinship systems highlighted ties among and through men as the primary basis for kin group membership and transmission of more valued property, especially land, yet recognized women as mothers and progenitors.

Many scholars of Maya prehistory believe that patrilineality is a deeply rooted, ancient feature of Maya society. They note that in contemporary Maya communities, lowland and highland, kin groups and households are structured by both patrilineal descent and patrilocal patterns of postmarital residence, where brides move into the household of their husbands' fathers. Other evidence of patrilineality includes the many indications that primogeniture was the primary means of succession for Maya Classic and Postclassic rulers and the emphasis in Maya languages on kin terminologies that reflect patrilineal descent.[73]

Although patriliny is often associated with gender asymmetry, prehistoric Maya households and kin groups may have been characterized by a flexible, rather than strict, system that recognized women's contributions to households of their reproductive capacities and productive labor.[74] While the Maya Classic and Postclassic elite emphasized male leadership and patrilineal chains of success to ruling positions, they also accorded some recognition to bilateral kinship. Like the Mexica and Ñudzahui, Maya rulers were ennobled by both their fathers *and* their mothers. Indeed, the word for "noble," *almehen*, was a word compounded of elements referring to a woman's offspring (*al*) and a man's sons (*mehen*). Women were primarily responsible for the worship of household ancestors, and worship in the late Postclassic often included reverence for female ancestors.[75]

The late Classic period might have been the time when two related but contradictory and persistent elements of Maya gender relations emerged. On the one hand, the growth of Maya urban centers, intensifying warfare, and the increasing importance and power of kings and nobles reinforced male dominance as both ideology and lived experience. On the other, women from the most powerful centers were prized as wives, some women may well have held leadership positions in smaller centers, and the household labor of noble and non-noble women became more valuable for exchange and tribute in the growing and more warlike Maya city-states. The "active but circumscribed" roles played by Maya women are reminiscent of Nahua gender concepts and practices, but the Maya apparently confined women's roles to a narrower range of contexts, and the parallelism evident in Nahua institutions did not exist among this other important Mesoamerican indigenous group.[76]

The Andes: Women and Supernatural and State Power

South America as a whole encompassed great variability in the types of cultures and economies that arose during the thousands of years of indigenous cultural development and florescence. Yet a fundamental cultural division in South America existed between highland cultures, located along the western side of the Andes, and the lowland cultures of central and eastern South America. The former experienced the development of complex civilizations and empires, with their large, dense populations, several times in that region. Among South America's Andean cultures, archaeologists have discovered an ancient tradition of female supernaturals, perhaps older than in Mesoamerica. Another contrast between Mesoamerica and highland South America is that in Mesoamerica work patterns were highly gendered and broadly similar across the regions described in this book, yet women's other roles varied, depending especially on the elaboration of markets and full-time specialization as well as military organization. As we move further south into the Andean region, we find more overlap in men's and women's work patterns and an ancient history of women holding institutionalized roles of authority.[77]

Gender roles in everyday life in the earliest cultures and first civilizations of the Andes prior to the rise and expansion of the Inka appear to have been relatively egalitarian. The discovery that images of female supernaturals, especially the Staff Goddess (see fig. 2.8), are very old in this part of Latin America, with the earliest image perhaps dating to 2250 B.C.E. (or more than 4,000 years ago, during the Peruvian Preceramic period) provides important evidence.

Associated also with such early cultures and art styles as Chavín and Yaya-Mama that date to about 1500 B.C.E., Andean peoples early on conceived of supernatural power as both male and female. For later periods, scholars must often contend with art styles, whether ceramic, textile, or sculptural, that are often rather abstract and highly stylized, even geometrical, in design (see figs. 2.9 and 2.10). Later cultures discussed in this chapter date to the Middle Horizon, beginning about C.E. 600, the late Intermediate (C.E. 1000–1476), and the late Horizon, ending in the early 1530s with the arrival of Francisco Pizarro and his band of fellow conquerors.[78]

One of the Andean cultures with a more naturalistic art style is the Moche culture of northern Peru (ca. C.E. 100–800). Well known in part because of its

FIGURE 2.8. A Chavín Staff Goddess image from the southern Peruvian coastal site of Carhua. (Drawing by Dwight T. Wallace, from *Paracas Art and Architecture*, edited by Ann Paul, University of Iowa Press, Iowa City, 1991, 76. Courtesy of University of Iowa Press.)

engaging and realistic art style, it is also renowned because this early complex culture, while not fully urban, featured several ceremonial centers, as well as a regional polity created through both warfare and the spread of an identifiable ideology and art style. Moche-style burials suggest the existence of two social strata, with elites interred in more elaborate burial sites than commoners. The Moche gave such burials to royal males who were accompanied by human sacrifices, as well as, perhaps, by the remains of their female ancestors. Some elite females, perhaps either priestesses or impersonators of an important female supernatural, also received special burials.[79]

Other images come from Moche ceramics, which offer literally thousands of depictions of people, rituals, deities, animals, and plants. Some of these images relate clearly to the everyday world, some to the supernatural world, and some to a domain of ancestors who appear to mediate between the two.[80] In scenes of the everyday, women are shown either working—making textiles or preparing food—or in depictions of childbirth and motherhood. They do not appear in battle scenes, and their depictions are generally less varied than

FIGURE 2.9. A Paracas textile from coastal Peru with mythical crea-
ture design, probably produced after 500 B.C. (From Ferdinand Anton,
Altindianische Textilkunst aus Peru, List/Seeman Verlage, Munich, 1984,
66. Courtesy of List/Seeman Verlage.)

those of men. In scenes of the ancestral and sacred worlds, images of women
again are more limited. They are shown in peripheries of scenes, as helpmates
to deities, for example, though some scenes feature female shamans as well as
a female supernatural who is depicted in the context of prisoner sacrifice and
the offering of blood (see fig. 2.11).[81]

A rather interesting aspect of Moche art is reflected in a subset of Moche
ceramics, those taking sexuality as their theme. Many ceramics depict or are
shaped as phalluses; others show couples engaged in sex. Moche craft producers portrayed a wide range of sexual practices, including same-sex male
couplings. While fewer in number, there are also vaginal images. Although a
phallic emphasis is discernible in Moche erotic art, the copulation scenes are
very natural and are neither violent nor degrading to women.[82] What these
images do evoke is a seeming emphasis on masculinity, with a secondary but
possibly linked emphasis on fertility (see fig. 2.12).

Apart from the Moche culture, other contemporaneous local cultures
and art styles, also in the northern region, offer images of prominent women,
perhaps carrying out specific political and religious roles. The Recuay-style
pottery of the Callejón de Huaylas region of north-central Peru features
images showing both men and women, sometimes a central male figure sur-
rounded by warriors and other attendants (who on occasion are female), and
sometimes individual portrait-like depictions of men or women alone or
in couples.[83] While men are generally shown with more ornate decorative
accoutrements such as headgear or earspools, images like the "Prominent
Woman" could indicate female authority (see fig. 2.13).

The site of Queyash Alto in the same area contains evidence of feasting
by high-ranking families or kin groups. Artifacts such as spindle whorls and
women's clothing pins (called *tupu* pins) may indicate areas within households
where women undertook work tasks such as weaving and food preparation
for feasting. Archaeologist Joan Gero also found that families buried women
under house floors, indicating their centrality in households and kin groups.

FIGURE 2.10. Above: An Inka textile, a shirt known as an *uncu*.
(Neg. no. 2A23893, courtesy of Department of Library Services,
American Museum of Natural History.) Facing page: A picture of a
quya wearing a woven garment with a similar geometric design. (From
Felipe Guaman Poma de Ayala, *La nueva crónica y buen gobierno*, Fondo
de Cultura Económica, Mexico City, 1980, 1:112.)

She speculates that even though images of female supernaturals are absent
from the site, women held power connected to the political and administrative aspects of ritualized feasting. In Gero's view, such activities depended
upon women's political as well as culinary skills, making women and men
interdependent in the feasting context.[84]

Female deities, discernible in other later pre-Inka Andean cultures and
archaeological sites such as Wari and Tiwanaku, provide further clues to the
existence of Andean ideas of gender interdependence and female power. These
sites were each the center of an important pre-Inka empire. The Tiwanaku
civilization of central Peru began to develop during the third century C.E.

LAOTAVA COÍA
MAMAÍVITOCA
IAN

Reyno lima xauxa chinchaycocha

mama

FIGURE 2.11. A Moche supernatural with long braids that are snakes presents a goblet of blood to a deity. (Drawing by Donna McClelland.)

FIGURE 2.12. A Moche erotic figurine. (Redrawn from Federico Kaufmann Doig, *Comportamiento sexual en el antiguo Peru*, Kompactos, Lima, 1978, p. 113.)

FIGURE 2.13. The Recuay "Prominent Woman." She appears alone on this vessel, but on others she appears with a male of equal size. (From Karen Olsen Bruhns, *Ancient South America*, Cambridge University Press, Cambridge, 1994, 192. Reprinted with the permission of Cambridge University Press and Karen Olsen Bruhns.)

While its primary deity was male, similar to the Chavín Staff God, female supernaturals can be found among Tiwanaku images but do not seem as central to this civilization's iconography as do such images for the somewhat later, but overlapping, Wari civilization (ca. C.E. 500–800) to the north. While a male deity received emphasis in early Wari images, a female deity began to be depicted soon thereafter. She was shown on ceramics and in textiles associated with maize and may well have had lunar associations, paired with the probable solar associations of the primary male supernatural. The civilizations succeeding Tiwanaku and Wari do not offer as many female supernatural images, though the Andean north coast, a region with some geographic overlap with the later Inka state, featured many images of women in figurines and on pottery.[85] Although Inka iconography, as represented on textile, ceramic, or stone, does not offer many female supernatural images, written sources—Spanish and indigenous—provide us with descriptions of Inka goddesses, as well as descriptions of women's activities and roles.

The spiritual world of the Inka consisted of at least two realms, one of gods and goddesses, the other a realm of sacred objects and places known as *wak'as* that included "ancestor mummies, mountains, rocks, and springs."[86] The most powerful deity, Wiracocha, was an androgynous creator deity whose place was at the top of the Inka cosmological order. Beneath Wiracocha, a series of gods existed, male and female, with Inti, the solar deity, and Illapa, the thunder deity, being the primary male gods. The Inka cosmology prominently featured female deities like Mamaquilla, the moon goddess (and wife of the sun), and Pachamama, the earth's mother. Pachamama's daughters, linked to specific crops and other valued goods, were also sacred: Saramama (tied to maize), Axomama (potatoes), Cocamama (coca), Coyamama (precious metals), and Sañumama (clay). Mamacocha, who was a sea deity, was also female. Andeans seem to have generally associated male gods with natural phenomena, placating them through sacrifices and offerings, and female deities with that which was necessary for human subsistence and survival, especially the earth, food, and water. The Inka grafted both their greater reverence for the Sun God, as well as a more hierarchical conceptualization of deities, onto a preexisting, cosmological structure. Because conquest had been an Andean reality for over a thousand years, this structure connected male deities (in particular, Illapa) and conquest. But until the Inka it did not feature the clearly organized male and female hierarchies that Inka rulers used as an ideological device to incorporate conquered peoples into their empire.[87]

Other Andean and Inka female supernaturals existed in the period prior to the Spanish conquest. Some were local goddesses connected to fertility, sexuality, the moon, and water, while others were wak'as, ancestral, sometimes mythical, women, who were worshiped as founding mothers.[88] One of these, Mama Huaco, daughter of the Sun and Moon, became the founding mother of the Inka dynasty. She was considered sower of the first corn and a fierce warrior implicated in the destruction of the Guallas, a group that opposed Inka conquest. Mama Huaco, as sister and wife of Manco Capac, the first supreme ruler or Inka, became the first *quya*, or queen, and tied the Inka supernatural realm to the everyday realm of men, and especially women.[89]

Like the hierarchy embedded in the Inka cosmology, the Inka conquest state, with its capital city of Cuzco, had a hierarchically organized politico-administrative structure. A male supreme ruler and his consort headed this structure. The quya, always a sister of the Inka, presided over women's religious organizations, especially during the month that Quya raymi was celebrated. This imperial festival honored both the Moon and the queen and coincided with the September equinox, when both the new agricultural cycle and rainy season began again. The ethnohistorian Irene Silverblatt argues that this "was a time when female concerns, as Andean society so defined them, were given voice."[90] Like other imperial rituals, Quya raymi included the parades of mummies of past Inkas and quyas, and the Inka people supported both the ancestral cults of deceased quyas and the living quyas through labor, lands, and offerings. These female leaders presided over female-centered rituals and a world of women that was parallel with, yet subordinate to, especially in political and military affairs, the world of men. While not paramount ruler, a quya could have authority over the king's domain in his absence. She also decided matters in cases when the Inka's highest council, composed of delegates from the four provincial divisions of the empire, was deadlocked. Local leaders known as *kurakas* replicated the more earthly, mundane powers of rulers. While often male, they were sometimes female, especially in the northern area of the Inka empire. Women called *capullanas,* who may have succeeded to their offices through their matrilines, were known to lead northern coastal ethnic groups at times.[91]

Women's sacred and earthly roles of authority were rooted in a kinship system that featured parallel lines of descent, one through men, another through women, within the *ayllu*, the basic Andean kinship unit. This unit might consist of extended families, larger kin groups within *señoríos* (seignorial domains), or ethnically defined communities as a whole, or even extend, "as the Incas would have it, to an empire."[92] While early colonial chronicles, most written by Spaniards, provide little information describing the activities of female kurakas within Andean communities, it is clear that the Inka reinforced, perhaps even heightened, the power of local headmen as the communities and regions they represented became parts of the Inka empire. Male power and authority increased as the growing imperial domain absorbed local ethnic groups and ayllu communities. This imperial expansion affected everyone in domains incorporated by the Inka.

Local peoples felt this impact primarily through changing patterns of labor. While Andeans differentiated between the types of labor carried out by women and men, with women more focused on weaving, food preparation, preparing of fields for cultivation, and childcare, and men on plowing fields, harvesting crops, herding llamas and alpacas, and combat, there was in fact overlap of male and female tasks. Both men and women farmed, each doing a particular set of tasks.[93] Weaving was another area where there was overlap. While weaving was considered a quintessentially female task, symbol-ized by the inclusion of cotton and spindles in shrines for female ancestors, boys and men could spin or weave rough cloth. Male specialist weavers, called *kumpi-kamayuq*, also produced fine cloth (*kumpi*), as did the *aqllas*, or Chosen Women. Even mining, in some areas, was carried out by families, with both men and women participating.[94]

Inka demands for labor appear, nevertheless, to have made the gender divison of labor more rigid, with men being called on for labor or military service and women increasing their output of yarn, 'awasqa or coarse cloth, and *chicha*, the maize beer often consumed in community feasts throughout the Andes past and present.[95] While men throughout the Inka empire could regularly expect to be called upon to provide labor for state uses (*mit'a*) in the army, for public works projects or transportation of goods, or crafts produc-tion, some women, the aqllas, might also be called upon to provide special services for the Inka state.

Representatives of the Inka selected girls between the ages of eight and ten from all over the Inka realm to come to the capital or other cities to carry out a variety of tasks. Some aqllas, those of Inka blood, were considered sacred. As wives of the Sun, they were expected to remain virgins throughout their lives. Others were consecrated to other gods or were chosen by the Inka to be among the Sun's secondary wives. The supreme ruler could also give them to close associates or the kurakas of Inka-controlled provinces as wives. Those who were less prized worked hard for the Inka state, caring for shrines, participating in rituals, preparing chicha for the gods, and, most important, weaving the fine textiles that circulated through the empire to be used for gifts or in ceremonies. Aqllas trained, worked, and lived in special state-con-structed housing, the *aqlla wasi*, found both in the Inka capital of Cuzco and regional capitals. Known as *mamaqunas*, some aqllas became priestesses who also served as the teachers of the young Chosen Women.[96]

The aqllas as a group represent the ability of Inka state power to con-trol women's sexuality as well as their labor power, but this institution also contained within it a female leadership hierarchy. While mamaqunas did not marry, provincial priestesses did, apparently sometimes passing their positions on to their daughters.[97] Like Nahua patterns, this hierarchy was not as deep as male hierarchies of authority and leadership, yet women clearly served in leadership positions. While most scholars do not see Andean women, within their respective strata, as the equals in power or authority of either noble or commoner men, they nevertheless recognize Andean women of the late prehispanic era as capable, even powerful, in their own right.[98] Even the sec-ondary wives of the Inka—whose positions surely depended upon provincial leaders' use of their daughters as political pawns—acted in political, even military, capacities.

The secondary wives and daughters of the penultimate ruler of the prehispanic era, Huayna Capac, illustrate the complexity of women's place. Undoubtedly privileged by receiving gifts of labor, houses, and perhaps lands as well, they experienced little real contact with their husbands and would be punished severely for any adulterous relationships. This was true even of the lowliest of such wives, those given by lower ranked provincial leaders. Yet one of Huayna Capac's secondary wives, Contarguacho (from the kingdom of Hatun Jauja), led an army allied with the Spanish to ward off an Inka-led uprising against them.[99] Her daughter, Quispe Sisa, became a concubine of Francisco Pizarro, Spanish conqueror of the Inka, when she was twelve or thirteen. She was baptized and given the name *doña* Inés Yupanqui (using the Spanish title of respect). But Peruvian ethnohistorian Waldemar Espinosa Soriano observes that she was never truly Pizarro's wife nor even a lover treated with real affection. Instead she functioned more like a servant and bore Pizarro two children, *don* Gonzalo and doña Francisca Pizarro.

Quispe Sisa was far from the only indigenous woman to come into intimate contact with a Spanish conqueror. One noted historian goes so far as to refer to the Spanish conquests in the Americas of the late fifteenth and early sixteenth centuries as "the conquest of women."[100] Why would these conquests be referred to this way? What did indigenous women, both noble and commoner, experience during and after this period of tremendous violence and culturally destructive consolidation of Iberian rule?

Conclusion

The groups focused on in this chapter present us with a surprisingly varied picture of gender relations. The Mexica cognatic kinship system underlay a tendency toward parallel gender institutions, yet male dominance existed and was heightened by the militarism of their society. While warlike, the Ñudzahui had no empire and had less developed systems of hierarchy, labor specialization, and exchange, so that while their highest leaders were, in a very real sense, male and female coleaders, there is little evidence of parallel-structured political, economic, or religious institutions. Prehispanic Maya society demonstrated the greatest degree of male dominance, yet this was a flexible dominance, variably expressed. The Maya patrilineal kinship structures, which emphasized ties from and through men and in which daughters left their natal households at or after marriage, are ancient and probably date back to the increasing stratification and intensifying warfare of the Classic period. The Maya, too, while highly skilled in agriculture and crafts production, had fewer full-time occupational specialists than did Nahuas, resulting in fewer opportunities for parallel institutions and positions. While Andean cultures varied in their depictions of female supernaturals and everyday roles, images of female power are very old. The Inka, also empire builders, represent the closest parallel to Nahua gender relations. Blending complementarity and subordination, elite and commoner women made major economic contributions, fulfilled socially recognized roles of authority, and enjoyed some degree of autonomy from fathers and husbands.

In the Americas, Europeans encountered an array of gendered systems of power and authority. Among a number of Circum-Caribbean peoples who included the Tainos of the Caribbean, the late prehispanic Panamanian societies ancestral to, among others, the San Blas Kuna, and the Sinú of northern Colombia, the Europeans even found female rulers. The Sinú, for example, treated their *cacica* (one leader in an indigenous tripartite authority structure, whose other leaders were male, and whom we know only as the "señora" [lady or madam] or "cacica" of Finzenú), with great reverence.[101] But as Iberians brought a more patriarchal gender system to the Americas, female systems of authority became weakened. The next chapter examines the gendered impact of the intense clash of cultures that occurred, as well as the consequences of the imposition of colonial rule for native women.

3

Colliding Worlds

Indigenous Women, Conquest, and Colonialism

That women played a variety of roles during the conquest and colonial periods almost goes without saying. However, one woman in particular has gone down in history as especially noteworthy during this period. She is Malinche, or doña Marina, or Malintzin, the variously named translator and sometime consort of the conqueror of the Nahuas of central Mexico, Hernán Cortés. Though no documents exist in which she narrates or interprets her life in her own voice, Spanish sources often refer to her somewhat ironically as *la lengua* (tongue). Her image and life illustrate in microcosm the ways that sexuality and gender were part of the process of conquest (see figs. 3.1 and 3.2). The illustrations, while different, recall some of the strength implicit in the Coyolxauhqui image discussed in the last chapter, but her life course tellingly foreshadows the conquerors' treatment of the indigenous women on whom they depended and with whom they had intimate relations. While Malintzin herself played an important public role in the events of conquest, other women experienced diminished public roles. And she gave birth to children who were among the first mestizo children of mainland Spanish America, helping to set off the development of mixed ethno-racial identities whose existence would complicate both gender and racial hierarchies.

This chapter explores this decline at the same time that it highlights a historical counterpoint, one in which native women demonstrated an admirable capacity to survive, adjust to, or resist myriad changes, barriers, and problems. While multifaceted transformational influences, especially new forms of labor extraction and a new religious belief system that stressed women's passivity, enclosure, purity, and honor, ended in a widespread dimi-

FIGURE 3.1. Malintzin watches as the Spanish arrive. (From
Florentine Codex, General History of the Things of New Spain,
translated by Arthur J. O. Anderson and Charles Dibble, University of
Utah Press, Salt Lake City, bk. 12, image no. 1. Courtesy of University
of Utah Press.)

nution of women's power and authority, women nevertheless were important, active presences in colonial societies. Through their work, their activities
in households as wives, mothers, and daughters, and their roles as community
elders and defenders, they used legal and extralegal means to protect both
themselves and others.[1]

The chapter seeks to describe the specificity of women's experiences
in the colonial world in relationship to work, family and sexuality, religion,
and politics and thereby to analyze the role of gender as a factor in conquest
and colonial rule. Images of the conquest are themselves gendered, not only
because Iberian conquerors brought to the Americas a masculine sensibility
that connected sexuality and conquest but also because indigenous participation in the conquests is symbolized most often not by the indigenous male
translators, who were actually more numerous during and after the conquest,
but by the female translator for Cortés, Malintzin.[2] Who was she? Why does
she carry such a heavy symbolic load?

FIGURE 3.2. Malintzin at Cortés's side as he receives gifts from one of a group of Tlaxcalan lords. (From Alfredo Chavero, *Lienzo de Tlaxcala*, in *Antigüedades mexicanas*, 1892, Oficina Tipográfica de la Secretaría de Fomento, Mexico City, pl. 28. Courtesy of the Benson Latin American Collection, University of Texas, Austin.)

Gender, Sex, and Violence in the Conquest Era

The very name of the young slave woman who lived and worked among the Gulf Coast Chontal Maya in the community of Potonchan is in doubt. While many writers assert that the Spanish gave her the name Marina because it closely matched her indigenous name Malinalli, Malina (or Malintzin, an honorific form used in indigenous-produced texts) more probably reflected a native pronunciation of the name "Marina," which was given to her by a priest in 1519.[3] Whatever her birth name, that she would become known by the Nahuatlized version of her name, Malintzin, is appropriate, because she was not Maya in origin but had been born among Gulf Coast Nahuatl speakers. Thought by Bernal Díaz del Castillo, a member of Cortés's expedition and author of the most informative source about her, to have been born to a noble family, Malintzin was given away after her father died and her mother remarried. She eventually ended up among Maya speakers who, in turn, gave her to Cortés in 1519.[4] Malintzin's early life was marked by loss of family and movement, a not uncommon experience for women before, during, and after the arrival of Europeans. Among Cortés and his group, her Maya-Nahuatl bilingualism became useful. Before she learned Spanish and some Spaniards learned Nahuatl, Cortés was forced to rely on a chain of translators, which included Malintzin, who translated from Nahuatl to Maya, and Gerónimo de Aguilar, a Spaniard who had been enslaved by Yucatec Maya after a ship-wreck in 1511, who translated from Maya to Spanish. Malintzin soon became trilingual by becoming fluent enough in Spanish to translate directly, though by then some Spaniards were also comfortable enough speaking Nahuatl to translate. She served as Cortés's primary translator throughout the conquest of the Mexica and even after, including on his ill-conceived march to Hondu-ras. However, as both Spanish and indigenous sources make clear, Malintzin's importance lay not only in her translation work but also in her loyalty to the Spanish cause.

That Malintzin was loyal to the Spanish cannot be doubted. While she aided the Spanish on several occasions, her role in the very bloody Span-ish massacre that took place in Cholula (after she reported to Cortés about Cholulan plans to aid a Mexica attack on the Spanish) is the event that forms the basis of the Mexican popular view of her as the very definition of an informer and traitor. But her role in the execution of Cuauhtemoc, the last Mexica supreme ruler, may even better illustrate her deep loyalty to the Span-ish, since not only was she present for his execution but she also helped two Franciscan friars as they ministered to him before his execution.[5]

Was the source of this loyalty love? Malintzin had relationships with two Spaniards, Alonso Hernández de Puertocarrero, to whom she was given by Cortés and stayed with for only a short time in 1519, and Cortés himself, with whom she had a son. Cortés then married her to a third, Juan Jaramillo—with whom she went on to have two more children—in what Cortés's secretary-chaplain, Francisco López de Gómara, viewed as an inappropriate wedding because the groom was intoxicated throughout. Did love play a role in these relationships? Was she driven by a very pragmatic will to survive? Or was she driven, at least in part, by an anti-Mexica desire to overthrow imperial domi-nation, perhaps born of bitterness over the several brutal turns her life had taken? Her actions, not inconsistent with an anti-Mexica sentiment, are the actions of a woman who made choices among the limited and unsatisfactory set of options presented by others—Nahua, Maya, Spanish—to her. And she could hardly be a traitor to the Mexican nation when no such nation existed. Passed from group to group and man to man, her role as translator was highly unusual for the time and rooted in her own exceptional abilities and the circumstances in which she found herself. Yet the pathos of her existence as object to be used and passed along, is undeniable and exemplifies the prag-matic, even uncaring, nature of most relations between Spanish conquerors and indigenous women.[6]

The actions of Cortés himself epitomize the often fleeting quality of relationships between the male conquerors and the female conquered. In addition to fathering four children with his Spanish wife and another out of wedlock with another Spanish woman, he was reported to have four mestizo children, each by a different mother. One of the women was Malintzin; another was Tecuichpochtzin, a daughter of Moteuczoma.[7] Such transitory relations were perhaps a variant of other, still more exploitative, and even violent, relationships between European conquerors and indigenous women caught up in the tumultuous events of the late fifteenth and sixteenth centuries.

The relations between Spanish men and native women took several forms. One, already mentioned, is the informal relationship that, while variable in length and depth of affection, often resulted in a child or children who may have been legitimated by their Spanish fathers and remembered with property in their wills. Such was the case with several of Cortés's mestizo children and with the children Pizarro had with Quispe Sisa. Those children whom conquerors legitimated did not live long with their native mothers. Malintzin's son, don Martín, was separated from his parents by the march to Honduras and was later taken by Cortés to Spain, where he lived most of the rest of his life. Pizarro's children—at least the two he had with Quispe Sisa, whom he subsequently legitimated—were taken from their mother's care and given to his half-brother and wife to raise according to Spanish custom.[8]

Other relationships resulted in marriages, legal and religious unions that were as stable as others of the same time period. However much affection may have motivated these marriages, status, wealth, and security probably played a greater role, as most involved native women born to noble families, especially those that owned landed estates. Sometimes native fathers presented their daughters to the Spanish conquerors, continuing a preexisting way of creating and maintaining political ties, in the hopes of solidifying alliances, as in the case of the Tlaxcalan leaders' donation of women, slave women, and their own daughters. In other cases, powerful Spaniards arranged marriages between indigenous women and some of their men, as Cortés did with Malintzin and Pizarro did with Quispe Sisa, marrying her to a man who had been his servant.[9] Combining elements of both spousal and parental roles, such arrangements continued well into the sixteenth century. In 1566, a wealthy Spanish resident of Cuzco, Arías Maldonado, promoted a marriage between his brother Cristóbal and his eight-year-old Inka stepdaughter doña Beatriz Clara Coya, granddaughter of Manco Inka (ally of and later rebel against the Spanish; see fig. 3.3). A formal betrothal and even intercourse took place. When the Maldonados were arrested, doña Beatriz went on to marry another Spaniard, don Martín García de Loyola, in a marriage arranged by the viceroy, don Francisco Toledo. In this instance, the use of coercive sex in the interest of fortune hunting is very clear.[10]

The women's views on any of these relationships remain unknown, though one historian speculates that the Guaraní women of a vast region stretching across northeastern South America willingly served Spaniards as sexual companions, interpreters, and laborers because they valued the gifts

FIGURE 3.3.   The marriage of doña Beatriz Clara Coya to don
Martín García de Loyola, as depicted in a painting in the Iglesia de
la Compañía del Cuzco. (Photo courtesy of the Emilio Harth-Terré
Collection, Latin American Library, Tulane University.)

of clothing and other items given by the Spanish.[11] Nor do we know how
the few Spanish women who married native men, virtually always from the
highest ranking royal families, perceived their relationships. Youth, family
pressure, and hopes of material benefit seem to have played a role in many
such arrangements. The children of these mixed marriages tended to be more
acculturated than their native peers and often married Spaniards.[12] Whatever the differences in culture, wealth, and power between partners, some of
these relationships endured, in sharp contrast to the third type of relationship,
which was brief and violent and in which sex served neither as expression of
affection nor tool of acculturation but instead as a weapon of war.

The full range of male-female relationships and violence committed specifically against women occurred early in the Caribbean, where informal
relationships, marriages, sexual coercion, and rape all took place. For some
Spaniards, marriages with high-ranking island women—while clearly inferior
in the eyes of fellow settlers to marriages with Spanish women—nevertheless offered the possibility of raising one's social status, wealth, and access to
labor within indigenous communities. For example, very early in the sixteenth century, the Spaniard Sebastián de Viloria hoped to marry Anacaona,
the Taino cacica, in order to become ruler of her group. But this scenario
proved uncommon, because on both the islands of the Caribbean as well as
on the mainland, Spaniards never lost their preference for Spanish wives. In

addition, the use of women as a tool of conquest led many native women to fear and reject European men, a rejection for which Anacaona herself paid with her life.[13]

While consensual sexual relations underlay some of the relationships already mentioned, Iberian notions of a New World sexual paradise of wild and welcoming women were vastly overstated. Descriptions of violent incidents suggest that European men treated coercion as a normal part of the range of sexual relations, and everywhere Iberians went, from the Caribbean to California to Peru, sexual violations occurred.[14] Although rape is a difficult term to define across cultures or time, it seems fair to say that Spanish and Portuguese chronicles contain many descriptions of coercive relations in which various kinds of pressure—psychological, social, physical—were brought to bear on sex acts.[15] The famous passage by Michele de Cuneo, an Italian nobleman who sailed with Columbus, illustrates such a relationship:

> While I was in the boat I captured a very beautiful Carib woman, whom the said Lord Admiral gave to me, and with whom, having taken her into my cabin, she being naked according to their custom, I conceived desire to take pleasure. I wanted to put my desire into execution but she did not want it and treated me with her finger nails in such a manner that I wished I had never begun. But seeing that (to tell you the end of it all), I took a rope and thrashed her well, for which she raised such unheard of screams that you would not have believed your ears. Finally we came to an agreement in such a manner that I can tell you that she seemed to have been brought up in a school of harlots.[16]

Even more violent than Cuneo's account is a passage by Diego de Landa in which he describes Maya women's pride in their modesty and chastity and then goes on to narrate a chilling incident.

> They prided themselves on being good and they had good reason to; for before they became acquainted with our nation, according to the old men who are complaining of it today, they were marvellously chaste. . . . Captain Alonso Lopez de Avila, brother-in-law of the *Adelantado* Montejo, had captured a young Indian woman, who was both beautiful and pleasing, when he was engaged in the war of Bacalar. She had promised her husband, who feared that he would be killed in the war, not to have relations with another than he; and so no persuasion was sufficient to prevent her giving up her life so as not to be defiled by another man, on which account they caused her to be put to death by dogs.[17]

Other Europeans condemned such behavior, most notably Bartolomé de las Casas, in his volume *Brevísima relación de la destrucción de las Indias*, a work depicting the Spanish in the Caribbean as murderers and rapists. The early chronicler of Peru, Pedro Cieza de León, criticized the conquerors and early settlers there for seizing and putting to their own uses the wives and daughters of native men.[18]

While it might be going too far to say that rape was a consciously used strategic tool in conquest and colonial rule, that sexual coercion was part of the process of Iberian exploration and conquest cannot be denied. Yet the frequency of sexual violence and the willingness of military leaders such as Cortés and Pizarro to distribute indigenous women among their close lieutenants suggest that conquerors indeed used "the phallus as an extension of the sword."[19] Seeing women as objects whose bodies could be conquered and who could be given as material reward was linked to another use of indigenous women, women as domestic servants. Francisco Pizarro's younger half-brother, Juan, for example, left his entire fortune to *his* younger brother, Gonzalo, leaving nothing to an indigenous woman from whom he "received service." She gave birth to a girl who may have been his daughter and whom he refused to recognize. For the Inka chronicler Guaman Poma, sexual abuse of women became part of the fabric of colonial life. He charged that women who performed labor connected to mining and domestic work in Spanish households were not only subject to labor abuse and theft of possessions by men of all ethnicities but also that they were frequently raped as well (see figs. 3.4 and 3.5). In Brazil, enslavement of and concubinage with indigenous women were closely connected.[20]

Before considering further how conquest was connected to the all-important resource for Spaniards, native labor, another aspect of native women's experiences during the conquest years must be discussed: their resistance to the sexual depredations of European conquerors and their resistance to European conquest. Although women and their kin often accepted relationships with Iberian men, women, their kin, and their communities resisted them as well. From rejection of individual sex acts, for which a woman risked harsh physical punishment, even death, to abortion, suicide, or communal resistance, clear evidence of frequent defiance exists. Women at times not only resisted the Iberian search for sexual satisfaction and subjugation but also sometimes participated in military resistance against European invaders. Natives destroyed the first Spanish community on Hispaniola, La Navidad, in 1493, leaving all its Spanish inhabitants for dead, as the community responded to Spanish attempts at coercive relations with local women. Even though the Mexica protected daughters of the nobility by shielding and taking them to safety during the conquest of Tenochtitlan, Cuauhtemoc ordered the women of Tlatelolco, where the final battles before the Mexica surrender were fought, to go up to the rooftops with shields and arms to threaten the Spanish with Mexica strength in numbers, when in fact their numbers were desperately low. A Tlatelocan woman (or women) helped the remaining desperate Tlatelolcan warriors by pouring water, presumably from a roof, onto the Spanish soldiers.[21]

In South America, Manco II called upon Inka women to act as decoys, again with the aim of making the fighting force appear larger to the Span-

FIGURE 3.4. Officials "looking at the shame" of an Andean Woman.
(From Felipe Guaman Poma de Ayala, *La nueva crónica y buen gobierno*,
Fondo de Cultura Económica, Mexico City, 1980, 2:467.)

FIGURE 3.5. A Dominican friar forcing a woman with a young child to weave. (From Felipe Guaman Poma de Ayala, *La nueva crónica y buen gobierno*, Fondo de Cultura Económica, Mexico City, 1980, 2:611.)

ish than it actually was.[22] The role of women supporting Inka forces, in fact, captured Spanish attention. Francisco Pizarro's brother, Hernando, ordered any women captured in fighting to be killed. An anonymous chronicler thought the order was intended to terrorize the Inka people, and that it did so effectively.[23] Francisco Pizarro executed a sister of Atahualpa living in his quarters who was suspected of aiding the Inka cause and whom Quispe Sisa (or doña Inés Yupanqui, as she was by then known) denounced to him. In sixteenth-century Paraguay, twenty-one Guaraní rebellions took place, due, in part, to mistreatment and abuse of Guaraní women and their labor. While some women resisted the invaders, others, like Malintzin and Quispe Sisa, supported them. Overall, women's military role during the conquests was similar to what it had been in the warfare prior to the European arrival: intermittent and less structured than male participation but not wholly uncommon.[24]

In the aftermath of Iberian victories, coercive, voluntary, and marital relations continued between indigenous women and Iberian men, but the colonial era would bring further changes in the lives and roles of women, especially in their labor patterns.

Laboring Women: Paying Tribute, Losing Authority

In most regions, urban and rural, indigenous women probably still arose to perform an array of early morning household tasks similar to those they would have performed in pre-European times. Grinding maize, preparing customary drinks such as *atole* (a maize-based Mesoamerican drink) or chicha, caring for small animals for household consumption, trade, or sale, and picking or sweeping up after their fellow household inhabitants marked women's labor patterns before Conquest as well as during the colonial period, especially in its earliest years. Yet from northern New Spain to Chile in the south, Latin America's native women worked harder but lost power and authority. This section of the chapter considers two questions: What kinds of work did women do? And did their access to power and authority, especially those forms rooted in labor-related hierarchies and ownership of property, change?

If women's work within households remained similar to what it had been prior to the arrival of Europeans, the labor they performed, whether household based or not, whether extracted through official or private means, or for the state or other purposes, changed in both its nature and amount. Scholars who examine a wide array of regions have found that women across Latin America worked harder during the colonial era.[25] Although the causes of women's labor burden, the commodities demanded by Iberians, and forms of labor organization varied by area, three basic reasons for this change stand out. First, there were drastic demographic changes. Second, an intensification of preexisting forms of labor adaptable to colonial economies occurred. Third,

Europeans assigned new types of work to indigenous women in addition to their traditional tasks.

The dramatic decline in native population throughout Latin America was both the backdrop to and cause of change in labor patterns, particularly during the early part of the colonial era. Even as the indigenous population fell due to disease and warfare, Spanish demands for labor increased. Their appetite for textiles for clothing and bedding for themselves and the growing *casta* (or mixed ethno-racial identities) and African populations, in particular, fueled a need to increase indigenous women's productivity, even as new kinds of extra-domestic textile production, often based primarily on male labor, came into being. Declining native populations had other effects on women, whose family responsibilities increased when they found themselves as single parents, a not uncommon consequence of greater male participation in the wars of conquest. Such a variable gender-related impact influenced family structures, although patterns of change varied by area.[26]

The type of women's labor with the greatest degree of continuity across colonial Latin America was weaving. While textile-related activities had more male participants in Andean regions and less in Mesoamerica during the prehispanic era, women's weaving predominated everywhere well into the sixteenth century.[27] Nonetheless, the types of cloth changed, and the amounts of time taken up by this production intensified. Many prehispanic sites of female labor outside of households (for example, temples, in the case of Mesoamerica, and aqlla wasi, in the case of the Andes) disappeared, eventually to be replaced in the seventeenth century by *obrajes*. These urban, sweatshop-like institutions existed primarily to produce textiles, and male labor predominated in them. Indigenous women, however, continued to produce cloth in households during the colonial period, especially in rural areas where obraje-based production did not penetrate. Household-based production provided cloth used by household members for local and long-distance markets and for tribute payments, which generally consisted of cotton cloth woven in a heavier and wider form to suit Iberian tastes, a type that entailed harder work.[28]

Women's marketing activities, especially in Mesoamerica, were also marked by continuity. From the Valley of Mexico to Oaxaca to the Yucatan, women of native origin predominated in local markets, both before and after the arrival of the Spanish. During the colonial period, women sold uncooked and prepared foods, beverages, textiles, and sometimes other wares in markets, from their homes, and on streets and roadways. They also occasionally participated in long-distance trade of profitable items, especially pulque.[29]

In central Mexico and Oaxaca, women were very active as pulque sellers. While it was primarily used as part of ritual celebrations or social gatherings, people drank pulque instead of water to quench thirst during the dry season and used it for medicinal purposes. Women drank it after childbirth to help their milk flow and to regain their strength. In the Mexico City region, late sixteenth- and early seventeenth-century laws aimed at controlling pulque sale and consumption explicitly recognized women as vendors, licensing small numbers of them to sell it over specified distances or areas.[30]

Women also predominated as sellers in colonial Andean markets, even though the existence of markets prior to the arrival of Europeans, especially in the central and southern Andes, is unclear.[31] In larger cities like Lima, indigenous women concentrated on sales of produce, whereas in smaller cities like Quito, Potosí, and Santiago de Chile, women sold a wide array of items, including food, textiles, and items like soap, jewelry, and paper. In mid-seventeenth-century Quito, the sale of nonfood items, especially those of Spanish style, precipitated deep conflicts with non-Indian grocers, *pulperos* (who owned small stores located in many urban neighborhoods), over who had the right to sell particular goods. Both profits and taxes were at stake, because indigenous sellers were exempt from the collection and payment of the *alcabala*, the sales tax city governments required pulperos to pay.[32] While market women were important for the distribution of agricultural and other commodities in many towns and cities, production and distribution in rural areas farther from central markets still took place, activities that often depended upon the sometimes extreme exploitation of female labor.

Even though forced labor, through the institutions of encomienda and *repartimiento* (rotational labor drafts), is typically thought of as a requirement placed upon indigenous males, women, too, labored to fulfill such obligations.[33] Women provided such labor in palaces and temples during the prehispanic period in many areas of Mesoamerica, and a certain similarity exists between prehispanic and colonial forms of compelled labor during the early postconquest years. In central Mexico, labor obligations yielded in part to exchange relations, especially in domestic service in Spanish households early in the colonial period. Employers sometimes paid the women in wages, sometimes in goods or room and board; some employers gave contracts, but most such relationships operated informally. In the Yucatan, native women, many from rural areas, provided rotational personal service labor for urban Spaniards throughout the colonial period.[34]

While female personal service may have been new to Andean societies, it is not hard to imagine lower status aqllas, distant female kin, or other types of female retainers or dependents performing such work in Inka noble households. Female personal service—rooted in both indigenous and Spanish associations between women and cooking, cleaning, and childcare tasks—occurred across the towns and cities of early colonial Spanish America. But in most places such labor ceased to be state-organized and became an individualized arrangement, highly susceptible to such extreme forms of coercion that it resembled involuntary servitude or slavery. Thus in its later forms, female labor bore little resemblance to prehispanic forms of labor service.[35]

Other kinds of work indigenous women performed were less traditional, including labor in and even ownership of mines, textile production in obrajes, and cigar and cigarette manufacture in tobacco factories. Most harshly of all, women worked as *tlamemes*, human carriers of a variety of goods. Female carriers were not common, but women did perform such labor in the Yucatan and Chile during the conquests and throughout the sixteenth century in parts of Central America. In some places, men began to do what indigenous men and women had previously considered to be women's work. Jesuit missionaries encouraged men to take over pottery making and to play a greater role in agriculture in the Paraguayan Guaraní missions, for example, in order to encourage greater adherence to Iberian ideas about gender roles.[36]

Non-elite rural and urban women bore the brunt of these demands in the century after the conquests. Policies exempted noblewomen from many of these requirements, and some profited from their associations with Spanish men as well as from the privatization of land ownership.[37] By the seventeenth century, so much compression in the native class structure had taken place that most indigenous women felt pressured by the need for cash or cloth for both basic survival and tribute payments, and many were subject to more extreme forms of exploitation.

The impact of tribute payment to Spanish officials almost certainly had a heavy impact on native women everywhere in Spanish America. While Andean women were formally exempt from such payments, the indigenous women of New Spain paid tribute. Single women, who became responsible for tribute payments as young as age fourteen, and widows were formally listed as half-tributaries, while tribute roles defined a full tributary as a man and his wife. Women as a category were not exempted from such payments until 1786, but, even then, such reforms were not fully enforced, with women continuing to owe payments at least into the 1790s.[38] Regardless of laws and policies, because colonial officials, Spanish or indigenous, could not meet tribute assessments without women's labor, the reality was that virtually everywhere in the Spanish empire, indigenous women worked to earn money or produce goods, generally cloth, that flowed into the tribute system. In regions such as Oaxaca, where women remained the primary textile producers, women probably provided the bulk of tribute payments to the Spanish, whose demands increased over time. Spaniards and indigenous community leaders across many regions sometimes pressured women intensely to produce goods for tribute.[39]

Domestic service was also almost inevitably abusive. Few women worked with contracts; therefore, employers subjected them to their whims regarding the kinds of labor they performed, whether they would be paid, and if so, in what form. While domestic service originated as a type of urban labor, Spanish officials and priests in towns and rural areas also required domestic labor, so it became a common type of work for native women everywhere. It also served as a magnet for rural women, drawing them into cities as a way to escape abusive husbands or find an income to support themselves or aid their families.[40] Depending on a household's needs, domestic labor included those tasks familiar to us such as cooking, cleaning, washing, and childcare, but in both Central America and Peru, domestic service also could include exploitation in more extreme forms. *Encomende-*

ros (holders of encomienda grants of tribute and labor) rented out women to sailors sailing from Central America to Peru for several months at a time; these women no doubt provided both domestic and sexual services. The men who rented out these often young women received rental payments based on their attractiveness. In seventeenth-century Guatemala, Spaniards commonly coerced, even kidnapped, widows to provide domestic service or perform other types of work, and indigenous parents signed contracts tying their pre-adolescent and adolescent daughters to periods of service, including working as wet nurses, in Spanish households, in exchange for money, clothing, and room and board. As widows, they continued to be responsible for tribute payments, and they had no husbands to speak up for them. In Peru, girls as young as six worked as domestic servants, and in the northern Border region, servants as young as one were listed on late eighteenth-century censuses. If not already working at such a young age (one must ask what useful labor they could have done), what the future held for these children is clear.[41]

Large numbers of women, younger and older, performed domestic service because wealthy Spaniards often required large numbers of servants (see fig. 3.6), and did not always want to pay them. Small debts could be used as a pretext for virtual imprisonment, though whether such debts even existed was sometimes debatable. In 1689 María Sisa, an Andean woman from Upper Peru (colonial Bolivia) sued a Spanish woman, doña Polonia Maldonado, over lack of payment of wages. In her two years of serving doña Polonia and her mother, María had received a chicken and three meters of cloth, but she had never been paid wages. After she fell ill and decided to leave her employment in this household, doña Polonia imprisoned María Sisa's son, claiming that María owed her payment for the chicken and cloth. While a constable set her son free, he did not order the payment of María Sisa's wages. Paraguayan officials received repeated orders during the seventeenth century to curb or eliminate abusive forms of female domestic service, suggesting that civil officials often failed to control such practices.[42]

Official involvement in virtual or actual imprisonment and involuntary servitude also occurred. During the sixteenth century in Central America, Mercedarian and Dominican friars kept women for domestic service in their houses. The Dominicans required these women to produce textiles that the friars then traded. They treated the female workers harshly and failed to pay wages.[43] Spanish officials, first encomenderos, later *corregidores* and *alcaldes mayores* (both civil officials who supervised districts), began to force indigenous women in Oaxaca to weave in the 1540s, a practice that continued throughout the colonial period. A bishop complained in 1779 about the circumstances of Zapotec women forced to weave who paid high prices for unspun cotton yet received unfairly low prices for the textiles they produced, getting as little as one-third to one-half of the value the textiles would bring if sold. The use and later intensification of forced weaving through the *repartimiento de mercancías* (a system of exchange that linked forced production with trade)

FIGURE 3.6.   A native official demands tribute from an elderly
woman. (From Felipe Guaman Poma de Ayala, *La nueva crónica y buen
gobierno*, Fondo de Cultura Económica, Mexico City, 1980, 2:832.)

also occurred in Chiapas, affecting highland Maya groups, especially the Tzeltal, Tzotzil, and Chol.[44]

Even the protective custody of women known as *depósito,* used in cases of premarital conflict, divorce, rape, or sexual misconduct, sometimes turned into a more coercive and exploitative practice. Primarily under ecclesiastical control, priests on occasion used depósito as a form of punishment for civil or sexual misdeeds. In the Toluca region west of Mexico City, priests sometimes forced women under the sanction of depósito to be housed in priests' living quarters. In this situation, abuses of labor occurred. In 1820, one priest was accused of rounding up both single women and widows, sheltering them in his own residence, and forcing them to spin and weave. All this continued without payment, going on until the women married. Women sometimes even received punishment for a husband's misdeeds. When an indigenous peddler failed to repay a loan of thirty pesos to a priest, again in the Toluca region, the priest placed the peddler's wife in depósito. Local officials in the Villa Alta district of Oaxaca fined women who did not produce required amounts of woven textiles and placed them in houses they owned if they did not pay fines.[45]

Compulsory female labor occurred throughout the colonial period, and the most extreme form—slavery—while rare, took place as well, primarily during the sixteenth century. Enslavement of indigenous women existed mainly in the Caribbean and Central America, especially Honduras and Nicaragua, but also in Brazil. Slavery also occurred on occasion in the core areas of Spanish America, with indigenous female slaves sometimes laboring as domestic servants but sometimes working in other types of establishments such as mines in New Spain, Peru, and elsewhere.[46] While the Spanish crown considered most of the native population of Spanish America to be free, the labor requirements of Spaniards, although increasingly driven by market rather than state requirements, fell on both men and women. Women usually fulfilled such requirements through household labor, but both need and coercion often pushed them into non-household-based workplaces where owners or overseers subjected them to a variety of abuses. In reference to Central America, William Sherman argued that of all the consequences of Spanish labor demands, the impact of early colonial compulsory labor on families and especially children was "perhaps the greatest social evil."[47] I believe his statement holds true across colonial Latin America.

Enslavement, compulsory labor, intensification of labor, and migration, male or female, all had an impact on native family life. So too did the loss of land held by communities and individuals. Just as the colonial labor system disadvantaged women in a variety of ways, the changing economic scene in regard to property ownership, especially land, also adversely affected women. In a few cases early on, individual sixteenth-century women actually profited. For example, Cortés rewarded Malintzin for her services with an encomienda, and some women descended from the Inka nobility profited from the privatization of land ownership by buying and selling land. On the other hand, when Spaniards married elite indigenous women, such marriages helped Spaniards gain land.[48]

At first the depopulation in the immediate post-Conquest period probably led to some increase in some women's access to material wealth, especially among Nahuas and Andeans, but this was not a lasting change.[49] Among colonial descendants of the Mexica, we can compare the 1585 testament of Angelina Martina, a merchant woman, and the twenty different plots of land she listed in her will, with the 1699 testament of Melchora de Santiago who left cacique lands ("tlalli cacicazgo") that could generate an income of about twenty pesos per year. Indeed, Melchora represented one of the 25 percent of seventeenth-century Mexico City's indigenous female will writers who owned *any* land (house plot or field) to bequeath to others, down from the over 40 percent of women writing wills who owned landed property in the sixteenth century.[50]

Ñudzahui cacicas continued to own extensive property holdings into the nineteenth century, though non-elite women's property ownership was concentrated in trade items such as textiles, wax, or pesos, with some ownership of house plots as well. Ñudzahui cacicas possessed amounts of land similar to that held by *caciques* (male leaders), but those non-elite women who held land owned house plots or maguey fields and owned somewhat less than men. Yucatec Maya women also owned and inherited land, but no sources indicate noblewomen with extensive landholdings. The land colonial Maya women owned generally consisted of house plots rather than fields.[51]

In central Mexico, indigenous women's loss of land appears to have increased during the late eighteenth and early nineteenth centuries. While the inheritance practices of the Spanish, who divided property equally among their male and female children, meant that native women held the right to inherit land, litigation from the Toluca Valley shows that women increasingly lost their holdings. Lawsuits over landholdings from that region suggest that men sought actively to dispossess women who were their sisters, sisters-in-law, or nieces from their small plots. They did so even though the agricultural labor performed by the region's women helped support their families and meet the economic requirements of daily and religious life, including the payment of tribute by widows. In colonial Ecuador, a type of serfdom known as *huasipunguerismo* developed, in which male laborers (*huasipungeros*) exchanged their labor for rights to use small plots of land on *haciendas* (large, landed estates). Women's rights to this land came solely through their ties to men. Thus, if a huasipungero died, a woman without an adult son would then be dispossessed.[52]

The Nahua and Andean peoples' loss of rights to land, a process that accelerated in the late eighteenth and nineteenth centuries, reinforced women's loss of authority and status more generally. The inheritance of use and ownership rights to land represented one pathway of women's autonomous access to resources. But just as the economic basis of their autonomy declined, so did their possibilities for holding positions of leadership. In Mexico City, female marketplace administrators disappeared, as did priestesses; in the Andes, the parallel female political hierarchy faded from public view.[53] Among the Ñudzahui, cacicas continued to hold political authority into the eighteenth century but lost power in a colonial political system in which they could not hold formal political offices. While we will return to the issue of changing political systems and their impact on women's power and authority, changing forms of labor and property ownership clearly had adverse effects on both elite and nonelite women. While markets may have represented an arena of continuity in women's economic roles, enabling them to help support their families and even sometimes to find economic self-sufficiency and autonomy (though markets also became a site for the expression of gendered and racial stereotypes in the later colonial and early national periods), most other female forms of work depended upon women's subservience and left them open to exploitation, often in extreme forms.

Family and Religious Life:
The Paradoxes of Purity and Enclosure

Single, married, and widowed women all made economic contributions to their households, and Spanish labor and taxation policies created a series of stresses with which native families across Spanish America had to deal. After conquest, the Iberian presence generally had an immediate impact on indigenous family life and gender relations. The conquests themselves brought death, dislocation, and disruption. But even in places like Brazil, where violent conquests did not play as great a role during the contact period, disease led to changes in family life. Although the forced labor systems of the sixteenth and early seventeenth centuries gave way in most areas of Spanish America to more individual and flexible labor arrangements, coercive and exploitative practices continued to affect native men, women, and children. At the same time, the new emphasis on ideas of honor, female purity, and enclosure reinforced male privilege and created a paradox for indigenous women, who, because of their work, did not and could not live the sheltered, enclosed lives idealized by Iberians.

It would be, however, a mistake to paint an overly rosy or idealized picture of native family life prior to the arrival of Europeans. Poverty, disruption of family life through war, violence against women, or the use of women to create or solidify kin group and political alliances all occurred and took their toll. But Iberian demands for labor and the introduction of new gender ideologies—especially as expressed through religion—led to significant changes in family life, with some of these changes having a negative impact on women. In regions like Central America and the Río de la Plata area, where official oversight and enforcement of laws and policies protecting indigenous women and family life were lax, enslavement and very exploitative forms of domestic service, such as the drafting of new mothers to serve as wet nurses, led to severe family disruption. Such disruption carried severe consequences, including marital breakup and even mothers killing their newborns or themselves or both, as well as other forms of resistance.[54]

In many areas, the effects of conquest, disease, and the imposition of increased tribute demands and labor drafts led to male outmigration, as men either complied with or sought to evade such tribute and labor demands. This migration then resulted in increased family disruption, as men left their families behind.[55] The forced resettlement of whole native communities through the policies of *congregacion* or *reducción* (as it was known in Peru) also contributed to the disruption of kinship structures and family life. While late prehispanic kinship structures varied, peoples across many regions appear to have had high proportions of multifamily households. These helped families meet the tribute and military demands, agricultural labor needs, and requirements of household-based or extra-household-based crafts production.[56] The tendencies of rulers and high-ranking nobles to take more than one wife also increased the size of households among the Nahua, Ñudzahui, Maya, and Inka and other Andean nobles.

Changes in labor patterns and the spread of new diseases immediately altered family size. However, in some areas, especially rural areas, indigenous groups were able to reconstitute traditional kinship systems and family and household structures. Such was the case among the Ñudzahui and the Maya.[57] In regions where either urbanism was more prevalent or where labor extraction or forced resettlement was especially intense, such reconstitution was less likely, and nuclear and single-parent households became more prevalent. During the sixteenth and seventeenth centuries (timing depending upon place), disease combined with other kinds of family and community disruption probably led to increased labor demands being placed upon women, thus in turn fueling further disruption and change.[58]

Another set of factors affecting indigenous family life and gender roles were Spanish beliefs about marriage and proper behavior for women. One area of family life on which the Catholic Church especially focused was marriage. Priests actively promoted chastity, monogamy, and marriage as the relationship of two individuals (rather than as a relationship between households or kin groups) as the only allowable family values.[59] Priests moved quickly to stamp out polygynous practices that traditionally conferred status by creating or affirming kinship and political or economic ties among regional elites. These practices also differentiated between nobles and nonnobles, since the latter generally had no more than one wife. The Franciscan friar Motolinía pointed out that multiple wives provided much-needed labor to produce goods for gifts or exchange among elite households of the cities of central Mexico. But he also noted that the practice embraced "sensuality" and was hard for men to give up.[60]

An early bigamy case from Coyoacan, near Mexico City, demonstrates that some men tried to continue such arrangements. Martín Xuchimitl had married four sisters before the Spanish conquest. Afterward, he legalized his marriage with one of them but continued his relationship with a second, the other two sisters having died. When he was found out, a religious court tried and sentenced him in 1539 to flogging and having his hair cut off. Among the Tarahumara in the north, male resentment over the loss of female labor was a factor leading to revolt. Colonial kurakas in Peru may have continued to engage in polygyny as a sign of their higher rank. Unfortunately, neither colonial chroniclers nor archival documents tell us how indigenous women felt about polygyny, but perhaps Nahua women's enthusiasm for church attendance related, at least in part, to a desire to end this practice. It is also possible that native people embraced both *cofradías* (confraternities) and compadrazgo because these institutions provided indigenous men and women the means to repair, at least in part, the strains felt by native families and communities as they adjusted to a colonial world with its policies of labor exploitation, new beliefs about marriage and ritual practices, and surveillance of family and community life.[61]

While requiring native groups to forego polygynous marriage arrangements, the Spanish Catholic emphasis on the role of free will in marital choice meant that partners were to be free to choose their spouses without parental or other interference. Yet priests in central Mexico worried that both families and matchmakers continued to play a role in the promotion of or objection to marriages.[62] They expressed such concerns well into the eighteenth century. These worries reflect clerical unease not only about whether or not Nahuas and others were, as individuals, freely choosing their partners but also about whether or not they respected the sanctity of marriage. Rural colonial Nahuas, for example, sometimes practiced a form of marriage in which after a betrothal, the future bridegroom lived with his future bride's family and worked for his in-laws. Upon the young man's relocation, sexual relations between the couple often commenced. One priest explained this practice by arguing that through sexual relations, the potential bridegroom discovered whether or not his bride was a virgin.[63] Known as *montequitl*, this practice could indicate either that virginity was not commonly required before marriage (except among noble families) either before or after the arrival of Europeans, or it could have been a response to the decline in both population and polygyny and the concomitant increased need for household-based labor. The labor of the prospective bridegroom (known as uxorilocal labor) could have compensated households for the loss of female work that resulted from a patrilocal marriage pattern, combined with the ending of polygyny. In central Peru, a somewhat similar custom, *sirvanacuy,* existed, though it was not solely uxorilocal. In fact in Peru, it was more common for a woman to move to her potential husband's family. Sirvanacuy does not appear to have been as much about providing labor as about allowing couples, and probably their families, to assess the strength and quality of the bond between the potential spouses.[64]

In both Mexico and Peru, priests tried to stop such practices. In the Toluca area, they confined women in depósito, with some priests routinely confining brides-to-be, indigenous and other. In central Peru both potential brides and grooms were subject to detention, usually in the church. While priests apparently succeeded in bringing an end to polygynous marriage practices in most areas, they were less successful in their attempts to make marriage an arrangement between two chaste individuals. Families and communities continued to play a role in arranging marriages, primarily because marriage was fundamentally tied to labor organization, particularly in rural indigenous communities, and a strict policing of chastity was neither practical nor particularly valued.[65]

Yet a rhetoric tying chastity to purity and honor did have some impact. The Catholic Church held the view that sexuality could only be expressed legitimately through heterosexual vaginal intercourse engaged in for the purpose of procreation. While friars addressed a message of chastity to both young men and women, they advised adolescent girls in particular to guard their virginity and to live lives of purity through enclosure.[66] In Peru, Viceroy Toledo intended the policy of reducción to encourage the surveillance of indigenous households by decreeing that their houses open out onto public streets, and he further declared that men and women were to have separate quarters within their houses. In the Jesuit missions among the Guaraní, priests created actual spaces of enclosure (coty-guazú, or cloister) where unattached women of any age could retreat, for shorter or longer periods, to "preserve their 'honor,' protect their virginity, and enjoy a 'good' social standing in the eyes of the missionaries," thus making the oversight and policing of honor and virginity easier.[67] But in many parts of Mesoamerica and the Andes, friars neglected to inform women about how they could enclose themselves or their daughters, given the intense pressures for women to work to provide tribute and service, often in locations outside their own households. Nevertheless, a concept of chastity that linked female virginity and virtue to male honor began to have an impact on native gender ideologies.[68]

A statement by doña Paula Mama Guaco Ñusta, a resident of Cuzco, exemplifies the rhetoric of honor as status used during the sixteenth century. She complained that a commoner woman insulted her by using dishonorable language, "ignoring the fact that I am the honorable wife of a Spaniard, and a woman of quality and nobility."[69] As time went on, a more gendered vocabulary that linked honor and status to sexuality began to appear, and by the eighteenth century, such concepts were relatively common. In both central Mexico and Peru, native husbands' repeated declarations of concern over the faithfulness of their wives, expressed the notion of wives as female guardians of rectitude and honor. Husbands' concerns about honor served as a cause of violence against wives, and such anxieties existed across the ethno-racial groupings and classes of colonial societies.[70] But indigenous men, expected to take on the more patriarchal masculine role associated with the Iberian gender system, found implementing such roles in a colonial world that discriminated against them particularly difficult. Expressions of concern about the sexual behavior of daughters and wives were one way that native men tried to recover their self-esteem; physical violence was another.[71]

High levels of violence, both beatings and murder, against native women occurred across many regions of colonial Latin America. This pattern is especially well documented for eighteenth-century central Mexico and the Andes.[72] Commenting on an earlier period, fray Diego de Landa believed that Maya men learned such behavior from the Spanish.

> Men who had children left their wives with the same ease, without any fear about another marrying them or returning to them themselves afterwards. In spite of all this, they are very jealous, and cannot bear with patience that their wives should be unfaithful to them; and now that they have seen that the Spaniards kill their wives in such a case, they have begun to maltreat theirs and even to kill them.[73]

Though violence against indigenous women was not uncommon, a study of gender relations among non-elites of the Morelos region of Mexico (south of Mexico City) shows that the indigenous sector of the area's population was no more prone to such violence than other sectors. Disputes among nonelites "focused on sexual claims and assertions" and accounted for almost 50 percent of such incidents of violence against women. Other participants claimed that issues of labor and economic obligation, physical mobility, women's verbal challenges to male authority, and complaints over past incidents of abuse caused men to lash out. Such reasoning accounted for nearly one-third of cases of violence against women in this area.[74] What were the deeper causes of such violence, and were these causes particular to indigenous groups, even if overall rates were similar across the general population?

Studies of familial violence in specific indigenous communities or regions show that some variations in patterns of causation existed. In the Toluca Valley, many late colonial cases of violence were rooted in indigenous wives' expressions of concern over whether their husbands were fulfilling their economic obligations and husbands' resentment over wives questioning their status. Casual comments or seemingly mild joking could provoke deadly violence.[75] In Pátzcuaro, while Purépecha wives were frequently targets of physical violence, sometimes their fathers were as well, a most unusual pattern. Whereas men of varying ethno-racial backgrounds in the Mexico City area complained about the interference of their mothers-in-law, Purépecha sons-in-law worried about the authority and influence of their wives' fathers. Felipe Castro Gutiérrez speculates that this authority may have been rooted in a prehispanic kinship structure in which succession to rulership as well as postmarital residence ran through maternal lines. This pattern of powerful fathers-in-law thus could have clashed with a Spanish gender system in which husbands were to be the patriarchs, especially in situations of stress and conflict exacerbated by male absence in repartimiento or waged labor on haciendas and mines.[76] In Oaxaca, indigenous husbands became angered to the point of violence by their perceptions of wives' disobedience or failures to manage economic affairs properly. In the Cuzco area, Quechua-speaking peoples demonstrate similarly high levels of violence against women, often familial in nature. The cases one researcher studied focused on sexual jealousy, honor, and desire, as when, for example, male adulterers beat or killed their wives to free themselves to be with lovers.[77] However causes may have varied by region and culture, it is noteworthy that among the Spanish and casta sectors of society, physical intimidation of women occurred often but only rarely led to public scandal. In other words, such behavior was considered a normal part of the fabric of daily life.

Episodes among the Purépechas and other indigenous groups had a public and highly emotional character. Perhaps the gap between Hispanic gender ideals and reality for indigenous people was particularly great. Men, especially, may have lived in fear of public exposure of any failure to live up to gender ideals of honor, including the ability to support a wife and family.[78] While virtually all examples of such violence describe male-on-female incidents, a petition from Leonor Magdalena, a Nahuatl-speaker and resident of Coyoacan, today a part of Mexico City, reminds us that, then as now, familial relations can be complicated. Filing a complaint against her daughter-in-law, Petronilla, Leonor accused her son's wife of lacking respect and described how "she intercepted me at the ravine and beat me, repeatedly kicked me, and gave me blows that almost split my head. And again on the day of Sacrament she beat me and ripped my blouse (huipil) and became like a crazy woman."[79] Did women, especially indigenous women, passively accept such violence?

Native women tried to manage the all-too-real threat of violence in a variety of ways. Before the fact, the primary ways women sought to ward off violence included amelioration or seeking aid from others recognized as authority figures. However, any distinction made between "before" and "after" an episode of violence is only theoretical, because violent episodes often occurred more than once. Evidence shows that in central Mexico, while any woman was a potential target for violence, poorer and non-Spanish women were frequent targets, as were women who lived in familial units, that is, women who lived in families and younger wives, more than older wives or widows.[80] Manuela Antonia of the pueblo Atlatlauca in the Valley of Toluca, for example, studiously tried to avoid trouble with her tense, insecure husband Paulino. Consistently seeking to perform her wifely duties by providing food, cleaning his clothing, and sleeping with him, she hoped to moderate his behavior despite his constant verbal provocation. Paulino nevertheless punched Manuela Antonia in the face and beat her with a poker after several days of household tension that started when she scolded two of their children. He further expected her to keep this beating quiet, as she had with previous incidents.[81]

Women also sought to signal to their husbands that they had allies by asking others, such as their mothers, fathers, brothers, community leaders, or even priests, to intervene on their behalf, often to avoid escalation of incidents.[82]

Sometimes such interventions helped, sometimes not. Rural Mesoamerican women such as those of the Toluca Valley or the Ñudzahui, Zapotec, or Mixe women of Oaxaca may have had greater community resources than did urban women, who often lived in smaller households and whose work less often was household based. In cities, a clearer distinction between public and private may have existed, whereas in rural areas, household life and community life were closely bound together, with work, meetings of town leaders, and community rituals often occurring in or near household settings.[83]

After an incident, women turned to the same kinds of allies for help and protection. If family and kin failed to effect a change for the better in a marital relationship, either the woman or members of her family might initiate judicial action. Men could be charged with the crime of battery, and family and friends might serve as witnesses. This communal response suggests that neither women nor indigenous communities passively accepted violence against women, though punishment for battery frequently was light, as husbands claimed drunkenness or accused wives of dishonorable behavior that undercut women's position. In central Peru, women's appeals to their brothers for help sometimes led to further violence, as brothers beat, even killed, violent husbands.[84] Yet native women also experienced intense economic and social pressures to bear brutal treatment silently. In the Toluca region, civil officials and priests generally sought to achieve reconciliation, and wives themselves sometimes tried to have charges that they or relatives had brought dropped. A reality for poor families, and indigenous families in particular because of their tribute and labor obligations, was that individuals and households coped with constant, heavy financial burdens. Because men's and women's work were often complementary, the labor of both was necessary to meet family and community obligations. Among the Purépecha, community officials rarely supported native women's attempts to use the judicial system, because needs for male labor for tribute or labor obligations were heavy. They preferred the use of informal means of self-help and even actively pressured one woman not to pursue her case, threatening to whip her if she did.[85]

While violence against women was primarily a family affair, workplace punishments also took place. For example, when a hacienda administrator in Tepetitlan, don Eugenio, whipped several women workers for going for wood instead of working, the women complained bitterly of their pain by saying "es mucho la mala vida que nos da" (he treats us very badly), using language similar to that used to describe domestic abuse. Female domestic servants were frequent targets subjected to exploitation, sexual abuse, and harsh punishments for failing to live up to expectations.[86]

Neither formal nor informal measures were always successful. Beatings continued, homicides occurred. In the small number of cases of men tried for the crime of killing their wives in Oaxaca, few were put to death. Courts there preferred to punish husbands with sentences of forced labor, whippings, or banishment, with forced labor for periods of two to eight years the most common sentence.[87] Compare these punishments with that of Teresa Sisa, an Andean woman who fled an unhappy first marriage, probably due to her husband's violence.

> A few years later, with her parents' blessing, she remarried. When Sisa and her new husband, because of his work, returned to the region where her first husband lived, she was recognized by her former in-laws. The church brought charges against her for being married twice. The second marriage was declared null, and Sisa was sentenced to be "punished exemplarily." She was mounted on a "beast of burden" and led through the streets, stripped to the waist except for a *corosa* (dunce cap), while a public crier called out her crime. After this public shaming she was lashed one hundred times. Sisa was also ordered to serve six months in a convent, after which she was to resume married life with her first husband, whom the church admonished not to hurt or maltreat her under threat of severe punishment.[88]

Given that legal, quasi-legal, and illegal acts of violence permeated colonial societies, we should not view native men as innately or culturally more prone to violence than other men. Instead, what becomes clear from both individual cases and historical literature is that colonial family life was stressful, particularly for native peoples who endured cultural and population loss, heavy burdens of tribute and labor, and frequent spousal separation (caused primarily by male absence) due to the demands of work. As eighteenth-century populations, both indigenous and other, began to grow rapidly, and as later colonial officials sought to increase tribute collections, as well as productivity, across all economic sectors, family violence appears to have intensified.[89] Is it any wonder that indigenous women turned to a variety of sources of power as a means of dealing with the violence that sometimes threatened their lives?

Understanding the spiritual, indeed magical, sources of women's attempts to exert power over their relationships, especially with the men in their lives, requires us to first consider women's roles in religion during the post-Conquest era. While religion, overall, constituted an important arena of transformation for native women and men, some aspects of those beliefs and symbols that were female centered continued to exist after the Conquest, as did some institutionalized roles for women, though the latter were much reduced in authority. Transformation in the gendered aspects of religious practices was tied to the more male-centered official belief system and authority structure of the Catholic Church. However important Marian devotion was in the Iberian church, Mary is at base the mother of Jesus and an intercessor between individuals and a male-conceptualized God.[90] Female deities of the prehispanic era, especially among Nahuas and Andean peoples, were powerful in their own right, symbolizing important foods and basic resources, fertility, and sexuality. During the sixteenth century, these powerful deities took on increasingly negative associations, as Iberians, because of their more dualistic worldview, linked them to evil, witches, even the devil.[91]

Spaniards portrayed colonial Nahua indigenous female deities as sinful and destructive. In addition, women's institutionalized roles in native temples began to decline, and ultimately disappeared. Female priestesses and religious functionaries like the aqllas lost their institutionalized positions in the colonial world, especially those centered in urban temples that ceased to exist after conquest.[92] There was little place for Latin America's indigenous people, male or female, in the priesthood or among the nuns who helped support colonial Catholic religious life, at least until the early eighteenth century, when a convent for Indian nuns sprang up in Mexico City. In more rural regions of central Mexico and in highland southern Mesoamerica, priests like Jacinto de la Serna feared that representations of earth goddesses intended to promote fertility continued to be worshiped in the guise of Marian devotion or in secret places such as caves.[93]

Scholars sometimes have emphasized that figures like the Virgin of Guadalupe of New Spain are syncretized images, blending elements of indigenous female deities with the Catholic Virgin. Yet the origins of the Virgin of Guadalupe as a cult figure remain somewhat obscure, since the earliest texts describe a Catholic Virgin, not a syncretized goddess. Colonial native language texts such as the late-sixteenth-century Nahuatl translation of a Spanish play, *Holy Wednesday*, or testaments referring to Mary depict a more autonomous, authoritative figure whose "son is less inclined to contradict her and treats her with more deference than do Spanish language texts." Ñudzahui colonial testaments, many of which date from the eighteenth century, contain numerous references to Mary as either a ruler or a deity, often paired with God as a coruler.[94]

Even though Catholicism considered submissiveness to be a desirable trait for indigenous women during the colonial era, early educational efforts aimed at quickly instilling the new religion's beliefs, practices, and values largely bypassed girls, as Spanish priests concentrated their educational efforts on boys. Women, however, participated actively in the spiritual and ritual realms of colonial life. Not only were indigenous women in central Mexico known for their piety and church attendance, they held some institutionalized roles such as sweepers (*tlachpanque*, in Nahuatl) or guardians of women (*cihuatepixque*) who had to ensure that girls and women attended services.[95] Another important female role within the churches of Nahua native communities took place within the cofradías that served as the most significant extra-familial resource for social welfare. Cofradías provided a variety of kinds of assistance for daily life—food, clothing, and shelter—as well as help with the costs associated with illness, death, and burial. The extant records of two central Mexican colonial Nahua cofradías, one in Mexico City, the other in Tula, show women not just as members but also as officers holding titles similar to prehispanic office titles. A small number of Chiapas confraternities also had female officers.[96] These female activities allowed for enactment of a female maternal and nurturing role that undoubtedly pleased Spanish churchmen, yet they express some continuity in both authoritative roles for women, as well as a gender-parallel structure of institutional governance, a parallelism seen in few other realms of indigenous colonial life.

Women also continued to serve as midwives, healers, and matchmakers, but friars and priests held more ambivalent attitudes toward such activities because they were intimately connected to a native domestic world they feared, and because such activities could so easily serve as a basis for idolatry and apostasy.[97] While the Spanish allowed midwives and curers to continue their functions throughout New Spain, they felt concern over what midwives might be doing beyond delivering babies. In Bartolomé de Alva's seventeenth-century *Guide to Confession*, he advises priests to ask midwives whether they have given "medicine [or] a potion to a young unmarried woman so that her baby would fall [stillborn] and be aborted," as well as asking how many times they had done so. This advice suggests that from Alva's point of view, the practice of abortion was relatively common and under women's control.[98] Among the highland Maya, female shamans pursued curing throughout the colonial period, and the Spanish viewed them as potential witches, *brujas*. Female religious practitioners in Peru also received intense scrutiny. Thus such activities, so necessary for young and old to survive the vicissitudes of everyday life, were only quasi-legitimate. Even in the eighteenth century, priests in central Mexico worried that matchmakers were still at work doing the business of creating family alliances rather than independent conjugal units.[99]

The female ritual activity that worried the Spanish the most involved the use of magic, generally referred to by the term *hechicería*. Hechicería involved the use of magical objects and unorthodox rituals to achieve a certain end, often related to love, illness, or revenge. While some magical practices used substances, forms, and terminology that were indigenous at root, the idea of ligature, tying magical objects together to achieve a certain end, especially to attract a particular man, was Spanish in origin. In both urban and rural areas across Spanish America, participation in magical practices often took place across class and ethno-racial and gender lines. But indigenous practitioners who were often, though not solely, women were common, and clients, whether of indigenous, mixed, or Spanish identities, thought them to be powerful.[100]

These magical acts represented a cross-class and cross-ethno-racial statement that asserted a kind of female power. At the same time, these transgressive acts reflected a lack of formal power as well. Such practices attracted the attention of authorities, especially religious, partly because of church concerns about idolatry and apostasy but also because these practices threatened to turn, in officials' eyes, into something even more worrisome. Both parish priests and the Inquisition persecuted midwives and healers, and they could be punished harshly by whipping, forced labor, or even death for a variety of idolatrous behaviors.[101] Love and other kinds of magic nonetheless persisted because they met individual and social needs and reflected the spirit of strength and possession of agency that often characterized women's work and family lives. This same strength also motivated women in the religious and political realms when they acted protectively for themselves, their families, and their communities.

A Rebellious Spirit

The political roles played by women in the late prehispanic period underwent change soon after the appearance of Spaniards. The Nahua woman who served as a marketplace judge became unemployed. The Ñudzahui *yya dzehe toniñe* (the Ñudzahui female ruler), or cacica, while keeping her position, saw her power decline. While she could continue to hold her title, she generally could not hold Spanish-recognized offices such as *gobernador* (governor) that became linked to indigenous offices and titles.[102] Nonetheless, some elite women continued to hold power and control wealth. In Oaxaca, for example, Ñudzahui aristocratic women remained wealthy and influential into the mid–eighteenth century. During the mid–sixteenth century, one Ana de Sosa of Tutepec, on Oaxaca's Pacific Coast, was so wealthy, holding twelve tributary communities and numerous fields and grazing lands, that she was richer than the region's Spanish *encomendero* (holder of a grant of tribute and labor) and probably the wealthiest woman in all of southern Mesoamerica.[103] In the Andes, female kurakas and the capullanas of the northern Peruvian coast still held these titles. In fact, the title of cacica seems to have proliferated in this area, generally to keep titles and assets within particular family lines. But as elsewhere, these women could not serve as governor and thus began to lose power. An Andean cacica complaining in 1699 to a visiting Spanish official about her status and her need for protection because of mistreatment by local, indigenous officials, said that

> I beg Your Grace, as such a Christian lord, that in your Ordinances you instruct that the Caciques and Cacicas be given an old man and an old woman and a young woman for their (household) service, Your Grace understanding that I am a poor woman, orphaned by father and mother and having no one to whom I can turn my eyes; and I also warn Your Grace that the Mayors and Officials come into my house without civility and circumspection . . . and for this they disrespect me with word and deed, even though they are Indians from my ayllos.[104]

Rather than asserting power, the cacica asks for a sort of patriarchal protection. Spanish gender codes and rules for succession to office, whereby a woman might serve only in the absence of a suitable male officeholder, contributed to a diminishing of the power that both noble and nonnoble women had exercised, but this occurred at a variable rate across Spanish America.[105]

While the female office-holder of the prehispanic period became more rare over time, in two of the most important political activities of the colonial period, activities through which indigenous populations interacted with and often directly confronted both individual Spaniards as well as the colonial government, women were very active. One realm of interaction was the judicial realm; the other was rebellions. The voluminous judicial records of Spanish America vividly illustrate women's presence in the judicial sphere. In drawing up wills, important legal documents that shaped the transmission of property, women influenced social relations through the flow of material items. They also expressed their feelings about close relationships, as when Ana Juana of Culhuacan in the southern Valley of Mexico used her will to call her third husband, Gabriel Itzmalli, "a great scoundrel" who "never gave me anything whatever, not money nor telling me 'poor you,' as did the three who died, two of whom were my husbands, because together we carried out the duties of life on earth."[106]

In legal cases, secular (civil and criminal) as well as religious, women appeared frequently as plaintiffs or defendants and also testified as witnesses. While all officials who worked in or supervised courts were male, whether Spanish or indigenous (with the latter typically holding the lowest status positions such as notary or interpreter), women brought civil or criminal lawsuits, or they might be defendants. As plaintiffs, defendants, or witnesses, they tended to participate in lower numbers than men, yet in each of these roles they were quite active, frequently speaking for themselves.[107]

However, in the center of Mexico, by the mid–seventeenth century, native women's legal status declined. Their husbands more often served as intermediaries for them; their rates of participation in property transactions decreased, at least in civil cases over property; and they served less frequently as guardians for children in lawsuits.[108] Nudzahui women's colonial legal activities changed less over time, but Zapotec women participated to a lesser extent in the colonial legal system, at least as witnesses, which has been linked to the distance between indigenous communities and the Spanish settlement of Villa Alta, where cases were tried. Further to the south, the market-women of Quito in colonial Ecuador, known as *gateras*, so successfully defended themselves in a series of mid-seventeenth-century suits brought by the pulperos, or grocers, that they succeeded in greatly enlarging the range of goods they could sell. They thus helped to transform the late seventeenth-century marketplace "into the unregulated sector which characterizes street markets today, in which women of all races participate."[109]

Paradoxes marked colonial native women's family lives and political activities. While families and kin were a resource for women in dealing with the economic burdens placed upon them and the violence that was a frequent part of their lives, that violence was often rooted in those very family relationships, especially those with husbands or lovers or both. While women had recourse to the legal system and their legal participation reveals their resilience, such intervention was frequently inadequate to lessen the abuse inflicted upon them. When such abuse came from officials, extrajudicial measures might be called for. Women were often active in a variety of protest actions, sometimes of a ritual nature, other times of a more secular nature.

Some protests were rooted in local issues and were neither anticlerical nor antistate, yet they demonstrate the existence early on of a "gendered etiquette of revolt," to use Steve Stern's term to refer to women's acts of protest aimed at legitimizing unrest by men, women, or communities.[110] In 1569 in Mexico City, a period during which tensions between the regular and secular clergy ran high, members of the secular clergy began to harass some Nahua *alcaldes* (civil officials) and Franciscan friars marching during the Feast of the Assumption. Native women and men both responded to the clerics by stoning them. The clerics in turn addressed a complaint to the viceroy, who had the alcaldes arrested. But when groups of indigenous people, among them many women, began to turn themselves in, the viceroy soon realized he could not arrest everyone and dropped the charges.[111]

While women took a similarly active role in a protest in the parish of Zacapan in Michoacan, this protest was aimed against a Franciscan friar, fray Gaspar Cuaco. Cuaco had jailed one Andrés Quaraqui for having a suspicious book in his possession. After a month, dissatisfied with the community's native officials, who had done nothing to free Quaraqui, a group of women took matters into their own hands, breaking into the jail and freeing him. When Spanish authorities sought to investigate, the women said that they had all been involved and took over the jail in protest. The authorities then arrested the women, and native male leaders testified against them, branding them as impudent and shameless ("atrevidas" and "desvergonzadas"). Authorities ultimately punished seven women, who each received fifty lashes, were exiled from the community for two months, and had to provide two months of service to the local hospital without pay. The actions of the Purépecha women, while perhaps rooted in this gendered form of protest in which the moral authority of women served to help legitimize a protest and protect communities from the backlash of authorities, went beyond it to reveal female political action aimed at Spanish authority, religious and secular, and perhaps even a rift with the men of their own community.[112]

In the Andes, women's protests with strong religious elements went farther still. The 1560s saw a movement of resistance emerge in parts of the central Andes, the Taki Onqoy, or "dancing sickness." Partially an expression of nostalgia for older ways, partially rebellion against the Spanish presence, over half the participants in this movement of religious revival were female. Perhaps Taki Onqoy's greatest significance lay in the rationale it helped provide for one of the strongest and longest lasting campaigns against idolatrous beliefs seen in Latin America, based on the European belief that idolatry, superstition, witchcraft, and sorcery ran rampant through indigenous communities.[113] Native men and women became caught up in the webs of accusations spun by the campaigns against idolatry. Records kept by clergy carrying out these campaigns provide strong evidence for continuity in the gender-parallel patterns of religious authority within Andean communities, a parallelism stronger than in the secular realm, where offices and titles either disappeared or were downgraded in authority. That parallelism may even have been reinforced by male absence, due to labor requirements or outmigration, thus leaving a greater space for female practitioners. But this space became more dangerous as Spaniards subjected male and female healers and practitioners to increased surveillance. The curandera Juana Icha, for example, was investigated by church authorities in central Peru in 1650. Accused of entering into pacts with a mountain deity who was also a devil, she admitted to having sexual relations with this figure and having asked him to intercede on behalf of fellow community members. Like Icha, those unlucky enough to be accused of any of a wide range of idolatrous practices became vulnerable to inquiries and serious punishment.[114]

While church authorities in most places accused more women than men of sorcery, both were subject to the extirpation campaigns. Yet their communities revered many of the accused women and viewed them as specialists with communally accepted authority. Some of them trained other women, including their daughters, to succeed them. Other Andean women chose to remain virgins who dedicated themselves to a spiritual life, but they devoted themselves to figures of local deities, or wak'as.[115] Such activities—sometimes supported, even encouraged, by kurakas—represent both a continuation of the parallel tradition of female authority and clear evidence of culturally sanctioned resistance to the loss of a still-viable spiritual world and the imposition of new beliefs and institutions of political economy. Important participants in activities of resistance, women continued action along parallel lines to men's, and some female roles in the religious realm intensified under colonial conditions.[116]

In both Mesoamerica and Peru, indigenous women also made important contributions to actions of protest and rebellion. Highly visible participants in rebellions across central Mexico, women not only commonly participated but also led as many as one quarter of such actions. When women led community uprisings, and most often these were aimed at civil authorities, they were "visibly more aggressive, insulting, and rebellious in their behavior toward outside authorities" than were men.[117] Female leadership of some protests in which both men and women participated suggests that while Stern's "etiquette" may have been a common pattern in collective violence, some women played real leadership roles, in which they contributed to planning and participated in actual fighting. Colonial authorities in the region of Quito noticed women's ardor as rebels during the eighteenth century and punished them severely. Yet neither in the northern Borderlands region nor in Maya areas do women appear to have participated as directly, though gendered etiquette appears to some extent in Maya-area revolts.[118]

In the Tzeltal Revolt of 1712 in the Cancuc area of highland Chiapas, for example, a revolt more extensive and planned than the short-lived revolts common to the central region, the visions of a young Maya woman, María

López, led her to instruct the community of Cancuc to build a shrine. Out of such a relatively commonplace beginning, and after the Catholic Church tried to put down this episode of cult worship, grew a lengthy, organized rebellion. While the *indizuela* ("little Indian girl," as the Spanish called her) continued speaking to the Virgin and a broader public, and called the indigenous population of the area to war, neither she nor other women seem to have played roles in the political and military decision-making that underlay a complex rebellion in which some five to six thousand Maya soldiers fought.[119]

Women were more active in the leadership of uprisings in the Andes, especially those of the late eighteenth century, including the Tupac Amaru rebellion of 1780–81 and the Tupac Katari rebellion of 1781. While some women participated in the rebel armies as camp followers, others "functioned as soldiers and even military commanders." The wives of the major leaders of these rebellions (José Gabriel Tupac Amaru and Julián Apasa Tupac Katari, respectively) were each important leaders in their own right. Micaela Bastidas Puyucahua, the wife of Tupac Amaru, served as a commander, and local leaders referred to her as Señora Gobernadora (governor), La Coya, or La Reina (Quechua and Spanish terms for queen).[120] The use of these titles displays a late colonial manifestation of an indigenous parallel-gender conceptualization. Her correspondence (with her husband and others) reveals her intelligence, strength, strategic skills, and commitment to her cause. Yet the complexity of the ethno-racial structuring of the colonial world also stands out, as Bastidas may well have been of mixed, probably mestiza identity. Bartola Sisa, wife of Tupac Katari, who worked as a trader from early in her life as well as a seamstress and washerwoman, likewise led troops, helped to strategize, and was also referred to as a quya. Other women joined Bastidas and Sisa in playing important leadership roles. These included Tomasa Titu Condemayta, cacica of Acos, who became an early supporter of Tupac Amaru's cause.[121]

Spanish authorities were appalled by the participation of the women, who were unable to use the usual gendered legal defense that emphasized feminine weakness and lack of education. Seen as excessively aggressive, even manly, the leading women of these rebellions received punishments as harsh as those of the men, and colonial authorities publicly executed the women, displaying their heads and limbs in several provinces. Yet Andeans supported the military roles of prominent female relatives of the male leaders, accepting participation in both leadership and support roles by female members of both leading indigenous families, as well as peasant women.[122]

The participation of women in rebellions across colonial Spanish America, while influenced by the gendered expectations of the Spanish, meant that a style of revolt relying on women to provide moral authority or legitimacy was useful and common. Nevertheless, deeper examination reveals that women frequently played more extensive roles in defending their communities and ways of life. While a variety of local issues provoked rebellious responses during the eighteenth century, the intensification of economic exploitation of indigenous communities through the forced sale of goods, coerced labor, and changing tax policies was an especially important factor. Such intensification led to increased male absence and greater work burdens on women, and often threw fragile household and community economies out of balance. Women participated in resistance activities planned and led primarily by men because women, too, bore the impact of such policies. Yet their styles of participation also depended on traditional, culturally patterned styles of authority and leadership, gendered traditions that reasserted themselves in novel circumstances.

Conclusion

This chapter began with the enigmatic image of Malintzin, whose short and tragic life encompassed so much change, foreshadowing a colonial period characterized by gendered transformations for indigenous populations. Some scholars believe that native women, especially those who lived in or migrated to cities, were often able to take advantage of new economic opportunities, while men endured "only an emasculating experience" during conquest and its aftermath.[123] Others argue that the burdens placed on women, particularly rural women, were heavier than those placed on men because, in addition to their labor burdens, men—Spanish and indigenous—sexually abused them.[124] This chapter shows each position to be neither wholly true nor false. Even though the balance of evidence suggests that forms of gender complementarity and parallelism declined, they did not altogether disappear. In part this is so because complementary conceptions of gender roles continued to characterize at least some aspects of everyday life among many indigenous groups, in part because where an indigenous individual sat in the native social hierarchy had a great impact on that person's life experiences and well-being throughout the colonial period.

But two other factors also proved significant for an analysis of the gendered impact of Iberian conquest and colonization. First, geographic location and cultural traditions matter deeply. Where a group lived, how Iberians chose to exploit that region, which particular group one belonged to, and that group's own gendered traditions shaped an individual's experiences. For example, the intense exploitation experienced by Central America's native peoples, including the region's women, differed from that of the Yucatec Maya, even though both places can be thought of as peripheries of the Spanish empire. Second, neither indigenous men nor women had a single "colonial" life course, not simply because class hierarchies shaped experiences even after class compression became marked but also because paradoxes often marked natives' lives. While Europeans imposed new forms of economic organization and belief systems, colonial control never came close to being complete, and spaces existed for the assertion of rights and identities. This chapter shows that gender had a bearing on how women and men experienced each of these aspects of colonial life, but culture and place, in combination with chronology, also gave shape to women's and men's lives.

T wentieth-century ethnographers have found that culture and place continued to influence both gender ideologies and women's and men's lived experiences, the subject of the next chapters. While scholars are still learning more about indigenous peoples and their histories during the nineteenth century, it is reasonable to argue that for most groups, especially the vast majority living in rural areas, their worlds seem to the contemporary observer more colonial than modern. How did nineteenth-century events—most importantly, the creation of independent nations—influence native peoples and gender roles?

For many of Latin America's indigenous groups, perhaps the most significant process affecting them in this period was a narrowing of spaces, geographic and cultural, for viable alternative ways to be indigenous, a process that began in the late eighteenth century and continued into the twentieth.[125] Access to land declined significantly, as collective land rights increasingly became a thing of the past. Across Latin America, including Brazil, new national governments sought to privatize communal holdings that proved especially helpful to large landowners seeking to increase the size of their estates. In addition to appropriating large amounts of land, elites—liberal or conservative—wielded old and new ways to coerce and exploit the labor and earning power of citizens of new nations such as Mexico, Peru, and Bolivia, though these changes occurred at different times and rates in different places. And even though the liberal state-building agenda (which dominated governments of many of the nations with large indigenous populations) officially eliminated the use of ethno-racial designations, hierarchical categorizations, while simplified, became more rigid. Indigenous communities and peoples thus endured greater impoverishment as their land base eroded and their legally recognized identity as "indios" officially disappeared. The newly empowered estate owner "'took charge' of 'his' indigenous workers, securing the reproduction of generations and providing protection; he administered a species of justice (at the hacienda courtyard . . .) and his powers stretched over individual and domestic life cycles, as well as the generational cycle of the population." In effect, entire indigenous populations in Latin America's new nations took on the "jural minor" status that Spanish law had defined for women and children.[126]

Civil codes governing family life in the new nations hewed closely to Iberian traditions, with men continuing to be the legal representatives of households. Husbands still administered both dowries and common property of married couples; they could restrict wives' employment and control their earnings. Nonetheless, women's labor in diverse types of work in both rural and urban settings continued to provide sustenance for their families and communities (though government records often failed to accurately record their work).[127] In most regions, men within indigenous communities increased their hold over use and ownership rights to the shrinking land base. When women did inherit land, poverty might force them to sell it, or courts might intervene to undermine women's inheritance, especially wives' inheritances from their husbands, as took place in highland Ecuador, for example.

But evidence also shows that indigenous women played important roles in the emerging market economies of the new nations of nineteenth-century Latin America. Native women in late nineteenth- and early twentieth-century southwestern Nicaragua saw an increase in their economic activities as artisans and merchants and, in small numbers, even began to own newly privatized plots of land. A wealthy female merchant, Antonia Lojo (of Poopó, near Oruro, Bolivia), owned a hacienda and was a major lender to both creole and indigenous individuals. Her 1843 will listed monetary and in-kind debts owed to her of over 2,400 pesos. Other Bolivian women, if not as wealthy as Lojo, either *chola* (urbanized, acculturated indigenous women) or mestiza, began to establish *chicherías* (bars or pubs for making and selling chicha and food that also offered music and dance) alongside roads, near markets, and on the outskirts of towns and cities. But the chicherías and their indigenous or mestiza owners held an ambiguous position. They were commercially successful; yet elites viewed these women and their businesses, like the indigenous domestic servants working throughout the cities of nineteenth-century Latin America, as sources of contagion, bringing dirt, disease, and dishonor to those in contact with them.[128]

In other realms, such as protest and rebellion, women's participation came to be more frequently expressed through supportive, background roles. Women's use of courts as a means to deal with problems such as domestic abuse or exploitative labor practices became less effective as their poverty, illiteracy, and lack of fluency in Spanish, as well as the tendency of nineteenth-century legal codes and courts to reinforce patriarchal familial relations, undermined colonial judicial protections. In the arts, writers and artists of the early national period began to depict indigenous women passively as beautiful virgins or as Virgin Mary figures representing the new nations or the Americas as a whole. Indigenous women came to be seen as intercessors par excellence and national symbols of fertility and abundance, as both artistic and print media conveyed gendered images that portrayed ethnic identity through female submissiveness (an image at odds with the treatment of urban indigenous women as dirty and diseased by elites and authorities in everyday life). National cultures, indigenous communities, even indigenous male leaders promoted this docile visual image well into the twentieth century.[129]

One exception to the more passive portrayals and patriarchal structures of authority within indigenous families and communities that developed in many areas across nineteenth-century Latin America occurred among the Mapuche population of Chile. There, "from the end of the nineteenth century to the present . . . the Mapuche religious world has been mainly represented by the *machi*, or women shamans."[130] As Mapuche men became farmers—a change from their former roles as hunters, fishermen, and breeders and traders of cattle—and as the pressures of modernization, education, and cultural change fell more on men than women, the concept and practice of tradition, especially traditional religion, became increasingly associated with women. The role of shaman (whose primary function was that of healer, though practitioners also began to practice divination and carry out public rituals by the end of the nineteenth century) became feminized, and female healers became more, not less, powerful. While this example appears unusual, given other kinds of political and cultural change in nineteenth-century Latin America, it may also be the case that as scholars reconstruct the histories of nineteenth-century indigenous communities in greater detail, we will gain a more nuanced understanding of women's roles and gender relations, equivalent to that provided by ethnographers for the twentieth century.

4

With Muted Voices

Mesoamerica's Twentieth-
and Twenty-First-Century Women

Rigoberta Menchú, as famous as she became by producing autobiographical texts and winning the 1992 Nobel Peace Prize, was not the first twentieth-century Mesoamerican indigenous woman to write her story. That honor belongs to doña Luz Jiménez (born Julia Jiménez González). She worked as a model for Diego Rivera and others among the international group of artists seeking to revolutionize Mexico's art, society, and culture during the 1920s and 1930s, an example of the *indigenismo* (Indianism) of elite Mexican intellectuals. They celebrated Mexico's native past yet tried to suppress indigenous identities and integrate native people and communities into the new national mainstream. Jiménez authored numerous folkloric texts, and most important, wrote an autobiographic volume entitled *De Porfirio Díaz a Zapata: Memoria náhuatl de Milpa Alta*.[1] However, while a reader can look up the book using Luz Jiménez's name, on the title page, its compiler, Fernando Horcasitas, is credited first as the translator and editor, and doña Luz is credited second for her "Nahuatl Recollections."

While Jiménez makes her presence felt strongly from page 1 of the book, a tension exists within the text over just whose story lies at the center of the book, doña Luz's or the town of Milpa Alta's. A similar tension can be found in Rigoberta Menchú's memoirs, especially the first volume entitled in English, *I, Rigoberta Menchú*, in which Menchú's own story and those of her family, her village Chimel, her people (the K'iche' Maya), and all Guatemalan Mayas compete for the reader's attention. The complexities of authorship of each of these volumes might account for the contradictory nature of each text. But maybe the compilers' choices (Horcasitas in the case of Jiménez, Elizabeth Burgos in the case of Menchú) also reflect both a popular and scholarly tendency to efface the voices of indigenous women. Such scholarly choices help to reinforce images of indigenous women, from both early and late in the twentieth century, as voiceless, outside of history, and as subjugated by, yet emblematic of, their families, communities, and cultures in their silent and hardworking way.[2]

The next chapters seek to move beyond such images. They focus on indigenous women in twentieth-and twenty-first-century Latin America, with this chapter covering Mesoamerica, and the next treating indigenous women of South and Central America. While ethnographers have supplied an almost overwhelming amount of information (in books and articles on a host of topics, not just those looking at gender and women specifically), until very recently, they often downplayed both women's economic productivity and their community-based, agrarian, or ethnic activism.

For Mesoamerica, the idea that indigenous women's productive activities have been confined to the domestic realm, carried out largely within their households in the service of household members, has been both powerful and persistent. Historian Arnold Bauer, for example, argues that the region was characterized for thousands of years by an almost unchanging gender division of labor shaped by the time-consuming requirements of a maize-driven agricultural economy and a tortilla-based diet. For Bauer, women's household labor centered around corn-grinding and tortilla-making and anchored an unchanging core of the indigenous economy dating back to 3000 B.C.E., that lasted into the late nineteenth century. In his view, the spread of the *molinos de nixtamal*, or mechanical mills, used to grind maize, allowed Mesoamerica's indigenous women to take on new productive activities that revolutionized their lives. Apart from failing to notice that Mesoamerican diets vary in the degree to which tortillas are eaten, Bauer's analysis assumes that the indigenous peasantry inevitably lived in nuclear family settings. He pictures mothers who were solely responsible for their family's food supply, downplaying ways that women in extended family households and through kinship and fictive kinship networks organized both tasks and the circulation of material items so that they could carry out the work of both production and reproduction. It is also important to point out that Andean women never used grinding stones the way Mesoamerican women did but nonetheless experienced some of the same kinds of domination as well as opportunities for agency.[3]

This chapter and the next will show the ways that indigenous women filled institutionalized economic and political roles in order to carry out tasks of production and reproduction. These roles carry authority and express women's agency by involving them in political and social conflicts and activities of resistance, even though gender dynamics, kinship and household structures, and patterns of land ownership often limit women's range of action within indigenous communities. The patriarchal political structures of nation-states, a carryover from both colonial political and legal structures and the liberal nation-building agenda of the nineteenth century, reinforced by political and economic changes of the twentieth, also influence gender roles and dynamics in these communities. The chapters show, too, that the degree to which women are politically active varies not only according to gender patterns within native communities but also to relations between communities and nation-states, and interventions by outside groups, religious or civil, governmental or nongovernmental.

Few scholars have attempted to assess and compare women's roles and gender patterns across modern Latin America.[4] Recent studies, however, emphasize that political ideologies early and economic changes later in the twentieth century undermined patterns of complementarity in indigenous gender relations. Anthropologist Brenda Rosenbaum contends, for example, that political changes meant to more fully incorporate indigenous communities into Mexican national political structures promoted male participation at the expense of women. This patriarchal political structure eroded women's agency at the same time that women served as the public face of subordinated indigenous peoples.[5] While true for much of the twentieth century, recent indigenous political movements, supported by democratizing activities occurring widely across Latin America, have served to promote and reinforce indigenous women's political activities. But women's political participation continues to be shaped by daily realities in which women spend large amounts of time performing productive labor and shouldering heavy reproductive responsibilities. These female roles have also been made more difficult by a changing, intensifying global economy that has burdened women in many indigenous communities with heavier workloads, a topic explored in depth in this chapter, by examining the histories of Nahua, Zapotec, and Maya women from the early twentieth century on.[6]

Nahua Women: Complementarity within Submissiveness

Robert Redfield captured the idea of the house-bound Nahua woman most poetically when he said: "While he [the Tepoztlán male] is led by the cycle of the sun, she [the Tepoztlán female] is the servant of another cycle—that of hunger and its satisfaction." Other ethnographers, especially those conducting fieldwork in the 1940s and 1950s, also stressed this notion of women's work as almost solely domestic (see fig. 4.1), as did Luz Jiménez herself, when she described how "men used to work and women made tortillas and cooked the food" in turn-of-the-century Milpa Alta. Anthropologist Oscar Lewis acknowledged, however, that Nahua women might on occasion perform either agricultural labor or work as domestic servants.[7]

In fact, Nahua women's work has not been only household based during the twentieth century, it has also varied regionally and changed over time. Understanding regional variations in women's work requires us first to comprehend how Nahua groups are spread over a large area of modern Mexico and the variations among Nahua communities. Contemporary Nahuas are the descendants of Nahuatl-speaking central Mexican highland groups who were divided into a number of separate ethnic groups, the best known among them

FIGURE 4.1. A Nahua woman from Hueyapan prepares corn meal
for tamales. (From Judith Friedlander, *Being Indian in Hueyapan*,
St. Martin's Press, New York, 1975, 75. Courtesy of Judith Friedlander.)

being the Mexica. Today's Nahua populations can be found as far north as the
state of San Luis Potosí, though much of the contemporary Nahua population resides in the central states of Hidalgo, Mexico, Puebla, Tlaxcala, and the
Distrito Federal. Nahuas also live in Guerrero to the west and Morelos and
Veracruz to the south and east.[8] Given that Nahua communities span such a
large area, encompassing a host of regions and environments, it is hardly sur-
prising that local economies vary, along with women's roles in them.

Many ethnographers, across a wide variety of regions, writing after Redfield and Lewis, began to report that Nahua women worked outside their
homes, most often as domestic servants. In 1976, ethnographer Doren Slade
further noted that Nahua women's situation was changing, "and women are
free to engage in many occupations that bring in good profits." Yet a careful reading of ethnographic reports makes clear that both within and outside
their own homes, Nahua women have long performed a variety of tasks with
income-earning potential, although they typically earn lower wages or profits
than do men.[9]

Among the most common income-earning activities for twentieth-century Nahua women have been food preparation and the closely linked tasks
of selling in local or regional markets and store-keeping. While weaving does
not dominate either women's domestic or income-earning work patterns
(as it does for Maya women, especially among highland groups), women do
weave both for household members and for sale.[10] Commercialized weaving
takes place in household-based settings or in urban-based textile factories. In
either case, women earn wages, although these are often low because they
frequently work part-time, but also because women tend to be assigned less
skilled tasks. In some areas, women participate in agriculture, helping in the
sowing or harvesting of maize or other cash crops, as well as working smaller
gardens near their homes. They also raise animals, though as Nahuas turn
to larger scale ranching, evidence of gender segregation within this activity
exists, with men controlling cattle ranching. In coastal Nahua municipalities
such as Pajapan (Veracruz), women also fish. Another important category of
work performed by women relates to the life cycle and health. Nahua women
serve as midwives, curers, and ritual specialists. Other women work as bakers,
butchers, or teachers.[11]

Age is a major influence on Nahua women's labor patterns. Younger,
unmarried women or older, widowed women can more easily undertake
work that requires mobility, either shorter term, perhaps traveling to a larger
town or city on a daily basis, or longer term, as in semipermanent or permanent migration. But other factors besides age can shape women's ways of
performing productive labor. Thus while middle-aged, married women tend
to be more house-bound, having daughters old enough to take on some
household and childcare activities can free some women to perform wage
labor. Older daughters may help fathers with domestic chores as well. Girls
from the Morelos village of Hueyapan occasionally accompanied fathers who
worked as seasonal laborers on large estates from the 1930s to 1950s in order
to provide domestic labor such as food preparation.[12]

But the type of marriage women enter into or whether—even when
they have children—they are married at all also influences their labor patterns.
Primary wives in polygynous marriages (which, while declining in number,
still exist), whom Nahua communities consider to be of better reputation
than secondary wives, tend to do work that can be carried out in domestic
settings, such as producing goods, for example food or crafts, for markets. Secondary wives and unmarried female heads of households may be forced by
circumstances to work outside their home, selling in the streets, near schools,
or in local markets.[13]

Economic changes over time, some dating back to the Porfiriato (a
period of economic change and modernization named for the Mexican
president Porfirio Díaz, who ruled for over thirty years, beginning in 1876)
also had gender-related consequences for labor, especially in more populated,
less remote Nahua regions. Textile factories were built in municipalities of
Tlaxcala in the late nineteenth century, drawing primarily male workers but,

at the same time, removing them from households that still had to survive. Women took up the slack. During the 1920s to the 1960s, as the pace of industrialization quickened, land redistribution began to make peasant agriculture more sustainable in some places during these years. For example, in the municipality of Xalatlaco on the southeastern edge of the Toluca Valley, women worked with men to cultivate family-held plots, and during harvest times, poorer women worked for wages on the lands of others. But beginning around 1960, population increase led to an increasing number of families without land. Because the costs of agricultural production rose much faster than crop prices, agricultural labor no longer sustained families, and men and women both began to seek other kinds of paid labor.[14]

Oscar Lewis pointed to another economic change occurring in the 1920s that he viewed as particularly significant for women: the establishment of commercial corn mills. Lewis, like Arnold Bauer, saw this as a positive change for Nahua women, even if men had reservations:

> The mills have been great time savers. Previously women spent from 4 to 6 hours a day in grinding corn, often getting up at four in the morning to prepare *tortillas* [unleavened corn meal cakes] for their husbands. Now women get more sleep, usually rising at six. The time saved is used in various ways, such as sewing, knitting, going to church more often and doing household chores. The added leisure has in many cases been turned towards gainful pursuits such as raising chickens, pigs and cows. Furthermore, many women became merchants on a small scale and regularly go to Cuernavaca to sell corn, beans, eggs, etc. The improved communication offered by the road and bus lines made this possible. Men assert that there has been an increase of adultery because of the fact that so many young married women go to Cuernavaca alone. Indeed, the husbands of these women are called "tonto" or fools for permitting their wives such liberties.[15]

More recent changes have led to an increased economic vulnerability for contemporary indigenous communities throughout Mesoamerica and are having a negative impact on Nahua communities and families.[16] Gulf Coast Nahua communities provide a particularly effective example of such changes because of the influence of the growing oil and cattle economies there. Land loss, outmigration, and increasing concentration of whatever capital exists in indigenous communities in male hands has undermined women's access to and control of land and wages. These patterns cause women to become more dependent on men for their economic survival, which then undermines whatever reciprocity existed between men and women. Nahua women have become increasingly impoverished; their access to land continued to decline in the 1990s, and their ability to influence the governing of their communities remained weak, even in the face of high rates of male outmigration. Yet in Xalatlaco, peasant (or "post-Nahua") women have increased access to a range of jobs, from teaching to secretarial work and even industrial jobs, and their earnings have correspondingly increased, which gives them somewhat greater authority within their families.[17]

Aside from wages, land ownership constitutes another aspect of women's and familial well-being and economic power, or lack thereof. While Nahua women of the Huasteca, Tlaxcala, and Puebla tend not to own very much land, because sons inherit more property (both land and houses) than do daughters, there are some areas, especially in Puebla, where land transmission is bilateral, as is Mexican inheritance law. The most common pattern for Nahua women, however, is that they inherit land (privately owned plots or shares in communally held lands, usually referred to *ejidos*) from their fathers in the absence of surviving sons or may inherit small amounts of property from their mothers or other kinswomen related through their mothers. Women may also inherit land from husbands, but this type of transfer is rare and usually takes place so that the widow can care for the land and the family until the children are old enough to farm it.[18]

In Pajapan on the Gulf Coast, women have experienced growing inequality with men in regard to land. Although some women have held rights to communally held lands of the municipality, these were women married to well-off Nahua ranchers. Others who pressed their cases for communal rights were widows or single mothers of young children. The spread of cattle ranching, however, has made many of the region's men land poor, but to the extent that Pajapan Nahuas retain land or other forms of wealth such as cattle, it is men who own and control such wealth, not women. This concentration, in combination with the male-dominated post-Revolutionary political structure, makes it difficult for women to assert rights to land or other economic or political claims.[19]

In moving from the economic sphere to that of politics and Nahua women's political activities, we must examine the contexts in which women can hold power, starting with the family and household. While the nuclear family is the most common residential and economic unit in Nahua communities, the three-generation unit of grandparents, married children, and their children remains an important social unit even today.[20] Patrilocal marriage, in which a young bride moves in with or near her husband's family and provides labor for the family under the direction of her mother-in-law, helps reinforce this structure. Where matrilocal residence occurs, it is relatively rare and takes place when a father has no sons and a young man has few prospects for inheriting land. On the Gulf Coast, young Nahua men customarily moved in with and provided up to a year's worth of labor for their prospective fathers-in-law prior to the actual marriage, though this practice began to break down with the growth of the cattle industry.[21]

The Nahua marriage pattern means that young brides typically endure a difficult period of adjustment during which they hold a position of extreme submission, though age brings changes in women's status in the household. Female submissiveness, especially in the early years of marriage, may also be reinforced by the common marital practice of *robo de la novia*, or "stealing the bride," in which a young man "'robs' a woman from her natal household and brings her to live with him in his father's house." Widely reported to occur among many Mesoamerican indigenous groups, not just Nahuas, this practice suggests coercion, but at times it allows partners to choose each other without parental interference and at less family expense.[22]

Female submissiveness does not preclude high levels of conflict between spouses. As Oscar Lewis noted in 1951, "according to the ideal culture patterns for husband-wife relations in Tepoztlán, the husband is an authoritarian, patriarchal figure who is head and master of the household and enjoys the highest status in the family," but Lewis also observed that the dominant husband–submissive wife pair is, to a large degree, a "social fiction." While the new wife faces a difficult period of adjustment, leaving the security of her own home and needing to please a demanding mother-in-law, she will someday probably be a mother-in-law, one who enjoys authority over her children, daughters-in-law, and occasionally even her husband.[23] Some evidence suggests that in recent decades central Mexican peasant communities have experienced a transformation in the patrilocal marriage system toward one in which married sons separate and form their own households sooner (a pattern called by anthropologists a neolocal postmarital residence pattern). In addition, women increasingly have other options, including bringing their husbands into their parents' home or separating from their husbands and living either with their parents or as single mothers. Some women even choose not to marry yet go on to have children, managing with the help of parents, siblings, other kin, or friends.[24]

Nahua women also take on more publicly recognized authority roles. These include specialized roles related to mothering, such as midwife, ritual roles expressing male/female complementarity, or ritual roles expressing female power. For example, the Nahua midwife (*amantecatl* in Nahuatl [N], *partera* in Spanish [S]), usually female, attends to births. Other women work as curers (*tepahtihqui* [N]; *curandera* [S]) or shamans (*tlamatiquetl* [N]) who attend to a variety of medical problems (see fig. 4.2). Midwives can play a ritual role in postbirth ceremonies, and another ritual role played by women is that of the marriage broker, or *siwatanke* (N).[25] In each case—midwife, curer, and marriage intermediary—the role echoes a socially recognized role dating back to the prehispanic era.

That echo is heard again in another set of socially and culturally recognized roles, roles complementary to ritual positions held by men. While adult men hold the religious offices that constitute today's *cargo* systems of indigenous Mesoamerica, in many areas, including Nahua regions, wives and other family members participate actively in the religious and social activities that are part of the system. While Nahua communities vary in the degree of elaboration and hierarchy of offices and sponsorship, Nahua wives play a critical role in enhancing their husbands' prestige. They gather information that may help their own husbands or hurt others in the competition for positions and

FIGURE 4.2. A female shaman from the Nahua community of
Amatlán interpreting corn kernel patterns during a divination session.
(From Alan Sandstrom, *Corn Is Our Blood*, University of Oklahoma
Press, Norman, 1991, 196. Copyright © by the University of Oklahoma
Press. All rights reserved. Reprinted by permission of the publisher.)

help their husbands with the lavish meals and gift giving that play a role in
the system. In Chignautla (Puebla), a cargo-holder's wife holds a title parallel
to her husband's (*mayordoma/mayordomo* [S]).[26]

Apart from sponsors, participants in an array of roles or rituals often
include women and men. For example, in Amatlán, the Huastecan Nahua
community studied by Alan Sandstrom, the yearly fertility ritual, known as
Tlakatelilis, includes many elements of parallel male/female participation or
symbolism, with these complementary activities or symbols necessary for the
completion of each stage of the ritual. In San Bernadino Contla (Tlaxcala),
wives of male ritual specialists or husbands of female specialists have specific
tasks to carry out that aid the successful enactment of these roles. Widows,
women who are separated, or single mothers in Nahua villages of the Balsas
River Valley (state of Guerrero) perform ritual tasks reserved especially for
these women, and their villages reward them by providing them with land
rights for houses, farming, and pasturing animals. Single women also sew or
help organize dance troupes of young girls whose dancing is necessary for
important ceremonies.[27]

Some female religious figures can be powerful in their own right. The
tlahuelpuchis ([N]; bruja/os [S], or witch) of rural Tlaxcala are overwhelmingly

female. Their actions, expressed primarily through infanticide, articulate the anguish daughters-in-law often experience because of patrilocal residence and the need to labor for and get along with their mothers-in-law. While most young wives can adjust well to the cultural norm, conflict between mothers- and daughters-in-law is not rare. This structurally predictable antagonism and witchcraft are closely correlated and symbolize the power of life and death that Nahua women have over their own children, a power they can—on occasion—use against their mothers-in-law, and perhaps against their husbands as well, who may not provide the emotional support their wives desire.[28]

Even though Nahua women have arenas in which they assert authority and power, such actions are both complementary yet subordinate to those of men, primarily because Nahua family and kinship configurations undermine female agency more than they promote it. The patrilocal marriage pattern, already noted, plays a prominent role in weakening female assertions of will. Two other factors also limit women's potential autonomy in family and community life: age at marriage and violence against women.

First, significant difference in the ages of spouses at first marriage has been a persistent characteristic of Nahua marriages through much of the twentieth century, especially among rural Nahuas. This common age difference reinforces male authority within the household because women have had "less time to learn habits of responsibility and independence which contributes to their weaker position in the family particularly during the early years of marriage." Second, male authority may also be expressed and reinforced by physical means, with men occasionally engaging in violence against their wives. Such violent male anger can be expressed when wives fail to perform household tasks to their husbands' satisfaction, when wives challenge their husbands' authority or spending, or when wives express jealousy over their husbands' attractions to other women. Female infidelity and expressions of autonomy, such as leaving the house for work, can also provoke beatings.[29]

But rates of violence in Nahua communities appear to vary. Larger, more acculturated Nahua or Nahua-descended communities seem to suffer from higher rates of violence and more tension in spousal relations (perhaps because women have more opportunities for independent action), with smaller, more isolated communities exhibiting warmer relations. While Nahua women have attempted some forms of political action during the twentieth century, few of these efforts target the issue of domestic violence, and little has been written about how contemporary Nahua women might mobilize familial or communal resources against such violence. Nonetheless, in more acculturated communities, rates of violence appear to be declining, because as women's monetary contributions increase, their willingness to tolerate physical abuse decreases.[30]

Even though their political roles, secondary to men's even in the prehispanic era, declined further during the colonial and postcolonial periods,

Nahua women have not been wholly lacking in authority and influence. Because the cargo system remains widespread and has both religious and political implications, women's roles within it—complementary to and necessary for husbands to carry out their positions—influence whether men hold offices and, when they do, how they carry out their appointed tasks. There are even rare cases where women hold cargo positions, for example, widows who hold them in place of their deceased husbands in Chignautla. There, a single woman in the early 1970s who met the customary requirements held an important cargo position. While she carried out the responsibilities of the office, helped by relatives and neighbors, she avoided some activities, especially those involving excessive drinking. Although this woman also kept away from some instances of religious politics, she had real influence, because she participated in the community's political discussions, and "recruitment decisions could not be made without her vote."[31]

Twentieth-century post-Revolutionary Mexican community political structures, centered on governing councils made up of and headed by men, undermined women's traditional forms of political participation by weakening the cargo system in which women had influence, could assert authority, and achieve prestige. Women's lesser familiarity with Spanish and the heavy burden of daily work that continues to shape their lives reinforce these structural impediments imposed by the Mexican government, even though all women gained the right to vote in 1953. Contemporary Nahua women in Pajapan, for example, participate at far lower rates than men in local political meetings or groups of any kind. In Ameyaltepec and San Agustin Oapan (Guerrero), men dominate public meetings, although female household heads can attend meetings where land is discussed, as do women whose husbands have migrated to the United States. Women also attend and actively participate in smaller, more informal meetings.[32] These lower rates of political participation in turn affect women's ability to organize and speak out on a range of issues. Nonetheless, indigenous women have tried to make their voices heard.

From the 1930s on, peasant women from a variety of regions in Mexico protested their lack of access to ejido lands. In addition, the "First Aztec Congress," held in 1940 in the town of Milpa Alta, raised some women's issues by expressing concern about the exploition of female manual labor, especially the situation of women taken to urban areas to work as domestic servants.[33] In 1972, the Interamerican Women's Commission (of the Organization of American States) met in San Cristóbal de las Casas, Chiapas. While Maya women predominated, women from a variety of indigenous groups spoke directly on the problems they viewed as most important to them, from work conditions and male outmigration to alcoholism and other health problems. The health problems of Nahua and other central Mexican indigenous women include malnutrition, high rates of maternal mortality, little access to state or national health services, and mistreatment—such as forced contraception or sterilization—when medical doctors have contact with them.[34]

The activism of today's indigenous women has historical roots both in the colonial period and in the twentieth century, as women have attempted to use evolving political structures—whatever the impediments may be—to at least raise their concerns. Nahua women have also formed cooperative units to produce and market crafts and deal with problems like domestic violence.[35] For example, some 200 Nahua women in the state of Puebla belong to the organization Maseualsiuamej Mosenyolchikahuanij (United Women Working Together), which participates in a variety of economic activities, such as an eco-tourism project, and serves as an advocacy group taking on issues like domestic violence and health and human rights in local, national, even international settings. Others involved in marketing cooperatives have found them to be educational and believe they can encourage greater community organization. A young Nahua woman says:

> The truth is that, before, we didn't know anything. Only now, since we've been in the organization, we've learned so much. We have woken up to so much. Because before, only men were organised; they ran the co-operative and everything and the women always stayed at home waiting for them. It's only now that women go to meetings too, and join in, and get organised. We already know what we want: to make our commmunities stronger.[36]

In addition, some 550 Nahua women from thirty-four communities in the states of Hidalgo and San Luis Potosí created a microbank to provide small loans to women to begin or sustain a variety of small business. Teenek women of the Sierra Gorda, where Nahuas are also located, fed up with high rates of male consumption of alcohol, forced the closure of illegal alcohol production facilities and have publicly burned hidden supplies. Marcelina Martínez of the town of San Rafael Tampaxal said, "A lot of men are not happy with this. . . . But, oh well. At least now they spend time with their families, so in the end things are better." But the development of women's co-ops or grass-roots movements to promote gender equality has not occurred to the extent it has elsewhere, especially in Maya areas, in part because the indigenous peoples of Mexico's central region are so dispersed, and in part because of the intense waves of change they have experienced.[37]

Beginning in the late nineteenth century and increasing during the Revolutionary era of the teens and 1920s, economic, cultural, and social changes have abounded. Accelerating again during the 1980s and 1990s, recent global economic shifts and armed struggles have impoverished and torn apart native communities like never before. While widespread agreement exists that events of the recent past have had a devastating impact, anthropologists do not agree on which earlier periods were the most crucial for change. Nutini and Isaac, for example, see the late nineteenth and first decades of the twentieth centuries as a particularly significant period, with economic and technological change very rapid, and social and religious change occurring much more slowly. For these ethnographers, causes of change include "the erosion of land

and the lack of cultivable lands, the establishment of textile factories in the region during the second half of the past century, the labor migration, and the improvement of forms of communication and transportation." Documenting the comparative impact of these changes on women and men over the twentieth century would not be a simple task, because most anthropologists remain so focused on the "ethnographic present." Nutini and Isaac show, however, that in the Tlaxcala region in the period from roughly 1880 to 1930, language, women's labor patterns, and the clothing they wore all demonstrated at least some degree of change, though some women remained more traditional, neither migrating to perform domestic labor nor changing their clothing, nor speaking Spanish instead of Nahuatl.[38]

Oscar Lewis, on the other hand, sees the era from the 1920s through the 1940s as the critical period of change. Transformations in population patterns and forms of communication and transportation, increased access to education, and the introduction of the automated corn-grinding mill were particularly important, in his view.[39] For Gulf Nahuas, Veronica Vázquez García argues that marked change came somewhat later, from the 1950s on, as cattle ranching and later the growing oil industry transformed the region's economy. Each of these new economic activities affected women, as agricultural land was converted to pasturage for animals and as the oil industry influenced local labor patterns. Women found whatever access to land they had declining, while their need for cash grew as the economy became increasingly monetarized. As larger numbers of men began to migrate out of the communities of the Pajapan region, greater numbers of women started to migrate as well.[40]

The migration of indigenous women to urban areas became relatively common in many parts of central Mexico. This pattern is especially characteristic of the second half of the twentieth century, because the number of women, single or married, who must fend for themselves and their children has increased as the growing impoverishment of rural communities worsens. Population pressure, shortages of arable land, and male outmigration may well be related factors contributing to a feminization of indigenous poverty, both rural and urban. The demographic, technological, and economic changes driving indigenous and rural impoverishment in the second half of the twentieth century led to a virtual superexploitation of women desperate to help themselves and their children and families by performing a variety of kinds of work for extremely low wages. This army of impoverished, displaced, single, married, or widowed indigenous women, the "Marías," can be found in the streets of Mexico City and many other urban areas. Many of them are Nahuas, others are Mazahuas or Otomís, and they and their children, who often accompany them, sell fruits or vegetables, gum, or crafts such as dolls in the city's markets, historical centers, and other tourist areas. In other regions, permanent male outmigration has left communities of extremely poor women and children in great need of social programs that would provide economic development and education. But government programs have proven to be a mixed blessing, with some Mazahua women complaining, for example, that doctors associated with the Mexican social program Oportunidades (Opportunities) treat them like servants. They "tell us to bring water so they can bathe. The doctors call those of us who don't speak Spanish stupid."[41]

Because Nahua and other central Mexican indigenous groups are exposed to a greater degree of integration into the market economy and are widely dispersed over a large landscape, the material factors driving economic and cultural change loom particularly large in understanding how women's lives, work patterns, political participation, and family lives have changed. While Nahua women experience a greater level of exposure to the dominant mestizo society, with accompanying language loss, their lack of educational access also hampers their efforts to better their own and their families' lives.[42] As we turn to southern Mesoamerica, we come to regions where stronger indigenous ethnic identities and political organizations exist and where native groups may be somewhat better equipped to appeal to outsiders for material and political support.

Oaxaca: Land of the "Matriarchs"?

If there is one group of women who excite the imaginations of an army of observers, it is the Zapotec women of the Isthmus of Tehuantepec in southern Mexico. They have been seen as exotic matriarchs, as feminist lesbians, even as Amazon-like "guardians of men . . . shaking their wombs, pulling the *machos* [men] towards them."[43] Subject of Beverly Chiñas's influential 1973 feminist ethnography, *The Isthmus Zapotec: Women's Roles in Cultural Context*, these "tiger beauties" (as naturalist Hans Gadow referred to them in 1908) had already been the subject of exoticizing image-making by nineteenth- and twentieth-century Mexican and foreign artists and writers such as Charles Brasseur, José Vasconcelos, and especially the writer and artist Miguel Covarrubias. He wrote of the *tehuanas* (Zapotec women of the Isthmus of Tehuantepec) that each was "a queen—a composite image of Egypt, Crete, India, and a gypsy camp. Zapotec poets never tire of writing in praise of the flowing lines, the stride and carriage, of their women" (see fig. 4.3).[44]

With these women's image of both physical beauty and strength, it is revealing that such a variety of observers also celebrated them as exotic sex objects. In fact the reality for Isthmus and other Zapotec women, as well as other indigenous women of Oaxaca (including groups such as the Mixtec, Mazatec, and Mixe), is that they work incredibly hard and are often the economic mainstays of their families, providing material and social support for the region's households and communities.

The modern state of Oaxaca lies at the northern and western end of the Mexican southern highlands and has long been home to a striking array of indigenous languages and cultures.[45] While archaeologists and ethnohistorians have concentrated their attentions on the Mixtecs of the western part of

Old lady and girl in everyday dress

FIGURE 4.3. Tehuana-style dress as shown by Miguel Covarrubias.
Note the similarity in composition to Frida Kahlo's famous 1939
painting "Las dos Fridas." (Illustration by Miguel Covarrubias, *Vogue*, Jan.
15, 1942, 53. Copyright © 1942 Condé Nast Publications, Inc.)

Oaxaca, it is the Zapotecs of the southern and eastern portions of the state
who grabbed the attention of twentieth-century ethnographers, focusing on
the Isthmus of Tehuantepec, yet also chronicling a variety of highland Zapotec communities in other parts of the state. Zapotec women and the gender
system serve as the subjects of an extensive ethnographic literature, a literature
that does not support an image of them as exotic sex symbols dominating

men in a matriarchal society. Women are powerful because of their important economic activities and because in Zapotec society women function in
parallel, semiautonomous female domains through which they hold socially
recognized roles of authority. But poverty, violence, social unrest, and a male-
dominant ideology continuously shaped women's lives throughout the twentieth century to such an extent that not only can we conclude that Zapotec
communities offer no examples of matriarchy, but also we must conclude that
women's power, real as it is, is lesser than Zapotec men's, though a contrast in
women's authority with Nahua and Maya women remains.[46]

Turning to the world of work, we find a strong female presence throughout the marketplaces of Oaxaca, demonstrating their important role in the
region's economic system. While marketing may be only one of the ways that
women contribute to the household and community economies of Oaxaca,
women tend to make up the dominant presence in the markets. Likewise,
they play an important role in the trade that brings goods to the markets.[47]
If women's place as sellers in highland markets has been noted, their place in
lowland Isthmus markets has been the stuff of legends:

> The most conspicuous asset of Tehuantepec is its women. Their cos-
> tume, beauty, and tropical allure have become legend among Mexi-
> cans in the way that the South Sea maidens appeal to the imagina-
> tion of Americans. It is these women, from the age of ten to eighty,
> who run the market, which, in a woman's town, is the most impor-
> tant of Tehuantepec's institutions . . . the women of Tehuantepec
> meet every morning and every evening for the things they enjoy
> most: selling, buying, gossiping, showing off their bright clothes, see-
> ing one another, and being seen.[48]

Their enduring work as sellers in Isthmus markets was first described in the
late sixteenth century and noted in ethnographies written throughout the
second half of the twentieth century.[49] Women of the urban and rural communities of the region sell a variety of goods, including fresh and cooked
foods (meats, fruits, vegetables, tortillas and breads, and dairy products), house-
wares, clothing, and jewelry. While sellers often process the goods they sell
themselves, especially food items, women frequently work as traveling merchants, buying, transporting, and selling a variety of products in smaller, rural
villages as well as larger towns and cities. Those who serve as middlewomen
reselling products processed or made by others are known as *viajeras*. They
can pursue a variety of buying and selling strategies, sometimes focusing on
selling locally produced foods or goods (mangos or fish, for example) in Oaxaca's larger marketplaces, sometimes taking Oaxaca-produced goods to other
regions. Viajeras differ from the home, street, or market sellers in their nearly
constant travel and their more economically and socially extensive trade networks, through which they not only buy and sell but also arrange shipping
and make their way around larger towns and cities. Women also sometimes
participate in higher prestige commercial exchange activities, which are more

FIGURE 4.4. Zapotec woman from the village of Teotitlán using a large foot-powered treadle loom. (From Lynn Stephen, *Zapotec Women*, University of Texas Press, Austin, 1991, 131. Courtesy of Lynn Stephen.)

heavily capitalized and in which men are generally more deeply involved, as part of trading teams or *comercias*.[50]

The merchant women of the highland weaving community of Teotitlán del Valle fit this latter profile. The village of Teotitlán (whose people are known as *teotitecos*), studied during the 1980s by ethnographer Lynn Stephen, offers a full picture of the labor patterns of *zapotecas* (Zapotec women) and how these have changed during the second half of the twentieth century. While the women of this community perform a variety of types of productive labor, many work as weavers, a traditional female occupation that has grown in importance as Teotitecos increasingly produce for tourist and export markets (see fig. 4.4). Most women live in households where the men, women, and children dedicate themselves to weaving, but about 10 percent of the community's households are merchant households that buy, sell, and oversee textile production. The women of these households "described themselves as managers or laborers working primarily in their husband's business" and generally hold higher status in the community, reflecting the greater wealth of their households. As the differences between households become more pronounced, this change in the class structure affects the gender system. Stephen reports that higher status women appear to be losing some of their traditional autonomy, and the complementary gender labor roles, once part of the household weaving system, also appear to be on the decline.[51]

These complementary work roles in Teotitlán and elsewhere in highland communities frequently include, in addition to weaving, participating in agricultural labor, especially the harvest, carrying water, and serving as medical and ritual specialists. But the economic and social forces intensifying weaving in Teotitlán have meant that many of Oaxaca's indigenous groups and communities are facing the incorporation of their laborers and production into expanding national and global markets. While Teotiteca weavers remained relatively well paid compared to men, elsewhere rural Oaxacan women's wages, like those of Nahua women, are extremely low, and men often perceive and identify women's work as labor that "helps out" rather than labor that is in itself productive, further undermining the cultural valuation of gendered labor patterns as complementary.[52]

Another factor shaping highland women's work experiences, especially from the 1950s on, has been outmigration. While men often made up a majority of outmigrants, in some areas, women migrated as well, with many of the younger women going to cities to work as domestic servants.[53] Even though employers frequently exploit them, some Zapotec women perceived urban work as easier because they no longer had to work in the fields in addition to doing housework, and they wanted the opportunity to earn a steady salary. A Zapotec woman who migrated to the United States in the 1980s commented that

> It's not quite as hard here as living in my village. There I was weaving a lot but I couldn't make enough money. There are a lot of customs in Teotitlán— weddings, engagements, other things—you have to buy a lot of things. They are all expensive. In contrast here, I am working and I'm not spending anything. I am working with my family. They take care of expenses, for eating.[54]

Of course, for the older and poorer women left behind, the loss of younger women's labor deprives them of help, thus increasing the demands placed upon them for productive and reproductive labor.[55]

As the twentieth century went on, couples changed their postmarital residence patterns, with a tendency toward generally brief patrilocal residence followed soon thereafter by a move to their own residence becoming more common. This shift meant that highland women's access to the cooperative female labor that allowed them to fulfill multiple household roles weakened. Isthmus Zapotec women enjoyed such access, especially when their relationships with their daughters-in-law were good ones, because the patrilocal phase lasted longer there. But many contemporary Isthmus couples also now prefer to form their own households as soon as possible.[56]

Just as kinship relations and household organization fail to lessen the impact of increasing market penetration and its accompanying class schisms and increased gender stratification, women's property ownership and inheritance rights do not blunt these changes. Zapotec women inherit land and animal herds through bilateral inheritance practices. But population pressure, the loss of lands to large agricultural producers (of coffee, for example), and the impact of outmigration and proletarianization of agricultural labor mean that the self-sufficient farming family, working either communal lands or lands owned by the husband or the wife, represents a much smaller number of families than was the case earlier in the twentieth century. Women also inherit clothing or gold jewelry, but these items usually serve as either investment or collateral and therefore are frequently pawned or sold rather than being passed on again. Such women's property, along with ownership of small animals like pigs and turkeys and labor contributions, played a crucial role in the politico-ritual economy of the Zapotec region for much of the twentieth century, but the ritual system has also declined somewhat in importance.[57]

While Nahua and Maya women often play an important but largely informal roles in the ceremonial life of their communities, Zapotec women experience greater public recognition for their roles, and they provide much of the labor and capital that maintains the ritual system. But while ritual feasting still takes place, its meaning has changed, shifting away from the focus on public rituals focused on saints and the civil-religious hierarchy as expressed through the *mayordomía* system toward a semipublic system of life-cycle rituals centered especially on weddings. In recent decades, growing class differentiation, waning interest on the part of many men, and the difficulties women experience translating ritual authority into political power has meant that an activity that once made an important contribution to women's status in Zapotec communities has now lessened in significance. At the same time, the civil political realm has assumed a central place, with little room for women in it.[58]

Although local governments throughout Mesoamerica treated men as the mayordomos for the civil-religious hierarchy, in Oaxaca even now most communities see men and women as joint office-holders, and women can fill in for male mayordomos if need be. Female participants gained respect, status, and community influence through holding these positions and carrying out their attendant responsibilities. They also contributed labor and material support through the system of *guelaguetza,* or reciprocal exchange of goods and labor necessary for the ritual system. While women's production, investment, and labor still continue to fuel the ritual system, such activities no longer translate into political influence or power in the wider community.[59]

In addition to roles as viajeras and mayordomas, roles that age, skill, and social prestige strongly influence, women often play three other authoritative roles in Zapotec communities—midwife, curandera, and *comadre* (godmother; female ritual cosponsor). Throughout the twentieth century, midwifery and curing were largely female occupations, and curers and midwives might be the same women, though men too worked as curers and occasionally delivered babies. Even with increased availability of Western medical—specifically obstetrical—care, women continue to prefer Zapotec midwives. This preference exists not only for reasons of cost but because midwives communicate in the Zapotec language, and Zapotecas view midwives as more experienced and knowledgeable about the birthing process.[60]

The other role through which authority and prestige accrue to women is that of comadre, a role that is part of the system of compadrazgo, or ritual kinship, in which men and women act as sponsors of children (never their own) at various important points in the life cycle. In Zapotec communities, women play a particularly important role in the compadrazgo system, even though community members prefer male-female pairs (often, but not always, husband and wife) as *compadres* (godparents). When a single individual holds the sponsorship, rather than a pair, chances are good that the individual is female. While a large number of life-cycle events and festivals can involve sponsorships (one anthropologist lists twenty-two for the community of Santa Catalina, a small village southeast of Oaxaca City with a population of about 500 people in 1979), the most important sponsorships involve baptism, marriage, confirmation, and communion.[61]

Compadrazgo may involve gifting or feasting and signifies a long-term relationship between the individuals and families involved. Since being asked to be a coparent conveys that the potential sponsor is a respected community member, people ask older and more prestigious community members more frequently. Women and men who take on this role accrue further prestige when they do so frequently. Such higher status individuals, as in the case of women curers and merchants, will have more financial obligations but will also gain allies, laborers, and more respect and prestige than other women. While community members prefer higher status couples, in fact, women are central to the functioning of the system because their social interactions, gifts, and labor maintain the system. Community members prefer better off women as comadres, and ritual spending is easier for them because it represents a smaller proportion of their household's income. As poorer women find their continuing participation in a practice that has promoted communal solidarity more difficult and as conversion to Protestantism increases in the region—requiring converts to forego participation in ritual kinship relationships—this pathway to authority for Zapotec women may be closed off, which also helps explain why Zapotec women resist conversion and men are the ones who convert first in this region.[62]

Another area where women have been active is that of contemporary politics, especially among the pro-democratizing forces of the region. In the colonial period, Zapotec women, like Nahua and other indigenous women, participated in colonial uprisings, including playing important roles in Tehuantepec insurrections in 1660 and 1715. While their public political participation decreased in the years after the Mexican Revolution, more recently, Zapotecas have begun to play an active role in local and regional political movements, although most of the formal political roles and offices remain in men's hands. Women's political activities often focus on local committees dealing with schooling and health issues, as well as in women's political action groups like the Unión de Mujeres Yalaltecas (Union of Yalálag Women), a group formed by women in that Zapotec community to democratize political power, long held by the town's caciques. The group chooses officers, has argued for a more inclusive community political process, and financially supports activities aimed at community development.[63]

Zapotec women have also participated in regional and national political parties and organizations, including the leftist political party COCEI (Coalition of Workers, Peasants, Students of the Isthmus) that dominates the city government of Juchitán. While men hold most of the leadership positions in the party and have always been the candidates for office, women make up half of the grassroots membership. Influential female members of COCEI include prominent female merchants and business owners as well as women whose husbands or sons have been particularly active. Women often march at the head of COCEI marches, though sometimes they walk separately from men or even "hold all-women protest marches. They also have their own separate political committee within the movement, which sometimes organizes special actions such as fundraisers and protest vigils."[64] Zapotec market-women even attacked a Oaxaca governor as well as police during a period of conflict with local and state governing officials in the late 1970s. Posters and book covers produced to attract support by the group commonly feature female imagery, showing them as strong, beautiful, and maternal. But COCEI, like the CNPA (National Coalition of the Plan of Ayala), a national peasant coalition representing more than twenty such regional organizations, encourages women to participate in protests, but does not address women's needs or issues. Because even Zapotec women face great difficulties articulating and enacting policies that address their concerns and needs, we must return to the question of whether this society ever was or is now matriarchal or matrifocal.[65]

While Zapotecs and others have bandied about notions of a Zapotec matriarchy, neither historical nor contemporary evidence supports the idea that women ever dominated Zapotec society. Instead, there is evidence that Zapotec women could be both authoritative and powerful, but this power tends to be enacted in women's spheres of action. Economically, women often held real power because of their work and financial contributions to households. Yet Isthmus women represent only one set of Zapotec gender arrangements. Intra-ethnic variation exists, and there are domains in which women's power was weaker than men's or was in decline, such as politics. In addition, certain characteristics of Zapotec family life negatively affect women's exercise of power.

For one thing, Zapotec women long married at very young ages. Ethnographers studying Zapotec communities from the 1930s through the 1960s found women marrying as young as eight or ten years old to young men some years older. Marriage at such young ages, with an interval between husband and wife of several years, indicates that women's position at the beginning of a marriage was a weak one, especially in cases where the bride moved to or near the husband's family's house. Some evidence, however, indicates that age at first marriage is increasing, with the young women of the Isthmus community of El Centro marrying around age sixteen.[66]

That the relationship has often signified subordination for women is also suggested by the fact that many women experience violence as part of their marriages. Anthropologist Elsie Clews Parsons observed in the 1930s that "Conjugal relations . . . are generally amiable; but if wives are not submissive and obedient they may be beaten, if not neglected or deserted."[67] Domestic violence, often tied to alcohol use, continues to be a problem that Zapotec women, for all their strength and power, face. While physical abuse of women and children is common, Zapotec women are more likely to contest that abuse than either Nahua or Maya women by bringing cases of domestic violence to local or regional authorities. Almost always male, such authorities take an anti-abuse position, but local authorities also stress reconciliation between marital partners, sometimes in response to pressure from husbands. Women's relatives, particularly their parents, try to help and support them through such difficult times, and in one interesting case from the mountain village of Talea a young wife left her husband's home because her mother-in-law frequently beat the young woman's husband, terrifying her. Family violence diminishes as spouses age however, and Zapotec women are not totally defenseless. The violence women endure sums up their situation. Far from matriarchs, yet refusing to give in to the power of patriarchs, Zapotec women are central actors not only in their families and community institutions but also in maintaining their ethnic identity, one sometimes expressed through a quest for community autonomy.[68]

Matriarchal, matrifocal, lesbian, submissive—writers and scholars have characterized these vivid, intense, hardworking women through any number of sometimes contradictory labels. While the political, ritual, even economic spheres of female activity grow more constricted, it remains the case, as Elsie Clews Parsons observed, that "the aspects of culture more closely associated with women—'remedies', weaving, cookery, and feasting—have outlasted the cultural activities of men—hunting, war, the ritual arts, and ceremonial and political organization."[69] In an early twenty-first century world where ethnic identity can increasingly be asserted and mobilized—in the case of Isthmus Zapotecs in their search for political power—Zapotec women play a crucial, double-sided role. Known for their important economic contributions and long-term political activism, they serve as particularly useful foot soldiers in the gendered etiquette of local protests and as key symbols of both COCEI ideology and Zapotec ethnic identity.

Maya Women: Working, Weaving, Changing

Just as the "strong but sexy" image of Zapotec women represents the Zapotec people in a variety of visual and written texts, so Maya women often represent the Maya people. In Guatemala, postcards with lovely, smiling images of Maya women—clad in exquisite, hand-woven *traje* (handmade clothing associated with specific Maya groups)—represent Maya culture, the women happily but silently reproducing and guarding it. Readers encounter similar images of mute female workers and weavers seeing to the survival of their culture through their largely domestic labors in many ethnographic descriptions. Such descriptions fail to account for more complex and variable realities such as the ways some women have discovered to critique and reshape their cultures and nation-states in a twenty-first-century world.[70]

Contemporary Maya women's experiences vary across diverse national and regional histories, economies, and environments. Primarily located in three nations—Mexico, Guatemala, and Belize—the Maya represent contemporary Mesoamerica'a largest indigenous group, numbering in the millions and linguistically and culturally differentiated into a wide variety of groups.[71] This section of the chapter focuses on Maya women of three areas: the Yucatec lowlands, Chiapas highlands, and Guatemalan highlands.

Ethnography in the early twentieth century took place primarily in communities of the Yucatan peninsula, much of it carried out by Robert Redfield and his close Mexican associate Alfonso Villa Rojas. While neither ethnographer paid great attention to the lives of Maya women, they each discussed the gender division of labor. In their fieldwork of the early 1930s in the town of Chan Kom in eastern Yucatan, Redfield and Villa Rojas noted that men did all the agricultural labor, except for small gardens cared for by women. While these ethnographers described some activities as shared, especially the weaving of henequen fibers into bags or hammocks, they emphasized the housebound nature of most women's tasks and stated that men held all secular and ritual offices. Further noting that men were the sole participants in public meetings, they observed that while marriage negotiators were men, women served as midwives.[72]

Later fieldwork carried out by ethnographers more influenced by and sympathetic to feminism paid more attention to the Yucatec Maya gender division of labor. As a consequence, a fuller picture of women's labor has emerged. Types of work performed by lowland Maya women include helping grow and harvest corn in the *milpas* (corn fields), operating the mechanized molinos, working vegetable gardens on houseplots, raising animals such as pigs, turkeys, and chickens, weaving, and embroidering, and in Chan Kom, baking and selling bread. Not only did women's labor appear less housebound than Redfield and Villa Rojas described, the mutual interdependence of Maya men and women in the Yucatan and other areas became clearer as well.[73] Anthropologists also began to pay more attention to the highland Maya where women specialize more in distinct crafts activities by town, generally weaving or pottery, with weaving differentiated by types of cloth, garment type, and design. Even though earlier ethnographers in Guatemala tended to discount Maya women's labor, one even asserting that women's work had "no economic value," patterns similar to those of the Yucatan existed. Maya women of Guatemala have long been economically active in and outside the home (see fig. 4.5) and may have been more active in area markets during much of the twentieth century than those in Chiapas.[74]

Weaving, however, constitutes an important part of women's work across the highlands and is an activity that serves as a source of both income and pride. Tzotzil Maya comment through song that women weave because they are women. In other words, men and women see weaving as part of the very essence of being a woman. While highland men have woven from the colonial period on, women specialize in weaving and wearing the most valuable items.[75] They make both items with the greatest cultural value within Maya communities and items with the greatest monetary value to outsiders, *ladinos* (people of mixed ethno-racial identities whose language and clothing reflect Hispanic rather that Maya influence) and tourists alike. Highland Maya men now wear traditional clothing less often, generally only for ceremonial purposes. Women still wear the distinctive traje signifying community and ethnic identity, though they increasingly wear mass-produced clothing or sometimes traje from a variety of communities, rather than only the styles or designs of their own communities. Given these changes, the overall market for hand-crafted, ethnically distinctive clothing is diminishing, even with increased tourist interest, because men now wear little of it, and an increasing number of women cannot afford these high-priced items.[76]

Such economic changes accelerated for all Maya communities in the eighties and nineties, with serious consequences for the gender division of labor. For Maya women of highland areas where greater integration into a market economy has coincided with the globalization of that economy, the changes have been particularly wrenching. But lowland Maya women have also experienced change, primarily the intensification of women's labor, sometimes through their traditional forms of labor, sometimes through the addition of new types of work.[77] The intensifying work patterns of Maya women of the municipality of Oxkutzcab (100 km south of Yucatan's major city of Mérida) illustrate these changes and the variable ways they can occur.

Two agricultural zones exist in the municipality, one devoted to traditional maize agriculture, the other devoted to commercial horticulture in which a variety of cash crops, especially fruits, are grown. The maize sector witnessed a prolonged crisis marked by a significant decline in yields, while the commercial sector has seen greater success. In the milpa communities, women have seen their agricultural labor intensify, in planting, harvesting, and preparation of maize as well as in crops like tomatoes that families try to sell in Oxkutzcab's market. The tendency of men to migrate to find salaried work

FIGURE 4.5. Woman from the Pokomam Maya community of
Chinautla, Guatemala, making pottery. (From Ruben Reina, *The Law
of the Saints*, Bobbs-Merrill, Indianapolis, 1966, after p. 172. Courtesy of
Ruben Reina.)

further intensifies women's labor. Younger women have begun to migrate as
well. They go to cities like Mérida and Cancún to work as domestic servants.
Yet neither of these work patterns allows women to better their positions in
their families or communities because any money they earn is turned over to
their families and spent immediately on necessities determined by husbands
and fathers.[78]

Women whose labor is more closely tied to the commercialized, horticultural sector of Oxkutzcab's economy have more possibilities to accumulate

and control capital. Women who sell the fruits and vegetables produced by their husbands are often able to keep a small portion of the profits for themselves that they can decide how to spend for household expenses, ceremonial functions, or purchases of small animals. A small number of these women become *revendedoras* (resellers) who buy local produce and then sell it to male commercial traders who are not from the local area, and a few become traders who sell a variety of produce grown in other areas of southern Yucatan.[79]

The revendedoras and traders hold considerable economic power within their families and households. Their husbands attend to family needs in women's absences, women make decisions about children's education, and wives occasionally convert title to the family's property to their names or decide how agricultural parcels will be used. These women report feeling pride in themselves and their Maya ethnic identity. But this economic power and self-esteem has not translated into political power. Women traders are limited to a local circuit of markets, and their roles in community political and economic institutions remains circumscribed.[80]

The social position of the women who stay closely connected to milpa agriculture is even more subordinated. Most of these women speak only Maya (as opposed to the more commercially active women who are often bilingual). They see their "Mayaness" as something negative, symbolizing poverty and backwardness. The younger women of both groups seem to prefer nonindigenous forms of work and styles of dress, but whether downplaying their ethnic identity offers any challenge to the multiple form of female subordination remains to be seen, since non-Maya women's position may well be worse.[81]

In Chiapas, women's labor shows a similar pattern of intensification but with less evidence of the development of market-based roles into entrepreneurship that might allow for capital accumulation, increase in self-esteem, and reinforcement of group identity. Chiapas Maya women use a variety of strategies to cope with a changing economy in which subsistence milpa agriculture and male income fail to meet the needs of families and households for food and cash. Sometimes women intensify their agricultural labor, sometimes they produce crafts to sell in local markets (most often woven textiles), and sometimes they sell their labor, usually working as domestics or agricultural laborers.[82] The particular strategies chosen depend both on the economic specialization of local communities as well as familial and personal factors. Ethnographer Brenda Rosenbaum's observation about Chamula women holds true for Maya women throughout highland Chiapas: "Women, particularly, seem exhausted by the tremendous effort of balancing home, a large number of children, highland milpas, and income-producing activities, while barely making ends meet." In the pottery-producing town of Amatenango del Valle, studied by anthropologist June Nash, men have begun to assist women in pottery making, long a female activity, as the prolonged agricultural crisis made both milpa and plantation agricultural labor less valuable.[83]

With most highland Maya families and communities struggling on a daily basis to support themselves, one way women have tried to cope with the low wages their labors earn—especially in the craft sector—is by forming or joining cooperatives. These provide credit to help supply material, and the women involved often receive social and emotional support to deal with the consequences of rapid economic and social change. The Mexican government's National Indigenous Institute (INI) formed the first cooperatives in the 1950s and 60s, with the earliest Chiapas cooperative appearing in Amatenango in 1973. In 1977 Sna Jolobil (House of the Weaver) formed out of a nonindigenous artists' group and became the first cooperative to be run by native women.[84] It remains the largest and most successful of the Chiapas cooperatives, with other co-ops often aligned with political parties or government agencies.

Co-ops help women receive fairer prices for their goods and teach skills in marketing, management, and politics. They provide women access to markets and credit as well as an arena that reinforces women's cultural, linguistic, and social ties. Payment, however, often arrives slowly, and husbands and other relatives sometimes resent women's earning power and the time they give to the work of organizing and maintaining cooperatives because these activities necessarily entail a more public presence for women. In Amatenango, such resentments became expressed violently when Petrona López, president of the local pottery cooperative, was murdered while running for the office of mayor in 1980. While the cooperatives cannot solve the enormous economic problems of Chiapas Maya women and families, they provide material aid and social solidarity and allow women to confront the economic and political problems of the region in a Maya way by stressing community and cooperation.[85]

In Guatemala, Maya women participate in a similar division of labor, and they face a similar range of problems as in Chiapas, including decreasing productivity of milpa agriculture, poverty, and low wages. But they do so in a political and cultural environment in which violence has been endemic throughout the second half of the twentieth century, and the larger society devalues Mayaness even more. Guatemalan Maya women's responses to the crisis in the subsistence economy have included intensification of their craft production, especially weaving, participation in waged plantation labor or in the agro-export sector, or working in *maquiladoras* (factories specializing in producing and/or processing goods for export).[86] Owners of the factories, often foreign, pay low salaries, force workers to work lengthy hours in poor conditions, and provide little job security. But none of these types of work affords women much opportunity to accumulate capital. As tourism increases, rural women respond by devoting greater amounts of time to weaving, something more urban Maya women—such as those from the town of San Pedro Sacatepéquez—have done for several generations.[87] But whether urban or rural, Guatemalan Maya women face severe economic problems as income from weaving of traje in many areas declines. While tourists may be interested in handwoven items, Guatemala's internal market for traje has decreased. Mechanized textile production based on sewing and knitting in small factories, usually owned by men, increasingly takes the place of household-based textile production. Women's control over production then decreases, and their wages remain very low. In some areas, like San Antonio Palopó, a small Kakchiquel-speaking community to the east of Lake Atitlán, men have begun to participate in commercialized weaving. Male participation pushes women out of their traditional roles, leading women to become more dependent on male income.[88]

While female weaving cooperatives have developed in some parts of rural Guatemala, these are fewer in number, smaller in scale, and frequently stimulated by development projects usually run either by the national government or non-Guatemalan charitable organizations. The smaller scale and short-lived nature of the Guatemalan cooperatives and development projects means they are even less able to provide support for Maya women in a rapidly changing world in which their incomes and social status are on the decline.[89]

Maya women's lesser access to real property in both highland and lowland areas—especially land—also contributes to their secondary social position. Throughout the twentieth century, most Maya groups favored sons over daughters in land inheritance.[90] While a few Maya communities do exhibit bilateral inheritance patterns, even when women inherit land, usually when there are no sons, they tend to receive small amounts or poorer quality land. Widows may also inherit land but generally do so in trust for minor sons, or they inherit a small share through which they can support themselves. Upon a widow's death, this share reverts to the husband's family. But even when women do inherit, given that the size of plots available for them is usually quite small, any economic advantages that accrue to them are minor.[91]

The patrilineal and patrilocal patterns of kinship and household structure that characterized lowland and highland Maya communities throughout the twentieth century mean that men have had greater access to property and power. In the first half of the twentieth century, most brides and grooms were in their young teens, with the bride often somewhat younger than the groom. However, it was common for young husbands-to-be or husbands to provide up to a year of service to the bride's father, labor that entailed a period of matrilocal residence. Only rarely did young men move to their wives' families' residence permanently, most often when the wife's family had no surviving sons.[92]

While marriages where the bride and groom form their own household right away (a neolocal postmarital residence pattern) became more common in the second half of the twentieth century and the age of marriage began to rise, Maya marriages, especially in the more traditional rural communities, retain a patrilineal quality. Sons remain tied to their fathers by the latter's power to distribute land and other resources, although parental control over marriage has clearly been declining. Parents, therefore, continue to influence spousal choice, but young women and men are not wholly without say, and elopements or love matches are becoming more common.[93] Even when marriages take place in the more traditional form, where the groom's parents take the lead in arranging it, if a young bride or her family becomes dissatisfied, separation or divorce may occur. In fact, many ethnographers characterize both traditional and contemporary Maya marriage as unstable. From disagreements with in-laws or polygyny to economic pressure and political and cultural instability, the forces leading to marital breakup are many, even though individual marital relations may provide companionship and emotional support.[94]

Maya women's work and family lives across all the regions suggest the complex blend of positive and negative valuations and experiences that characterize their lives and relationships with men.[95] On the positive side, women's work is highly valued, there are culturally sanctioned roles with authority that they can play, and their communities acknowledge them (especially in the more traditional areas) as symbols of community and ethnic identity. Women's labor is highly valued because Maya cultural beliefs stress the importance of work, and men's and women's work is seen as fundamentally complementary, as each sex depends so much on the work of the other.[96]

Women also play roles in ritual and the delivery of traditional forms of health care, especially in relation to birth, that carry authority and allow them to wield power. While Maya men have tended to dominate in the public performance of ritual throughout the twentieth century, the complementarity of the organization of work can also be seen in ritual. As Redfield and Villa Rojas explained, "the worship of the pagan rain and maize gods tends to fall into the hands of the men, while the Catholic rituals are more often in charge of the women; and ... public or community rituals are led by men, but domestic rituals by women." In the highlands in particular, women frequently prepare foods for fiestas and in some areas share extensively in the preparations and ritual connected to the community cargos, though males dominate in public ritual performances.[97] Women play other roles that span the traditional ritual and healing aspects of everyday life in lowland and highland communities. As shamans, witches, curers, and midwives, they act in publicly authoritative ways and help assure the biological and cultural continuity of their communities, even though male ritual practitioners are more visible. Such roles may be enhanced as women age and gain more prestige. K'iche' Maya refer to older women as *nan* (mother) and offer some deference, though less than that given to middle-aged and older men. Communities also treat midwives as esteemed figures, according them deference, which is especially paid—in some communities—by the children whom they delivered.[98]

Many anthropologists believe that there is another way in which women play a crucial public role, that is, preserving local forms of ethnic identity. Both community insiders and outsiders closely associate highland Maya women, who are strongly identified as more culturally conservative through language and clothing, with community identity. All three factors—women's role in production and marketing, their complementary participation in ritual and healing, and their association with ethnic identity—serve as sources of power and underlie some degree of complementarity in the social roles of women and men.[99] But that complementarity is powerfully undercut by a number of factors, including greater overall male activity in the public realm, patterns of sexuality and violence, and differences in the overall health and nutrition of Maya women and men.

Observers note that deference to authority from younger to older and from female to male constitutes an important principle governing Maya social relationships throughout the twentieth century across the regions inhabited by Maya groups. Anthropologists also frequently report male dominance of public speaking at many types of gatherings, public or domestic, political or religious; lower rates of female voting; and considerable levels of tension between men and women. This tension, exacerbated by changing economic patterns, can manifest itself in the area of sexuality and sometimes through domestic violence.[100]

Women's lack of knowledge about menstruation and sexuality prior to the commencement of sexual relations or marriage (since virginity is not often highly stressed in contemporary Maya communities) has been reported for a large number of Maya groups, as have young ages at marriage and parental tendencies to disregard daughters' feelings about prospective husbands. All these factors may be connected to the brittle marital relations already mentioned, with conflict, separation, and divorce relatively common. Beliefs and tales indicate that, although Maya women associate sexuality with pleasure, antagonism between women and men is also common.[101] Alcohol abuse frequently exacerbates marital tensions, as do male absence due to labor migration, perceived threats to male honor, and the economic pressures of the current period.

Rape is another form of violence against women that has worsened under the conditions of conflict that mark many Maya areas, especially in the highlands. Women appeal to their fathers, brothers, or local authorities for support, but they have a notable lack of success in using the judicial system to prosecute rapists.[102] One exception to this pattern is the Chiapas community of Amatenango, where June Nash reports that, if a woman could prove her right to be where an attack or abuse took place, town authorities would find in her favor, and her relatives "were then allowed to publicly beat the accused in the town hall." While female-on-female violence occurs (most commonly in markets), such conflicts are far fewer in number. Though such fighting expresses enmity, it does not have the disciplinary aspect that domestic violence often has, and acts of violence and rape cannot always be easily distinguished from political violence toward women.[103]

Violence raises the issue of health problems faced by Maya women. Among these are the continuing tendency to begin having children at young ages, often between the ages of fifteen and twenty, with little prenatal care. Apart from high rates of maternal mortality, adolescent pregnancy and breastfeeding often lead to deficiencies in calcium and phosphorous, anemia, and hypertension, the combination of which can leave women with serious long-term health problems. Malnutrition exacerbates those conditions related to reproduction that are endured by Maya women. Their access to contraception and abortion remains minimal across rural areas generally, but this pattern is especially prevalent in areas like Chiapas and other mostly poor, mostly indigenous regions.[104] Both are subjects of religious and social controversy due to the doctrines of the Catholic Church and Protestant sects, though some Protestant groups encourage the use of birth control. The forced sterilizations that have taken place in the highlands of Chiapas and Guatemala have made rural women fearful and resentful toward Western gynecological and obstetrical care and knowledge. Relations between traditional practitioners and doctors and nurses representing national medical institutions are also troubled. Rural women, thus, often lack access to modern health care, and their experiences with alcohol—either their own abuse or more commonly the abuse of alcohol by the men in their lives—also negatively influence their health and well-being.[105]

The combination of the worsening social and economic conditions within all kinds of Maya communties—lowland, highland, urban, rural, Catholic, Protestant, traditional, and newly formed—with the increasing presence of governmental agencies, NGOs, and a variety of activists means that many Maya communities and groups actively seek a political voice. Motivated by concerns about the economic well-being of their families and communities, women have been pushed toward social action of various kinds. But their ability to draw on a Maya ideology of complementarity, as well as the existence of female roles with authority in certain domains, also propels them. Maya women have been active agents in dealing with social problems and cultural changes, as they face a new century in which rapid change seems to be the norm rather than the exception.[106]

What changes have had the greatest impact on Maya women and gender roles? One set has to do with the economy and women's patterns of work. Maya women, lowland and highland, became increasingly linked to the global economic nexus during the late twentieth century, and indigenous families and communities have experienced dislocations in subsistence-based work patterns that bring an increased workload for women and children. Another change affecting communities and their members has to do with the intensification of class difference.[107] The sale of women's crafts is often a critical factor that allows some families to become significantly better off. These activities give some women real economic power and autonomy within their families, but this power does not translate into broader power or influence in communities or regions, though women may express more openly their desires as to whom or whether they marry. A recent study of the town of San Pedro Sacatepéquez, a commercial center in the western Guatemalan highlands, shows that women have responded to changing economic conditions by creating new commercial activities, including smuggling low-priced goods

FIGURE 4.6. Woman from the Chiapas village of Amador
Hernández confront police during a 1999 protest against building a
road. (Courtesy of AP/Wide World Photos.)

from southern Mexico and reselling them (at cheaper prices than other sellers) and selling secondhand clothes (usually castoffs from the U.S.), an activity
that can be quite profitable.[108]

The high levels of political violence endured in the highlands of Chiapas
and Guatemala have also had a negative impact. Political violence reached
such a level of intensity that women spoke out, joined, or formed organizations to counter the destruction of life, property, and the very communal
bonds that hold villages and towns together. The gendered nature of political
violence also shaped women's emerging political activism. Both the armed
conflict in Chiapas (1994–) and the civil war in Guatemala (1975–85) exacerbated the problem of violence against women, with increases in rape, beatings,
and killings of indigenous women.[109] Of course the state and its paramilitary
representatives actually direct much of the violence at men. But the high
levels of violence also affect women and children, especially because women
have at times acted as shields in defense of their communities against armies
and paramilitary groups (see fig. 4. 6).

Social dislocations, due to moves by refugees into established communities, *colonias* (communities of exile, often resulting from forced expulsions),
or refugee camps where living conditions are poor and rates of violence

against women are high, lead to the breakdown of traditional forms of social control.[110] A horrifying incident took place in Acteal, Mexico on December 22, 1997, in which a right-wing paramilitary group massacred forty-five individuals, members of a pro-democracy group known as Las Abejas (The Bees). Thirty-two of those murdered were female, including five pregnant women and fourteen young girls. Acteal suggests that women who participate in prodemocracy movements are just as likely, perhaps even more likely, to be targeted as men.[111]

Guatemala's deadly counterinsurgency violence (resulting from the state's targeting the large indigenous sector of its population as subversive) led to another serious social problem: the large number of widows left to head families. These women have had to try to survive in the postwar years, a period marked by continuing political tension and economic decline of indigenous communities. Prior to the civil war in Guatemala, widowhood was relatively rare, because women's lives tended to be shorter than men's.[112] In the postwar years, indigenous women have suffered serious economic, social, physical, and psychological problems as they cope with the losses of husbands and sons. The factionalism within many communities, which worsened in connection with the counterinsurgency violence, has made finding social and economic support from kin or community members problematic. State action designed to erase memory hindered the postwar healing process and reinforced increased factionalism. While some widows turned to alcohol out of despair, others sought comfort in solidarity with other women through informal or formal organizations whose goals may be both benevolent (to help widows with their economic and social problems) and political. Indigenous women have, in fact, turned to a variety of organizations with social and political influence and in so doing have taken a more public role than ever before.[113]

While certain women, such as Comandante Ramona of the EZLN (Zapatista Army of National Liberation) or Rigoberta Menchú, closely associated with Guatemala's CUC (Peasant Unity Committee), became symbols of indigenous women's potential as political activists and leaders, such individual actions should be seen as part of a wider trend toward female collective political action, often in groups that are solely or primarily female.[114] Sometimes women of local communities band together to protest the actions of local landowners, paramilitary groups, or local officials. Others ally themselves with movements that are part of the emergence of a civil society struggling in favor of more democratic and open political systems in both Mexico and Guatemala. Still others join political parties or groups, like the EZLN, that either represent or struggle against national and local power structures.[115]

The EZLN specifically targeted the recruitment of women in rural communities as they began to organize in the 1980s because of a belief that women could persuade their husbands and ultimately whole communities to join the movement. The recruitment efforts aimed at women were successful, with perhaps as many as 40 percent of EZLN soldiers being female.[116] Women's presence in the EZLN and indigenous rights organizations led to the inclusion of women's issues in a variety of meetings and documents. The "Revolutionary Law of Women," a text distributed by the EZLN in January 1994, illustrates the way Zapatista women articulated a desire for more egalitarian gender relations in both the army and their home communities, by encouraging men and women to rethink customs and traditions that denigrate or damage women physically or emotionally. The text asserts women's rights in the areas of labor, political expression, health, and education, demands that rape and violence against women be punished, and affirms their place in and responsibility for the EZLN's revolutionary struggle.[117]

While parties and rights organizations tend toward a mixed-gender composition, other organizations—such as cooperatives or formal women's organizations like the Grupo de Mujeres (Women's Group) of San Cristóbal de las Casas, founded in 1989 and made up of both indigenous and nonindigenous women—include mostly women. The GAM (Mutual Support Group), begun by urban, ladina, Guatemalan women in 1984, soon saw its membership swell, with large numbers of indigenous women joining because disappearances affected them in large numbers. In 1990, Guatemalan refugee women in Mexico formed the organization Mamá Maquín, one of several started to help refugee women. The group helped the United Nations High Commissioner on Refugees to conduct a survey of women's needs in some sixty refugee camps and aided the development of programs focused on job skills, education, health, and human rights. Named for one of the first women killed when the military began to massacre Mayas during the civil war, since the refugees' return to Guatemala, the group has concentrated on health, land rights, free trade, and globalization, particularly as these issues concern women.[118]

Another important type of organization is the widows groups that emerged in Guatemala. Such groups formed on both the local and national levels, with CONAVIGUA (National Coalition of Guatemalan Widows), which began in the department of El Quiché, Guatemala, in 1988, being the largest and longest lasting.[119] Membership in these groups allows women to search for communal solutions to the economic, social, even psychological problems they encounter as part of the endemic political conflict. Such membership allows women to experience a higher degree of gender and ethnic solidarity than before, yet competition and even conflict sometimes mars relations within groups, as women struggle for access to scarce forms of aid and with the changes in their own lives that widowhood brings.[120]

If global economic and political forces have the greatest impact on Maya women and communities, new cultural forces, especially educational and religious, also influence their lives. These forces have been impinging on Maya women's lives since the mid–twentieth century, though they intensified during the 1980s.[121] Indigenous women have long lagged behind other sectors of Mexican and Guatemalan society in their access to education and literacy. A number of factors lead to indigenous girls' school attendance falling behind that of the general population, other girls, or indigenous boys at all levels (with female attendance dropping even more sharply in the upper grades). A Tzotzil woman named María described her education, saying:

> I finished up to third grade. I learned Spanish from my teachers at school. They were federal bilingual teachers, and they were good teachers. They only spoke Spanish to us. At first, since we only spoke Tzotzil, we couldn't make sense of what they said. But little by little we understood. It was a good experience. We stopped going to school, though, because my father couldn't afford our education any more.[122]

Other reasons for women's lower rates of education include household needs for female labor and doubts about the value of education in regions where rural indigenous people see themselves as having little social or economic mobility, as well as government policies that encourage families to send sons to school rather than daughters.[123]

Yet Mayas in many areas have begun to embrace education for young women as well as young men, in order to increase family and community access to literacy, quantitative, and technological skills.[124] While some educated girls become teachers or nurses, most use new skills to diversify their families' economic activities in more traditional ways (such as intensifying craftwork); but schooling sometimes undermines certain traditional values. For example, educated girls may eschew traditional forms of clothing, which then weakens the market for a major female economic activity—the production of indigenous styles of cloth and clothing.[125] As Maya women become increasingly bilingual, they may shift from their role as transmitters of traditional languages to become promoters of the national language. When Maya women of two Yucatec communities—Xocen and Dzitás—became increasingly bilingual, language change in each community then proceeded very rapidly, because adolescents and children soon became only Spanish speakers.

Literate Maya women have also used their own languages in drama and poetry to give voice to their criticisms of contemporary political and social problems. Two Chiapas Maya women, Petrona de la Cruz Cruz and Isabel Juárez Espinosa, started FOMMA (Fortitude of the Maya Woman), a theater and self-help group encouraging literacy, job skills, and self- expression. Maya women in Chiapas and Guatemala also participate in photography projects that document both the impact of the high levels of violence they and their communities have endured as well as changing ways of life. Maya women, far from always being culturally conservative, sometimes promote the turn away from traditional, often syncretic, forms of Catholicism toward Protestantism, which began to attract larger numbers of converts in Chiapas in the 1970s and in Guatemala in the 1980s.[126]

The turn to Protestantism in indigenous communities began for multiple reasons. While the presence of foreign missionaries no doubt played a role, conversion can be both a political statement of protest, accompanied by a refusal to participate in the entrenched power structure or pay the religious taxes in many communities, and a personal statement of desire to leave behind poverty, alcoholism, and despair.[127] Women often initiate conversion after a crisis with a husband or child. Once a husband sees that his wife is serious, he may follow her decision, but it is a decision with real consequences, because the result can be either voluntary or forced exclusion from the community of origin. Such a move often leads to a life spent scrambling to survive for both men and women—in urban environments, where further change in gender roles (such as authority structures within urban Maya households), language patterns, dress, and identity often occurs, or in rural peasant communities, where Maya from a variety of areas have formed agricultural colonies. While Maya women dominate both the conversion process and church attendance, they play little role in church hierarchies, since the evangelizing Protestant sects tend to conceive of leadership as solely male.[128] Thus, even in cultural changes in which Maya women play an active, but often unrecognized, role, gender relations display the complex blend of complementarity and patriarchy that marked male-female relations in families, work, and communities throughout the twentieth century.

Conclusion

It is ironic that Maya women, whose communities have exhibited less gender parallelism than Nahua or Zapotec women's, are the most politically active of these three ethnic groups. To some extent their activism rests on the base of complementarity in male-female roles that can be found across Maya communities. But the roots of women's activism lie also in the extreme suffering generated in Chiapas by the ongoing, low-intensity warfare between local political groups tied to the Mexican national state and its former long-term governing party (PRI, Institutional Revolutionary Party) and forces struggling for democracy and representation and in Guatemala by the civil war of the 1970s and 1980s. These political conditions attracted the attention not only of ethnographers but also of urban-based national organizations, as well as international groups, that have supported local democratizing efforts, including those of women. Neither Nahua nor Zapotec women have attracted nearly as much attention; women in these groups seem more isolated from forms of political support that might help them to gain a greater voice in local or national affairs. Nonetheless, the rise of Maya female activism, in combination with other factors, like economic change, the increased presence and support of multiethnic regional, national, and international women's groups, and even liberation theology and its persistent questioning of inequality (including, on occasion, gender inequality), mean that women's issues across indigenous Mesoamerica receive growing support through a proliferation of grassroots women's groups. These groups are creating new forms of dialogue with men, peasant groups, and national and international feminist groups.[129]

Thus globalization can be said to have a variable, even paradoxical, impact. On the one hand, it seriously undermines the economic viability of indigenous communities and households, in some cases leading to a feminization of poverty that carries with it extreme deprivation and exploitation. Yet, in political and cultural terms, it enhances indigenous women's voices and political power. The extent to which this enhancement takes place depends, to some extent, on the degree of attraction the outside world feels for a particular ethnic group. It is also fair to say that neither national nor international feminist or aid organizations have been able to effect much change thus far in indigenous women's access to land, capital, or credit, though patterns of access to land for indigenous women are beginning to change. Nor have they had much success in changing the conditions of poor health and domestic violence with which many native women must contend. Yet a woman from the Zapatista-led Chiapas community of Oventic recognized that women have made progress, even as they continue to seek more rights: "We have only just begun to learn to be free, that we don't need to ask permission from the men all the time. You still see women walking behind the men, it's true, but when you have been struggling for so long you learn to be patient."[130]

Globalization also brings with it a growing media power to disseminate representations of indigenous women. While arguments about the veracity of Rigoberta Menchú's first book or images of Maya women defending their communities appear in the *New York Times*, perhaps the more stereotypical image of the Huichol woman, María Isabel, played by a nonindigenous actress in the popular Mexican *telenovela* (soap opera) *"Si Tu Supieras María Isabel"* (If You Knew Maria Isabel), had the greater impact. Seen by more people, it undoubtedly reinforced demeaning ethnic stereotypes about indigenous women that are the heritage of nineteenth-century ideologies, however much such ideologies and images may be dressed up and romanticized.[131] Bettering these conditions will depend on the development of greater gender equity in both rural and urban political structures. Local and national indigenous groups giving voice to women's concerns and objectives could strengthen this process.

5

Fighting for Survival through Political Action and Cultural Creativity

Indigenous Women in Contemporary South and Central America

If globalization, modernizing aid, and political and cultural changes—especially war, urbanism, and changing ethno-racial categorizations—often carry negative consequences for South and Central America's indigenous women, there female autonomy and activism sometimes found their fullest expression in native Latin America. In parts of the Andes, where women's political energies express themselves very directly and openly, this is especially the case. No one expressed these energies and her ideas better than Bolivian Domitila Barrios de Chungara (see fig. 5.1), political activist and wife of a miner, who described herself and her beliefs by saying:

> I'm proud to have Indian blood in my heart. And I'm also proud of being the wife of a miner. I'd like everyone to be proud of what they are and what they have, of their culture, their language, their music, their way of being, and not accept influences from abroad so much, try to imitate other people who, ultimately, have given little of worth to our society.[1]

A range of visual images—from the almost naked, exotic, sexual-yet-not-sensual Yanomami women depicted by Napolean Chagnon and his collaborators in their well-known ethnographic films of the Amazon to the serious and dignified Kuna women of Panama depicted in many photographs[2]—also exhibits the variety and dynamism of female roles. Like the words of Barrios

FIGURE 5.1. Photograph of Domitila Barrios de Chungara.
(From Domitila Barrios de Chungara, *Let Me Speak!* Monthly Review
Press, New York, 1978, 7. Reprinted by permission of Monthly
Review Press.)

de Chungara, the visual and written image of the savvy, sometimes irate, chola
market women of Peru and Bolivia captures well the economic and cultural
struggles in which indigenous and other women have been engaged. Discussion of the chola offers us a pathway into the worlds of work, family, and
political struggle of Andean women.

Women in the Andes: Revolutionizing Tradition in the
Highland Cultures of Ecuador, Peru, and Bolivia

From the nineteenth century on, the term *chola* has served as an important, generally negative, cultural marker. It signifies a fundamentally
indigenous but fluid urban female identity. Seen as both a "dark-eyed temptress" who is also a "dirty Indian," cholas are most identified with markets.
Whether the marketplace is "in the capital city or in smaller provincial centers, [it] constitutes the border marking the separation between the urban
and rural spheres and the nexus in which they intersect." That border, so
often crossed by female sellers and shoppers, mediates many other divisions in Andean societies, especially upper class/lower class, clean/dirty, non-
Indian/Indian.[3]

The chola women who fill the markets, clean and cook for the houses,
and pose for the postcards and covers of travel magazines and cookbooks
for the middle and upper classes of the towns and cities across the Andes
remind us that Andean indigenous groups remain a large and vital presence
in today's Andean nations. Indigenous women have a long history of working, participating in the public and political life of their communities, and
shouldering responsibility for the maintenance of family, kin groups, and
communities. Women have also played an important role in the resistance of
indigenous and peasant peoples to ongoing modernizing and nationalizing
projects that result in the impoverishment and weakening of the region's
indigenous identities. Women's work has played a key role both in maintaining indigenous communities and in negotiating and ameliorating many of
the sweeping economic, political, and cultural changes faced by rural communities, along with the large numbers of migrants, male and female, flood-
ing cities like Lima, Ayacucho, Quito, and La Paz. Although Andean native
peoples, whether they are Quechua- or Aymara-speaking, share many cultural practices and characteristics, there are many differences among them
as well, which reflect not only the varying impacts of local environments,
urbanism, and economic change and development but also differences in
the histories of the three nation-states—Ecuador, Peru, and Bolivia—where
Andean groups are concentrated.[4]

Ethnographies done by two North American anthropologists also influential in Mesoamerican ethnographic studies of the first half of the twentieth
century, Elsie Clews Parsons and Ralph Beals, recorded the broad range of
work done by women in the 1940s to the mid-1960s in Ecuador. Parsons
worked in Peguche, near the town of Otavalo, Ecuador. She stressed that both
men and women farmed, women spun, and men wove but also observed
that households lacked a rigid division of labor and implied that—at least
within households—there was rough equality in women's and men's roles
and authority, a theme taken up by later ethnographic studies of Ecuador.
Ralph Beals also found a flexible division of labor in the larger, more urban-

FIGURE 5.2. An Otavaleñan indigenous woman inspects the field before she begins planting maize and beans. (From Rudi Colloredo-Mansfield, *The Native Leisure Class*, University of Chicago Press, Chicago, 1999, after p. 162. Courtesy of University of Chicago Press.)

ized community of Nayón, which lies in the vicinity of Ecuador's capital, Quito. Not only did women and men both farm and care for animals, but the community expected women to contribute economically to their families by selling in markets, as well as overseeing their families' business interests in Quito when their husbands were away. Later studies show that native women across the Andes continued their hardworking ways. They persisted in sharing power and authority within their families and households, even if domestic

FIGURE 5.3. An Otavaleñan man weaves on a backstrap loom. (From Rudi Colloredo-Mansfield, *The Native Leisure Class*, University of Chicago Press, Chicago, 1999, after p. 162. Courtesy of University of Chicago Press.)

violence as well as local and national political structures that afforded women a lesser public voice sometimes undermined that authority.[5]

Recent Ecuadorian ethnography still describes a flexible and rather egalitarian division of labor in agriculture, animal husbandry, and weaving (see figs. 5.2 and 5.3), yet ethnographers report some changes, as intensifying participation in local and national labor markets, more often by men, leads to a more rigid division of labor.[6] This emerging division of labor, in which men have greater access to waged labor, often through outmigration, increases the burden on women. It also increases wage and status differences between men and women (especially since women's cash earnings often come from the sale of crafts, an activity increasingly seen as domestic and therefore not as work), and it may trap women—even when they work—in an image of being more domestic and traditional. A well-known Quito hotel, the Hotel Rey, for example, specifically recruited women from the indigenous community of Quimsa based upon the idea that they were more native and more traditional, yet more exotic, than indigenous men. Dressed in the hotel's version of authentic Quimseña clothing, women were employed in jobs where the hotel management virtually displayed them, particularly to male guests and customers in the hotel's restaurants and bars. Trapping Quimseñas in an ongoing exhibition of cultural authenticity, Quito elites often try to hire the community's young women to work as servants in their homes, employment that reinforces ethnic, class, and gender hierarchies.[7]

To the south, the native populations of Peru and Bolivia characteristically evidence a somewhat more rigid division of labor, one that is more complementary than overlapping. In Peru, men's participation in agriculture is commonly greater than women's, including on the haciendas that used coercive labor practices from the colonial period well into the 1970s.[8] Yet in subsistence agriculture, women in many of the indigenous regions and communities of Peru and Bolivia manage, and even control, their families' agricultural production and its profits. In addition to bartering and selling in local markets, cooking, spinning, weaving, and caring for young children, the indigenous women of Peru often care for cows, sheep, llamas, pigs, and goats that they or their families own. Weaving and caring for animals, however, can be tasks shared with men and children, respectively, with men throughout the Andes often participating in, even dominating, in some cases, the production of woven textiles. At times of the year when communal labor is performed to repair or build roads, schools, or water systems, women may work on such projects and participate in reciprocal exchanges of labor to help feed work crews or participants in ritual events.[9]

But women do not confine their labor to Peru's rural areas. While men leave the countryside at higher rates than do women, women also migrate. As temporary or permanent migrants, they work as domestic servants in homes, as vendors in markets or on the streets, or in factories. In the larger cities, cholas dominate urban markets, as they have for generations, though they do not usually control the long-distance trading and wholesaling that brings commodities—especially valuable ones such as meat—into markets to be sold. Cholas thus perform complementary yet differentiated tasks, while men have greater access to the higher paying, higher prestige positions, a pattern of hierarchy that has become more common in the countryside as well.[10]

Such changes have also been occurring in Bolivia, where male outmigration from rural areas has left rural indigenous women to cope with a greater number of tasks. While men traditionally performed the heavier agricultural tasks and tended to rear and care for pack animals, with women planting seeds and overseeing the distribution and consumption of the harvests, as well as raising other kinds of animals, a more hierarchical structure may be seen in mining and urban indigenous families. Among the latter, women's economic contributions (as defined by the ability to earn cash income) vary from very substantial to minor, and the definition of their work as menial undermines perceptions of a complementary division of labor. Even the prosperous chola market women of La Paz have found transforming their economic power into political power a daunting task, though urban Andean women, especially in Bolivia, have undertaken collective action to better their working conditions. For indigenous women in the countryside, a heavier workload combined with gender and racial ideologies, as expressed by national governments and media, results in their devaluation. While the cooperatives common among

Maya women have not been as popular, whether located in rural or urban areas or traveling between both, not only do women have a long and continuous history of labor but also they have often achieved a significant degree of control over the goods or wages resulting from their work.[11]

This control extends to property, because native women of the Andes have more extensive inheritance rights than do Mesoamerican indigenous women. Ecuador's indigenous women are widely reported to inherit land bilaterally, with male and female children inheriting the property of each parent, along with any jointly owned property, in equal shares. While indigenous communities in Peru and Bolivia evidence bilateral inheritance patterns as well, men usually inherit land in greater amounts, and women also have been reported to have lesser access to irrigation water. Yet even in those communities or regions where male ownership of land predominates, women often serve as the household managers, responsible not just for doing the housework but also overseeing the distribution and consumption of the items produced by household members.[12]

This predominance in the management of household wealth and affairs occurs throughout the Andes even though postmarital residence patterns, at least for the early stages of marriage, are patrilocal. This is regardless of whether kinship systems are reported to be predominantly bilateral (that is, centered on nuclear families and with little tracing or use of lines of descent), as in Ecuador and much of Peru, or patrilineal, as in parts of Bolivia. But even where patrilineal descent ideologies are important in structuring descent and community political relations, matrilineal forms of inheritance and an ideology of the household as female-centered also exist.[13] Thus Andean kinship systems tend to reinforce women's control over household resources and their authoritative roles within households, especially as women advance through the life cycle. While both girls and boys and teenagers contribute significant labor to households in rural and urban areas, as women marry (generally around the age of twenty) their household responsibilities and authority increase. Middle-aged women not only hold management roles in their families and households but also play leadership roles in their communities, even as state structures emphasize male political roles. Later, as widows, women usually face fewer conflicts over their authority.[14] But before exploring the roles of Andean indigenous women beyond the family, we must consider aspects of family life that undermine their authority and power, namely, domestic violence, patterns of sexuality, and health problems specific to women.

Even though many observers agree that male and female roles within Andean households are complementary and that women exercise authority over resources, reports of domestic violence are widespread. What is not clear, because no scholar has systematically examined the question for any of the Andean countries or regions, is whether rates of domestic violence are higher, lower, or the same among other ethnic or racial groups; nor do scholars agree on underlying causes. They often link alcohol to occurrences of family violence. But while drinking and intoxication—a common part of rituals and celebrations of all kinds in Andean indigenous communities—may allow conflict and frustration to be more openly expressed, alcohol abuse is more a symptom of conflict than its root cause.[15] What factors lead to the drinking and domestic violence that express and exacerbate the conflicts that family members have?

Three elements help explain why domestic violence is relatively common among indigenous Andean groups: the family configuration; the context of poverty and exploitation in which indigenous communities exist; and the broader role of violence in Andean indigenous cultures. Andean families and households are often small, highly interdependent groups in which members focus many, even all, their emotional ties; families are only part of larger kin units to a limited degree. Such a breeding ground for intimacy, Andean experts Ralph and Charlene Bolton point out, may also breed spousal and parent-child conflict. Men's feelings that women have too much power in the home, an inversion of what national cultures through law, the media, and social expectations communicate as the culturally appropriate patriarchal system, as well as spouses' worries over the fidelity of their partners, lead to conflict. The exploitation that males so often experience in their work, which echoes the colonial gender dynamic, and the fact that their hard labor, often under circumstances in which they are separated from their families and homes, only leads to more poverty and exacerbates feelings of frustration and anger. These feelings can only be expressed within the family, but unfortunately the drive to reassert masculinity may be expressed in damaging ways.[16]

Yet family violence is only one type of violence to be found among Andean cultures and therefore should be considered within the broader context of patterns of conflict within the indigenous world. Violence begins early, and is sometimes a part of Andean children's experience of discipline, since parents teach respect through physical punishment. Courtship and marriage rituals, sometimes linked to the initiation of both drinking and sexual relations, may also include token violence between the families of the bride and groom and even the bride and groom themselves, perhaps because marriage is viewed in part as an abduction, and because institutionalized fighting, or *tinku*, continues to be a part of community ritual and feasts.[17] Violence within marriages, as a form of punishment for work transgressions and crimes and as a part of political struggles and rebellions, constitutes a persistent and common part of Andean life. Domestic violence and spousal abuse thus take place within a claustrophobic family structure, a context of often extreme poverty, and a cultural climate marked by frequent violence, both ritual and real. Political instability and an increasingly militarized drug war, in which indigenous women become targets of abuse and rape, is an additional factor reinforcing male-on-female violence.[18]

Indigenous women and their families do not passively accept spousal violence. While men may joke about *amor andino* (Andean love), women seldom do. They turn to friends and family to try to get help, and even to police or courts in more extreme cases. Yet women with children who separate from their husbands do not find it easy to survive on their own, whether they work in farming, markets, or factories. Such separations often wind up being only temporary, because "when the drinking, the dancing, the fighting and beating are over, both women and men go back to work."[19] In other words, because the complementarity of spousal economic roles remains such a vital part of individual and community survival, the pressure to maintain even unsatisfactory marriages can be very strong.

Another aspect of family life that affects women's lives and well-being is sexuality. Although there is little indication of parental or community emphasis on premarital virginity, and both men and women associate sexuality with pleasure, indigenous women receive little information on menstruation or sexuality prior to courtship or marriage, and rural women have generally had little access to birth control information. Until recently, abstinence has been a major form of birth control that can feed into the cycle of male infidelity and male and female jealousy that, in part, underlies spousal abuse. For female migrants to cities, sexual harassment as part of their work experiences is common, and the association of indigenous women with looser sexual mores becomes more common in multiethnic work environments like Quito's Hotel Rey. The hotel does not simply buy Quimseña labor, it appropriates Quimseña femininity and sexuality to enhance its appeal to businessmen and tourists.[20]

Sexuality connects to the issue of indigenous women's health and the roles women play in safeguarding their own, their families', and their communities' well-being. While statistical studies on this subject are rare, the ethnographic literature indicates that rural and indigenous women suffer from an array of health problems related to poverty, malnutrition, and pregnancy and childbirth. Poverty and geography often limit rural women's access to modern medical care. Even in cities, migrant women frequently suffer from limited access to clinics or hospitals.[21] Their efforts to control pregnancies also meet with varying degrees of success because they tend to rely on abstinence. Although urban women may have access to nurses or clinics, practitioners sometimes provide incorrect information, or the techniques and supplies they give may not work effectively. The Peruvian health ministry has, however, proved stunningly successful at raising the rates of sterilization of poor and indigenous women in recent years. And while husbands participate in the birthing process, especially during difficult births, and may even be supportive of women's efforts to find reliable birth control techniques, women continue to function as primary caretakers for family and community health throughout the Andes, a role that offers them a pathway to community respect and authority.[22]

Beyond the family, women in indigenous communities across the Andes frequently serve as midwives and curers, though men serve as curers as well. Women also hold other ritual specialist positions, especially that of *yatiri*, or diviner. Learning through apprenticeship, female yatiri have a special and respected role in conserving communities' ritual lore and practices, particularly those tied to daily life. A Bolivian woman, doña Matilde Colque, described how much she desired to become a yatiri, saying "I've always wanted to cure, ever since I was a young girl," and relating how her mother and brother taught her to read coca to effect cures. However, especially in the Ecuadorian Andes, men are thought of as the most powerful ritual specialists. Men also tend to hold political positions within rural indigenous communities, but communities expect office-holders' wives to take on certain tasks, especially ritual tasks connected to community well-being that express male/female complementarity.[23]

Just as the ritual realm expresses both complementarity and gender hierarchy, so too does the political realm. If women's political roles have often been informal, women have nonetheless been active in the creation and furthering of political movements throughout the twentieth century that express the identity and demands of indigenous peoples. As in Mesoamerica, the formal political structures of nation, region, and local community all give institutionalized roles to men rather than women. Most observers agree that women may have some influence behind the scenes but that, in addition to dominating office holding, husbands represent the family unit publicly. But some incremental change is beginning to take place. Small numbers of rural women in Peru and other Andean nations are running for and winning election to community governing councils and provincial and national legislatures, as well as other kinds of elective positions. Perhaps the best-known indigenous woman elected to a national legislature is Nina Pacari of Ecuador. Lawyer, CONAIE (Confederation of Indigenous Nationalities of Ecuador) activist, and legislator, she currently serves as Ecuador's minister of foreign affairs.[24]

Indigenous women throughout the Andes also have a striking twentieth-century history of taking political action. This sometimes takes place in traditional female realms, as when the indigenous women in Quimsa, Ecuador, in the early 1980s, protested and got rid of a primary school director. Even though rural women manifest low levels of participation in formal political structures, they have proven to be well aware of the political issues facing their communities. Sometimes they play roles in strikes, rebellions, or wars in which male participation dominates.[25] Women's high level of political consciousness in fact fueled political activism across the twentieth-century nations of the Andes.

In 1940s Ecuador, an indigenous woman, Dolores Cacuango, headed the FEI (Ecuadorian Federation of Indians, an important, early forerunner to CONAIE) and participated in many strikes and other political actions. In the 1970s and 1980s, more women, especially the younger women of many rural communities, began to participate in regional and national organizations aimed at creating economic, political, and social change. During the January 2000 uprising against then president Jamil Mahuad, CONAIE and other indigenous groups allied themselves with the military, and women participated in the demonstrations against Mahuad, as well as in the leadership of indigenous rights groups.[26]

In Peru and Bolivia, where indigenous women had little tradition of participation in the formal political structures of indigenous communities, they nonetheless participated in grassroots efforts to recoup land from haciendas, joined peasant unions struggling over land rights and labor conditions, fought in wars such as the 1930s Chaco War between Bolivia and Paraguay, agitated for and against political movements such as Sendero Luminoso (Shining Path) in Peru, and participated in mining strikes. In cities, market women's, cooks', and domestic workers' unions exist along with other urban self-help associations such as mothers' clubs (though the clubs have now spread widely beyond urban areas). In Lima, the Micaela Bastidas Community, a self-help organization of indigenous women, includes women from a variety of native groups who migrated there from all over Peru.[27] At the same time, women's peasant and union organizations often grew out of or in conjunction with larger umbrella organizations dominated by men. One such group was the Bartolina Sisa Federation of Peasant Women of Bolivia, founded in 1980, which was based on the belief of a prominent male peasant union leader, Geñaro Flores, that women could aid peasant struggles in a more active and organized way. Aymara women of highland Bolivia were extremely active in the federation, which played a crucial role in expressing peasant women's demands for land and greater economic equality, as well as greater equality in their marriages. In addition, Bartolina women protested the roles they were permitted in the larger male-dominated peasant confederation, namely cooking and recruiting other female members, because they wanted to speak out and help set policy.[28]

Female activists faced male criticism over the degree of autonomy to which they were entitled. But they also found that when indigenous women's groups tried to work in conjunction with nonindigenous women's groups, ethnic differences and discrimination became apparent. As early as the 1920s in Bolivia, when urban indigenous women tried to participate in feminist meetings, they were discouraged from making presentations by upper class women. Contemporary rural and urban indigenous women continue to suffer from the ethnic and class differences separating them from other women for whom they work in houses and markets. These social differences reinforce the poverty and inequities from which subaltern women and their families suffer. Police frequently harass urban market women, often using racially discriminatory language. For example, in one incident described by Lima market woman Asunta to anthropologist Linda Seligmann, a policeman who was demanding to see Asunta's market license called her an "Indian whore." Female customers also verbally abuse the vendors, drawing attention to their ethnicity and poverty, calling them "smelly," "vulgar," or "insolent."[29]

In situations where women's groups and leaders try to cooperate, ethnic and class differences make this a real challenge. One illustration comes from the human rights groups that developed in Peru to protest the violence and injustices perpetrated by both the Peruvian state and Sendero Luminoso (Shining Path) beginning in the early 1980s. Many of these groups protested the disappearance of family members; both members and leaders were predominantly female. In the case of María, who was bilingual and illiterate and led the group known as ANFASEP (National Association of Family Members of the Detained-Disappeared), and Teresa, who was mestiza, had received some schooling, and led COFADER (Committee of Family Members of the Detained-Disappeared), both with disappeared children, tensions grew when Teresa was elected to the board of FEDEFAM (Latin American Federation of Associations of Family Members of the Detained-Disappeared), representing Peru at a variety of international human rights meetings. María's leadership allowed her organization to serve families and children in desperate circumstances, yet she received less encouragement to use those skills in national and international contexts, and the strains that developed between the two groups eliminated any possibility that they could work together.[30]

Even with interethnic tensions among women's groups, Andean indigenous women continued to show a strong preference for female-dominated action groups in both urban and rural areas (fig. 5.4). Whether forming women's committees in the countryside of Ecuador or Peru or continuing efforts to form a lasting household workers' union in La Paz, Bolivia, activist indigenous women continue to demand work and social rights in a wide variety of settings.[31] Do the persistence of their demands and the female-centered organizations through which they pursue their causes reflect the complementarity that so many Andean and other observers see as central to indigenous gender relations?

If gender complementarity prevails most clearly among Ecuador's indigenous peoples, complementary forms of work, religious ideology and ritual, and social organization are strong in Peru and Bolivia as well. As one observer notes about Bolivia's Aymara-speaking K'ultas, they "carry out all their rituals in gender parallel, men libating male deities, altars, animals, and souls, while women libate the feminine realm." While parallelism, complementarity, and androgeny have ancient roots in the Andes, examples from everyday life abound in today's rural and urban areas, and as Andean peoples themselves acknowledge in the Aymara expression about male-female interdependence, "in this world everything is a pair."[32]

Yet politically, socially (especially in relation to patterns of familial and spousal violence), and economically, Andean women also experience subordination, both within and beyond their ethnic groups. As Justina Quispe, an office-holder in rural Peru, says:

> [M]y life has changed a lot since becoming director, I have been alone on this path . . . but I also say with a lot of worry that in spite of all the unfolding struggle, that [as] peasant women and women of the [urban] working class areas, we are still marginalized in our house, in our communities and even more in the offices of city governments. . . . They treat us with indifference, they don't respond to our questions . . . as if we don't exist.[33]

FIGURE 5.4. A peasant woman from Huancavelica tries to speak before a meeting of the Peasant Confederation of Peru. (Photo by Ernesto Jimenez, from Carol Andreas, *When Women Rebel*, Lawrence Hill, Westport, Conn., 1985, 59. Courtesy of Carol Andreas.)

Such patterns of subordination are not new, yet evidence exists to suggest that gender subordination is intensifying. For example, when political supporters of Alberto Fujimori, Peru's former president, wanted to insult his opponent, current president Alejandro Toledo, during the spring and summer 2000 presidential campaign, they referred to Toledo's wife, Eliane Karp, as a "servinacuy-camarada." The term "servinacuy" refers to the indigenous custom of trial marriage, so the foreign-born Karp was likened to indigenous women in racially insulting terms and the legitimacy of her marriage called into question by referring to her as Toledo's "comrade." Even though Andeans root their notions of complementarity more in ideas of flexibly blending differences and Mesoamericans more in ideas of combining opposites, in both areas deepening gender hierarchies are becoming more apparent. While Andean native women, rural and urban, serve as symbols of persistent ethnicity, because they are left behind when men migrate, continue to speak their languages at higher rates, and wear clothing styles identified as indigenous, they nonetheless have been experiencing deep change, especially in the last fifty years.[34]

For Andeans, transformative change has been a long-term process, but the pace of change sped up rapidly in the second half of the twentieth century. States and international agencies started promoting economic development in rural areas, often with uneven results, and globalization reached into the remotest areas in its search for resources and its efforts to reshape local market and labor relations. These phenomena have had a largely negative impact on indigenous women. In rural areas, development programs often focus on men, empowering them economically to some degree, particularly through land reform and politics, which then negatively influences women's authority and participation in decision-making within households and communities. To the extent that such programs do include women, they offer training in gender-specific skills such as sewing or nursing. Even when individual women benefit, their training reinforces traditional roles. Where national and international programs encourage or demand male participation in the market economy, the use of medical doctors and hospitals, or advise rural farmers (often increasingly female because of the impact of migration) to use commercial pesticides, women's authority, as achieved through higher status positions such as midwife, declines, as does their health and economic well-being.[35]

Migration constitutes another important form of change and is linked in basic ways to the economic changes caused by structural transformations and development programs. Though predominantly a male phenomenon, in some regions women also make up a large proportion of the migrants. In either case, migration has a deep impact on Andean women's lives. Men typically migrate for a variety of reasons, including the search for wages (because subsistence farming can no longer support families and communities in virtually all regions) and the desire to learn new skills or seek more education. While women left behind may experience a short-term gain in political participation and authority, over the longer term, rural women work harder to make up for the loss of labor, have less access to male income, lose companionship and their partner in parenting, and increasingly find their household and agricultural labor defined as "domestic" and therefore devalued.[36]

When women migrate, their behavior differs in some significant ways from that of men. Female migrants are typically younger, have a narrower range of employment possibilities from which to choose, and often end up working as domestic servants or in markets. They send a greater proportion of their salaries home to help their families, and their urban stays are more frequently short term. While many young women who migrate are single, mothers with young children are also on the move, often to escape abusive marriages. Migrant girls as young as five or six work as maids, as street vendors, or in markets. Many older adolescents and young women in their twenties find the difficulties of language difference, loneliness, and confronting an oppressive racial hierarchy in urban mestizo or white homes demoralizing. In addition, they are forced to negotiate the employer-employee relationship, in which employers demand long hours of intensive labor and childcare and frequently attempt to indoctrinate their servants in urban ideas about time management.[37] While many indigenous women, facing the daunting challenges of rural-to-urban migration, return to their villages, some stay on and experience new influences and opportunities, especially in the areas of religion and education, though these influences are also at work in the countryside.

One way migrants cope with the dramatic effects of migration is to turn to new, more participatory religions such as Pentecostalism, which appeals to poorer Latin Americans, urban and rural, especially in times of life crisis.[38] Vacilia Choque, a first-generation Aymara woman who migrated to La Paz, Bolivia, and within a few years began attending services at a local evangelical Protestant Church, Cristo es la Respuesta (Christ Is the Answer), is typical of the first- or second-generation migrants often attracted to Pentecostalism or other evangelical sects. Through guidance and the chance to socialize with others in similar situations, these churches, their ministers, and activities help migrant women deal with many of the problems in their lives—illness, alcoholism, domestic abuse—playing the role that family and neighbors would have played in their home villages. While men join such churches as well, many of the members are women. Even if the church hierarchies are always male, women participate in a wide variety of church activities, including "proselytizing on the streets, visiting needy church members in their homes, attending family services, and traveling to church meetings in other cities and foreign countries." Women's church attendance and the religious activism of some can transform them from symbols of persistence to agents of cultural change.[39]

Indigenous migrant women have also struggled for access to another cultural resource that they see as having the potential to help them and their children live better lives: schooling. For servants in La Paz, the only available education has been designed to train them to be better maids. In urban areas of Peru, indigenous women seeking reading skills frequently attend night schools. In rural areas, while schooling has become more available for indigenous communities, women often face formidable obstacles in obtaining even a primary school education, due to both ideological and material factors.

Not only do parents question how much and what types of schooling are appropriate for girls but also families must calculate how to spend whatever meager resources they might have for education. In making these calculations, they often choose sons. What this means is that, despite exceptions like the Saraguaro of highland Ecuador, among whom both men and women were attending postsecondary institutions and beginning to complete degrees in the early 1980s, indigenous women have less education than men and are more frequently monolingual and illiterate.[40]

Peasant women in Bolivia began to struggle in the late 1970s and 1980s to change this situation, realizing that although the Bolivian revolution of 1952 led to increased access to education in the countryside, girls' educational participation remained very low. Through women's peasant organizations and congresses, rural women—many indigenous—began to demand to learn various skills, especially reading, writing, and weaving, as well as technical training in agriculture and herding and political education. While Bolivia's literacy rate has risen, indigenous women there and elsewhere remain disadvantaged because of the many factors that impede their access to educational institutions.[41] Indigenous women in other parts of South and Central America face even more severe challenges, as their cultures not only confront the economic, political, and social changes of the twentieth and twenty-first centuries but must fight for their very cultural survival.

Women in the Tropical Lowlands of South America: Egalitarian Political Structures, Female Subordination, and the Fight for Cultural Survival

Lowland cultures, less well known than the highland cultures of the Andes and Mesoamerica and quite diverse culturally and linguistically, faced unprecedented assaults on their very identity and right to exist in the twentieth century. Individual groups are often small in number, live on lands that are resource rich in minerals, and have histories of intense warfare with their neighbors. In addition to confronting many of the same issues presented by political instability and global economic transformation faced by indigenous women of other parts of Latin America, lowland women face the political problems specific to their communities. But they face these challenges from a weaker position in relation to both men in their own societies and to nation-states. The latter have offered women fewer routes toward political participation and little significant aid, such as development projects aimed at women's economic, educational, and health problems.

To the extent that lowland women can be said to have an image either inside or outside their own nation-states, misogyny shapes how they are perceived. Napolean Chagnon, a well-known and controversial anthropologist, commented about Yanomami women, for example, that by the time they are thirty they have "lost their shape" because of the children they have borne . . . and they seem to be much more often in "bad moods" than men. They seem, in these moods, to have developed a rather unpleasant attitude toward life in general and toward men in particular. To the outsider, the older women seem to chronically speak in what sounds like a "whine,"frequently punctuated with contemptuous statements and complaints.

While his views were put in an extreme way, few ethnographers gave deeper attention to gender roles until the 1970s.[42]

Also telling were the Italian- and English-language publications of Helena Valero's memoir, an account of this Brazilian woman's capture in 1932, when she was twelve or thirteen, and her more than fifty years of life among the Namowei Yanomami of Venezuela. Even though the text is written in first person, in Valero's voice, Italian researcher Ettore Biocca saw himself as Valero's biographer and, in a sense, appropriated authorship. Just as significantly, the best known of the Yanomami ethnographers, especially Chagnon and Jacques Lizot, failed to credit Valero until recently as the first individual of European descent to travel and live among this famous Amazonian group, so anxious were they to see themselves as the first white men to do so (see fig. 5.5).[43]

Valero's effacement from the ethnographic record was nearly total. Yet she had profound knowledge about Yanomami ways of life, knowledge that would have challenged the image of the war-obsessed, male-dominant culture that Chagnon created for English-speaking anthropological and popular audiences. To go beyond this overly simplified portrait, we must look at the complex and varied lowland cultures stretching from Surinam and Guyana in eastern South America through Brazil, Venezuela, and parts of Colombia, extending into eastern Ecuador, Peru, and parts of Bolivia. Smaller and more differentiated in linguistic and cultural patterns than highland South American peoples, despite variations in the organization of lowland gender hierarchies, certain gendered patterns nonetheless exist. These include a relatively uniform and complementary, though changing, division of labor; household, kinship, and community configurations that separate men and women and that feature some patterned violence, symbolic and real, toward women; relatively little institutionalization of political or religious roles of authority for women; and less attention given to the contemporary plight of women in the current context of rapid cultural change.

Intense anthropological study of South American lowland cultures began in the 1930s and 1940s with the studies of German ethnographer Curt Nimuendajú. Nimuendajú's perceptive ethnographies observed differences in women's activities and roles among a variety of Brazilian groups. The *Handbook of South American Indians*, published in 1946, paid less attention to questions of gender. But anthropologist Robert Lowie, writing generally about the cultures of the tropical rainforest, briefly noted diversity in women's sta-

FIGURE 5.5.   Helena Valero with her second husband, Akawe, her
father, and three of her children. (Photo by Father Luigi Cocco, from
Ettore Biocca, *Yanoáma: The Narrative of a White Girl Kidnapped by
Amazonian Indians*, Dutton, New York, 1970, 377.)

tuses, varying from being virtual slaves to their husbands to "set[ting] the
tone" among the Palikur of Brazil and French Guiana. Claude Levi-Strauss's
classic ethnographic tour guide to Brazil's indigenous peoples, *Tristes Tropiques*,
also gave little time to matters of gender, although he noted women's authoritative behavior among some groups and also perceived the problems raised
by polygyny and shortages of marriageable women, a topic taken up in great
detail by later ethnographers. Stressing the importance of male leadership and
men's hunting, he saw women primarily as cooks and sexual partners,[44] but

FIGURE 5.6. Yanomami woman returns home from a visit with a
distant community carrying children and a basket with palm leaves used
to repair roofs and other items. (From William J. Smole, *The Yanoama
Indians: A Cultural Geography*, University of Texas Press, Austin, 1976,
171. Copyright © 1976. By permission of the University of Texas Press.)

ethnographers who followed would find more complex patterns of labor and
political organization.

Throughout the twentieth century, most lowland peoples' gender divisions of labor clearly segregated work, with males tending to hunt, fish, and
clear land for gardens. They also had a significantly higher degree of interaction with local or regional market networks, through which labor, horticultural items, or crafts could be sold. Women often gathered, grew, harvested,
and processed plant foods, especially manioc and plantains, performed an
array of household tasks as well as childcare, and made a variety of craft
items usually for their own or other households within their communities,
including pottery and woven items (see figs. 5.6, 5.7, and 5.8). Some overlap
in productive tasks existed. Men dominated hunting, but women hunted
smaller animals and often controlled, and still do, the distribution of meat
that hunters brought back, along with the products of their plant processing, and in some Amazonian groups, men could be found weaving.[45] The
precise division of labor, however, depended to a large extent on whether
communities emphasized hunting, fishing, or horticulture or some com-

FIGURE 5.7. Kalapalo women process manioc. (From Ellen Basso,
The Kalapalo of Central Brazil, Holt, Rinehart, and Winston, New York,
1973, 32. Courtesy of Ellen Basso.)

bination as the main activity or activities. Among the Canelos Quichua of
the Ecuadorian rainforest, for whom slash-and-burn agriculture was particularly important, men and women grew different crops. These rainforest
Quichua men grew plantains and corn; women grew manioc and other
root crops.[46]

Another aspect of lowland labor patterns that affects gender relations
is the degree to which men and women work alone or in groups. For the
Brazilian Mundurucú, "women's work is always done in combination, or in
companionship, with other women." Their work was often household based,
and because the large Mundurucú households were organized around a core
of related women, a pattern reinforced by their tendency toward matrilocal
postmarital residence patterns in the more traditional villages, women frequently worked together, especially to process manioc. Mundurucú women's
work groups perform labor-intensive tasks cooperatively and may even help
them cope with male dominance,[47] but other groups, notably the Gê and
Bororo peoples of central Brazil, feature more male cooperative organization
of work than female. While most ethnographers report work as quite gender
segregated, men and women do participate together in some tasks, especially
fishing and planting. Among the Sanumá, a Yanomami subgrouping in the
northwestern Yanomami region on the Brazilian-Venezuelan border, studied
by Brazilian anthropologist Alcida Ramos, male and female tasks can be inter-

FIGURE 5.8. Canelos Quichua women, including Clara Santi
Simbaña in the foreground, making pottery for a 1972 ayllu festival.
(From Norman E. Whitten, *Sacha Runa*, University of Illinois Press,
Urbana, 1976, 92. Courtesy of Norman E. Whitten.)

changeable if need be. Across the lowlands, because the food and other items
produced by women stay within their families and communities, attempts to
form self-help groups that could market goods more widely have not met
with as much success as they have with Andean and Maya women. Lowland
women also frequently begin their work lives at younger ages and spend more
hours per day working than do men.[48]

The complementarity inherent in the lowland organization of work tasks
does not readily translate into social or political authority for women. Nor
can women stake much claim on material resources, since lowland peoples
have traditionally placed less emphasis on individual ownership of houses,
land, or other items than Andean or Mesoamerican peoples. Women, nonetheless, sometimes identify strongly with gardens and the manioc plants they
grow and process, even giving birth there.[49] Across the lowlands, women
generally bring few valued resources at marriage and do not receive them
through inheritance. In fact, many groups see women themselves as a resource,
a sometimes scarce resource, whose labor, companionship, and childbearing
capacities must be negotiated over or even fought for. The idea of women as
a resource has implications for lowland kinship, marriage, and political systems, even if men's "fierceness" and misogyny is sometimes overemphasized
in Amazonian ethnographic writing.[50]

The patrilineal kinship systems of many areas of lowland South America
generally do not involve the tracing of genealogies of much depth, nor do

they strongly structure inheritance or corporate residential or political group-ings. What patrilineality does do is accord men a dominant status, often in conjunction with rules that define who can or cannot marry whom, with marriage creating many significant ties among men, especially brothers, and brothers-in-law. Among northwestern Amazonian peoples, especially those of the Vaupés region of Brazil-Colombia border, men commonly marry women from different villages who also speak different languages.[51] Thus, these peo-ples emphasize both kin *and* linguistic group exogamy. Because these groups also emphasize marriage patterns in which women marry into their hus-bands' households and villages, the social structure reinforces ties among close male relatives, especially brothers, who form the core of local descent groups. Among the Yanomami, on the other hand, marriage creates enduring ties of reciprocity and solidarity among brothers-in-law, who can be such close friends that they express their feelings physically, for example lying together in hammocks embracing each other, or as political allies who help their vil-lages cement relations organized around trading, feasting, exchanging women, and military alliances.[52]

Postmarital residence patterns affect women's lives as well. When brides tend to live with their husband's family (a pattern for which anthropolo-gists working with lowland peoples prefer the term virilocality), mothers and daughters find the separation that marriage brings quite difficult because of the close relationship they often share. Anthropologist Kenneth Good, who married a Yanomami woman named Yarima of the Hasupuweteri village of southeastern Venezuela, reports the following exchange with his future mother-in-law after she sent Yarima with food to share with him:

> Later that day when I passed her mother's shelter, I said jokingly, "Is your daughter already betrothed? I'd like to marry her someday."
>
> "No, she's not betrothed," came the answer. "But
> I don't want you to marry her."
>
> "Oh, why not?"
>
> "Because you'd take her far away downriver, and I'd never see her again. I'd miss her too much. No, she's not going to be your wife."
>
> "Oh," I said, teasing her some more, "you know I wouldn't take her anywhere. I'd live right here and do son-in-law service for you. I'd hunt for you and bring you game."
>
> "No"—she laughed—"I doubt you'd do that. You'd take her away."

Because daughters leave their households of birth (her mother's words having proved prophetic, as Yarima moved to New Jersey and had three children with Good—though she ultimately returned to Venezuela, leaving Good and the children behind), they take up residence as outsiders, not just in new house-holds but often in new communities, where they must provide labor and children for their husbands and families. This cluster of practices leads women to lose autonomy and status upon marriage.[53]

In other lowland areas, uxorilocal marriage, in which husbands join their wives' families, is more common. Paradoxically, uxorilocal residence often combines with patrilineal kinship structures and ideologies that accord men superiority, but these societies still allow women greater solidarity and more areas of control and authority than among groups like the Yanomami. Uxorilocal postmarital residence patterns occur frequently across lowland South America, from the Mundurucú of north-central Brazil to the Shipibo and Mai Huna of western and eastern lowland Peru, respectively. Among these peoples, women have a lot of say within their households, which are often female spaces, because men—while ostensibly joining the wife's household—frequently spend a lot of their time in men's houses, where they plan and carry out much of their economic, religious, and social lives.[54]

If uxorilocality produces greater female household authority for and solidarity among women, other pan-lowland characteristics of marriage contribute to the generally lower status held by women. The early age at marriage for women and often tense nature of marital relations, combined with the tendency to treat women less as people and more as resources to be negotiated over, reinforce male dominance. Women enter into their first marriages young, with many lowland women being married off in early adolescence, at age thirteen or fourteen. But these marriages, generally contracted by parents and occurring between young women and men, usually several years older but sometimes significantly older, often do not last. It frequently takes several tries for more stable couplings to develop, and many of the same factors that lead to women marrying young help explain the unstable nature of marriage.[55]

Many lowland peoples experienced some degree of shortage of women due to war, disease patterns, female infanticide, and polygyny. While shortages of women could theoretically lead to a higher value placed on women and wives, in fact antagonism between the sexes seems to have been the outcome. In the virilocally oriented societies, wives are considered outsiders who bond as much with each other as they do with their spouses. Helena Valero's account of her relationship with her first mother-in-law and set of co-wives emphasizes the wives working together. She observes that by obeying her husband's senior wife, "it led me to get on better with him." In uxorilocally oriented societies, men and women lead somewhat separate lives. Each partner in a marriage may take lovers, and parent-child relations, especially same-sex parent-child relations, often appear to be closer than spousal relations.[56]

While forms of marriage in which couples themselves decide to marry, usually through elopement, are becoming more common, the power to make matches still lies with families, especially with fathers and brothers, whose political and economic interests shape marriage decisions.[57] Among groups who consider marriageable women to be scarce, not only do women have little say over who they will marry but forms of marriage by capture have been practiced in the past and still continue to some extent. Well documented for the Yanomami, this practice occurred elsewhere, especially among the Barasana, living along the Pirá-Paraná River of southeastern Colombia, as well other Tukano groups to the east on the Colombia-Brazil border.[58] Virilocal marriage patterns and conflictual relations with neighboring peoples characterized these northern Amazonian groups. As among the Yanomami, marriage by capture further reinforced the notion of women as outsiders who held low status within their households and communities of marriage. In the Vaupés region, where marriage by capture was once relatively common, anthropologist Jean Jackson reports being told that the practice had disappeared, but it is remembered and remains a "theme and fantasy" that reflects how marriage reinforces gender inequality in groups that, in other ways, were relatively egalitarian. Judith Shapiro, speaking about the Yanomami, captures this paradox beautifully when she points out how "women are at the same time highly coveted and profoundly despised."[59] This inequality is also evident in that husbands frequently resort to violence as a way to discipline their wives.

Violence was endemic in many parts of indigenous lowland South America because war helped to define both the political identity of groups along with the leadership hierarchy among men. Being captured and often married into enemy groups, losing fathers, husbands, and sons, and the frequent disruptions war brought to village life all had a heavy impact on women. War also helped to create an environment in which violence against women flourished and still does, even though older warfare practices have for the most part declined or disappeared. Some of this violence against women is political in nature, but most of it is domestic and male-on-female, though examples of violent behavior by women are not hard to find. Curt Nimuendajú described threats embedded in ceremonial contexts that intimidated Xerente women.[60] If eastern and northern lowlands groups exhibit a greater tendency toward violence as a part of community and family life, elsewhere ideas about and threats of violence, only seldom enacted, nevertheless contribute to the status differences between men and women. Ethno-racial and gender hierarchies associated with the laws, policies, and popular cultures of modern nation-states and increasingly globalized networks of exchange and communication reinforce hierarchical gender ideologies within indigenous communities.

Among eastern and northern lowland groups, two types of violence against women occur, but both share in common the idea of male violence as punishment for female misbehavior. Among groups such as the Mundurucú and the Mehinaku of central Brazil, mythical explanations of hierarchical gender roles emphasize that if women see sacred instruments kept hidden in men's houses, they will be subject to gang rape as punishment, though anthropologists report that the practice of gang rape is dying out. In the Vaupés, ideas of gang rape as punishment exist and reflect tensions in affinal and spousal relations, but actual rapes of this kind are rare.[61] Among the Yanomami, who lack men's houses and myths about sacred instruments, women also experience high levels of violence, some of the violence accompanying war, as rape of captured women was common. But violent beating, burning, cutting of earlobes, or cutting off of ears all are punishments for specific misdeeds. When Helena Valero's husband Husiwë grew angry because one of their dogs died, choking on meat that he had prepared, he took out his anger on Helena and hit her so hard with a stick that he broke her arm. While her mother-in-law and other women scolded Husiwë and cared for her, Valero's account of her own and other women's marital lives depicts domestic violence as a nearly daily occurrence.[62]

To the west, rape associated with war or mythical explanations of gender roles occurs among fewer groups, but marriage—as elsewhere in lowland cultures—is conflict ridden, and people sometimes conceive of it as a battle.[63] As in warfare, both sides fight, which means that women participate in the physical conflict. But the weapons at their disposal are literally the "weapons of the weak." Reports exist of women beating their husbands, because the wives retaliate during a fight husbands have started or feel aggrieved (the former is the more common scenario), and examples of women withdrawing their domestic and sexual services abound. Women also seek help from fathers, brothers, and other women, including mothers, mothers-in-law, other female relatives, or friends. Kin clearly can sometimes moderate domestic violence, with older women having authority and influence to do so.[64] But men are both physically stronger and have greater access to weaponry among the groups in which war was an important feature of political and daily life.

Women, nonetheless, seek to help themselves or receive help from others, and as they move through the life cycle, their marriages become more stable and their position within households improves. While most groups do not carry out elaborate wedding ceremonies, menstrual seclusion and ritual is very common. Ranging in time from about a week to three years (in the case of the Brazilian Kalapalo), such rites exist even among groups that have no puberty ceremonies for men. They mark the biological changes that take place in women's bodies and the beginning of more stable unions that will produce children. In societies with age sets (groups based on closeness of age, rather than kinship, that go through life-cycle ceremonies together and often retain close ties throughout members' lives), women sometimes belonged to a female version, but ceremonies associated with women's aged-based groups were less elaborate, and their activities did not reinforce women's political participation.[65] Even with the loss of functions for men's groupings, the marking of the beginning of women's most active years sexually and economically continues, if only in an attenuated form.

Just as lowland women actively participate in the economic endeavors that are key to survival, so too do they play active and energetic sexual roles. Women across lowland societies become sexually active at young ages, usually soon after they begin to menstruate. In many groups, young adolescent girls and boys then begin a period of sexual experimentation and trial marriage that ends when a couple settles into a more permanent relationship, often tied to pregnancy and childbirth.[66] Even after marriage, in some groups both husbands and wives may take lovers or participate in extramarital sex. Among the Sharanahua of Peru, women could send men on a "special hunt" when meat was short. During these hunts either partner might have a brief affair, and neither spouse could express jealousy of the affairs of the other. Among the Canela, a Gê-speaking group of northeastern Brazil, women or men can initiate extramarital sex in private contexts or on ceremonial occasions. The group's pattern of intense social bonding and its highly valued ethic of generosity underlie these extramarital encounters. A Yanomami woman, on the other hand, might take lovers but could expect violent punishment from her husband or brothers or both.[67]

Although women experience some degree of sexual freedom, especially during adolescence, lowland groups continue to regulate women's sexuality more than men's. Among some peoples, a category of sexually active women existed that Curt Nimuendajú called "wantons," women who were not married, took numerous lovers, and were sometimes associated with men's houses or groups. They did so into the 1970s, when ethnographer Dennis Werner found a group of Mekranoti women known as *kupry*, "unmarried women who have had children out of wedlock and who specialize in providing sexual services for the community's men in return for payments of meat, beads, and other small items." Yet however actively both lowland women and men participate in marital and extramarital lovemaking, many groups—and particularly men—see female sexuality as dangerous, even polluting. Menstrual blood in particular may be viewed as contaminating, with the vagina conceptualized as potentially castrating.[68] This negative imagery contains notions of female power that echo the myths commonly told among many lowland peoples of central and northern Brazil, as well as the Vaupés region, that say that powerful women once ruled. Though men overthrew them, according to the myths, women are still perceived as retaining the powers of both creation and destruction, powers that must be tamed by initiation rituals in which men steal the sacred flutes and appropriate female reproductive powers by imitating menstruation.[69] Before discussing whether this potential power supports female roles of authority, it is necessary to consider the implications of childbearing and other female health-related issues.

The few detailed accounts of childbirth that exist suggest that childbirth was and is frequently a lonely experience, with women often giving birth unattended. Among the Siriono of Bolivia, studied in the 1930s by Allen Holmberg, who witnessed eight births, other women were present at birth, but they provided little help or support. In other groups, husbands or midwives or both may be present, but even when attended by midwives, lowland women have little access to modern medical assistance if it is needed during pregnancy or childbirth.[70] Lowland women also suffer from an array of diseases and work-related conditions, and domestic violence, war, and male drinking also prove injurious to female health. However, women themselves often treat these diseases, injuries, or conditions, because they grow the plants that are used medicinally, and they sometimes serve as curers for other members of their communities.

Female self-injury also occurs. High rates of attempted and actual female suicide occur among Peru's Aguaruna. Such actions serve as both expression of unhappiness with the vulnerabilities and constraints an individual woman may feel in marriage and as a means, the only way apparently, a woman has of garnering support from her own male relatives to pressure her husband for a divorce or to influence him not to take a second wife. An Aguaruna woman explained to ethnographer Michael Brown that "sometimes women kill themselves when their husbands become angry and yell at them." This plaintive expression of powerlessness brings into question lowland women's authority, roles, and power and the extent to which they can hold recognized positions in birthing, curing, religion, or politics.[71]

The ethnographic literature lacks systematic exploration of women's roles as midwives and curers, but what is clear is that to the extent they serve as curers, they do so largely within their own families. Their ability to act as shamans or participate in community-wide rituals was and remains limited. Female shamans exist among some groups, but their role is often circumscribed. Among the Peruvian Mai Huna, for example, whose female shamans must be older women because fertile women cannot drink the hallucinogenic *yagé*, female shamans carry out only a curing role. The more numerous male shamans, on the other hand, played a more aggessive role in encouraging success in warfare, though intergroup warfare no longer exists in this region. They still encourage community self-defense and enact a greater role in community rituals than do the female shamans. Among the Canelos Quichua, however, female visionary power, often expressed in ceramics women produce for ceremonies, complements the shamanic power of men.[72]

Across the lowlands, women's ritual roles are similar to their shamanic roles; when they participate in or carry out important ceremonies, this participation is more limited than men's, and usually consists of helping men carry out their more extensive ceremonial responsibilities. These ritual roles range from singing and dancing at important occasions, like the female naming ceremony held by the Mekranoti of Brazil, the return of hunters, intra- or intercommunity feasting, and male or female initiation ceremonies and mortuary rituals. Among the western lowland groups of Ecuador and Peru, the wives of ritual leaders play important roles by preparing food and carrying out other ceremonial preparations, but their ceremonial participation remains lesser and often takes place under male direction or supervision. This secondary ritual role is mirrored in the political realm.[73]

It must be remembered that lowland societies, past and present, generally do not feature highly elaborated or specialized leadership roles, and many societies value individual autonomy and freedom. Within this context, women often carry some authority within households and influence husbands, brothers, and sons by expressing their political opinions. In those groups with uxorilocal residence patterns, like the Mundurucú of Brazil, where men spent much of their time in men's houses, the household was a female-centered space where the eldest woman had considerable authority, but this arrangement has now largely broken down. Among the Peruvian Cashinahua, female leaders (often the wives of male leaders) attend to women's concerns and sometimes speak at meetings attended by both men and women, but neither men nor women expect them to be fierce in the way male community leaders should be, nor do they interact much with the formal political system as constructed by the Peruvian state.[74] The Brazilian Kalapalo, whose leadership roles are primarily filled by males, also depend on village mediators, called *anetaw*, who can represent the village in ceremonial events with other villages, mediate relationships among village households, and help organize reciprocal gift-giving within or between villages. This is an inherited position, which men gain from their fathers and women their mothers, but female anetaw are far less active than the men who hold this position, because women must be quiet in public, and they can "never appear publicly as formal representatives of their village groups during intervillage ceremonies, as do men."[75] While wives of leaders often carry some authority or influence, lowland women's primary pathway to political influence is through the expression of their views to male relatives. This influence increases with age. Among the Yanomami, older women not only had influence within their households but also played some, albeit limited, role in political affairs. They urged men on to violence by calling for vengeance. They also moved among enemy villages to serve as messengers and sometimes even recovered the dead bodies of men slain in warfare.[76]

If women exercise less power in the everyday practices of ritual and politics, they nonetheless exhibit some degree of spiritual power. Many groups associate gardens with female supernatural power, female deities, or love magic. Jívaro women of eastern Ecuador sing to the earth mother goddess, Nugkuí,

> I am a woman of Nugkuí
> Therefore I sing,
> So that the manioc will grow well.
> For when I do not sing,
> There is not much production.
> I am of Nugkuí
> Therefore I harvest faster than others.[77]

Myths of female power that explain how men came to hold the dominant position they do across most lowland groups also abound. These myths usually have in common three elements: that women either invented or once owned the group's secret ritual objects, often musical instruments; that those who control the objects, whose existence is supposed to be a secret, gain power and positions of authority; and that men eventually won a battle for knowledge of and control over these objects. That knowledge and control made women "the subject of male terrorism," by forbidding women to participate in important political and religious events on pain of violent punishment, often gang rape. Seemingly more a charter for male domination than a historical record of earlier forms of female power, these myths explain male power but also express masculine anxieties about the insecurity of both marital and affinal relations.[78] If male/female economic relationships are in many ways complementary and male dominance of social life, though widespread, is accompanied by anxiety over that dominance, is it possible to speak of gender complementarity or parallelism, as in other parts of native Latin America?

Lowland societies vary somewhat in the degree to which women manifest power and authority,[79] and most ethnographers report that both men and women view women's economic contributions positively, recognizing male and female labor as complementary. But this recognition does not form a basis for women to hold positions of authority or exercise power, particularly in the political sphere, and sexual antagonism is a real part of everyday life for many groups. Lowland men often seek to control both women's work and creative powers through forms of political practice and spiritual belief that denigrate and exclude women, but they also feel ambivalence because their control over the women in their lives does not come easily. At best, women's roles combine elements of both subordination and autonomy, through which, especially as they age, they influence household and community decision-making and place some limits on male dominance. But they cannot play an equivalent public role to men in or beyond their communities.[80] Little basis thus exists for women to play complementary or parallel social roles, and because men often view women in stereotyped, negative ways, women's subordinated position and negative image also shape the impact of contemporary patterns of change.

While lowland peoples have experienced varying degrees of economic penetration and pressures to acculturate from the sixteenth century on, as elsewhere, change accelerated in the second half of the twentieth century as efforts to increase resource extraction and appropriate land and labor, especially the low-waged labor of men, grew. An increasing number of Catholic and Protestant missionaries also appeared, bringing with them not only new religious and cultural ideologies but also trade goods and schooling, both of which have influenced women's lives and gender relations.

Rubber production, gold mining, and growing integration of remote areas into regional, national, and global marketing and media systems all have had a significant impact on lowland peoples throughout the Amazon rainforest and beyond. Among the Mundurucú, men's increased participation in the rubber trade, beginning in the 1920s, led to deep changes in their way of life. Families moved out of the savannah to riverine communities whose social structure became markedly different from that of the more traditional communities. Riverine villages lack men's houses; thus men live in nuclear family households. The gender division of labor also changed; rather than working in the traditional, cooperative male or female work groups, husband and wife became the central unit in work, especially in gardening. Mundurucú women often instigated these changes because of their desires to live in a nuclear family setting and to have greater access to trade goods such as metal pots and pans, knives, and western-style clothing and jewelry. While the husband-wife unit has strengthened and husbands consult wives about family decisions, the cohesion of women as a group has declined, as has the power of senior women, since men play the role of head of household in the riverine settlements.[81]

In other areas of Brazil and Venezuela, economic and social changes came with the arrival of ranchers and gold miners, whose presence has brought disease, violence, and new trade goods. Close to one-fourth of the Brazilian Yanomami population died between 1987 and 1989, when thousands of *garimpeiros*, gold miners, infiltrated the Brazilian-Venezuelan border area, bringing disease, especially malaria, and violent confrontation. Where indigenous men also begin to join in the gold mining effort, their absence increases women's work load, as has the desire for trade goods, reinforcing changes away from hunting and other traditional forms of male labor toward waged labor. Brazil's army also has had an impact on Yanomami communities and women, as it began to build bases along the Brazil-Venezuela border, intruding into lands reserved for the Yanomami. Aside from land loss and an increase in tensions in already stressed communities, individual soldiers have had amorous relationships with Yanomami women. These relationships have led to the birth of children, about whom the Yanomami are ambivalent, because of the strong emphasis they place on their ethnic identity, and contributed to the spread of venereal diseases, such as gonorrhea and syphilis. Other groups have complained about forced sterilization, connecting the practice to genocide.[82]

Among Peru's and Ecuador's lowland peoples, the growth of regional marketing systems in which native men play an especially prominent long-distance trading role has meant that women and children perform more subsistence labor, and the increased access to manufactured goods that comes with male wages and mobility means that women have slowed or stopped their traditional forms of pottery and textile production. As these changes occur, women become more dependent on husbands who, even when often absent, gain greater control over the household economy. Peruvian laws designed to integrate indigenous communities into the modern nation-state's political system also disadvantage women. They rarely hold offices and only occasionally represent lowland communities to organizations concerned with indigenous rights. Lowland indigenous women in Ecuador increasingly find that as individual property ownership becomes more common, ownership of land and livestock has become concentrated in male hands.[83] In addition, as national governments, along with Catholic and Protestant missionaries, try to make education more available in remote lowland regions, women become disadvantaged in this way as well.

While girls have begun to attend primary schools in greater numbers, very few complete a primary education. Even fewer go on for secondary or postsecondary education, with one consequence being that almost no indigenous female teachers exist. Large numbers of women continue to speak indigenous languages rather than Portuguese or Spanish, and women's illiteracy rates remain high. Women themselves desire more practical types of education, emphasizing reading and learning (or relearning) crafts skills such as the weaving of cotton textiles. But evidence from the northwest Brazilian states of Acres and Amazonas shows that these wishes often remain frustrated because of the dispersed nature of many groups and the difficulties of balancing household responsibilities with school attendance.[84] Yet lowland women desire education and try to form self-help groups, especially mothers' clubs, to aid in their struggles to better their own economic and social positions as well as those of their children, families, and communities.

Missionaries, NGOs, and government agencies charged with overseeing indigenous affairs have at times encouraged self-help groups among lowland women, either cooperatives for economic development or mothers' clubs. The latter have tried to foster reading skills and trained lowland women to produce crafts items that can be sold either locally or marketed to nonindigenous citizens or tourists. The clubs have also lobbied for increased access to health care, especially for those women who desire birth control and for young children, who often suffer from malnutrition.[85] Shipibo women of northeastern Peru, on their own, formed a cooperative to sell ceramics, textiles, and jewelry in urban markets. Because they never lost their role in agricultural production and retained control over the sale of their artisanal production, Shipibo women sustained a higher level of economic autonomy than most other tropical lowland women. Shipibo and other women have also struggled to participate in indigenous congresses and regional governments so that female perspectives might be heard.[86]

But the devastating impact of development schemes, especially the recent Brazilian gold rush, combined with highly dispersed settlement patterns and great variability of lowland languages and cultural patterns, means that lowland women have not been able to organize themselves politically to anywhere near the same extent as either highland South American or Mesoamerican women have, despite lowland women's efforts to do so. And in Brazil, Venezuela, and Colombia especially, lowland women are also hampered by national governments whose agendas place very little value on their needs or the needs of indigenous peoples generally.[87] Similar problems plague the efforts of many native women in Central America, particularly in those countries where indigenous people make up a smaller percentage of the population, to organize and lobby for improvements in their economic and social position.

Indigenous Women in Central America: Searching for Empowerment in Diverse Circumstances

Central America's indigenous peoples, with the exception of the Kuna of Panama, tend to be even less well known than highland or lowland peoples. Like lowland groups, many are very dispersed within the individual nation-states of Central America. Fragmented into small communities scattered across rural landscapes, the specific dynamics within and issues facing native communities often remain unrecognized among the social and economic conditions of the rural poor. Central America and the Circum-Caribbean also present us with the challenge of integrating the stories of peoples and women of mixed ethno-racial heritage whose identity is less mestizo (like the post-Nahuas described in chapter 4) than Afro-indigenous. While a variety of Central American peoples will be mentioned, this part of the chapter focuses primarily on three groups: the Garifuna (also known either as the Garinagu or, more commonly, Black Carib) of Belize, Guatemala, Honduras, and Nicaragua; the Miskito of Nicaragua, Honduras, and Costa Rica; and the San Blas, or island, Kuna of Panama. Anthropologists have given the most attention to these peoples because these are the largest groups, the history of each group's ethnogenesis is interestingly complex, rooted in the multicultural colonial dynamics of the conquest and migration of native peoples and enslavement of African peoples, and each has some history of autonomy.[88] Miriam Miranda, a Garifuna activist member of the Honduran Iseri Lidawamari (New Dawn) movement, which defends land rights and cultural identity, writes about Garifuna identity:

> We are the Garifuna, descendants of black Africans brought to this continent and of the native people of the Caribbean. Our Caribbean ancestors have sometimes simply been called "island Caribs," because they were Arawak and Carib people who intermarried. We believe that our African ancestors were shipwrecked, enabling them to escape slavery and to live peacefully on the islands, intermarrying with the island people.

This sense of mixed identity includes language as well: "Our language reflects our history. It has strong Arawak roots from our Arawak grandmothers, Carib roots from our grandfathers, and African sounds from our Black ancestors."[89]

Because ethnographers gravitated to other parts of Middle and South America, largely ignoring many Central America native groups, indigenous women of many groups received even less attention. Early ethnographers—even those writing in the mid-1940s for the *Handbook of South American Indians*—scarcely noticed their existence, let alone the patterns of gender relations in work, family, or political or religious life.[90] As in other regions, while women have been left out of national government plans, however meager, to incorporate indigenous communities more fully into national public life and market expansion, the appearance of women's cultural conservatism belies a more complex reality. This cultural conservatism can be a lucrative asset for tourism, which is an increasingly important niche in local economies, as the Kuna in particular have discovered. Not only do women often bear the brunt of change and modernization, since they form the stable social and economic core of households and indigenous communities across Central America, but women have also been quiet agitators for change and managers of its pace.[91]

FIGURE 5.9. Garifuna woman preparing cassava bread. (From
Virginia Kerns, *Women and the Ancestors*, 2nd ed., University of Illinois
Press, Urbana, 1997, illus. no. 19. Courtesy of Virginia Kerns.)

In work, Central American women's roles vary yet have often been crucial to familial and community survival in the twentieth and twenty-first centuries. Plantations, slavery, sailing, and piracy shaped gendered labor patterns,
and men either were coerced into or actively sought kinds of work in which
they resided for long periods of time elsewhere than their natal communities.
But it was really in the nineteenth and early twentieth centuries that today's
patterns of ethnic identities, locations, and gender divisions of labor came into
being.[92] At that time, a division of labor that for many native Central Americans was similar to that of lowland South America began to shift. That older
division of labor, in which men hunted, fished, cleared fields, and generally
performed the heavier labor and women carried out most of the rest of the
plant-growing and harvesting tasks, as well as most household-based labor
and child-rearing, and manufactured essential craft items, was common across
the entire region. It still can be found in those areas, usually inland, where
subsistence-based activities continue to predominate, even as market penetration grows (see fig. 5.9).[93]

But especially along the coasts, the impact of long-term male outmigration (long-term in that men have been departing for wage-paying jobs for

generations and that they leave their communities and families of birth and marriage more or less permanently), increasing involvement in a cash-based economic nexus, and growth in tourism all led to transformations in the gender organization of work, especially in the second half of the twentieth century. One consequence of these changes is that women have also begun to migrate, work in local paying jobs, or spend greater amounts of time producing craft items for tourists. Kuna women, for example, produce beautiful *molas*, or blouses made with panels of layered cloth, cut and sewn to reveal geometric designs and highly stylized images.[94] These economic changes have significant repercussions for indigenous family life, whether in urban or rural areas. They affect the nature of male/female relations, the socializing of children, and even relations among women. Women's work also changes rather dramatically as they advance through the life cycle, with senior Kuna women, for example, serving more as household managers and less as mola-makers and older Garifuna women finding ways to earn cash, especially in the absence of financial support from a male partner.[95]

For many Circum-Caribbean indigenous peoples, male absence, due primarily to outmigration for purposes of work, shaped family and kinship structures, and women's roles became central. The Garifuna, Miskito, and Kuna all construct their family lives around core groups of women. Men marry into these female-centered households, and women's ties to their children are deep and long-lasting, more than to their husbands or partners, from whom separation or divorce is relatively easy. Even though some variation exists—for example, the Maya of Belize and the Guaymí of Panama exhibit family configurations that we could term more "Mesoamerican" (young age at marriage, a tendency toward patrilocal postmarital residence, a more male-centered authority structure within and beyond the household)—female-centered households proved to be adaptive and persistent across a range of indigenous groups, especially Atlantic coastal peoples. They enabled female kin networks to care for children and the elderly. Women thus became and remain the focus of affection and exchange; they often owned houses and land; and they carried out the redistribution of food, other goods, and even money within households and among larger kin networks.[96] If their household authority has not always translated into broader forms of political power, their authoritative familial roles correlate with relatively lower levels of domestic violence, more female control over sexuality, and communally recognized authoritative roles in healing and religion.

The theme of domestic violence does not show up very much in the literature on Central American indigenous peoples, although clearly such behavior exists. Among the Garifuna, for whom the most reporting of intrafamilial violence occurs, men can be violent toward their partners or wives (part of a pattern of emotionally abusive, even controlling, male behavior that increases in urban settings), but women have resources to rely on that protect them from the most physically damaging forms of abuse. Garifuna women reject beating as an appropriate form of behavior, older women help to police potentially or actually violent situations, and women can leave households in which violence toward them has taken place.[97]

Another set of issues having to do with women's well-being—physical and emotional—are the patterns of sexuality that shape their romantic and procreative lives and the health problems common to women who live in poverty and lack access to medical care. Patterns of sexuality, like family structures and domestic violence, are variable. The Garifuna place a very high value on male *and* female sexuality, and both women and men view sexuality as "natural, desirable, and even healthful."[98] If women's sexuality among the Garifuna is more controlled than men's, this control comes less from male authority or proprietary rights in women and more from surveillance by middle-aged women, who enforce a moral code that discourages young women from being unfaithful. Women enforce this code because of their belief that children suffer if their mothers are unfaithful and irresponsible. Garifuna women also criticize Maya women for marrying and bearing children too young.[99] Nineteenth-century Moravian missionaries among the Rama and Miskito of Nicaragua made concerted efforts to repress older patterns of sexuality that allowed both men and women a certain amount of sexual freedom. While the Moravians succeeded in requiring the Rama to begin their marriages with a church ceremony, they were less successful in instilling monogamy as a cultural value. For the Miskito, missionary efforts to repress female sexuality enjoyed greater success, but this repression came at some cost to women's physical and psychological health.[100]

The Kuna, too, evidence greater control over female sexuality, and women's roles generally are more constrained than men's in comparison, especially, with the Garifuna. The Kuna, however, manifest a number of gender roles not seen elsewhere in Central America, classifying individuals as male, female, male-like (*macharetkit*), or, more commonly, female-like (*omekit*). The omekit, who "are usually identified as such as children," while not dressing like women, perform the labor of women by making molas.[101] They sometimes marry women but usually have sexual relations with men, with these homosexual relations being more accepted by Kuna men of San Blas than by Kuna men who have spent significant periods of time in Panama City. Rural and urban Kuna women, in contrast, both had a positive attitude about omekits, believing "that any woman who had an omekit son was very lucky indeed." The term "macharetkit," on the other hand, seems to refer either to tomboys or women who may carry out male roles in labor, rather than a role involving both identity and sexual orientation.[102]

The variable social structures and sexualities of Central America also influence patterns of health and well-being, with women and children in particular bearing the burdens of poverty, malnutrition, lack of clean drinking water and sanitary kitchen and bathroom facilities, and male absence. Other factors that contribute to poor health, especially in rural areas, include lack of access to vaccines and crowded households in which large numbers of people live, often in close proximity to animals who can transmit diseases to their human companions. While indigenous women's life expectancy is higher than that of men, they rarely have detailed knowledge about reproductive processes or contemporary forms of contraception. Rates of infant, child, and maternal mortality are high, and while the herbal medicines and forms of local knowledge women rely on can be effective at times, chronic malnutrition and disease lead to large numbers of malnourished, frequently ill children and adults and populations with high death rates.[103]

Miskito women in Nicaragua and Honduras have responded to the physical and emotional stresses they endure by developing a contagious, sometimes epidemic syndrome known as *grisi siknis*. Its victims "lose consciousness, believe that devils beat them and have sexual relations with them, and run off through the village and into the bush." Violent behavior can also be a part of attacks of grisi siknis, with victims—almost always young women—picking up knives or machetes and running around, though the victims generally do not aim weapons at specific people. Men and boys attempt to restrain the victims, but some young men who pursue the women to subdue them have been known to participate in gang rapes of them. While Miskito curers tend to be male, female practitioners, whether traditional midwives, curers, or modern nurses, are common among many indigenous groups of Central America.[104]

In coastal and urban areas, birth has become more medicalized, but midwives still play a role in prenatal and postnatal care. Among the Kuna of the island of Ailagandi, by the late 1970s no women were becoming midwives, but Kuna female health professionals, trained in western medical practices, were attending most normal births, and maternal and infant mortality rates declined significantly because of the presence of trained attendants and better infant nutrition. Curanderas continue to practice across a range of groups, but they struggle against the problems of poverty, malnutrition, and chronic diseases, along with the introduction of new diseases like AIDS.[105]

Central American indigenous women play other kinds of authoritative roles, especially in ritual, but males' roles in ritual and politics clearly outweigh women's, except among the Garifuna. The ritual roles of Garifuna women have been increasing over the second half of the twentieth century, as female shamans (*buwiyes*) and older women became more dominant, due to male absence and the declining interest of younger generations in funeral and healing rituals. Older women believe that healing rituals, particularly those aimed at righting the relationship between a dead ancestor and his or her descendants, help to protect their children and grandchildren. Women can pester relatives to sponsor rituals they believe necessary, or they can organize ceremonials themeselves, raising funds, recruiting participants, and leading the singing and dancing that are part of the ceremonies.[106]

For the Miskito and the Kuna, ritual practices are usually led by male religious specialists, but among the Kuna the most important and most public ceremonies center on the female life cycle. They practice menstrual seclusion upon a girl's first menses: "over the course of four days she is secluded in a ritual enclosure, has her hair shorn, is painted all over . . . is repeatedly bathed with sea water, and finally her parents sponsor a feast."[107] A longer public ceremony, usually called an *inna*, takes place about a year later and announces that a young woman is now marriageable. This is a more elaborate affair involving the entire village. Women "cleanse our communities to prepare for ceremonies," men and women contribute materials or labor for the chicha-brewing, and participate in the drinking, singing, dancing, and oratory, the latter a major part of Kuna public life. While male ritual specialists predominate in the chicha preparation and in the speaking that forms a critical part of these ceremonies, neither the birth nor puberty of boys is marked ceremonially, perhaps because of mother-centered households and the way Kuna mythology emphasizes the importance of women's procreative role. But while inna ceremonies continue to be carried out, men must sometimes rely on the more traditional villages to organize the ceremonies for their daughters, since they may be working in Panama City or the Canal Zone to pay for them. Contemporary parents now sometimes give innas for younger girls, treating them less as celebrations of female fecundity and more as symbols for the display of material success, as well as celebrations of Kuna ethnic identity.[108]

As for women's political roles, as elsewhere, women have less access to political positions and less influence in the public life and decision-making processes of indigenous communities, though they are not wholly without a voice. In addition to their important roles as organizers and participants in Garifuna rituals, older women participate in village governing councils (though men outnumber women), and they help to oversee community moral codes, policing the sexuality of younger Garifuna women and protecting children, both young and adult, from supernatural threats. In Nicaragua, rural women across the country participate in unions and peasant organizations organized around land and labor issues, but indigenous women's attempts to participate in local institutions of governance is a little-studied topic. Kuna patterns of governance have received more attention, in part because of their success in maintaining a semiautonomous political system within the Panamanian nation-state, and in part because of the speech practices associated with this system, which lie at the center of Kuna public and political life.[109]

Every Kuna village has a "gathering house" (*onmakket neka*) in which a variety of political events can be held. The most common such gathering occurs several evenings a week, includes both male and female attendees, and consists of a variety of discussions and chanting, through which community issues are aired and crimes and conflicts may be adjudicated. At these meetings, chants or orations by chiefs focus on Kuna mythico-historical themes. Through such chanting, leaders intend these chants to reinforce community cohesion and adherence to Kuna behavioral norms.[110] All-male and mostly female gatherings also take place, but the traditional female gatherings featured chiefs and other male leaders chanting to women about their appropriate household roles and demeanor.

However, by the 1970s, new kinds of female-centered gatherings began to occur. On one island, these were organized and led solely by women and focused on their tasks in the village or the mola cooperative. Women also became more active as lower level officials in the *congresos* (or governing councils), formerly all male, found in Kuna communities.[111] Men monopolized the chanting and speaking roles at community meetings and still do (though to a lesser extent), but they frequently inform and consult female household members about community issues. Kuna women actively sought and seek ways to communicate their ideas, as when, for example, Amma, a member of the Kuna women's mola cooperative and resident of the island of Tupile, was returning to her island from Panama City. While waiting at the airport, she used the opportunity to scold two Kuna political leaders for their failure to include any of the co-op leaders in a regional economic development planning meeting that had recently taken place.[112] Women also have forms of expression that are unique to them. These include lullabies and tuneful weeping that help mark the early socializing of infants and the death of community members, as well as the molas, which can be considered a form of female visual expressiveness.[113] While neither Kuna nor other Central American indigenous women have the history of political participation or action that Andean women do, their persistent centrality to household affairs, even when the division and content of labor varies (as it does between the Garifuna and the Kuna), means that women—at least in the larger indigenous groupings—have a history of autonomy. This history is linked to women's status within these societies and how that status is changing due to the impact of the ever deeper penetration of global market systems.

The devaluation of female gender identity with little recognition of women's labor value or attention to their opinions about community affairs continues to mark women's experiences among groups such as the Miskito and Lenca. Yet the status of other Central American indigenous women, as shaped by age, ethnicity, and intensifying patterns of change, is a more complex question. Men do not view or treat women as their equals, but as women move through the life cycle, and especially by middle age, they gain greater autonomy. They express this autonomy through freedom of movement, the exertion of control over the activities of younger women in particular, and by exercising ritual authority that influences the well-being of their immediate families, broader kin networks, and entire communities.[114]

Kuna men, for example, certainly do not see women as their equals. Gathering house orations commonly express the view that women are weak, quarrelsome, and in need of the direction and moral authority provided by men. Women occupy fewer ascribed or achieved statuses, and their travel remains restricted by the male-dominated congresos.[115] Yet ethnographers consistently report that Kuna women have strong, colorful personalities, that within the household women and men share authority, and that women's substantial property rights in land and houses, as well as their roles in depicting, even embodying "Kunaness" through their designing and wearing of molas, ensures them a strong position. Because Kuna women arguably hold a status that is "stronger than other indigenous or peasant women in Latin America," the question of how Kuna men and women, as well as those of other Central American indigenous peoples, respond to the inexorable forces of change is an important one.[116]

Plenty of evidence exists to suggest that both the material and ideological changes that accompanied the incorporation of indigenous peoples into the newly forming Central American nations of the nineteenth century and the emerging global economy of the late twentieth and early twenty-first centuries have involved Central American indigenous men more centrally than women. Undoubtedly, men have profited through their greater opportunities to find wage-paying jobs and ability to serve as middlemen in the sales of agricultural products or crafts produced by women. Nor has the integration of local and national political structures served indigenous women well.[117] Yet Garifuna women have taken on increased roles of authority as shamans and as organizers of important life-cycle rituals; Miskito women remain at the core of family life, performing both subsistence and wage labor and managing the daily affairs of households; and Kuna women have seen a range of new opportunities open up for them, even as family structures show evidence of shifts that may well endanger island women and children's economic well-being. Kuna women in particular have experienced access to education, modern health care, and new occupations. While this has been truer of urban Kuna women, especially migrants to Panama City, it is also true for women on the less traditional islands.[118]

Kuna women's access to education has, however, also been greater than that of other indigenous Central American women. Indigenous women across the region evidence higher rates of illiteracy and lower rates of bilingualism than other women or indigenous men. Women's rates of secondary and postsecondary education are much lower than men's in every area, except among the Kuna. While Kuna leaders were originally reluctant to allow girls to attend primary schools, by the 1940s, girls were attending primary schools on several islands. By the mid-1970s, a few Kuna women were attending universities, and the number of female teachers and trained health personnel was increasing. Women who received more education often preferred to remain in urban areas rather than return to the coastal islands. However, incorporation into a global economy is proving to be a double-edged sword.[119]

Both the increasing involvement of the Kuna in tourism and their longer term incorporation into global economic networks have gendered consequences. Both tourism and mola-making and distribution open up new roles for women, such as hotel and resort employment, or leadership positions in the mola cooperative that organizes sales for women across the San Blas region. Such roles provide women with both more power and author-

FIGURE 5.10.   Kuna woman and child in customary clothing as
the child learns to embroider. (From *The Art of Being Kuna*, edited by
Mari Lyn Salvador, Fowler Museum of Cultural History, University of
California, Los Angeles, 1997, 152. Courtesy of Mari Lyn Salvador.)

ity and more income. Yet tourism traps women by making them the symbols par excellence of a supposed Kuna traditional ethnicity, all the more
ironic because there is nothing about "traditional" Kuna women's clothing
(the molas, jewelry, *saburet* or wraparound skirt, and *muswe*, headscarf) that was
and is not either imported or produced locally from imported materials (see
fig. 5.10). As Kuna households and families, especially the increasing number
headed by single women, become ever more economically dependent on
mola production, women become increasingly vulnerable to shifts in national

and international tastes, as well as exploitation of their designs and mass production at factories that make similar items at cheaper prices.[120]

One way that Kuna women seek to counter these trends is through the formation of a multi-island mola cooperative, which raises funds, organizes labor, markets women's craft production, and protects it from outside competition. Starting with eight chapters in the mid-1960s, by 1985 the mola cooperative included seventeen chapters, with a total membership of over one thousand women.[121] It has strengthened women's leadership roles, as they have sought funding from national and international organizations, tried to outlaw any sales of non-Kuna-produced molas, and dealt with the emergence of competing Kuna mola-producing groups. The original co-op continues to survive, and its leaders play a growing role in Kuna public life by speaking out at congreso meetings, with some women becoming "active junior officials in their village *congressos.*" Kuna women have recently begun to turn to the Internet to market their molas internationally. The Kuna woman who does the bookkeeping at the Panama City office of the mola co-op comments that the website "has helped us a lot and we like it. . . . This is the only thing that allows many of the women in the islands to feed their children."[122]

Garifuna and other Central America indigenous women have also formed cooperatives, mothers' clubs, and other associations to increase women's business activities and to sponsor projects relating to women's and children's health needs and educational goals. Miskito women focus less on cooperative efforts to engage in economic development and more on preserving and defending traditional cultural practices. They also participated in the postwar peace and autonomy processes, through which Miskito men active against the Sandinistas were repatriated and Miskito communities adjusted to new political realities. One of these new realities was the birth of a small Miskito women's movement, concentrating on matters of health, education, and indigenous rights.[123] While it is clear that the formation of successful and long-lasting cooperative ventures, economic and political, depends on patterns of cooperative production and decision-making already in existence (the success of Maya and Kuna women's cooperatives bearing this out), the encounter between indigenous women and outside activist groups and funding agencies has borne some fruit in empowering some of Central America's indigenous women.

Conclusion

Central and South American women increasingly seek their own solutions to the economic and social problems and possibilities of the twenty-first century. Andean women historically have been the most active in resisting forms of change or exploitation that they viewed as too damaging to customary familial, communal, or gender relations, even as they used or created new organizational forms to resist change. Central American native women, especially Garifuna and Kuna, whose ethnicities have in some cases been the products of more recent patterns of ethnogenesis, have benefited from their own histories of autonomy. Both Andean and Central American women seek to take advantage of newer forms of political action in which indigenous people themselves decide on courses of action and development projects and search for governmental or NGO support, defining to a greater extent than elsewhere in Latin America how such support, financial or otherwise, will be given and used.

It is the women of Brazil, Venezuela, and other parts of the tropical low-lands who appear to be most isolated from contemporary forms of female activism. Lacking traditions of autonomy or political activism in their own cultures, they participate in the new supranational indigenous women's orga-nizations to a lesser extent than do Andean, Kuna, or Maya women. Their isolation within their own societies and nation-states remains deep. Whether international organizations, indigenous or nonindigenous, can reach out in ways that will provide women with tools for taking on the health, educa-tional, and economic development issues that affect them, yet allow them to maintain cultural integrity, is as yet unclear. The paradoxical impact of globalization identified for Mesoamerica—with the feminization of poverty yet the simultaneous enhancement of women's political power—also can be observed in Central and South America. But the constraints on women's developing political power are real. This and the previous chapter have shown that global, national, and local structures of economic, political, and gender power concentrate authority and wealth in male hands. Even as the higher-level structures reach into or affect local power configurations, women con-tinually challenge the distribution of resources and power on a variety of fronts, using old and new tools of resistance in order to do so.

6

Indigenous Women

Creating Agendas for Change

This book has emphasized a number of themes in the lives of Latin American indigenous women. First, the chapters demonstrate that women have a very long history of performing productive labor and that the amount of work they do has increased over time. Second, images of women as active and associated with important cultural beliefs or as symbols of identity have an ancient, often unrecognized, history. Third, while the degree to which women participate in political activism varies, in many areas—past and present—women have played roles in community political and religious structures of authority and in agitating for change. Fourth, families, households, and kinship structures have offered women sanctuary and support, emotional and material, yet male-female and parent-child relations can be marked by tension, even violence. Finally, the preceding two chapters, in particular, show the varied and sometimes contradictory impact of globalization. It speeds up change, enmeshes indigenous communities and families ever more deeply in market-oriented forms of production and exchange, intensifies the exploitation of female labor, and undermines complementarity in male/female relations, yet it brings with it new forms of political organization and access to international aid and worldwide media. To a greater extent than ever before, native women can help shape their own images and give voice to their ideas, hopes, and agendas for change in a variety of contexts and forums, regional, national, and international. Yet the question remains as to whether or not globalization has enhanced or undermined indigenous women's agency.

Before answering this question, it is important to return to the two faces of agency discussed in the first chapter. It is agency in the sense of political action that often stands out in this book, and many times those actions were or are defensive in nature. Women's engagement with carrying out the projects—economic, political, religious, familial—necessary for daily community and household life has also been chronicled here. Historian Greg Grandin argues that, at least for the Q'eqchi Maya women he writes about, their sense of their own historical agency may be more episodic than men's, speculating that "[b]ecause they are excluded from current politics, their recollections tend to dilute their own sense of agency, and political commitment fades from their stories."[1] His notion that women's own memories downplay their activism may well be true more broadly, but we must also remember that the degree of women's agency in daily life as well as in times of great stress and change is contingent and varies by place, time, and ethnicity. While certain factors, especially the exclusion of women from decision-making and violence, political and interpersonal, work to suppress indigenous women's agency, other factors, including the separation of male and female spheres, the existence of arenas of self-expression, and women's often central role in the production and distribution of valuable commodities support their ability to construct and shape daily life.

In assessing globalization and female agency across Latin America, characterized as it is by so many different indigenous groups and histories, we should note that three trends that began in the 1990s seem likely to accelerate early in the twenty-first century and will have a significant impact on the present and future of indigenous women. These include the growing tendency toward activism in varied, innovative forms at and beyond the local level; the increase in numbers of and roles for female indigenous leaders; and women's increasing ability to make their voices heard and to play a greater role in shaping their own images.

The roles played by indigenous women as activists in local communities and across regions have become widely known, in large part due to the activism shown by women of the EZLN and related groups devoted to the causes of indigenous rights and democratization in southern Mexico. As described in chapter 4, indigenous women have questioned gender inequality in their communities as well as in groups engaging in political activism. Showing a willingness to question tradition, activist women have raised issues such as domestic violence, land distribution, and customary patterns of decision-making in government, on the streets, and in community and regional meetings. Women even briefly took over a Chiapas radio station to broadcast concerns about indigenous and women's rights.[2] At the regional level, innovative strategies include starting organizations to address new kinds of issues and problems. Somewhat similar to the cooperatives that began springing up in many parts of Latin America from the 1970s on, indigenous curers and midwives, male and female, in Chiapas have, for example, formed COMPITCH (Council of Indigenous Traditional Midwives and Healers of Chiapas). This alliance, made up of representatives from twelve organizations, works to confront the issue of biopiracy (government- and corporate-sponsored efforts to find plants and traditional cures with commercial medical or other applications), to help sustain traditional medical practices, and to aid curers and midwives with their needs for materials and equipment. Likewise, a group of Mexican women, many of them members of indigenous communities in southern Mexico, met in August 2002 in Oaxaca, Mexico, to discuss the gender implications of the Plan Puebla Panama, developed by Mexico's president, Vicente Fox, to stimulate economic development from Puebla, Mexico, to Panama in Central America. The women discussed protecting natural resources and how to control the impact of *maquiladoras* (foreign-owned or run factories where imported parts are assembled for export) and tourism. Whether the women who attended the conference agreed that the proposal will lead to economic development or not, they asserted that women must struggle as a group to be included in the programs of the global financial institutions already investing in the plan.[3]

Activist indigenous women are also carrying their demands and programs for change beyond their localities and regions to both national and international levels. In Mexico, indigenous women from all over the country have begun pressing their demands for political, cultural, and economic rights, especially for the right to representation in indigenous congresses. At the Third National Indigenous Congress held in Nurio, Michoacán, in early March 2001, a women's session took place, despite disruption by men. As Cándida Jiménez of the National Council of Indigenous Women delicately put it, "it was a little difficult; [because of] this custom of the indigenous pueblos that the men have had more [political] opportunities than the women." The women's session focused on proposed changes to the Mexican constitution that would have given greater legal and cultural autonomy to indigenous groups and communities, with the women maintaining they could discuss both gender issues as well as the legal and cultural issues on which the meeting primarily focused.[4]

Native women in Mexico and elsewhere are finding that the formation of female groups, made up of representatives of many different ethnicities, communities, and regions, can be a successful strategy to obtain legal remedies for the broad range of issues concerning women. Mexican journalist Rosa Rojas described an interview with three members of the organization AMMOR (Mexican Association of Organized Women in Network, a group that includes indigenous and nonindigenous women) who emphasized the difficulties women have ("la bronca que es siempre," the struggle it always is) finding ways to discuss women's and gender issues in mixed-gender groups.[5] In Guatemala, Maya women from many groups and regions have joined together publicly to demonstrate, to form new, national-level groups that support democratization and an increase in women's presence in government at all levels, and to voice the particular social needs of indigenous women. They have also joined with nonindigenous rural and urban women to press the human rights, cultural, and gender-related agenda that is of importance to them. Costa Rican indigenous women of varying localities and ethnicities participate in that country's Commission of Indigenous Women.

In Ecuador, native women promote gender issues in national indigenous congresses and are forming groups and holding their own meetings, such as the First Congress of Amazonian Women, held in September 1996. This meeting addressed a wide range of issues, including those of resource ownership, environmental despoilment by petrochemical and logging companies, and biopiracy. The delegates also supported efforts by regional and national indigenous organizations to interact more forcefully with the ministry dealing with indigenous affairs. Furthermore, they asked the national Amazonian indigenous congress (Confederation of the Nationalities Indigenous to the Amazon of Ecuador, or CONFENAIE) to require all organizations sending groups to its meetings to send delegations composed of equal numbers of male and female delegates. In Colombia, women of a variety of ethnic backgrounds formed ANMUCIC (National Association of Peasant, Black, and Indigenous Women of Colombia) to advocate for gender equity in development projects and land reform and provide political and social support for women and families in the areas of the country most affected by the ongoing political violence.[6]

Peru has witnessed a similar development in which both highland and lowland women participate in nationally organized workshops and conferences addressing both general issues relating to discrimination, multiculturalism, and multilingualism and many of the gender-related issues already mentioned. In one such workshop, women expressly protested the caricatured and stereotyped images through which they are presented, arguing that modern means of communication, especially television, depict them in undignified ways. And in Chile, Mapuche women launched a group, Keyukleayñ Pu Zomo (Women in Action or Solidarity among Women), at the very moment, in 1991, when Chile's transition to democracy was occurring. Coming from urban and rural areas and working with other Mapuche women's groups, along with non-Mapuche women's groups, Keyukleayñ Pu Zomo focused on political and educational goals relating to female political representation, adult literacy, and economic development. The group and its founder, Rosa Isolde Reuque Paillalef, also became active in the preparations by Chilean activists for the International Women's Conference in Beijing in 1995 and in conferences held in Chile during and after the Beijing meeting.[7]

At the Beijing meeting, indigenous women from many parts of the world promulgated a declaration of some fifty points, some of which criticized the Beijing Draft Platform for Action for ignoring the conditions under which indigenous women live. The declaration argued that the draft platform failed to address the impact of globalization and overlooked the roles of western media, educational systems, and religions in undermining indigenous cultural diversity. The document covers native women's demands in several areas, especially with respect to land rights, access to education and health care, and control over foreign investment and plans for economic development, as well as the need to stop both domestic violence and human rights violations.[8] A variety of meetings attended by indigenous women from the western hemisphere, including Latin America, have also been held during the 1990s and beyond. A series of conferences of native women from North,

Central, and South America—known as the First through Fourth Continental Encuentros (encounters) of Indigenous Women of the First Nations
of Abya Yala (continent of life), held in 1995 (Ecuador), 1997 (Mexico), 2000
(Panama), and 2003 (Peru)—have helped reinforce indigenous women's
capacities to exert leadership at all levels of political organization. These
meetings, along with others such as the Summit of Indigenous Women of
the Americas, sponsored by both the Inter-American Development Bank
and the Rigoberta Menchú Foundation, which met in Oaxaca, Mexico, in
December 2002, also served to reinforce women's commitment to struggles
by indigenous peoples to assert rights nationally and internationally, as well
as women's sense of ethnic identity.

The issues of greatest concern at the international level include the
impact of globalization, especially in relation to both the economic rights
of women and the environmental impact of economic development; ending political violence in areas where military and paramilitary groups disrupt
everyday life; and gaining greater political representation and legal and social
rights for women. These issues have, however, proven to be controversial. The
2002 Oaxaca summit, for example, provoked a response from a committee
of the Episcopal Mexican Conference (made up of bishops and archbishops
of the Mexican Catholic Church) who accused the participants of attempt-
ing to impose concepts of sexual and reproductive rights that would undermine the values of maternity and human life in indigenous communities
and cultures, as well as "indirectly" seeking to incite violence. The delegates
rejected the accusations as without foundation. Indeed, the final document
promulgated by the summit called for governments to guarantee indigenous
women's access to health care in ways that respect indigenous belief systems
and to eliminate forced sterilization, but did not directly address sexual and
reproductive rights.[9]

These movements cannot exist without leaders, and while Rigoberta
Menchú continues to be the best known Latin American indigenous female
activist, she follows in the footsteps of others like Ecuadorian Dolores Cacuango, who founded bilingual schools, organized strikes and unions, and
founded and served as the first president of the Ecuadorean Federation of
Indians.[10] The number of women participating in local, regional, and national
governments, as well as in organizations and meetings occurring at all levels,
has been increasing, and this increase will probably continue.

One of the places indigenous women's activism is most apparent is in
Guatemala. While it is tempting to assume that Rigoberta Menchú provided
a model that other women chose to follow, other factors were also significant. These include the explosion of new groups with male and female participation (sometimes together but often apart) dedicated to creating a more
active civil society in Guatemala, the very public role of women in leadership positions in Mexico's EZLN, and perhaps most important, the way that
Guatemalan indigenous women had to fill the leadership void in villages
and in communities of internally and externally displaced peoples because

men were disproportionately victims of the civil war. Rosalina Tuyuc, of the Kaqchiquel community of Acatenango, Chimaltenango, and former president of CONAVIGUA, was elected to Guatemala's congress and served as its vice president, where she introduced important legislation for women, including a bill to create an Office for the Defense of the Rights of Indigenous Women. Other Maya women became active in political parties, and Otilia Lux de Cotí, K'iche', served on Guatemala's Truth Commission (also known as the CEH, or Historical Clarification Commission) and later became minister of culture in the Alfonso Portillo government. She remains in that office serving Oscar Berger, who became Guatemala's president in January 2004, and who also appointed Rigoberta Menchú "goodwill ambassador to the [1996] peace accords," the United Nations–brokered agreement that ended the long and devastating civil war.[11]

In other parts of Latin America, similar patterns occur, with indigenous women emerging from feminist and indigenous activist groups to hold governmental and other types of positions. These positions provide women with forums to work on legislation and to voice their own views as well as those of their communities. In Mexico, Xóchitl Gálvez, an Otomí woman who currently heads Mexico's Office of Development for Indigenous Communities, has described the multiple forms of discrimination from which she suffered, commenting: "This is really triple discrimination: being poor, being a woman and being indigenous." Myrna Cunningham, a doctor and member of the Nicaraguan Miskito community, served as president of the University of the Autonomous Regions of the Nicaraguan Caribbean Coast (URACCAN). She continues to participate actively in a variety of international congresses and forums; for example, she presented the views of NGOs and indigenous and civil society groups to the World Conference against Racism held in Durban, South Africa, in September 2001. Paulina Arpasi, Aymara-speaker from the Puno region, was elected to Peru's congress in April 2000, the first Aymara woman to hold such a position. In Lima, she has been treated more as a "picturesque anecdote" than a politician with a depth of experience forged in her community and through her leadership of the Peasant Confederation of Peru (CCP). But her expertise in indigenous issues, along with the economic issues of the rural peasantry, helps her believe that she can serve as a force for change, even in the face of discrimination. Other indigenous South American politicians include Nina Pacari, former vice president of Ecuador's congress and current foreign minister, Remedios Loza of Bolivia, who served in the country's legislature and briefly ran for the Bolivian presidency in the summer of 2002, and Isabel Ortega, of Aymara and Quechua descent, who serves in Bolivia's congress. She has described how guards would try to deny her entry into the congressional building: "The guards would say, 'How can you come in'? And then they pushed me out. . . . They would say 'An Indian is coming into the palace.'"[12]

Whether working in or leading the many different activist groups that have sprung up around indigenous women's issues or serving in elective offices, native women have made their voices heard in local, regional, national, and international institutions and forums as never before. They use their positions to press a variety of demands and have begun to reshape how they are perceived and treated in and beyond their communities. But in some cases, native women find themselves downplaying their ethnicity to highlight their gender identity. Emphasizing gender over ethnicity can be, in certain times and places, a successful strategic essentialism that makes use of public perceptions of women as outsiders who represent a moral authority that will be used to clean up governments associated with fraud and corruption. Rosario Novelo Canche, a Yucatec Maya woman who ran for and served as mayor of the town of Teabo, used the slogan "Del corazón de una mujer" (From the heart of a woman), which stressed her gender, presumably reminding voters of associations they may draw between women and caring and compassion, while downplaying her Maya identity.[13]

But the opposite, highlighting ethnicity and downplaying gender differences and subordination, occurs too. In 1996, for example, a *canton* (equivalent to a county) in Ecuador's Cañar province elected a female mayor. The canton has a mixed indigenous and mestizo population, and in order to gain some degree of acceptance from mestizos, this Quichua mayor (identified only by the pseudonym "María" by anthropologist Emma Cervone) took to having her husband accompany her in public, rejected alliances with any indigenous women or women's groups, and emphasized the gender-complementary aspects of Quichua culture. In doing so, she deemphasized the existence of gender hierarchy both in the political realm, in which indigenous women have less access to formal political power or authority, and in the home, in which men sometimes use domestic violence to curtail women's activities outside of it. María stressed, instead, the beneficial features of a "traditional" ethnic identity, giving it "more positive meanings and associations. Tradition becomes associated with '*lo propio*,' that of one's own. In this way 'tradition,' that which is indigenous, is presented as the only just and balanced alternative to Western forms of injustice and destruction."[14]

While it is too early to evaluate the success of women's groups and activists across the many countries and issues they are addressing, one issue to which many Latin American governments have responded is women's demands for greater land rights. Women's participation as activists, bureaucrats, or politicians in social movements, the state, and at the international level led to agreements such as the 1979 Convention to End All Forms of Discrimination against Women, which all Latin American countries ratified by 1990. Such changes led many nations to begin revising their constitutions and legal codes to both strengthen women's property rights and accommodate the multiethnic, pluricultural nature of their citizenries.[15] To expand women's property rights, legislatures have generally concentrated on joint titling of lands, so that both husbands and wives have legal rights of ownership, and on establishing rights of ownership for female heads of household. As a result, rural women across Latin America, some indigenous, own or will own more land than ever before, though considerable variation by country exists in the proportions of women benefiting from these legal changes. Of those nations with the largest indigenous populations, Guatemala has made the most progress toward both joint titling of land (for both married couples and men and women in consensual unions) and titling of land for female heads of household. Mexico and Peru have made the least progress, because the rush to individualize ownership of formerly collectively owned lands due to neoliberal economic reforms has largely left women behind. While Bolivia arguably created the strongest legal framework for both land redistribution and collective ownership by indigenous communities, and recent legislation explicitly says that women have rights to land, the relevant law calls neither for joint titling nor any specific effort to legitimize land titles for female heads of household.[16]

Another area where the same coalitions of activists, bureaucrats, and politicians have made progress in changing legal codes is in the area of domestic violence. Nongovernmental, governmental, and international organizations all brought pressure to bear, especially during the 1990s, to encourage Latin American governments to create legal frameworks that would offer women protection and recourse against domestic and sexual violence. The result was that virtually all Latin American countries now have laws that criminalize domestic violence, and some countries, particularly Bolivia and Costa Rica, attempt to provide legal and social services relating to women's and family issues. But the targeting of indigenous women by armies or paramilitaries who use rape as a weapon of war and the increasing number of girls and women who turn to prostitution, due to coercion by fighters or miners or out of economic desperation, represent significant new problems in many indigenous communities to which legal codes will need to respond.[17]

Indigenous women's activism, even when combined with increased access to land rights, has not yet translated into significantly greater amounts of political power within traditional power structures at any level. Activists at the local level sometimes find that at the national level both mixed and female indigenous organizations and meetings emphasize the defense of indigenous and communal land rights over other issues, including those relating to gender. Some female indigenous activists and leaders privilege ethnic identity because they reject feminism, seeing it as a western, middle-class movement irrelevant to their concerns. Having witnessed nonindigenous feminists in their own countries discriminate against indigenous women and suspecting that demands for reproductive rights could be linked to genocide, some activists and leaders prefer to highlight ethnicity. Others simply believe that native communities and groups gain more when men and women work together politically.[18] Domitila Barrios de Chungara argued at the 1975 United Nations–sponsored World Conference of the International Women's Year in Mexico City that for Latin American women "the first and main task isn't to fight against our compañeros [companions], but with them to change the system we live in for another, in which men and women will have the right to live, to work, to organize." Mapuche women believe that the Chilean agency charged with addressing women's political, economic, and social issues, SERNAM (National Women's Service), fails to recognize that Mapuche women's issues are not the same as those of other Chilean women and that some of the discrimination they face comes from non-Mapuche Chilean women.[19]

But many indigenous women, activists and others, have demonstrated an increasing willingness to question traditional gender roles within their communities and groups, particularly as these relate to the distribution of land and political power, the imposition of marriage partners, the need for more educational access, and the occurrence of domestic violence and high rates of health problems because these are the issues that matter most to them in their daily lives. As part of that questioning, some women have also begun to create their own historical and cultural record, writing stories, plays, songs, and poems, taking photographs and making videos, and collecting testimonies. Given the different kinds of communities, social statuses, and forms of struggle that exist across the many areas in which indigenous women live, these important records surely will provide a variety of women's voices and perspectives upon which future activists and scholars can draw.[20]

New ways to redefine tradition and embrace or control change will emerge from the intersection of locally defined concerns and agendas with global economic and communications networks. Juana Catinac Xom, the K'iche' director of Guatemala's Office of the Ombudsman for Indigenous Women, pointed to the particular importance of training and education for indigenous women, because "only in this way will we have human resources for the future." If globalization has worsened gender inequalities for women in many parts of the world, as a recent report commissioned by the International Labor Organization conclusively argues, the scope and scale of Latin America's indigenous women's activism and assertions of agency, while rooted in their history, is also unprecedented. Women's demands for representation, rights, and education have had and will have far-reaching consequences for the organization of daily life in indigenous communities, the politics of indigenous and women's groups, and the policies of twenty-first-century Latin American nation-states.[21]

ORGANIZATIONS
MENTIONED IN THE TEXT
AND THEIR ACRONYMS

AMMOR   Asociación Mexicana de Mujeres Organizadas en Red (Mexican Association of Organized Women in Network; Mexico)

ANFASEP   Asociación Nacional de Familiares de Secuestrados, Detenidos y Desaparecidos del Perú (National Association of Family Members of the Detained-Disappeared; Peru)

ANMUCIC   Asociación Nacional de Mujeres Campesinas, Negras e Indígenas (National Association of Peasant, Black, and Indigenous Women of Colombia; Colombia)

CCP   Confederación de la Campesina del Perú (Peasant Confederation of Peru; Peru)

CEH   Comisión para el Esclarecimiento Histórico (Historical Clarification Commission; Guatemala)

CENDOC-Mujer   El Centro de Documentación sobre la Mujer (Center for Documentation about Women; Peru)

CNMI   Coordinadora Nacional de Mujeres Indígenas (National Coordinating Committee of Indigenous Women; Mexico)

CNPA   Coodinadora Nacional Plan de Ayala National (Coalition of the Plan of Ayala; Mexico)

COCEI   Coalición Obrera Campesina Estudiantil del Istmo (Coalition of Isthmus Workers, Peasants, and Students; Mexico)

COCOPA   Comisión de Concordía y Pacificación (Commission on Concord and Pacification; Mexico)

COFADER   Comité de Familiares de Detenidos, Desaparecidos, Refugiados (Committee of Family Members of the Detained-Disappeared; Peru)

COMPITCH   Consejo de Organizaciones de Médicos y Parteras Indígenas Tradicionales (Council of Indigenous Traditional Midwives and Healers of Chiapas; Mexico)

CONAVIGUA   Coordinadora Nacional de Viudas de Guatemala (National Coalition of Guatemalan Widows; Guatemala)

CONAIE	Confederación de Nacionalidades Indígenas de Ecuador (Confederation of Indigenous Nationalities of Ecuador; Ecuador)
CONFENAIE	Confederación de Nacionalidades Indígenas del Amazonia Ecuatoriana (Confederation of the Nationalities Indigenous to the Amazon of Ecuador; Ecuador)
CUC	Comité de Unidad Campesina (Peasant Unity Committee; Guatemala)
EPR	Ejército Popular Revolucionario (Revolutionary Popular Army; Mexico)
EZLN	Ejército Zapatista de Liberación Nacional (Zapatista Army of National Liberation; Mexico)
FEDEFAM	Federación Latinoamericana de Asociaciones Familiares de Detenidos-Desaparecidos (Latin American Federation of Associations of Family Members of the Detained-Disappeared; Peru)
FEI	Federación Ecuatoriana de Indios (Ecuadorian Federation of Indians; Ecuador)
FOMMA	Fortaleza de la Mujer Maya (Fortitude of the Mayan Woman; Guatemala)
GAM	Grupo de Apoyo Mutuo (Mutual Support Group; Guatemala)
INI	Instituto Nacional Indígenista (National Indigenous Institute; Mexico)
INRA	Instituto Nacional de Reforma Agraria (National Institute of Agrarian Reform; Bolivia)
PRI	Partido Revolucionario Institucional (Institutional Revolutionary Party; Mexico)
SERNAM	Servicio Nacional de la Mujer (National Women's Service; Chile)
URACCAN	Universidad de las Regiones Autónomas de la Costa Caribe Nicaragüense (University of the Autonomous Regions of the Nicaraguan Caribbean Coast; Nicaragua)

GLOSSARY

The following abbreviations are used for languages: A (Aymara), E (English), G (Garifuna), Gê (Gê languages), Gu (Guaraní), K (Kuna), L (Lenca), M (Maya languages), MH (Mai Huna), Mi (Miskito), Mp (Mapudugun), N (Nahuatl), Ñ (Ñudzahui), Q (Quechua), P (Portuguese), S (Spanish), Sh (Sharanahua), T (Taino), Tu (Tupian), Z (Zapotec).

Al (M) woman's children
Alcabala (S) colonial sales tax
Alcaldes or Alcaldes mayores (S) civil officials
Almehen (M) noble
Amantecatl (N) midwife
Aqllas (Q) chosen women
Aqlla wasi (Q) state housing for aqllas
Atole (N) maize-based thick drink
Atrevidas (S) impudent or daring women
'Awasqa (Q) coarse cloth
Ayllu (Q) basic unit of kinship and locality in the Andes
Ayuntamiento (S) town council
Bracero (S) temporary laborer
Bruja/os (S) witches
Buwiyes (G) female shamans
Cacera (S) semiformal commercial relationships
Cacica (T) female indigenous leader
Caciques (T) male indigenous leaders
Calli (N) house
Calmecac (N) school primarily for children of nobles
Camarada (S) female comrade
Cantón (S) county
Capullanas (Q) female leaders in northern Andes
Cargo (S) hierarchically organized civil-religious or religious system
Casta (S) person of mixed ethno-racial identity
Chicha (Q) maize beer
Chicherías (Q) chicha bars or pubs

Chola/o (unknown) people, especially women, in the Andes with an urban, indigenous identity

Chuchcajaw (M) "father-mother," male lineage heads

Cihuacuacuiltin (N) higher level priestesses

Cihuatecutli (N) high-ranking noblewoman

Cihuatepixque (N) female neighborhood guards

Cihuatiachcahuan (N) female "older brothers," female officials in song houses

Cihuatl (N) woman

Cihuatlamacazque (N) lower level priestesses

Cihuatlaxicaleque (N) female neighborhood leaders

Cofradías (S) confraternities

Colonias (S) colonies, communities of exile

Comadre/s (S) godmother/s

Comercias (S) sales teams

Compadres (S) godparents

Congregación (S) forced resettlement of colonial indigenous communities

Congresos (S) Kuna governing councils

Coty-guazu (Gu) enclosure or cloistering of indigenous women in missions

Cuicacalli (N) song house

Corregidores (S) colonial civil officials

Curandera (S) female curer

De pollera (Q/S) wearing clothing associated with cholas

De vestido (S) wearing urban, acculturated clothing

Depósito (S) protective custody for women

Don/Doña (S) Spanish title of respect for men or women

Desvergonzadas (S) shameless women

Ejidos (S) communally owned lands

Encomenderos (S) holders of encomienda grants

Encomienda (S) grant of labor and tribute

Encuentros (S) encounters

Estupro (S) rape or violation (often referring to acts that result in the loss of virginity)

Garimpeiros (P) gold miners

Gateras (Q) marketwomen in colonial Quito

Gobernador/a (S) governor (male or female)

Grisi siknis (Mi/E) gender- and stress-related syndrome found among the Miskito

Guelaguetza (Z), reciprocal exchange of goods and labor

Hacienda (S) large, landed estate

Hechicería (S) sorcery, witchcraft

Huasicamía (Q) serf-like female domestic service

Huasipungerismo (Q) form of serfdom in colonial Ecuador

Huasipungero (Q) serf-like colonial laborers

Huehuetlatolli (N) elders' words

Huipiles (N) women's shift-like shirts

Ichpochtlayacanque (N) female administrators in song houses

Indigenismo (S) Indianism

Indizuela (S) little Indian girl

Inna (K) female puberty ritual

Joyera (S) female jewelry maker
Kumpi (Q) fine cloth
Kumpi-kamayuq (Q) male weavers
Kupry (Gê) female sexual partners
Kurakas (Q) local leaders
La coya (Q/S) the queen
La lengua (S) the tongue
La reina (S) the queen
Ladinos (S) people of mixed ethno-racial identity who identify more with national
    rather than indigenous culture
Lo propio (S) one's own
Macharetkit (K/S) masculine women
Machi (Mp) female shaman
Machos (S) men
Mamaqunas (Q) priestesses
Maquiladoras (S) factories that produce or process export goods
Mayordoma/o (S) a title in the cargo system, a post that sponsors festivals
Mayordomía system (S) another term for cargo system
Me-kuprí-ya (Gê) translated by Nimuendajú as "wantons"
Me-kuprú (Gê) translated by Da Matta as "promiscuous women"
Mehen (M) man's sons
Mestiza/o (S) mixed identity whose primary components are indigenous and
    Spanish
Milpas (N/S) corn fields
Mingas (Q) reciprocal work groups
Mit'a (Q) labor draft
Molas (K) blouses with intricate embroidered designs made by Kuna women
Molinos de nixtamal (N/S) mechanized corn mills
Montequitl (N) period of bride service provided by husband to wife's family
Mucahua (Q) chicha serving bowls
Muswe (K) headscarf
Nan (M) mother
Nawawa kusi (Sh) stinging nettles
Ñandahi (Ñ) commoners
Nele (L) seers
Obrajes (S) sweatshops (often for textiles) in colonial urban areas
Omekit (K) feminine men
Onmakket neka (K) gathering house
Partera (S) midwife
Pauahtuns (M) male deities holding up four corners of the earth
Polleras (Q) heavy pleated skirts in multiple colors
Pulperos (S) small store owners
Pulque (N) fermented drink made from maguey plant
Quya (Q) queen
Rapto (S) abduction
Reducción (S) forced resettlement of colonial indigenous communities
Regador (S) representative to town council
Repartimiento (S) rotational labor draft

Revendedora (S) female resellers
Robo de la novia (S) stealing the bride
Saburet (K) wraparound skirt
Señora (S) lady, madam
Señoríos (S) seigniorial domains
Servinacuy (Q) trial marriage
Siwatanke (N) marriage broker
Tayu (Ñ) married couple
Tehuanas (S) Zapotec women of Isthmus of Tehuantepec
Telenovela (S) soap opera
Telpochcalli (N) school for children of commoners
Telpochtlatoque (N) youth leaders in song houses
Teoteca/os (N) women, people of Teotitlán
Tepahtiqui (N) curer
Tepixque (N) neighborhood guards
Tiachcahuan (N) older brothers, male officials in song houses
Tianquizpan tlayacanque (N) marketplace administrators
Tlachpanque (N) sweepers
Tlahuelpuchis (N) witches
Traje (S) customary, handmade clothing
Tupu (Q) kind of pin to hold women's clothing together
Tlalli cacicazgo (N/T) cacique lands
Tlamatiquetl (N) shaman
Tlamemes (N) human carriers
Tlatoani (N) Mexica supreme leader
Tlatocacihuatl (N) female supreme leader
Tlaxicaleque (N) neighborhood leaders
Tortillas (S) unleavened cornmeal cakes
Viajeras (S) traveling saleswomen
Violación (S) violation, rape
Wak'as (Q) sacred objects and places
Warmi (Q) woman
Yagé (Mh) hallucinogenic drink
Yatiri (A) diviner
Yuhui (Ñ) reed mat
Yuhuitayu (Ñ) rulership
Yya (Ñ) nobility
Yya toniñe (Ñ) male ruler
Yya dzehe toniñe (Ñ) female ruler
Zapotecas (N) Zapotec women

NOTES

1. Introducing the Indigenous Women of Latin America

1. Silverblatt 1987. Important literature on women and the rise of states is described in Silverblatt 1988 and 1991.

2. See Anton 1973; Bossen 1984; and Rosenbaum 1996 for comparative works on indigenous women in Middle and South America. For overviews or collections of essays on North American indigenous women, see Niethammer 1977; Green 1980; Albers and Medicine 1983; Albers 1989; Klein and Ackerman 1995; Shoemaker 1995; Johnston 1996; and Ford 1997.

3. Examples include Benería 1982; Benería and Feldman 1992; Bose and Acosta-Belen 1995; Deere 1990; Deere and León 1982; Deere, Humphries, and León 1982; Leacock and Safa 1986; Marchand and Parpart 1995; Mies, Bennholdt-Thomsen, and von Werlhof 1988; Momsen and Kinnaird 1993; and Nash and Fernández-Kelly 1983.

4. Mohanty 1991 discusses the ways scholars have systematically silenced women of the so-called Third World and failed to chronicle their agency and activism.

5. Gayle Rubin distinguishes between sex and gender (1975); Judith Butler argues that sex *is* gender (1990: 6–13); and Kamala Visweswaran describes how various forms of hierarchy and discrimination shape gender performances (1997: 59–60), leading me to argue that identity is as much inscribed, through a complex interplay of social and biological forces, as it is performed.

6. Allman, Geiger, and Musisi 2002: 3–4.

7. Meisch 1991.

8. Ortner 2001: 78–9. Also see Ortner 1996: 6–12, 16–8, as well as Sahlins 1981; Guha 1983; and many of the essays in Montoya, Frazier, and Lessig 2002.

9. See Gailey 1987a for a thorough discussion of this literature and the many explanations offered to explain gender asymmetry.

10. Quinn 1977: 182; also see Mukhopadhyay and Higgens 1988; Meigs 1990; and Crown 2000a. For Ortner's discussion of status, see 1996: 140–7 (quotation on 140).

11. Monaghan 2001: 287–8 (quotation on 287). Also see Harris's seminal article (1978) on this concept.

12. Silverblatt 1987: 5–7, 31–8, 47–66; Kellogg 1988: 676; and Wood and Haskett 1997: 317–9.

13. Silverblatt 1987: 46, 66; Harris 1978. Also see Stern, who points to the need to analyze the dynamic relations among "gender conflict and subordination," "gender complementarity and parallelism," and "cross-gender unity as well as gender differentiation" (1999: 621).

14. Good 2000: 124–7, 139–40, 145–8. Some ethnographers use the concept "post-Nahua" to describe communities that have ceased speaking Nahuatl yet continue to organize family and social life in ways that they and others consider to be indigenous (Mulhare 1998; Robichaux 2003).

15. See Taylor 1951 and Gonzalez 1969, who heavily stress the "black" identity of the Garifuna or the Black Carib, as they were generally known until recently. Bateman, on the other hand, asserts that, in comparison to the Black Seminole of Florida and Oklahoma, the Black Carib became "more Indian" as newly arrived African men raided Island Carib villages for women, who then transmitted indigenous cultural practice and language to children born of these unions (1990: 9–10). Peter Wade (1997) emphasizes that Latin American racial and ethnic identities are diverse and changing, not homogeneous and fixed, and Mary Weismantel discusses the complexities of ethno-racial identities in the indigenous Andes (2001: xxviii–xli; also see Abercrombie 1996). Other scholarship that helped me think about ethnicity, race, and indigenism includes Díaz Polanco 1997; Fogelson 1998; Warren 1998; Niezen 2003; and several of the essays in Applebaum, Macpherson, and Rosemblatt 2003 (especially those by Chambers, Sanders, and Wade).

16. McGrew 1992: 63. Also see his more extensive definition (65–6) and Appadurai, who argues for the existence of forms of globalization from "above" and "below," the latter emerging out of the struggles of the poorer 80 percent of the world's population to achieve democracy, autonomy, and greater economic well-being (2001: 3). An anthropologically oriented overview of studies of globalization can be found in Tsing 2001.

17. I am drawing on and expanding Walter D. Mignolo's brief definition of globalization (1998: 32). Mignolo notes how both Wallerstein and Elias described processes crucial to the complex of changes that contemporary scholars define as "globalization" (see Wallerstein 1974 and Elias 1978). For discussion of when globalization began, see Abu-Lughod 1989 and Frank 1990. For insights into the gendered ambiguities entailed in this "civilizing process," see Stoler 2002.

18. For description of these more recent transformative processes operating on a truly worldwide scale, see McGrew 1992; Sklair 1995; and Hopkins 2002.

19. Dickenson 1997: 116–21.

20. Hochschild 2000. Benería 2003 and Ehrenreich and Hochschild 2003 provide accessible general discussions of women and globalization. Chapters 4 and 5 include extensive references to literature on globalization as it effects indigenous women throughout Latin America.

21. For a discussion of the changing gender division of labor, emphasizing women's increasing autonomy and participation in political movements, see Sassen 1998: 91–3, 99–100. For more pessimistic views, see Tinker 1990; Ward 1990; Sethie 1999; and Louie 2001. The essays in *Feminism and Globalization* 1996 provide a nuanced treatment of both the impact of globalization on women and the dialogues between and among feminists across national boundaries about globalization and gender.

22. Brysk 2000; Niezen 2003; and Deere and León 2001a: ch. 7.

23. Frank and Gills 1993: 4.

24. Dillehay 2000: chs. 1 and 2. Also see Meltzer 1995.

25. De Terra, Romero, and Stewart 1949: 95; Heizer and Cook 1959; and Weaver 1993: 9–10.

26. Zihlman 1981; Gero 1991; Pringle 1998; and Bruhns and Stothert 1999: ch. 1.

27. Bruhns and Stothert 1999 explore the gendered nature of these changes, especially in chs. 4–6, on the development of horticulture, agriculture, and social complexity. For the impact of the transition to food production on physical well-being, see Cohen and Armelagos 1984. For the U.S. southwest, in particular the Grasshopper Pueblo of Arizona, see Ezzo's discussion of gendered changes in work, patterns of food consumption, and increasing status differences between men and women (1993: 77–80).

28. Spielmann 1995: 96.

29. For Oaxaca, see Reynolds 1986; and Whallon 1986. On the chronology of Guilá Naquitz, see Flannery 1986: 38–9. For Ecuador, see Damp 1979: ch. 5; and Zeidler 1984: 481–567.

30. Sheets 1992: 56, 59–60, 89–97, 102–8. For discussion of a possible female shaman at Ceren, see Sweely 1999: 166–7, 169. Also see Marcus and Flannery's discussion of gendered work areas at the Archaic period Oaxaca site of Guilá Naquitz (1996: 54–5). Stothert discusses the possible existence of female shamans in Formative Ecuador (2003: 360–1, 400–405).

31. A classic statement of the "fertility" interpretation for figurines can be found in Roosevelt (1988). For explanations emphasizing female figurines as objects symbolizing social power, see Rice 1981; Cyphers Guillén 1993; and Joyce 2000a: ch. 2. Richard Lesure has argued, on the other hand, that Early Formative figurines (1400–1000 B.C.), with their depictions of either young females or elders (usually male but sometimes female), symbolize the ability of elders to control female labor and perhaps give women in marital exchanges (1997: 244–7). Di Capua (1994) argues that Formative figurines from the Valdivia site in Ecuador were used to represent both women's maturation and life-cycle transitions.

32. Marcus and Flannery 1996: 85. Also see Marcus 1998 (especially chs. 2, 3, and 19); and 1999.

33. Saenz Samper 1993.

34. On women's emerging roles as potters in the American Southwest, see Crown and Wills 1995. On women's possible roles in the emergence of trade networks in central Mexico, see Cyphers Guillén 1984; 1993; and 1994.

35. This point of view dates back to Engels 1972 and has been updated by feminist scholars such as Gailey 1987b; Leacock 1981; 1983; Lerner 1986; Sacks 1974; 1979; and Silverblatt 1987; 1988.

36. See descriptions of individual burials in García Moll et al. 1991: 27–84. Also see Joyce 1999 and 2000a: 30–4.

37. On San José phase (1150–850 B.C.) burials at the site of Tomaltepec, see Whalen 1981. For analysis of figurines and burials, at the nearby site of Fábrica San José, see Drennan 1976. Marcus and Flannery provide an overview of Preclassic burials in the region (1996: 96–9, 105–6, and 113–7).

38. Quotation from Marcus and Flannery 1996: 117. Also see 170 and 240.

39. Quilter 1989: 59, 64–5, 168–70 (table 3, "Burials by Sex").

40. Ubelaker (1984) fails to find skeletal evidence for increased gender hierarchy while social complexity was increasing in early prehistoric Ecuador. For a comparative discussion of many burials from early coastal Andean sites, see Quilter 1989: ch. 6. Also see Bruhns and Stothert (1999: ch. 3), who review much evidence

on Archaic and/or Formative figurines and burials, especially for Chile, Peru, and Ecuador. Interestingly, burial evidence from both Tlatilco in central Mexico and Paloma in coastal Peru indicates that these societies may have paid more attention to age than gender in early forms of social differentiation (Joyce 2000a: 31–4; Quilter 1989: 63, 83).

2. Of Warriors and Working Women

1. In this chapter (and throughout the book), I strive to use terminology and spellings that reflect as accurately as possible contemporary knowledge of linguistic and ethnic patterns in the various areas. Of all the relevant terms, "Nahua" and "Aztec" may well be the most vexing, because they do not refer to any specific known, ethnically defined group of people but instead can refer either to the Nahuatl-speaking peoples of Postclassic highland central Mexico or to those ethnic groups constituting the Aztec or Triple Alliance empire of late Postclassic times (consisting of the Mexica of Tenochtitlan, the Acolhua of Texcoco, and the Tepanec of Tlacopan). While archaeologists continue to use the term "Aztec," historians increasingly use "Nahua," which has the advantage of referring to the languages and dialects spoken, but this term too is one of convenience that does not reflect the complex ethnicities of the region. When speaking broadly, I use "Nahua"; when focusing more specifically, I refer to the largest and most important group, the Mexica. Likewise, rather than "Mixtec" I use "Ñudzahui," as well as some Quechua, rather than hispanicized, spellings, in the section on Andean women and gender relations (though scholars differ on usage and spelling), but I leave some terms (generally for places and personal names) in commonly used forms.

2. Quotation from Cordell 1989: 17. The archaeological cultures include the Hohokam, Mogollon, and Anasazi. The linguistic groupings include Uto-Aztecan, Tanoan, Keresan, Zunian, and Athapaskan language families or languages, and the tribal or ethnic groups include the O'odham (also known as the Pima and Papago), the Tarahumara, the Yaqui, the Tepehuan, Puebloan peoples, and the Apache and Navajo.

3. Little Borderlands archaeological or ethnohistorical writing has examined gender, but the topic is now receiving attention. See Foote and Schackel 1986; Howell 1995; Sparks 1995; Spielman 1995; Crown and Fish 1996; Deeds 1997; Ford 1997; Rautman 1997; Shaffer, Gardner, and Powell 2000; Hays-Gilpin 2000; and the many nuanced essays in Crown 2000b, especially Louise Lamphere's "Gender Models in the Southwest: A Sociocultural Perspective." For a summary of literature examining the status(es) of Navajo women, about whom much has been written, see Denetdale 1999: ch. 2.

4. Quotation from R. Millon 1992: 259; also see Taube 1983; C. Millon 1988; R. Millon 1988; Berlo 1992; and Pasztory 1997: 84–91, 104. Cowgill argues against the idea of a single supreme Goddess (1997: 149–51). The Goddess should not be seen, however, as having only benign associations. Clara Millon discusses her military associations, saying that "the domain of the goddess seems to include the institution of heart sacrifice" (1988: 123).

5. R. Millon 1981: 213, 216–7, 229–31 (the phrase "sacralized polity" appears on 217); Sugiyama 1992; and Pasztory 1997: 119–20, 200, 220–2.

6. On the apartment compounds generally, see R. Millon 1981: 206; 1993: 29–30. On kinship (patrilineal or cognatic systems, and how these might have been organized in Teotihuacan) and skeletal evidence, see R. Millon 1981: 208. His argument is supported and amplified in Sempowski and Spence 1994: chs. 18–21. Also see Storey 1992: ch. 4.

7. Pasztory 1997: 86.

8. Sempowski and Spence 1994: 260; Storey 1992: 98.

9. For general works on Aztec culture and history see Caso 1979; Berdan 1982; Rodríguez-Shadow 1990; Smith 1996; and Carrasco 1999.

10. Rodríguez-Shadow 1997: 69–70.

11. *Florentine Codex* (hereafter cited as FC) 1950–82: 3:43; 4:3–4; 6:171–3; 6:201; Durán 1967: 2:57; Hassig 1988: 30–1; Berdan 1982: 105. Note that years of composition (approximate) or first publication are included in the bibliography.

12. For a discussion of Nahua warfare and military organization see Hassig 1988: especially chs. 2–8.

13. FC 1950–82: 6:209–18.

14. For the Tlatelolcan women see Durán 1967: 2:263; Klein 1994: 219. For the fighting Toltec women, see Alva Ixtlilxochitl 1975–7: 1:281. On the Tepanec women fighting, see Durán 1967: 2:pl. 11. For the horseback-riding woman, see Durán 1967: 2:573–4. Also see Klein (1993: 41–2) for a recounting and analysis of several of these incidents, and note the example of a Ñudzahui "Warrior Princess," cited by Nash (1978: 353), who fought to protect her father's realm in the year 1038 after being insulted by enemies of her father during her wedding (*Codex Selden:* plates 7, 8, p. 87).

15. Klein 1988; 1993; 1994.

16. While Todorov asserts that "the worst insult . . . that can be addressed to a man is to treat him as a woman" (1984: 91), Burkhart argues that such comments could be interpreted less as demeaning to women and more as insulting to men by pointing out that they were unfit (1997: 347 n. 79).

17. *Codex Mendoza* 1992: 3:fs. 57v–58r. The women who served as priestesses were primarily of the noble stratum. For women's work, in addition to primary sources such as the FC or the *Codex Mendoza*, summarized in Hellbom (1967: 126–45), also see Rodríguez-Shadow 1997, especially chs. 3 and 4; Brumfiel 1991; Kellogg 1995a; 1995b: ch. 3; Anderson 1997; Sousa 1998: 175–99; and Goldsmith Connelly 1999.

18. FC 1950–8: 10:2; Burkhart 1997: 29.

19. FC 1950–82: 10:5. Note that where English translations exist, I have relied on those; all other translations are mine.

20. Carrasco 1984: 43–4; Gillespie 1989: 19–21; Schroeder 1992: 70; and Klein 1993: 46–50.

21. FC 1950–82: 10:130, 132.

22. For gendered naming patterns, see Cline 1986: 117–22; Lockhart 1992: 117–30; and Horn 1997: 107–108. On kinship, see Kellogg 1986a; 1995b: ch. 5; and Cline 1986: ch. 5.

23. On the marketplace judges, see FC 1950–82: 8:67–9. For female crafts producers, see Durán 1967: 1:130.

24. For female officials in the cuicacalli, see FC 1950–82: 2:97. Eloise Quiñones Keber notes that FC (Book Four) describes the paired deities Oxomoco (female)

and Cipactonal (male) as the inventors of the 260-day ritual calendar known as the *tonalpohualli* and as the originators of day sign reading (2002: 253–5). On priestesses see FC 1950–82: 2:215–6; Durán 1967: 2:544; Clavijero 1976: 206; Nicholson 1971: 436–7; Brown 1983; and Alberti Manzanares 1993: ch. 3.

25. For definitions and discussions of the terms, see Durán 1967: 1:189; Cline 1986: 54; and Lockhart 1992: 44. For early colonial uses of these terms, see Archivo General de la Nación, México, Tierras 42:exp. 5: 3r (also cited as AGNT with file and case number); AGNT 2729–20: 3v; and AGNT 59–3: 18r. Klein argues (1988; 1993; 1994) that because the terms for female officials are based on the terms for male officials, such terminology is actually evidence of male dominance. For me, keys to understanding Mexica gender patterns are recognizing that, while there was gender asymmetry, pathways to authority existed for Mexica women, as well as acknowledging the many ways, linguistically and socially, Nahuas expressed complementarity of male and female. One of the best examples comes from Klein's own work in her discussion of the male symbol par excellence, the shield, which paradoxically may well be a "fundamentally feminine symbol" because it was "a visual metaphor for the female body itself" (1993: 41). She also argues that images of males are never shown with female symbolism, yet apart from the ambiguous meaning of the shield, Milbrath cites evidence of male deities, especially those with lunar and pulque associations, depicted with female accouterments (1995: 48–50). But also see Klein 2001 for a detailed discussion of gender ambiguity in Nahua symbols, ceremonies, and beliefs.

26. FC 1950–82: 10:46. Also see Schroeder 1992: 81–2; Bell 1992: ch. 5.

27. Motolinía 1971: 134–5. Cline 1986; Kellogg 1986b; 1995b: 116–7; 1997; and Horn 1997. On Nahua inheritance practices in the eighteenth century, see Loera y Chávez 1977; and Wood 1997.

28. Durán 1967: 1:57; FC 1950–82: 7:31.

29. FC 1950–82: 4:59.

30. FC 1950–82: 4:25.

31. Estas son las leyes 1941: 281; Pomar 1891: 32–3; Alva Ixtlilxochitl 1975–77: 1:385; Motolinía 1971: 355–6. On Aztec crime and punishment, see Offner 1983: ch. 6; on punishment and gender, see Rodríguez-Shadow 1997: 218–9. On the punishment of younger men, see Hassig 1988: 34–7, 110–1.

32. See analysis of instances of rape and violence against women in prehispanic central Mexico in Lipsett-Rivera 1997: 561–7. For marketwomen's fighting, see Durán 1967: 2:255; Clendinnen 1991: 159.

33. FC 1950–82: 4:108–9. Also see a description of women's character under the sign One House, in which women are depicted as capable of considerable verbal aggression (FC 1950–82: 4: 95).

34. FC 1950–82: 4:79. On women's ability to provoke warfare, see the FC 1950–82: 2:61–2.

35. Burkhart 1989: 131–3; Sousa 1998: 356–60. Several of the *huehuetlatolli* (elders' words; ancient words of knowledge) collected by Sahagún, especially those for a young man or woman before marriage, depict sexuality as potentially pleasurable for both sexes. But each partner was also obligated to wait until marriage and carry out his or her social responsibilities, maintaining the Mexica ideal of moderate behavior (FC 1950–82: 6: chs. 18–22). Also see Clendinnen 1991: 163–8, 180–2. On sexuality, also see Evans 1998 and 2001: 255–64. López Austin (1982: 160–3), Quezada (1977), and Rodríguez-Shadow (1997: 184–5) emphasize the negative, even polluting, con-

notations of sexual activity and argue that women's virginity was highly valued. On male homosexuality, see Kimball 1993; Trexler 1995; and C. Taylor 1997. There are almost no clear references to female same-sex attractions, though the FC mentions female same-sex acts in a brief passage (1950–82: 10:56), and Bierhorst mentions in passing "lesbian songs" as among a group of songs performed by men in women's clothing (1985: 95–6).

36. An image of a Mexica female scribe can be found in the *Codex Telleriano-Remensis* (1995: f. 30r), and Bruhns and Stothert speculate that the parallel administrative and authority structures of the Mexica make the existence of female scribes likely (1999: 163). Those contending that Mexica culture, or that of the Nahuas generally, was marked by gender asymmetry (with some arguing that extreme forms of male dominance existed) include Delgado 1964; MacLachlan 1976; Blanco 1977; Nash 1978; Klein 1988; 1993; 1994; Brumfiel 1996; 2001; Rodríguez-Shadow 1997; 1999; and McCaa 1996; 1998. Others who argue either that forms of male dominance were tempered by complementary and parallel forms of ideology and social organization or that complementary is more fundamental than asymmetry include Hellbom 1967; Ladd 1979; Kellogg 1988; 1995a; 1995b: ch. 3; 1997; McCafferty and McCafferty 1988; Garza Tarazona 1991; Quezada 1996; Burkhart 1997; Evans 1998; and Joyce 2000a: ch. 5.

37. Complicating the Mexica pantheon was its character as assimilative rather than proselytizing (Berdan 1982: 125). Insightful general discussions of Aztec religion can be found in Caso 1979 and Nicholson 1971. See Milbrath 1995 on the "bisexual" nature of Mexica lunar deities. For the complex images of female deities, see Carrera 1979; and Alberti Manzanares 1993.

38. Sullivan 1982: 7; Lewis 1997; González Torres 1979; and McCafferty and McCafferty 1999.

39. For Cihuacoatl, see Klein 1988: 237; for Tlazolteotl, see Burkhart 1989: 92.

40. On the Mexica cosmos as composed of male and female elements, see López Austin 1998. See Rodríguez-Shadow 1997: ch. 7 for a discussion of Mexica goddesses as subordinated and reinforcing of a patriarchal gender hierarchy. On the Coyolxauhqui image in particular, see Klein 1994: 225–7 and Brumfiel 1996: 156–60.

41. The quote is from Klein 1994: 225. For the story of Coyolxauhqui, see the FC 1950–82: 3:1–5.

42. Brumfiel 1996: 146. Also see Klein's discussion of the placement of female images, especially of Coyolxuahqui and Cihuacoatl, in subordinate positions (1988: 241–4).

43. Smith 1983a: 243.

44. Serra Puche 2001.

45. McCafferty and McCafferty 1994a: 167; Jansen and Pérez Jiménez 1998.

46. Ethnohistoric sources for the Ñudzahui are discussed in Spores 1967; 1984; 1997; Sousa 1997; 1998; and Terraciano 2001: ch. 1. Mixtec codices are analyzed by Nuttall 1975; Spinden 1935; Caso 1979; and McCafferty and McCafferty 1994b; and their material remains are discussed in McCafferty and McCafferty 1994b; and Hamann 1997.

47. On the balancing of forces, see Spores 1984: 86–7; and Terraciano 1994: 394. On the male sky and female earth, see Terraciano 1994: 394 and Sousa 1997: 201. On the symbols of rulership, see Smith 1983a: 244 and Terraciano 2001: 158–9, 165–9, who also discusses terms for rulers.

48. On the preference for male succession, see Spores 1974: 303. On patterns of female succession, see Terraciano 2001: 174–82. Also see Hamann 1997; Sousa 1997: 201; Spores 1997; and Marcus 2001: 317–24.

49. Spores 1967: 152–3; 1984: 72; Sousa 1998: 306–8; and Terraciano 2001: 165–81.

50. On depictions of female rulership in Ñudzahui codices, see Smith 1983b: 263–4. On female rulers protecting the rights of succession of both sons and daughters, see Spores 1967: 134, 135; Spores 1997; and Terraciano 2001: 175–6.

51. Sousa 1997: 202.

52. On women's sociopolitical authority at levels of organization below the yuhuitayu, see Terraciano 1994: 397. On women as religious practitioners, see Terraciano 2001: 286, 314. For the flexibility of this social status, see Dahlgren de Jordán 1966: 268–71; Spores 1967: 9; and 1984: 72–4. On noblewomen's supervision of the production of crafts, see Terraciano 2001: 137.

53. Sousa 1997: 201–4; Terraciano 2001: 151, 220–4, 352–5.

54. Sousa 1997: 211; 1998: 165–75; Terraciano 2001: 139–40.

55. On women and household exchanges of goods and services, see Sousa 1997: 211. For prehispanic Ñudzahui society and its military organization, see Spores 1984: ch. 3. To the south and east of the Ñudzahui lay another important ethnic group, the Zapotec, who captured many ethnographers' interest, in part because of the apparently high status of women, and who are dealt with at length in chapter 4. While gender complementarity existed in most realms of Zapotec life, paramount rulers, high governing officials, and deities were primarily male in the prehispanic period (Whitecotton 1977: 142–64).

56. Schele and Miller 1986: 143; Josserand 2002. In addition to Schele and Freidel 1990, cited hereafter, readers can find a broad overview of prehispanic Maya culture in Coe 1999.

57. Bruhns 1988: 106; Joyce 1992a: 63–5, 68; Joyce 1996: 169–70; also see Proskouriakoff 1964; and Joyce 2000a: ch. 3. The latter volume incorporates information cited in articles by Joyce cited hereafter.

58. Joyce Marcus (1976: 157–70) postulates that noblewomen of major centers may have married ruling men of secondary centers and then "played important political roles at dependencies" (170). Variation in patterns of office-holding among both centers and regions is likely; thus her suggestion is certainly possible, given the way such women are shown either alone or as central figures standing over captives at some sites. However, while women are frequently depicted as paired with men, they are rarely placed with them on the front side of stelae (160–3). Also see Marcus 2001: 330 on the circumstances under which noblewomen might rule among the Maya as well as Molloy and Rathje 1974; and on probable variations in gender patterns among the Maya, see Joyce 1993. On women rulers at Palenque, Yaxchilán, and Copán, see Bruhns 1988: 106; and Josserand 2002: 147–8.

59. Schele and Miller 1986: 143; Stone 1988; Joyce 1992b; 1996; Haviland 1997: 1–2; Josserand 2002; and Krochock 2002. Concepts of complementarity probably had deep roots among the Maya, whose ancient 260-day divinatory calendar may have been based on the measurement of the length of an average pregnancy, with this calendar also having strong lunar associations (Earle and Snow 1985).

60. Joyce 1992a: 66–8; Stone 1988: 75–6, 81, 86; and Tate 1999: 92–3. While sexual characteristics, male or female, are rarely depicted in public art (see Stone 1988 for an example of a more sexually graphic image in a more private setting), the Emblem

Glyph (a glyph signifying the person identified as noble and often an office-holder) for Chichén Itzá contains an image of male genitalia (Schele and Freidel 1990: 363), and Krochock discusses penis imagery at Chichen Itzá, especially at the Temple of the Phalli (2002: 162–4). On sexual symbols in Maya art, see Strecker (1987). Also see Joyce (1996, 2000b), who argues that prehispanic Maya art associates the female gender with creation and the male gender with sexuality (the latter often expressed, in her view, through homoeroticism, a subject also explored through Maya prehispanic and colonial images and texts in Sigal 2000).

61. Schele and Freidel 1990: 84–5. Other sites mentioned as possibly having had a female ruler at some point in their histories include Naranjo, Piedras Negras, Cobá, Caracol, and Calakmul (Marcus 1976: 152–60; Schele and Miller 1986: 143; Kahn 1990: 14; and Graham 1991). On Maya conceptions of rulership as combining male and female elements, with female rulers symbolically masculinized through names and titles, see Hewitt 1999.

62. Quotation from Marcus 1976: 169. Also see Schele and Freidel 1990: 220–5; and Marcus 2001: 324–7.

63. On the intensification of Maya warfare later in the Classic period and its association with the nobility, see Schele and Freidel 1990: 130–215. On the images from Cobá, Calakmul, and the Usumacinta region, see Marcus 1976: 162, 169.

64. See Schele and Miller 1986: pl. 78 and their explanation of the Chichén Itzá image, 223; also see Thompson 1970: 209–49; and Sigal 2000: ch. 5. For the dating of the Temple of the Warriors, see Schele and Freidel 1990: 356, 500 n. 26. A recently discovered tomb at the Guatemalan site of Waka contains the burial of a female ruler who may have lived between A.D. 650 and 750, buried with, in addition to sumptuous grave goods, what could have been her war helmet (Wilford 2004).

65. Thompson 1939.

66. Schele and Freidel 1990: 413, 502 n. 44; Vail and Stone 2002: 210–5, 226. Ralph Roys observes that as patroness of weaving, Ixchel, is shown with spiders (1972: 78), a symbol also associated with Teotihuacan's Great Goddess.

67. Kahn 1990: 314.

68. Blom 1983: 305–7; Kahn 1990: 142–80.

69. Kahn 1990: 302–8, 320–1.

70. On female religious functionaries, see Roys 1972: 81; Edmonson 1993: 78–9; and Joyce 1996: 185–6. On the Ix Mol (a term Alfred Tozzer translated as "conductress") see Tozzer 1941: 159 and Landa 1985: 141–2. López de Cogolludo (1971: 2:257) says that there were nunneries for women who did not wish to marry but gives no information about women as priestesses or any hierarchy of female religious activity, contrary to Blom's statement (1983: 307–8).

71. Pohl and Feldman 1982: 302–6; Pohl 1991; Izquierdo 1989: 11; Joyce 1992a: 66–7; Hendon 1992; 1997; McAnany 1995: 139–40; and Hunt and Restall 1997.

72. Landa 1985: 99; McAnany 1995: 140.

73. N. Hopkins (1988) argues for patrilineality as a long-term feature of Maya society, dating back to the Classic period, and summarizes the literature on this topic. Also see Schele and Freidel 1990: 84–5. On primogeniture, see Schele and Freidel 1990: 84, 431, n. 44. On patrilineality and kin terminologies, see R. Hill 1992: 32–3.

74. On patriliny and male dominance among the Maya, see Haviland 1997: 10. On the topic more generally, see Sanday 1981: 176–9.

75. On ennoblement through fathers and mothers, see Schele and Miller 1986: 275; and Hendon 1991: 912. On the meaning of *almehen*, see McAnany 1995: 2; and

Restall 1997: 88. Restall says that *mehen* usually refers to a man's son, rather than his offspring generally. McAnany notes that in modern Maya communities, terms for lineage heads, as for example among the highland K'iche', translate as "father-mother" (*chuchkajaw*). She argues that this meaning "indicates that the contribution of the female to lineage leadership and ritual is deeply encoded linguistically" (1995: 25). For possible matri- and patrilineal descent patterns among Classic, Postclassic, and colonial Maya elites, see discussion and sources in Jones 1998: 78–81, 445–7 ns. 44, 49, and 51. On ancestor worship, see Landa 1985: 100. Also see McAnany 1995: 24–33.

76. Hunt and Restall 1997: 242.

77. Bruhns 1994 provides a thorough, state-of-the-art overview of the prehistory of South America. Works with a greater emphasis on the pre-Inka and Inka cultures and civilizations of Peru include Lumbreras 1983, Moseley 1992; Rostworowski de Diez Canseco 1998; and D'Altroy 2002.

78. Lyons 1978: 98–103; Niles 1988; Bruhns 1994: 126–30; Mendieta Parada 1995; Spotts 2003; and Gourd Lord 2003. For South American chronologies, see Bruhns 1994: 10–1 and Bruhns and Stothert 1999: 25.

79. Donnan and Castillo 1992; Bruhns 1994: 195; and Bruhns and Stothert 1999: 183–6.

80. Arsenault 1991: 317; also see Hocquenghem 1987.

81. Hocquenghem and Lyon 1980; Benson 1988; Arsenault 1991; and Donnan and Castillo 1992.

82. Kaufmann Doig 1978.

83. Bruhns 1994: 190–1; Gero 2001: 26–48.

84. Gero 1992: 23–4.

85. Lyon 1978: 111–4.

86. Malpass 1996: 105.

87. Silverblatt 1987: 21–5, 41–53; Rostworowski de Diez Canseco 1995: 6; and Cajías de la Vega et al. 1994: 56–61.

88. Lyon 1978: 117–9; Alaperrine-Bouyer 1987; Damian 1995: 108–20; and Mendieta Parada 1995: 19, 21.

89. Sarmiento de Gamboa 1947: 129–31; Guaman Poma de Ayala 1980: 1:121; Lyon 1978: 117; Silverblatt 1987: 50, 57; and Dransart 1992: 150–2.

90. Silverblatt 1987: 65.

91. Murúa 1946: 352; Silverblatt 1987: 17–9, 57–61, 151; and Rostworowski de Diez Canseco 1995: 10–2.

92. Silverblatt 1987: 217. Also see Zuidema 1977 for a detailed discussion of Inka kinship structures, but see Rowe, who argues that Inka descent was traced patrilineally, that is, through fathers (1963: 254).

93. Murra 1962: 711; Silverblatt 1987: 9–14.

94. Murra 1962: 714; Costin 1993: 5–6; 1996: 124–5; Bruhns 1991: 424; and Graubart 2000a: 541–2. Murra (1989: 289) cites evidence of a cloth manufactory of the Inka era employing 1,000 male weavers who wove fine cloth full-time.

95. Silverblatt 1987: 15; Hastorf 1991; and Costin 1993: 15–9.

96. Cobo 1890–95: 4:145–8; Silverblatt 1987: 81–7, 104–5; Murra 1989: 290–1; and Rostworowski de Diez Canseco 1995: 13–4. See Graubart (2000b), who argues that notions of acllas as virginal were colonial reworkings of Andean traditions that overemphasized similarities between acllas and nuns.

97. Silverblatt 1987: 37.

98. In addition to works already cited, Kendall (1973: 88–9) sees adult women as playing a variety of socially recognized roles. Valcárcel, on the other hand, arguing against a preponderance of evidence, finds that Inka women were subjugated, experiencing a variety of forms of exploitation and humiliation. He does point out that women were excluded from testifying in legal cases (1985: 67; Guaman Poma de Ayala 1980: 1:162), and Rowe finds that women could be punished more harshly than men for the crime of adultery (1963: 271).

99. Espinosa Soriano 1976: 251, 261–2; Silverblatt 1987: 18; and Rostworowski de Diez Canseco 1995: 10.

100. Mörner 1967: 21–7.

101. On the Taínos, see Sued-Badillo 1979: ch. 4; and Wilson 1990: 116–41. For ancient Panamanians see Helms 1976a: 20–8; 1980; and on the Sinú, see Steward and Faron 1959: 223; and Saénz Samper 1993 (especially 79–81).

3. Colliding Worlds

1. Stephanie Wood's essay "Gender and Community Influence in Mesoamerica: Directions for Future Research" (1998a) was especially helpful in thinking about colonial indigenous women's agency, an important theme throughout this chapter; also see Schroeder 1997. On Spanish gender ideologies of Golden Age Spain, see Lavrin 1978; 1989; Arrom 1985: ch. 2; Perry 1990: ch. 1; and Dopico Black 2001, especially her discussion of the sixteenth-century moralizing text *La perfecta casada*, by Fray Luis de León, with its emphasis on women's need of containment and enclosure, or, as León put it, "as men were meant to mix in public, so women were made for seclusion" (quoted at 90).

2. On images of conquest, see Montrose 1993; Lewis 1996. On the connections among masculinity, sexuality, and conquest see Krippner-Martínez 1990; Herren 1991; Hurtado 1999; Barbosa Sánchez 1994; Gutiérrez 1994; and Powers 2002. On male and female translators, no female translators are mentioned for the conquest of the Maya or the Inka (Chamberlain 1966: 37–8; Restall 2003: ch. 2; and Hemming 1970: 25). The references to female translators, other than Malintzin, that I have come across include a woman named María who translated for Bartolomé de las Casas on the Caribbean island of Cubagua in 1521 (Saco 1932: 2:227). In the north, don Juan Oñate brought a Pueblo woman with his expedition in the hopes that she would be seen as "'a second Malinche'" (Oñate, quoted in Gutiérrez 1994: 57). He also desired that she serve him in the additional capacities of lover and diplomat. His hopes seem to have been dashed when it became apparent that she spoke only one indigenous language, Tano, and not the multiple languages necessary for coping with the complex language patterns of the Pueblo groups (57; also see Foote and Schackel 1986: 22). An indigenous woman of unknown ethnicity helped translate for several Spaniards who sailed from Vera Cruz to Florida in 1549 (Dobyns 1983: 265–6). After the Spanish conquests, indigenous women—at least in Mesoamerica—did not participate in the growing business of translation for political or legal purposes or in the turn toward scribal writing of indigenous languages with Spanish orthography (Schroeder 1997: 7–8; Karttunen 1998: 435).

3. For the Marina/Malinalli argument, see Cypess 1991: 2, 33. For a more plausible explanation of how she received the name Marina, see Karttunen 1994: 506. But as Jeanette Peterson has pointed out, the association of "Marina" with "Malinalli" may not have been entirely accidental (but *not* because Marina was picked to closely

match the indigenous name). The "twisted grass" meaning has strong associations with the skin, hair, and brooms of the powerful Mexica earth goddesses (1994: 195–6). Furthermore, Malintzin may have been subtly imaged as a warrior goddess, at least in the mid-sixteenth-century images of the Lienzo de Tlaxcala (196–9).

4. Díaz del Castillo 1955: 1:121; Karttunen 1994: 5.

5. For a description of incidents where she helped the Spanish (including her presence at the execution of Cuahtemoc), see Karttunen 1994: 7–8, 19. Her loyalty, combined with the fact that she bore Cortés a child, serve as the basis for the highly negative Mexican view that emerged in the post-Independence and, especially, post-Revolutionary periods. Cypess 1991 and Núñez Becerra 1996 trace how this view has been expressed in Mexican literature. Several Mexican-American feminist scholars have sought to portray Malintzin in a more sympathetic light. See, for example, Cotera 1976: 31–6; del Castillo 1977; Alarcón 1989; and Hurtado 1999. Also see the sympathetic, popular biography by Lanyon (1999), along with a collection of essays analyzing her as a historical and literary figure in Glantz (1994). A detailed analysis of Malintzin imagery appears in Maturo (1994). Hassig (1998) provides an in-depth analysis of the events surrounding the Cholula massacre. He raises doubts about whether it happened in the way Cortés (and others) describe and questions the importance of Malintzin's role.

6. López de Gómara 1943: 2:132–3; Somonte 1969: 131; and Karttunen 1997: 312.

7. For Cortés's amorous history, see Karttunen 1997: 306. Tecuichpotzin had her own complex marital history. Possibly married to Cuitlahuac (who ruled briefly after Moteuczoma), she married Cuauhtemoc, the last Mexica tlatoani, who was executed in 1525. Soon thereafter, she married a Spaniard, Alonso de Grado. At the age of fifteen (if the year of her birth was 1510, as López de Meneses speculates), she then joined the growing line of Cortés's partners and gave birth to his daughter, doña Leonor Cortés. She subsequently married twice more, both times to Spaniards, bearing one child with Pedro Gallego de Andrade and five children with Juan Cano de Saavedra (López de Meneses 1948; Pérez-Rocha 1998). A daughter of Huayna Capac, doña Beatriz Huayllas Ñusta, also had three Spanish partners. After a relationship with the conqueror Mancio Sierra de Leguizamo, she then married Pedro de Bustinza, who was later executed for his association with Gonzalo Pizarro. Next she married Diego Hernández, formerly a tailor, whom she "considered beneath her dignity" (Hemming 1970: 291).

8. Karttunen 1994: 305–7. In addition to the two children Pizarro had with Quispe Sisa, Francisca and Gonzalo, he had two more, Francisco and Juan, with Atahualpa's sister Añas, who later married the chronicler Juan de Betanzos (Hemming 1970: 269, 291). Also see Mannarelli 1990: 234; 1994: ch. 1.

9. Muñoz Camargo 1986: 195–7; Carrasco 1997: 102; Stern 1993: 170–3; and Hemming 1970: 180, 269.

10. Hemming 1970: 312–3; Rostworowski 1970: 155–8; and Mannarelli 1990: 235–6. For the text of doña Beatriz Clara Coya's will (a text in which her references to her husband, don Martín García de Loyola, are certainly restrained), see Dunbar Temple 1950: 118–22.

11. Ganson 1994: 62; also see Ganson 2003. Susnik, on the other hand, argues that while some Guaraní women voluntarily entered into relations with Spaniards, others were given by their families in exchange for goods like metal axes, and still others were taken violently (1965: 1:13). Service points out that in colonial Paraguay, relationships of concubinage or intermarriage were very common between Spanish

men and Guaraní women. These relations created a mestizo society in which the Guaraní language is still commonly spoken and is an official language along with Spanish (1971: 20, 24, 30–8).

12. Carrasco 1997: 102. In the 1555 will of Hernando de Tapia, for example, himself married to a Spanish woman, he left explicit instructions that his legitimate daughters marry Spaniards (AGNT 37–2: 78v–94v). Also see Hemming's brief description of three Tupinamba men taken from Brazil to France in 1612 who, during the course of their two-year stay, married French women with whom they returned to Brazil in 1614 (1995: 207–8). Whatever the nature of these relations, without denying that attractions on both sides were possible, little evidence supports Hemming's notion that "the women themselves were often attracted by the dashing foreigners" (1970: 180) or Ricardo Herren's that "la sexualidad de los españoles parece haber sido más rica que la de los varones indios" (1991: 100), though the benefits of such contact, especially economic, must have been clear (Graubart 2000c: 250–1).

13. Herren 1991; Wood 1998b.

14. While both Herren (1991) and Wood (1998b) discuss sexual violence in colonial Latin America broadly, on California, specifically, see Castañeda 1990: ch. 2; 1993; Hurtado 1999: ch. 1; and Bouvier 2001: chs. 1 and 6. For the northern Borderlands generally, see McDonald 2000: 156–64.

15. In her classic work *Against Our Will*, Susan Brownmiller offers a legally oriented "female definition" of rape: "if a woman chooses not to have intercourse with a specific man and the man chooses to proceed against her will, that is a criminal act of rape" (1975: 18). Other attempts to define rape are discussed by Linda Brookover Bourque (1989; also see Wood 1998b: 10–8). Other literature on male violence toward women is cited in Castañeda 1993: 32 n. 61. While medieval and early Spanish law did not clearly define rape, it recognized coercive sex in a variety of contexts (*rapto*, *violación*, and *estupro*; see Lipsett-Rivera 1997: 567–8; also see Barahona 2003: ch. 3 on Spanish law and legal cases involving coercive sex). This topic has many contemporary implications, because rape and other forms of gendered sexual violence have served as a tool of repression used by recent military regimes, particularly in Argentina, Chile, and Uruguay. See Bunster 1993 and Taylor 1997.

16. Passage quoted in Sale 1990: 140. For a general discussion of the relationship between sexuality and coercion in the conquest period, see Wood 1998: 11–8.

17. Tozzer 1941: 127; Landa 1985: 98. See Todorov's discussion of this passage (1984: 246–7) along with the dedication of his book. Also see Restall's discussion of the passage (1995: 577–9).

18. Cited in Hemming 1970: 265.

19. Barbosa Sánchez 1994: 93. Wood argues that European men not only saw the sexual coercion of women as part of conquest but as key to a "new, multilayered power structure" (1998b: 10).

20. Hemming quotes Juan Pizarro's will (1970: 182, 198–9). Busto Duthurburo discusses this relationship, suggesting that the woman was a close relative of Manco Inka (1965: 103–4). On Brazil, see Hemming 1995: 41. For Peru, see Guaman Poma de Ayala 1980: 2:489, 496, 498, 538; and Silverblatt 1987: 138–43.

21. On La Navidad, see Sale 1990: 139, 150–1. On Tenochcan and Tlatelolcan women's resistance against the Spanish, see the *Codex Azcatitlan*, cited in Klein 1994: 222. Also see Durán 1967: 2:568; FC 1950–82: 12:117; and Wood 1998b: 11–2.

22. Hemming 1970: 240.

23. *Relación del sitio del Cuzco* 1879, quoted and cited in Hemming 1970: 204, 574, note to p. 204.

24. Hemming 1970: 211. On Paraguay, see Ganson 1994: 63–75. For a report on indigenous women in colonial Venezuela fighting alongside men against the Spanish, see Alvarez de Lovera 1994: 82.

25. Foote and Schackel 1986: 22–4; Deeds 1997: 259; Villanueva 1985: 26–7; Clendinnen 1982: 432; Farriss 1984: 172; Patch 1993: 86–8, 90, 253; Sherman 1979: ch. 14; Stark 1985: 5–10; Silverblatt 1987: 127–38; Zulawski 1990; and Larson 1998: 199–200.

26. On changing patterns of textile production, see Bazant 1964: 495; Villanueva 1985: 22–7; and Salvucci 1987. Gauderman discusses male textile producers in the larger workshops of the Quito region (1998: 260–2; also see Gauderman 2003). Gibson (1964: 141) and Wachtel (1977: 91) find gender imbalances, with more women than men for colonial central Mexico and Peru (though Wachtel is referring specifically to the sixteenth century, whereas Gibson is referring to the entire period), while Deeds argues that in the north "women of childbearing age, along with children, were at particularly high risk during epidemics" (1997: 260; also see Jackson 1994: 108). On Peru, also see Cook 1981: 251–3.

27. For a description of male weavers in eighteenth-century Upper Peru, see Larson 1998: 261.

28. Deeds 1997: 259; Villanueva 1985; Terraciano 2001: 239–43; Clendinnen 1982: 432; Farriss 1984: 172, 271; Patch 1993: 86–8; Sherman 1979: 313, 324–5; Silverblatt 1987: 134–5; Premo 2000: 77–84; Graubart 2000c: 100–103, 146–8; Hemming 1995: 423; and 1987: 159. The use of women in Paraguayan Jesuit missions to grow cotton may have been related to textile production (Ots Capdequí 1930: 338; Susnik 1965: 1:179–80). On women's production of textiles in eighteenth-century Guaycuruan missions of the Gran Chaco (spanning much of today's Paraguay and including parts of southeastern Bolivia and northeastern Argentina), see Saeger 2000: 65–6. On women's work as spinners, encouraged by Jesuits in the missions of the Moxos region of modern-day Bolivia, see Block 1994: 167.

29. Arrom 1985: 158–9; Kanter 1993: 171; Pescador 1995: 618; Horn 1998: 71, 74, 76; Terraciano 2001: 239, 343; and Clendinnen 1982: 436.

30. Taylor 1979: 38, 53, 58; Terraciano 1994: 399–401.

31. Gauderman 1998: ch. 5; also see Ramírez 1995.

32. Gauderman 1998: 181–3, 191–9. Burkett finds a similar pattern for the city of Potosí of Andean women selling a wide array of goods, including those of Spanish origin (1978: 113). Also see Poloni 1992: 204–2; Mangan 1999: 108–27, 250–5; and Larson 1998: 203.

33. Zavala 1984: 1:300, 320–2; 2:280–3; *Fuentes para la historia de México* 1939–46: 1:21–2; *Colección de documentos para la historia de México* 2:100; *Códice Osuna* 1947: 339; and Farriss 1984: 52–3.

34. Farriss 1984: 203; Hunt and Restall 1997: 236.

35. McDonald 2000: 73–82, 126–8; Burkett 1978: 109; and Rostworowski de Diez Canseco 1995: 13. In colonial Venezuela, Paraguay, and Chile, state-sponsored forms of such labor lasted longer. See Alvarez de Lovera 1994: 87–9; Service 1971: 20, 35; and Flusche and Korth 1983: 58–61.

36. For women working in sixteenth- and seventeenth-century Andean mines, see Larson 1983: 178, 182. For an example of a female owner of a small silver mine in Peru, see Zulawski 1990: 106–7 (also see Stern 1993: 165–9). On women in obrajes

see Salvucci 1987: 105 and Gauderman 1998: 260–2. On women's labor in the tobacco factory of Mexico City, see Deans-Smith 1992: 175–8; and Pescador 1995: 620. On women carriers in the Yucatan and Central America, see Clendinnen 1982: 431; Ots Capdequí 1930: 338; and Sherman 1979: 121, 322–3. For brief comments on missionaries' imposition of a different gender division of labor that placed more responsibility onto men in the far North, Baja California in particular, see Jackson 1999: 77–8. On men's role in agriculture in the Guaraní missions, see Ganson 1994: 205, 208–12.

37. See, for example, Silverblatt 1987: 114–6.

38. Ots Capdequí 1930: 346; Gibson 1964: 200–201, 207–8; and Silverblatt 1987: 129. Stern says that female heads of Andean households were specifically exempt (1993: 152, 163). Also see Premo 2000: 77–8. In New Spain, attempts to reform the practice of women's payment of tribute were uneven. In 1755, colonial officials attempted to force single women to pay tribute after a period of some thirty-three years when they had customarily been excused (though married women and widows had not been so excused), and a lawsuit resulted (Zavala 1984: 7:21). Attempts by officials in 1770 to rationalize tribute payments by holding all adult men up to the age of fifty responsible and excusing women regardless of their marital status are also mentioned by Zavala but were countermanded by royal policy (60).

39. Terraciano 1994: 405; 2001: 239–41. Cases even exist of married women jailed for failure to make tribute payments, placed there by a native official in Toluca, west of Mexico City, in 1799. Not only was one of the women jailed but also the native governor ordered that an enema be administered to her (Kanter 1993: 286–8).

40. Pescador 1995: 617–9; Hunt and Restall 1997: 236; Glave 1987: 54–62; and Vergara Ormeño 1997: 142–5, 153. Pescador also points out that, while mixed-race or indigenous employers existed, they were rare but gives the example of a native stonemason employing a native woman for food preparation (618).

41. On Guatemalan wet nurses, see Herrera 1997: 367–8 (see also Herrera 2003); Komisaruk 2000: 117–8; and Webre 2001. On the economic responsibilities of widows, see Sherman 1979: 310–1, 336. On the young ages of servants in Peru and the northern Borderlands, see Vergara Ormeño 1997: 137 and McDonald 2000: 68–70, respectively. Malvido (1980: 546) ties rural, primarily indigenous, child abandonment in the late seventeenth- and early eighteenth-century region of Tula, near Mexico City, to gender and notes that more female infants than male were abandoned. She argues that not only was male agricultural labor highly valued within indigenous communities but also abandoned female infants had potential labor value as servants or as obraje workers who spun or wove for nonindigenous employers.

42. The case of María Sisa is described in Zulawski 1990: 104–5. The orders to Paraguayan officials can be found in *Colección de documentos para la historia de la formación social de Hispanoamérica, 1493–1810* 1953–62: 2:216, 277, 680, 718.

43. Sherman 1979: 308, 325. On similar accusations in seventeenth-century central Peru, see Vergara Ormeño 1997: 140–1.

44. Chance 1989: 109–10; Gosner 1997: 225.

45. Kanter 1993: 302, 304–5. For a study of depósito as an urban institution that shows its protective and coercive sides, see Penyak 1999. He finds that in the Mexico City region, both Spanish and indigenous women "were equally likely to be placed in depósito and then sent to jail, or vice versa" (1999: 96). Chance cites an intendant's statement about the confinement of women who failed to pay fines for not meeting allotments of woven mantas (1989: 110).

46. For the Caribbean and Central America, see Saco 1932: 1:171, 262; Sherman 1979: 41, 70; and Monteiro 1994: 83–4. In mid-sixteenth-century Panama, the governor Sancho de Clavijo ordered many indigenous slaves, predominantly female, into depósito. In this case, depósito functioned as a sort of protective custody, with the women usually lodged with married Spanish women who had honorable reputations ("de buena fama") until the Spanish monarch could order them freed (Saco 1932: 2:59–60). For examples in Mexico City, see notarial documents described and quoted in Millares Carlo and Mantecón 1945–46, such as the one referring to the use of fifty slaves, "machos y henbras," in a mine owned by two Spaniards, Pedro de Villalobos and Alvaro Maldonado (1: doc. no. 15:28). Many of these documents are summarized in Ladd (1979: 29–45). On Peru, see Burkett 1978: 110, and on what is now the Southern Cone, see Saco 1932: 2:216–7. It should also be recognized that the outlawing of the enslavement of indigenous people as part of the 1542 New Laws had a greater impact on New Spain and Peru than Central America and outlying regions. For the story of an enslaved indigenous woman in early eighteenth-century northern Brazil, see Sweet 1981.

47. 1979: 315.

48. See Silverblatt's discussion of noblewomen and land in the Andes (1987: 113–6). Also see Carrasco 1997: 97–9.

49. Cline 1986: 164–5; Kanter 1995; Wood 1997: 180; Kellogg 1998: 51–3; and Silverblatt 1987: 113–9, 134. Graubart argues that indigenous men and women in early colonial Lima and Trujillo (at least those who wrote wills) obtained and owned house plots and other kinds of land at about equal rates into the seventeenth century and that women gained new forms of access to wealth (2000c: 193–4).

50. For Angelina Martina's will, see AGNT 49–5. For Melchora de Santiago's, see Newberry Library/Ayer Collection 1481B-3l.

51. Terraciano provides discussion of two seventeenth-century Ñudzahui women's wills with evidence of extensive ownership of trade goods (1994: 406–407, 413–5; 2001: 216–24, 242–5). Also see Spores 1984: 109, 116. Yucatec Maya women's property is described in Hunt and Restall 1997: 245–6. For a late sixteenth-century Purépecha cacica actively seeking to increase the size of her inherited landed fortune, see López Sarrelangue 1965: 187–9, and for an Andean example of an indigenous female employer of means, see Stern 1993: 166.

52. For Toluca, see Kanter 1995: 610–1. On colonial Ecuador, see Stark 1985: 9–10. Note that the term "huasipungero" combines the Quechua words for house (*wasi*) and door or doorway (*punku*; Crapo and Aitken 1986: 35, 43).

53. Kellogg 1997: 136; Silverblatt 1987: ch. 8.

54. Saco 1932: 2:216–8, 224–7; Sherman 1979: 311–22, 336.

55. Kellogg 1995b: 195–211; Farriss 1984: 172–4; Burkett 1978: 109–10; and Cook 1981: 251. Spores asserts, however, that while early colonial Oaxaca experienced dramatic population decline, little disruption in family life occurred (1984: 113).

56. Late prehispanic kinship structures varied from the cognatic system of the Mexica or the Maya emphasis on patriliny to the Inka use of parallel lines of descent (an ambilateral descent system). Kellogg 1986a; 1995b: 180–4; Farriss 1984: 132–3; Restall 1998: 357; and Rowe 1963: 223 discuss changing kinship structures.

57. Spores 1984: 108–9, 113; Farriss 1984: 170–1; and Restall 1998: 358–9. But Farriss also argues, however, that the "material security" of Yucatec Maya extended families was weakened by missionary attempts to create households structured around a single married couple, Spanish tribute assessments defining the married

man as the unit of taxation, and the bilateral inheritance system (1984: 169–70). She notes clerical pressure to marry young and points to the heavy tribute and labor burdens on younger married couples, noting women's onerous existence "when pregnancies were frequent but brought no relief from the fixed quotas of cotton cloth they were required to produce on their own backstrap looms" (172, 259). See Klein (1986), who argues that while highland Maya women married quite young, they retained some control over spousal choice, as well as goods they brought to their marriages.

58. On complex patterns of family change in northern Mexico, see Reff 1991: 240–2; Jackson 1994: 108–9; Radding 1997: ch. 4; and Bouvier 2001: ch. 6. Seventeenth- and eighteenth-century data suggest that for Mexico City's indigenous residents, nuclear family households had become the predominant form (Kellogg 1995b: 195–201; Pescador 1995: 621). For Central America, see Sherman 1979: 336. For the colonial Andes, see Glave 1987: 48–54. Larson and Zulawski point out that families sometimes migrated together, especially to Potosí (Larson 1983: 178; Zulawski 1990: 100–101), though single women dominated in migration to Lima (Vergara Ormeño 1997: 153). Both types of migration would have undermined the formation of large, multifamily households. Hemming (1995: 114, 482) describes sixteenth- and seventeenth-century Jesuit attempts to transform native family forms in Brazil but does not assess how successful these were. For a clear discussion of compadrazgo and how it functioned in the Yucatan, see Farriss 1984: 106, 257–9.

59. I draw here on the title and arguments presented in Silverblatt 1998. Also see Gonzalbo 1987 and Burkhart 2001a on Spanish family values as communicated to indigenous populations, especially by the Church.

60. Motolinía's 1971 discussion of "sensuality" is on 189; also see 148–52.

61. On the difficulties of foregoing the practice of polygyny, see Burkhart 1989: 105, 150–1; Osorio 1990: 314; and Stavig 1995: 603–5. For the Coyoacan case, see Quezada 1996: 255–6, and on the Tarahumara, see Deeds 1997: 262. Silverblatt discusses the link between polygyny and status in the Andes (1998: 82). On Nahua women's church attendance, see Gibson 1964: 111, and on cofradía membership, see Schroeder 1997: 10–11. Sousa cites the case of a Nahua woman who denounced her husband for polygyny to the Inquisition in 1540 (1998: 260–1). For the potential of congregación and reducción for the policing of behavior, see Gibson 1964: 282–3; Farriss 1984: 160; Abercrombie 1998: 248–52, 262; and Larson 1998: 67–8. The literature on confradías and compadrazgo is better developed for Mesoamerica. On cofradías, see Chance and Taylor 1985; for compadrazgo, see Mintz and Wolf 1950; and Farriss 1984: 250, 257–9.

62. See Seed's discussion (1988: chs. 2, 7, 235–6) of the role of free will and the changing role of parents, especially fathers, in colonial marriage. On the role of families and matchmakers, see Gruzinski 1989: 109.

63. Pérez, cited in Gruzinski 1989: 109.

64. Kanter 1993: 157. While bride service in the early years of Yucatec Maya marriage sometimes occurred (Restall 1998: 360), whether coresidence during the betrothal period took place is unclear. On sirvanacuy, see Stavig 1995: 602–12.

65. Kanter 1993: 161; Stavig 1995: 611.

66. Lavrin 1989: 51–4; Burkhart 1989: 136–7; 2001; Overmyer-Velázquez 1998; and Silverblatt 1998: 71.

67. Toledo's 1573 "Instrucción para los visitadores" is quoted in part in Abercrombie 1998: 248. For the Guaraní, the quotation is from Ganson 1994: 210; and

on missions in California, see Bouvier 2001: 82. For the potential of congregación and reducción to police behavior, see Gibson 1964: 282–3; Farriss 1984: 160; Abercrombie 1998: 248–52, 262; and Larson 1998: 67–8.

68. On the rhetoric tying female virtue to male honor, see Seed 1988: chs. 4, 6; Krippner-Martínez 1990: 188–94; and Gutiérrez 1991: chs. 5–7. For interesting examples of the languages of both honor and purity of bloodlines by indigenous people, in this case by members of the Tlaxcalan frontier colony of San Esteban de Nueva Tlaxcala near the city of Saltillo in northern Mexico, see Offutt 1997: 278–81.

69. She is quoted in Silverblatt 1987: 119.

70. Kanter 1993: 174; Stern 1995: chs. 4 and 7; and Stavig 1995.

71. On the patriarchal nature of colonial Spanish American gender ideology and relations, see Kanter 1993: 7–14, 153–98; and Stern 1995: chs. 2, 7, and 11; and Castro Gutiérrez 1998: 15. For a critique, see Gauderman 1998: ch. 2.

72. Kanter 1993: 174–5; Castro Gutiérrez 1998; Taylor 1979: 79, 84–5, 87; Sousa 1996; 1998: 322–35; Terraciano 1998a; and Stavig 1995: 616–20; 1999: 31–6. On high rates of male on female violence and murder among the colonial Guaraní, see Ganson 1994: 358–9. She also mentions a small number of cases of women killing (or having killed) their husbands (360).

73. Tozzer 1941: 100; Landa 1985: 82.

74. Boyer 1989; Stern 1995: 53, 78. Taylor has suggested that violence against women in indigenous peasant communities in Oaxaca—especially homicides—made up a greater proportion of homicides overall than was the case in Mexico City (1979: 79), but Stern's larger sample and statistical analysis does not seem to bear this out (1995: tables 9.1, 9.3, 9.5, 10.1, and 12.2).

75. Kanter 1993: 173–91.

76. On mothers-in-law in Mexico City, see Arrom 1985: 247–9. On the Purépecha, see Castro Gutiérrez 1998: 8, 10, 13.

77. For Oaxaca, see Sousa 1998: 323. On the Andes, see Stavig 1995: 616–7.

78. Castro Gutiérrez 1998: 16.

79. Transcription and translation of this 1613 Nahuatl document can be found in Lockhart 2001: 128–9.

80. Stern discusses both amelioration and what he refers to as the "pluralization of patriarchs" (1995: 99–101); also see Sousa 1998: 323–4. On the general characteristics of women who endured domestic violence, see Stern (53–62).

81. Kanter 1993: 177–9.

82. While Mesoamerican women appealed to parents and brothers, Stavig observes that central Andean women tended to turn to their brothers (1995: 619). Saeger finds that Guaycuruan women sought out mission priests in cases of domestic violence (2000: 106).

83. Sousa 1996: 3–4.

84. For Mesoamerica, see Sousa 1998: 328–9; n.d.; Kanter 1993: 175–97; also see Stern 1995: 101. On Peru, see Stavig 1995: 605, 619. For a rare case of a woman herself murdering her husband in response to his cruel treatment, see Deeds 1997: 269. On native women's reluctance to initiate physical aggression against men, see Kanter 1993: 184–5.

85. On pressures to reconcile, see Kanter 1993: 193–7; Castro Gutiérrez 1998: 18; and Stavig 1995: 620–1.

86. Women quoted in Zavala 1984: 7:107. On the harsh treatment of female servants, see the discussion in the preceding section of this chapter on women's work, exploitation, and punishment.

87. Sousa 1998: 334. Also see Lipsett-Rivera 1996 on the crime of uxoricide (wife-killing) in central Mexico generally during the period 1750 to 1856. Like Sousa, she finds leniency in punishment of men (1996: 336).

88. Stavig 1995: 621. Also see Deeds's discussion of the ten-year sentence given a Tarahumara woman for killing her abusive husband who had, at least according to his wife's account, among other things, bound her hands and feet and left her outside in the freezing cold before departing for an evening of drinking. It was after this incident that the woman, María Gertrudis Ysidora de Medina, killed him (1997: 266–7).

89. For Mexico, this is shown especially clearly by Stern (1995: 49). On Peru, Stavig says that domestic violence was common in the late colonial period (1995: 600–601).

90. See entries discussing Mary's life and interpretations of its meanings and images in the *New Catholic Encyclopedia*, 9: 335–86; also see Pelikan 1996.

91. Burkhart 1998: 95; Klein 1995; and Silverblatt 1987: 179–86.

92. Klein 1995: 259–62; Kellogg 1997: 138–40; and Silverblatt 1987: 155–6.

93. For indigenous women as nuns see Gallagher 1978; Muriel 1963; Lavrin 1999; and Burns 1999. On accusations about the worship of earth goddesses, see Aramoni Calderón 1992: 88–92.

94. Madsen 1960: 28–9, 221; Campbell 1982: 7–8. On images of Mary in Nahuatl texts and for the quote, see Burkhart 1996: 89; also see Burkhart 2001b. On Ñudzahui testaments, see Terraciano 1998b: 129–31. On the Andes, see Mendieta Parada 1995: 32–3. On the origins of Guadalupe texts, see Sousa, Poole, and Lockhart 1998.

95. Burkhart 1996: 81; Schroeder 1997: 9–11.

96. Gibson 1964: 127–32; Schroeder 1997: 10–1; Sell n.d.; and, on Chiapas, Gosner 1997: 223.

97. Duviols 1986: lxxii; Burkhart 1997: 27.

98. Alva 1999: 103.

99. For the highland Maya, see Gosner 1997: 222. For Peru, see Silverblatt 1987: 109. On central Mexico, see Gruzinski 1989: 109.

100. Deeds 1997: 263; Behar 1989: 179, 185, 193; Anzures y Bolaños 1983: 73–9; Quezada 1989b: 114–20; Lewis 2003: chs. 4–6; Few 1995: 632; Lane 1998: 482–7; Mannarelli 1985: 144; 1998: ch. 2; Silverblatt 1987: 175; Mills 1997: 118; and Osorio 1999: 207–15. Griffiths (1996: 11–2) provides definitions of a series of witchcraft- and sorcery-related terms, and Quezada (1996: 46–70) and Mills (1997: 113–24) argue that Nahuas and Andeans also drew on love magic traditions that predated the arrival of the Spanish. Also see Glass-Coffin's list of eighteenth and early nineteenth-century cases of hechicería from Trujillo in northern Peru in which indigenous practitioners represent as least half of those tried (1999: 234–5).

101. Quezada 1989a: 108–10. On female shamans' loss of power in Guaycuruan missions, see Saeger 2000: 99, 108.

102. Kellogg 1997: 107; Spores 1997; and Terraciano 2001: 182–4, 186–90, 363. For examples of colonial cacicas primarily among Nahuas, see Fernández de Recas (1961). In a 1798 case in colonial Venezuela that stretched out until 1809, when

it ended inconclusively, Dionisia Quintero complained to the Fiscal Protector de Indias, trying to reclaim a cacicazgo for her son. Acting as head of her family (though she was not a widow) and as a community leader, she used a colonial court system in a time and place when it had little sympathy for indigenous assertions of defense of community, lands, or identity (Alvarez de Lovera 1994: 94–7).

103. Spores 1997: 188–9.

104. Statement of doña Agustina Cususoli, in Zevallos Quiñones 1989, quoted in Graubart 2000c: 300.

105. Arrom 1985: 58–61; Spores 1997: 186; Silverblatt 1987: 150–3; Rostworowski de Diez Canseco 1995: 12; Graubart 2000c: 281, 297–8, 301–21; and Alvarez de Lovera 1994: 80–3.

106. Cline 1986: 112–7; Wood 1997; Kellogg 1998; Powers 1998; and Graubart 2000c: chs. 3 and 4. The testament of Ana Juana, 1580, is transcribed and translated in Cline and León-Portilla 1984: 80–5 (quotes on 83).

107. On indigenous women and the Spanish legal realm across a variety of places from north to south, see Deeds 1997; Kellogg 1984; Sousa 1997; 1998: 322–35; and Gauderman 1998: ch. 5. In addition to Gauderman's discussion of a very specific example of women's legal activities in Quito, Silverblatt—while not focused on law per se—provides many examples of female legal participation (1987: chs. 6–10), as does Graubart 2000c.

108. Kellogg 1984; 1995b: 111–2.

109. Sousa 1997: 208; Gauderman 1998: 173–9, 190–9 (quote on 190).

110. 1995: 206.

111. Burkhart 1998: 375–6.

112. Castro Gutiérrez 1998: 9. On the importance of women's defense of their communities in colonial central Mexican protests, see Wood 1998a. This form of protest is strikingly familiar, given its use in the recent past in many parts of Latin America. See, for example, Alvarez 1990; Andreas 1985; Blondet 1990; Bouvard 1994; Feijoó 1989; Feijoó and Gogna 1990; and Navarro 1989.

113. For women as Taki Onqoy participants, see Stern 1993: 55. Works treating the history of religious change and the campaigns to extirpate idolatry include Duviols 1977, 1986; MacCormack 1985, 1991; Griffiths 1996; and Mills 1997. On Taki Onqoy, in addition to Stern's discussion (1993: 51–79), see Millones (1990); Varón Gabai (1990); and Mumford (1998), who provides a discussion of sources and critique of the historiography.

114. Silverblatt 1987: 183–8, 197; Griffiths 1996: 116–8, 126–7, 130–1; and Flores Espinosa 1999.

115. Mannarelli 1985: 142; Silverblatt 1987: 186, 200, 203–7; Griffiths 1996: 250; and Glass-Coffin 1999: 210.

116. Silverblatt 1987: ch. 10. Poole and Harvey (1988) have called for more nuanced definitions of resistance and critiqued Irene Silverblatt's use of the concept, arguing that what she is describing is less resistance and more "traditionalism" expressed in an individualistic rather than collective fashion (291–2). While I agree with their call for more careful definitions and studies of resistance, assertion of a non-Catholic belief system with significant roles for female actors in the context of extirpation campaigns can be seen as an expression of agency that sometimes took a collective form.

117. Taylor 1979: 116. Eric Van Young makes a similar point about women's involvement in early nineteenth-century protests and speculates that they "were

more likely to be involved in collective violence where the ostensible issues were tribute and labor obligations, and men more likely to be involved where land was the major question" (2001: 430).

118. Haskett 1997; Gosner 1997: 228–9; Dunn 1995; and Moreno Yánez 1977: 135, 195, 255–6. For an example of some Maya women leading a revolt in the town of Tecpán, Guatemala in 1759, see Patch 2002: ch. 3; and on women's roles and aggressive behavior in the Tehuantepec Rebellion of 1661, see Rojas 1964: 25–7.

119. Gosner 1992: 122–31.

120. Quotation from Campbell 1985: 167, also see 173–5. For the rebellions generally, see Valcárcel 1947; Fisher 1966; and Campbell 1987. On the term "quya," also see chapter 2. See Stark 1985: 11–4 for a description of women's violent behavior, including killing two nonindigenous tax collectors, in an uprising in colonial Ecuador.

121. Fisher 1966: 107, 209–11; Valencia Vega 1978: 49–50; and Campbell 1985: 171, 186; and Stavig 1999: 245–6.

122. Fisher 1966; Valencia Vega 1978: ch. 12; and Campbell 1985: 188–90.

123. The quotation about emasculation comes from Eleanor Burkett writing on early colonial Peru (1978: 119). Also see Salomon 1988; Kellogg 1997; and Hunt and Restall 1997.

124. For the Andes, see Silverblatt 1987: 111, 124, 138–47, 155; and Zulawski 1995: 151–6. On Mexico, see Barbosa Sánchez 1994: 93.

125. See Salomon's discussion of "ways to be an urban Indian" (1988: 326), from which my discussion takes off. On the "long nineteenth century," see Dore 2000. Also see Dore 1997: 604, 610–1; Aguirre 1996: 412–5; and Hames 1996: ch. 1 for discussions of nineteenth-century racism and processes of hybridity and identity formation that helped create rural peasantries and urban working classes with ambiguous racial identities that reinforced social distinctions between white creoles and indigenous and mixed groups.

126. Quotation from Guerrero 2003: 285. On land loss, tribute policies, and changing racial designations see Halperin-Donghi 1985; Bauer 1986: 158–9; Hale 1968: 219–36; 1989: 221; Rugeley 1996: 63–8; Mulhare 2004; Mallon 1983: 10, 28, 38; 1995: 91–103; Rappaport 1990: 81–6; Moscoso 1992; O'Connor 1997: 87–9; Poole 1988; Thurner 1997: 46–53; Platt 1982; Langer 2001; Block 1994: 172–3; and Wright with Carneiro da Cunha et al. 1999. For a general overview of the policies of nineteenth-century nations toward indigenous groups, see Reina and Velasco 1997.

127. For the intensification of patriarchy in nineteenth-century law codes, see Deere and León 2001a: 38–40. See Chassen-López 1994: 38–40 on women, labor, and record-keeping in early twentieth-century Oaxaca; also see Stephen (1991: 93–7), who demonstrates the gendering of census categories and the frequent undercounting of female laborers for the district of Tlacolula and town of Teotitlan, also in Oaxaca, in the early twentieth century.

128. On women's declining land rights, see Mallon 1994: 8–9; Grandin 2000: 39–40; O'Connor 1997: 195–8, 302–10; and 2002. Chassen-López argues that women increased their share of land ownership, from large estates to small plots, in late nineteenth- and early twentieth-century Oaxaca but also shows the vulnerability of their holdings in a legal system that privileged male ownership and responsibility for female relatives. On women's economic activities that aided the development of nineteenth-century regional economies, see Mallon 1995: 69–70; Reina 1997: 351–4; Grandin 2000: 38–41; Dore 1997: 603–5; Borchart de Moreno 1991; Mos-

coso 1995; Larson 1998: 364–5; Hames 1996: ch. 4; and Langer 2001, who discusses the testament of Antonia Lojo. Santos-Granero and Barclay (2000: 41–2, 271–2) describe the capture and virtual enslavement of indigenous women in northeastern (Amazonian) Peru during the rubber boom of the late nineteenth and early twentieth centuries. For chola and mestiza women and the new chicherías, see Larson 1998: 364–9 and Gotkowitz 1998: 267–73. On negative images of indigenous, chola, and mestiza women, see Chambers 1999: 206–215; Gotkowitz 1998: 294–314; 2003; and Stephenson 1999: 141–6. Few (2002) describes attempts by colonial authorities in Santiago de Guatemala to control the disorderly behavior of urban women of the popular classes with a range of ethno-racial identities.

129. On women and courts, see González Montes and Iracheta Cenegorta 1987; Chenaut 1993: 184–5; 1997: 134–5; 143–6; Moscoso 1992; and O'Connor 1997: 298–310. On images, see Mallon 1994: 8; 1995: 77–9; Platt 1993: 169–74; and Poole 1988; 2004: 52–3, 61–9, 74–9.

130. Degarrod 1998: 339; Bacigalupo 2004.

4. With Muted Voices

1. See Menchu 1984, 1998; Jiménez 1968,1972; and Karttunen 1994: 192–214. Author of another book of Nahua tales, Jiménez also wrote some stories with Anita Brenner, for which she received no credit (MacMasters 1999; G. Hernández 2000). For a brief discussion of the very few other female Nahua writers, see Karttunen, who also discusses the small number of contemporary female Maya writers (1998: 441–2). On the Mexican version of indigenismo, see Knight 1990.

2. On the writing of *I, Rigoberta Menchú*, see Stoll 1999: chs. 13 and 14; and several of the essays in Arias 2001. Also on Rigoberta Menchú and Maya women as symbols of identity, see Nelson 1999: 162–9, 271–81. On the production of testimonies, or "autobiographies," see Behar 1993 (especially the introductory chapter) and Mallon 2001.

3. Bauer 1990: 3, 16–7; Bruhns 1991: 422; also see Keremitsis 1983.

4. None of the volumes of the *Handbook of Middle American Indians* (1964–76), for example, treat the subject of gender, though the occasional essay touches upon the subject either generally (see Colby 1967 for a thematic article on psychological patterns among Mesoamerican peoples that refers in places to gender roles) or specifically (as in essays treating individual groups with sections on the division of labor and kinship). With the rise of the most recent women's movement in the 1960s, a variety of scholars began to write about gender more systematically, but only a few articles or books offer comparison. An ambitious, though unsystematic, attempt at cross-cultural comparison can be found in a 1975 special issue of the Mexican-published journal *América Indígena*. Its wide-ranging articles on Mesoamerican, South American, and Central American women illustrate the increasing attention given to women, as the issue attempts to counter an ethnographic literature that fails to acknowledge the deep historical roots of women's productive labor and political action. Also see Anton 1973; Bossen 1983; Rosenbaum 1996; and Rubio Orbe 1975.

5. Rosenbaum 1996: 323, 338, 343–5; Bossen 1983: 36, 45–7. The notion of women as more Indian is de la Cadena's (1995), for Peru, but can be applied to Mesoamerica, where beginning early in the twentieth century, photographers of indigenous women began to use their images to symbolize the identity of whole

groups. For examples, see Poole 2004. Also see Mathews 1985 and Stephen 1991: ch. 7, as well as further discussion of women's political activism in this and the next two chapters.

6. González Montes 1994a. For information on the conditions of extreme poverty that many of Mexico's indigenous communities currently endure, see Ballinas 2000; and Thompson 2001.

7. Quotation from Redfield 1930: 85; quotation from Jiménez 1972: 3. Also see Lewis 1951: 98–9, 101–2; and 1960: 55, 88. For critiques of the failure of ethnographers to acknowledge the labor of indigenous women in central Mexico, see Rodríguez 1975 and Rothstein 1983.

8. Madsen 1969: 602. See Good 2000 and Sandstrom 2000 for recent surveys of literature on Nahua communities across central Mexico. Mexican census information for the year 2000 suggests the number of Nahuas, based on the number of Nahuatl speakers, is at least 1,500,000. (Figures are available online. See Mexico, Instituto Nacional de Estadística, Geografía e Informática [INEGI] at: www.inegi. gob.mx or see XII Censo General de Población y Vivienda 2000 [2002].)

9. Slade 1976: 176. While Nahuas typically have a fairly rigid division of labor, in which men's and women's activities differ and are often carried out separately, as is common elsewhere in Mesoamerica, there is some variation among central Mexican groups. Mazahuas of the central region, while maintaining a gender-based division of labor, stressed to ethnographer Alicja Iwańska the interchangeability of male and female work roles (1971: 51–3). A similar pattern with a more cooperative division of labor stressing some task sharing has also been reported for Teeneks of the Huastec region of Veracruz (Dietiker-Amslër 1993: 152, 154–7) and for Totonacs of Puebla and Veracruz (Harvey and Kelly 1969: 663). Among the Wixárika (also known as Huichols), especially those of northern Jalisco, while male and female tasks are differentiated, men and women do help each other, especially in agriculture and weaving (Schaefer 2002: 58, 107, 109). On Nahua women as domestic servants, see for example Taggart 1975: 160. On their employment outside the home, see Arizpe 1975a: 581.

10. Lewis 1944: 299, 301, 304; 1951: 101; Van Zantwijk 1960: 30; Nutini 1968: 48, 189–90; Arizpe 1973: 83; Friedlander 1975: 9, 12–4, 40–2; Taggart 1975: 161; Huber 1990: 159; Slade 1992: 103; Good 1993: 253–5; Frye 1996: 26; and Vázquez García 1997: 180.

11. Redfield 1930: 152; Lewis 1944: 299; 1951: 98; 1963: 323; Madsen 1960: 49; Nutini 1968: 44–5, 188–90; Friedlander 1975: 21–2, 42–3; 1994: 125; Taggart 1975: 159; González Montes 1988: 68; 1994b: 178–9; Huber 1990; Sandstrom 1991: 139–40; Chevalier and Buckles 1995: 260–1; and Vázquez García 1997: 169.

12. Lewis 1951: 413; Nutini 1968: 84; Taggart 1975: 160; Sandstrom 1991: 177, 365; and on daughters from Hueyapan accompanying fathers, see Friedlander 1975: 61–2.

13. Vázquez García 1997: 184–8.

14. Nutini and Isaac 1974: 407; González Montes 1994b: 176–9.

15. Lewis 1944: 304. Also see Nutini and Isaac (1974: 412–420), as well as Steve Stern's discussion of the corn mills (1995: 332–5). Lourdes Arizpe points out that other technological changes, such as electricity in homes, meant that women could work harder and longer at other household tasks (1975a: 580). Also see Friedlander (1975: 7) for a Nahua informant's brief discussion of the time saved.

16. The following discuss general patterns across various areas of Mesoamerica: Annis 1987; Arizpe 1988; Cook and Binford 1990; Ehlers 1990; and Nash 1993.

17. Arizpe 1975a: 578–81; Chevalier and Buckles 1995: 240–1; and Vázquez García 1996: 67–71. On "post-Nahuas," see Mulhare 2003: 268–9. On women's changing economic roles in Xalatlaco, see González Montes 1994b: 177, 186–7.

18. On patrilineal patterns of inheritance, especially of land, see Sandstrom 1991: 183–4; Dietiker-Amslër 1993; and Slade 1976: 176; 1992: 136. On bilateral inheritance, see Montoya Briones 1964: 85; Arizpe 1973: 92. Variation within a single region is discussed in Taggart 1983: 24, 35. For widows inheriting, see González Montes 1988: 69–73; Robichaux 1988; and Sandstrom 1991: 183–4. Also see Robichaux 1997 for a discussion of indigenous patterns of postmarital residence and ultimogeniture in both Tlaxcala and Mesoamerica.

19. Chevalier and Buckles 1995: 238–41; Vázquez García 1996: 78–81; 1997: 172–3. On women's legal rights to ejidos, see Arizpe and Botey 1987: 70; Brunt 1992: 79–81; Deere and León 2001a: 69–73, 150–6, 257, 273–4, 284–7; and Stephen 2002a: 3–4.

20. Madsen 1969: 624; Sandstrom 1991: 166–73.

21. Redfield 1930: 139–40; Lewis 1951: 76; Madsen 1960: 101; Montoya Briones 1964: 87–9; Nutini 1968: 188; Arizpe 1973: 163; Nutini and Bell 1980: 40, 44; Taggart 1983: 27, 35, 48; Slade 1976: 176; 1992: 128; Sandstrom 1991: 179–80; Tirado 1991: 33–5; Chevalier and Buckles 1995: 232–3; and Vázquez García 1996: 64. On Gulf Coast bride service, see Chevalier and Buckles 1995: 232.

22. For the quotation, see Slade 1992: 128. On robo, see D'Aubeterre Buznego 2003; Goloubinoff 2003. For an extensive description of robo in Tarascan communities of the 1940s, see Beals 1998 (1946; the year of first publication is included once so that readers understand the chronology of ethnographic publications): 178–80. For a discussion emphasizing the coercive elements of robo, see Nutini 1968: 264–8. On the Isthmus of Tehuantepec, rapto, or abduction, according to the Juchiteco writer and journalist Andrés Henestrosa, occurred either because the parents of a potential bride rejected a particular groom (and she then voluntarily eloped with him), or a man wished to have proof of his potential bride's virginity (1993: 130–1). Writing from a female perspective, Ruiz Campbell says that women see the practice as a "shameful and denigratory action" (1993: 139).

23. For quotation, see Lewis 1951: 319. On the early stages of marriage, see Nutini 1968: 86, 184; Nutini and Bell 1980: 41; Friedlander 1975: 27–31; Rothstein 1983: 12; Sandstrom 1991: 144–5, 179–80; and Nutini and Roberts 1993: 250–2.

24. González Montes 1991; 1994b: 185–8; 1994c; and Mulhare 1998 An important area influencing the husband-wife relationship is, of course, sexuality. Little work exists on patterns of native women's sexuality, and that which does mostly focuses on the Maya. It has been suggested, however, that Nahua women remain subject to strongly held ideas about sexual honor, sex as enjoyable is not much encouraged for Nahuas, male or female, and women still have relatively little access to contraception or information about venereal diseases or other sex- or gender-related health issues (Lewis 1951: 290–1, 325–8, 362; Sandstrom 1991: 144; and Castañeda Salgado 1997).

25. Redfield 1930: 152; Madsen 1960: 90; Van Zantwijk 1960: 43; Taggart 1975: 97–8; Huber 1990: 160; Sandstrom 1991: 233–5, 296; and Huber and Sandstrom 2001. Also see Huber on Nahuatl terms for curers (1990: 160, 173 n. 5). Good finds male marriage go-betweens in the Balsas River Valley Nahua villages she studied (1993: 407–11).

26. Nutini 1968: 191; Sandstrom 1991: 313–5; and Slade 1975: 135–6, 146.

27. For Tlakatelilis, see Sandstrom 1982; for San Bernardino Contla, see Nutini 1968: 192–3; for Balsas River villages, see Good 1993: 317–22.

28. On infanticide, see Nutini and Roberts 1993: 249–50. On tensions in Nahua marriages as expressed between mothers- and daughters-in-law, also see Taggart 1983: 24. For husbands' fears of wives practicing sorcery against them in 1940s Tepoztlán, see Lewis 1951: 324.

29. Quotation is from Taggart 1983: 26. Also see Redfield 1930: 139; Lewis 1951: 328–9; Madsen 1960: 88; Nutini 1968: 86, 184; Taggart 1975: 97; 1983: 26, 48; Huber 1990: 166; Good 1993: 402; Chevalier and Buckles 1995: 233–4, 256; and González Montes 1998: 31.

30. Lewis 1963: 328–9; Ingham 1989: 62–3; Sandstrom 1991: 144; and González Montes 1994c: 115. Soledad González Montes has also studied domestic violence in the municipality of Cuetzalan in the Sierra Norte region of Puebla. She finds high rates of male-on-female domestic violence, arguing that about 40 percent of women who have lived with a man at some point experience physical abuse, to the point where such behavior is considered a normal part of marriage. But people also see women as having the right to turn to authorities, medical or politico-legal, to protect themselves (1998; discussion of rates, 29). For the more acculturated area González Montes studied (Xalatlaco), see 1994b: 188; also see González Montes and Iracheta Cenegorta 1987.

31. For quotation, see Slade 1975: 145 (also see 135–6, 144). Slade does not explain whether the woman was widowed or never married.

32. Mathews 1985; Stephen 1991: ch. 7; Rosenbaum 1996: 337–8; Vázquez García 1996: 71–3; and Good 1993: 34, 358 n. 7.

33. For women protesting lack of ejido lands, see Vázquez García 1996: 77–8; and on the First Aztec Congress, see Karttunen 1994: 206.

34. Rendón 1975; González Montes 1998: 20, 23–5; Townsend et al. 1999: 141–2; Harrison 2001: 277; Molina Ramírez 2002; Aguirre 2003; Gómez Mena 2003; Peters 2003; and Rojas 2003a.

35. Townsend et al. 1999: 9–10, 88; International Funding and Indigenous Self-Development 1999; and Ojeda-Macias n.d.

36. Quoted in Townsend et al. 1999: 95. On Maseualsiuamej Mosenyolchikahuanij, see Freeman and Garelli 2002; Sierra 2002.

37. Peters 2003; and Pérez U. 2004.

38. Quotation from Nutini and Isaac 1974: 404 (also see 400–420).

39. Lewis 1944: 303–4.

40. Chevalier and Buckles 1995: 4–5; Vázquez García 1996: 66–9; 1997: 175.

41. Arizpe 1975a: 581; 1975b; Bar Din 1992: 157–9; Vázquez García 1997: 174–5; Salazar 2000; quote in Rojas 2002a.

42. Las mujeres indígenas 1997; Reyes Razo 1999.

43. Poniatowska 1993: 134; also see Poniatowska 1989. For a very misleading comment about Zapotec women of the famous Isthmus town of Juchitán as all being lesbians, see Bennholdt-Thomsen 1989: 4. On Mixtec women, see Bailey 1958 and on Huave women, see Dalton and Musalem Merhy 1992. For articles on Nahua, Zapotec, and Mixtec women (as well as women of other ethnic groups), see Aranda B. 1988.

44. For the "tiger beauties" quotation, see Gadow, quoted in Campbell 1994: 71. On exoticizing image-makers, see Campbell 1994: 236. For the tehuanas as queens, see Covarrubias 1946: 246.

45. West 1964a: 62–5; West 1964b: 317–22; and Stephen 1991: 64. Oaxaca's Zapotec-speaking population, according to the 2000 Mexican census, is 347,020.

46. Stephen 1991: 119; Campbell 1994: 232–6, 289 n. 18; and Rubin 1997: 232, 268.

47. On the range of women's economic activities, see Cook and Binford 1990: 154–5.

48. Covarrubias 1946: 150. Also see Parsons 1936: 61–5; de la Fuente 1949: 107; Sault 1985a: 72–4; Stephen 1991: 61; and Bennholdt-Thomsen 1989.

49. For Zapotec women in colonial markets, see Torres de Laguna cited in Campbell 1994: 234. On the twentieth century, see Chiñas 1992 [1973]; Stephen 1991; and Campbell 1994: 234.

50. Chiñas 1976: 186; 1992: 33–4, 173, 184–5. Also see her example of a viajera selling Oaxaca-made items to the largely male workers of an isolated hydroelectric project in Chiapas (1976: 181–3). Campbell argues that the arrival of chain stores in Juchitán has been bad for most women sellers there (1994: 94).

51. Stephen 1991: 119–24, 148–55 (quotation on 148).

52. Parsons 1936: 29–31, 43, 53, 61–4; de la Fuente 1949: 104–9; Nader 1969: 345; Jopling 1973; Brueske 1976: ch. 3; Sault 1985a: 71–6; Stephen 1991: 146. Note also that Cook and Binford find evidence of matrilineal transmission of female crafts work, especially palm plaiting in Oaxaca (1990: 158, 173). On the devaluation of rural women's work, see Young 1978 and Cook and Binford 1990: 157, 188–9.

53. Young 1978: 141–3; Ornelas López 1988; and Hirabayashi 1993: 64–5. For a discussion of the impact of male outmigration on women in a Zapotec community, particularly in relationship to the United States's *bracero* (temporary laborer) program with Mexico, see Stephen 1991: 27–8, 109–17.

54. Quoted in Stephen 1991: 54–5.

55. Hirabayashi 1993: 65–6; Young 1978: 146–7, 150–1.

56. Parsons 1936: 66; Nader 1969: 347–8; Sault 1985a: 279–82; and Chiñas 1992: 21, 54.

57. On women's property, see Parsons 1936: 54, 485; de la Fuente 1949: 159; Young 1978: 133–43; Chiñas 1992: 27; and Stephen 1991: 71, 103–7, 109–11. Stephen 1991 also discusses the decline in significance of the ritual system.

58. Mathews 1985; Stephen 1991: 179–83, 208–9; and Chiñas 1992: 64–70.

59. Parsons 1936: 192–3; Mathews 1985: 290, 296; Stephen 1991: 157–61, 176–7, 194–202; Chiñas 1992: 46, 64; and Rios 1999. For an example of a woman elected to the position of *regador* (representative to the *ayuntamiento*, or town council) as part of an Institutional Revolutionary Party council in San Juan Evangelista, see Chiñas 1992: 121.

60. Parsons 1936: 63–4, 74–5, 115–31, 304; de la Fuente 1949: 108–9; O'Nell and Selby 1968: 104 n. 2; Chiñas 1992: 56; Sokoloff 1993; Sesia 1997; and Huber and Sandstrom 2001: 165. There is also evidence from the Oaxaca area that indigenous women face discrimination ranging from scorn and maltreatment to pressure for sterilization when they seek care from medical doctors at area clinics and hospitals (Aguirre 1999).

61. Sault 1985a: ch. 2 (on the town, see x and 50); 2001: 126–7; El Guindi 1986: 47–8; and Stephen 1991: 190–1.

62. Sault 1985a: 434–5; 1985b: 229, 234–9; 2001: 118, 120, 132–3; Stephen 1991: 192–4, 207.

63. Parsons 1936: 165; Chiñas 1992: 13; Mathews 1985: 291–2; Stephen 1991: 216–21, 232–6; and Campbell 1994: 20–1, 231. A fascinating example of the twentieth-century reemergence of the Mixtec tradition of female rulers can be found in Chassen-López (1998: 114, 116–7): rebelling Mixtecs in the Pinotepa Nacional chose a queen as ruler as part of a Mixtec rebellion against local ranchers that broke out in Oaxaca during the early years of the Mexican Revolution.

64. Campbell 1994: 230–1. Note also that in the text acronyms are defined in English and both Spanish and English meanings are listed prior to the endnotes.

65. For Zapotec marketwomen attacking a governor, see Campbell 1990: 322–3. On COCEI's use of female imagery, see Magallón Cervantes 1988; Stephen 1991: 241–2; Campbell 1994: 232–3; and Rubin 1997: 232. Chiñas (based on Tanner 1974) defines matrifocal cultures as those in which the mother's role is central organizationally, economically, and psychologically, gender relations are relatively egalitarian, and where girls and women behave assertively (1992: ch. 8).

66. Parsons 1936: 100; O'Nell and Selby 1968: 104 n. 5; Nader 1969: 357; and Chiñas 1992: 51.

67. Parsons 1936: 112.

68. On Zapotec women and domestic violence, see especially Nader 1990: 191–203; also see Chiñas 1992: 101; and Campbell 1994: 292 n. 21. Kearney, writing on the highland community of Ixtepeji, points out that Zapotec folklore suggests that women can use food preparation with poison as a means to overcome male dominance in sexuality and violence (1972: 113 n. 2). On localism and ethnic identity, see Stephen 1991: 15–21. Also see Campbell 1994: 233–8; and Rubin 1997: 228–31. Violence against women in the form of wife beating has been reported to be common among the Amuzgo, a nearby group of southeastern Guerrero and western Oaxaca (Ravicz and Romney 1969: 423, 429). It is also important to note that abortion is a contentious issue in indigenous communities. In Talea, while women can challenge abuse through legal means, as cases of abortion show, "a woman has no right over her reproductive capacity. Backed by village law, abortion is dealt with in the most repressive manner, which violates women's privacy and rights over their own bodies. Such treatment is not found in any cross-sex complaints about men, as in paternity, physical abuse, abandonment, or adultery issues" (Nader 1990: 217).

69. 1936: 536. On Zapotec culture as matrifocal, see Chiñas 1992: 87–107. On Zapotec women as submissive, see O'Nell and Selby 1968: 99, and for discussions of female and male pathways of gender identity and sexuality, see Chiñas 1995 and Stephen 2002b.

70. Nelson 1999: 170–1; also see Rosenbaum 1992: 157. Note also that it is interesting that so much ethnography depicts Maya women as silent domestic workers when, according to Diane Nelson, ladino men in Guatemala frequently assert that native women there are sexually aggressive, particularly toward white men (1999: 224). For a relatively recent example of Maya women depicted largely as laborers in the domestic realm, see Gossen 1999: 24.

71. Estimates of Maya population for each relevant country exist but vary (partly because determining the characteristics that define the identity is so difficult). The Yucatan Peninsula may have a Maya population approaching one million (based on statistics from the 2000 Mexican census for the states of Yucatan, Quintana Roo, Campeche, and Tabasco, the precise figure being 856,537; for Chiapas, Mexico, Neil Harvey gives a figure for the Maya population of close to 700,000, based on 1990 Mexican census figures (1998: 71; 2000 census figures show over 800,000 indig-

enous language speakers in the state); and for Guatemala, Diane Nelson suggests a Maya population that could range from 45 to 70 percent of its approximately eleven million people (1999: 7). For relatively conservative figures, with a total of roughly four million (across the relevant countries), also based on linguistic evidence, see Wearne 1996: app. 1: 206–12.

72. 1934: 68–9. Redfield did acknowledge that change was occurring. Some communities, he observed, had a wider range of female curers, which he viewed as a negative consequence of modernization. In his words, "the secularization of the folk medicine results in great measure from the fact of transfer of the functions of healing from a man who is a priest as well as a shaman to a woman who is only a healer and practitioner of beneficent magic" (1941: 314). He also noted that some women's work, particularly in curing and textile production and decoration, began to be paid for in money, which, he argued, would lead to a gain in public presence and self-confidence for women (1941: 174–5; 1950: 65–135). Also see Lombardo Otero 1944 for a discussion of how economic changes in the 1930s and 1940s affected highland Tzeltal women.

73. On Yucatec Maya women's work, see Elmendorf 1976: 15, 37, 99–103; Holmes 1978: 61; Nimis 1982; and Kintz 1998. For patterns elsewhere, see Brown 1999; Guiteras-Holmes 1961: 50; Devereaux 1987: 89; Black 1988: 91; Rosenbaum 1993: 40; and Zur 1998: 51. On the division of labor of the Lacandon Maya in the Chiapas lowlands, see McGee (1990: 25–6), who shows that while work is conceptualized as highly gender differentiated, with men farming and hunting and women performing domestic labor, in fact, there is considerable overlap in work of all kinds.

74. Quotation from Tax [1953] 1963: 25; also see Bunzel 1952: 25. But note that Tax's own detailed data (most of it from the 1930s) shows that in addition to their contribution to the subsistence economy, women contributed cash through their agricultural work harvesting milpa-grown corn and in what he terms "truck gardens," where plants like beans, garlic, onions, and other vegetables were grown, with much of this produce to be harvested and marketed by both men and women. Tax also wrote about Maya, male and female, who provided field labor for other, largely ladino landowners, with the women workers making about half the male wage (92–3, 101). Carey (2002) found indigenous women workers on coffee plantations paid as little as 8–9 cents per day, with men paid 40 cents per day, during the 1950s and 1960s. Bossen (1984: 66–70) found significant rates of female participation in plantation wage labor from the highland community T'oj Nam that she studied during the 1970s. She observed women being paid roughly equivalent wages to men. Rigoberta Menchú has written about her experience picking coffee as her mother both picked and cooked food for Maya workers on a coffee plantation (1984: 30–7). For Chiapas, Devereaux discusses Zinacantecas of the seventies, whom she portrays as reluctant to engage in trade that took them any distance from their home communities (1987: 93, 103). Rosenbaum observes that during the eighties, while Chamula women sold food in markets in Chamula or San Cristóbal, they were often reluctant to leave their communities for outside employment unless forced by economic circumstances (1992: 161; 1993: 18–9, 122–4). On highland women's labor patterns, also see H. de Pozas 1959; Nash 1970: 48; Gossen 1974: 40; Collier 1975: 43, 46; McVey-Dow 1986: 114–5; Haviland 1978: ch. 5; and Cabrera Pérez-Armiñán 1992: 43, 51–3.

75. Guiteras-Holmes 1961: 51; Bossen 1984: 60; Pancake 1992: 122–4; Schevill 1991: 11; and Hendrickson 1995: 151, 206 n. 2.

76. Nash 1995: 14–6; Brodman 1994; Rosenbaum 1993: 18; Hendrickson 1995: 35–8, 62–6, 89, 118–9; 1996: 162–3; Otzoy 1996: 146–7; Nelson 1999: 182; Ehlers 1990: 128–30; and 2000: xxxii–xxxiii.

77. García and Gomáriz 1989: 2:61–2; Flood 1994.

78. Lazos Chavero 1995. For a description of women's work and health patterns in the eastern Yucatec communities of Yalcobá, also a traditional milpa community still using slash-and-burn agriculture, in which women's position is highly subordinated, see Daltabuit Godás 1992. Hamilton and Fisher (2003) argue, for highland Guatemala, that nontraditional export agriculture can have a positive impact on gender relations, particularly in terms of women's participation in economic decision-making within households.

79. Lazos Chavero 1995: 119–20.

80. Lazos Chavero 1995: 123, 128.

81. Lazos Chavero 1995: 117, 127. Also see Maynard 1974; and Bossen 1984: 311–316. On the loss of ethnic identity and intensification of family problems such as alcoholism and domestic abuse among the Chontal Maya of Tabasco, see Uribe Iniesta and May May 1993.

82. McVey-Dow 1986; Rus 1990: 13; O'Brian 1992; 1994; Garza Caligaris et al. 1993: 21–2; Eber and Rosenbaum 1993; Nash 1993; Rosenbaum 1993: 121–5, 130; and Rovira 1997: 40–2.

83. Quotation from Rosenbaum 1993: 122; also see Nash 1993: 142.

84. Cruz H. 1987; Eber and Rosenbaum 1993: 166–7; and O'Brian 1994: 160–1.

85. Morris 1991; Nash 2001: 178–9; Rovira 1997: 166–74; Kampwirth 2002: 104–5; Eber 1999; and Castro Apreza 2003. Eber and Rosenbaum discuss some of the problems with cooperatives (1993: 168–73). On Petrona López's murder, see Nash 1993: 127–9; 1995: 161; and 2001: 98. For a participant's account of J'olom Mayatik (Maya Weavers), a cooperative that separated from Sna Jolobil, see Ortiz's interview with Lorenza (2001: 88–95).

86. These categories come from Bossen 1984: ch. 3.

87. Bossen 1984: ch. 3; Anderson and Garlock 1988: 34; Ehlers 1990; 1991; Dary Fuentes 1991; and Carey 2001: 108–9. The migration of highland Maya women, particularly Kaqchiquel of Guatemala's western highlands to the Pacific Coast to work on coffee plantations, began in the late nineteenth century (Carey 2002). Maya merchant women from the town of Palin, somewhat similar to the Zapotec female merchants described by Chiñas, have been discussed by Maynard (1974: 91–2).

88. Ehlers 1990: 110–30. Also see her revised introduction in Ehlers 2000. On Palopó, see Ehlers 1991: 6–8. Men dominated wool weaving in Momostenango (a center for such production) in Guatemala's western highlands, though women and children participated as well in the family-organized enterprises (Carmack 1995: 156–8, 252–3).

89. Bossen 1984: 74–5, 110–2; Hamerschlag 1985; Ehlers 1993; and Green 1999: 101–5, 131–47.

90. Redfield 1950: 57; Elmendorf 1976: 98; Lazos Chavero 1995: 108, 110–1; Guiteras-Holmes 1961: 38; Villa Rojas 1969a: 211; Haviland 1978: 85–6; Collier 1973: 176–9; Collier 1975: 88–9, 102–5; Wagley 1941: 70; Bunzel 1952: 18; Reina 1966: 43; Brintnall 1979: 83; Bossen 1984: 113; Carmack 1995: 155, 255–6; and Zur 1998: 59.

91. Villa Rojas 1969b: 263–6; Lazos Chavero 1995: 110–1; Pozas 1977 [1959]: 1:179, 181; Nash 1970: 32, 103; Collier 1973: 176; Collier 1975: 102; Rosenbaum 1993: 18, 49–50 (note her argument that bilateral inheritance patterns still work to

the advantage of Chamula women because, due to their land rights, they are "more independent and less submissive than women in neighboring communities such as Zinacantán and Oxchuc, where only men inherit and patrilineages tend to be stronger"); and Tax 1963: 69, 79–80.

92. Redfield and Villa Rojas 1934: 87; Lombardo Otero 1944: 51–6; Villa Rojas 1945: 89; Guiteras Holmes 1961: 70, 128–9; Wagley 1941: 14–5; and Bunzel 1952: 25.

93. Elmendorf 1976: 90–1; Lazos Chavero 1995: 99–104; Juaréz 2001; Collier 1968: 156–7, 180–2, 186; Nash 1993: 139–40; Rosenbaum 1993: 49, 89–91, 100–103; Nash 1993: 140; Siverts 1993; O'Brian 1994: 91–2; Maynard 1974: 90; Brintnall 1979: 83; Bossen 1984: 113–5; and Black 1988: 94–5.

94. On instability, see Holmes 1978: 237–8; Woodrick 1995; Juaréz 2001; Collier 1968: 180; Rosenbaum 1993: 10; Bunzel 1952: 129–32; Bossen 1984: 117–8; Black 1988: 96; Zur 1998: 56–7. On polygyny, see Pozas 1977: 1: 164–6 and Rosenbaum 1993: 113–5. On Maya marriages as companionate and more stable than among non-Mayas (though ethnographers report that open displays of affection are rare), see Rosenbaum 1993: 50; Maynard 1974: 95; and Black 1988: 96. Kray emphasizes that community members in the Yucatecan pueblo, Dzitnup, see marriage as a life-long relationship that is to be taken extremely seriously (1997: 103).

95. McClusky reviews the literature and convincingly argues that while Maya gender relations are constituted by both complementary and hierarchical relations, the hierarchical elements, especially male control over more financial resources, the sexual double standard, and the common occurrence of domestic violence outweigh the complementary ones (2001: 42–6). On gender hierarchy and sexual antagonism among the Lacandon of eastern Chiapas, see Boremanse 1998: 53–7.

96. Elmendorf 1976: 107; Holmes 1978: 2, 354; Devereaux 1987: 89, 92, 109–10; Eber and Rosenbaum 1993: 163; Eber 1995: 33, 240–1; 1999: 10–1; Rosenbaum 1993: 40, 136; O'Brian 1994: 91, 95; Maynard 1974: 87, 96; Bossen 1984: 59; and Ehlers 1990: 6. Some ethnographers report that while gender complementarity, particularly in work, is valued among Maya groups, a reality that both sexes recognize is that it is harder for husbands to survive without wives than vice versa (Pozas 1977: 2:161; Collier 1973: 199; Eber and Rosenbaum 1993: 164; Eber 1995: 68).

97. Guiteras-Holmes 1961: 99; Cancian 1965: 46, 212–3; Nash 1970: 102; Rosenbaum 1993: 158–66; Eber 1995: 104–6; and Reina 1966: 101, 103, 105, 111, 114–7.

98. For quotation, see Redfield and Rojas 1934: 69. Also see Redfield 1941: 314; 1950: 65; Elmendorf 1976: 16; Vogt 1969: 420, 425; Pozas 1977: I: 159–60; Haviland 1978: 252–4; Eber 1995: 77, 157–92; Rovira 1997: 94–5; Gossen 1999: 183; Reina 1966: 238–42, 273; Paul and Paul 1975; Paul 1978; Cosminsky 1982: 207–9; 2001: 180, 186; Orellana 1987: 65–71; Cabrera Pérez-Armiñán 1992: 54–5; Carmack 1995: 306–7; and Jordan 1993: ch. 2.

99. Holmes 1978: 353; Lazos Chavero 1995: 127; Rosenbaum 1992; 1993: 30–6; Gossen 1999: 172, 204; Paul 1974: 298; Smith 1995: 738–9; Warren 1998: 108; Zur 1998: 64; Bastos 1999; and Nelson 1999: chs. 5 and 6.

100. Redfield 1941: 123, 143; Elmendorf 1976: 5, 17; Cancian 1965: 33; Laughlin 1991: 88; Gossen 1974: 40–3; Rosenbaum 1993: 70–1, 171; Ehlers 1990: 134–8; 1991: 6–7; Hendrickson 1995: 132; and Carmack 1995: 306–8, 320–3. While women have the right to vote in national elections in Mexico, Guatemala, and Belize, the ability of most indigenous women to vote in national and local elections remains limited (Hernández Castillo 2001: 138; Nash 2001: 50–1, 55; Carey 2001: 228; Forster 2001: 2; and McClusky 2001: 33).

101. Elmendorf 1976: 65–7; Holmes 1978: 224–5; Pozas 1977: 1:142; Blaffer 1972: 113–21; Gossen 1974: 42–3; Devereaux 1987: 100–101; Rosenbaum 1993: 50–2, 106; Barrios Ruiz and Pons Bonals 1995: 46–7, 109–11, 112–4, 128–9; Marión 1997: 77–8; Kampwirth 2002: 88–9; Bunzel 1952: 120; Paul 1974; Maynard 1974: 94; Black 1988: 96; Ehlers 1990: 150–3; and Hendrickson 1995: 127–130.

102. Elmendorf 1976: 50; Holmes 1978: 245–6; Lombardo Otero 1944: 27; Collier 1973: 159–61, 180, 183–9, 193; Rendón 1975: 588; Laughlin 1991: 88; Garza Caligaris and Ruiz Ortiz 1992: 70–5; Rosenbaum 1993: 51–2, 108–9; Eber 1995: 196–7, 205–6; Freyermuth Enciso and Fernández Guerrero 1995; Rovira 1997: 35–6; Rojas 1999; Bunzel 1952: 128–9; Reina 1966: 264–6; Bossen 1984: 125–7; Zur 1998: 57; Forster 2000; and McClusky 2001. On women's lack of success with the judicial system, see McClusky 2001.

103. Quotation from Nash 2001: 274 n. 33. Also see Collier 1973: ch. 9; Rosenbaum 1993: 174–5; and Bossen 1984: 125–7.

104. Daltabuit Godás 1992: 150–1, 210–1; Lazos Chavero 1995: 99–100; Freyermuth and Fernández 1997; Freyermuth Enciso 1998: 69–71; Barrios Ruiz and Pons Bonals 1995: 26–7; Rovira 1997: 216–22; Palomo 2001; Muñoz 2002; Ehlers 1990: 37–8; Smith-Ayala 1991: 26; Glittenberg 1994: 39–40; and Piedrasanta Herrera 1997. Evidence on the serious problem of malnutrition among Mexico's indigenous children can be found in Cruz 2002 and Roman 2003; on Guatemala, see Gonzalez 2002. Kampwirth provides some evidence (a doctor's interview) that younger indigenous women in Chiapas are beginning to use contraception in greater numbers (2002: 88).

105. Rendón 1975: 589–90; Daltabuit et al. 1994: 75; Barrios Ruiz and Pons Bonals 1995: 44–5, 76, 79–80, 119–24; Eber 1995; Rovira 1997: 216–23; Freyermuth Enciso 1998: 78; González 1999; Güémez Pineda 2000: 332; Cosminsky 2001: 201–10; Bossen 1984: 124; García and Gomáriz 1989: I: 249–50; Smith-Ayala 1991: 26, 35–6 n. 28; Cabrera Pérez-Armiñán 1992: 55–6; Fabri 1995: 70; and Hurtado and Sáenz de Tejada 2001.

106. For Maya women's experiences in a variety of settings in Chiapas, see Eber and Kovic 2003; also see Marión 1997.

107. Nash 2001: 58–9, 100–101.

108. While references to the occasional female council member can be found in the ethnographic literature, in general Maya women's formal political participation, during much of the twentieth century, was minimal, though, like Nahua women, through family relationships and the sharing of cargo responsibilities, they carried some political influence (Elmendorf 1976: 16–7, 80; Lazos Chavero 1995: 122–30; Collier 1974; Devereaux 1987: 104; Nash 1993: 127–9; 1995: 16–7; Rosenbaum 1993: 123–42, 157–8, 174; Bossen 1984: 74–8, 99–100; and Ehlers 1990: 38–41, 136–8, 160–2). Also see Ehlers's restudy of San Pedro Sacatepéquez and her discussion of new women's economic activities (2000: xxxix–li).

109. García and Gomáriz 1989: 2:85–6; Hernández Castillo 1997; Castro Apreza 1998; del Valle 1998; Figueroa Mier 1998; Rojas 1999; 2002b; 2002c; Nash 2001: 137–8, 192–5, 247–8; and Speed 2003. On the impact of army and paramilitary terror on children and families during the civil war in Guatemala, see Violencia contra la niñez 1999.

110. On women acting as shields and defenders, see Preston 1998a; 1998b; 1998c; and Mexican General Accuses Bishop 1998. On life in colonias and refugee camps, see O'Brian 1992; Rojas 1994; Rovira 1997: 148–51; and Eber 1999: 14–5. Stephen

2002a: 199–213 includes important testimony from individuals of indigenous communities of eastern Chiapas about the intimidation of women and the long-term impact on all community members of army surveillance. Also see Ortiz 2001: 217–24. On Guatemalan Maya women in Mexican refugee camps during the 1990s, see Sayavedra 2001.

111. Conclusiones al trabajo 1998; Garza et al. 1998; Garza and Hernández 1998; Hernández Castillo 1998: 15; McCaughan 1998; Eber 1999: 14–5; and Nash 2001: 194–5. For a list of the individuals killed, see Ortiz 2001: 191–2. For the responses of the women of Acteal to the massacre, see Morquecho 2000 and Weiser 2001.

112. Zur 1998: 59.

113. Zur 1998; Green 1999.

114. On Ramona and other female EZLN leaders, see Rovira 1997: 199–214; Stephen 2002a: 183–93, 338–9. On the roles and public appearances of female EZLN leaders during the group's visit to Mexico City and address to the national legislature, in March 2001, see Aponte, Becerril, and Pérez Silva 2001 and Las comandantas del EZLN 2001. On Rigoberta Menchú, in addition to her own books (1984, 1998), also see Beverly 1999: ch. 4; Nelson 1999: ch. 5; and Stoll 1999. For analysis of the Menchú/Stoll controversy, featuring both academic comments from a variety of points of view, as well as newspaper articles and columns responding in the aftermath of the *New York Times* article that revealed the conflict to a wider public audience, see Arias 2001. On women's increasing demands for change, see Hernández Castillo 2001: 181–6, 219–24. On the social and economic changes underlying the mobilization of women, see Kampwirth 2002: 90–4.

115. Rovira 1997; Preston 1998a; Eber 1999; Stephen 2002a: ch. 7; and Menchú 1984.

116. Stephen discusses the targeted recruitment of women (2002a: 135). Nash says that some 40 percent of the EZLN's 15,000 soldiers are women (2001: 180). Capozza (1999) and Kampwirth (2002: 90) argue that women make up one-third of the EZLN's membership.

117. English-language versions of the laws can be found in Ortiz 2001: 225–6; Kampwirth 2002: 112–3; Stephen 2002a: 180; or Eber and Kovic 2003: 23. Also see El grito de la luna 1994; Hernández Castillo and Garza Caligaris 1995; Hernández Castillo and Stephen 1999; Indigenous Women's Proposals 1996; N. Harvey 1998: 223–6; Coordinadora Nacional de Mujeres Indígenas 1993; and Nash 2001: 180–1.

118. Laughlin 1991; Freyermuth Enciso and Fernández Guerrero 1995; Eber 1995: 237–9; 1999; Myers 1997; Bedregal 1998; Nelson 1999: 163–9; Petrich 2000; Nash 2001: 178–84, 199–200; and Hooks 1993: 90. Among the relatively few non-Maya examples of indigenous women's activities or groups I have found (though the number of such groups is surely growing) are Mixtec and Zapotec women with ties to the Ejército Popular Revolucionario (EPR, or the Popular Revolutionary Army), a guerilla group operating in a variety of areas of Mexico, as well as the Colectivo de Mujeres Indígenas Tlapanecas (Indigenous Tlapanec Women's Collective; see Gutiérrez 1999, 2000; Rojas 2000a). Brief descriptions of unnamed Nahua groups can be found in Townsend *et al* 1999: 9–10, and Hernández Castillo describes the CNMI (National Coordinating Committee of Indigenous Women), an organization that includes women from at least twenty indigenous communities from throughout Mexico (2002: 42–3). On Mamá Maquín, see Garcia 1996; Returned Refugee Women Gather Strength 2003; and Organización de Mujeres Guatemaltecas "Mamá Maquín" 2003.

119. Schirmer 1993; Hooks 1993: 126–31; Zur 1998: 2, 23–4 n. 6, 185–6; and Green 1999: 105–7. Also see CONAVIGUA's website, which describes their history and major projects, at http://members.tripod.com/CONAVIGUA/.

120. Zur 1998: 147–9; Green 1999: 107–8.

121. Redfield 1950: 134–5; Elmendorf 1976: 4, 119–25; Rosenbaum 1993: 185; Eber 1995: ch. 10; Bossen 1984: 131; and Green 1999: 43–5.

122. Quoted in Ortiz 2001: 38.

123. Velázquez 1987: 311, 323–7; Rovira 1997: 159–64; Collier 1999: 59; Kampwirth 2002: 85–6; Bossen 1984: 106–9; and García and Gomáriz 1989: 1:207, 235–6.

124. Note that figures for Guatemalan women suggest a rate of illiteracy for indigenous women double that of ladinas (Warren 1998: 229 n. 35). The serious problems facing girls and women in obtaining access even to primary schooling, especially in the rural and most indigenous areas of Guatemala, are discussed by Montenegro 1998. For Belize, see McClusky 2001: 198–202.

125. Ehlers 1990: 76–7, 79–80; Glittenberg 1994: 31–2; and Hendrickson 1995: 107.

126. On language change in Xocen and Dzitáas, see Terborg 1996: 122–4, 133. For the beginnings of the shift to Protestanism, see Collier 1999: 56; Green 1999: 150; also see Stoll 1990. An interview with Juárez Espinoza provides an account of her life, the founding of FOMMA, and some of her experiences with the group (Ortiz 2001: 81–8). For an example of the playwriting of Cruz and Juárez, see Juárez Ch'ix and Cruz Cruz 1992. Bautista Vázquez 2003 is another play by a Maya woman, dealing with the problems of contemporary Maya children living in the colonías surrounding San Cristobal de las Casas. On Maya women's photography projects, see Ortiz 2001: 75–9; Snow 2001; and Asociación de la Mujer Maya 2000.

127. Kray 1997: ch. 7; Rosenbaum 1993: 181; Collier 1999: 57; Green 1993: 161; 1999: 156, 160–3; and Bossen 1984: 105.

128. Goodman 2001: 72, 92, 190–1, 493–4; McVey-Dow 1986: 130–1; O'Brian 1994: 76, 108–10; Eber 1995: 221–3; Collier 1999: ch. 2; Kovic 2003: 138–42; Robledo Hernández 2003; Rostas 2003: 178–87; Ehlers 1990: 70–1; and Bastos 1999. The gender hierarchy promoted by Protestant sects contrasts with the traditional role of women in cargos and with the possible naming of female deacons by outgoing Bishop Samuel Ruíz García in Chiapas in January 2000, an act that higher church officials criticized (Rojas 2000b). While Ruíz later denied that he ordained the women, with one investigator (noted historian Jean Meyer) saying that the wives of the deacons participated in the ceremony because this was Maya custom, and with Felipe Arizmendi, Ruíz's successor, saying that journalists misunderstood the blessing of the deacons' wives (Turati 2000; Pensamiento 2000), the inclusion of the women in the ceremony remains significant. Writing on a Zapotec village, Sault demonstrates ways Protestantism reinforces male dominance by undermining women's roles of authority and abilities to function outside the household (2001: 131–5).

129. Hernández Castillo 2002: 41; Kampwirth 2002: 2, 4, 96–8.

130. Mistry 2004.

131. Rohter 1998. For a picture of Maya women confronting Mexican police in the village of Amador Hernádez, see Preston 1999 (and fig. 4.6 here). On the soap opera *Si Tú Supieras María Isabel*, see Gonzáles and Rodríguez 1998. On nineteenth-century Latin American fiction, especially the romanticized yet demeaning portrayal of indigenous women, see Sommer 1991.

5. Fighting for Survival through Political Action and Cultural Creativity

1. 1979: 19. See also 1978: 17.

2. Criticism of stereotypical and negative images of Yanomami women (and men) created by Chagnon and other ethnographers and filmmakers can be found in Ramos 1987 and Tiffany and Adams 1993. A list of the ethnographic films that Chagnon helped make, which were then shown to several generations of U. S. anthropology undergraduates, can be found in Chagnon 1992 [1968]: 257–9. See citations later in the chapter to the works of Mari Lyn Salvador on Kuna women, their clothing, and the textiles they produce that feature many photographic images. Note that for most subsequent endnotes in the first part of this chapter, sources are cited for Ecuador, Peru, and Bolivia and then are cited chronologically for each country. While Web searching was done for newspaper articles, most newspaper citations for the Andean section come from the CD-ROM *Warmi: 25 años de información sobre la mujer en la prensa escrita: 1970–1996*, produced by CENDOC-Mujer, Lima, Peru.

3. Quotations from Weismantel 2001: xxvi (also see 90–104) and Seligmann 1989: 698–703; also see de la Cadena 2000: 220–1; Stephenson 1999: 3–5; Sikkink 2001; Weismantel 2001: chs.1–2; and Paulson 2002: 140–3.

4. Weismantel 1988: 120–2; Crain 1996; Barrios de Chungara 1978: 32–5; and Stephenson 1999: 150–7. Historical and ethnographic overviews of highland and lowland peoples discussed in the first two sections of this chapter can be found in Salomon and Schwartz 1999. Albo (1999: 767) provides population figures for Andean indigenous populations and says that Ecuador, Peru, and Bolivia have native inhabitants numbering 2,564,000; 6,025,000; and 3,526,000, respectively (with Peru's and Bolivia's figures including both Quechua and Aymara peoples).

5. Parsons 1945: 19, 27, 51, 60–1, 184 and Beals 1966: 106. Also see Sikkink 2001: 217.

6. On the enduringly flexible division of labor, see Punín de Jiménez 1975: 559; Stark 1979: 2; Alberti 1986: 72–3; Phillips 1987: 113–6; Belote and Belote 1988: 106; Crain 1991: 83; 1994: 86; and Hamilton 1992: 371–2; 1998: 47–8, 91–3, 110, 145–8, 157–8.

7. On Quimseñas and the Hotel Rey, see Crain 1996. On the impact of increasing male outmigration as well as development projects privileging men as the primary agricultural laborers, see Belote and Belote 1988: 110–2; Poeschel Rees 1988: 108, 112–21; Weismantel 1988: 174–7; 1997: 48–51; Hamilton 1992: 353–4; and 1998: 27–30. For a more positive view, arguing that the expanding nexus of labor and commercial transactions will not disadvantage all rural Ecuadorian women, see Hamilton 1998: 239–42.

8. Babb 1976: 2; Deere 1976: 51–2; and Skar 1979: 455.

9. On the division of labor, see Flores Ochoa 1968: 93; Mayer 1974: 62–4; Núñez del Prado Béjar 1975a; 1975b; Babb 1976: 2–3; Skar 1978; 1979; 1981; Isbell 1978: 56–7; Bourque and Warren 1981: 117–8; Allen 1988: 72–80; Tapia and de la Torre 1993: 19–26; and Bolin 1998: 59, 120–1. Ecuador, especially, has a strong tradition of male involvement in weaving, as men may weave even women's clothes (Parsons 1945: 27, 184; Salomon 1973: 467; Meisch 1987: 76, 80; and Poeschel Rees 1988: 51–2). In other parts of the Andes, a more mixed pattern of both genders spinning and weaving is common, though weaving as a primarily female task has also been reported. For the mixed-gender pattern, see, on Peru, Skar 1979: 455; Allen 1988: 73, 76; Femenias 1991: 187; and Bolin 1998: 119. For Bolivia, see Arnold 1988: 82–3. On

the Quechua generally, see Mishkin 1946: 2: 431. For female predominance in weaving, see Flores Ochoa 1968: 98–9 on Peru. This pattern appears to be most common in Bolivia; see Suárez Guerra 1975: 526; Bastien 1978: 103; and Rivera Cusicanqui 1990: 160–2. For women's participation in public works projects or reciprocal exchanges of labor, see Mishkin 1946: 419–20; D. Hopkins 1988: 179–80; and Bolin 1998: 121.

10. Babb 1976: 8, 34–5; Skar 1978: 58–9; Radcliffe 1985: 97, 99–102; Bunster and Chaney 1989: 31–2; Seligmann 1989: 703, 705; and de la Cadena 2000: 214–5.

11. For indigenous women and agriculture in Bolivia, see Fortún 1972: 938–42; Miranda Baldivia 1975: 312–3; Suárez Guerra 1975: 521, 526; Muñoz 1984: 365–70; Arnold 1988: 82–3; Rivera Cusicanqui 1990: 154–5, 160–2. Both Rivera Cusicanqui (1990: 154–5) and Stephenson (1999: 15–7) point to the exploitative nature of women's labor in agriculture and domestic service on the haciendas. For a Peruvian Quechua-speaking woman's account of her work history and the hard labor involved in hacienda agriculture and urban domestic service, see Valderrama Fernández and Escalante Gutiérrez 1996: ch. 13. A similar pattern of women's domestic service on Ecuador's haciendas (known as *huasicamía*) has also been reported for Ecuador (Phillips 1987: 108). On women in markets, see Mishkin 1946: 2: 435; Buechler and Buechler 1971: 14–7; 1992: 4, 59; Buechler 1997; and Miles and Buechler 1997. See the Buechlers' interesting discussion of *cacera* ties (or semiformalized, commercial relationships) among urban and between urban and rural indigenous women (1971: 16). On migrant women's work in cities, see Medinaceli 1989: 66–7, 87–91; and Gill 1994. On women's labor patterns in mine-working families, see Barrios de Chungara 1978: 32–4, 102–12, 200–201; and Nash 1976: 6; 1979: 86 230, 334. While women's political activities will be discussed further later, see Medinaceli 1989: 94–6, 107–14; and Buechler and Buechler 1992: 217–30, who describe cooperative political strategies.

12. On inheritance in Ecuador's indigenous communities, see Parsons 1945: 38; Beals 1966: 70; Belote and Belote 1977: 106–7; 1988: 105; Stark 1979: 2; Alberti 1986: 96; Poeschel Rees 1988: 43; Hamilton 1998: 64, 202–3; and McKee 1999: 176–7. Stark points out that huasipungo land use rights flowed to and through men, but that land reform has led such lands to be inherited bilaterally, a conclusion Hamilton's more recent research on the impact of land reform reinforces (Stark 1979: 4–5; Hamilton 1998: 202–3). On bilateral inheritance in Peru and Bolivia, see Mishkin 1946: 2: 422, 455–6; Hickman and Stuart 1977: 53; Skar 1979: 454; 1981: 41; Allen 1988: 85; Bastien 1978: 42–3, 115; Nash 1979: 68; and Arnold 1988: 61. Lambert treats bilateral inheritance across the Andes (1977: 9). Some ethnographers find evidence of a parallel inheritance pattern; on Peru, see Isbell 1977: 94; 1978: 79; on Bolivia, see Arnold 1991: 12. On the preference for males as heirs to and owners of land, see for Peru, Babb 1976: 6; Bourque and Warren 1981: 120–1; de la Cadena 1995: 335; on Bolivia, see Buechler and Buechler 1971: 41, 45; and Abercrombie 1998: 341–2. On women and irrigation rights, see Bourque and Warren 1981: 120–1; for women and household management, in Ecuador, see Hamilton 1998: 174. For Peru, see Núñez del Prado Béjar 1975a; 1975b. For Bolivia, see Arnold 1991: 13–4.

13. On kinship systems throughout the Andes, see Lambert 1977. On Ecuador, see Parsons 1945: 33; Beals 1966: 42; Belote and Belote 1977: 106–7; 1988: 106; Poeschel Rees 1988: 64–5; and Hamilton 1998: 64, 142–3, 201. On Peru, see Flores Ochoa on male predominance in descent and kinship among a southern pastoral people (1968: 67–8); and on other rural, indigenous, and what might be termed

"postindigenous groups" (recalling use of this concept for contemporary Nahuas in ch. 4), see Bolton 1977: 222, 224; Babb 1976: 29; Isbell 1978: 79; Bourque and Warren 1981: 99; Skar 1993: 130; and de la Cadena 1995: 335–6. On Bolivia's rural, indigenous families, see Carter 1977; Bastien 1978: 118–9, 193; Arnold 1988; 1991: 7–9, 12; and Abercrombie 1998: 341–2. On patterns of informal relationships and marriage among mining families and urban migrant women, see Nash 1979: 69, 74–5; and Medinaceli 1989: 77–8.

14. On the labor of children and adolescents, see Buechler and Buechler 1971: 24–33. For age at marriage, see Mishkin 1946: 2: 459. On widowhood and women's authority, see Núñez del Prado Bejar 1975b: 625. Also see Hamilton (1998: 198–201) on middle-aged women's authority.

15. On Ecuador, see Stølen 1987; 1991; Poeschel Rees 1988: 101–2; Harrison 1989: 127–35; Sánchez Parga 1990; Hamilton 1998: 106–7; and McKee 1999. While Hamilton hypothesizes that rates of domestic violence are lower in indigenous communities, McKee asserts that they are similar across ethnic and racial groups in the central Andean community of Las Flores, Ecuador. The ethnic makeup of communities and regions may well influence rates of abuse, as Andreas asserts for Peru. She argues that violence toward women is most common in areas where mestizo influence is greatest (1985: 65). Also on Peru, see Bolton and Bolton 1975 and P. Harvey 1994. For a more acculturated community, see Bourque and Warren 1981: 106–9 and on family conflict among urban market women, see Babb 1998: 138. On Bolivia, see Harris 1994. On violence in mining families, see Barrios de Chungara 1978: 49, 59–61; Nash 1979: 77–8. Note also that while female-on-male domestic violence may occur, reports of it are rare (see Harris 1994: 60; and P. Harvey 1994: 75 for examples), and female-on-female violence also is rare and seemingly more associated with markets than any other context (Babb 1998: 161–2). Women may resort to more indirect means, such as witchcraft, to influence male behavior, at least in some areas (P. Harvey 1994: 75). On alcohol, see Sánchez Parga 1990: 42–4; Weismantel 1988: 182; McKee 1999: 180–1; Bourque and Warren 1981: 106; P. Harvey 1994: 71, 83–5; Estremadoyro 2002; and Harris 1978: 34–5.

16. Bolton and Bolton 1975: 33–5. On Andean family life and its repercussions for men, see Sánchez Parga 1990: 40–1. On the role of exploitation and poverty, see Nash 1979: 77–8. McKee (1999: 176–9) makes the argument that the need for men to recover honor is not simply because women have more authority in the household. She finds this need has a material basis as well, because while men often wait for their inheritance, particularly with land, women often receive theirs at marriage. Even if women's holdings are smaller or plots of poorer quality, "a wife's inherited land often constitutes the sole real property claimed by the newly married pair" (177), thus putting men in an economically asymmetrical situation, which, even if only short term, may strain the marital relationship. On concerns over fidelity, see Bolton and Bolton 1975: 34; P. Harvey 1994: 75; and 1998.

17. P. Harvey 1994: 70, 73; 1998: 77–9; Harrison 1989: 129; Harris 1994: 52–8; and Briggs 1995: 32–42.

18. Harris 1994: 41–2; Von Struensee 2002.

19. Quotation from Harris 1994: 60; also see 73; Estremadoyro 2001; along with Asunta Quispe Huamán's description of how, despite fights with her husband in which he hit her and her daughter, "even though we sometimes fight and insult each other, we're doing fine together" (Valderrama Fernández and Escalante Gutiérrez 1996: 129).

20. On sexuality, see Parsons 1945: 53, 60; Carter 1977: 180; Nash 1979: 61; Harris 1980: 78–9; Bourque and Warren 1981: 112; Gill 1994: 74; and Crain 1996: 145–8.

21. Bourque and Warren 1981: 64–5; Andreas 1985: 64–5; Llanos Cervantes 1992; and Guerra García Campos 1995.

22. On birth control see Bourque and Warren 1981: 88–90, 112; Nash 1979: 61–3; Llanos Cervantes 1992: 117–8; Hamilton 1998: 62, 197–8; and Muchos mujeres aún sienten vergüenza 2002. On forced sterilization in Peru, particularly in the years between 1996 and 2000, see Elton 1998; Johansen n.d.; McDermott 2002; and Peru's Apology 2002. Elton (1998) says that "in 1997, state doctors performed 110,000 tubal ligations—up from 30,000 the year before." On husbands and birth, see Bourque and White 1981: 92–3 and Llanos Cervantes 1992: 134. For an example of husbands' support of women's desires for birth control, see Hamilton 1998: 197–8. On women as the primary health agents, see Sánchez Parga 1992: 73.

23. Colque is quoted in Rivera Cusicanqui 1990: 169. On women as curers, diviners, and midwives throughout the Andes, see Buechler and Buecher 1971: 102; Babb 1976: 3; Bastien 1978: 1, 48, 62; Taller de Historia Oral Andina 1986: 31, 47; Poeschel Rees 1988: 77–8; Finerman 1989; and Llanos Cervantes 1992: 127. On male ritual specialists as more powerful, see Poeschel Rees 1988: 79 and Weismantel 1988: 191. Also see Tschopik on the Aymara of Peru and Bolivia (1946: 2: 563–5; 568–70). On office-holders' wives' ritual tasks, see Miranda Baldivia 1975: 515–6; Isbell 1978: 174; Skar 1979: 458; and Arnold 1988: 156. Belote and Belote find that among the Ecuadorian Saraguaro, men and women both sponsor fiestas but do so separately rather than jointly (1988: 107). Rösing has also studied gender identity and ritual, finding a complex system of gender symbolism with many elements of complementarity (2003).

24. On male dominance of formal political structures in Ecuador, see Belote and Belote 1988: 108; Poeschel Rees 1988: 128; and Crain 1994: 87–8. An exception can be found in the community of Chanchaló, studied by anthropologist Sarah Hamilton in the early 1990s, where women make up "independent voting members of the comuna [political community]. They participate equally with men both in public debate, which often concerns community development, and in the labor of community maintenance" (1998: 200). On Bolivia, see Harris 1980: 73. For women and elective office in rural Peru, see Miloslavich Túpac 1999: 93–7, 100; and on Nina Pacari, see Rodas 2003.

25. Bourque and Warren 1981: 151; Crain 1994: 89–92.

26. Albó discusses Cacuango (1999: 803). On the formation of women's groups within organizations, see Belote and Belote 1988: 112–3; Moya 1989: 221–9; Carrere 1997; and Hamilton 1998: 199–200. On women in Ecuador, see Rivera Zea n.d.; Bedregal 2000; El poder indígena 2000; and Rojas 2000c.

27. For an overview of Andean women's political roles, see Lapiedra 1985: 54–9. On women's participation in land reclamations, see Andreas 1985: 56–7 and Radcliffe 1990: 239–40. On women in peasant unions see Andreas 1985: 77–86; Radcliffe 1990, 1993; Mejia et al 1984; Taller de Historia y Participación de la Mujer 1986; Tuya 1987; and León 1990. On women's actions either in support of or, especially in rural areas, in opposition to Sendero, see Castro 1994; del Pino H. 1998: 180; and Coral Cordero 1998: 355–73. For women's support of and participation in worker actions in mining regions, see Barrios de Chungara 1978: 40–2; and Nash 1979: xviii–xix, 13, 113, 242–3. On urban indigenous women and unions, see Babb 1998: 165; Seligmann 1989: 711, 714; 1993: 199, 202; Medinaceli 1989:

94–6, 110–4; Wadsworth and Dibbits 1989: 79, 170–1; Gill 1994: 32–3, 35, 126–9; and Stephenson 1999: 11–2, 129–32. On mothers' clubs in rural and urban areas see Mujeres asumen rol 1992; Seligmann 1993: 201; Coral Cordero 1998: 358–9; Barrios de Chungara 1978: 40–2; and Muñoz 1984: 374, 386–7. On the Micaela Bastidas Community, see "Micaela Bastidas" logró 1991. For women's participation in recent upheavals in Bolivia protesting neoliberalism, and in the process overthrowing President Gonzalo Sánchez Morales in 2003, see Bedregal 2003a; 2003b; and Rivera Cusicanqui 2003.

28. León 1990; Zurita Vargas 2003; and Organizaciones sociales n.d.

29. See Medinaceli 1989: 149–52 on indigenous and elite women discussing feminist politics. Asunta's account of this incident is quoted in Seligmann 1989: 711. Also see the interchange witnessed and described by Linda Seligmann (1993: 189–90) between market woman Elizabeth Anchaya and "upper-class `white' mestiza" Faustina Mendoza in Cuzco's main market; see also Valderrama Fernández and Escalante Gutiérrez 1997: 133.

30. The story of María's and Teresa's competition for leadership in coordinating Peruvian efforts to deal with the thousands of detained and disappeared is told in Muñoz (1998). For discussions of class differences within urban and rural settings and how these affect women, see Bourque and Warren 1981: ch. 6 and de la Cadena 2000: 229–30. On the impact of race within families, see Rivera Zea 1992.

31. For women's committees in rural Ecuador and Peru, see Hamilton 1998: 201 and Bolin 1998: 189, 224. On indigenous women's increased political power as a result of their struggles against Sendero, and especially the formation of active and effective mother's clubs, see Krauss 1999. For cholas' efforts to form a household workers' union in La Paz during the 1980s, see Gill 1994: 126–9.

32. Quotation on parallelism from Abercrombie 1998: 335. Quotation on interdependence from Rivera Cusicanqui 1990: 181. Ethnographers who see egalitarianism, parallelism, and complementarity among Ecuadorian groups include Alberti 1986: 3; Belote and Belote 1988; Poeschel Rees 1988: 102; Harrison 1989: 121; and Hamilton 1998: 27–30, 92–3, and 96–7, though Hamilton sees power and authority more as shared rather than complementary (96–7, 166, 192–4). For Peru, see Núñez del Prado Béjar 1975a: 398; Babb 1976: 8; Isbell 1976; 1978: 206–7; 1997; Allen 1988: 72–8; Skar 1993: 129; and Bolin 1999: 194–5. On Bolivia, see Harris 1978; 1980: 72; Arnold 1988: 3; 1991: 46; and Gill 1994: 25.

33. Quispe quoted in Afirmando la ciudadanía 1998: n.p. Also see McKee 1999: 171–2 on Ecuador; Allen 1988: 81 and de la Cadena 1995: 330, 333 on Peru; and Choque Quispe 1998 on Bolivia.

34. Quotation on Karp from Clemente 2000. On the perception of indigenous women as more indigenous than men (an idea held by both indigenous communities and the wider society), see de la Cadena 1995; and Crain 1996. On how women's clothing often displays their ethnicity, even in urban areas, see in addition to Crain 1996, Gill 1994: 104–6; and Stephenson 1999: 152–6. Sofía Velazquéz, a Bolivian marketwoman who was an important informant for and told her life story to anthropologists Hans and Judith-Maria Buechler, explained that wearing the *polleras* (heavy, pleated skirts of multiple colors, several often worn together) associated with the chola image could make her job of selling easier and help her to be more successful. While the chola identity is more ascribed than achieved, her discussion of what it means to be "de pollera" (wearing the skirt and other clothing associated with cholas) and "de vestido" (the more acculturated urban style) makes it clear that

clothing and its labels refer less to a fixed ethno-racial identity and more to a flexible social role (Buechler and Buechler 1996: 173; also see Forero 2004). On women and indigenous languages, especially in more remote rural areas, see Flores Ochoa 1968: 39 and Bolin 1998: 6.

35. On the impact of development programs in Ecuador, see Alberti 1986: 153–4; Belote and Belote 1988: 110; Poeschel Rees 1988: 108; Hamilton 1992; 1998: 10–1, 24–5, 199. For Peru, see Babb 1976: 18; Skar 1978: 59; and Radcliffe 1993: 204–5. On Bolivia, see Fortún 1972: 943. The impact of male outmigration on women's economic well-being is discussed later. On the impact of the nation-state on rural women's status, especially as use of hospitals and medical doctors becomes more common, see Bourque and White 1981: 110–1. For the dangers of pesticide use for women in a farming community, specifically Chanchaló and the *cantón* (county) of Salcedo in the central Ecuadorian Andes, see Hamilton 1998: 99, 158–9.

36. The best general discussion of the gendered experiences and impacts of migration is to be found in Bourque and Warren 1981: 196–204. On the overall negative impact of male outmigration, see Poeschel Rees 1988: 113–4; and Weismantel 1988: 182–3 on Ecuador. For Peru, see Skar 1978: 59; and Andreas 1985: 61. Hamilton argues, however, that male outmigration does not negatively impact women's household authority and participation in decision-making in Chanchaló, Ecuador (1998: 213–34), though comparing rates of male outmigration may help explain some differences in its impact. On female migrants' experiences, in addition to Gill 1994, see Hamilton 1992; and Zuñiga 1988.

37. On female migration, see Isbell 1978: 180–1; Radcliffe 1985; and Gill 1994: 60–5. For a Peruvian example, see Valderrama Fernández and Escalante Gutiérrez 1996: 112–4. On the lives of young Aymara women in La Paz, see Gill 1994: ch. 3. Arteaga Montero describes urban Aymara women and their struggles with poverty, domestic violence, and efforts to get an education (1990). For a discussion of the high numbers of Mapuche female migrants in Chile, see Rebolledo 1995a and 1995b.

38. Gill 1990: 709–12.

39. Quotation from Gill 1990: 713; also see Gill 1993: 189–90. On Aymara women and the growth of Pentecostalism in La Paz, see Gill 1990; 1993; and 1994: ch. 7. For women's turn to Protestantism in a rural Peruvian Quechua community, see Allen 2002 [1988]: 218–29.

40. On the Saraguaro, see Belote and Belote 1988: 111–2. For negative attitudes toward female education within indigenous communities, see Alberti 1986: 115–8, and Weismantel 1988: 36. On women's lower levels of schooling and literacy, see Poeschel Rees 1989: 77; and Hamilton 1998: 56 on Ecuador. For rural Peru, see Bourque and Warren 1981: 188–90; and Zúñiga 1989: 297–304. On the north-central city and administrative center of Huaraz, Peru, and urban market women's struggles against illiteracy, see Babb 1998: 25–6, 134–5, 148–54. For Bolivia, see Ardaya S. 1989; and Gill 1994: 31–2, 40–1, 120–3; and on South America generally, see Pinella Cisneros 1995; several of the essays in D'Emilio 1989; Hernández and Murguialday 1992: 92–3; and Messina 2001.

41. Stromquist 1992; 1996; also see Zúñiga 1988; Añaños Castilla 1993; and Barrig 2001 for figures on women and literacy for Peru and Bolivia. On rural Bolivian women's educational demands, see Múñoz 1984: 383–4.

42. Quotation from Chagnon 1992: 126. The image of Yanomami women as repulsive had its greatest impact among North American college students and read-

ers of popular science journals, since Chagnon's work has not been translated into Portuguese (Ramos 1985: 299).Two important books that brought greater attention to women's roles were Janet Suskind's *To Hunt in the Morning* (1973, about the Sharanahua of Peru) and Yolanda Murphy's and Robert Murphy's *Women of the Forest* (1974, about the Mundurucú of Brazil).

43. Biocca 1970. A Spanish-language version of Valero's life is both more detailed and told in a far more lively and vivid voice than the Biocca version, yet the Spanish-language version is little cited in the immense English-language literature on the Yanomami (see Valero 1984). Note also Judith Shapiro's criticism of Biocca, saying that he "might have behaved in a manner more appropriate to his role as ghost writer by acknowledging on both cover and title page that the true author of this book is named Helena Valero" (1971: 1333), as well as Tierney's discussion of Valero's life and treatment in the writings of western anthropologists (2000: 91, 244–9). A later edition of the Biocca volume features a jacket blurb from Chagnon and an introduction by Lizot (Biocca 1996).

44. See Nimuendajú 1939; 1979 [1942]; and 1946 on the Apinayé, Timbira, and Xerente of eastern Brazil, respectively; Lowie 1946: 3:30; and Levi-Strauss 1974 [1955]: 288–9, 311–3.

45. Lowland South American ethnography features extensive descriptions of the gender division of labor. In this and other notes, I cite works across the modern nation-states of the region, organized east to west and chronologically, identifying both the specific group and country referred to by the ethnographer at first use, unless the work is comparative. Note also that estimating lowland populations is quite difficult. Using average figures provided by Maybury-Lewis (1999: 875) for seven countries, a total population of just over 1,100,000 is suggested. Among accounts describing female distribution of both plant foods and meat, see Murphy and Murphy 1974: 131–2; Crocker and Crocker 1994: 177–8 (Canela/Brazil); Langdon 1984: 20 (Siona/Peru); Holmberg 1969 [1950]: 126 (Siriono/Bolivia); Jackson 1988: 22 (Tukano/Colombia); Halbmayer 1997: 84–5 (Yukpa/Venezuela-Colombia border); Seymour-Smith 1991: 637 (Jivaroans/Ecuador and Peru); Siskind 1973: 87 (Sharanahua/Peru); and Kensinger 1997: 116 (Cashinanhua/Peru). In the western lowlands, where horticulture plays a greater role and hunting a lesser one, the gender divisions of labor are more flexible, with tasks often overlapping. Due to the extent of market penetration, there are differences in the degree of control over rights to distribution or profits that women maintain (Stocks and Stocks 1984, Candoshi, Cocamilla, Shipibo/Peru; Tizón 1994: 111–5, Ashéninka/Peru). For studies discussing women's craftswork, especially pottery-making and weaving, see Fejos 1943: 113–6 (Yagua/Peru); Girard 1958: 188–9, 234–5; Murphy 1960: 66 (Mundurucú/Peru); Murphy and Murphy 1974: 128–9; Gregor 1985: 25 (Mehinaku/Brazil); Dole 1974: 4 (Amahuaca/Peru); Kelekna 1981: 52–3; Olschewski 1992: 68, 132–6 (Airo-Pai/Peru); and Johnson 2003: 81–4 (Matsigenka/Peru). Whitten shows how pottery production, especially ceremonial pottery, can be a form of self-expression for women, who make, among other items, highly decorated chicha serving bowls called *mucahua*, each of which "tells some secret story relating to the life situation of the maker" (1976: 91; also see Whitten 1981; 2003, Canelos Quichua/Ecuador).

46. While Kloos (1969: 900, Moroni River Caribs/Surinam) emphasizes the existence of a flexible division of labor, most ethnographers of Brazilian lowland peoples, as well as those of the Yanomami of the Brazilian-Venezuelan border region, stress that tasks are conceived of and performed in a gender-segregated way, though

NOTES TO PAGES 146-147

Ramos argues for some interchangability of tasks among Brazil's Sanumá, a Yano-mami group (1995: 30–2). For Brazil, see Murphy 1959: 91–2; 1960: 66, 114–9 (Mun-durucú); Murphy and Murphy 1974: 60–2, 126–30; Gregor 1977: 23–4; 1985: 23–4, 80–1; and on the Bororo, Novaes 1986: 40–3, 100–107. On Yamomami peoples, see Chagnon 1992: 70–1; Shapiro 1972: 127–32; and Restrepo G. 1993: 40–2. For the Barasana peoples of Colombia, see C. Hugh-Jones 1979: 170, 174–80, 200–201 and S. Hugh-Jones 1979: 30–1. Jean Jackson, writing on related Tukanoan-speaking peoples, notes that while hunting is largely a male activity, women can contribute "by relaying information about game noticed en route to their fields or on trips to abandoned fields and longhouse sites to collect fruit" (1983: 46–7). Romanoff (1983) has reported that Matses women of the Peruvian Amazon hunt with their husbands on about half of the daily hunts and that their participation increases hunts' yields. On Jivaroan groups in eastern Ecuador, see Harner 1972: 49–53, 68–9, Kelekna 1981: 16, 41–5; 1994: 228–30; and on the Quichua of Ecuador's Curaray region see Reeve 1988: 40–1, 176–7, 180, 183, especially on women's participation in recipro-cal work groups known as *mingas*. On lowland Peruvian peoples, see Fejos 1943: 103–4; Siskind 1973: 39–40, 73–4, 110–1; Johnson and Johnson 1975: 639, 642–3; and Johnson 2003: ch. 2 on the Matsigenka; and Stocks and Stocks 1984, which com-pares traditional and changing gendered labor patterns among the Candoshi, Coca-milla, and Shipibo. Also on Peru, see Dradi 1987 on the Chayahuita; McCallum 1989: 188–9 on the Cashinahua; and Bellier 1991: 2:56–8, 68, 77, 114–9 on the Mai Huna. For male entry into broader labor and commodity markets, see Murphy and Murphy 1974: 182–3; Whitten 1976: 77; Stocks and Stocks 1984; and Fabián 1994 (Asháninka/Peru), who all suggest greater participation by and control over money-earning tasks by men. The topic of changes in the gender division of labor with integration in global markets, especially outside of lowland Peru, much explored for Mesoamerican and Andean highland peoples, is less explored for lowland peoples, but also see discussion of changes in women's roles hereafter. Whitten discusses agri-culture and men's and women's crops (1976: 38).

47. Quotation from Murphy and Murphy 1974: 130. Also see Turner 1979: 155 (Gê and Bororo/Brazil); Ramos 1995: 30–1; and Lizot 1985: 70 (Yanomami/Brazil).

48. While women and cultural change will be discussed further on in the chap-ter, on self-help projects, see Barclay 1985: 297–9 and Restrepo G. 1993: 53–5. On the socialization of girls into work earlier than boys, see Nimuendajú 1979: 56–7; Murphy 1960: 118–9; Chagnon 1992: 127; and Henley 1982: 73, 83 (Panaré/Ven-ezuela). Gregor suggests that among the Mehinaku, adult women's workday is at least double in length that of men (1985: 23–4; also see Goldman 1963: 58, Cubeo/Colombia and Brazil). Other authors point to the arduousness of women's garden-ing and food-processing tasks. On weeding, see Harner (1972: 52); on chicha prepa-ration (here made from fermented manioc), see Whitten 1976: 82–8. Orna Johnson and Allen Johnson argue, on the other hand, that among the Matskigenka, male work is more demanding both in hours and calorie expenditure (1975: 643).

49. Bant and Basurto 1991: 20; Århem 1998: 101 (Makuna/Colombia and Brazil). For examples of fields and houses flowing from and through women, see Nim-uendajú 1939: 128; and 1946: 59. Among the Xerente, men own the houses and land (Nimuendajú 1979: 35).

50. On the scarcity of Yanomami women and its importance in Yanomami life, see Chagnon 1992: 7–8. Also see Siskind 1973: 77–8; Kensinger 1989; and Men-

tore 1987: 514 (Waiwai/Guiana). For a critique of Amazonian ethnography that deconstructs its "bipolar imaginary," both the "fierce" image as well as the opposite (and not always convincing) "gentle" image, see Santos-Granero 2000 (quoted terms on 268).

51. On the patrilineal structure of many lowland kinship and descent systems, see Shapiro 1987: 302–4; also see Chernela 1993: 73–4 (Wanano/Brazil); and Jackson 1983: 120; 1996: 94–8. For the Tapirapé, a Tupí-Guaraní speaking group of central Brazil, as formerly matrilineal, see Wagley 1977: 99. For matrilineal peoples, see Nimuendajú 1946; J. C. Crocker 1969: 238; 1985: ch. 2; and Novaes (1986: 89). On a lowland cognatic system, see Morton 1983–84: 234 (Waiwai/Guiana), and for examples of lowland bilateral kinship sytems, see Basso (1973: 52) on the Kalapalo of Brazil and Harner (1972: 97).

52. On homosexual relations between Yanamami brothers-in-law, see Shapiro 1972: 106; 1976: 92–3. On affinal and alliance relations, see Chagnon 1992: 160.

53. Yarima's mother is quoted in Good 1991: 64, also see 329–37; Tierney 2000: 252–6; and Jackson 1988: 23.

54. Other groups emphasizing matrilocal or uxorilocal residence include the Tapirapé and Bororo peoples of Brazil (see Wagley 1977: 93 on the Tapirapé and Turner 1979: 158–9 and Novaes 1986: 49 on the Gê and Bororo groups). In Ecuador, lowland groups like the Jívaro and the Achuar also emphasize uxorilocal postmarital residence (Harner 1972: 79; Kelekna 1981: 147). A variety of Peruvian lowland groups practice these female-centered forms of postmarital residence, including the Sharanahua (Siskind 1973: 80), Chayahuita (Dradi 1987: 71), Mai Huna (Bellier 1991: 1:96–7), and Shipibo (Hern 1992: 506), as did the Siriono (Holmberg 1969: 217). Murphy and Murphy (1974: 56–7) and Gregor (1985: ch. 6) discuss men's houses among the Mundurucú and Mehinaku, respectively. Also see Murphy 1960: 80–2 and Murphy and Murphy 1974: 123–7 on collective forms of manioc production and Ferguson 1992: 212 on warfare as factors shaping female-centered domestic units.

55. On the fragility of marriage, see Århem 1987: 138 (Makuna/Colombia and Brazil). Groups with especially young ages at marriage, particularly for prepubescent women (sometimes including the betrothal of female infants) include the Akwê-Shavante of southwestern Brazil (Maybury-Lewis 1967: 88–9); the Yanomamo (Shapiro 1972: 112–3; Lizot 1985: 56; and Ramos 1995: 128); the Achuar, Yagua, Sharanahua, and Amahuaca of Ecuador and Peru (Kelekna 1981: 147; Fejos 1943: 76; Siskind 1973: 77–8; Dole 1974: 19); and the Waiwai of Guiana (Mentore 1987: 515). The settling-down process is well described by Henry for the Kaingáng of southern Brazil (1964: 24–5).

56. Christine Hugh-Jones refers to Vaupés women's "outsider status during adult married life" (1978: 44). Also see Århem 1987: 135. Helena Valero describes how feelings of female solidarity pervade Yanomami life. Even if women's relationships are not emotionally close, they help and protect each other in a variety of ways (1984: 160–5, quotation, on 161). On the unstable and frequently brittle nature of marriage among many lowland groups, see J. C. Crocker 1985: 113–4; Murphy and Murphy 1974: 150–60; Shapiro 1972: 112, 123–6; Ramos 1995: 129–30; C. Hugh-Jones 1979: 93–4; and Harner 1972: 106–7. For an example of a lowland group where more stable, closer marital ties are the norm, see Johnson and Johnson 1975: 637–8; and Johnson 2003: 92–6. Jackson has noted that marriage among Vaupés groups, while it is neither much marked ceremonially nor features deep intimacy that can readily be

observed by outsiders, tends to grow more monogamous and more stable after an initial period in which young spouses may not stay with their initial partners (1983: ch. 7; 1984: 179 n. 7).

57. On the role of parents in marriage decisions, see Murphy and Murphy 1974: 48; Shapiro 1972: 112–3; Chagnon 1992: 122; Jackson 1984: 124–9; and Kelekna 1981: 69. Also see Kelekna 1994: 236–7; Dole 1974: 19; and Shapiro 1987 on the political significance of affinity across the Amazon. On changing marriage patterns, see Murphy and Murphy 1974: 148, 197; Brown 1986a: 136 (Aguaruna/Peru); and Gow 1989: 575 (Piro/Peru). Among the Airo-Pai, the older pattern of bride service and virilocal postmarital residence is more mixed as uxorilocality and neolocality become more common (Olschewski 1992: 126–7).

58. For wife-capture among the Yanomami, see Chagnon 1992: 160–1; Shapiro 1972: 175; and 1976: 94. For the Vaupés, in addition to Jackson's discussion, cited hereafter, see C. Hugh-Jones 1979: 95–6; Århem 1981: 160–1; and 1987: 165–6. For the Aguaruna, a Jívaro group of Peru, see Bant 1994: 85.

59. Quotation from Jackson 1990–91: 35, also see 37–8; Shapiro 1971: 1332.

60. Both Ferguson (1995: 321–2, 338) and Chagnon (1997 [1968]: 238) discuss changes in Yanomami warfare amid a general pattern of decline. See Nimuendajú's discussion of ritual threats of violence toward women intended to intimidate them in 1979: 66–7. Another example of violence as intimidation can be found in Robert Murphy's discussion of rape as punishment, in which he gives the following account:

> Adolescent girls who run away from the school conducted by the Cururú Mission, for example, are frequently apprehended in their flight and raped. All men join in on these occasions, without recognition of clan or moiety affiliations to their victim. One case was related in which a true parallel cousin took part in the rape of a girl who had fled the mission. At the conclusion of the act, he brought her back to the priests with appropriate and sanctimonious comments on the problem of wayward girls. (1960: 109)

Also see Wagley's chilling account of a gang rape of a disabled women suffering from an epileptic attack (1977: 251–2). On violence against women in contexts of racism and the gender hierarchy associated with nation-states and the increasing economic exploitation of tropical rainforest environments, see Muratorio 2001.

61. Murphy 1960: 108–9; Murphy and Murphy 1974: 92–4; Gregor 1985: 100–104; and Jackson 1988: 26–7; 1990–91: 27, 35–7; also see Bamberger 1974.

62. Chagnon 1992: 124–5, 190; Valero 1984: 305–7; also see Shapiro 1972: 117, 180–2; Lizot 1985: 71; and Restrepo G. 1993: 34–5.

63. Siskind characterized Sharanahua male/female relations as "a semi-playful semi-hostile battle" (1973: 108). Reports of violent wife beatings, stabbings, and shootings occur among the Jívaro, Achuar, Amuesha, and Mai Huna. See Harner 1972: 96, 107, 181–2; Kelekna 1994: 238–9; Santos Granero 1991: 238; and Bellier 1991: 1:107, respectively. Tizón has argued that for the Asháninka, physical violence toward wives is relatively rare and is often fueled by alcohol when it occurs (1994: 114). For lowland groups, reports of alcohol-related violence are not as pervasive as in Mesoamerica or highland South America, though it seemed to play a role among some groups, notably the eastern Timbira and Siriono (Nimuendajú 1946: 128; Holmberg 1969: 95).

64. Charles Wagley describes a case among the 1940s Tapirapé of a wife retaliating against her continually unfaithful husband (1977: 163). Even Yanomami women occasionally retaliate, but the brutality with which they are treated is well documented (Ramos 1995: 127, 131). Among the Sharanahua of Peru, women have been known to attack men with stinging nettles, known as *nawawa-kusi*, in retaliation for male misbehavior, but men's greater strength gives them an advantage in ritualized or real violence (Siskind 1973: 98–109). On the role of kin and female leaders in ameliorating the rare cases of violence among the Cashinahua, see McCallum 2001: 115–6.

65. On menstrual seclusion and ceremonies, see Basso 1973: 71–3; Seeger 1981: 114–5 (Suya/Brazil); Donner 1982: 128–9 (Yanomami/Venezuela); Good 1991: 152; Restrepo G. 1993: 28–9; Overing 1986: 148 (Piaroa/Venezuela); Guss 1989: 47–9 (Yekuana/Venezuela); J. Hill 1992: 90–2, 133–53 (Wakuenaí/Venezuela); Reichel-Dolmatoff 1971: 43–4 (Desana/Colombia); C. Hugh-Jones 1979: 134–6; Harner 1972: 92–4; Holmberg 1969: 212; Kloos 1969: 900–902; and Morton 1983–84: 236–7. Bellier points out that in the area of Ecuador she studied, such rituals ceased as of the 1970s (1991: 1:219). Readers should note that critics of Donner 1982 point to the book's extreme subjectivity, and some doubt has been raised about its authenticity (Picchi 1983; Donovan 2003), but in this case her information is in line with that of other sources. On stable unions and children, see Bamberger 1974: 278–9. Maybury-Lewis 1967: ch. 4 provides discussion and examples of both male and female age sets.

66. Useful discussions of heterosexual relations include, on Brazilian lowland peoples, Henry 1964: 19; Maybury-Lewis 1967: 84–5; J. C. Crocker 1969; W. Crocker 1984; 1985 (Canela/Brazil); and Gregor 1973; 1985: 33–5. On the Yanomami, see Lizot 1985. On indigenous groups in Colombia, see Goldman 1963: 30, 182–3; Buenaventura-Posso and Brown 1980: 123 (Bari); and Jackson 1988: 24–5. For Peru, see Siskind 1973: 58, 96–105.

67. For the "special hunts" of the Sharanahua, see Siskind 1973a: 105. For Canela extramarital sex, see Crocker and Crocker 1994: ch. 4. Lizot (1985: 68–9) discusses punishment for Yanomami women taking lovers.

68. 1984a: 395 (Mekranoti/Brazil). On Apinayé "wantons" (*me-kupri-ya*) see Nimuendajú 1939: 81; 1946: 130–1. Da Matta refers to the Apinayé *me-kuprú* as "promiscuous women," though he translates the term literally as either "women of the plaza" or "public women" (1982: 91–2). Also see J. C. Crocker 1969 on "men's house associates" among the eastern Bororo. On negative menstrual and vaginal imagery, see Basso 1973: 63–4; Murphy and Murphy 1974: 94–5; C. Hugh-Jones 1979: 137–8; and Gregor 1985: 160–1.

69. On myths that emphasize men's houses, sacred instruments, and male power over women, see Villas Boas and Villas Boas 1973: 119–21; Murphy and Murphy 1974: ch. 4; Bamberger 1974; Nadelson 1981 (Mundurucú/Brazil); Gregor 1985: 98–105, as well as the many of the essays in Gregor and Tuzin 2001a. This topic is explored further later. On sexuality as pleasurable but disruptive and potentially dangerous, see Brown 1986a: 138. On male appropriation of female creative powers, see S. Hugh-Jones 1979: 185–92, 212–3, 222–6, 250–1; Jackson 1996: 90, 98, 104–5; and Gregor 1985: 198–9.

70. In addition to Holmberg's account of witnessing eight births (1969: 178–92), also see Helena Valero's accounts in Biocca 1970: 160–1 and Valero 1984: 444. Johnson's description of childbirth among the Matsigenka describes how husbands,

extended family members, and close neighbors may provide help during and after a birth (2003: 98–100).

71. Quotation from Brown 1986b: 323. Also see Brown 1986a and Bant 1994: 43–5, as well as Harner 1972: 182–3, on female suicide among the Jívaro and Bellier 1991: 1:159 on the Mai Huna. Halbmayer argues that among the Yukpa, a Carib-speaking people on the Venezuelan-Colombian border, male rates of suicide are higher and reflect men's inability to negotiate marital conflicts, as well as their maintenance of "masculine ideals of ignoring death and demonstrating recklessness in front of a situation of social impotence" (1997: 99–100).

72. Bellier 1991: 1:154–8. Other groups for whom female shamans have been reported include the Kaingáng (Henry 1964: 76), Tapirapé, (Wagley 1977: 187, 197), Canela (Crocker and Crocker 1994: 41–50, 176), Jívaro (Harner 1972: 122; Perruchon 1997: 61–5), and Cashinanhua (Kensinger 1989: 25). The Mai Huna pattern of fewer and less powerful female shamans holds true in all cases except among the Akawaio of Guiana, whose female shamans were reported to be as powerful as the males (Colson 1977: 44). Also see Land 1975: 495; Whitten 1981: 751–61; and 2003: 81–5.

73. On female naming ceremonies, see Werner 1984b: 167–9, 176–81, who also discusses female ritual participation when men return from hunting among the Mekranoti. Yanomami women participate in both intercommunity feasting and mortuary rituals (Shapiro 1976: 97–8; Tierney 2000: 102). Among the Barasana, a female guardian cares for male inititates, bringing them food and water (S. Hugh Jones 1979: 85), and Buenaventura-Posso and Brown describe community singing rituals held by the Bari in which both women and men participate (1980: 120). On women and ceremonial preparations, see Whitten 1976: 169; Dradi 1987: 91–3; and Descola 2001: 99–101. See Muratorio for an interesting discussion of how Napo Quichua women of lowland Ecuador have reinterpreted the Catholic figures of the Virgin Mary and Eve, associating each figure with the importance and power of motherhood as conceptualized in their belief system. The women reimagine the Virgin Mary in particular as a mother of a powerful shaman, because mothers of shamans can "transmit part of their own powers to their sons through breastfeeding" (1995: 327).

74. On the Mundurucú, see Murphy 1960: 120–1. For the Cashinahua, see McCallum 1989: 223–4, 247, 252–6, 265, 279. For a similar description of female leadership patterns among the Kayapo of central Brazil, see Fisher 2001. Also see J. C. Crocker 1985: 87–8 on Bororo women's authority, especially that of dominant women of the matri-centered households who influence household affairs, including coordinating the household's use of male and female labor, but whose broader authority only comes through influencing senior men in community affairs.

75. Basso 1973: 135.

76. On women's societies, see Nimuendajú 1979: 12, 35; and Werner 1984c: 398. On the role of chiefs' wives in the village, see Seeger 1981: 177. Gregor refers to Mehinaku female chiefs but does not elaborate on their roles, except to say that they only deal with matters concerning women (1985: 111). On wives' behind-the-scenes, household-based political influence, see Graham 1995: 145–7, on Brazilian Xavante women's expressions of opinions about community affairs only in domestic contexts; Bellier 1991: 1:148, 151–4, on the Mai Huna; and Anderson 1985, who discusses gender roles and politics across the Amazon. Chagnon 1992: 126; Smole 1976: 82; and Lizot 1985: 71 discuss the political roles of older Yanomami women,

and Ramos argues that Sanumá women can express their views in village meetings and that, while males speak publicly for the family or community, women participate in decision-making (1979: 185–7).

77. Song quoted in Harner 1972: 72. On women's supernatural power and female deities, see Brown on Nugkui, the Aguaruna female deity who "gives life to cultivated plants" (1986a: 105; also see Harner 1972: 70–9). On the association of motherhood with origin in the Siona cosmos, see Langdon (1984: 17). The Siona also believe that shamans, who are men, have a spiritual mother, the Yagé Mother, who appears in visions and from whom shamans must be reborn (17). Jackson notes the existence of powerful female beings, often associated with creation, across the South American lowlands (1988: 30). On Cubeo female love magic, see Goldman 1963: 183.

78. For examples and analyses of many versions of these myths, see Bamberger 1974 (quotation on 275) and Jackson 1988: 30–3. For a particularly dramatic and violent version, see Chapman 1982: 66–70 (Selk'nam/Argentina). On male anxiety, see Gregor 1985: chs. 6–8 and Gregor and Tuzin 2001b.

79. Groups that manifest evidence of egalitarian relations include the Canela (W. Crocker 1985: 191; 1984: 67, 72, 90), Piaroa (Overing 1986), Bari (Buenaventura-Posso and Brown 1980), Sharanahua (Siskind 1973: 108–9), Amuesha (Santos Granero 1986: 124), and Airo-Pai (Olschewski 1992: 67–8, 112).

80. Seymour-Smith (1991) discusses limits on female power. On sexual antagonism see Murphy 1959; Murphy and Murphy 1974: 87–97; Gregor 1985: 22, 93, 131–9, 161–2, 182–3; Kelekna 1994; and Jackson 1990–91. For an example of ways women can contest male dominance, see Descola 1996: 186–9 (Achuar/Ecuador). Anne Chapman discusses at length the antagonism between the genders and the patriarchal worldview of Selk'nam men, a group who lived in Tierra del Fuego in extreme southern Argentina. They did not conform to the patterns of egalitarianism many anthropologists argue exist among hunting, fishing, and gathering peoples, but they were also in extreme crisis, in the process of ceasing to exist as Chapman studied them in the 1960s and 1970s (1982: 60–2, 65, 153–6). Also see Tizón 1994: 106; Kensinger 1997: 109–11; del Pino H. 1998: 169–78 and Manrique 1998: 212–5. The essays in Perrin and Perruchon 1997 discuss limits placed upon gender complementarity in a variety of lowland societies.

81. On change among the Mundurucú, see Murphy 1960: 155–9; and Murphy and Murphy 1974: ch. 7.

82. Ramos 1995: 277. Chagnon discusses the impact of the Brazilian gold rush on the Yanomami in the latest edition of his famous ethnography (1997: ch. 8; also see Brazil: Indigenous Women Abused 1993; and Chernela 2001). For broad overviews of the history and impact of development and modernization has had in the Brazilian Amazon, see Davis 1977; Hemming 1987; Hecht and Cockburn 1989; and Dean 1995. Historical studies that trace the impact of economic and political change on specific groups include Santos Granero and Barclay 2000 and Garfield 2001. Århem 1998: 161–2 discusses gold mining on the Makuna, another Tukanoan-speaking people of the Vaupés region of Colombia. On the actions of the Brazilian army, see Rohter 2002a. On forced sterilization, see Carnell 1999; Johansen n.d.; and Women Stage Demonstrations 2001.

83. Dradi shows women's increasing dependence on husbands for the Chayahuita of north-central Peru (1985: 310–4; 1987: 112–3). On the negative impact of market penetration for women among Peru's lowland peoples, also see Stocks and

Stocks 1984, whose comparison concluded that while some variations could be found in the extent to which women lost control over the sale of products they produced, the general tendency toward decreased autonomy was widespread. Tizón (1984, 1994) reaches a similar conclusion for the Asháninka, who suffered additionally from the impact of the Sendero Luminoso presence in their region, which disrupted family and community economic and social life. Seymour-Smith argues for Jivaroan peoples that

> As trade goods and cash become increasingly important, accumulation as a goal begins to rival redistribution as a source of prestige for political leaders and those seeking leadership. Thus the traditional balance, in Jivaroan societies as least, between the "female" discourse of social harmony and the male discourse of competitiveness, potential conflict and affinity becomes more heavily weighted on the male side. (1991: 643)

Also see Arvelo-Jiménez for a description of the male monopoly on "jobs within the bureaucratic structure created by the Venezuelan government to integrate the Ye'Kuana into the mainstream" (2000: 743). On the concentration of property in male hands, see Tizón 1994: 116–7 for a Peruvian example. Perruchon describes this process across a variety of Ecuadorian Shuar-speaking groups (1997: 50); also see Muratorio 1998: 410–1.

84. On lowland women and education, see Buenaventura-Posso and Brown 1980: 126; Maybury-Lewis 1985: 32 (Xavante/Brazil); Dradi 1989; Lindenberg M. 1989; and Kensinger 1997: 118. The latter finds some increase in the number of Cashinahua women, ages fourteen to forty, who have learned to read and write both their own language and Spanish. For illiteracy rates for Peruvian lowland indigenous women (the only nation for which I could find figures specifically on lowland indigenous women), see Dradi 1987: 98; Fabián 1994: 297; and Rivas 1994: 228 (Cocama/Peru). On the disruptiveness of the last wave of political violence in Peru, particularly for rural schools, see Fabián 1994: 304. Restrepo G. argues that Salesian missionaries have encouraged both boys and girls to attend primary school among the Venezuelan Yanomami of the Ocama, Mavaca, and Platanal zones (1993: 50–2). For newspaper accounts of the violence, disease, health problems, and virtual enslavement caused by the Sendero Luminoso presence among the Asháninkas, see Ejército y marina 1994; Estaban esclavizados 1994; Estaban cautivos 1994; and Mattos 1994.

85. On women's self-help groups, see Lindenberg M. 1989 for Brazil; Restrepo G. 1993: 54–5 on female-centered cooperative projects among Venezuelan Yanomami; and Stocks and Stocks 1984: 73–4; Fabián 1994: 298, 308–10; and Barclay 1985: 297–300 for such activities among Peruvian lowland women. A list of U.S. Agency for International Development (USAID) grants from the Office of Women in Development to women weavers, horticulturalists, and honey producers in lowland Bolivia can be found in "USAID: Women in Development: NGO Small Grants Program: Bolivia" (2002). For Cocama women's lack of access to modern medical care, see Rivas 1994: 235. On the lack of access to modern forms of birth control and health and reproductive education in lowland Peru, see Mujer amazónica 1992. Also see Alderete et al. 1992: 115–21 for a listing of both lowland and highland indigenous women's organizations.

86. Stocks and Stocks 1984: 72–4; La mujer indígena en contextos andino-amazónicas 1990; Mujeres nativas 1990; I Congreso de Mujeres Indígenas 1994;

and Indigenous Women Are Getting Organized 2001 all discuss the first efforts of women from a variety of indigenous ethnicities to promulgate demands and organize meetings. For recent efforts in Brazil to form cooperatives to expand production and marketing of rainforest products, see Rohter 2002b.

87. See Maybury-Lewis 1999 for extensive discussion of the relationship between lowland indigenous communities and the nation-states in which they reside. Patricia Lyon discusses women's loss of traditional forms of social protection even as they gained a bit of autonomy, particularly in marriage choices, and shows how devastating the loss of cultural identity may be for lowland women (1984, Wachipaeri/Peru). The Venezuelan government's refusal to include women in its attempts to empower indigenous communities has helped fuel female outmigration. Their movement to cities is often permanent and strikes at the heart of the ability of Ye'kuana culture to persist, since women have long been charged with safeguarding cultural continuity in times of change (Arvelo-Jiménez 2000: 743).

88. For a brief discussion of anthropological approaches to Central America, see Loveland 1982a. For an overview of the history of indigenous peoples of the region, see Helms 1976b. For more detailed historical accounts, see Gonzalez 1988: chs. 1–3 (Garifuna/Central America); Helms 1971: 14–33 (Miskito/Nicaragua); Falla 1979 (Kuna/Panama); and Howe 1998 (Kuna/Panama). Tice discusses the significance of the term "San Blas," which refers to a region made up of a series of islands inhabited by the Kuna along Panama's northeastern coast (1995: 2–3). Overviews of indigenous peoples of Central America in the second half of the twentieth century can be found in Torres de Araúz 1980; Spahni 1981; and Rivas 1993. It is also the case that while the Kuna are probably related to northern South American native peoples (with some Kuna communities still found in Colombia), this coastal group is one of the largest among Central America's native peoples and offers the greatest contrast with the Mesoamerican and highland and lowland South American peoples already discussed. While reliable population figures for indigenous and Afro-indigenous peoples are hard to come by, the Kuna population is at least 50,000; the Garifuna and Miskito may number as many as 200,000 each. About half of all Garifuna live in Honduras, and three-quarters of Miskitos reside in Nicaragua (Población Indígena n.d.; Holston 1999; Garifuna Community n.d.; Garifuna Settlement and Migration Patterns n.d.; Williams 2001; Languages of Nicaragua 2004; and Miskito People n.d.) Other groups mentioned in this part of the chapter include the Lenca and Tolupan of Honduras, Rama of Nicaragua, and the Embera and Guaymí of Panama. While brief reference is made to Maya women of Belize, Maya women in Guatemala are not covered, nor are Afro-descended peoples of other parts of Latin America, such as maroon communities of coastal northern South America and the Afro-indigenous peoples of Colombia and Ecuador, who are somewhat less studied, especially in terms of gender.

89. Quotations from Miranda 1993: 1–2.

90. Stout, for example, evinces little interest in Kuna women in his 1948 article in the *Handbook of South American Indians*, even though their role as symbol of Kuna ethnic identity had begun to evolve in the 1920s, as the Panamanian government attacked their style of dress and the Kuna practice of holding elaborate female puberty ceremonies (Howe 1998: 147–8, 154–5, 178–81; also see Falla n.d.). Important early ethnographic descriptions of the Kuna include Nordenskiöld 1938 and Puig 1910.

91. For discussion of women as the conservative element transmitting persistent identities among Central American indigenous peoples, see Kerns 1982: 38–9; Rivas 1993: 81; Helms 1970: 205; 1971: 23–4, 109; Kane 1994: 188; Young 1971: 12; Holloman 1975; Swain 1978: 8, 150; and 1989: 88, 102–3. Also see Helms 1976c for a discussion of the long-term impact of male outmigration on these groups from the colonial period on.

92. For discussion of the history of the rise of the female-centered household among the Garifuna, Miskito, and the San Blas Kuna, see Helms 1976c. On Garifuna family forms and women's roles in them, see Gonzalez 1969: 60–77; Kerns 1997 [1983]: 108–29; on the Miskito, see Helms 1970: 199–205; Helms 1971: 24; and on the Kuna, see Nordenskiöld 1938: 28–34; Torres de Ianello 1957: 48; Swain 1978: 96, 105–6; Costello 1982; and Tice 1995: 44–5, 172–5.

93. Useful discussions of the evolving gender divison of labor among the Garifuna can be found in Gonzalez 1969: 32–50; 1988: 28, 108–3, 140 n. 1); and Kerns 1997: 22–34. Christine Loveland's discussion of the impact of market penetration on the Rama of eastern Nicaragua (1982b: 11–2) also applies to the Miskito. For the Kuna, Tice discusses the history and gendered impact of market forces (1995: chs. 4–6). Detailed descriptions of the gender division of labor as it existed in the second half of the twentieth century can be found in Taylor 1951: 55–6 (Garifuna); Kerns 1982 (Garifuna); Kerns 1997: 32–60, 68–73 (Garifuna); Cosminsky and Scrimshaw 1982 (Garifuna); Gamio de Alba 1957: 42 (Lenca); Conzemius 1984 [1932] (Miskito); Helms 1971: 101, 118, 123 (Miskito); Rivas 1993: 416–7 (Miskito); Young 1971: 93, 154–6, 158–9 (Guaymí); Torres de Ianello 1957: 32–3, 37 (Kuna); Tice 1995: chs.4 and 5 (Kuna); and Kane 1994: 132–3, 136–7, 180 (Embera). On adolescent girls and women as petty traders in rural Garifuna villages, see Palacio 1982: 94–101.

94. Though change will be described further later, see the sources cited earlier on the history of the gender divison of labor for a discussion of the impact of market forces. Gonzalez 1988 and Tice 1995 pay particular attention to this issue. For the history of mola making, see Salvador 2003.

95. Tice explains that the change in women's work over the course of the life cycle was caused largely by the commercialization of mola production (1995: 146–7). On Garifuna women's need to earn cash, particularly in the absence of male partners and as they age, see Gonzalez 1969: 50–2; 1988: 110–3; Palacio 1982: 46–8, 78–81; and Khan 1989. It is also important to note that across Central America, women have inheritance rights, usually inheriting from parents (with few bequests between spouses), but inheritance may not be the most common way of gaining property rights, and male access to the most valuable forms of property—especially land—is usually greater (Kerns 1997: 76; Young 1971: 96; Kane 1994: 86–7; Torres de Ianello 1957: 42–3; Salvador 1978: 6; Swain 1978: 108–9; and Stier 1982: 525).

96. On Maya women and family life in Belize, see McLaurin 1996: 41–6, 66–8. On the Guaymí, see Young 1971: 126, 140, 172–4. While Garifuna men and women own houses, few own land (Kerns 1997: 76). Guaymí and Embera women have property rights through inheritance, but these are reported to be weaker than men's (Young 1971: 96; Kane 1994: 186–7, 214 n. 11). Women's property rights are extensive among the Kuna, as they own houses, land, shares in the mola cooperative, and gold jewelery, yet men have an advantage in land ownership, and female migration may weaken women's inheritance of houses (Torres de Ianello 1957: 43; Holloman 1976: 137–8; Salvador 1978: 6; Costello 1982: 86; and Stier 1982: 525).

97. For discussion of domestic abuse among the Garifuna, see Gonzalez 1969: 63; Kerns 1997: 79; 1992a; Miranda 1993: 6; McLaurin 1996: 4, 37, 80–1, 83–4, 102–3; and Gargallo 2000: 95–6. Belize and other Central American countries passed legislation criminalizing domestic violence, making it easier for women to seek help from police or judicial authorities. For Belize, see McLaurin 1996: 187, 189–90, 204 (note. no.1). For legislation passed in Costa Rica, El Salvador, and Nicaragua, see Cancel n.d.; also see Villanueva 1999; Human Rights 1999; and En la casa 2000.

98. Kerns 1997: 91.

99. For middle-aged Garifuna women's enforcement of a moral code, see Kerns 1992b: 97. Belizean Maya women marry around age fourteen, and Garifuna women begin to have children in their later teen years, with most having their first child by age twenty (Kerns 1997: 98–9).

100. For Moravian missionaries among the Rama, see Loveland 1982b: 9–10, 19. On the Miskito, see García 1997: 209–12.

101. Tice 1995: 73; also see Sherzer and Sherzer 1976: 28–9.

102. Quotation in Tice 1995: 74.

103. Rivas discusses the health conditions of indigenous women in Honduras (1993: 469–70). His comments are applicable generally to native peoples across Central America. For health conditions among the Garifuna of Honduras, see Rivas 1993: 275–8. For the Lenca, see 121–30. In addition, the Lenca suffer from high rates of alcoholism, which affect both men and women. On alcoholism among younger Garifuna men and older women, see Gonzalez 1988: 186–7. On the Miskito of Nicaragua and Honduras, see Flores Andino 1975: 569–70; Rivas 1993: 442–3; and Gonzalez 2001. On Panama's Kuna population—generally healthier than other Central American groups—see Swain 1978: 212, 219–20; and 1982: 108. For recent attempts by Planned Parenthood to provide both educational and reproductive health–related services to Nicaraguan coastal indigenous and Afro-indigenous peoples, see Planned Parenthood Family Planning 2001.

104. Dennis 1985: 293–8; and García 1997. Spirit possession also occurs among the Garifuna, again primarily among young women, but it takes place as an accepted part of ancestor-focused ritual (Taylor 1951: 122–4; Ghidinelli and Massajoli 1984: 512; and Gonzalez 1988: 89).

105. Swain (1978: 211–2) discusses Kuna midwives and birth attendants. She finds that children's mortality rates decreased in Ailigandi because of the Children's Feeding Center, where the community's congresos requires that children under the age of six be fed (1982: 108). Female curers are reported for the Garifuna of Belize, Guatemala, and Honduras (Kerns 1997: 160–1; Gonzalez 1988: 85–6, 89); the Lenca of Honduras (Nuñez 1975: 567); and as "seers" (nele), or diagnosticians, though not curers, among the Kuna (Stout 1947: 32 and Sherzer 1983: 60–1). Rivas notes that AIDS was beginning to spread in Garifuna communities, a development likely to affect other Central American indigenous peoples, especially coastal communities, where men and women come and go with great frequency and among whom knowledge about or willingness to engage in safer sexual practices is low (1993: 278); also see Miranda 1993: 6. On midwives among the Garifuna of Belize, see Cosminsky 1970: 108.

106. On change in the gender makeup and roles of Garifuna practitioners, compare Taylor 1951: 110, 117–8, 122 to Kerns 1997: 150–87. Also see Coelho 1981 [1955]: 146–52 and Gonzalez 1988: 85–94.

107. Howe 1986: 131. Note also that a birth inna of one day's duration used to be performed but no longer is on most islands (Tice 1995: 30). On women's subordinate roles in Miskito community feasting and in Moravian congregations, see Helms 1971: 106, 202–3.

108. The quotation describing Kuna ceremonial preparations is in Alderete et al. 1992: 83. On inna ceremonies, see Stout 1948: 262; Torres de Ianello 1957: 51–2; Swain 1978: 117–22; Sherzer 1983: 147–52; Howe 1986: 131–2; and Tice 1995: 29–30. For a discussion of Mu, a Kuna female creator deity, see Stout 1947: 40–1. On men financing others to perform innas, see Sherzer 1983: 153.

109. For Garifuna's women's roles of authority, see Kerns 1997: 67, 194–5; and 1992b: 97, 106–7. For rural Nicaraguan women, see Pérez Aleman 1990: 28–9, 31–2; and Babb 2001: 214.

110. Sherzer 1983: 72–90.

111. Nordenskiöld 1938: 54; Sherzer 1983: 104; Howe 1986: 47; and Swain 1989: 97.

112. Tice 1995: 20–1.

113. Helms 1981; Sherzer 1983: 70.

114. On the Miskito, see Helms 1971: 97, 109. Also see Young 1971: 12–5, 18–9 on Guaymi women and Loveland on the long-term impact of missionary discourse on Rama women (1982b: 19). Rivas (1993: 83–7) discusses Lenca women's status. On the higher social status of Garifuna men, see Gonzalez 1969: 62–3. On the autonomy and role of women in social control and societal well-being, see Kerns 1997: 191–4 and 1992b: 106–7. For a comparison of Maya and Garifuna women that argues that Maya women are much more subordinated, see Cosminsky 1970: 118.

115. Brennan argues that Kuna men see women as "slightly less intelligent" than themselves (1973: 61); also see Sherzer and Sherzer 1976: 31; and Howe 1986: 29, 62, 230–1. On achieved and ascribed statuses, see Stout 1947: 31–3; and Swain 1978: 143–50. For traveling, see Tice 1995: 175.

116. Ethnographers who emphasize the relatively higher status of Kuna women include Nordenskiöld 1938: 40; Torres de Ianello 1957: 3, and Howe 1986: 29, though Howe also points to women's subordinated public role. The quotation is from Howe and Hirschfeld 1981: 299.

117. For an overall assessment of the impact of change on indigenous Central American women, see Loveland 1982a. For discussion of the impact of Protestant missionaries in the nineteenth and twentieth centuries, see Loveland 1982b: 4, 9–11; and Miranda 1993: 4. On the negative impact of change on specific groups, see Miranda 1993 and Gargallo 2000 on the Garifuna. On the Lenca, see Rivas 1993: 82–6; on rural Nicaraguan women generally, see Pérez Alemán 1990: 23; on the Rama, see Loveland 1982b; on the Guaymí and Embera, see Bort and Young 1982 and Kane 1994: 183–9, respectively; on the Kuna, see Stout, who documents the negative impact Panamanians had on Kuna women's lives early in the twentieth century (1947: 85–6). For contemporary Kuna women and change, see Costello 1982; Swain 1978: 158–9, 182–3, 219–41, 257–9; 1982; 1989; and Tice 1995: 52–3, 170–85.

118. For Garifuna women's increased ritual role, see Kerns 1997: 187–9; and on a Garifuna female student leader, see Hooks 1993: 105–8. For Miskito women and change, see Helms 1976c: 147–8; on Kuna women and new occupations, see Swain 1978: 225–6, 257–9; and Costello 1982: 85–6. For changing Kuna family structures, see Tice 1995: 171–5. On other aspects of change for Kuna women, see Tice 1995:

chs. 8–10. Also see Costello's discussion of female migration to urban areas and the changes in work and education patterns for women that result (1982: 71–4, 82–6).

119. For indigenous women's illiteracy and lack of access to schooling, see Rivas 1993: 466–7. Also see McLaurin 1996: 104 on Belizean women's lack of access to secondary education. For Nicaragua and Panama, see Flores Andino 1975: 570 on Miskito women's virtually total lack of access to primary education and Young 1971: 18 on Guaymí women's illiteracy and monolingualism. On the Kuna, see Stout 1947: 88–90; Swain 1978: 110, 200–202; 1982: 111–2; Costello 1982: 71–3; and Howe 1986: 230.

120. Hirschfeld 1977: 111; Salvador 1978: 10–1; Swain 1989; and Tice 1995: 184–7. Also see Wright 1995: 254–8, who discusses the Miss Garifuna beauty pageants that have become a popular vehicle for the celebration and bolstering of Garifuna ethnic identity and observes that they highlight "ethnic knowledge" over beauty.

121. Tice 1995: 101–3. Also on the early history of the Kuna mola cooperative, see Hatley 1976: 75–8; and Swain 1989: 95–6. Brennan explains how the *sociedad* (voluntary association) structure organizing labor and the accumulation of capital laid a basis for the formation of the mola cooperative (1973: 91–2, 105–6).

122. Quotation from Swain 1989: 96–7; also see Alderete et al. 1992: 83–6; Tice 1995: 107–14; and Machlis 1998. The Web address is www.peoplink.org. The bookkeeper is quoted in Jeffrey n.d.

123. On Garifuna efforts to form cooperatives and other groups, see Kerns 1997: 204; and Rivas 1993: 302, 309. ASOMUGA: Antecedentes 2003 discusses the Association of Guatemalan Garifuna Women, founded in 1997, which focuses on sexual abuse, alcohol and drug addiction, AIDS prevention, and strengthening identity. Tolupan and Lenca women in Honduras have been active in organized activities that expand on women's traditional concerns over health and literacy, as well as in peasant groups acting to defend land rights (Rivas 1993: 135–7, 463–4; Indígenas exigen 1998; also see Collinson 1990: 180–5).

6. Indigenous Women

1. Grandin 2004:139.

2. In addition to the discussion of Chiapas women's political activism in chapter 4, on highland Maya women's willingness to question tradition, see Hernández Castillo 1995; Ortiz Elizondo and Hernández Castillo 1996: 64–5; Hernández Castillo 2001: 219–24; and Stephen 2002a: 195–6. For the radio station takeover by thousands of women, many indigenous, see Zapatista Women Briefly Take Mexican Radio Station 2000, as well as Por su contribución 1999, an article describing the work of five Guatemalan indigenous women to create radio programming for women, children, and Guatemalan refugees living on the Mexican side of its border with Guatemala. For examples of indigenous women's local and regional activism and leadership in highland and lowland Ecuador, see Mujeres contracorriente 1998.

3. COMPITCH's organizing statement (Reglamento COMPITCH 2002) can be found online at: www.laneta.apc.org/sclc/noticias/compitch-reglamento.htm. Discussions of the group's formation, and especially their successful struggle against the ICBG Maya project, can be found in Galán 2001; Belejack 2001; and Weinberg 2001. On the August 2002 conference, see Rosen 2002: 7. Also see Ferrer 2004, who describes a group of Zenú women of northern Colombia who started an organization to grow and market medicinal plants.

4. Jiménez quotation in Rojas and Pérez 2001. Also see Gargallo 2001.

5. Rojas 2003b. Also see Gómez Mena 2002 on multiethnic groups that include indigenous and nonindigenous Mexican women that work to strengthen women's land rights.

6. For Guatemala, see González Moraga 2001; Quirós Robinson 2000; and Mujeres instalarán Tribunal 1999. For Costa Rica, see Rodríguez Lobo 1998. On the Ecuadorian Amazonian women's conference sponsored by the Regional Coalition of Women of the Ecuadorian Amazon, see 50% de los miembros del CONFENIAE son mujeres 1996; also see Ecuador: las mujeres en el levantimiento indígena 2001. ANMUCIC's origins is discussed in Deere and León 2001a: 86, 192-8; also see Asociación Nacional de Mujeres Campesinas, Negras e Indígenas de Colombia n.d.; S.O.S. por mujeres campesinas 2003; and Colombia: Abduction and Torture of Black Women Activists 2003.

7. On congresses in Peru, see Pronunciamiento de las mujeres indígenas del Peru 1999; and Seminario de mujeres indígenas 1995. For Chile, see Reuque Paillalef 2002: 230, who discusses Keyukleanyñ Pu Zomo; Richards 2003; and Marín 2004, who describes a variety of Mapuche women's groups and female leaders.

8. Beijing Declaration of Indigenous Women 1995.

9. Encuentro de mujeres indígenas 1991; Boves 1998; Olowaili Declaration 2000; Alvarez et al. 2002; Nicholas-MacKenzie n.d.; and Rojas 2003c.

10. On Cacuango, see Albó 1999: 802-803; Ayala Marín n.d.; and En Ecuador, raíces vivas n.d.

11. On indigenous women's participation in Guatemalan politics generally, see Jimeno 2001; n.d. On Tuyuc, see Brigadas Internacionales de Paz: un trabajo de conciencia n.d.; Guatemala Day of Action n.d., and L. Hernández 2000. On Lux de Cotí, see Truth Commission Asks More 1998; Palabras de la comisionada Otilia Lux de Cotí 1999; Molina Mejía 2000: 11; and Discurso de la Licenciada Otilia Lux de Cotí 2002. For Menchú's new governmental role, see Llorca 2004; and Peace Role for Guatemalan Activist 2004. For testimonies by a variety of Maya and non-Maya activists, see Stoltz Chinchilla 1998.

12. Quotation from Galvéz in Pantin 2002; also see de la Torre 2001. On Arpasi, see Paulina Arpasi: primera vez 2001; Perú: campesina al Congreso 2001; La Franchi 2001; and Ugaz and Fernández Stoll 2002. For Pacari and Loza, see Fraser 2001. On Cunningham, see Acciones de los estados 2001; Giving Voice to Indigenous People 2002; and Cunningham 2001. For Ortega, including the quotation, see Forero and Rohter 2003. Bunster discusses the life history of a female Mapuche leader particularly active on the issue of land rights (1976).

13. Martin 1998: 564; also see Re Cruz 1998.

14. Cervone 2002: 184, quotation on 192.

15. Deere and León 2001a: 184-5; 2001b: 31-3. On efforts by Latin American governments to recognize legally the variable cultures and ethnicities, especially indigenous, within many countries, see Stavenhagen 1988; Stavenhagen and Iturralde 1990; and Sánchez 1996.

16. Deere and León 2001a: chs. 5-7 (see especially 174-8, a discussion of Bolivia's 1996 Ley INRA [Law, National Institute of Agrarian Reform]); Deere and León 2001b.

17. For overviews of the problem of domestic violence across Latin America, see Facts about Gender-Based Violence 1998; En la casa 2000; Susskind 2000; Creel 2001; and Making Violence against Women Count 2004. For information on legis-

lation and social programs, see Legislaciones n.d.; Human Rights Practices for 1998 Report: Bolivia 1999; Ley Integral 2002; and Alméras et al 2002. For the problems of rape and prostitution as these affect indigenous women, see Cameron 1996; Susskind 2000; Campbell 2001; Von Struensee 2002; Declaration from the First Indigenous Women's Summit 2002; Kelly 2003; Levine 2003; and Indigenous Women Today 2004.

18. Deere and León 2001a: 236–63; Cervone 2002; and Radcliffe 2002. For a Mexican example relating to the way women's concerns expressed at the local level do not get addressed at higher levels, see Lynn Stephen's account of the development of the 1996 proposals by the Commission on Concord and Pacification (COCOPA) and endorsed by the EZLN (2002a: 196–7).

19. Quotation from Barrios de Chungara 1978: 199. She also gives an account of her interchanges with Betty Friedan and two unnamed Mexican delegates, to whom Barrios de Chungara pointed out the class differences among women and the need for feminists to pay more attention to the struggles of men, women, and families in the world's poorer countries (201–4). Rigoberta Menchú also expressed doubts about the wisdom of indigenous women focusing solely on women's issues (1984: 221–2) but evinces more sympathy in her second memoir for women's issues, especially the problem of violence against women during times of war (1998: 179–81). For Mapuche women and SERNAM, see Richards 2003: 50–1. For a general analysis of the complexities of women's politics in late twentieth-century Latin America, see Alvarez 1998.

20. Eber and Kovic 2003 describe this process for Chiapas, but the many sources of testimony and oral history used in chapters 4 and 5 show that women are creating their own historical record in many parts of indigenous Latin America.

21. Catinac Xom quoted in González Moraga 2001. On the worldwide impact of globalization on women's work patterns, see *A Fair Globalization* 2003: 165–5; and Milmo 2004. On the global scale of women's activism, apart from many sources consulted in chapters 4 and 5, see Benería 2003: 164–5; and Desai 2002.

BIBLIOGRAPHY

Documents, Chronicles, and Codices

Dates in brackets represent either approximate date of composition or first publication.

Alva, Bartolome de. 1999. *A Guide to Confession Large and Small in the Mexica Language 1634.* Edited by Barry D. Sell and John Frederick Schwaller, with Lu Ann Homza. University of Oklahoma Press, Norman [ca. 1634].

Alva Ixtlilxochitl, don Fernando de. 1975–77. *Obras históricas.* 2 vols. Edited by Edmundo O'Gorman. UNAM, Mexico City [ca. 1600–1640].

Archivo General de la Nación (Mexico), Tierras. Land documents cited as AGNT by file and case number.

Clavijero, Francisco Javier. 1976. *Historia antigua de México.* Editorial Porrua, Mexico City [1780–81].

Cobo, Bernabé. 1890–95. *Historia del Nuevo Mundo.* 4 vols. E. Rasco, Seville [1653].

Codex Azcatitlán. 1949. *Códice Azcatitlan.* Société des Américanistes, Paris [16th century].

Codex Mendoza. 1992. *Codex Mendoza.* Edited by Frances Berdan and Patricia Anawalt. 4 vols. University of California Press, Berkeley [1542].

Codex Selden. 1964. *Codex Selden 3135 (A. 2).* Sociedad Mexicana de Antropología, Mexico City [mid–sixteenth century].

Codex Telleriano-Remensis. 1995. *Codex Telleriano-Remensis: Ritual, Divination, and History in a Pictorial Aztec Manuscript,* by Eloise Quiñones Keber. University of Texas Press, Austin [ca. 1562].

Códice Osuna. 1947. *Códice Osuna: Reproducción facsimilar de la obra del mismo titulo, editada en Madrid, 1878.* Ediciones del Instituto Indigenista Interamericano, Mexico City [ca. 1560s].

Colección de documentos para la historia de la formación social de Hispanoamerica, 1493–1810. 1953–62. Compiled by Richard Konetzke. 3 vols. Consejo Superior de Investigaciones Cientificas, Madrid.

Colección de documentos para la historia de México. 1858–66. Edited by Joaquín García Icazbalceta. 2 vols. J. M. Andrade, Mexico City.

Díaz del Castillo, Bernal. 1955. *Historia verdadera de la conquista de la Nueva España.* 2 vols. Editorial Aramor, Mexico City [1568].

Durán, fray Diego. 1967. *Historia de las indias de Nueva España y islas de tierra firme*. 2 vols. Editorial Porrua, Mexico City [1581].

El grito de la luna (Documento del taller—Los Derechos de las Mujeres en Nuestras Costumbres y Tradiciones). 1994. *Ojarasca* 35(6): 27–34.

Estas son las leyes que tenían los indios de la Nueva España. 1941. In *Nueva colección de documentos para la historia de México, Pomar-Zurita-Relaciones Antiguas (Siglo XVI)*. Edited by Joaquín García Icazbalceta. Editorial Salvador Chávez Hayhoe, Mexico City [1543].

Florentine Codex. 1950–82. Compiled by fray Bernadino de Sahagún. Translated and edited by Arthur J. O. Anderson and Charles E. Dibble. No. 14, 13 pts. School of American Research and University of Utah Press, Salt Lake City [1569].

Fuentes para la historia del trabajo en Nueva España. 1939–46. Edited by Silvio A. Zavala and María Castelo. 8 vols. Centro de Estudios Historicos del Movimiento Obrero Mexicano, Mexico City.

Gadow, Hans. 1908. *Through Southern Mexico: Being an Account of the Travels of a Naturalist*. Scribner's, New York.

Guaman Poma de Ayala, Felipe. 1980. *Nueva crónica y buen gobierno*. Edited by John V. Murra and Rolena Adorno. 3 vols. Siglo Veintiuno, Mexico City [1613].

Indigenous Women's Proposals to the National Indigenous Congress. 1996. *Cultural Survival* (spring): 52–3.

Landa, fray Diego de. 1985. *Relación de las cosas de Yucatán*. Edited by Miguel Rivera. Historia 16, Madrid [1566].

López de Cogolludo, fray Diego. 1971. *Los tres siglos de la dominación española en Yucatan o sea historia de esta provincia*. 2 vols. Akademische Druck-u. Verlagsanstalt, Graz [1654].

López de Gómara, Francisco. 1943. *Historia de la conquista de México*. 2 vols. Editorial Pedro Robredo, Mexico City [1552].

Millares Carlo, A., and J. I. Mantecón. 1945–46. *Indice y extractos de los Protocolos del Archivo de Notarías de México, D.F.* 2 vols. El Colegio de México, Mexico City.

Motolinía, fray Toribio (de Benavente). 1971. *Memoriales o libro de las cosas de la Nueva España y los naturales de ella*. Universidad Nacional Autónoma de México, Mexico City [1541].

Muñoz Camargo, Diego. 1986. *Historia de Tlaxcala*. Historia 16, Madrid [ca. 1576–95].

Murúa, fray Martín de. 1946. *Historia del origen y genealogía real de los reyes incas*. Edited by Constantino Bayle. Consejo Superior de Investigaciones Científicas, Instituto Santo Toribio de Mogrovejo, Madrid [1590].

Newberry Library. Testaments from the Ayer Collection. Cited by MS number.

Nuttall, Zelia. 1975. *Codex Nuttall: A Picture Ms. from Ancient Mexico: The Peabody Museum Facsmile*. Dover, New York [1902].

Pomar, Juan Bautista. 1891. Relación de Tezcoco. In *Nueva colección de documentos para la historia de México*, edited by Joaquín García Icazbalceta, 3 vols., 3:1–69. Imprenta de Francisco Díaz de León, México City [1582].

Relación del sitio del Cuzco y principio de las guerras civiles del Perú hasta la muerte de Diego de Almagro. 1879. In *Colección de libros españoles raros ó curiosos* 13:1–195. Imprenta de M. Ginesta, Madrid [1539].

Sarmiento de Gamboa, Pedro. 1947. *Historia de los Incas*. Biblioteca Emece, Buenos Aires [1572].

Torres de Laguna, Juan. 1983. *Descripción de Tehuantepec.* H. Ayuntamiento Popular, Juchitán, Oaxaca [1580].

Tozzer, Alfred M. 1941. *Landa's Relación de las cosas de Yucatan.* Peabody Museum Papers, vol. 18. Peabody Museum of Archaeology and Ethnology, Cambridge, Mass. [1566].

Newspapers, Websites, and Listservers

Note: The Mexican newspapers *Excelsior, La Jornada*, and *Reforma* were researched on the Web; they are available online at the following addresses: www.excelsior. com.mx, www.jornada.unam.mx, and www.reforma.com. The Peruvian newspaper references primarily come from the the CD-ROM *Warmi: 25 años de información sobre la mujer en la prensa escrita: 1970–1996*, produced by CENDOC-Mujer, Lima, Peru, and include articles from *Cambio, El Comercio, El Peruano, Reforma, La República*, and *VSD* (a magazine published with *La República*). Note also that while most newspapers were consulted through their websites or the Warmi CD-ROM, the print editions of the *New York Times* and *Houston Chronicle* were used. For newspaper citations from the web, I give only the date of publication..

50% de los miembros del CONFENIAE son mujeres y tenemos nuestra propia voz: El Primer Congreso de Mujeres de la Amazonia. 1996, September 17. CONFENIAE. Available online at: www. unii.net/confeniae/espanol/mujeres. Accessed May 25, 2002.

Acciones de los estados fomentan la desintegración social y cultural. 2001, March. *Women's Human Rights net.* Available online at: www.whrnet.org/wcar_es/key_docs/foro_americas.htm. Accessed October 18, 2002.

Aguirre, Aleyda. 2003. Prevenir mortalidad de madres indígenas obligacíon del Estado: Kinal y CNMI. *La Jornada*, Triple Jornada section, June 2.

———. 1999. El personal de salud maltrata y desprecia a las indígenas: Cándida Jiménez, promotora de derechos de las mujeres. *La Jornada*, Triple Jornada section, November 1.

Alméras, Diane, Rosa Bravo, Vivian Milosavljevic, Sonia Montaño, and María Nieves Rico. 2002. Violencia contra la mujer en relación de pareja: América Latina y el Caribe. Una propuesta para medir su magnitud y evolución. *CEPAL/ECLAC: Unidad Mujer y Desarrollo*, June. Available online at: www.eclac.cl/publicaciones/UnidadMujer/4/LCL1744/1c/1744e.pdf. Accessed June 24, 2004.

Añaños Castilla, Norma. 1993. La mujer campesina. *El Comercio*, March 7.

Aponte, David, Andrea Becerril, and Ciro Pérez Silva. 2001. *La comandanta Esther* dio a conocer cuatro puntos que allanan el camino para el diálogo. *La Jornada*, Política section, March 29.

Asociación Nacional de Mujeres Campesinas, Negras e Indígenas de Colombia. n.d. *Iniciativa de Mujeres Columbianas por la Paz.* Available online at: www .mujeresporlapaz.org/article.php3?id_article=15. Accessed June 29, 2004.

ASOMUGA: Antecedentes. 2003, October 1. *Asociación de Mujeres Garífunas Guatemaltecas.* Available online at: www.geocities.com/asomugagua/spa-ASOMUGA .htm. Accessed June 8, 2004.

Ayala Marín, Alexandra. n.d. El protagonismo de las indígenas: Gran paralización de protesta contó con la decidida participación de las mujeres indígenas. *Mujeres en ed.* Available online at: www.nodo50.org/mujeresred/ecuador-indigenas.html. Accessed October 23, 2002.

.linas, Victor. 2000. Con graves carencias sociales sobrevive 66.5% de la población. *La Jornada*, section. Primera Plana, February 26.

arrera, Lourdes. 1999, February 2. La falta de espacios de expresión para las mujeres indígenas, tema de *Frontera Sur: El retorno de lo reprimido.* CONACULTA. Available online at: www.jmvelasco.cnart.mx/cnca/nuevo/diarias/220299/220299 .html. Accessed November 2, 2000.

Bedregal, Ximena. 2003a. "De revolución hablan pero sigue la escalvitud hacia las mujeres." Interview with Florentina Alegre. *La Jornada*, Triple Jornada section, November 3.

———. 2003b. Indias, mineras, amas de casa, feministas, putas, "hemos estado al frente todos los días." *La Jornada*, Triple Jornada section, November 3.

———. 2000. De Seattle a Quito: [Las] campañas suenan! El protagonismo de las indígenas ecuatorianas. *La Jornada*, Triple Jornada section, February 7.

———. 1998. Teatreras y escritoras indígenas reconstruyen su mundo. *La Jornada*, Doble Jornada section, November 2.

Beijing Declaration of Indigenous Women. 1995, September/October. *Third World Network.* Available online at: www.twnside.org.sg/title/indig-cn.htm. Accessed September 25, 2002.

Belejack, Barbara. 2001. The Professor and the Plants: Prospecting for Problems in Chiapas. *Texas Observer*, online ed., June 22. Available online at: www.texas .observer.org/showArticle.asp?ArticleID=22. Accessed on October 16, 2002.

Boves, Paloma. 1998. II encuentro continental: Asumen las indígenas la forja de su propio destino. *La Jornada*, Doble Jornada section, January 5.

Brazil: Indigenous Women Abused. 1993. *NativeNet.* Available online at: http:// nativenet.uthscsa.edu/archive/nl/9306/0039.html. Accessed May 15, 2003.

Brigadas Internacionales de Paz, Guatemala. N.d. Un trabajo de conciencia: Entrevista con Rosalina Tuyuc. *Peace Brigades International.* Available online at: www .peacebrigades.org/guatemala/cap9903l.html. Accessed October 18, 2002.

Cameron, Sara. 1996. Fragile Environment . . . Vulnerable Children: Child Rights and Primary Enviromental Care in the Amazon. Web page available online at: www.saracameron.org/index_files/page0075.htm. Accessed June 29, 2004.

Campbell, Colin. 2001. Amerindian Researcher Brings Grassroots Views on Mining to Fore. *IDRC Reports*, November 1. *International Development Research Centre.* Available online at: http://web.idrc.ca/en/ev-26041–201–1-DO_TOPIC.html. Accessed June 29, 2004.

Cancel, Cecil Marie. N.d. Asuntos de la mujer en el Tercer Mundo, Enfoque especial en América Latina: Violencia contra la mujer. Web encyclopedia available online at: http://women3rdworld.miningco.com/library/espanol/blviolencia. htm. Accessed on July 18, 2001, site now discontinued.

Capozza, Korey L. 1999. The Masked Women of Mexico. *WIN*, June, distributed to H-Women mailing list, June 1. Available online at: www.h-net.org/~women.

Carnell, Brian. 1999. Population News—April 26, 1999. *Population News*, April 26. Available online at: http://overpopulation.com/population_news/1999/ popnews_04_26_1999.html. Accessed June 2, 2004.

Carrere, Ricardo. 1997. Mujeres indígenas contra exploración petrolera. *Revista del Sur*, November. Available online at: www.revistadelsur.org.uy/revista.073/ ambiente.htm. Accessed on June 20, 2001.

Castro Apreza, Inés. 1998. Los cotidianos acteales: Mujeres entre la violencia y la participación política, article distributed to Chiapas95 mailing list, February 23. Available online at: www.eco.utexas.edu/~archive/chiapas95.

Chernela, Janet. 2001, December. The Yanomami of Brazil: Human Rights Update. *American Anthropological Association*. Available online at: www.aaanet.org/committees/cfhr/rptyano10.htm. Accessed May 15, 2003.

Clemente, José. 2000. Fujimori intensifica "Guerra sucia" contra Toledo en segunda vuelta. *La Republica* (Peru), Política section, April 17. Available online at www.larepublica.com.pe/diario/politica.htm. Accessed April 17, 2000.

Colombia: Abduction and Torture of Black Women Activists. 2003. *Aviva: Action Alert*, September. Available online at: www.aviva.org/action.htm. Accessed September 23, 2003.

Las comandantas del EZLN explicaron en su propia voz por qué participan en la marcha hacia el Distrito Federal. 2001. *La Jornada*, Triple Jornada section, March 6.

Conclusiones al trabajo de observación realizado por la Comisión Civil Internacional de Observación de los Derechos Humanos. 1998. Article distributed to Chiapas95 mailing list, March 29. Available online at: www.eco.utexas.edu/~archive/chiapas95.

Coordinadora Nacional de Mujeres Indígenas. 1999. Carta entregada a la Alta Comisionada de las Naciones Unidas para los Derechos Humanos, Mary Robinson. *La Jornada*, Triple Jornada section, December 6.

Creel, Liz. 2001. Domestic Violence: An Ongoing Threat to Women in Latin America and the Caribbean. *Population Reference Bureau*, October. Available online at: www.prb.org/Template.cfm?Section=PRB&template=/ContentManagement/ContentDisplay.cfm&ContentID=4744. Accessed June 23, 2004.

Cruz, Angeles. 2002. Se *africaniza* la desnutrición en México. *La Jornada*, Contraportada section, February 20.

———. 2000. Sin acceso a los anticonceptivos, mujeres de zonas rurales: Conapo. *La Jornada*, Primera Plana section, July 23.

Cunningham, Myrna. 2001. Statement by Myrna Cunningham of International Steering Committee in Presenting the NGO Declaration and Programme of Action to the Chair of the WCAR Plenary, October 3, 2001. *World Conference against Racism*. Available online at: http//wcar.alrc.net/mainfile.php/Statements/67/. Accessed October 18, 2002.

De la Torre, Ana Laura. 2001. Mujeres indígenas: Profetas en su tierra. *Univision.com*, April 20. Available online at: www.alminuto.com/content/es007EB759.htm. Accessed June 20, 2002.

Declaration from the First Indigenous Women's Summit of the Americas. 2002, December 4. *Red de Salud de las Mujeres Latinoamericanas y del Caribe*. Available online at: www.reddesalud.org/english/sitio/info.asp?Ob=1&Id=80. Accessed June 29, 2004.

Del Valle, Sonia. 1998. Las muertas vivas de Chiapas: Testamonio de una justicia pendiente. *La Jornada*, Doble Jornada section, January 5.

Discurso de la licenciada Otilia Lux de Cotí, Ministra de Cultura y Deportes, en ocasión del Primer Foro Permanente de las Cuestiones Indígenas. 2002, May 15. *Permanent Missions to the United Nations*. Available online at:www.un.int/guatemala/spanish/intervenciones/social/1_ForoIndígena.htm. Accessed October 18, 2002.

ovan, Corey. 2003. Real Ethnography vs. Anthropologically Inspired Fiction: *Shabono* and *Yanoáma* Compared. *Sustained Action*. Available online at: www.sustainedaction.org/Explorations/Shabono%20and%20Yanoama%20compared.htm. Accessed June 1, 2004.

ército y marina retiran bases en varias zonas. 1994. *La República*, September 18.

poder indígena en Ecuador. 2000. *Reforma*, Internacional: Otras regiones section, July 1.

Elton, Catherine. 1998. Peru's Family Planning Became Coerced Sterilization. *Christian Science Monitor*, online ed., February 20. Available online at: www.csmonitor.com.

Encuentro de mujeres indígenas. 1991. *El Peruano*, March 26.

En Ecuador, raíces vivas de la rebelión indígenas. n.d. *Paginas Seminario Sureño*. Available online at: www.paginass.com/articulo.php?idArticulo=130. Accessed October 23, 2002, site now discontinued.

En la casa: Domestic Violence in Latin America. 2000, March 2. *National Radio Project*. Available online at: www. radioproject.org/archives/2000/0009.html. Accessed July 18, 2001.

Estaban cautivos en cuartel clandestino de Sendero. 1994. *La República*, July 6.

Estaban esclavizados en campamentos de Sendero. 1994. *La República*, September 18.

Estremadoyro, Julieta. 2001. Domestic Violence in Andean Communities of Peru. *LGD (Law, Social Justice and Global Development)*, June. Available online at: http://elj.warwick.ac.uk/global/issue/2001–1/estremadoyro.html. Accessed October 14, 2002.

The Facts about Gender-Based Violence. 1998. International Planned Parenthood Federation, November. Available online at: www.ippf.org/resource/gbv/ma98/1.htm. Accessed June 23, 2004.

A Fair Globalization: Creating Opportunities for All. 2004, February. *International Labor Organization*. Available online at: www.ilo.org/public/english/wcsdg/docs/report.pdf. Accessed June 29, 2004.

Ferrar, Yadira. 2004. Colombia: Indigenous Women Reclaim Traditional Medicine. *Inter Press Service News Agency*, October 14. Available at: www.ipsnews.net/print.Asp?idnews=25857. Accessed October 15, 2004.

Forero, Juan. 2004. Even the Upscale Wear Indian Dress, but Not in the Office. *New York Times*, October 14, A 4.

Forero, Juan, and Larry Rohter. 2003. Native Latins Are Astir and Thirsty for Power. *New York Times*, March 22, A2.

Fraser, Barbara J. 2001. Indigenous Groups Seek Self-Determination. *Digital Freedom Network*, October 30. Available online at: http://dfn.org/focus/americas/indigenous-groups.htm. Accessed October 21, 2002.

Freeman, Hannah, and Joseph Garelli. 2002. Women's Work in Mexico. *emagazine.com*. Available online at: www.emagazine.com/view/?156. Accessed January 15, 2005.

Galán, José. 2001. Impiden médicos tradicionales uso lucrativo de plantas mexicanas. *La Jornada*, Política section, December 2.

García, Margarita. 1999. Liberado presunto violador de niña indígena: "Ya era sexualmente activa" arguyen magistrados. *La Jornada*, Triple Jornada section, July 5.

Garcia, Sandra. 1996. On the Outside, Looking In. *Flashpoint! Electronic Magazine*, July. Available online at: www.webcom.com/hrin/magazine/july96/guatewom.html. Accessed October 22, 2003, site now discontinued.

Gargallo, Francesca. 2001. La voz de las mujeres en el Tercer Congreso Nacional Indígena: Una reflexión sobre la política de las mujeres. *La Jornada*, Triple Jornada section, April 1.

The Garifuna Community. n.d. *Garifuna.com*. Available online at: www.garifuna. com. Accessed August 3, 2004.

Garifuna Settlement and Migration Patterns. n.d. Jason DeFay Garifuna research page. Available online at: http://weber.ucsd.edu/~jdefay/PopulationEst.doc. Accessed August 3, 2004.

Garza, Anna María, and Rosalva Aída Hernández. 1998. Women in the Violence of Counterrevolution, article distributed to Chiapas95 mailing list, January 27. Available online at: www.eco.utexas.edu/~archive/chiapas95.

Garza, Anna María, Rosalva Aída Hernández, Marta Figueroa, and Mercedes Olivera. 1998. In Acteal Micaela Heard Them Shout: "We Need to Finish Off the Seed," article distributed to Chiapas95 mailing list, January 26. Available online at: www.eco.utexas.edu/~archive/chiapas95.

Giving Voice to Indigenous People. 2001, February 28. *Red Global de Aprendizaje para el Desarollo/Global Development Learning Network*. Available online at: http://Inweb18.worldbank.org/External/lac/lac.nsf/0/51800128B15E0B2985256B6E007D2433?OpenDocument. Accessed October 18, 2002.

Gómez Mena, Carolina. 2003. En areas indígenas, a mortalidad maternal llega a triplicar la media nacional: Experta. *La Jornada*, Sociedad y Justicia section, May 15.

———. 2002. Instan mujeres rurales al gobierno a hacer realidad la equidad de género. *La Jornada*, Sociedad y Justicia section. October 16.

Gonzáles, Patrisia, and Roberto Rodríguez. 1998. "Indigenous Women Strengthen Freedom in Mexico," article distributed to Chiapas95 mailing list, April 9. Available online at: www.eco.utexas.edu/~archive/Chiapas95.

Gonzalez, David. 2002. Malnourished to Get Help in Guatemala: U.N. Food Agency Acts in Emergency. *New York Times*, March 20, A3.

———. 2001. For Nicaragua's Atlantic Indians, Autonomy Means Neglect. *New York Times*, September 28, A8.

González, Roman. 1999, December 7–13. Esterilizaciones forzadas: Crimen "con consentimiento." *Comunicación e Información de la Mujer*. Available online at: www.cimac.org/mx/noticias/semanal/s99120201.html. Accessed July 25, 2002.

González Moraga, Miguel. 2001. Mujeres mayas a la lucha política. *Prensa Libre*, 25 February. Article available online at: www.geocities.com/tayacan_2000/aportes.mujeresmayas.html. Accessd June 22, 2001.

Gourd Lord. 2003. *Archaeology* 56(3), online ed. Available online at: www.archaeology/org/0305/newsbriefs.gourd.html. Accessed March 1, 2004.

Guatemala Day of Action: Rosalina Tuyuc and Other Members of *Coordinadora Nacional de Viudas de Guatemala* (CONAVIGUA). n.d. *Amnesty International USA*. Available online at: www.amnestyusa.org/countries/guatemala/actions/peace_accords/tuyuc/html. Accessed October 18, 2002, article now discontinued.

Guerra García Campos, Antenor. 1995. La salud reproductiva en las poblaciones indígenas. *El Peruano*, September 14.

Gutiérrez, Maribel. 2000. Comité de Viudas de El Charco: Luchar por el castigo a los responsables y por indemnización. *La Jornada*, Triple Jornada section, March 3.

———. 1999. Colectivo de mujeres indígenas tlapanecas. *La Jornada*, Triple Jornada section, January 4.

Hernández, Gloria. 2000. Luz Jiménez: Transmisora y traductora de conocimiento. *La Jornada*, Triple Jornada section, February 7.

Hernández, Leonor. 2000, February 10. "El estado se cierra a la participación indígena en las instituciones": Rosalina Tuyuc, ex vicepresidenta del Congreso de Guatemala, en Palma. Article available online at: www.uib.es/premsa/febrero00/dia-10/193315.htm. Accessed October 18, 2002.

Holston, Mark. 1999. Threads of Tradition among the Kuna. *The World and I Online.* Available online at: www.worldandi.com/public/1999/november/kuna.html. Accessed August 3, 2004.

Human Rights Practices for 1998 Report: Bolivia. 1999. *Bureau of Democracy, Human Rights, and Labor, U.S. State Department.* Available online at: www.usemb.se/human/human1998/bolivia.html. Accessed June 24, 2004.

Human Rights: Violence against Women. 1999. *Radio Netherlands*, April 21. Available online at: www.rnw.nl/humanrights/html/violence.html. Accessed July 18, 2000.

Indígenas exigen cumplimiento de promesas gubernamentales. 1998. *La Prensa* (Honduras), Nacionales section, October 13. Available online at: www.laprensahn.com.

Indigenous Women Are Getting Organized. 2001. *Conselho Indigenista Missionário.* Available online at: www.wald.org/cimi/2001/cimie451.htm. Accessed May 15, 2003.

Indigenous Women Today: At Risk and a Force for Change. 2004. *United Nations Permanent Forum on Indigenous Issues*, August 9. Available online at: www.un.org/hr/indigenousforum/women.html. Accessed June 29, 2004.

International Funding and Indigenous Self-Development. 1999. *Living Traditions: Abya Yala Fund Newsletter*, spring. Available online at: http://ayf.nativeweb.org/isd.htm. Accessed October 8, 2001.

Jeffrey, Paul. n.d. Fair Trade Offers Central American Producers a Better Deal. *General Board of Global Ministries, United Methodist Church.* Available online at: www.gbgm-umc.org/honduras/articles/fairtrad/html. Accessed July 12, 2001.

Jimeno, Clara. n.d. Women's Participation and the Right to Development: The Contribution of Guatemalan Women to Strengthen Civil Society. *Participatory Development Forum.* Available online at: www.pdforum.org/jimeno141.html. Accessed October 18, 2002.

Johansen, Bruce E. n.d. Stolen Wombs: Indigenous Women Most at Risk. *Rat Haus Reality Press.* Available online at: www.ratical.org/ratville/stolenWombs.html. Accessed September 27, 2002.

Krauss, Clifford. 1999. A Revolution Peru's Rebels Didn't Intend. *New York Times*, August 29, A1.

LaFranchi, Howard. 2001. After 500 Years, a Political Revival. *Christian Science Monitor*, online ed., June 1. Available online at: www.csmonitor.com.

La mujer indígena en contextos andino-amazónicos. 1990. *VSD*, June 25.

Languages of Nicaragua. 2004. *SIL International, Ethnologue.* Available online at: www.ethnologue.com/show_country.asp?name=Nicaragua. Accessed August 4, 2004.

Legislaciones. n.d. *Red Feminista Latinoamericana y del Caribe contra la Violencia Doméstica y Sexual.* Available on line at: www. koalaweb.cl/redfem/sitio/pagina. asp?p=6. Accessed June 24, 2004.

Levine, Alia. 2003. Obstacles to Women's Health: Indigenous Women's Reproductive Health in Latin America. *Sexing the Political* 3(1). Available online at: www.sexingthepolitical.com/2003/one/obstacles.htm. Accessed June 29, 2004.

Ley Integral: Tras leyes, otros paises. 2002. *Red Feminista*. Available online at: www.redfeminista.org/Ley_integral_otros_paises.asp. Accessed June 24, 2004.

Llorca, Juan Carlos. 2004, January 17. Nobel Laureate to Join Guatemala Government. *Resource Center of the Americas*. Available online at: www.americas.org/item_550. Accessed January 24, 2004.

Machlis, Sharon. 1998. Third World Crafters Go Online, August 14. Available online at: www.cnn.com/TECH/computing/9808/14/crafters.idg/. Accessed July 12, 2001.

MacMasters, Merry. 1999. Luz Jiménez es "la mujer más pintada de México," sostiene Blanca Garduño. *La Jornada*, Cultura section, November 24.

Making Violence against Women Count: Facts and Figures—A Summary. 2004. *The Religious Consultation on Population, Reproductive Health and Ethics*, May 3. Available online at: www.religiousconsultation.org/Special_Features/Amnesty_International_violence_vs_women.htm. Accessed June 24, 2004.

Marín, Llanca. 2004. La matria mapuche y el patriarcado occidental. *La Jornada*, Triple Jornada section, November 1.

Mattos, Francisco. 1994. Niños huérfanos asháninkas sufren trauma de guerra. *La República*, September 11.

McCaa, Robert. 1998. The Geometry of Gender among Aztecs: "Earthly Names," Marriage, and the Household. Unpublished paper on webpage available online at: www.hist.unm.edu/~rmccaa/AZTCNAM2/nahuanms.htm. Accessed November 23, 2000.

McDermott, Jeremy. 2002. Peru Regime Sterilised Poor. *The Age*, July 26. Available online at: www.theage.com.au. Accessed September 27, 2002.

McGaughan, Michael. 1998. Mexican Forces Resent "Uppity" Europeans, article distributed to Chiapas95 mailing list, April 29. Available online at: www.eco.utexas.edu/~archive/chiapas95.

Messina, Graciela. 2001. State of the Art of Gender Equality in Basic Education in Latin America (1999–2000). OREALC/UNESCO Santiago. Available online at: www.unesco.cl/www.unesco.cl/medios/biblioteca /documentos/estado_arte_igualdad_genero_ed_basica_lac_eng.pdf?menu=/esp/prelac/docdig/. Accessed September 27, 2002.

Mexican General Accuses Bishop of Links to Zapatistas. 1998. *Houston Chronicle*, January 10, A22.

Mexico, Instituto Nacional de Estadística, Geografía e Informática. 2000. Census for 2000 available online at www.inegi.gob.mx. Accessed May 20, 2004.

"Micaela Bastidas" logró llegar a la autogestión. 1991. *El Comercio*, April 13.

Milmo, Cahal. 2004. Exploitation Is the Price of Cheaper Food, Says Oxfam. *Common Dreams News Center*, Februrary 9. Available online at: www.commondreams.org/headlines04/0209–02.htm. Accessed February 9, 2004.

The Miskito People: Name, Population, Location, Education and Literacy. n.d. *Miskito Strategy Team, International Mission Board, Southern Baptist Convention*. Available online at: www.miskitomissions.com/The%20Miskito%20People%20name%20population.htm. Accessed August 3, 2004.

Mistry, Gretchen. 2004. Slow Progress for Zapatistas as Revolution Loses Mexican Support. *Independent*, online ed., January 3. Available online at: http://news.independent.co.uk.

Molina Ramírez, Tania. 2002. Parteras y curanderas, cuidadores de la salud en las comunidades indígenas. *La Jornada*, Triple Jornada section, October 7.

Montenegro, Nineth. 1998, May. La educación de la niñez guatemalteca ingrediente indispensable para la paz, el crecimiento económico, el desarollo y la competitividad global. Unpublished paper available online at: www.c.net.gt/ceg/doctos/nine9805.html. Accessed July 31, 2000, site now discontinued.

Morquecho, Gaspar. 2000. Pese a la miseria y alto riesgo en que viven las familias desplazadas, las mujeres recrean el sentido de comunidad. *La Jornada*, Triple Jornada section.

Muchas mujeres aún sienten vergüenza ante los médicos (Correo del Sur). 2002, June 14. *Boliviahoy.com*. Available online at: www.boliviahoy.com/modules/news/article.php?storyid=961. Accessed September 26, 2002, article now discontinued.

Mujer amazónica. 1992. Mujer amazónica y planificación familiar. *El Peruano*, November 25.

Mujeres asumen rol. 1992. Mujeres asumen rol vital en sus comunidades. *El Peruano*, June 27.

Las mujeres indígenas en Morelos. 1997, February. *Comisión Independiente de Derechos Humanos de Morelos*. Available online at: www.axon.com. mx/org/cidhmor/public/nekocred.htm. Accessed August 8, 2000, site now discontinued.

Mujeres instalarán Tribunal de Conciencia. 1998, December 4. *Contrainformación en red/nodo50.org*. Available online at: www.nodo50.org/mujeresred/guatemala-tribunal.htm. Accessed September 27, 1999.

Mujeres nativas piden participar en gobiernos regionales. 1990. *El Peruano*, December 9.

Muñoz, Alma E. 2002. Padecen anemia 40% de mujeres indígenas: INI. *La Jornada*, Sociedad y Justicia section, June 21.

Myers, Robert. 1997. Mayan Women Find Their Place Is on the Stage. *New York Times*, section 2, September 28, 4.

Nicholas-MacKenzie, Lea. n.d. Indigenous Women and Beijing+5. *Canadian Feminist Alliance for International Action*. Available online at: www.fafia.org/Bplus5/news5_e.htm. Accessed October 16, 2002.

Ojeda-Macias, Nancy. n.d. Ethnic Tourism: The Case of Cuetzalan, Mexico. Unpublished paper available online at: www.msu.edu/user/schmid/ethnic.htm. Accessed October 8, 2001.

Olowaili Declaration. 2000, March 8. *International Centre for Human Rights and Democratic Development*. Available online at: www.ichrdd.ca/english/commdoc/publications/indigenous/olowailiE.html. Accessed July 12, 2001.

Organización de Mujeres Guatemaltecas "Mamá Maquín." 2003. *Pacificar.com*. Available online at: www.pacificar.com/imprimir.hlvs?id=1282. Accessed January 15, 2005.

Organizaciones sociales de mujeres. n. d. *Red EuroSur*. Available online at: www.eursur.org/FLACSO/mujeres/bolivia/orga1.htm. Accessed September 27, 1999, site now discontinued.

Palabras de la comisionada Otilia Lux de Cotí con ocasión de la entrega del Informe de la Comisión para el Esclarecimiento Histórico. 1999. Speech available online at: www.c.net.gt/ceg/doctos/lux0225.html. Accessed July 31, 2000, site now discontinued.

Pantin, Laurence. 2002. Indigenous Women Convene Summit in Mexico. *Women's eNews*, December 2. Available online at: www.womensenews.org/article.cfm/dyn/aid/1129. Accessed April 9, 2003.

Paulina Arpasi: Primera vez en la historia del Perú, que una aymara, es elegida congresista. 2001, May. *Aymara Net*. Available online at: www.AymaraNet.org/AymaraToday001.html. Accessed June 20, 2001.

Peace Role for Guatemala Activist. 2004. *BBC News: World Edition*, January 18. Available online at: http://news.bbc.co.uk/2/hi/americas/3407041.stm. Accessed January 24, 2004.

Pensamiento, Daniel. 2000. Defiende Obispo Arizmenda a Samuel Ruíz. *Reforma*, Nacional: Estados y Regiones section, May 5.

Pérez, U., Matilde. 2004. Crean microbanco en las Huasteca. *La Jornada*, Política section, April 6.

Peru's Apology for Forced Sterilization Feared Part of a Strategy to Limit Family Planning Options. 2002, July 26. *PLANetWire.org*. Available online at: www.planetwire.org/details/3036. Accessed September 27, 2002.

Perú: Campesina al Congreso. 2001, May 14. *BBC Mundo.com*. Available online at: http://news.bbc.co.uk/hi/spanish/latin_america/newsid_1329000/1329754.stm. Accessed October 21, 2001.

Peters, Gretchen. 2003. Mexican Women Say "No Mas" to Booze. *Christian Science Monitor*, online ed., March 31. Available online at: www.csmonitor.com. Accessed April 6, 2003.

Petrich, Blanche. 2000. Aprendimos que tenemos derechos: "Una comunidad, sin su organización de mujeres, no es comunidad" sostienen indígenas guatemaltecas retornadas del exilio mexicano. *La Jornada*, Triple Jornada section, January 3.

Pinella Cisneros, Jimena. 1995. Hilaria Supa hizo sentir voz de mujer indígena en Beijing: "Las Mujeres no tenemos acceso a la educación." *El Comercio*, October 8.

Planned Parenthood Family Planning International Assistance: Investing in Women, Their Families, and the Future. 2000, May 14. *Planned Parenthood Family Planning International Assistance—Programs in Nicaragua*. Available online at: www.plannedparenthood.org/fpia/nicaragua.html. Accessed July 12, 2001.

Población Indigena. n.d. *Red EuroSur*. Available online at: www.eurosur.org/FLACSO/mujeres/panama/demo-5.htm. Accessed August 3, 2004.

Por su contribución a la educación y el trabajo comunitario refugiadas guatemaltecas ganan el Premio Nacional a la Juventud Indígena. 1999. *La Jornada*, Triple Jornada section, December 6.

Preston, Julia. 1999. Road Dispute Revives Zapatista Fight. *New York Times*, August 31, A8.

———. 1998a. Mexican Indian Women Protest Army's Search for Weapons. *New York Times*, January 12, A3.

———. 1998b. Mexico Army to Arrest Chiapas Police. *New York Times*, January 14, A4.

———. 1998c. Observers from Italy Draw Ire of Mexico. *New York Times*, May 8, A7.

Pronunciamiento de las mujeres indígenas del Perú. 1999, November 27. *Red Cientifica Peruana.* Available online at: http://ekeko2.rcp.net.pe/chirapaq/pronunc .htm. Accessed June 20, 2001, site now discontinued.

Quirós Robinson, Adriana. 2000. Mujeres indígenas de Guatemala exigen fin de discriminación y respeto a derechos. *La Nación* (Costa Rica), Internacional section, May 24. Available online at: www.nacion.com.cr.

Reglamento COMPITCH. 2002, May 21. *LaNeta.* Available online at: www.laneta/ apc.org/sclc/noticias/compitch-reglamento.htm. Accessed October 16, 2002.

Reyes Razo, Miguel. 1999. Duele el alma y el corazón se encoge con tanta pobreza. *Excelsior,* Primera Plana section, June 20.

Ríos, Guadalupe. 1999. Las Velas, simbiosis de fe católica y prácticas ancestrales en Juchitán. *La Jornada,* Cultura section, May 29.

Rivera Cusicanqui. 2003. Bolivia: Metáforas y retóricas en el levantamiento de octubre. *La Jornada,* Triple Jornada section, November 3.

Rivera Zea, Tarcila. n.d. Blanca Chancoso, Quichua del Ecuador: La triple opresión de la mujer indígena. Cited as *Varios periódicos* (*Warmi* CD-ROM).

Rodas, Cristina. 2003. Nina Pacari Vega. *Cosas.com,* January. Available online at: www .cosas.com.ec/ene2003/paginas/gente/gente2.htm. Accessed May 26, 2004.

Rodríguez Lobo, Mayela. 1997. Desagravio indígena. *La Nación* (Costa Rica), Revista Dominical section, January 4. Available online at: www.nacion .com.cr.

Rohter, Larry. 2002a. Discovering Amazon Rain Forest's Silver Lining. *New York Times,* September 10, A8.

———. 2002b. A New Intrusion Threatens a Tribe in Amazon: Soldiers. *New York Times,* October 1, A1 (continued on 10).

———. 1998. Nobel Winner Accused of Stretching Truth. *New York Times,* December 15, A1 (continued on 10).

Rojas, Rosa. 2003a. Documenta DeSer 209 casos de violación a derechos sexuales y reproductivos de mujeres en Oaxaca. *La Jornada,* Triple Jornada section, July 7.

———. 2003b. Las aguantadoras del campo exigen sus derechos: Demandan ser dueñas de su tierra. *La Jornada,* Triple Jornada section, February 3.

———. 2003c. La Cumbre de Mujeres Indígenas de las Américas. *La Jornada,* triple Jornada section, January 6.

———. 2002a. Progesa-Oportunidades: Permite la supervivencia pero también el control político y social de las indígenas. *La Jornada,* Triple Jornada section, July 1.

———. 2002b. Sin castigo, violaciones de militares a indígenas; La actuación de la CNDH, entredicho: ONG. *La Jornada,* Política section, January 27.

———. 2002c. Cuestionan actuación de la justicia militar en el caso de dos indígenas violadas en Guerrero. *La Jornada,* Política section, January 28.

———. 2000a. Mujeres indígenas zapotecas en lucha por la libertad de sus familiares. *La Jornada,* Triple Jornada section, March 4.

———. 2000b. Cuestiona la jerarquía católica la ordenación de diáconas indígenas. *La Jornada,* Triple Jornada section, February 7.

———. 2000c. Las indígenas del Ecuador luchan por sus derechos como mujeres, como pueblos indios y contra el neoliberalismo: Vicenta Chuma. *La Jornada,* Triple Jornada section, August 7.

———. 1999. Tres mil mujeres repudian la violencia de la guerra, la doméstica y la institucional en Chiapas. *La Jornada,* Triple Jornada section, December 6.

Rojas, Rosa, and Matilde Pérez. 2001. Piden en Nurio sensibilidad al Legislativo. *La Jornada*, Política section, March 3.

Roman, José Antonio. 2003. UNICEF: 70% de los niños indígenas padece desnutrición. *La Jornada*, Sociedad y Justicia section, November 21.

Salazar, Claudia. 2000. Pierde tradiciones el pueblo mazahua. *Reforma*, Ciudad de Mexico, medio ambiente, section, May 8.

Seminario de mujeres indígenas. 1995. *El Comercio*, March 5.

Sierra, María Teresa. 2002. The Challenge to Diversity in Mexico: Human Rights, Gender and Ethnicity. *Max Planck Institute for Social Anthropology Working Papers.* Available on line at: www.eth.mpg.de/pubs/wps/pdf/mpi-eth-working-paper-0049.pdf. Accessed January 15, 2005.

S.O.S. por mujeres campesinas: Amenazadas lideres de ANMUCIC. 2003. *Quechua Network*, August 13. Available online at: www.quechuanetwork.org/news_template.cfm?news_id=952&lang=s. Accessed September 23, 2003.

Spotts, Peter N. 2003. Religion in the Americas began 2250 BC. *Christian Science Monitor*, online ed., April 17. Available online at: www.csmonitor.com/2003/0417/p02s02-woam.html. Accessed March 1, 2004.

Stromquist, Nelly P. 1996, April 24. Gender and Democracy in Education in Latin America. *Council on Foreign Relations, Working Group on Educational Reform.* Available online at: www.foreignaffairs.org/conference/stromquist/html. Accessed August 9, 2000, article now discontinued.

Susskind, Yifat. 2000, May. Violence against Women in Latin America. *Madre.* Available online at: www.madre.org/art_violence_ep.html. Accessed June 24, 2004.

Thompson, Ginger. 2002. Vatican Seeks to Curb Mexico's Indian Deacons. *New York Times*, March 12, A10.

———. 2001. Mexican Rebels' Hopes Meet Hard Indian Reality. *New York Times*, March 3, A4.

Truth Commission Asks More of Government. 1998. *Cerigua Weekly Briefs*, no. 2, January 8. Available online at: www.hartford-hwp.com/archives/47/154.html. Accessed October 18, 2002.

Turati, Marcela. 2000. Niegan ordenación de mujeres. *Reforma*, Nación, sociedad y ciudadanos section, May 4.

Tuya, Hugo. 1987. Promesas sin cumplir: Mujeres del campo. *Cambio*, February 27.

Ugaz, Paola, and Diego Fernández Stoll. 2002, May 28. Ley contra discriminación en debate. *Agenciaperu.com.* Available online at: www.agenciaperu.com/sociedad/2002/may/discriminacion.htm. Accessed October 21, 2002.

USAID: Women in Development: NGO Small Grants Program: Bolivia. 2002. *USAID.* Available online at: www.usaid.gov/wid/activities/sgpboli.htm. Accessed September 25, 2002, document now discontinued.

Von Struensee, Vanessa. 2002. War on Drugs, War on Women: Bolivia, July 25, 2002. *Partners International.* Available online at: http://lists.partners-intl.net/pipermail/women-east-west/2002-July/001741.html. Accessed September 25, 2002, site now discontinued.

Weiser, Ursula. 2001. Las mujeres de Acteal exigen justicia, fin del desplazamiento y ser tomadas en cuenta en las decisiones que afectan su vida. *La Jornada*, Triple Jornada section, January 8.

Wilford, John Noble. 2004. In Guatemalan Jungles, a Bumper Crop of Maya Treasure. *New York Times*, May 11, D3.

Williams, Kent C. 2001. Afromestizo: The Third Root: African Heritage of Central America. *Lest We Forget.* Available online at: www.bjmjr.com/afromestizo/nicaragua.htm. Accessed August 4, 2004.

Women Stage Demonstrations thoughout Brazil. 2001. *Wald.org.* Available online at: www.wald.org/cimi/2001/cimie451.htm. Accessed May 15, 2003.

Zapatista Women Briefly Take Mexico Radio Station. 2000, Article distributed to Chiapas95 mailing list, March 9. Available online at: www.eco.utexas.edu/~archive/chiapas95.

Zurita-Vargas, Leonida. 2003. Coca Culture. New York Times, October 15, A23.

Theses and Dissertations

Alberti, Amalia Margherita. 1986. *Gender, Ethnicity, and Resource Control in the Andean Highlands of Ecuador.* Ph.D. diss., Stanford University.

Alberti Manzanares, Pilar. 1993. *El concepto sobre la mujer azteca deducido a través de las diosas en México prehispánico.* Ph.D. diss., Universidad Complutense de Madrid.

Arnold, Denise Y. 1988. *Matrilineal Practice in a Patrilineal Setting: Rituals and Metaphors of Kinship in an Andean Ayllu.* Ph.D. diss., University of London.

Bell, Karen Elizabeth. 1992. *Kingmakers: The Royal Women of Ancient Mexico.* Ph.D. diss., University of Michigan.

Brennan, Nancy Sue. 1973. *Cooperativism and Socialization among the Cuna Indians of San Blas.* M.A. thesis, University of California, Los Angeles.

Brueske, Judith M. 1976. *The Petapa Zapotecs of the Inland Isthmus of Tehuantepec, Oaxaca, Mexico: An Ethnographic Description and an Exploration into the Status of Women.* Ph.D. diss., University of California, Riverside.

Campbell, Howard. 1990. *Zapotec Ethnic Politics and the Politics of Culture in Juchitán, Oaxaca (1350–1990).* Ph.D. diss., University of Wisconsin.

Carrera, Magali Marie. 1979. *The Representation of Women in Aztec-Mexica Sculpture.* Ph.D. diss., Columbia University.

Castañeda, Antonia. 1990. *Presidarias y pobladoras: Spanish-Mexican Women in Frontier Monterey, Alta California, 1770–1821.* Ph.D. diss., Stanford University.

Damp, Jonathan. 1979. *Better Homes and Gardens: The Life and Death of the Early Valdivia Community.* Ph.D. diss., University of Calgary.

Denetdale, Jennifer R. Nez. 1999. *Remembering Juanita through Navajo Oral Tradition: Out of the Shadow of Chief Manuelito.* Ph.D. diss., Northern Arizona University.

Ganson, Barbara Anne. 1994. *Better Not Take My Manioc: Guaraní Religion, Society, and Politics in the Jesuit Missions of Paraguay, 1500–1800.* Ph.D. diss., University of Texas, Austin.

Gauderman, Kimberly. 1998. *Women Playing the System: Social, Economic, and Legal Aspects of Women's Lives in Seventeenth-Century Quito.* Ph.D. diss., University of California, Los Angeles.

Good, Catharine. 1993. *Work and Exchange in Nahuatl Society: Local Values and the Dynamics of an Indigenous Economy.* Ph.D. diss., Johns Hopkins University.

Gotkowitz, Laura. 1998. *Within the Boundaries of Equality: Race, Gender, and Citizenship in Bolivia (Cochabamba, 1880–1953).* Ph.D. diss., University of Chicago.

Graubart, Karen. 2000c. *Con nuestro trabajo y sudor: Indigenous Women and the Construction of Colonial Society in 16th and 17th Century Peru.* Ph.D. diss., University of Massachusetts.

Hamerschlag, Kari. 1985. *Indigenous Women's Craft Groups in the Guatemalan Highlands: Constraints and Opportunities for Empowerment through Organization.* M.A. Thesis, University of California, Berkeley.

Hames, Gina L. 1996. *Honor, Alcohol, and Sexuality: Women and the Creation of Ethnic Identity in Bolivia, 1870–1930.* Ph.D. diss., Carnegie-Mellon University.

Haviland, Leslie. 1978. *The Social Relations of Work in a Peasant Community.* Ph.D. diss., Harvard University.

Herrera, Robinson Antonio. 1997. *The People of Santiago: Early Colonial Guatemala, 1538–1587.* Ph.D. diss., University of California, Los Angeles.

Holmes, Barbara Ellen. 1978. *Women and Yucatec Kinship.* Ph.D. diss., Tulane University.

Jopling, Carol F. 1973. *Women Weavers of Yalalag: Their Art and Its Process.* Ph.D. diss., University of Massachusetts.

Kahn, Anna Lee. 1990. *A Thematic Study of the Female Figures in Late Classic Maya Vessel Paintings.* Ph.D. diss., University of Texas, Dallas.

Kanter, Deborah A. 1993. *Hijos del pueblo: Family, Community, and Gender in Rural Mexico, the Toluca Region, 1730–1830.* Ph.D. diss., University of Virgina.

Kelekna, Pia. 1981. *Sex Asymmetry in Jivaroan Achuara Society: A Cultural Mechanism Promoting Belligerence,* Ph.D. diss., University of New Mexico.

Komisaruk, Catherine Helen. 2000. *Women and Men in Guatemala, 1765–1835: Gender, Ethnicity, and Social Relations in the Central American Capital.* Ph.D. diss., University of California, Los Angeles.

Kray, Christine Anne. 1997. *Worship in Body and Spirit: Practice, Self, and Religious Sensibility in Yucatán.* Ph.D. diss., University of Pennsylvania.

Mangan, Jane E. 1999. *Enterprise in the Shadow of Silver: Colonial Andeans and the Culture of Trade in Potosí, 1570–1700.* Ph.D. diss., Duke University.

Maturo, Carol. 1994. *Malinche and Cortes, 1519–1521: An Iconographic Study.* Ph.D. diss., University of Connecticut.

Mayer, Enrique José. 1974. *Reciprocity, Self-Sufficiency and Market Relations in a Contemporary Community in the Central Andes of Peru.* Ph.D. diss., Cornell University.

McCallum, Cecilia. 1989. *Gender, Personhood and Social Organization among the Cashinahua of Western Amazonia.* Ph.D. diss., London School of Economics, University of London.

McDonald, Debra Shawn. 2000. *Negotiated Conquests: Domestic Servants and Gender in the Spanish and Mexican Borderlands, 1598–1860.* Ph.D. diss., University of New Mexico.

McVey-Dow, Vicki. 1986. *Indian Women and Textile Production: Adaptation to a New Environment in Chiapas, Mexico.* Ph.D. diss., University of Colorado.

O'Brian, Robin. 1994. *The Peso and the Loom: The Political Economy of Maya Women's Work in Highland Chiapas, Mexico.* Ph.D. diss., University of California, Los Angeles.

O'Connor, Erin E. 1997. *Dueling Patriarchies: Gender, Indians, and State Formation in the Ecuadorian Sierra, 1860–1925.* Ph.D. diss., Boston College.

Olschewski, Luisa Elvira Belaunde. 1992. *Gender, Commensality and Community among the Airo-Pai of West Amazonia (Secoya, Western Tukanoan Speaking).* Ph.D. diss., London School of Economics.

Palacio, Joseph Orlando. 1982. *Food and Social Relations in a Garifuna Village.* Ph.D. diss., University of California, Berkeley.

Sault, Nicole L. 1985a. *Zapotec Godmothers: The Centrality of Women for "Compadrazgo" Groups in a Village of Oaxaca, Mexico (Ritual Kinship, Peasants, Life-Cycle Ceremonies)*. Ph.D. diss., University of California, Los Angeles.

Shapiro, Judith Rae. 1972. *Sex Roles and Social Structure among the Yanomama Indians of Northern Brazil*. Ph.D. diss., Columbia University.

Sousa, Lisa M. 1998. *Women in Native Societies and Cultures of Colonial Mexico (Nahua, Mixtec, Zapotec, Mixe)*. Ph.D. diss., University of California, Los Angeles.

Swain, Margaret Byrne. 1978. *Ailigandi Women: Continuity and Change in Cuna Female Identity*. Ph.D. diss., University of Washington.

Terraciano, Kevin. 1994. *Ñudzahui History: Mixtec Writing and Culture in Colonial Oaxaca*. Ph.D. diss., University of California, Los Angeles.

Zeidler, James Anthony. 1984. *Social Space in Valdivia Society: Community Patterning and Domestic Structure at Real Alto, 3000–2000 B. C.* Ph.D. diss., University of Illinois.

Articles and Books

Abercrombie, Thomas. 1998. *Pathways of Memory and Power: Ethnography and History among an Andean People*. University of Wisconsin Press, Madison.

———. 1996. Q'agchas and la Plebe in "Rebellion": Carnival vs. Lent in Eighteenth-Century Potosí. *Journal of Latin American Anthropology* 2(1): 62–111.

Abu-Lughod, Janet. 1989. *Before European Hegemony: The World System A.D. 1250–1350*. Oxford University Press, New York.

Afirmando la ciudadania de las mujeres. 1998. Lima: Centro Amauta de Estudios y Promoción de la Mujer.

Alaperrine-Bouyer, Monique. 1987. Des femmes dans le manuscrit de Huarochirí. *Bulletin de l'Institut Français d'Etudes Andines* 16 (3–4): 97–101.

Alarcón, Norma. 1989. *Traddutora, Traditora*: A Paradigmatic Figure of Chicana Feminism. *Cultural Critique* 13 (fall): 57–87. Special issue: The Construction of Gender and Modes of Social Division, edited by Donna Przybylowicz, Nancy Hartsock, and Pamela McCallum.

Albers, Patricia. 1989. From Illusion to Illumination: Anthropological Studies of American Indian Women. In *Gender and Anthropology: Critical Reviews for Research and Teaching*, edited by Sandra Morgen, 132–70. American Anthropological Association, Washington, D.C.

Albers, Patricia, and Beatrice Medicine. 1983. *The Hidden Half: Studies of Plains Indian Women*. University Press of America, Washington, D.C.

Albó, Xavier. 1999. Andean People in the Twentieth Century. In *The Cambridge History of the Native Peoples of the Americas*, vol. 3, *South America Part 2*, edited by Frank Salomon and Stuart B. Schwartz, 765–871. Cambridge University Press, Cambridge.

Alderete, Wara, Gina Pacaldo, Xihuanel Huerta, and Lucilene Whitesell, eds. 1992. *Daughters of Abya Yala: Native Women Regaining Control*. Book Publishing Company, Summertown, Tenn.

Allen, Catherine J. 2002. *The Hold Life Has: Coca and Cultural Identity in an Andean Community*. 2nd ed. Smithsonian Institution Press, Washington, D.C. [1988].

———. 1988. *The Hold Life Has: Coca and Cultural Identity in an Andean Community*. Smithsonian Institution Press, Washington, D.C.

Allman, Jean, Susan Geiger, and Nakanyike Musisi. 2002. Women in African Colonial Histories: An Introduction. In *Women in African Colonial Histories*, edited by Jean Allman, Susan Geiger, and Nakanyike Musisi, 1–15. Indiana University Press, Bloomington.

Alvarez, Sonia E. 1998. Latin American Feminisms "Go Global": Trends of the 1990s and Challenges for the New Millennium. In *Cultures of Politics, Politics of Cultures: Re-visioning Latin American Social Movements*, edited by Sonia E. Alvarez, Evelina Dagnino, and Arturo Escobar, 293–324. Westview Press, Boulder, Colo.

————. 1990. *Engendering Democracy in Brazil: Women's Movements in Transition Politics*. Princeton University Press, Princeton.

Alvarez, Sonia E., Elisabeth Jay Friedman, Erika Beckman, Maylei Blackwell, Norma Stoltz Chinchilla, Nathalie Lebon, Marysa Navarro, and Marcela Ríos Tobar. 2002. Encountering Latin American and Caribbean Feminisms. *Signs* 28(2): 537–79.

Alvarez de Lovera, María. 1994. *La mujer en la colonia: Situación social y jurídica*. Fondo Editorial Tropykos, Caracas.

América Indígena. 1975. *América Indígena*. 35(3): 459–646. Special issue: *La mujer indígena*.

Anderson, Arthur J. O. 1997. Aztec Wives. In *Indian Women of Early Mexico*, edited by Susan Schroeder, Stephanie Wood, and Robert Haskett, 55–85. University of Oklahoma Press, Norman.

Anderson, Jeanine. 1985. Los sistemas de género y el desarollo de la selva. *Shupihui*, nos. 35–6: 335–45.

Anderson, Marilyn, and Jonathan Garlock. 1988. *Granddaughters of Corn: Portraits of Guatemalan Women*. Curbstone Press, Willimantic, Conn.

Andreas, Carol. 1985. *When Women Rebel: The Rise of Popular Feminism in Peru*. Lawrence Hill, Westport, Conn.

Annis, Sheldon. 1987. *God and Production in a Guatemalan Town*. University of Texas Press, Austin.

Anton, Ferdinand. 1973. *Woman in Pre-Columbian America*. Translated by Marianne Herzfeld and George A. Shepperson. Abner Schram, New York.

Anzures y Bolaños, María del Carmen. 1983. *La medicina tradicional en México: Proceso histórico, sincretismos y conflictos*. UNAM, Mexico City.

Appadurai, Arjun. 2001. Grassroots Globalization and the Research Imagination. In *Globalization*, edited by Arjun Appadurai, 1–21. Duke University Press, Durham, N.C.

Applebaum, Nancy P., Anne S. Macpherson, and Karin Alejandra Rosemblatt, eds. 2003. *Race and Nation in Modern Latin America*. University of North Carolina Press, Chapel Hill.

Aramoni Calderón, Dolores. 1992. De diosas y mujeres. *Mesoamérica* 23: 85–94.

Aranda B., Josefina, ed. 1988. *Las mujeres en el campo: Memoria de la Primera Reunión Nacional de Investigación sobre Mujeres Campesinas en México*. Instituto de Investigaciones Sociológicas de la Universidad Autónoma Benito Juárez de Oaxaca, Oaxaca de Juaréz, Oaxaca, Mexico.

Ardaya S., Isabel. 1989. Bolivia (Situación educativa de la mujer indígena). In *Mujer indígena y educación en América Latina*, edited by Anna Lucia D'Emilio, 129–66. UNESCO/I. I. I, Santiago.

Århem, Kaj. 1998. *Makuna: Portrait of an Amazonian People*. Smithsonian Institution Press, Washington, D.C.

————. 1987. Wives for Sisters: The Management of Marriage Exchange in Northwest Amazonia. In *Natives and Neighbors in South America: Anthropological Essays*, edited by Harald O. Sklar and Frank Salomon, 130–77. Göteborgs Etnografiska Museum, Göteborg, Sweden.

————. 1981. *Makuna Social Organization: A Study in Descent, Alliance and the Formation of Corporate Groups in the North-Western Amazon.* Uppsala Studies in Cultural Anthropology no. 4. Acta Universitatis Upsaliensis, Uppsala, Sweden.

Arias, Arturo. 2001. *The Rigoberta Menchú Controversy*, edited by Arturo Arias. University of Minnesota Press, Minneapolis.

Arizpe, Lourdes. 1988. La participación de la mujer en el empleo y el desarollo rural en América Latina y el Caribe: Trabajo de síntesis. In *Las mujeres en el campo: Memoria de la Primera Reunión Nacional de Investigación sobre Mujeres Campesinas en México*, edited by Josefina Aranda B., 25–61. Instituto de Investigaciones Sociológicas de la Universidad Autónoma Benito Juárez de Oaxaca, Oaxaca de Juárez, Oaxaca, Mexico.

————. 1977. Women in the Informal Labor Sector: The Case of Mexico City. *Signs* 3(1): 25–37.

————. 1975a. Mujer campesina, mujer indígena. *América Indígena* 35(3): 575–85.

————. 1975b. *Indígenas en la ciudad de México: El caso de las "Marías."* SepSetentas, Mexico City.

————. 1973. *Parentesco y economía en una sociedad nahua: Nican pehua Zacatipan.* INI/SEP, Mexico City.

Arizpe, Lourdes, and Carlota Botey. 1987. Mexican Agricultural Development Policy and Its Impact on Rural Women. In *Rural Women and State Policy: Feminist Perspectives on Latin American Agricultural Development*, edited by Carmen Diana Deere and Magdalena León, 67–83. Westview Press, Boulder, Colo.

Arnold, Denise Y. 1991. The House of Earth-Bricks and Inka-Stones: Gender, Memory, and Cosmos in Qaqachaka. *Journal of Latin American Lore* 17(1): 3–69.

Arnold, Denise Y., with Juan de Dios Yapita. 1997. La lucha por la dote en un ayllu andino. In *Mas allá del silencio: Las fronteras de género en los Andes*, vol. 1, *Parentesco y género en los Andes*, edited by Denise Y. Arnold, 345–83. ILCA, La Paz.

Arrom, Silvia. 1985. *The Women of Mexico City, 1790–1857.* Stanford University Press, Stanford.

Arsenault, Daniel. 1991. The Representation of Women in Moche Iconography. In *The Archaeology of Gender: Proceedings of the Twenty-Second Annual Conference of the Archaeological Association of the University of Calgary*, edited by Dale Walde and Noreen D. Willows, 313–26. University of Calgary Archaeological Association, Calgary.

Arteaga Montero, Vivian. 1990. La mujer aymara urbana. In *Seminario de estudio: Etnicidad, género y política en América Latina* (course readings), edited by Marisol de la Cadena, 1–38. Instituto de Estudios Peruanos, Lima.

Arvelo-Jiménez, Nelly. 2000. Three Crises in the History of Ye'kuana Cultural Continuity. *Ethnohistory* 47 (3–4): 731–46.

Asociación de la Mujer Maya Ixil. 2000. *Voces e imágenes: Mujeres maya ixiles de Chajul/Voices and Images: Mayan Ixil Women of Chajul.* ADMI, Chajul, El Quiché, Guatemala.

Babb, Florence E. 2001. *After Revolution: Mapping Gender and Cultural Politics in Neoliberal Nicaragua.* University of Texas Press, Austin.

————. 1998. *Between Field and Cooking Pot: The Political Economy of Marketwomen in Peru.* Rev. ed. University of Texas Press, Austin [1989].

————. 1976. *The Development of Sexual Inequality in Vicos, Peru.* Special studies series, Council on International Studies. Department of Anthropology, State University of New York, Buffalo.

Bacigalupo, Ana Mariella. 2004. The Struggle for Mapuche Shamans' Masculinity: Colonial Politics of Gender, Sexuality, and Power in Southern Chile. *Ethnohistory* 51(3):489–533.

Bailey, Helen Miller. 1958. *Santa Cruz of the Etla Hills.* University of Florida Press, Gainesville.

Bamberger, Joan. 1974. The Myth of Matriarchy: Why Men Rule in Primitive Society. In *Women, Culture, and Society,* edited by Michelle Zimbalist Rosaldo and Louise Lamphere, 263–80. Stanford University Press, Stanford.

Bant, Astrid A. 1994. Parentesco, matrimonio e intereses de género en una sociedad amazónica: El caso Aguaruna. *Amazonia Peruana* 12 (24): 77–103.

Bant, Astrid A., and Rosario Basurto. 1991. La mujer amazónica en la producción: ¿Complementariedad o dominación masculina? *Chacarera: Boletín de la Red Rural,* no. 8: 19–21.

Barahona, Renato. 2003. *Sex Crimes, Honour, and the Law in Early Modern Spain: Vizcaya, 1528–1735.* University of Toronto Press, Toronto.

Barbosa Sánchez, Araceli. 1994. *Sexo y conquista.* UNAM, Mexico City.

Barclay, Fredrica. 1985. "Para civilizarlas mejor": Reflexiones acerca de programas de desarrollo para mujeres en sociedades amazonicas. *Shupihui,* nos. 35–6: 289–302.

Bar Din, Anne. 1992. La población indígena en la ciudad de México: algunos de sus problemas y éxitos. *América Indígena* (1 and 2): 153–67.

Barrig, Maruja. 2001. Latin American Feminism: Gains, Losses and Hard Times. *NACLA: Report on the Americas* 34(5): 29–35.

Barrios de Chungara, Domitila, with David Aceby. 1985. *Aquí También Domitila.* Siglo Veintiuno, Mexico City.

Barrios de Chungara, Domitila, with Moema Viezzer. 1978. *Let Me Speak! Testimony of Domitila, a Woman of the Bolivian Mines.* Translated by Victoria Ortiz. Monthly Review Press, New York.

Barrios Ruiz, Walda, and Leticia Pons Bonals. 1995. *Sexualidad y religión en los Altos de Chiapas.* CONACYT and UNACH, Tuxtla Gutiérrez, Chiapas, Mexico.

Basso, Ellen B. 1973. *The Kalapalo Indians of Central Brazil.* Holt, Rinehart and Winston, New York.

Bastien, Joseph W. 1978. *Mountain of the Condor: Metaphor and Ritual in an Andean Ayllu.* West, St. Paul.

Bastos, Santiago. 1999. Concepciones del hogar y ejercicio del poder. El caso de los mayas de Ciudad de Guatemala. In *Divergencias del modelo tradicional: Hogares de jefatura femenina en América Latina,* edited by Mercedes González de la Rocha, 37–75. CIESAS and Plaza y Valdés Editores, Mexico City.

Bateman, Rebecca. 1990. Africans and Indians: A Comparative Study of the Black Carib and Black Seminole. *Ethnohistory* 37(1): 1–24.

Bauer, Arnold. J. 1990. Millers and Grinders: Technology and Household Economy in Meso-America. *Agricultural History* 64(1): 1–17.

————. 1986. Rural Spanish America, 1870–1930. In *Cambridge History of Latin America,* vol. 4 (1870–1930), edited by Leslie Bethel, 151–86. Cambridge University Press, Cambridge.

Bautista Vázquez, Ruperta. 2003. Indigenous Children: We Are Not to Blame. In *Women of Chiapas: Making History in Times of Struggle and Hope*, edited by Christine Eber and Christine Kovic, 71–9. Routledge, London.

Bazant, Jan. 1964. Evolución de la industria textil poblana (1544–1845). *Historia Mexicana* 13(4): 473–516.

Beals, Ralph L. 1998. *Cherán: A Sierra Tarascan Village*. University of Oklahoma Press, Norman [1946].

———. 1966. *Community in Transition: Nayón-Ecuador*. Latin American Studies, vol. 2, Latin American Center, University of California, Los Angeles.

Behar, Ruth. 1993. *Translated Woman*. Beacon Press, Boston.

———. 1989. Sexual Witchcraft, Colonialism, and Women's Powers: Views from the Mexican Inquisition. In *Sexuality and Marriage in Colonial Latin America*, edited by Asunción Lavrin, 178–206. University of Nebraska Press, Lincoln.

Bellier, Irene. 1991. *El temblor y la luna: Ensayo sobre las relaciones entre las mujeres y los hombres Mai Huna*. 2 vols. Ediciones ABYA-YALA, Quito.

Belote, Jim, and Linda Belote. 1977. The Limitation of Obligation in Saraguro Kinship. In *Andean Kinship and Marriage*, edited by Ralph Bolton and Enrique Mayer, 106–16. Special publication no. 7, American Anthropological Association, Washington, D.C.

Belote, Linda, and Jim Belote. 1988. Gender, Ethnicity, and Modernization: Saraguro Women in a Changing World. *Michigan Discussions in Anthropology*, 102–17. Department of Anthropology, University of Michigan, Ann Arbor.

Benería, Lourdes. 2003. *Gender, Development, and Globalization: Economics As If All People Mattered*. Routledge, London.

———. 1982. *Women and Development: The Sexual Division of Labor in Rural Societies*. Praeger, New York.

Benería, Lourdes, and Shelley Feldman, eds. 1992. *Unequal Crises, Persistent Poverty, and Women's Work*. Westview Press, Boulder, Colo.

Benfer, Robert A. 1990. The Preceramic Period Site of Paloma, Peru: Bioindications of Improving Adaptation to Sedentism. *Latin American Antiquity* 1(4): 284–318.

———. 1984. The Challenges and Rewards of Sedentism: The Preceramic Village of Paloma, Peru. In *Paleopathology at the Origins of Agriculture*, edited by Mark Nathan Cohen and George J. Armelagos, 531–58. Academic Press, Orlando.

Bennholdt-Thomsen, Veronika. 1989. Women's Dignity Is the Wealth of Juchitán, Oaxaca, Mexico. *Anthropology of Work Review* 10(1): 3–10.

Benson, Elizabeth P. 1988. Women in Mochica Art. In *The Role of Gender in Precolumbian Art and Architecture*, edited by Virginia E. Miller, 63–74. University Press of America, Lanham, Md.

Berdan, Frances F. 1982. *The Aztecs of Central Mexico: An Imperial Society*. Holt, Rinehart and Winston, New York.

Berlo, Janet C. 1992. Icons and Ideologies at Teotihuacán: The Great Goddess Reconsidered. In *Art, Ideology and the City of Teotihuacan*, edited by Janet C. Berlo, 129–68. Dumbarton Oaks, Washington, D.C.

Beverley, John. 1999. *Subalternity and Representation: Arguments in Cultural Theory*. Duke University Press, Durham, N.C.

Bierhorst, John. 1985. *Cantares Mexicanos: Songs of the Aztecs*. Stanford University Press, Stanford.

Biocca, Ettore. 1996. *Yanoáma: The Story of Helena Valero, A Girl Kidnapped by Amazonian Indians, As Told to Ettore Biocca*. Translated by Dennis Rhodes. New ed. Kodansha International, Tokyo [1970].

———. 1970. *Yanoáma: The Narrative of a White Girl Kidnapped by Amazonian Indians*. Translated by Dennis Rhodes. Dutton, New York.

Black, Nancy J. 1988. Anthropology and the Study of Quiche Maya Women in the Western Highlands of Guatemala. In *Lucha: The Struggles of Latin American Women*, edited by Connie Weil, 75–111. Prisma Institute and Minnesota Latin American series no. 2, Minneapolis.

Blaffer, Sarah C. 1972. *The Black-Man of Zinacantan: A Central American Legend*. University of Texas Press, Austin.

Blanco, Iris. 1977. Participación de las mujeres en la sociedad pre-hispanica. In *Essays on La Mujer*, edited by Rosaura Sanchez and Rose Martinez Cruz, 48–81. Anthology no. 1, Chicano Studies Center Publications, University of California, Los Angeles.

Block, David. 1994. *Mission Culture on the Upper Amazon*. University of Nebraska Press, Lincoln.

Blom, Franz. 1983. *Cherchez La Femme* Maya, or Woman's Place among the Ancient Maya. In *Antropología e historia de los Mixe-Zoques y Mayas: Homenaje a Franz Blom*, edited by Lorenzo Ochoa and Thomas A. Lee, Jr., 305–20. UNAM, Mexico City.

Blondet, Cecilia. 1990. Establishing an Identity: Women Settlers in a Poor Lima Neighborhood. In *Women and Social Change in Latin America*, edited by Elizabeth Jelin, 12–46. Zed Books, London.

Bolin, Inge. 1998. *Rituals of Respect: The Secret of Survival in the High Peruvian Andes*. University of Texas Press, Austin.

Bolton, Ralph. 1977. The Qolla Marriage Process. In *Andean Kinship and Marriage*, edited by Ralph Bolton and Enrique Mayer, 217–39. Special publication no. 7, American Anthropological Association, Washington, D.C.

Bolton, Ralph, and Charlene Bolton. 1975. *Conflictos en la familia andina*. Translated by Jorge A. Flores Ochoa and Yemira D. Nájar Vizcarra. Centro de Estudios Andinos, Cuzco.

Borchart de Moreno, Christiana. 1991. La imbecilidad del sexo: Pulperas y mercaderas quiteñas a fines del siglo XVII. In *Historia de la mujer y la familia*, edited by Jorge Núñez Sánchez, 17–35. Editorial Nacional, Quito.

Boremanse, Didier. 1998. *Hach Winik: The Lacandon Maya of Chiapas, Southern Mexico*. Institute for Mesoamerican Studies, Albany.

Bort, John R., and Philip D. Young. 1982. New Roles for Males in Guaymí Society. In *Sex Roles and Social Change in Native Lower Central American Societies*, edited by Christine A. Loveland and Franklin O. Loveland, 88–102. University of Illinois Press, Urbana.

Bose, Christine E., and Edna Acosta-Belén. 1995. *Women in the Latin American Development Process*. Temple University Press, Philadelphia.

Bossen, Laurel. 1984. *The Redivision of Labor: Women and Economic Choice in Four Guatemalan Communities*. State University of New York Press, Albany.

———. 1983. Sexual Stratification in Mesoamerica. In *Heritage of Conquest: Thirty Years Later*, edited by Carl Kendall, John Hawkins, and Laurel Bossen, 35–71. University of New Mexico Press, Albuquerque.

Bourque, Linda Brookover. 1989. *Defining Rape*. Duke University Press, Durham, N.C.

Bourque, Susan C., and Kay Warren. 1981. *Women of the Andes: Patriarchy and Social Change in Two Peruvian Towns*. University of Michigan Press, Ann Arbor.

Bouvard, Marguerite. 1994. *Revolutionizing Motherhood: The Mothers of the Plaza de Mayo*. Scholarly Resources, Wilmington, Del.

Bouvier, Virginia M. 2001. *Women and the Conquest of California, 1542–1840: Codes of Silence*. University of Arizona Press, Tucson.

Boyer, Richard. 1989. Women, *La Mala Vida*, and the Politics of Marriage. In *Sexuality and Marriage in Colonial Latin America*, edited by Asunción Lavrin, 252–86. University of Nebraska Press, Lincoln.

Briggs, Lucy T. 1995. *Manuela Ari: An Aymara Woman's Testimony of Her Life*, edited and prepared by Lucy T. Briggs and completed by Sabine Dedenbach-Salazar Sáenz. Holos, Bonn.

Brintnall, Douglas E. 1979. *Revolt against the Dead: The Modernization of a Mayan Community in the Highlands of Guatemala*. Gordon and Breach, New York.

Brodman, Barbara. 1994. Paris or Perish: The Plight of the Latin American Indian in a Westernized World. In *On Fashion*, edited by Shari Benstock and Suzanne Ferriss, 267–83. Rutgers University Press, New Brunswick.

Brown, Betty Ann. 1983. Seen but Not Heard: Women in Aztec Ritual—The Sahagún Texts. In *Text and Image in Pre-Columbian Art: Essays on the Interrelationship of the Verbal and Visual Arts*, edited by Janet C. Berlo, 119–54. BAR Press, Oxford.

Brown, Denise Fay. 1999. Espacios mayas de familia y comunidad: Una relación de interdependencia. *Mexican Studies/Estudios Mexicanos* 15(2): 322–42.

Brown, Michael F. 1986a. *Tsewa's Gift: Magic and Meaning in an Amazonian Society*. Smithsonian Institution Press, Washington, D.C.

———. 1986b. Power, Gender, and the Social Meaning of Aguaruna Suicide. *Man* (n.s.) 21 (2): 311–28.

Brownmiller, Susan. 1975. *Against Our Will: Men, Women, and Rape*. Simon and Schuster, New York.

Bruhns, Karen Olsen. 1994. *Ancient South America*. Cambridge University Press, Cambridge.

———. 1991. Sexual Activities: Some Thoughts on the Sexual Division of Labor and Archaeological Interpretation. In *The Archaeology of Gender: Proceedings of the Twenty-Second Annual Conference of the Archaeological Association of the University of Calgrary*, edited by Dale Walde and Noreen D. Willows, 420–9. University of Calgary Archaeological Association, Calgary, Canada.

———. 1988. Yesterday the Queen Wore . . . An Analysis of Women and Costume in the Public Art of the Late Classic Maya. In *The Role of Gender in Precolumbian Art and Architecture*, edited by Virginia E. Miller, 105–34. University Press of America, Lanham, Md.

Bruhns, Karen Olsen, and Karen E. Stothert. 1999. *Women in Ancient America*. University of Oklahoma Press, Norman.

Brumfiel, Elizabeth M. 2001. Asking about Aztec Gender: The Historical and Archaeological Evidence. In *Gender in Pre-Hispanic America: A Symposium at Dumbarton Oaks*, edited by Cecelia F. Klein, 57–85. Dumbarton Oaks Research, Washington, D.C.

————. 1996. Figurines and the Aztec State: Testing the Effectiveness of Ideological Domination. In *Gender and Archaeology*, edited by Rita P. Wright, 143–66. University of Pennsylvania, Philadelphia.

————. 1991. Weaving and Cooking: Women's Production in Aztec Mexico. In *Engendering Archaeology: Women and Prehistory*, edited by Joan Gero and Margaret Conkey, 224–51. Blackwell, Oxford.

Brunt, Dorien. 1992. *Mastering the Struggle: Gender, Actors and Agrarian Change in a Mexican Ejido*. CEDLA, Amsterdam.

Brysk, Allison. 2000. *From Tribal Village to Global Village: Indian Rights and International Relations in Latin America*. Stanford University Press, Stanford.

Buechler, Hans C., and Judith-Maria Buechler. 1996. *The World of Sofía Velasquez: The Autobiography of a Bolivian Market Vendor*. Columbia University Press, New York.

————. 1992. *Manufacturing against the Odds: Small-Scale Producers in an Andean City*. Westview Press, Boulder, Colo.

————. 1971. *The Bolivian Aymara*. Holt, Rinehart and Winston, New York.

Buechler, Judith-Maria. 1997. The Visible and Vocal Politics of Female Traders and Small-Scale Producers in La Paz, Bolivia. In *Women and Economic Change: Andean Perspectives*, 75–87, edited by Ann Miles and Hans Buechler. Society for Latin American Anthropology publication series, vol. 14, Society for Latin American Anthropology and American Anthropological Association, Washington, D.C.

Buenaventura-Posso, Elisa, and Susan E. Brown. 1980. Forced Transition from Egalitarianism to Male Dominance: The Bari of Colombia. In *Women and Colonization: Anthropological Perspectives*, edited by Mona Etienne and Eleanor Leacock, 109–33. Praeger, New York.

Bunster, Ximena. 1993. Surviving beyond Fear: Women and Torture in Latin America. In *Surviving beyond Fear: Women, Children, and Human Rights in Latin America*, edited by Marjorie Agosin, 98–125. White Pine Press, Fredonia, New York.

————. 1976. The Emergence of a Mapuche Leader: Chile. In *Sex and Class in Latin America*, edited by June Nash and Helen Icken Safa, 302–19. Praeger, New York.

Bunster, Ximena, and Elsa M. Chaney. 1989. *Sellers and Servants: Working Women in Lima, Peru*. Bergin and Garvey, Granby, Mass.

Bunzel, Ruth. 1952. *Chichicastenango: A Guatemala Village*. University of Washington Press, Seattle.

Burkett, Eleanor. 1978. Indian Women and White Society: The Case of Sixteenth-Century Peru. In *Latin American Women: Historical Perspectives*, edited by Asunción Lavrin, 101–28. Greenwood Press, Westport, CT.

Burkhart, Louise. 2001a. Gender in Nahuatl Texts of the Early Colonial Period: Native Tradition and the Dialogue with Christianity. In *Gender in Pre-Hispanic America*, edited by Cecilia F. Klein, 87–107. Dumbarton Oaks, Washington, D.C.

————. 2001b. *Before Guadalupe: The Virgin Mary in Early Colonial Nahuatl Literature*. IMS monograph 13, Institute for Mesoamerican Studies, State University of New York, Albany.

————. 1998. Pious Performances: Christian Pageantry and Native Identity in Early Colonial Mexico. In *Native Traditions in the Post-Conquest World*, edited by Elizabeth Hill Boone and Tom Cummins, 361–81. Dumbarton Oaks, Washington, D.C.

————. 1997. Mexica Women on the Home Front: Housework and Religion in Aztec Mexico. In *Indian Women of Early Mexico*, edited by Susan Schroeder,

Stephanie Wood, and Robert Haskett, 25–54. University of Oklahoma Press, Norman.

———. 1996. *Holy Wednesday: A Nahua Drama from Early Colonial Mexico*. University of Pennsylvania Press, Philadelphia.

———. 1989. *The Slippery Earth: Nahua-Christian Moral Dialogue in Sixteenth-Century Mexico*. University of Arizona Press, Tucson.

Burns, Kathryn. 1999. *Colonial Habits: Convents and the Spiritual Economy of Cuzco, Peru*. Duke University Press, Durham, N.C.

Busto Duthurburo, José Antonio del. 1965. Una huérfana mestiza: La hija de Juan Pizarro. *Revista Histórica* 28: 103–6.

Butler, Judith. 1990. *Gender Trouble: Feminism and the Subversion of Identity*. Routledge, New York.

Cabrera Pérez-Armiñán, María Luisa. 1992. *Tradición y cambio de la mujer k'iche': Kib'antajik pe, uk'exik pe ri k'iche' ixoqib'*. IDESAC, Guatemala.

Cajías de la Vega, Magdalena, Patricia Fernández de Aponte, Florencia Durán de Lazo de la Vega, Pilar Mendieta Parada, and Ana María Seoane de Capra. 1994. In *La mujer en las sociedades prehispanicas de Bolivia: Investigaciones históricas, identidad y memoria*. Centro de Información y Desarollo de las Mujer, La Paz, Bolivia.

Campbell, Ena. 1982. The Virgin of Guadalupe and the Female Self-Image: A Mexican Case History. In *Mother Worship: Theme and Variations*, edited by James J. Preston, 5–24. University of North Carolina Press, Chapel Hill.

Campbell, Howard. 1994. *Zapotec Renaissance: Ethnic Politics and Cultural Revivalism in Southern Mexico*. University of New Mexico Press, Albuquerque.

Campbell, Leon G. 1987. Ideology and Factionalism during the Great Rebellion, 1780–1783. In *Resistance, Rebellion, and Consciousness in the Andean Peasant World, Eighteenth to Twentieth Centuries*, edited by Steve J. Stern, 110–39. University of Wisconsin Press, Madison.

———. 1985. Women and the Great Rebellion in Peru, 1780–1783. *Americas* 42(2): 163–96.

Cancian, Frank. 1965. *Economics and Prestige in a Maya Community: The Religious Cargo System in Zinacantan*. Stanford University Press, Stanford.

Carey, David, Jr. 2002. Empowered through Labor and Buttressing Their Communities: Mayan Women and Coastal Migration. Paper presented at the annual meeting of the Conference on Latin American History, San Francisco, January 3–6.

———. 2001. *Our Elders Teach Us: Maya-Kaqchikel Historical Perspectives: Xkib'ij kan qate' qatata'*. University of Alabama Press, Tuscaloosa.

Carmack, Robert M. 1995. *Rebels of Highland Guatemala: The Quiche-Mayas of Momostenango*. University of Oklahoma Press, Norman.

Carrasco, Pedro. 1999. *The Tenochca Empire of Ancient Mexico: The Triple Alliance of Tenochtitlan, Tetzcoco, and Tlacopan*. University of Oklahoma Press, Norman.

———. 1997. Indian-Spanish Marriages in the First Century of the Colony. In *Indian Women of Early Mexico*, edited by Susan Schroeder, Stephanie Wood, and Robert Haskett, 87–103. University of Oklahoma Press, Norman.

———. 1984. Royal Marriages in Ancient Mexico. In *Explorations in Ethnohistory: Indians of Central Mexico in the Sixteenth Century*, edited by H. R. Harvey and Hanns J. Prem, 41–82. University of New Mexico Press, Albuquerque.

Carter, W. E. 1977. Trial Marriage in the Andes? In *Andean Kinship and Marriage*, edited by Ralph Bolton and Enrique Mayer, 177–216. Special publication no. 7, American Anthropological Association, Washington, D.C.

Caso, Alfonso. 1979. *Reyes y reinos de la Mixteca*. Vol. 2. *Diccionario biográfico de los señores mixtecos*. Fondo de Cultura Económica, Mexico City.

———. 1970. *The Aztecs: People of the Sun*. Translated by Lowell Dunham. University of Oklahoma Press, Norman.

Castañeda, Antonia. 1993. Sexual Violence in the Politics and Policies of Conquest: American Women and the Spanish Conquest of Alta California. In *Building with Our Hands: New Directions in Chicana Studies*, edited by Adela de la Torre and Beatríz M. Pesquera, 15–33. University of California Press, Berkeley.

Castañeda Salgado, Martha Patricia. 1997. El cuerpo y la sexualidad de las mujeres nauzontecas. In *Mujeres y relaciones de género en la antropología latinoamericana*, edited by Soledad González Montes, 121–39. El Colegio de México, Mexico City [1993].

Castro, Daniel. 1994. "War Is Our Daily Life": Women's Participation in Sendero Luminoso. In *Confronting Change, Challenging Tradition: Women in Latin American History*, edited by Getrude M. Yeager, 219–25. Scholarly Resources, Wilmington, Del.

Castro Apreza, Yolanda. 2003. J'Pas Joloviletik-Jolom Mayaetik-K'inal Antzetik: An Organizational Experience of Indigenous and Mestiza Women. In *Women of Chiapas: Making History of Times of Struggle and Hope*, edited by Christine Eber and Christine Kovic, 207–18. Routledge, London.

Castro Gutiérrez, Felipe. 1998. Condición femenina y violencia conyugal entre los purépechas durante la época colonial. *Mexican Studies/Estudios Mexicanos* 14(1): 5–21.

Cervone, Emma. 2001. Engendering Leadership: Indigenous Women Leaders in the Ecuadorian Andes. In *Gender's Place: Feminist Anthropologies of Latin America*, edited by Rosario Montoya, Lessie Jo Frazier, and Janise Hurtig, 179–96. Palgrave Macmillan, New York.

Chagnon, Napolean A. 1997. *Yanomamö*. 5th ed. Harcourt Brace, Fort Worth, Tex. [1968].

———. 1992. *Yanomamö*. 4th ed. Harcourt Brace Jovanovich, Fort Worth, Tex. [1968].

Chamberlain, Robert S. 1966. *The Conquest and Colonization of Yucatan, 1517–1550*. Octagon Books, New York.

Chambers, Sarah. 1999. *From Subjects to Citizens: Honor, Gender, and Politics in Arequipa, Peru, 1780–1854*. Pennsylvania State University Press, University Park.

Chance, John. 1989. *Conquest of the Sierra: Spaniards and Indians in Colonial Oaxaca*. University of Oklahoma Press, Norman.

Chance, John, and William B. Taylor. 1985. Cofradías and Cargos: An Historical Perspective on the Mesoamerican Civil-Religion Hierarchy. *American Ethnologist* 12(1):1–26.

Chapman, Anne. 1982. *Drama and Power in a Hunting Society: The Selk'nam of Tierra del Fuego*. Cambridge University Press, Cambridge.

Chassen-López, Francie. 1998. Maderismo or Mixtec Empire? Class and Ethnicity in the Mexican Revolution, Costa Chica of Oaxaca, 1911. *Americas* 55(1): 91–127.

———. 1994. "Cheaper Than Machines": Women and Agriculture in Porfirian Oaxaca, 1880–1911. In *Women of the Mexican Countryside, 1850–1990*, edited by Heather Fowler-Salamini and Mary Kay Vaughan, 27–50. University of Arizona Press, Tucson.

Chenaut, Victoria. 1997. Honor y ley: La mujer totonaca y el conflicto judicial en la segunda mitad del siglo XIX. In *Familiares y mujeres en México: Del modelo a la diversidad*, edited by Soledad González Montes and Julia Tuñón, 111–62. El Colegio de México, Mexico City.

———. 1993. La costa totonaca: Divorcio y sociedad en el Porfiriato. In *Huasteca: Selección de trabajos pertenicientes al V y VI Encuentros de Investigadores de la Huasteca*, vol. 1, *Espacio y tiempo: Mujer y trabajo*, edited by Jesús Ruvalcaba and Graciela Alcalá, 177–98. CIESAS, Mexico City.

Chernela, Janet M. 1993. *The Wanano Indians of the Brazilian Amazon: A Sense of Space*. University of Texas Press, Austin.

Chevalier, Jacques M., and Daniel Buckles. 1995. *A Land without Gods: Process Theory, Maldevelopment and the Mexican Nahuas*. Zed Books, London.

Chiñas, Beverly. 1995. Isthmus Zapotec Attitudes toward Sex and Gender Anomalies. In *Latin American Male Homosexualities*, edited by Stephen O. Murray, 293–302. University of New Mexico Press, Albuquerque.

———. 1992. *The Isthmus Zapotecs: A Matrifocal Culture of Mexico*. Rev. ed. Harcourt Brace Jovanovich, Fort Worth, Tex. [1973].

———. 1976. Zapoteca *Viajeras*. In *Markets in Oaxaca*, edited by Scott Cook and Martin Diskin, 169–88. University of Texas Press, Austin.

———. 1973. *The Isthmus Zapotecs: Women's Roles in Cultural Context*. Holt, Rinehart and Winston, New York.

Choque Quispe, María Eugenia. 1998. Colonial Domination and the Subordination of the Indigenous Woman in Bolivia. Translated by Christine Taff with Marcia Stephenson. *Modern Fiction Studies* 44(1): 10–23. Special issue: Contested Spaces in the Caribbean and the Americas, edited by Aparajita Sagar and Marcia Stephenson.

Clendinnen, Inga. 1991. *Aztecs: An Interpretation*. Cambridge University Press, Cambridge.

———. 1987. *Ambivalent Conquests: Maya and Spaniard in Yucatan, 1517–1570*. Cambridge University Press, Cambridge.

———. 1982. Yucatec Maya Women and the Spanish Conquest: Role and Ritual in Historical Reconstruction. *Journal of Social History* 15 (spring): 427–42.

Cline, S. L. 1986. *Colonial Culhuacan, 1580–1600: A Social History of an Aztec Town*. University of New Mexico Press, Albuquerque.

Cline, S. L., and Miguel Leon-Portilla. 1984. *The Testaments of Culhuacan*. Latin American Center Publications, University of California, Los Angeles.

Coe, Michael. 1999. *The Maya*. 6th ed. Thames and Hudson, New York [1966].

Coelho, Ruy Galvao de Andrade. 1981. *Los negros caribes de honduras*. Translated by Guadalupe Carías Zapata. Editorial Guaymuras, Tegucigalpa, Honduras.

Cohen, Mark Nathan, and George J. Armelagos. 1984. *Paleopathology at the Origins of Agriculture*, edited by Mark Nathan Cohen and George J. Armelagos. Academic Press, Orlando.

Colby, Benjamin N. 1967. Psychological Orientations. In *Handbook of Middle American Indians*, vol. 6, *Social Anthropology*, edited by Manning Nash, series edited by Robert Wauchope, 416–31. University of Texas Press, Austin.

Collier, George A., with Elizabeth Lowery Quaratiello. 1999. *Basta! Land and the Zapatista Rebellion in Chiapas*. Rev. ed. Food First Books, Oakland, Calif. [1994].

———. 1975. *Fields of the Tzotzil: The Ecological Bases of Tradition in Highland Chiapas*. University of Texas Press, Austin.

Collier, Jane Fishburne. 1974. Women in Politics. In *Woman, Culture and Society*, edited by Michelle Zimbalist Rosaldo and Louise Lamphere, 89–96. Stanford University Press, Stanford.

―――. 1973. *Law and Social Change in Zinacantan*. Stanford University Press, Stanford.

―――. 1968. *Courtship and Marriage in Zinacantan, Chiapas, Mexico*. Publication no. 25: 139–201, Middle American Research Institute, New Orleans.

Collinson, Helen. 1990. *Women and Revolution in Nicaragua*, edited by Helen Collinson. Zed Books, London.

Colloredo-Mansfeld, Rudi. 1999. *The Native Lesiure Class: Consumption and Cultural Creativity in the Andes*. University of Chicago Press, Chicago.

Colson, Audrey Butt. 1977. The Akawaio Shaman. In *Carib-Speaking Indians: Culture, Society and Language*, edited by Ellen B. Basso, 43–65. University of Arizona Press, Tucson.

I Congreso de Mujeres Indígenas. 1994. I Congreso de Mujeres Indígenas. *Amazonía Peruana* 12(24): 367–74.

Conzemius, Eduard. 1984. *Miskitos y Sumus: Estudio etnográfico sobre los indios de Honduras y Nicaragua*. Translated by Jaime Incer. Libro Libre, San José, Costa Rica [1932].

Cook, Noble David. 1981. *Demographic Collapse: Indian Peru, 1520–1620*. Cambridge University Press, Cambridge.

Cook, Scott. 1982. *Zapotec Stoneworkers: The Dynamics of Rural Simple Commodity Production in Modern Mexican Capitalism*. University Press of America, Lanham, Md.

Cook, Scott, and Leigh Binford. 1990. *Obliging Need: Rural Petty Industry in Mexican Capitalism*. University of Texas Press, Austin.

Coral Cordero, Isabel. 1998. Women in War: Impact and Responses. In *Shining and Other Paths: War and Society in Peru, 1980–1995*, edited by Steve J. Stern, 345–74. Duke University Press, Durham, N.C.

Cordell, Linda. 1989. Durango to Durango: An Overview of the Southern Heartland. In *Columbian Consequences*, vol. 1, *Archaeological and Historical Perspectives on the Spanish Borderlands West*, edited by David Hurst Thomas, 17–40. Smithsonian Institution Press, Washington, D.C.

Cosminsky, Sheila. 2001. Maya Midwives of Southern Mexico and Guatemala. In *Mesoamerican Healers*, edited by Brad R. Huber and Alan R. Sandstrom, 179–210. University of Texas Press, Austin.

―――. 1982. Childbirth and Change: A Guatemalan Study. In *Ethnography of Fertility and Birth*, edited by Carol P. MacCormack, 205–29. Academic Press, London.

―――. 1970. Birth Rituals and Symbolism: A Quiche Maya–Black Carib Comparison. In *Ritual and Symbol in Native Central America*, edited by Philip Young and James Howe, 105–23. Anthropological papers no. 9, Department of Anthropology, University of Oregon, Eugene.

Cosminsky, Sheila, and Mary Scrimshaw. 1982. Sex Roles and Subsistence: A Comparative Analysis of Three Central American Communities. In *Sex Roles and Social Change in Native Lower Central American Societies*, edited by Christine A. Loveland and Franklin O. Loveland, 44–69. University of Illinois Press, Urbana.

Costello, Richard W. 1982. New Economic Roles for Cuna Males and Females: An Examination of Socioeconomic Change in a San Blas Community. In *Sex Roles and Social Change in Native Lower Central American Societies*, edited by Christine A. Loveland and Franklin Loveland, 70–87. University of Illinois Press, Urbana.

Costin, Cathy Lynn. 1996. Exploring the Relationship between Gender and Craft in Complex Societies: Methodological and Theoretical Issues of Gender Attribution. In *Gender and Archaeology*, edited by Rita P. Wright, 111–40. University of Pennsylvania Press, Philadelphia.

———. 1993. Textiles, Women, and Political Economy in Late Prehispanic Peru. *Research in Economic Anthropology* 14: 3–28.

Cotera, Martha P. 1976. *Diosa and Hembra: The History and Heritage of Chicanas in the U.S.* Information Systems Development, Austin.

Covarrubias, Miguel. 1946. *Mexico South: The Isthmus of Tehuantepec*. Knopf, New York.

Cowgill, George. 1997. State and Society at Teotihuacan, Mexico. In *Annual Review of Anthropology*, edited by William H. Durham, E. Valentine Daniel, and Bambi B. Schieffelin, 26:129–61. Annual Reviews, Palo Alto.

Crain, Mary M. 1996. The Gendering of Ethnicity in the Ecuadorian Andes: Native Women's Self-Fashioning in the Urban Marketplace. In *Machos, Mistresses, Madonnas: Contesting Power of Latin American Gender Imagery*, edited by Marit Melhaus and Kristi Anne Stolen, 134–58. Verso, London.

———. 1994. Unruly Mothers: Gender Identities, Peasant Political Discourses, and Struggles for Social Space in the Ecuadorean Andes. *PoLAR* (Political and Legal Anthropology Review) 15(2): 85–97.

———. 1991. Poetics and Politics in the Ecuadorean Andes: Women's Narratives of Death and Devil Possession. *American Ethnologist* 18(1): 67–89.

Crapo, Richley H. and Percy Aitken. 1986. *Bolivian Quechua Reader and Grammar-Dictionary*. Karoma, Ann Arbor.

Crocker, Jon Christopher. 1985. *Vital Souls: Bororo Cosmology, Natural Symbolism, and Shamanism*. University of Arizona Press, Tucson.

———. 1969. Men's House Associates among the Eastern Bororo. *Southwestern Journal of Anthropology* 25(1): 236–60.

Crocker, William H. 1985. Extramarital Sexual Practices of the Ramkokamekra-Canela Indians: An Analysis of Socio-Cultural Factors. In *Native South Americans: Ethnology of the Least Known Continent*, rev. ed., edited by Patricia J. Lyon, 184–95. Waveland Press, Prospect Heights, Ill. [1974].

———. 1984. Canela Marriage: Factors in Change. In *Marriage Practices in Lowland South America*, edited by Kenneth M. Kensinger, 63–98. University of Illinois Press, Urbana.

Crocker, William H., and Jean Crocker. 1994. *The Canela: Bonding through Kinship, Ritual, and Sex*. Harcourt Brace, Fort Worth, Tex.

Crown, Patricia L. 2000a. Gendered Tasks, Power, and Prestige in the Prehispanic American Southwest. In *Women and Men in the Prehispanic Southwest*, edited by Patricia Crown, 3–41. School of American Research, Santa Fe.

———, ed. 2000b. *Women and Men in the Prehispanic Southwest: Labor, Power, and Prestige*. School of American Research, Santa Fe.

Crown, Patricia L., and W. H. Wills. 1995. The Origins of Southwestern Ceramic Containers: Women's Time Allocation and Economic Intensification. *Journal of Anthropological Research* 51(2): 173–86.

Crown, Patricia L., and Suzanne K. Fish. 1996. Gender and Status in the Hohokam Pre-Classic to Classic Tradition. *American Anthropologist* 98(4): 803–17.

Cruz H., María de los. 1988. La mujer indígena y el trabajo artesanal. In *Las mujeres en el campo: Memoria de la Primera Reunión Nacional de Investigación sobre Mujeres*

Campesinas en México, edited by Josefina Aranda B., 275–82. Instituto de Investigaciones Sociológicas de la Universidad Autónoma Benito Juárez de Oaxaca, Oaxaca de Juaréz, Oaxaca, Mexico.

Cypess, Sandra Messinger. 1991. *La Malinche in Mexican Literature: From History to Myth*. University of Texas Press, Austin.

Cyphers Guillén, Ann. 1994. Las mujeres de Chalcatzingo. *Arqueología Mexicana* 2(7): 70–3.

———. 1993. Women, Rituals, and Social Dynamics at Ancient Chalcatzingo. *Latin American Antiquity* 4(3): 209–24.

———. 1984. The Possible Role of a Woman in Formative Exchange. In *Trade and Exchange in Early Mesoamerica*, edited by Kenneth G. Hirth, 115–23. University of New Mexico Press, Albuquerque.

Dahlgren de Jordán, Barbro. 1966. *La Mixteca: Su cultura e historia prehispánica*. 2nd ed. UNAM, Mexico City [1954].

Daltabuit Godás, Magalí. 1992. *Mujeres mayas: Trabajo, nutrición y fecundidad*. UNAM, Mexico City.

Daltabuit Godás, Magalí, Luz María Vargas, Enrique Santillán, and Héctor Cisneros. 1994. *Mujer rural y medio ambiente en la Selva Lacandona*. UNAM and Centro Regional de Investigaciones Multidisciplinarias, Cuernavaca, Morelos, Mexico.

Dalton, Margarita, and Guadalupe Musalem Merhy. 1992. *Mitos y realidades de las mujeres huaves*. Comunicación Social Difusión Institucional, Oaxaca, Mexico.

D'Altroy, Terence N. 2002. *The Incas*. Blackwell, Malden, Mass.

Da Matta, Roberto. 1982. *A Divided World: Apinayé Social Structure*. Harvard University Press, Cambridge, Mass.

Damian, Carol. 1995. From Pachamama to the Virgin Mary: What the Spanish Never Saw. In *Andean Art: Visual Expression and Its Relation to Andean Beliefs and Values*, edited by Penny Dransart, 109–30. Avebury, Brookfield, Vt.

Dary Fuentes, Claudia. 1991. *Mujeres tradicionales y nuevos cultivos*. FLACSO, Guatemala.

D'Aubeterre Buznego, María Eugenia. 2003. Los multiples significados de robarse la muchacha: El robo de la novia en un pueblo de migrantes del estado de Puebla. In *El matrimonio en Mesoamerica ayer y hoy: Unas miradas antropológicas*, edited by David Robichaux, 249–64. Universidad Iberoamericana, Mexico City.

Davis, Shelton H. 1977. *Victims of the Miracle: Development and the Indians of Brazil*. Cambridge University Press, Cambridge.

Dean, Warren. 1995. *With Broadax and Firebrand: The Destruction of the Brazilian Atlantic Forest*. University of California, Berkeley.

Deans-Smith, Susan. 1992. *Bureaucrats, Planters, and Workers: The Making of the Tobacco Monopoly in Bourbon Mexico*. University of Texas Press, Austin.

Deeds, Susan M. 1997. Double Jeopardy: Indian Women in Jesuit Missions of Nueva Vizcaya. In *Indian Women of Early Mexico*, edited by Susan Schroeder, Stephanie Wood, and Robert Haskett, 255–72. University of Oklahoma Press, Norman.

Deere, Carmen Diana. 1990. *Household and Class Relations: Peasants and Landlords in Northern Peru*. University of California Press, Berkeley.

———. 1976. Rural Women's Subsistence Production in the Capitalist Periphery. *Review of Radical Political Economics* 8: 9–18.

Deere, Carmen Diana, and Magdalena León. 2001a. Institutional Reform of Agriculture under Neoliberalism: The Impact of the Women's and Indigenous Movements. *Latin American Research Review* 36(2): 31–63.

———. 2001b. *Empowering Women: Land and Property Rights in Latin America*. University of Pittsburgh Press, Pittsburgh.

———. 1982. Peasant Production, Proletarianization, and the Sexual Division of Labor in the Andes. In *Women and Development: The Sexual Division of Labor in Rural Societies*, edited by Lourdes Benería, 29–64. Praeger, New York.

Deere, Carmen Diana, Jane Humphries, and Magdalena León. 1982. Class and Historical Analysis for the Study of Women and Economic Change. In *Women's Roles and Population Trends in the Third World*, edited by Richard Anker, Mayra Buvenic, and Nadia H. Youssef, 87–114. Geneva: International Labour Organization.

Degarrod, Lydia Nakashima. 1998. Female Shamanism and the Mapuche Transformation into Christian Chilean Farmers. *Religion* 28(4):339–50.

De la Cadena, Marisol. 2000. *Indigenous Mestizos: The Politics of Race and Culture in Cuzco, Peru, 1919–1991*. Duke University Press, Durham, N.C.

———. 1995."Women Are More Indian": Ethnicity and Gender in a Community near Cuzco. In *Ethnicity, Markets, and Migration in the Andes: At the Crossroads of History and Anthropology*, edited by Brooke Larson and Olivia Harris, with Enrique Tandeter, 329–48. Duke University Press, Durham, N.C.

De la Fuente, Julio. 1949. *Yalalag: Una villa zapoteca serrana*. Museo Nacional de Antropología, Mexico City.

Del Castillo, Adelaida R. 1977. Malintzin Tenépal: A Preliminary Look into a New Perspective. In *Essays on La Mujer*, edited by Rosaura Sánchez and Rosa Martinez Cruz, 124–49. Chicano Studies Center Publications, University of California, Los Angeles.

Del Pino H., Ponciano. 1998. Family, Culture, and "Revolution": Everyday Life with Sendero Luminoso. In *Shining and Other Paths: War and Society in Peru, 1980–1995*, edited by Steve J. Stern, 158–92. Duke University Press, Durham, N.C.

D'Emilio, Anna Lucia, editor. 1989. *Mujer indígena y educación en América Latina*. UNESCO/I.I.I., Santiago.

Dennis, Philip A. 1985. *The Culture-Bound Syndromes: Folk Illnesses of Psychiatric and Anthropological Interest*, 289–306. In *Grisi Siknis in Miskito Culture*, edited by Ronald C. Simons and Charles C. Hughes. Reidel, Dordrecht.

Desai, Manisha. 2002. Transnational Solidarity: Women's Agency, Structural Adjustment, and Globalization. In *Women's Activism and Globalization: Linking Local Struggles and Transnational Politics*, edited by Nancy A. Naples and Manisha Desai, 15–22. Routledge, London.

Descola, Phillipe. 2001. The Genres of Gender: Local Models and Global Paradigms in the Comparison of Amazonia and Melanesia. In *Gender in Amazonia and Melanesia: An Exploration of the Comparative Method*, edited by Thomas A. Gregor and Donald Tuzin, 91–114. University of California Press, Berkeley.

———. 1996. *The Spears of Twilight: Life and Death in the Amazonian Jungle*. Translated by Janet Lloyd. New Press, New York.

De Terra, Javier Romero, and T. D. Stewart. 1949. *Tepexpan Man*. Viking Fund Publications in Anthropology no. 11, New York.

Devereaux, Leslie. 1987. Gender Difference and the Relations of Inequality in Zinacantan. In *Dealing with Inequality: Analyzing Gender Relations in Melanesia and Beyond*, edited by Marilyn Strathern, 89–111. Cambridge University Press, Cambridge.

Díaz Polanco, Hector. 1997. *Indigenous Peoples in Latin America: The Quest for Self-Determination.* Translated by Lucías Rayas. Westview Press, Boulder, Colo.

Di Capua, Costanza. 1994. Valdivia Figurines and Puberty Rituals. *Andean Past* 4: 229–79.

Dickinson, Torry D. 1997. Selective Globalization: The Relocation of Industrial Production and the Shaping of Women's Work. In *Research in the Sociology of Work: The Globalization of Work*, vol. 6, edited by Randy Hodson, 109–29. JAI Press, Greenwich, Conn.

Dietiker-Amslër, Marianne. 1993. Mujer y tierra en la Huasteca. In *Huasteca I: Espacio y tiempo, Mujer y trabajo: selección de trabajos pertenecientes al V y VI encuentros de investigadores de la Huasteca*, edited by Jesús Ruvalcaba and Graciela Alcalá, 149–76. CIESAS, Mexico City.

Dillehay, Thomas D. 2000. *The Settlement of the Americas: A New Prehistory.* Basic Books, New York.

Di Peso, Charles. 1979. Prehistory: Southern Periphery. In *Handbook of North American Indians*, vol. 9, *Southwest*, edited by Alfonso Ortiz, general editor William C. Sturtevant, 152–61. Smithsonian Institution, Washington, D.C.

Dobyns, Henry F. 1983. *Their Number Become Thinned: Native American Population Dynamics in Eastern North America.* University of Tennessee Press, Knoxville.

Dole, Gertrude. 1974. The Marriages of Pach: A Woman's Life among the Amahuaca. In *Many Sisters: Women in Cross-Cultural Perspective*, edited by Carolyn J. Matthiasson 3–35. Free Press, New York.

Donnan, Christopher, and Luis Jaime Castillo. 1992. Finding the Tomb of a Moche Priestess. *Archaeology* 45(6): 38–42.

Donner, Florinda. 1982. *Shabono.* Delacorte Press, New York.

Dopico Black, Georgina. 2001. *Perfect Wives, Other Women: Adultery and Inquisition in Early Modern Spain.* Duke University Press, Durham, N.C.

Dore, Elizabeth. 2000. One Step Forward, Two Steps Back: Gender and the State in the Long Nineteenth Century. In *Hidden Histories of Gender and the State in Latin America*, edited by Elizabeth Dore and Maxine Molyneux, 3–32. Duke University Press, Durham, N.C.

———. 1997. Property, Households and Public Regulation of Domestic Life: Diriomo, Nicaragua 1840–1900. *Journal of Latin American Studies* 29(3): 591–611.

Dradi, María Pia. 1989. La mujer chayahuita (Mujer indígena y educación en América Latina). In *Mujer indígena y educación en América Latina*, edited by Anna Lucía D'Emilio, 86–105. UNESCO/I. I. I, Santiago.

———. 1987. *La mujer chayahuita: ¿Un destino de marginación?* INP and Fundación Friedrich Ebert, Lima.

———. 1985. Masculino-Femenino: Entre el equilibrio y la subordinación (el caso de la sociedad Chayahuita). *Shupihui*, nos. 35–6: 303–36.

Dransart, Penny. 1992. Pachamama: The Inka Earth Mother of the Long Sweeping Garment. In *Dress and Gender: Making and Meaning*, edited by Ruth Barnes and Joanne B. Eicher, 145–63. Berg, New York.

Drennan, Robert D. 1976. *Fábrica San José and Middle Formative Society in the Valley of Oaxaca.* Vol. 4 of *Prehistory and Human Ecology of the Valley of Oaxaca*, edited by Kent V. Flannery. Memoirs of the Museum of Anthropology, no. 8. University of Michigan, Ann Arbor.

Dunbar Temple, Ella. 1950. El testamento inédito de doña Beatriz Clara Coya de Loyola, hija del Inca Sayri Túpac. *Fénix* (Lima) 7: 111–22.

Dunn, Alvis E. 1995. A Cry at Daybreak: Death, Disease, and Defense of Community in a Highland Ixil-Maya Village. *Ethnohistory* 42(4): 595–606. Special issue: Women, Power, and Resistance in Colonial Mesoamerica, edited by Kevin Gosner and Deborah E. Kanter.

Duviols, Pierre, ed. 1986. *Cultura andina y represión. Procesos y visitas de idolatrías y hechicerías Cajatambo, siglo XVII.* Centro de Estudios Rurales Andinos "Bartolomé de las Casas," Cusco.

———. 1977. *La destrucción de las religiones andinas: Conquista y colonia.* Translated by Albor Maruenda. UNAM, Mexico City.

Earle, Duncan M., and Dean R. Snow. 1985. The Origin of the 260-Day Calendar: The Gestation Hypothesis Reconsidered in Light of Its Use among the Quiche-Maya. In *Fifth Palenque Round Table, 1983,* edited by Virgina M. Fields, general editor Merle Greene Robertson, 241–4. Pre-Columbian Art Research Institute, San Francisco.

Eber, Christine. 1999. Seeking Our Own Food: Indigenous Women's Power and Autonomy in San Pedro Chenalhó, Chiapas (1980–1998). *Latin American Perspectives* 26(3): 6–36.

———. 1995. *Women and Alcohol in a Highland Maya Town: Water of Hope, Water of Sorrow.* University of Texas Press, Austin.

Eber, Christine, and Brenda Rosenbaum. 1993. That We May Serve beneath Your Hands and Feet: Women Weavers in Highland Chiapas, Mexico. In *Crafts in the World Market: The Impact of Global Exchange on Middle American Artisans,* edited by June Nash, 155–79. State University of New York Press, Albany.

Eber, Christine, and Christine Kovic, eds. 2003. *Women of Chiapas: Making History in Times of Struggle and Hope.* Routledge, London.

Edmonson, Munro. 1993. The Mayan Faith. In *World Spirituality: An Encyclopedic History of the Religious Quest,* vol. 4, *South and Mesoamerican Native Spirituality: From the Cult of the Feathered Serpent to the Theology of Liberation,* edited by Gary H. Gossen, with Miguel León-Portilla, 65–86. Crossroad, New York.

Ehlers, Tracy Bachrach. 2000. *Silent Looms: Women and Production in a Guatemalan Town.* Rev. ed. University of Texas Press, Austin [1990].

———. 1993. Belts, Business, and Bloomingdale's: An Alternative Model for Guatemalan Artisan Development. In *Crafts in the World Market: The Impact of Global Exchange on Middle American Artisans,* edited by June Nash, 181–96. State University of New York, Albany.

———. 1991. Debunking Marianismo: Economic Vulnerability and Survival Strategies among Guatemalan Wives. *Ethnology* 30(1): 1–16.

———. 1990. *Silent Looms: Women and Production in a Guatemalan Town.* Westview Press, Boulder, Colo.

Ehrenreich, Barbara, and Arlie Russell Hochschild. 2003. *Global Woman: Nannies, Maids, and Sex Workers in the New Economy.* Metropolitan Books, New York.

El Guindi, Fadwa. 1986. *The Myth of Ritual: A Native's Ethnography of Zapotec Life-Crisis Rituals.* University of Arizona Press, Tucson.

Elias, Norbert. 1978. *The Civilizing Process.* Translated by Edmund Jephcott. Urizen Books, New York.

Elmendorf, Mary. 1976. *Nine Mayan Women: A Village Faces Change.* Schenkman, Cambridge, Mass.

Engels, Friedrich. 1972. *The Origin of the Family, Private Property, and the State.* Pathfinder Press, New York [1884].

Espinosa Soriano, Waldemar. 1976. Las mugeres secundarias de Huayna Capac: Casos de señorialismo feudal en el imperio Inca. *Revista del Museo Nacional* (Lima) 42: 247–98.

Evans, Susan. 2001. Aztec Noble Courts: Men, Women, and Children of the Palace. In *Royal Courts of the Ancient Maya*, vol. 1, *Theory, Comparison, and Synthesis*, edited by Takeshi Inomata and Stephen D. Houston, 237–73. Westview Press, Boulder, Colo.

———. 1998. Sexual Politics in the Aztec Palace: Public, Private, and Profane. *Res* 33 (spring): 167–83.

Ezzo, Joseph A. 1993. *Human Adaptation at Grasshopper Pueblo, Arizona: Social and Ecological Perspectives*. International Monographs in Prehistory Archaeological series no. 4, Ann Arbor.

Fabián, Beatriz. 1994. La mujer asháninka en un contexto de violencia política. *Amazonía Peruana* 12(24): 287–315.

Fabri, Antonella. 1995. Maya Women and the Politics of Health. *Cultural Survival* 19(1): 70–2.

Falla, Ricardo. 1979. *El tesoro de San Blas: Turismo en San Blas*. Ediciones Centro de Capitación Social, Panama City.

Falla, Ricardo. N.d. *Historia kuna, historia rebelde: La articulación del archipelago kuna a la nación panameña*. Ediciones Centro de Capitacion Social, Panama City.

Farriss, Nancy M. 1984. *Maya Society under Colonial Rule: The Collective Enterprise of Survival*. Princeton University Press, Princeton.

Feijoó, María del Carmen. 1989. The Challenge of Constructing Civilian Peace: Women and Democracy in Argentina. In *The Women's Movement in Latin America*, edited by Jane S. Jaquette, 72–94. Unwin and Hyman, Boston.

Feijoó, María del Carmen, and Monica Gogna. 1990. Women in the Transition to Democracy. In *Women and Social Change in Latin America*, edited by Elizabeth Jelin, 79–114. Zed Books, London.

Fejos, Paul. 1943. *Ethnography of the Yagua*. Viking Fund Publications in Anthropology no. 1, New York.

Femenias, Blenda. 1991. Regional Dress of the Colca Valley, Peru: A Dynamic Tradition. In *Textile Traditions of Mesoamerica and the Andes: An Anthology*, edited by Margot Blum Schevill, Janet Catherine Berlo, and Edward B. Dwyer, 179–204. Garland, New York.

Feminism and Globalization: The Impact of the Global Economy on Women and Feminist Thought. 1996. *Indiana Journal of Global Legal Studies* 4(1). Special issue.

Ferguson, R. Brian. 1995. *Yanomami Warfare: A Political History*. School of American Research, Santa Fe.

———. 1992. A Savage Encounter: Western Contact and the Yanomami War Complex. In *War in the Tribal Zone: Expanding States and Indigenous Warfare*, edited by R. Brian Ferguson and Neil L. Whitehead, 199–227. School of American Research Press, Santa Fe.

Fernández de Recas, Guillermo S. 1961. *Cacicazgos y nobiliario indígena de la Nueva España*. Instituto Bibliográfico Mexicano, Mexico.

Few, Martha. 2002. *Women Who Live Evil Lives: Gender, Religion, and the Politics of Power in Colonial Guatemala*. University of Texas Press, Austin.

———. 1995. Women, Religion, and Power: Gender and Resistance in Daily Life in Late-Seventeenth-Century Santiago de Guatemala. *Ethnohistory* 42(4): 627–37.

Figueroa Mier, Martha. 1998. De homicidio calificada a genocidio: cuestionamientos jurídicos en torno a la masacre de Acteal. In *La otra palabra: mujeres y violencia en Chiapas, antes y después de Acteal*, edited by Rosalva Aída Hernández Castillo, 106–13. CIESAS, COLEM, and CIAM, Mexico.

Finerman, Ruthbeth. 1989. The Forgotten Healers: Women as Family Healers in an Andean Indian Community. In *Women as Healers: Cross-Cultural Perspectives*, edited by Carol Shepherd McClain, 24–41. Rutgers University Press, New Brunswick, N.J.

Fisher, Lillian E. 1966. *The Last Inca Revolt, 1780–1783*. University of Oklahoma Press, Norman.

Fisher, William H. 2001. Age-Based Genders among the Kayapo. In *Gender in Amazonia and Melanesia: An Exploration of the Comparative Method*, edited by Thomas A. Gregor and Donald Tuzin, 115–40. University of California Press, Berkeley.

Flannery, Kent. 1986. Guilá Naquitz in Spatial, Temporal, and Cultural Context. In *Guilá Naquitz: Archaic Foraging and Early Agriculture in Oaxaca, Mexico*, edited by Kent V. Flannery, 31–42. Academic Press, Orlando.

Flood, Merielle K. 1994. Changing Gender Relations in Zinacantán, Mexico. *Research in Economic Anthropology* 15: 145–73.

Flores Andino, Francisco A. 1975. La muger miskita. *América Indígena* 35(3): 569–74.

Flores Espinosa, Javier F. 1999. En brazos de la divinidad. Historia de una mujer y su huaca (Canta, 1650). In *Mujeres y género en la historia del Perú*, edited by Margarita Zegarra, 15–37. CENDOC-Mujer, Lima.

Flores Ochoa, Jorge A. 1968. *Pastoralists of the Andes: The Alpaca Herders of Paratía*. Translated by Ralph Bolton. Institute for the Study of Human Issues, Philadelphia.

Flusche, Della M., and Eugene H. Korth. 1983. *Forgotten Females: Women of African and Indian Descent in Colonial Chile, 1535–1800*. Blaine Ethridge Books, Detroit.

Fogelson, Raymond D. 1998. Perspectives on Native American Identity. In *Studying Native America: Problems and Prospects*, edited by Russell Thornton, 40–59. University of Wisconsin Press, Madison.

Foote, Cheryl J., and Sandra K. Schackel. 1986. Indian Women of New Mexico, 1535–1680. In *New Mexico Women: Intercultural Perspectives*, edited by Joan M. Jensen and Darlis A. Miller, 17–40. University of New Mexico Press, Albuquerque.

Ford, Ramona. 1997. Native American Women: Changing Statuses, Changing Interpretations. In *Writing the Range: Race, Class, and Culture*, edited by Elizabeth Jameson and Susan Armitage, 42–68. University of Oklahoma Press, Norman.

Forster, Cindy. 2001. *The Time of Freedom: Campesino Workers in Guatemala's October Revolution*. University of Pittsburgh Press, Pittsburgh.

———. 1999. Violent and Violated Women: Justice and Gender in Rural Guatemala, 1936–1956. *Journal of Women's History* 11(3): 55–77.

Fortún, Julia Elena. 1972. La mujer aymara en Bolivia. *América Indígena* 32(3): 935–47.

Frank, Andre Gunder. 1990. A Theoretical Introduction to 5,000 Years of World System History. *Review* (Ferdinand Braudel Center) 13(2): 155–248.

Frank, Andre Gunder, and Barry K. Gills. 1993. The 5,000 Year World System: An Interdisciplinary Introduction. In *The World System: Five Hundred Years or Five Thousand?* edited by Andre Gunder Frank and Barry K. Gills, 3–55. Routledge, London.

Freyermuth Enciso, Graciela. 1998. Antecedentes de Acteal: Muerte materna y control natal, ¿genocidio silencioso? In *La otra palabra: Mujeres y violencia en Chiapas, antes y después de Acteal*, edited by Rosalva Aída Hernández Castillo, 63–83. CIE-SAS, COLEM, and CIAM, Mexico.

Freyermuth, Graciela, and Mariana Fernández. 1997. Factores culturales en el registro de la muerte de mujeres en dos municipios de los altos de Chiapas. In *Género y salud en el sureste de México*, edited by Esperanza Túñon Pablos, 33–54. ECO-SUR and Universidad Juárez Autónoma de Tabasco, Mexico.

Freyermuth Enciso, Graciela, and Mariana Fernández Guerrero. 1995. Migration, Organization, and Identity: The Case of a Women's Group from San Cristóbal de las Casas. *Signs* 20(4): 970–95.

Friedlander, Judith. 1975. *Being Indian in Hueyapan: A Study of Forced Identity in Contemporary Mexico*. St. Martin's Press, New York.

Frye, David. 1996. *Indians into Mexicans: History and Identity in a Mexican Town*. University of Texas Press, Austin.

Gailey, Christine. 1987a. Evolutionary Perspectives on Gender Hierarchy. In *Analyzing Gender: A Handbook of Social Science Research*, edited by Beth B. Hess and Myra Marx Ferree 32–67. Sage, Newbury Park, Calif.

———. 1987b. *From Kinship to Kingship: Gender Hierarchy and State Formation in the Tongan Islands*. University of Texas Press, Austin.

Gallagher, Ann Miriam. 1978. The Indian Nuns of Mexico City's *Monasterio* of Corpus Christi, 1724–1821. In *Latin American Women: Historical Perspectives*, edited by Asunción Lavrin, 150–72. Greenwood Press, Westport, Conn.

Gamio de Alba, Margarita. 1957. *La mujer indígena de Centro America: sumaria recopilación acerca de sus condiciones de vida*. Instituto Indigenista Interamericano, Mexico City.

Ganson, Barbara. 2003. *The Guaraní under Spanish Rule in the Río de la Plata*. Stanford University Press, Stanford.

García, Ana Isabel, and Enrique Gomáriz. 1989. *Mujeres centroamericanas*. Vol. 1. *Ante la crisis, la guerra y el proceso de Paz*. Vol. 2. *Effectos del conflicto*. Universidad para la Paz, San José, Costa Rica.

García, Claudia. 1997. Identidad femenina y pensamiento religioso tradicional: algunos comentarios acerca de la posesión femenina entre los miskitos de Nicaragua. *América Indígena* 57(3–4): 203–15.

García Moll, Roberto, Daniel Juárez Cossío, Carmen Pijoan Aguade, María Elena Salas Cuesta, and Marcela Salas Cuesta. 1991. *Catálogo de entierros de San Luis Tlatilco, México, Temporada IV*. Serie Antropología Física-Arqueología, INAH, Mexico City.

Garfield, Seth. 2001. *Indigenous Struggle at the Heart of Brazil: State Policy, Frontier Expansion, and the Xavante Indians, 1937–1988*. Duke University Press, Durham, N.C.

Gargallo, Francesca. 2000. Los garífuna de Centroamérica: Reubicación, sobrevivencia y nacionalidad de un pueblo afroindoamericano. *Política y Cultura* (UAM, Xochimilco), Fall, no. 14: 89–107.

———. 1993. Las culturas afroamericanas de Belice: Criollos y garífunas en la identidad pluriétnica de su país. In *Presencia africana en Centroamerica*, edited by Luz María Martínez Montiel, 61–102. Consejo Nacional para la Cultura y las Artes, Mexico City.

Garza Caligaris, Anna María, and Juana María Ruiz Ortiz. 1992. Madres solteras indígenas. *Mesoamérica* 23: 67–77.

Garza Caligaris, Anna María, María Fernanda Paz Salinas, Juana María Ruiz Ortiz, and Angelino Calvo Sánchez. 1993. *Sk'op Antzetik: una historia de mujeres en la selva de Chiapas*. Universidad Autónoma de Chiapas, Tuxtla Gutiérrez, Chiapas, México.

Garza Tarazona de González, Silvia. 1991. *La mujer mesoamericana*. Editorial Planeta Mexicana, Mexico City.

Gauderman, Kimberly. 2003. *Women's Lives in Colonial Quito: Gender, Law, and Economy in Spanish America*. University of Texas Press, Austin.

Gero, Joan M. 2001. Field Knots and Ceramic Beaus: Interpreting Gender in the Peruvian Early Intermediate Period. In *Gender in Pre-Hispanic America: A Symposium at Dumbarton Oaks*, edited by Cecelia F. Klein, 15–55. Dumbarton Oaks, Washington, D.C.

————. 1992. Feasts and Females: Gender Ideology and Political Meals in the Andes. *Norwegian Archaeology Review* 25(1): 15–30.

————. 1991. Genderlithics: Women's Roles in Stone Tool Production. In *Engendering Archaeology: Women and Prehistory*, edited by Joan M. Gero and Margaret W. Conkey, 163–93. Blackwell, Oxford.

Ghidinelli, Azzo, and Pierleone Massajoli. 1984. Resumen etnográfico de los caribes negros (garifunas) de Honduras. *América Indígena* 44(3): 485–518.

Gibson, Charles. 1964. *The Aztecs under Spanish Rule: A History of the Indians of the Valley of Mexico, 1519–1810*. Stanford University Press, Stanford.

Gill, Lesley. 1994. *Precarious Dependencies: Gender, Class, and Domestic Service in Bolivia*. Columbia University Press, New York.

————. 1993. Religious Mobility and the Many Words of God in La Paz, Bolivia. In *Rethinking Protestantism in Latin America*, edited by Virginia Garrard-Burnett and David Stoll, 180–98. Temple University Press, Philadelphia.

————. 1990. "Like a Veil to Cover Them": Women and the Pentecostal Movement in La Paz. *American Ethnologist* 17(4): 708–21.

Gillespie, Susan D. 1989. *The Aztec Kings: The Construction of Rulership in Mexica History*. University of Arizona Press, Tucson.

Girard, Rafael. 1958. *Indios selváticos de la Amazonía Peruana*. Libro Mex, Mexico.

Glantz, Margo, ed. 1994. *La Malinche, sus padres y sus hijos*. UNAM, Mexico City.

Glass-Coffin, Bonnie. 1999. Engendering Peruvian Shamanism through Time: Insights from Ethnohistory and Ethnography. *Ethnohistory* 46(2): 205–38.

Glave, Luis Miguel. 1987. Mujer indígena, trabajo doméstico y cambio social en el virreinato peruano del siglo XVII: La ciudad de La Paz y el Sur Andino en 1684. *Bulletin de l'Institut d'Etudes Andines* 16(3–4): 39–69.

Glittenberg, Jody. 1994. *To the Mountain and Back: The Mysteries of Guatemalan Highland Family Life*. Waveland Press, Prospect Heights, Illinois.

Goldman, Irving. 1963. *The Cubeo: Indians of the Northwest Amazon*. University of Illinois Press, Urbana.

Goldsmith Connelly, Mary. 1999. Barriendo, tejiendo y cocinando: El trabajo doméstico en la sociedad azteca. In *Chalchihuite. Homenaje a Doris Heyden*, edited by María de Jesús Rodríguez-Shadow and Beatriz Barba de Piña Chán, 213–25. INAH, Mexico City.

Goloubinoff, Marina. 2003. ¿Por qué se roba la novia? Las razones de una costumbre negada pero viva. In *El matrimonio en Mesoamérica ayer y hoy: Unas miradas antropológicas*, edited by David Robichaux, 237–48. Universidad Iberoamericana, Mexico City.

Gonzalbo, Pilar. 1987. Tradición y ruptura en la educación femenina del siglo XVI. In *Presencia y transparencia: La mujer en la historia de México*, by Carmen Ramos Escandón et al., 33–60. El Colegio de México, Mexico City.

Gonzalez, Nancie L. (Solien). 1988. *Sojourners of the Caribbean: Ethnogenesis and Ethnohistory of the Garafuna.* University of Illinois, Urbana.

———. 1969. *Black Carib Household Struture: A Study of Migration and Modernization.* University of Washington Press, Seattle.

González Montes, Soledad. 1998. La violencia doméstica y sus repercusiones en la salud reproductiva en una zona indígena (Cuetzalan, Puebla). In *Los silencios de la salud reproductiva: violencia, sexualidad y derechos reproductivos,* 17–54. Asociación Mexicana de Población y La Fundación John D. y Catherine T. MaCarthur, Mexico City.

———. 1994a. Mujeres, trabajo y pobreza en el campo mexicano: Una revisión crítica de la bibliografía reciente. In *Las mujeres en la pobreza,* edited by Javier Alatorre, Gloria Careaga, Clara Jusidman, Vania Salles, Cecilia Talamante, and John Townsend, 179–214. El Colegio de México, Mexico.

———. 1994b. Intergenerational and Gender Relations in the Transition from a Peasant Economy to a Diversified Economy. In *Women of the Mexican Countryside, 1850–1990,* edited by Heather Fowler-Salamini and Mary Kay Vaughan, 175–91. Tucson: University of Arizona Press.

———. 1994c. Del matrimonio eterno a las mujeres que no aguantan: Cambios recientes en familias rurales. In *La pareja o hasta que la muerte nos separe ¿Un sueño imposible?* edited by María Teresa Döring, 105–21. Fontamara, Mexico City.

———. 1991. Los ingresos no agropecuarios, el trabajo remunerado femenino y la transformación de las relaciones intergenéricas e intergeneracionales de las familias campesinas. In *Textos e pre-textos: Once estudios sobre la mujer,* edited by Vania Salles and Elsie McPhail, 225–57. El Colegio de México, Mexico City.

———. 1988. La reproducción de la desigualdad entre los sexos: Prácticas e ideología de la herencia en una comunidad campesina (Xalatlaco, Estado de México, 1920–1960). In *Las mujeres en el campo: Memoria de la Primera Reunión Nacional de Investigación sobre Mujeres Campesinas en México,* edited by Josefina Aranda B., 65–81. Instituto de Investigaciones Sociológicas de la Universidad Autónoma Benito Juárez de Oaxaca, Oaxaca de Juárez, Oaxaca, Mexico.

González Montes, Soledad, and Pilar Iracheta Cenegorta. 1987. La violencia en la vida de las mujeres campesinas: El distrito de Tenango, 1880–1910. In *Presencia y transparencia: La mujer en la historia de México,* by Carmen Ramos Escandón et al., 111–41. El Colegio de México, Mexico City.

González Torres, Yolotl. 1979. El panteón mexica. *Antropología e historia* 25: 9–19.

Good, Catharine. 2000. Indigenous Peoples in Central and Western Mexico. In *Supplement to the Handbook of Middle American Indians,* edited by John D. Monaghan, series edited by Victoria Reifler Bricker, 120–49. University of Texas Press, Austin.

Good, Kenneth (with David Chanoff). 1991. *Into the Heart: One Man's Pursuit of Love and Knowledge among the Yanomama.* Simon and Schuster, New York.

Goodman, Felicitas D. 2001. *Maya Apocalypse: Seventeen Years with the Women of a Yucatan Village.* Indiana University Press, Bloomington.

Gosner, Kevin. 1997. Women, Rebellion, and the Moral Economy of Maya Peasants in Colonial Mexico. In *Indian Women of Early Mexico,* edited by Susan Schroeder, Stephanie Wood, and Robert Haskett, 217–30. University of Oklahoma Press, Norman.

————. 1992. *Soldiers of the Virgin: The Moral Economy of a Colonial Maya Rebellion.* University of Arizona Press, Tucson.

Gossen, Gary H. 1999. *Telling Maya Tales: Tzotzil Identities in Modern Mexico.* Routledge, New York.

————. 1974. *Chamulas in the World of the Sun: Time and Space in a Maya Oral Tradition.* Harvard University Press, Cambridge, Mass.

Gotkowitz, Laura. 2003. Trading Insults: Honor, Violence, and the Gendered Culture of Commerce in Cochabamba, Bolivia, 1870s–1950s. *Hispanic American Historical Review* 83(1): 83–118.

Gow, Peter. 1989. The Perverse Child: Desire in a Native Amazonian Subsistence Economy. *Man* (n.s.) 24(4): 567–82.

Graham, Elizabeth. 1991. Women and Gender in Maya Prehistory. In *The Archaeology of Gender: Proceedings of the Twenty-second Annual Conference of the Archaeological Association of the University of Calgary,* edited by Dale Walde and Noreen D. Willows, 470–8. Calgary Archaeological Association, Calgary,.

Graham, Laura R. 1995. *Performing Dreams: Discourses of Immortality among the Xavante of Central Brazil.* University of Texas Press, Austin.

Grandin, Greg. 2004. *The Last Colonial Massacre: Latin America in the Cold War.* University of Chicago Press, Chicago.

————. 2000. *The Blood of Guatemala: A History of Race and Nation.* Duke University Press, Durham, N.C.

Graubart, Karen. 2000a. Weaving and the Gender Division of Labor in Early Colonial Peru. *American Indian Quarterly* 24(4): 537–61.

————. 2000b. Indecent Living: Indigenous Women and the Politics of Representation in Early Colonial Peru. *Colonial Latin American Review* 9(2): 213–35.

Green, Linda. 1999. *Fear as a Way of Life: Mayan War Widows in Rural Guatemala.* Columbia University Press, New York.

————. 1993. Shifting Affiliation: Maya Widows and *Evangélicos* in Guatemala. In *Rethinking Protestantism in Latin America,* edited by Virginia Garrard-Burnett and David Stoll, 159–79. Temple University Press, Philadelphia.

Green, Rayna. 1980. Review Essay: Native American Women. *Signs* 6(2): 248–67.

Gregor, Thomas A. 1985. *Anxious Pleasures: The Sexual Lives of an Amazonian People.* University of Chicago Press, Chicago.

————. 1977. *Mehinaku: The Drama of Daily Life in a Brazilian Village.* Chicago: University of Chicago Press.

Gregor, Thomas A., and Donald Tuzin, eds. 2001a. *Gender in Amazonia and Melanesia: An Exploration of the Comparative Method.* University of California Press, Berkeley.

————. 2001b. The Anguish of Gender: Men's Cults and Moral Contradiction in Amazonia and Melanesia. In *Gender in Amazonia and Melanesia: An Exploration of the Comparative Method,* edited by Thomas A. Gregor and Donald Tuzin, 309–36. University of California Press, Berkeley.

Griffiths, Nicholas. 1996. *The Cross and the Serpent: Religious Repression and Resurgence in Colonial Peru.* University of Oklahoma Press, Norman.

Gruzinski, Serge. 1989. Individualization and Acculturation: Confession among the Nahuas of Mexico from the Sixteenth to the Eighteenth Century. In *Sexuality and Marriage in Colonial Latin America,* edited by Asunción Lavrin, 96–117. University of Nebraska Press, Lincoln.

Güémez Pineda, Miguel. 2000. La concepción del cuerpo humano, la maternidad y el dolor entre mujeres mayas yukatekas. *Mesoamérica* (Antiqua, Guatemala) 39: 305–22.

Guerrero, Andrés. 2003. The Administration of Dominated Populations under a Regime of Customary Citizenship: The Case of Post-Colonial Ecuador. In *After Spanish Rule: Postcolonial Predicaments of the Americas*, edited by Mark Thurner and Andrés Guerrero, 272–309. Duke University Press, Durham, N.C.

Guha, Ranajit. 1983. *Elementary Aspects of Peasant Insurgency in Colonial India.* Oxford University Press, Delhi.

Guiteras-Holmes, Calixta. 1961. *Perils of the Soul: The World View of a Tzotzil Indian.* Free Press of Glencoe, Glencoe, Ill.

Guss, David M. 1989. *To Weave and Sing: Art, Symbol, and Narrative in the South American Rain Forest.* University of California Press, Berkeley.

Gutiérrez, Ramon A. 1994. A Gendered History of the Conquest of America: A View from New Mexico. In *Gender Rhetorics: Postures of Dominance and Submission in History*, edited by Richard C. Trexler, 47–63. Medieval and Renaissance Texts and Studies, Binghamton, N.Y.

———. 1991. *When Jesus Came, the Corn Mothers Went Away: Marriage, Sexuality, and Power in New Mexico, 1500–1846.* Stanford University Press, Stanford.

H. de Pozas, Isabel. 1959. La posición de la mujer dentro de la estructura social tzotzil. *Revista de Ciencias Políticas y Sociales* 5(18): 565–75.

Halbmayer, Ernst. 1997. La construcción cultural de las relaciones de género entre los Yukpa. In *Complementariedad entre hombre y mujer: relaciones de género desde la perspectiva amerindia*, edited by Michel Perrin y Marie Perruchon, 77–108. Ediciones ABYA-YALA, Quito.

Hale, Charles A. 1989. *The Transformation of Liberalism in Late Nineteenth-Century Mexico.* Princeton University Press, Princeton.

———. 1968. *Mexican Liberalism in the Age of Mora, 1821–1853.* Yale University Press, New Haven.

Halperin-Donghi, Tulio. 1985. Economy and Society in Post-Independence Spanish America. In *Cambridge History of Latin America*, vol. 3 (From Independence to c. 1870), edited by Leslie Bethell, 299–345. Cambridge University Press, Cambridge.

Hamann, Byron. 1997. Weaving and the Iconography of Prestige: The Royal Gender Symbolism of Lord 5 Flower's/Lady 4 Rabbit's Family. In *Women in Prehistory: North America and Mesoamerica*, edited by Cheryl Claassen and Rosemary A. Joyce, 153–72. University of Pennsylvania Press, Philadelphia.

Hamilton, Sarah. 1998. *The Two-Headed Household: Gender and Rural Development in the Ecuadorean Andes.* University of Pittsburgh Press, Pittsburgh.

———. 1992. Visible Partners: Women's Labor and Management of Agricultural Capital on Small Farms in the Highlands of Central Ecuador. *Urban Anthropology* 21(4): 353–83.

Hamilton, Sarah, and Edward Fisher. 2003. Non-Traditional Agricultural Exports in Highland Guatemala: Understanding of Risk and Perceptions of Change. *Latin American Research Review* 38(3): 82–110.

Handbook of Middle American Indians. 1964–76. Series edited by Robert Wauchope. 16 vols. University of Texas, Austin.

Harner, Michael J. 1972. *The Jívaro: People of the Sacred Waterfalls.* Doubleday, Garden City, N.Y.

Harris, Olivia. 1994. Condor and Bull: The Ambiguities of Masculinity in Northern Potosí. In *Sex and Violence: Issues in Representation and Experience*, edited by Penelope Harvey and Peter Gow, 40–65. Routledge, London.

————. 1980. The Power of Signs: Gender, Culture and the Wild in the Bolivian Andes. In *Nature, Culture and Gender*, edited by Carol P. MacCormack and Marilyn Strathern, 70–94. Cambridge University Press, Cambridge.

————. 1978. Complementarity and Conflict: An Andean View of Women and Men. In *Sex and Age as Principles of Social Differentiation*, edited by J. S. La Fontaine, 21–40. Academic Press, London.

Harrison, Margaret E. 2001. Mexican Physicians, Nurses, and Social Workers. In *Mesoamerican Healers*, edited by Brad R. Huber and Alan R. Sandstrom, 270–306. University of Texas Press, Austin.

Harrison, Regina. 1989. *Signs, Songs, and Memory in the Andes: Translating Quechua Language and Culture*. University of Texas Press, Austin.

Harvey, H. R., and Isabel Kelly. 1969. The Totonac. In *Handbook of Middle American Indians*, vol. 8, *Ethnology*, pt. 2, edited by Evon Z. Vogt, series edited by Robert Wauchope, 638–81. University of Texas Press, Austin.

Harvey, Neil. 1998. *The Chiapas Rebellion: The Struggle for Land and Democracy*. Duke University Press, Durham, N.C.

Harvey, Penelope. 1998. Los "hechos naturales" de parentesco y género en un contexto andino. In *Gente de carne y hueso: las tramas de parentesco en los Andes*, vol. 2, *Parentesco y género en los Andes*, edited by Denise Y. Arnold, 69–82. ILCA, La Paz, Bolivia.

————. 1994. Domestic Violence in the Peruvian Andes. In *Sex and Violence: Issues in Representation and Experience*, edited by Penelope Harvey and Peter Gow, 66–89. Routledge, London.

Haskett, Robert. 1997. Activist or Adulteress? The Life and Struggle of Doña Josefa María of Tepoztlan. In *Indian Women of Early Mexico*, edited by Susan Schroeder, Stephanie Wood, and Robert Haskett, 145–63. University of Oklahoma Press, Norman.

Hassig, Ross. 1998. The Maid of the Myth: La Malinche and the History of Mexico. *Indiana Journal of Hispanic Literatures* 12: 101–33.

————. 1988. *Aztec Warfare: Imperial Expansion and Political Control*. University of Oklahoma Press, Norman.

Hastorf, Christine. 1991. Gender, Space, and Food in Prehistory. In *Engendering Archaeology: Women and Prehistory*, edited by Joan M. Gero and Margaret W. Conkey, 132–59. Blackwell, Oxford.

Hatley, Nancy Brennan. 1976. Cooperativism and Enculturation among the Cuna Indians of San Blas. In *Enculturation in Latin America: An Anthology*, edited by Johannes Wilbert, 67–94. Latin American Center Publications, University of California, Los Angeles.

Haviland, William. 1997. The Rise and Fall of Sexual Inequality: Death and Gender at Tikal, Guatemala. *Ancient Mesoamerica* 8(1): 1–12.

Hays-Gilpin, Kelley. 2000. Beyond Mother Earth and Father Sky: Sex and Gender in Ancient Southwestern Visual Arts. In *Reading the Body: Representations and Remains in the Archaeological Record*, edited by Alison E. Rautman, 165–86. University of Pennsylvania Press, Philadelphia.

Hecht, Susannah, and Alexander Cockburn. 1989. *The Fate of the Forest: Developers, Destroyers, and Defenders of the Amazon*. Verso, London.

Heizer, Robert F., and Sherburne F. Cook. 1959. New Evidence of Antiquity of Tepexpan and Other Human Remains from the Valley of Mexico. *Southwestern Journal of Anthropology* 15(1): 36–42.

Hellbom, Anna-Britta. 1967. *La participación cultural de las mujeres indias y mestizas en el México precortesano y postrevolucionario*. Ethnographical Museum, Stockholm.

Helms, Mary W. 1981. *Cuna Molas and Cocle Art Forms: Reflections on Panamanian Design Styles and Symbols*. Working Papers in the Traditional Arts, no. 7, ISHI, Philadelphia.

———. 1980. Succession to High Office in Pre-Columbian Circum-Caribbean Chiefdoms. *Man* 15(4): 718–31.

———. 1976a. Competition, Power, and Succession to Office in Pre-Columbian Panama. In *Frontier Adaptations in Lower Central America*, edited by Mary W. Helms and Franklin O. Loveland, 25–35. ISHI, Philadelphia.

———. 1976b. Introduction. In *Frontier Adaptations in Lower Central America*, edited by Mary W. Helms and Franklin O. Loveland, 1–22. ISHI, Philadelphia.

———. 1976c. Domestic Organization in Eastern Central America: The San Blas Cuna, Miskito, and Black Carib Compared. *Western Canadian Journal of Anthropology* 6(3): 133–63.

———. 1971. *Asang: Adaptations to Culture Contact in a Miskito Community*. University of Florida Press, Gainesville.

———. 1970. Matrilocality, Social Solidarity, and Culture Contact: Three Case Histories. *Southwestern Journal of Anthropology* 26(2): 197–212.

Hemming, John. 1995. *Red Gold: The Conquest of the Brazilian Indians*. Rev. ed. Papermac, London [1978].

———. 1987. *Amazon Frontier: The Defeat of the Brazilian Indians*. Harvard University Press, Cambridge, Mass.

———. 1970. *The Conquest of the Incas*. Harcourt Brace Jovanovich, New York.

Hendon, Julia A. 1997. Women's Work, Women's Space, and Women's Status among the Classic-Period Maya Elite of the Copan Valley, Honduras. In *Women in Prehistory: North America and Mesoamerica*, edited by Cheryl Claassen and Rosemary A. Joyce, 33–46. University of Pennsylvania Press, Philadelphia.

———. 1992. Hilado y tejido en la época prehispanica: Tecnología y relaciones sociales de la producción textil. In *La indumentaria y el tejido mayas a través del tiempo*, edited by Linda Asturias de Barrios and Dina Fernández García, 7–16. Museo Ixchel del Traje Indígena, Guatemala.

———. 1991. Status and Power in Classic Maya Society: An Archaeological Study. *American Anthropologist* 93(4): 894–918.

Hendrickson, Carol. 1996. Women, Weaving, and Education in Maya Revitalization. In *Maya Cultural Activism in Guatemala*, edited by Edward F. Fischer and R. McKenna Brown, 156–64. University of Texas Press, Austin.

———. 1995. *Weaving Identities: Construction of Dress and Self in a Highland Guatemala Town*. University of Texas Press, Austin.

Henestrosa, Andres. 1993. The Forms of Sexual Life in Juchitán. In *Zapotec Struggles: Histories, Politics, and Representations from Juchitán, Oaxaca*, edited by Howard Campbell, Leigh Binford, Miguel Bartolomé, and Alicia Barabas, 129–33. Smithsonian Institution Press, Washington, D.C.

Henly, Paul. 1982. *The Panare: Tradition and Change on the Amazonian Frontier*. Yale University Press, New Haven.

Henry, Jules. 1964. *Jungle People: A Kaingang Tribe of the Highlands of Brazil*. Vintage Books, New York.

Hern, Warren M. 1992. Shipibo Polygyny and Patrilocality. *American Ethnologist* 19(3): 501–22.

Hernández, Teresita, and Clara Murguialday. 1992. *Mujeres indígenas, ayer y hoy: Aportes para la discusión desde una perspectiva de género.* Talasa Ediciones, Madrid.

Hernández Castillo, Rosalva Aída. 2002. Zapatismo and the Emergence of Indigenous Feminism. *NACLA: Report on the Americas* 35(6): 39–43.

———. 2001. *Histories and Stories from Chiapas: Border Identities in Southern Mexico.* Translated by Martha Pou. University of Texas Press, Austin.

———. 1998. Antes y después de Acteal: Voces, memorias y experiencias desde las mujeres de San Pedro Chenalhó. In *La otra palabra: Mujeres y violencia en Chiapas, antes y después de Acteal,* edited by Rosalva Aída Hernández Castillo, 15–36. CIESAS, COLEM, and CIAM, Mexico.

———. 1997. Between Hope and Adversity: The Struggle of Organized Women in Chiapas since the Zapatista Uprising. *Journal of Latin American Anthropology* 3(1): 102–20.

———. 1995. Reinventing Tradition: The Women's Law. *Cultural Survival Quarterly* 19–20 (spring): 24–5.

Hernández Castillo, Rosalva Aída, and Anna María Garza Caligaris. 1995. En torno a la ley y la costumbre: Problemas de antropología legal y género en los Altos de Chiapas. In *Tradiciones y costumbres jurídicas en comunidades indígenas de México,* edited by Rosa Isabel Estrada Martínez and Gisela González Guerra, 215–24. Comisíon Nacional de Derechos Humanos, Mexico.

Hernández Castillo, Rosalva Aída, and Lynn Stephen. 1999. Indigenous Women's Participation in Formulating the San Andrés Accords. *Cultural Survival* 23 (spring): 50–1.

Herren, Ricardo. 1991. *La conquista erótica de las Indias.* Planeta, Barcelona.

Herrera, Robinson. 2003. *Natives, Europeans, and Africans in Sixteenth-Century Santiago de Guatemala.* University of Texas Press, Austin.

Hewitt, Erika A. 1999. What's in a Name: Gender, Power, and Classic Maya Women Rulers. *Ancient Mesoamerica* 10(2): 252–62.

Hickman, John M., and William T. Stuart. 1977. Descent, Alliance, and Moiety in Chucuito, Peru: An Explanatory Sketch of Aymara Social Organization. In *Andean Kinship and Marriage,* edited by Ralph Bolton and Enrique Mayer, 43–59. Special publication no. 7, American Anthropological Association, Washington, D.C.

Hill, Jonathan D. 1992. *Keepers of the Sacred Chants: The Poetics of Ritual Power in an Amazonian Society.* University of Arizona Press, Tucson.

Hill, Robert M. 1992. *Colonial Cakchiquels: Highland Maya Adaptations to Spanish Rule, 1600–1700.* Harcourt, Brace, Jovanovich, Fort Worth, Tex.

Hirabayashi, Lane Rio. 1993. *Cultural Capital: Mountain Zapotec Migrant Associations in Mexico City.* University of Arizona Press, Tucson.

Hirschfeld, Lawrence A. 1977. Art in Cunaland: Ideology and Cultural Adaptation. *Man* (n.s.), 12(1): 104–23.

Hochschild, Arlie Russell. 2000. Global Care Chains and Emotional Surplus Value. In *Global Capitalism,* edited by Will Hutton and Anthony Giddens, 130–46. New Press, New York.

Hocquenghem, Anne Marie. 1987. *Iconagrafía mochica.* Pontificia Universidad Católica del Perú, Fondo Editorial, Lima.

Hocquenghem, Anne Marie, and Patricia J. Lyon. 1980. A Class of Anthropomorphic Supernatural Females in Moche Iconography. *Ñawpa Pacha* 18: 27–48.

Holloman, Regina E. 1976. Cuna Household Types and the Domestic Order. In *Frontier Adaptations in Lower Central America*, edited by Mary W. Helms and Franklin O. Loveland, 131–49. ISHI, Philadelphia.

―――. 1975. Ethnic Boundary Maintenance, Readaptation and Societal Evolution in the San Blas Islands of Panama. In *Ethnicity and Resource Competition in Plural Societies*, edited by Leo M. Despres, 27–40. Mouton, The Hague.

Holmberg, Allan R. 1969. *Nomads of the Long Bow: The Siriono of Eastern Bolivia*. Natural History Press, Garden City, N.Y. [1950].

Hooks, Margaret. 1993. *Guatemalan Women Speak*. EPICA, Washington, D.C.

Hopkins, A. G., ed. 2002. *Globalization in World History*. Norton, New York.

Hopkins, Diane Elizabeth. 1988. Ritual, Sodality and Cargo among Andean Women. In *Manipulating the Saints: Religious Brotherhoods and Social Integration in Postconquest Latin America*, edited by Albert Meyers and Diane Elizabeth Hopkins, 175–195. WAYASBAH, Hamburg.

Hopkins, Nicholas A. 1988. Classic Mayan Kinship Systems: Epigraphic and Ethnographic Evidence for Patrilineality. *Estudios de Cultura Maya* 17: 87–121.

Horn, Rebecca. 1998. Testaments and Trade: Interethnic Ties among Petty Traders in Central Mexico (Coyoacan, 1550–1620). In *Dead Giveaways: Indigenous Testaments of Colonial Mesoamerica and the Andes*, edited by Susan Kellogg and Matthew Restall, 59–83. University of Utah Press, Salt Lake City.

―――. 1997. Gender and Social Identity: Nahua Naming Patterns in Postconquest Central Mexico. In *Indian Women of Early Mexico*, edited by Susan Schroeder, Stephanie Wood, and Robert Haskett, 105–22. University of Oklahoma Press, Norman.

Howe, James. 1998. *A People Who Would Not Kneel: Panama, the United States and the San Blas Kuna*. Smithsonian Institution Press, Washington, D.C.

―――. 1986. *The Kuna Gathering: Contemporary Village Politics in Panama*. University of Texas Press, Austin.

Howe, James, and Lawrence A. Hirschfeld. 1981. The Star Girls' Descent: A Myth about Men, Women, Matrilocality, and Singing. *Journal of American Folklore* 94(373): 292–322.

Howell, Todd L. 1995. Tracking Zuni Gender and Leadership Roles across the Contact Period. *Journal of Anthropological Research* 51(2): 125–47.

Huber, Brad R. 1990. The Recruitment of Nahua Curers: Role Conflict and Gender. *Ethnology* 29(2): 159–76.

Huber, Brad R., and Alan R. Sandstrom. 2001. Recruitment, Training, and Practice of Indigenous Midwives: From the Mexico-United States Border to the Isthmus of Tehuantepec. In *Mesoamerican Healers*, edited by Brad R. Huber and Alan R. Sandstrom, 139–78. University of Texas Press, Austin.

Hugh-Jones, Christine. 1979. *From the Milk River: Spatial and Temporal Processes in Northwest Amazonia*. Cambridge University Press, Cambridge.

―――. 1978. Food for Thought: Patterns of Production and Consumption in Pirá-Paraná Society. In *Sex and Age and Principles of Social Differentiation*, edited by J. S. La Fontaine, 41–66. Academic Press, London.

Hugh-Jones, Stephen. 1979. *The Palm and the Pleiades: Initiation and Cosmology in Northwest Amazonia*. Cambridge University Press, Cambridge.

Hunt, Marta Espejo-Ponce, and Matthew Restall. 1997. Work, Marriage, and Status: Maya Women of Colonial Yucatan. In *Indian Women of Early Mexico*, edited by

Susan Schroeder, Stephanie Wood, and Robert Haskett, 231–52. University of Oklahoma Press, Norman.

Hurtado, Albert L. 1999. *Intimate Frontiers: Sex, Gender, and Culture in Old California.* University of New Mexico Press, Albuquerque.

Hurtado, Elena, and Eugenia Sáenz de Tejada. 2001. Relations between Government Health Workers and Traditional Midwives in Guatemala. In *Mesoamerican Healers,* edited by Brad R. Huber and Alan R. Sandstrom, 211–42. University of Texas Press, Austin.

Ingham, John M. 1989. *Mary, Michael, and Lucifer: Folk Catholicism in Central Mexico.* University of Texas Press, Austin.

Isbell, Billie Jean. 1997. De inmaduro a duro: Lo simbólico femenino y los esquemas andinos de género. In *Más allá del silencio: Las fronteras de género en los Andes,* vol. 1, *Parentesco y género en los Andes,* edited by Denise Y. Arnold, 253–300. ILCA, La Paz.

———. 1978. *To Defend Ourselves: Ecology and Ritual in an Andean Village.* Institute of Latin American Studies, Austin.

———. 1976. La otra mitad esencial: un estudio de complementariedad sexual andina. *Estudios Andinos* 5(1): 37–53.

Iwańska, Alicja. 1971. *Purgatory and Utopia: A Mazahua Indian Village of Mexico.* Schenkman, Cambridge, Mass.

Izquierdo, Anna Luisa. 1989. La condición de la mujer en la sociedad maya prehispánica. In *Seminario sobre la participación de la mujer en la vida nacional,* edited by Patricia Galeana de Valadés, 7–15. UNAM, Mexico City.

Jackson, Jean E. 1996. Coping with the Dilemmas of Affinity and Female Sexuality: Male Rebirth in the Central Northwest Amazon. In *Denying Biology: Essays on Gender and Pseudo-Creation,* edited by Warren Shapiro and Uli Linke, 89–127. University Press of America, Lanham, Md.

———. 1992. The Meaning and Message of Symbolic Sexual Violence in Tukanoan Ritual. *Anthropological Quarterly* 65(1): 1–18.

———. 1990–91. Rituales tukano de violencia sexual. *Revista Colombiana de Antropologia* 18: 25–52.

———. 1988. Gender Relations in the Central Northwest Amazon. *Antropologica* 70: 17–38.

———. 1984. Vaupés Marriage Practices. In *Marriage Practices in Lowland South America,* edited by Kenneth M. Kensinger, 156–79. University of Illinois Press, Urbana.

———. 1983. *The Fish People: Linguistic Exogamy and Tukanoan Identity in Northwest Amazonia.* Cambridge University Press, Cambridge.

Jackson, Robert H. 1999. *Race, Caste, and Status: Indians in Colonial Spanish America.* University of New Mexico Press, Albuquerque.

———. 1994. *Indian Population Decline: The Missions of Northwestern New Spain, 1687–1840.* University of New Mexico Press, Albuquerque.

Jansen, Maarten and Gabina Aurora Pérez Jiménez. 1998. Dos princesas mixtecas en Monte Albán. *Arqueología mexicana* 5(29): 28–33. Special issue: *La mujer en el mundo prehispánico.*

Jiménez, Doña Luz. 1972. *Life and Death in Milpa Alta: A Nahuatl Chronicle of Díaz and Zapata.* Translated and edited by Fernando Horcasitas. University of Oklahoma Press, Norman.

———. 1968. *De Porfirio Díaz a Zapata: Memoria náhuatl de Milpa Alta*. Compilation and translation by Fernando Horcasitas. UNAM, Mexico City.

Jimeno, Clara. 2001. Implementation of the Gender Demands Included in the Guatemala Peace Accords: Lessons Learned. In *Women Resist Globalization: Mobilizing for Livelihood and Rights*, edited by Sheila Rowbotham and Stephanie Linkogle, 180–98. Zed Books, London.

Johnson, Allen. 2003. *Families of the Forest: The Matsigenka Indians of the Peruvian Amazon*. University of California Press, Berkeley.

Johnson, Orna R., and Allen Johnson. 1975. Male/Female Relations and the Organization of Work in a Machiguenga Community. *American Ethnologist* 2(4): 634–48.

Johnston, Carolyn Ross. 1996. In the White Woman's Image? Resistance, Transformation, and Identity in Recent Native American Women's History. *Journal of Women's History* 8(3): 205–18.

Jones, Grant D. 1998. *The Conquest of the Last Maya Kingdom*. Stanford University Press, Stanford.

Jordan, Brigette. 1993. *Birth in Four Cultures: A Crosscultural Investigation of Childbirth in Yucatan, Holland, Sweden, and the United States*, 4th ed., rev. and exp., edited by Robbie Davis-Floyd. Waveland Press, Prospect Heights, Ill. [1978].

Josserand, J. Kathryn. 2002. Women in Classic Maya Hieroglypic Texts. In *Ancient Maya Women*, edited by Traci Arden, 114–51. AltaMira Press, Walnut Creek, Calif.

Joyce, Rosemary A. 2000a. *Gender and Power in Prehispanic Mesoamerica*. University of Texas Press, Austin.

———. 2000b. A Pre-Columbian Gaze: Male Sexuality among the Ancient Maya. In *Archaeologies of Sexuality*, edited by Robert A. Schmidt and Barbara L. Voss, 263–83. Routledge, London.

———. 1999. Social Dimensions of Pre-Classic Burials. In *Social Patterns in Pre-Classic Mesoamerica*, edited by David C. Grove and Rosemary A. Joyce, 15–47. Dumbarton Oaks, Washington D.C.

———. 1996. The Construction of Gender in Classic Maya Monuments. In *Gender and Archaeology*, edited by Rita P. Wright, 167–95. University of Pennsylvania Press, Philadelphia.

———. 1993. Images of Production and Reproduction in Pre-Hispanic Southern Central America. *Current Anthropology* 34(3): 255–74.

———. 1992a. Images of Gender and Labor Organization in Classic Maya Society. In *Exploring Gender through Archaeology: Selected Papers from the 1991 Boone Conference*, edited by Cheryl Claassen, 63–70. Prehistory Press, Madison, Wisc.

———. 1992b. Dimensiones simbolicas del traje en monumentos clásicos mayas: La construcción del género a través del vestido. In *La indumentária y el tejido mayas a través del tiempo*, edited by Linda Asturias de Barrios y Dina Fernández García, 29–38. Ediciones del Museo Ixchel, Guatemala.

Juárez, Ana María. 2001. Four Generations of Maya Marriages: What's Love Got to Do with It? *Frontiers* 22(2): 131–53.

Juárez Ch'ix, Isabel, and Petrona de la Cruz Cruz. 1992. La desconfiada (diálogo dramático). *Mesoamérica* 23: 135–41.

Kampwirth, Karen. 2002. *Women and Guerrilla Movements: Nicaragua, El Salvador, Chiapas, Cuba*. Pennsylvania State University Press, University Park.

Kane, Stephanie C. 1994. *The Phantom Gringo Boat: Shamanic Discourse and Development in Panama*. Smithsonian Institution Press, Washington, D.C.

Kanter, Deborah. 1995. Native Land Tenure and Its Decline in Mexico, 1750–1900. *Ethnohistory* 42(4):607–16.

Karovkin, Tanya. 2001. Reinventing the Communal Tradition: Indigenous Peoples, Civil Society, and Democratization in Andean Ecuador. *Latin American Research Review* 36(3): 37–67.

Karttunen, Frances. 1998. Indigenous Writing as a Vehicle of Postconquest Continuity and Change in Mesoamerica. In *Native Traditions in the Postconquest World*, edited by Elizabeth Hill Boone and Tom Cummins, 421–47. Dumbarton Oaks, Washington, D.C.

———. 1997. Rethinking Malinche. In *Indian Women of Early Mexico*, edited by Susan Schroeder, Stephanie Wood, and Robert Haskett, 291–312. University of Oklahoma Press, Norman.

———. 1994. *Between Worlds: Interpreter, Guides, and Survivors*. Rutgers University Press, New Brunswick, N.J.

Kaufmann Doig, Federico. 1978. *Comportamiento sexual en el antiguo Peru*. Kompactos, Lima.

Kearney, Michael. 1972. *The Winds of Ixtepeji: World View and Society in a Zapotec Town*. Holt, Rinehart and Winston, New York.

Kelekna, Pia. 1994. Farming, Feuding, and Female Status: The Achuar Case. In *Amazonian Indians from Prehistory to the Present: Anthropological Perspectives*, edited by Anna Roosevelt, 225–48. University of Arizona Press, Tucson.

Kellogg, Susan. 1998. Indigenous Testaments of Early-Colonial Mexico City: Testifying to Gender Differences. In *Dead Giveaways: Indigenous Testaments of Colonial Mesoamerica and the Andes*, edited by Susan Kellogg and Matthew Restall, 37–58. University of Utah Press, Salt Lake City.

———. 1997. From Parallel and Equivalent to Separate but Unequal: Tenochca Mexica Women, 1500–1700. In *Indian Women of Early Mexico*, edited by Susan Schroeder, Stephanie Wood, and Robert Haskett, 123–43. University of Oklahoma Press, Norman.

———. 1995a. The Woman's Room: Some Aspects of Gender Relations in Tenochtitlan in the Late Pre-Hispanic Period. *Ethnohistory* 42(4): 563–76.

———. 1995b. *Law and the Transformation of Aztec Culture, 1500–1700*. University of Oklahoma Press, Norman.

———. 1988. Cognatic Kinship and Religion: Women in Aztec Society. In *Smoke and Mist: Mesoamerican Studies in Memory of Thelma D. Sullivan*, edited by J. Kathryn Josserand and Karen Dakin, 2:666–81. British Archaeological Reports Press, Oxford.

———. 1986a. Kinship and Social Organization in Early Colonial Tenochtitlán. In *Supplement to the Handbook of Middle American Indians*, vol. 4, *Ethnohistory*, edited by Ronald Spores, series edited by Victoria Reifler Bricker, 103–21. University of Texas Press, Austin.

———. 1986b. Aztec Inheritance in Sixteenth-Century Mexico City: Colonial Patterns, Prehispanic Influences. *Ethnohistory* 33(3): 313–30.

———. 1984. Aztec Women in Early Colonial Courts: Structure and Strategy in a Legal Context. In *Five Centuries of Law and Politics in Central Mexico*, edited by Ronald Spores and Ross Hassig, 25–38. Publications in Anthropology, no. 30, Vanderbilt University Press, Nashville, Tenn.

Kelly, Patty. 2003. "I Made Myself from Nothing": Women and Sex Work in Urban Chiapas. In *Women of Chiapas: Making History in Times and Struggle and Hope*, edited by Christine Eber and Christine Kovic, 81–97. Routledge, London.

Kendall, Ann. 1973. *Everyday Life of the Incas*. Putnam, New York.

Kensinger, Kenneth M. 1997. Cambio de perspectivas sobre las relaciones de género. In *Complementariedad entre hombre y mujer: Relaciones de género desde la perspectiva amerindia*, edited by Michel Perrin and Marie Perruchon, 109–24. Ediciones ABYA-YALA, Quito.

———. 1989. Hunting and Male Domination in Cashinahua Society. In *Farmers as Hunters: The Implications of Sedentism*, edited by Susan Kent, 18–26. Cambridge University Press, Cambridge.

Keremitsis, Dawn. 1983. Del metate al molino: La mujer mexicana de 1910 a 1940. *Historia Mexicana* 33(2): 285–302.

Kerns, Virginia. 1997. *Women and the Ancestors: Black Carib Kinship and Ritual*. 2nd ed. University of Illinois Press, Urbana [1983].

———. 1992a. Preventing Violence against Women: A Central American Case. In *Sanctions and Sanctuary: Cultural Perspectives on the Beating of Wives*, edited by Dorothy Ayers Counts, Judith K. Brown, and Jacqueline C. Campbell, 125–38. Westview Press, Boulder, Colo.

———. 1992b. Female Control of Sexuality: Garífuna Women at Middle Age. In *In Her Prime: New Views of Middle-Aged Women*, edited by Virginia Kerns and Judith K. Brown, 2nd ed., 95–111. University of Illinois Press, Urbana [1985].

———. 1982. Structural Continuity in the Division of Men's and Women's Work among the Black Carib (Garifuna). In *Sex Roles and Social Change in Native Lower Central American Societies*, edited by Christine A. Loveland and Franklin O. Loveland, 23–43. University of Illinois Press, Urbana.

Khan, Aisha. 1987. Migration and Life-Cycle among Garifuna (Black Carib) Street Vendors. *Women's Studies* 13(3): 183–98.

Kimball, Geoffrey. 1993. Aztec Homosexuality: The Textual Evidence. *Journal of Homosexuality* 26(1): 7–24.

Kintz, Ellen R. 1998. The Yucatec Maya Frontier and Maya Women: Tenacity of Tradition and Tragedy of Transformation. *Sex Roles* 39 (7/8): 589–601.

Klein, Cecilia. 2001. None of the Above: Gender Ambiguity in Nahua Ideology. In *Gender in Pre-Hispanic America: A Symposium at Dumbarton Oaks*, edited by Cecelia F. Klein, 183–253. Dumbarton Oaks, Washington, D.C.

———. 1995. Wild Woman in Colonial Mexico: An Encounter of European and Aztec Concepts of the Other. In *Reframing the Renaissance: Visual Culture in Europe and Latin America, 1450–1650*, edited by Claire Farago, 244–63. Yale University Press, New Haven.

———. 1994. Fighting with Femininity: Gender and War in Aztec Mexico. *Estudios de Cultura Náhuatl* 24: 219–53.

———. 1993. The Shield Women: Resolution of an Aztec Gender Paradox. In *Current Topics in Aztec Studies: Essays in Honor of Dr. H. B. Nicholson*, edited by Alana Cordy-Collins and Douglas Sharon, 39–64. San Diego Museum papers 30, San Diego Museum of Man, San Diego.

———. 1988. Rethinking Cihuacoatl: Aztec Political Imagery of the Conquered Woman. In *Smoke and Mist: Mesoamerican Studies in Memory of Thelma D. Sullivan*, edited by J. Kathryn Josserand and Karen Dakin, 2:237–77. BAR Press, Oxford.

Klein, Herbert. 1986. Familia y fertilidad en Amatenango, Chiapas, 1785–1816. *Historia Mexicana* 36(2): 273–86.

Klein, Laura F., and Lillian A. Ackerman, eds. 1995. *Women and Power in Native North America*. University of Oklahoma Press, Norman.

Kloos, Peter. 1969. Female Initiation among the Maroni River Caribs. *American Anthropologist* 71(5): 898–905.

Knight, Alan. 1990. Racisim, Revolution, and *Indigenismo*: Mexico, 1910–1940. In *The Idea of Race in Latin America, 1870–1940*, edited by Richard Graham, 71–113. University of Texas Press, Austin.

Kovic, Christine. 2003. Demanding Their Dignity as Daughters of God: Catholic Women and Human Rights. In *Women of Chiapas: Making History in Times of Struggle and Hope*, edited by Christine Eber and Christine Kovic, 131–46. Routledge, London.

Kovic, Christine, and Christine Eber. 2003. Introduction to *Women of Chiapas: Making History in Times of Struggle and Hope*, edited by Christine Eber and Christine Kovic, 1–27. Routledge, London.

Krippner-Martínez, James. 1990. The Politics of Conquest: An Interpretation of the *Relación de Michoacán*. *Americas* 47(2): 177–97.

Krochock, Ruth J. 2002. Women in Hieroglyphic Inscriptions of Chichén Itzá. In *Ancient Maya Women*, edited by Traci Arden, 152–70. AltaMira Press, Walnut Creek, Calif.

Ladd, Doris M. 1979. *Mexican Women in Anahuac and New Spain: Aztec Roles, Spanish Notary Revelations, Creole Genius*, Institute for Latin American Studies, University of Texas, Austin.

Lambert, Bernd. 1977. Bilaterality in the Andes. In *Andean Kinship and Marriage*, edited by Ralph Bolton and Enrique Mayer, 1–27. Special publication no. 7, American Anthropological Association. Washington, D.C.

Land, Ney. 1975. Variantes del papel desempeñado por la mujer en las comunidades indígenas brasileñas. *América Indígena* 35(3): 491–501.

Lane, Kris. 1998. Taming the Master: *Brujería*, Slavery, and the *Encomienda* in Barbacoas at the Turn of the Eighteenth Century. *Ethnohistory* 45(3): 477–507.

Langdon, E. Jean. 1984. Sex and Power in Siona Society. In *Sexual Ideologies in Lowland South America*, edited by Kenneth M. Kensinger, 16–23. Working papers on South American Indians, no. 5, Bennington College, Bennington, Vt.

Langer, Erick D. 2001. The Testament as Narrative: Gender and Trade in Early Nineteenth-Century Bolivia. Paper read at the annual meeting of the American Historical Association, Washington, D. C., January 4–7.

Lanyon, Anna. 1999. *Malinche's Conquest*. Allen and Edwards, St. Leonards, New South Wales, Australia.

Lapiedra, Aurora. 1985. Roles y valores de la mujer andina. *Allpanchis* 25–26: 43–65.

Larson, Brooke. 1998. *Cochabamba, 1550–1900: Colonialism and Agrarian Transformation in Bolivia*. Exp. ed. Duke University Press, Durham, N.C [1988].

———. 1983. Producción doméstica y trabajo femenino indígena en la formación de una economia mercantil colonial. *Historia Boliviana* 3(2): 173–88.

Laughlin, Miriam. 1991. Arts: The Drama of Maya Women. *Ms.*, July/August, 88–9.

Lavrin, Asunción. 1999. Indian Brides of Christ: Creating New Spaces for Indigenous Women in New Spain. *Mexican Studies/Estudios Mexicanos* 15(2): 225–60.

————. 1989. Sexuality in Colonial Mexico: A Church Dilemma. In *Sexuality and Marriage in Colonial Latin America*, edited by Asunción Lavrin, 47–95. University of Nebraska Press, Lincoln.

————. 1978. In Search of the Colonial Women in Mexico: The Seventeenth and Eighteenth Centuries. In *Latin American Women: Historical Perspectives*, edited by Asunción Lavrin, 23–59. Greenwood Press, Westport, Conn.

Lazos Chavero, Elena. 1995. De la candela al mercado: El papel de la mujer en la agricultura comercial del sur de Yucatán. In *Relaciones de género y transformaciones agrarias*, edited by Soledad González Montes y Vania Salles, 91–133. El Colegio de México, Mexico City.

Leacock, Eleanor B. 1983. Interpreting the Origins of Gender Inequality: Conceptual and Historical Problems. *Dialectical Anthropology* 7(4): 263–84.

————, ed. 1981. *Myths of Male Dominance*. Monthly Review Press, New York.

Leacock, Eleanor B., and Helen I. Safa and contributors. 1986. *Women's Work: Development and the Division of Labor by Gender*. Bergin and Garvey, South Hadley, Mass.

León, Rosario. 1990. Bartolina Sisa: The Peasant Women's Organization in Bolivia. In *Women and Social Change in Latin America*, edited by Elizabeth Jelin, 115–34. Zed Books, London.

Lerner, Gerda. 1986. *The Creation of Patriarchy*. Oxford University Press, New York.

Lesure, Richard G. 1997. Figurines and Social Identities in Early Sedentary Societies. In *Women in Prehistory: North America and Mesoamerica*, edited by Cheryl Claassen and Rosemary A. Joyce, 227–48. University of Pennsylvania Press, Philadelphia.

Levi-Straus, Claude. 1974. *Tristes Tropiques*. Translated by John and Doreen Weightman. Atheneum, New York [1955].

Lewis, Laura A. 2003. *Hall of Mirrors: Power, Witchcraft, and Caste in Colonial Mexico*. Duke University Press, Durham.

————. 1997. Temptress, Warrior, Priestess or Witch? Four Faces of Tlazolteotl in the Laud Codex. In *Códices y documentos sobre México: Segundo simposio*, vol. 2, edited by Salvador Rueda Smithers, Constanza Vega Sosa, and Rodrigo Martínez Baracs, 179–91. INAH, Mexico City.

————. 1996. The "Weakness" of Women and the Feminization of the Indian in Colonial Mexico. *Colonial Latin American Review* 5(1): 73–94.

Lewis, Oscar. 1951. *Life in a Mexican Village: Tepoztlán Restudied*. University of Illinois Press, Urbana.

————. 1944. Social and Economic Changes in a Mexican Village: Tepoztlan, 1926–1944. *América Indígena* 4(4): 281–314.

Lindenberg M., Nietta. 1989. Brasil (Eperiencias educativas en Brasil, Chile y México). In *Mujer indígena y educación en America Latina*, edited by Anna Lucía D'Emilio, 313–38. UNESCO/I. I. I, Santiago.

Lipsett-Rivera, Sonya. 1997. The Intersection of Rape and Marriage in Late-Colonial and Early-National Mexico. *Colonial Latin American Historical Review* 6(4): 559–90.

————. 1996. La violencia dentro de las familias formal e informal. In *Familia y vida privada en la historia de Iberoamérica*, edited by Pilar Gonzalbo Aizpuro and Cecilia Rabell Romero, 325–40. El Colegio de México and UNAM, Mexico City.

Lizot, Jacques. 1985. *Tales of the Yanomami: Daily Life in the Venezuelan Forest*. Translated by Ernest Simon. Cambridge University Press, Cambridge [1976].

Llanos Cervantes, Elvira. 1992. El embarazo en mujeres aymaras migrantes: un estudio en zonas urbanopopulares al oeste de La Paz. In *Mujeres de los Andes: Condiciones de vida y salúd*, edited by Anne-Claire Defossez, Didier Fassin, and Mara Viveros, 111–40. IFEA and Universidad Externado de Colombia, Colombia.

Lockhart, James. 2001. *Nahuatl as Written: Lessons in Older Written Nahuatl, with Copious Examples and Texts*. Stanford University Press and UCLA Latin American Center Publications, Stanford and Los Angeles.

———. 1992. *The Nahuas after the Conquest: A Social and Cultural History of the Indians of Central Mexico, Sixteenth through Eighteenth Centuries*. Stanford University Press, Stanford.

Loera y Chávez, Margarita. 1977. *Calimaya y Tepemexalco: Tenencia y transmisión hereditaria de la tierra en dos comunidades indígenas (época colonial)*. INAH, Mexico.

Lombardo Otero, Rosa María. 1944. *La mujer tzeltal*. Mexico.

López Austin, Alfredo. 1998. La parte feminina del cosmos. *Arqueología Mexicana* 5(29): 6–13. Special issue, *La mujer en el mundo prehispánico*.

———. 1982. La sexualidad entre los antiguos nahuas. In *Familia y sexualidad en Nueva España: Memoria del primer simposio de historia de las mentalidades: "Familia, Matrimonio y sexualidad en Nueva España,"* 141–76. Fondo de Cultura Económica, Mexico City.

López de Meneses, Amada. 1948. Tecuichpochtzin, hija de Moteczuma (¿1510?–1550). *Revista de Indias* 9: 471–96.

López Sarrelangue, Delfina Esmeralda. 1965. *La nobleza indígena de Pátzcuaro en la época virreinal*. UNAM, Instituto de Investigaciones Históricas, Mexico City.

Louie, Miriam Ching Yoon. 2001. *Sweatshop Warriors: Immigrant Women Take on the Global Factory*. South End Press, Cambridge, Mass.

Loveland, Christine A. 1982a. Introduction to *Sex Roles and Social Change in Native Lower Central American Societies*, edited by Christine A. Loveland and Franklin O. Loveland, xi–xix. University of Illinois Press, Urbana.

———. 1982b. Rama Men and Women: An Ethnohistorical Analysis of Change. In *Sex Roles and Social Change in Native Lower Central American Societies*, edited by Christine A. Loveland and Franklin O. Loveland, 3–22. University of Illinois Press, Urbana.

Lowie, Robert. 1946. Eastern Brazil: An Introduction. In *Handbook of South American Indians*, edited by Julian H. Steward, vol. 1, *The Marginal Tribes*, 381–97. Bureau of American Ethnology, Bulletin 143, Smithsonian Institution, Washington, D.C.

Lumbreras, Luis G. 1983. *Los origines de la civilización en el Peru*. 6th ed. Editorial Milla Batres, Lima [1972].

Luykx, Aurolyn. 1997. Discriminación sexual y estrategias verbales femininas en contextos escolares bolivianos. In *Más allá del silencio: Las fronteras de género en los Andes*, vol. 1, *Parentesco y género en los Andes*, edited by Denise Y. Arnold, 189–231. CIASE, ILCA, La Paz.

Lyon, Patricia. 1984. Change in Wachipaeri Marriage Patterns. In *Marriage Practices in Lowland South America*, edited by Kenneth M. Kensinger, 252–63. Illinois Studies in Anthropology, no. 14, University of Illinois Press, Urbana.

———. 1978. Female Supernaturals in Ancient Peru. *Ñawpa Pacha* 16: 95–140.

MacCormack, Sabine. 1991. *Religion in the Andes: Vision and Imagination in Early Colonial Peru*. Stanford University Press, Stanford.

———. 1985. "The Heart Has Its Reasons": Predicaments of Missionary Christianity in Early Colonial Peru. *Hispanic American Historical Review* 65(3): 443–66.

MacLachlan, Colin. 1976. The Eagle and the Serpent: Male over Female in Tenochtitlan. *Proceedings of the Pacific Coast Council of Latin American Studies* 5: 45–56.

Madsen, William. 1969. The Nahua. In *Handbook of Middle American Indians*, vol. 8, *Ethnology*, pt. 2, edited by Evon Z. Vogt, series edited by Robert Wauchope, 602–37. University of Texas Press, Austin.

———. 1960. *The Virgin's Children: Life in an Aztec Village Today*. University of Texas Press, Austin.

Magallón Cervantes, María del Carmen. 1988. Participación de la mujer en las organizaciones campesinas: Algunas limitaciones. In *Las mujeres en el campo: Memoria de la Primera Reunión Nacional de Investigación sobre Mujeres Campesinas en México*, edited by Josefina Aranda B., 411–24. Instituto de Investigaciones Sociológicas de la Universidad Autónoma Benito Juárez de Oaxaca, Oaxaca de Juárez, Oaxaca, México.

Mallon, Florencia E. 2001. Bearing Witness in Hard Times: Ethnography and *Testimonio* in a Postrevolutionary Age. In *Reclaiming the Political in Latin American History: Essays from the North*, edited by Gilbert M. Joseph, 311–55. Duke University Press, Durham, N.C.

———. 1995. *Peasant and Nation: The Making of Postcolonial Mexico and Peru*. University of California Press, Berkeley.

———. 1994. Exploring the Origins of Democratic Patriarchy in Mexico: Gender and Popular Resistance in the Puebla Highlands, 1850–1876. In *Women of the Mexican Countryside, 1850–1990*, edited by Heather Fowler-Salamini and Mary Kay Vaughan, 3–26, University of Arizona Press, Tucson.

———. 1983. *The Defense of Community in Peru's Central Highlands: Peasant Struggle and Capitalist Transition, 1860–1940*. Princeton University Press, Princeton.

Malpass, Michael A. 1996. *Daily Life in the Inca Empire*. Greenwood Press, Westport, Conn.

Malvido, Elsa. 1980. El abandono de los hijos—una forma de control del tamaño de la familia y del trabajo indígena—Tula (1683–1730). *Historia Mexicana* 29(4): 521–61.

Mannarelli, María Emma. 1994. *Pecados públicos: La ilegitimidad en Lima, siglo XVII*. Ediciones Flora Tristán, Lima.

———. 1990. Sexualidad y desigualdades genéricas en el Perú del siglo XVI. *Allpanchis* 35–36: 225–48.

———. 1985. Inquisición y mujeres: Las hechiceras en el Perú durante e siglo XVII. *Revista Andina* 3(1): 141–54.

Manrique, Nelson. 1998. The War for the Central Sierra. In *Shining and Other Paths: War and Society in Peru, 1980–1995*, edited by Steve J. Stern, 193–223. Duke University Press, Durham, N.C.

Marchand, Marianne H. and Jane L. Parpart, eds. 1995. *Feminism/Postmodernism/Development*. Routledge, London.

Marcus, Joyce. 2001. Breaking the Glass Ceiling: The Strategies of Royal Women in Ancient States. In *Gender in Pre-Hispanic America: A Symposium at Dumbarton Oaks*, edited by Cecilia F. Klein, 305–40. Dumbarton Oaks, Washington, D.C.

———. 1999. Men's and Women's Ritual in Formative Oaxaca. In *Social Patterns in Pre-Classic Mesoamerica*, edited by David C. Grove and Rosemary A. Joyce, 67–96. Dumbarton Oaks, Washington, D.C.

———. 1998. *Women's Ritual in Formative Oaxaca: Figurine-making, Divination, Death and the Ancestors*. Memoirs no. 33, Museum of Anthropology, University of Michigan, Ann Arbor.

———. 1976. *Emblem and State in the Classic Maya Lowlands: An Epigraphic Approach to Territorial Organization.* Dumbarton Oaks, Washington, D.C.

Marcus, Joyce, and Kent V. Flannery. 1996. *Zapotec Civilization: How Urban Society Evolved in Mexico's Oaxaca Valley.* Thames and Hudson, London.

Marión, Marie Odile. 1997. *Entre anhelos y recuerdos.* Plaza y Valdés, Mexico City.

Martin, Kathleen R. 1998. "From the Heart of a Woman": Yucatec Maya Women as Political Actors. *Sex Roles* 39 (7/8): 559–71.

Mathews, Holly. 1985. "We Are Mayordomo": A Reinterpretation of Women's Roles in the Mexican Cargo System. *American Ethnologist* 12(2): 285–301.

Maybury-Lewis, David. 1999. Lowland Peoples of the Twentieth Century. In *The Cambridge History of the Native Peoples of the Americas*, vol. 3, pt. 2, edited by Frank Salomon and Stuart B. Schwartz, 872–947. Cambridge University Press, Cambridge.

———. 1967. *Akwẽ-Shavante Society.* Clarendon Press, Oxford.

Maybury-Lewis, Pia. 1985. Un paso adelante y dos atrás: La mujer Xavante de 1958 a 1982. *Extracta* (Lima) 4: 31–3.

Maynard, Eileen. 1974. Guatemalan Women: Life under Two Types of Patriarchy. In *Many Sisters: Women in Cross-Cultural Perspective*, edited by Carolyn J. Matthiasson, 77–98. Free Press, New York.

McAnany, Patricia A. 1995. *Living with the Ancestors: Kinship and Kingship in Ancient Maya Society.* University of Texas Press, Austin.

McCaa, Robert. 1996. Matrimonio infantil, *cemithualtin* (familias complejas) y el antiguo pueblos nahua. *Historia Mexicana* 46(1): 3–70.

McCafferty, Sharisse D., and Geoffrey D. McCafferty. 1999. The Metamorphosis of Xochiquetzal: A Window on Womanhood in Pre- and Post-Conquest Mexico. In *Manifesting Power: Gender and the Interpretation of Power in Archaeology*, edited by Tracy L. Sweely, 103–25. Routledge, London.

———. 1994a. The Conquered Women of Cacaxtla: Gender Identity or Gender Ideology? *Ancient Mesoamerica* 5(1): 159–72.

———. 1994b. Engendering Tomb 7 at Monte Albán: Respinning an Old Yarn. *Current Anthropology* 35(2): 143–65.

———. 1988. Powerful Women and the Myth of Male Dominance in Aztec Society. *Archaeological Review from Cambridge* 7: 45–59.

McCallum, Cecilia. 2001. *Gender and Sociality in Amazonia: How Real People Are Made.* Berg, Oxford.

McClusky, Laura J. 2001. "*Here, Our Culture Is Hard*": Stories of Domestic Violence from a Mayan Community in Belize. University of Texas Press, Austin.

McGee, R. Jon. 1990. *Life, Ritual, and Religion among the Lacandon Maya.* Wadsworth, Belmont, Calif.

McGrew, Anthony. 1992. A Global Society? In *Modernity and Its Futures*, edited by Stuart Hall, David Held, and Tony McGrew, 61–116. Polity Press, Cambridge.

McKee, Lauris. 1999. Men's Rights/Women's Wrongs: Domestic Violence in Ecuador. In *To Have and to Hit: Cultural Perspectives on Wife Beating*, 2nd ed., edited by Dorothy Ayers Counts, Judith K. Brown, and Jacquelyn C. Campbell, 168–86. University of Ilinois Press, Urbana [1992].

McLaurin, Irma. 1996. *Women of Belize: Gender and Change in Central America.* Rutgers University Press, New Brunswick, N.J.

Medinaceli, Ximena. 1989. *Alterando la rutina: Mujeres en las ciudades de Bolivia, 1920–1930.* CIDEM, La Paz.

Meigs, Anna. 1990. Multiple Gender Ideologies and Statuses. In *Beyond the Second Sex: New Directions in the Anthropology of Gender*, edited by Peggy Reeves Sanday and Ruth Gallagher Goodenough, 101–12. University of Pennsylvania Press, Philadelphia.

Meisch, Lynn. 1991. The Missing Half: Pre-Hispanic and Contemporary Traditions of Andean Males as Spinners and Weavers. Paper presented at the Forty-Seventh International Congress of Americanists, New Orleans, July 7–11.

———. 1987. *Otavalo: Weaving, Costume and the Market*. Ediciones Libri Mundi, Quito.

Mejia, Lucila, Irma García, Marcela Valdivia, Celinda Sosa, Lidia Anti, Florentina Alegre, Jacinta Mamani, and Bernardina Laura. 1984. *Las hijas de Bartolina Sisa*. HISBOL, La Paz.

Meltzer, David J. 1995. Clocking the First Americans. In *Annual Review of Anthropology*, edited by William H. Durham, E. Valentine Daniel, and Bambi Shieffelin, 24: 21–45. Annual Reviews, Palo Alto, Calif.

Menchú, Rigoberta. 1984. *I, Rigoberta Menchú: An Indian Woman in Guatemala*. Edited by Elisabeth Burgos-Debray. Translated by Ann Wright. Verso, London.

———. 1998. *Crossing Borders*. Translated and edited by Ann Wright. Verso, London.

Mendieta Parada, Pilar. 1995. Lo femenino en las concepciones míticas y religiosas del mundo prehispanico. In *Palabras del silencio: Las mujeres latinoamericanas y su historia*, edited by Martha Moscoso, 15–35. Ediciones ABYA-YALA, Quito.

Mentore, George P. 1987. Waiwai Women: The Basis of Power and Wealth. *Man* (n.s.) 22(3): 511–27.

Mies, Maria, Veronika Bennholdt-Thomsen, and Claudia von Werlhof. 1988. *Women: The Last Colony*. Zed Books, London.

Mignolo, Walter. 1998. Globalization, Civilization Processes, and the Relocation of Languages and Cultures. In *The Cultures of Globalization*, edited by Fredric Jameson and Masao Miyoshi, 32–53. Duke University Press, Durham, N.C.

Milbrath, Susan. 1995. Gender and Roles of Lunar Deities in Postclassic Central Mexico and Their Correlations with the Maya Area. *Estudios de Cultura Náhuatl* 25: 45–93.

———. 1988. Birth Images in Mixteca-Puebla Art. In *The Role of Gender in Precolumbian Art and Architecture*, edited by Virginia Miller, 153–77. University Press of America, Lanham, Md.

Miles, Ann, and Hans Buechler. 1997. Introduction: Andean Perspectives on Women and Economic Change. In *Women and Economic Change: Andean Perspectives*, edited by Ann Miles and Hans Buechler, 1–12. Society for Latin American Anthropology Publication Series, vol. 14, Society for Latin American Anthropology, Washington, D.C.

Millon, Clara. 1988. A Reexamination of the Teotihuacan Tassel. In *Feathered Serpents and Flowering Trees: Reconstructing the Murals of Teotihuacan*, edited by Kathleen Berrin, 114–34. Fine Arts Museums of San Francisco, San Francisco.

Millon, René. 1993. The Place Where Time Began: An Archaeologist's Interpretation of What Happened in Teotihuacan History. In *Teotihuacan: Art from the City of the Gods*, edited by Kathleen Berrin and Esther Pasztory, 15–43. Thames and Hudson, New York.

———. 1992. Teotihuacan Studies: From 1950 to 1990 and Beyond. In *Art, Ideology, and the City of Teotihuacan*, edited by Janet C. Berlo, 339–430. Dumbarton Oaks, Washington, D.C.

————. 1988. Where Do They All Come From? The Provenance of the Wagner Murals from Teotihuacán. In *Feathered Serpents and Flowering Trees: Reconstructing the Murals of Teotihuacan*, edited by Kathleen Berrin, 78–113. Fine Arts Museums of San Francisco, San Francisco.

————. 1981. Teotihuacán: City, State, and Civilization. In *Supplement to the Handbook of Middle American Indians*, vol. 1, *Archaeology*, edited by Jeremy A. Sabloff, series edited by Victoria Reifler Bricker, 198–243. University of Texas Press, Austin.

Millones, Luis. 1990. *El retorno de las huacas. Estudios y documentos sobre el Taki Onqoy, siglo XVI*. Instituto de Estudios Peruanos and Sociedad Peruana de Psicoanálisis, Lima.

Mills, Kenneth. 1997. *Idolatry and Its Enemies: Colonial Andean Religion and Extirpation, 1640–1750*. Princeton University Press, Princeton.

Miloslavich Túpac, Diana. 1999. Comentarios. In *Mujeres, pueblos indígenas y poblaciones rurales: Democracia y gobiernos locales*, edited by Luis Chirinos Segura, 93–100. Ediciones Flora Tristan, Lima.

Mintz, Sidney W., and Eric R. Wolf. 1950. An Analysis of Ritual Co-Parenthood (Compadrazgo). *Southwestern Journal of Anthropology* 6(4): 341–68.

Miranda, Miriam. 1993. Jamolali Jiñariñu—A Woman's Voice: Black Indigenous Struggle for Survival in Honduras. *Bridges: Quaker International Affairs Reports* 93(4): 1–9.

Miranda Baldivia, Gloria. 1975. La mujer aymara en Bolivia. *América Indígena* 35(3): 511–17.

Mishkin, Bernard. 1946. The Contemporary Quechua. In *Handbook of South American Indians*, edited by Julian H. Steward, 7 vols., vol. 2, *The Andean Civilizations*, 411–70, Bureau of American Ethnology, bulletin 143, Smithsonian Institution, Washington, D.C.

Mohanty, Chandra Talpade. 1991. Under Western Eyes: Feminist Scholarship and Colonial Discourses. In *Third World Women and the Politics of Feminism*, edited by Chandra Talpade Mohanty, Ann Russo, and Lourdes Torres, 51–80. Indiana University Press, Bloomington.

Molina Mejía, Raúl. 2000. Uneasy Allies: The Far Right Comes to Power. *NACLA: Report on the Americas* 33(5): 11–12.

Molloy, John P., and William L. Rathje. 1974. Sexploitation among the Late Classic Maya. In *Meosamerican Archaeology: New Approaches*, edited by Norman Hammond, 431–44. University of Texas Press, Austin.

Momsen, Janet H., and Vivian Kinnaird. 1993. *Different Places, Different Voices: Gender and Development in Africa, Asia and Latin America*. Routledge, London.

Monaghan, John. 2001. Physiology, Production, and Gendered Difference: The Evidence from Mixtec and Other Mesoamerican Societies. In *Gender in Pre-Hispanic America: A Symposium at Dumbarton Oaks*, edited by Cecelia F. Klein, 285–304. Dumbarton Oaks, Washington, D.C.

Monteiro, John Manuel. 1994. *Negros da terra: Índios e bandeirantes nas origins de São Paulo*. Companhia das Letras, São Paulo.

Montoya, Rosario, Lessie Jo Frazier, and Janise Hurtig, eds. 2002. *Gender's Place: Feminist Anthropologies of Latin America*. Palgrave Macmillan, New York.

Montrose, Louis. 1993. The Work of Gender in the Discourse of Discovery. In *New World Encounters*, edited by Stephen Greenblatt, 177–217, University of California Press, Berkeley.

Moreno Yáñez, Segundo. 1977. *Sublevaciones indígenas en la Audiencia de Quito: Desde comienzos del siglo XVIII hasta finales de la colonia.* Centro de Publicaciones Pontificia Universidad Católica del Ecuador, Quito.

Mörner, Magnus. 1967. *Race Mixture in the History of Latin America.* Little Brown, Boston.

Morris, Walter F., Jr. 1991. The Marketing of Maya Textiles in Highland Chiapas, Mexico. In *Textile Traditions in Mesoamerica and the Andes: An Anthology,* edited by Margot Blum Schevill, Janet Catherine Berlo, and Edward B. Dwyer, 403–33. Garland, New York.

Morton, John. 1983–4. Women as Values, Signs and Power: Aspects of the Politics of Ritual among the Waiwai. *Antropologica* 59–62: 223–61.

Moscoso, Martha. 1995. La historia de las mujeres en el Ecuador. In *Palabras del silencio: las mujeres latinoamericanas y su historia,* edited by Martha Mosoco, 383–99. Ediciones ABYA-YALA, Quito.

———. 1992. Mujer indígena y sociedad republicana: Relaciones étnicas y de género en el Ecuador, siglo XIX. In *Mujeres de los Andes: Condiciones de vida y salud,* edited by Anne-Claire Defossez, Didier Fassin, and Mara Viveros, 223–43. IFEA and Universidad Externado de Colombia, Colombia.

Moseley, Michael E. 1992. *The Incas and Their Ancestors: The Archaeology of Peru.* Thames and Hudson, London.

Moya, Ruth. 1989. Ecuador (Situación educativa de la mujer indígena). In *Mujer indígena y educación en America Latina,* edited by Anna Lucía D'Emilio, 167–231. UNESCO/I. I. I, Santiago.

Mujeres contracorriente. 1998. *Mujeres contracorriente: Voces de líderes indígenas.* Fondo para Equidad de Género, Acdi, Ecuador.

Mukhopadhyay, Carol C., and Patricia J. Higgens. 1988. Anthropological Studies of Women's Status Revisited: 1977–1987. In *Annual Review of Anthropology,* edited by Bernard J. Siegel, Alan R. Beals, and Stephen A. Tyler, 17: 461–95. Annual Reviews, Palo Alto, Calif.

Mulhare, Eileen. 2004. Social Organization and Property Reform in Nineteenth-Century Rural Mexico. *Continuity and Change* 19(1): 105–40.

———. 2003. Respetar y confiar: Ideología de género versus comportamiento en una sociedad post nahua. In *El matrimonio en Mesoamérica ayer y hoy: Unas miradas antropológicas,* edited by David Robichaux, 267–90. Universidad Iberoamericana, Mexico City.

———. 1998. When Daughters Return or Remain: Women and the Natal Household in Rural Mexico. Paper presented at the Symposium on Family and Kinship in Mexico and Mesoamerica, Universidad Iberoamericana, Mexico City, February 11–12 (rev. August 1999).

Mumford, Jeremy. 1998. The Taki Onqoy and the Andean Nation: Sources and Interpretations. *Latin American Research Review* 33(1): 150–65.

Muñoz, Blanca. 1984. La participación de la mujer campesina en Bolivia: Un estudio del Altiplano. In *Bolivia: La fuerza histórica del campesinado,* edited by Fernando Calderón and Jorge Dandler, 363–99. Centro de Estudios de la Realidad Económica y Social, La Paz.

Muñoz, Hortensia. 1998. Human Rights and Social Referents: The Construction of New Sensibilities. In *Shining and Other Paths: War and Society in Peru, 1980–1995,* edited by Steve J. Stern, 447–69. Duke University Press, Durham, N.C.

Muratorio, Blanca M. 2001. Violence against Women in Indigenous Communities of the Ecuadorian Upper Amazon: History and Culture in a Context of Globalization. Paper read at the annual meeting of the American Society for Ethnohistory, Tucson, October 17–21 .

———. 1998. Indigenous Women's Identities and the Politics of Cultural Reproduction in the Ecuadorian Amazon. *American Anthropologist* 100(2): 409–20.

———. 1995. Amazonian Windows to the Past: Recovering Women's Histories from the Ecuadorian Upper Amazon. In *Articulating Hidden Histories: Exploring the Influence of Eric R. Wolf*, edited by Jane Schneider and Rayna Rapp, 322–35. University of California Press, Berkeley.

Muriel, Josefina. 1963. *Las indias caciques de Corpus Christi*. UNAM, Mexico City.

Murphy, Robert F. 1960. *Headhunter's Heritage: Social and Economic Change among the Mundurucú Indians*. University of California Press, Berkeley.

———. 1959. Social Structure and Sex Antagonism. *Southwestern Journal of Anthropology* 15(1): 89–98.

Murphy, Yolanda, and Robert F. Murphy. 1974. *Women of the Forest*. Columbia University Press, New York.

Murra, John. 1989. Cloth and Its Function in the Inka State. In *Cloth and Human Experience*, edited by Annette B. Weiner and Jane Schneider, 275–302. Smithsonian Institution Press, Washington, D.C.

———. 1962. Cloth and Its Function in the Inca State. *American Anthropologist* 64(4): 710–28.

Nadelson, Leslee. 1981. Pigs, Women, and the Men's House in Amazonia: An Analysis of Six Mundurucú Myths. In *Sexual Meanings: The Cultural Construction of Gender and Sexuality*, edited by Sherry B. Ortner and Harriet Whitehead, 240–72. Cambridge University Press, Cambridge.

Nader, Laura. 1990. *Harmony Ideology: Justice and Control in a Zapotec Mountain Village*. Stanford University Press, Stanford.

———. 1969. The Zapotec of Oaxaca. In *Handbook of Middle American Indians*, vol. 7, *Ethnology*, pt. 1, edited by Evon Z. Vogt, 329–59, series edited by Robert Wauchope. University of Texas Press, Austin.

Nash, June. 2001. *Mayan Visions: The Quest for Autonomy in an Age of Globalization*. Routledge, New York.

———. 1995. The Reassertion of Indigenous Identity: Mayan Responses to State Intervention in Chiapas. *Latin American Research Review* 30(3): 7–41.

———. 1993. Maya Household Production in the World Market: The Potters of Amatenango del Valle, Chiapas, Mexico. In *Crafts in the World Market: The Impact of Global Exchange on Middle American Artisans*, edited by June Nash, 1–24. State University of New York Press, Albany.

———. 1979. *We Eat the Mines and the Mines Eat Us: Dependency and Exploitation in Bolivian Tin Mines*. Columbia University Press, New York.

———. 1978. The Aztecs and the Ideology of Male Dominance. *Signs* 4(2): 349–62.

———. 1976. *Dos mujeres indígenas*. Serie: Antropólogia Social 14, Instituto Indigenista Interamericano, Mexico City.

———. 1970. *In the Eyes of the Ancestors: Belief and Behavior in a Maya Community*. Yale University Press, New Haven.

Nash, June, and María Patricia Fernández-Kelly. 1983. *Women, Men and the International Division of Labor*, edited by June Nash and María Patricia Fernández-Kelly. State University of New York Press, Albany.

Navarro, Marysa. 1989. The Personal Is Political: *Las Madres de Plaza de Mayo*. In *Power and Popular Protest: Latin American Social Movements*, edited by Susan Eckstein, 241–58. University of California Press, Berkeley.

Nelson, Diane M. 1999. *A Finger in the Wound: Body Politics in Quincentennial Guatemala*. University of California Press, Berkeley.

New Catholic Encyclopedia 1967–89. 18 vols. McGraw-Hill, New York.

Nicholson, H. B. 1971. Religion in Pre-Hispanic Central Mexico. In *Handbook of Middle American Indians*, vol. 10, pt. 1, *Archaeology of Northern Mesoamerica*, edited by Gordon F. Ekholm and Ignacio Bernal, series edited by Robert Wauchope, 395–446. University of Texas Press, Austin.

Niethammer, Carolyn. 1977. *Daughters of the Earth: The Lives and Legends of American Indian Women*. Macmillan, New York.

Niezen, Ronald. 2003. *The Origins of Indigenism: Human Rights and the Politics of Identity*. University of California Press, Berkeley.

Niles, Susan. 1988. Pachamama, Pachatata: Gender and Sacred Space on Amantani. In *The Role of Gender in Precolumbian Art and Architecture*, edited by Virginia E. Miller, 135–51. University Press of America, Lanham, Md.

Nimis, Marion M. 1982. The Contemporary Role of Women in Lowland Maya Livestock Production. In *Maya Subsistence: Studies in Memory of Dennis E. Puleston*, edited by Kent V. Flannery, 313–25. Academic Press, New York.

Nimuendajú, Curt. 1979. *The Šerente*. Translated by Robert H. Lowie. AMS Press, New York [1942].

———. 1946. *The Eastern Timbira*. Translated and edited by Robert H. Lowie. University of California Publications in American Archaeology and Ethnology, vol. 41, University of California Press, Berkeley.

———. 1939. *The Apinayé*. Translated by Robert H. Lowie, edited by Robert H. Lowie and John M. Cooper. Anthropological series no. 8, Catholic University of America, Catholic University of America Press, Washington, D.C.

Nordenskiöld, Erland. 1938. *An Historical and Ethnological Survey of Cuna Indians*. Comparative ethnological studies 10, Göteborgs Museum, Etnografiska Avdelningen, Göteborg.

Novaes, Sylvia Caiuby. 1986. *Mulheres Homens e Heróis: Dinâmica e Permanência através do Cotidiano da Vida Bororo*. FFLCH-USP, São Paulo.

Núñez, Olga Marina. 1975. Generalidades sobre la mujer indígena de Honduras. *América Indígena* 35(3): 565–73.

Núñez Becerra, Fernanda. 1996. *La Malinche: De la historia al mito*. INAH, Mexico City.

Núñez del Prado Béjar, Daisy Irene. 1975a. El rol de la mujer campesina quechua. *América Indígena* 35(2): 391–401.

———. 1975b. El poder de decisión de la mujer quechua andina. *América Indígena* 35(3): 623–30.

Nutini, Hugo G. 1968. *San Bernardino Contla: Marriage and Family Structure in a Tlaxcalan Municipio*. University of Pittsburgh Press, Pittsburgh.

Nutini, Hugo G., and Betty Bell. 1980. *Ritual Kinship: The Structure and Historical Development of the Compadrazgo System in Rural Tlaxcala*. Vol. 1. Princeton University Press, Princeton.

Nutini, Hugo G., and Barry L. Isaac. 1974. *Los pueblos de habla náhuatl de la región de Tlaxcala y Puebla*. Translated by Antonieta S. M. de Hope. INI, Mexico.

Nutini, Hugo G., and John M. Roberts. 1993. *Bloodsucking Witchcraft: An Epistemological Study of Anthropomorphic Supernaturalism in Rural Tlaxcala*. University of Arizona Press, Tucson.

O'Brian, Robin. 1992. Un mercado indígena de artesanías en los Altos de Chiapas: Persistencia y cambio en las vidas de las vendedoras mayas. *Mesoamérica* 23: 79–84.

O'Connor, Erin. 2002. Widows' Rights Questioned: Indians, the State, and Fluctuating Gender Ideas in Central Highland Ecuador, 1870–1900. *Americas* 59(1): 87–106.

O'Nell, Carl, and Henry A. Selby. 1968. Sex Differences in the Incidence of Susto in Two Zapotec Pueblos: An Analysis of the Relationships between Sex Role Expectations and a Folk Illness. *Ethnology* 7(1): 95–105.

Offner, Jerome A. 1983. *Law and Politics in Aztec Texcoco*. Cambridge University Press, Cambridge.

Offutt, Leslie S. 1997. Women's Voices from the Frontier: San Esteban de Nueva Tlaxcala in the Late Eighteenth Century. In *Indian Women of Early Mexico*, edited by Susan Schroeder, Stephanie Wood, and Robert Haskett, 273–89. University of Oklahoma Press, Norman.

Orellana, Sandra L. 1987. *Indian Medicine in Highland Guatemala: The Prehispanic and Colonial Periods*. University of New Mexico Press, Albuquerque.

Ornelas López, José Luz. 1988. Deterioro de las ocupaciones tradicionales y migración de mujeres zapotecas: Santo Domingo del Valle, Tlacolula, Oaxaca. In *Las mujeres en el campo: Memoria de la Primera Reunión Nacional de Investigación sobre Mujeres Campesinas en México*, edited by Josefina Aranda B., 113–21. Instituto de Investigaciones Sociológicas de la Universidad Autónoma Benito Juárez de Oaxaca, Oaxaca de Juárez, Oaxaca, Mexico.

Ortiz, Teresa. 2001. *Never Again a World without Us: Voices of Mayan Women in Chiapas, Mexico*. EPICA, Washington, D.C.

Ortiz Elizondo, Hector, and Rosalva Aida Hernández Castillo. 1996. Constitutional Amendments and New Imaginings of the Nation: Legal Anthropological and Gendered Perspectives on "Multicultural Mexico." *PoLAR (Political and Legal Anthropology Review)* 19(1): 59–69.

Ortner, Sherry. 2001. Specifying Agency: The Comaroffs and Their Critics. *Interventions* 3(1): 76– 84.

————. 1996. *Making Gender: The Politics and Erotics of Culture*. Beacon Press, Boston.

Osorio, Alejandra. 1999. *El callejón de la soledad*: Vectors of Cultural Hybridity in Seventeenth-Century Lima. In *Spiritual Encounters: Interactions between Christianity and Native Religions in Colonial America*, edited by Nicholas Griffiths and Fernando Cervantes, 198–229. University of Birmingham Press, Birmingham, England.

————. 1990. Seducción y conquista: Una lectura de Guamán Poma. *Allpanchis* 35–36: 293–332.

Ots Capdequí, José María. 1930. El sexo como circunstancia modificativa de la capacidad jurídica en nuestra legislación de Indias. *Anuario de Historia del Derecho Español* 7: 311–80.

Otzoy, Irma. 1996. Maya Clothing and Identity. In *Maya Cultural Activism in Guatemala*, edited by Edward F. Fischer and R. McKenna Brown, 141–55. University of Texas Press, Austin.

Overing, Joanna. 1986. Men Control Women? The "Catch-22" in the Analysis of Gender. *International Journal of Moral and Social Studies* 1(2): 135–56.

Overmyer-Velazquez, Rebecca. 1998. Christian Morality Revealed in New Spain: The Inimical Nahua Woman in Book Ten of the *Florentine Codex*. *Journal of Women's History* 10(2): 9–37.

Palomo, Nellys. 2001. Las miradas del presente, futuro del mañana, la población infantil indígena en México. *Fem* 25(217): 22–4.

Pancake, Cherri M. 1992. Fronteras de género en la producción de tejidos indígenas. In *Fronteras de género en la producción de tejidos indígenas*, 119–28. Museo Ixchel del Traje Indígena de Guatemala, Guatemala.

Parsons, Elsie Clews. 1945. *Peguche: Canton of Otavalo, Province of Imbabura, Ecuador: A Study of Andean Indians*. University of Chicago Press, Chicago.

———. 1936. *Mitla Town of the Souls and Other Zapoteco-Speaking Pueblos of Oaxaca, Mexico*. University of Chicago Press, Chicago.

Pasztory, Esther. 1997. *Teotihuacan: An Experiment in Living*. University of Oklahoma Press, Norman.

Patch, Robert. 2002. *Maya Revolt and Revolution in the Eighteenth Century*. M. E. Sharpe, Armonk, New York.

———. 1993. *Maya and Spaniard in Yucatan, 1648–1812*. Stanford University Press, Stanford.

Paul, Lois. 1978. Careers of Midwives in a Mayan Community. In *Women in Ritual and Symbolic Roles*, edited by Judith Hoch-Smith and Anita Spring, 129–49. Plenum Press, New York.

———. 1974. The Mastery of Work and the Mystery of Sex in a Guatemalan Village. In *Woman, Culture and Society*, edited by Michelle Zimbalist Rosaldo and Louise Lamphere, 281–99. Stanford University Press, Stanford.

Paul, Lois, and Benjamin Paul. 1975. The Maya Midwife as Sacred Specialist: A Guatemalan Case. *American Ethnologist* 2(4): 707–26.

Paulson, Susan. 2002. Placing Gender and Ethnicity on the Bodies of Indigenous Women and in the Work of Bolivian Intellectuals. In *Gender's Place: Feminist Anthropologies of Latin America*, edited by Rosario Montoya, Lessie Jo Frazier, and Janise Hurtig, 135–154. Palgrave MacMillan, New York.

Pelikan, Jaroslav. 1996. *Mary through the Centuries: Her Place in the History of Culture*. Yale University Press, New Haven.

Penyak, Lee M. 1999. Safe Harbors and Compulsory Custody: *Casas de Depósito* in Mexico, 1750–1865. *Hispanic American Historical Review* 79(1): 83–99.

Pérez Alemán, Paola. 1990. *Organización, identidad y cambio: Las campesinas en Nicaragua*. CIAM, Managua.

Pérez-Rocha, Emma. 1998. *Privilegios en lucha: La información de doña Isabel Moctezuma*. INAH, Mexico City.

Perrin, Michel, and Marie Perruchon, eds. 1997. *Complementariedad entre hombre y mujer: Relaciones de género desde la perspectiva amerindia*. Ediciones ABYA-YALA, Quito.

Perruchon, Marie. 1997. Llegar a ser una Mujer-Hombre: Chamanismo y relaciones de género entre los shuar. In *Complementariedad entre hombre y mujer: Relaciones de género desde la perspectiva amerindia*, edited by Michel Perrin and Marie Perruchon, 47–75. Ediciones ABYA-YALA, Quito.

Perry, Mary Elizabeth. 1990. *Gender and Disorder in Early Modern Seville*. Princeton University Press, Princeton.

Pescador, Juan Javier. 1995. Vanishing Woman: Female Migration and Ethnic Identity in Late-Colonial Mexico City. *Ethnohistory* 42(4): 617–26.

Peterson, Jeannette. 1994. *¿Lengua o Diosa?* The Early Imaging of Malinche. In *Chipping Away on Earth: Studies in Prehispanic and Colonial Mexico in Honor of Arthur J. O. Anderson and Charles E. Dibble*, edited by Eloise Quiñones Keber, 187–202. Labyrinthos, Lancaster, Calif.

Phillips, Lynne. 1987. Women, Development, and the State in Rural Ecuador. In *Rural Women and State Policy: Feminist Perspectives on Latin American Agricultural Development*, edited by Carmen Diana Deere and Magdalena León, 105–24. Westview Press, Boulder, Colo.

Picchi, Debra. 1983. Review of *Shabono*, by Florinda Donner. *American Anthropologist* 85(3): 674–5.

Piedrasanta Herrera, Ruth. 2001. Panorama de los problemas de salud y atención de las mujeres en los municipios fronterizos de Huehuetenango, Guatemala. In *Mujeres en las fronteras: Trabajo, salud y migración (Belice, Guatemala, Estados Unidos y México)*, edited by Esperanza Tuñón Pablos, 165–85. El Colegio de la Frontera Norte, ECOSUR, El Colegio de Sonora, and Plaza y Valdés, Mexico City.

Pino H., Ponciano del. 1998. Family, Culture, and "Revolution": Everyday Life with Sendero Luminoso. In *Shining and Other Paths: War and Society in Peru, 1980–1995*, edited by Steve J. Stern, 158–92. Duke University Press, Durham, N.C.

Platt, Tristan. 1993. Simón Bolívar, the Sun of Justice and the Amerindian Virgin: Andean Conceptions of the *Patria* in Nineteenth-Century Potosí. *Journal of Latin American Studies* 25(1): 159–85.

———. 1982. *Estado boliviano y ayllu andino: Tierra y tributo en el norte de Potosí*. Instituto de Estudios Peruanos, Lima.

Poeschel Rees, Ursula. 1989. La mujer salasaca (Enfoques socioantropológicos). In *Mujer indígena y educación en America Latina*, edited by Anna Lucía D'Emilio, 281–313. UNESCO/I. I. I, Santiago.

———. 1988. *La mujer salasaca: Su situación en una época de reestructuración económico-cultural*. Ediciones ABYA-YALA, Quito.

Pohl, Mary. 1991. Women, Animal Rearing, and Social Status: The Case of the Formative Period Maya of Central America. In *The Archaeology of Gender: Proceedings of the Twenty-Second Annual Conference of the Archaeological Association of the University of Calgary*, edited by Dale Walde and Noreen D. Willows, 392–99. University of Calgary Archaeological Association, Calgary.

Pohl, Mary, and Lawrence H. Feldman. 1982. The Traditional Role of Women and Animals in Lowland Maya Economy. In *Maya Subsistence: Studies in Memory of Dennis E. Puleston*, edited by Kent V. Flannery, 295–311. Academic Press, New York.

Poloni, Jacques. 1992. Mujeres indígenas y economia urbana: El caso de Cuenca durante la colonia. In *Mujeres de los Andes: Condiciones de vida y salud*, edited by Anne-Claire Defossez, Didier Fassin, and Mara Ontiveros, 202–21. IFEA and Universidad Externado de Colombia, Colombia.

Poniatowska, Elena. 1993. Juchitán, a Town of Women. In *Zapotec Struggles: Histories, Politics, and Representations from Juchitán, Oaxaca*, edited by Howard Campbell, Leigh Binford, Miguel Bartolomé, and Alicia Barabas, 133–6. Smithsonian Institution Press, Washington, D.C.

———. 1989. *Juchitán de las Mujeres*. Photographs by Graciela Iturbide and text by Elena Poniatowska. Ediciones Toledo, Oaxaca City, Mexico.

Poole, Deborah A. 2004. An Image of "Our Indian": Type Photography and Racial Sentiments in Oaxaca, 1920–1940. *Hispanic American Historical Review* 94(1): 37–82.

————. 1988. A One-Eyed Gaze: Gender in Nineteenth-Century Illustration of Peru. *Dialectical Anthropology* 13: 333–64.

Poole, Deborah A., and Penelope Harvey. 1988. Luna, sol y brujas: Estudios andinos e historiografía de resistencia. *Revista Andina* 6(1): 277–98.

Powers, Karen. 2002. Conquering Discourses of "Sexual Conquest": Of Women, Language, and *Mestizaje*. *Colonial Latin American Review* 11(1): 7–32.

————. 1998. A Battle of Wills: Inventing Chiefly Legitimacy in the Colonial North Andes. In *Dead Giveaways: Indigenous Testaments of Colonial Mesoamerica and the Andes*, edited by Susan Kellogg and Matthew Restall, 183–213. University of Utah Press, Salt Lake City.

Pozas, Ricardo. 1977. *Chamula*. 2 vols. INI, Mexico City.

Premo, Blanca. 2000. From the Pockets of Women: The Gendering of the Mita, Migration, and Tribute in Colonial Chucuito, Peru. *Americas* 57(1): 63–94.

Pringle, Heather. 1998. New Women of the Ice Age. *Discover* 19(4, April): 62–9.

Proskouriakoff, Tatania. 1964. Portraits of Women in Maya Art. In *Essays in Pre-Columbian Art and Archaeology*, by Samuel K. Lathrop, et al., 81–99. Harvard University Press, Cambridge, Mass.

Puig, Manuel María. 1910. *Los indios cunas de San Blas: Su orígen, tradiciones, costumbres, organización social, cultura y religion*. Los Talleres de "El Independiente," Colón, Panama.

Punín de Jiménez, Dolores. 1975. La mujer saraguro en el hogar. *América Indígena* 35(3): 559–63.

Quezada, Noemí. 1996. *Sexualidad, amor y erotismo: México prehispánico y México colonial*. Plaza y Valdés, Mexico City.

————. 1996b. Mito y género en la socieda mexica. *Estudios de Cultural Náhuatl* 26: 21–40.

————. 1989a. *Amor y magia amorosa entre los aztecas: Supervivencia en el México colonial*. 3rd ed. UNAM, Mexico City [1975].

————. 1989b. *Enfermedad y maleficio: El curandero en el México colonial*. UNAM, Mexico City.

————. 1977. Creencias tradicionales sobre embarazo y parto. *Anales de Antropología* 14: 307–26.

Quilter, Jeffrey. 1989. *Life and Death at Paloma: Society and Mortuary Practices in a Preceramic Peruvian Village*. University of Iowa Press, Iowa City.

Quinn, Naomi. 1977. Anthropological Studies on Women's Status. *Annual Review of Anthropology*, edited by Bernard J. Siegel, Alan R. Beals, and Stephen A. Tyler, 6: 181–225. Annual Reviews, Palo Alto, Calif.

Quiñones Keber, Eloise. 2002. Painting Divination in the *Florentine Codex*. In *Representing Aztec Ritual: Performance, Text, and Image in the Work of Sahagún*, edited by Eloise Quiñones Keber, 252–76. University Press of Colorado, Boulder.

Radcliffe, Sarah A. 2002. Indigenous Women, Rights and the Nation-State in the Andes. In *Gender and the Politics of Rights and Democracy in Latin America*, edited by Nikki Craske and Maxine Molyneux, 149–72. Palgrave, New York.

————. 1993."People Have to Rise Up—Like the Great Women Fighters": The State and Peasant Women in Peru. In *"Viva": Women and Popular Protest in Latin America*, edited by Sarah A. Radcliffe and Sallie Westwood, 197–218. Routledge, London.

————. 1990. Multiple Identities and Negotiation over Gender: Female Peasant Union Leaders in Peru. *Bulletin of Latin American Research* 9(2): 229–47.

————. 1985. Migración femenina de comunidades campesinas: Un estudio de caso, Cusco. *Allpanchis* 25–26: 81–119.

Radding, Cynthia. 1997. *Wandering Peoples: Colonialism, Ethnic Spaces, and Ecological Frontiers in Northwestern Mexico, 1700–1850*. Duke University Press, Durham, N.C.

Ramírez, Susan E. 1995. Exchange and Markets in the Sixteenth Century: A View from the North. In *Ethnicity, Markets, and Migration in the Andes: At the Crossroads of History and Anthropology*, edited by Brooke Larson and Olivia Harris with Enrique Tandeter, 135–64. Duke University Press, Durham, N.C.

Ramos, Alcida R. 1995. *Sanumá Memories: Yanomami Ethnography in Times of Crisis*. University of Wisconsin Press, Madison.

————. 1987. Reflecting on the Yanomami: Ethnographic Images and the Pursuit of the Exotic. *Cultural Anthropology* 2(3): 284–303.

————. 1979. On Women's Status in Yanoama Societies. *Current Anthropology* 20(1): 185–7.

Rappaport, Joanne. 1990. *The Politics of Memory: Native Historical Interpretation in the Colombian Andes*. Cambridge University Press, Cambridge.

Rautman, Alison E. 1997. Changes in Regional Exchange Relationships during the Pithouse-to-Pueblo Transition in the American Southwest. In *Women in Prehistory: North America and Mesoamerica*, edited by Cheryl Claassen and Rosemary A. Joyce, 100–118. University of Pennsylvania Press, Philadelphia.

Ravicz, Robert, and A. Kimball Romney. 1969. The Mixtec. In *Handbook of Middle American Indians*, vol. 7, *Ethnology*, pt. 1, edited by Evon Z. Vogt, series edited by Robert Wauchope, 367–400. University of Texas Press, Austin.

Rebolledo, Loreto. 1995a. Los cambios de "personalidad" en mujeres mapuche migrantes. In *Otros pieles: género, historia y cultura*, edited by Maruja Barrig and Narda Henríquez, 57–71. Pontificia Universidad Católica del Perú, Lima.

————. 1995b. Factores de clase: Género y étnia en la migracíon de mujeres mapuche. In *Mujeres: Relaciones de género en la argicultura*, edited by Ximena Valdés, Ana María Artega, and Catalina Artega, 407–23. CEDEM, Santiago.

Re Cruz, Alicia. 1998. Maya Women, Gender Dynamics, and Modes of Production. *Sex Roles* 39(7–8): 572–87.

Redfield, Robert. 1950. *A Village That Chose Progress: Chan Kom Revisited*. University of Chicago Press, Chicago.

————. 1941. *The Folk Culture of Yucatan*. University of Chicago Press, Chicago.

————. 1930. *Tepoztlan, A Mexican Village: A Study of Folk Life*. University of Chicago Press, Chicago.

Redfield, Robert, and Alfonso Villa Rojas. 1934. *Chan Kom: A Maya Village*. University of Chicago Press, Chicago.

Reeve, Mary-Elizabeth. 1988. *Los quichua del Curaray: El proceso de formación de la identidad*. Ediciones ABYA-YALA, Quito.

Reff, Daniel T. 1991. *Disease, Depopulation, and Culture Change in Northwestern New Spain, 1518–1764*. University of Utah Press, Salt Lake City.

Reichel-Dolmatoff, Gerardo. 1971. *Amazonian Cosmos: The Sexual and Religious Symbolism of the Tukano Indians*. University of Chicago Press, Chicago.

Reina, Leticia. 1997. Etnicidad y género entre los zapotecas del Istmo de Tehuantepec, Mexico. In *La reindianizacíon de América, siglo XIX*, edited by Leticia Reina, 340–57. Siglo Veintiuno, Mexico City.

Reina, Leticia, and Cuauhtémoc Velasco. 1997. Introduction to *La reindianización de América, siglo XIX*, edited by Leticia Reina, 340–57. Siglo Veintiuno, Mexico City.

Reina, Ruben E. 1966. *The Law of the Saints: A Pokomam Pueblo and Its Community Culture*. Bobbs-Merrill, Indianapolis.

Rendón, Silvia. 1975. Espectancias de mujeres indígenas para el mejoramiento social de sus comunidades de origen. *América Indígena* 35(3): 587–97.

Restall, Matthew. 2003. *Seven Myths of the Spanish Conquest*. Oxford University Press, New York.

———. 1998. The Ties That Bind: Social Cohesion and the Yucatec Maya Family. *Journal of Family History* 23(4): 355–81.

———. 1997. *The Maya World: Yucatec Culture and Society, 1550–1850*. Stanford University Press, Stanford.

———. 1995."He Wished It in Vain: " Subordination and Resistance among Maya Women in Post-Conquest Yucatan. *Ethnohistory* 42(4): 577–94. Special issue: Women, Power, and Resistance in Colonial Mesoamerica, edited by Kevin Gosner and Deborah E. Kanter.

Returned Refugee Women Gather Strength: Interview with Pantaleona Morales González of Mamá Maquín. 2003. *Report on Guatemala* 24(1): 9–13.

Reuque Paillalef, Rosa Isolde. 2002. *When a Flower Is Reborn: The Life and Times of a Mapuche Feminist*. Edited and translated by Florencia E. Mallon. Duke University Press, Durham, N.C.

Richards, Patricia. 2003. Expanding Women's Citizenship? Mapuche Women and Chile's National Women's Service. *Latin American Perspectives* 30(2): 41–65.

Rice, Patricia C. 1981. Prehistoric Venuses: Symbols of Motherhood or Womanhood? *Journal of Anthropological Research* 37(4): 402–14.

Rivas, Ramón D. 1993. *Pueblos indígenas y Garífuna de Honduras: Una caracterización*. Editorial Guaymuras, Tegucigalpa, Honduras.

Rivas, Roxani. 1994. La mujer cocama del Bajo Ucayali: Matrimonio, embarazo, parto y salud. *Amazonía Peruana* 12(24): 227–42.

Rivera Cusicanqui, Silvia, comp. 1990. Indigenous Women and Community Resistance: History and Memory. In *Women and Social Change in Latin America*, edited by Elizabeth Jelin, 151–83. Zed Books, London.

Rivera Zea, Tarcila. 1992. Testimonio: La nieta del indio Santos Zea. *Chacarera: Boletín de la Red Rural* (Peru) 9: n.p.

Robichaux, David. 2003. La formación de la pareja en la Tlaxcala rural y el origen de las uniones consuetudinarias en la Mesoamérica contemporánea: Un análisis etnográfico y etnohistórico. In *El matrimonio en Mesoamérica ayer y hoy: Unas miradas antropológicas*, edited by David Robichaux, 205–236. Universidad Iberoamericana, Mexico City.

———. 1997. Residence Rules and Ultimogeniture in Tlaxcala and Mesoamerica. *Ethnology* 36(2): 149–71.

———. 1988. Hombre, mujer y la tenencia de la tierra en una comunidad de habla náhuatl de Tlaxcala. In *Las mujeres en el campo: Memoria de la Primera Reunión Nacional de Investigación sobre Mujeres Campesinas en México*, edited by Josefina Aranda B., 83–100. Instituto de Investigaciones Sociológicas de la Universidad Autónoma Benito Juárez de Oaxaca, Oaxaca de Juárez, Oaxaca, Mexico.

Robledo Hernández, Gabriella Patricia. 2003. Protestantism and Family Dynamics in an Indigenous Community of Highland Chiapas. In *Women of Chiapas: Mak-*

ing History in Times of Struggle and Hope, edited by Christine Eber and Christine Kovic, 161–70. Routledge, London.

Rodríguez, Catalina. 1975. El trabajo de la mujer campesina entre los tarascos. *América Indígena* 35(3): 599–608.

Rodríguez-Shadow, María J. 1997. *La mujer azteca.* 3rd ed. Universidad Autónoma del Estado de México, Toluca, Estado de México, Mexico [1988].

———. 1990. *El estado azteca.* Universidad Autónoma del Estado de México, Toluca, Estado de México, Mexico.

Rojas, Basilio. 1964. *La rebelión de Tehuantepec.* Sociedad Mexicana de Geografía y Estadística, Mexico.

Rojas, Rosa, ed. 1994. *Chiapas ¿y las mujeres qué?* Ediciones la Correa Feminista, Mexico.

Romanoff, Steven. 1983. Women as Hunters among the Matses of the Peruvian Amazon. *Human Ecology* 11(3): 339–43.

Roosevelt, Anna C. 1988. Interpreting Certain Female Images in Prehistoric Art. In *The Role of Gender in Precolumbian Art and Architecture*, edited by Virginia E. Miller, 1–34. University Press of America, Lanham, Md.

Rosen, Fred. 2002. Survival and Resistance in Mexico. *NACLA: Report on the Americas* 36(2): 7.

Rosenbaum, Brenda. 1996. Women and Gender in Mesoamerica. In *The Legacy of Mesoamerica: History and Culture of a Native American Civilization*, by Robert M. Carmack, Janine Gasco, and Gary H. Gossen, 321–52. Prentice Hall, Englewood Cliffs, N.J.

———. 1993. *With Our Heads Bowed: The Dynamics of Gender in a Maya Community.* Institute for Mesoamerican Studies, State University of New York, Albany.

———. 1992. Mujer, tejido e identidad étnica en Chamula: Un ensayo histórico. In *Indumentaria y el tejido mayas a través del tiempo*, edited by Linda Barrios and Dina Fernández, 157–69. Museo Ixchel, Guatemala City.

Rösing, Ina. 2003. *Religión, ritual y vida cotidiana en los Andes. Los diez géneros de Amarete.* Translated by Rafael Puente. Interamericana, Madrid.

Rostas, Susanna. 2003. Women's Empowerment through Religious Change in Tenejapa. In *Women of Chiapas: Making History in Times of Struggle and Hope*, edited by Christine Eber and Christine Kovic, 171–87. Routledge, London.

Rostworowski de Diez Canseco, María. 1999. *History of the Inca Realm.* Translated by Harry B. Iceland. Cambridge University Press, New York.

———. 1995. *La mujer en el Peru prehispanica.* Instituto de Estudios Peruanos, Peru.

———. 1970. El repartimiento de Doña Beatriz Coya en el valle de Yucay. *Revista de Historia y Cultura*, no. 4: 153–267.

Rothstein, Frances. 1983. Women and Men in the Family Economy: An Analysis of the Relations between the Sexes in Three Peasant Communities. *Anthropological Quarterly* 56(1): 10–23.

Rovira, Guiomar, ed. 1997. *Mujeres de maíz.* Ediciones Era, Mexico City.

Rowe, John. 1963. Inca Culture at the Time of the Spanish Conquest. In *The Andean Civilizations*, vol. 2, *Handbook of South American Indians*, edited by Julian H. Steward, 183–410. Cooper Square, New York [1946].

Roys, Ralph L. 1972. *The Indian Background of Colonial Yucatan.* University of Oklahoma Press, Norman [1943].

Rubin, Gayle. 1975. The Traffic in Women: Notes on the "Political Economy" of Sex. In *Toward an Anthropology of Women*, edited by Rayna Reiter, 157–210. Monthly Review Press, New York.

Rubin, Jeffrey W. 1997. *Decentering the Regime: Ethnicity, Radicalism, and Democracy in Juchitán, Mexico.* Duke University Press, Durham, N.C.

Rubio Orbe, Gonzalo. 1975. La mujer indígena. *América Indígena* 35(3): 459–75.

Rugeley, Terry. 1996. *Yucatán's Maya Peasantry and the Origins of the Caste War.* University of Texas Press, Austin.

Ruiz Campbell, Obdulia. 1993. Representations of Isthmus Women: A Zapotec Woman's Point of View. In *Zapotec Struggles: Histories, Politics, and Representations from Juchitán, Oaxaca*, edited by Howard Campbell, Leigh Binford, Miguel Bartolomé, and Alicia Barabas, 137–42. Smithsonian Institution Press, Washington, D.C.

Rus, Diana L. 1990. *La crisis económica y la mujer indígena: El caso de Chamula, Chiapas.* Instituto de Asesoría Antropológica para la Región Maya, San Cristóbal de las Casas.

Sacks, Karen. 1979. *Sisters and Wives: The Past and Future of Sexual Equality.* Greenwood Press, Westport, Conn.

———. 1974. Engels Revisited: Women, the Organization of Production, and Private Property. In *Woman, Culture and Society*, edited by Michelle Z. Rosaldo and Louise Lamphere, 207–22. Stanford University Press, Stanford.

Saco, José Antonio. 1932. *Historia de la esclavitud de los indios en el Nuevo Mundo.* 2 vols. Cultural S. A., Havana.

Saeger, James Schofield. 2000. *The Chaco Mission Frontier: The Guaycuruan Experience.* University of Arizona Press, Tucson.

Saénz Samper, Juanita. 1993. Mujeres de barro: Estudio de las figurinas cerámicas de Montelíbano. *Boletín de Museo del Oro* (Bogotá) 34–35: 76–119.

Sahlins, Marshall. 1981. *Historical Metaphors and Mythical Realities: Structure in the Early History of the Sandwich Islands Kingdom.* University of Michigan Press, Ann Arbor.

Sale, Kirkpatrick. 1990. *The Conquest of Paradise: Christopher Columbus and the Columbian Legacy.* Knopf, New York.

Salomon, Frank. 1988. Indian Women of Early Quito as Seen through Their Testaments. *Americas* 44(3): 325–41.

———. 1973. Weavers of Otavalo. In *Peoples and Cultures of Native South America: An Anthropological Reader*, edited by Daniel R. Gross, 463–92. Doubleday, Garden City, New York.

Salomon, Frank, and Stuart B. Schwartz, eds. 1999. *The Cambridge History of the Native Peoples of the Americas*, vol. 3, pts. 1 and 2, *South America*. Cambridge University Press, Cambridge.

Salvador, Mari Lyn. 2003. Kuna Women's Arts: Molas, Meaning, and Markets. In *Crafting Gender: Women and Folk Art in Latin America and the Carribbean*, edited by Eli Bartra, 47–72. Duke University Press, Durham, N.C.

———. 1997. Looking Back: Contemporary Kuna Women's Arts. In *The Art of Being Kuna: Layers of Meaning among the Kuna of Panama*, edited by Mari Lyn Salvador, 151–211. Fowler Museum of Cultural History, University of California, Los Angeles.

———. 1978. *Yer Dailege! Kuna Women's Art.* Maxwell Museum of Anthropology, University of New Mexico, Albuquerque.

Salvucci, Richard J. 1987. *Textiles and Capitalism in Mexico: An Economic History of the Obrajes, 1539–1840.* Princeton University Press, Princeton.

Sánchez, Enrique, ed. 1996. *Derechos de los pueblos indígenas en las contituciones de América Latina*. Disloque Editores, Santefé de Bogotá, Colombia.

Sánchez Parga, José. 1992. Cuerpo y enfermedad en las representaciones indígenas de los Andes. In *Mujeres de los Andes: Condiciones de vida y salúd*, edited by Anne-Claire Defossez, Didier Fassin, and Mara Viveros. IFEA and Universidad Externado de Colombia, Colombia.

————. 1990. *¿Por que golpearla? Etica, estetica y ritual en los Andes: Estudios y analisis*. CAAP, Quito.

Sandstrom, Alan R. 2000. Contemporary Cultures of the Gulf Coast. In *Supplement to the Handbook of Middle American Indians*, vol. 6, *Ethnology*, edited by John D. Monaghan, series edited by Victoria Reifler Bricker, 83–119. University of Texas Press, Austin.

————. 1991. *Corn Is Our Blood: Culture and Ethnic Identity in a Contemporary Aztec Indian Village*. University of Oklahoma Press, Norman.

————. 1982. The Tonantzi Cult of the Eastern Nahua. In *Mother Worship: Theme and Variations*, edited by James J. Preston, 25–50. University of North Carolina Press, Chapel Hill.

Sanford, Victoria. 2003. *Buried Secrets: Truth and Human Rights in Guatemala*. Palgrave MacMillan, New York.

Santos Granero, Fernando. 2000. The Sisyphus Syndrome, or the Struggle for Conviviality in Native Amazonia. In *The Anthropology of Love and Anger*, edited by Joanna Overing and Alan Passes, 268–87. Routledge, London.

————. 1991. *The Power of Love: The Moral Use of Knowledge amongst the Amuesha of Central Peru*. Athlone Press, London.

————. 1986. The Moral and Social Aspects of Equality amongst the Amuesha of Central Peru. *Journal de la Société des Américanistes* 72: 107–31.

Santos Granero, Fernando, and Frederica Barclay. 2000. *Tamed Frontiers: Economy, Society, and Civil Rights in Upper Amazonia*. Westview Press, Boulder, Colo.

Sassen, Saskia. 1998. *Globalization and Its Discontents*. New Press, New York.

Sault, Nicole L. 2001. Godparenthood Ties among Zapotec Women and the Effects of Protestant Conversion. In *Holy Saints and Fiery Preachers: The Anthropology of Protestantism in Mexico and Central America*, edited by James W. Dow and Alan R. Sandstrom, 117–46. Praeger, Westport, Conn.

————. 1985b. Baptismal Sponsorship as a Source of Power for Zapotec Women in Oaxaca, Mexico. *Journal of Latin American Lore* 11(2): 225–43.

Sayavedra, Gloria. 2001. Mirando al sur del Sur: Las mujeres guatemaltecas refugiadas en Chiapas. In *Mujeres en las fronteras: Trabajo, salud y migración (Belice, Guatemala, Estados Unidos y México)*, edited by Esperanza Tuñón Pablos, 121–42. El Colegio de la Fontera Norte, ECOSUR, El Colegio de Sonora, and Plaza y Valdés, Mexico City.

Schaefer, Stacy B. 2002. *To Think with a Good Heart: Wixárika Women, Weavers, and Shamans*. University of Utah Press, Salt Lake City.

Schele, Linda, and Mary Ellen Miller. 1986. *The Blood of Kings: Dynasty and Ritual in Maya Art*. Kimball Art Museum, Fort Worth, Tex.

Schele, Linda, and David Freidel. 1990. *A Forest of Kings: The Untold Story of the Ancient Maya*. Morrow, New York.

Schevill, Margot Blum. 1991. The Communicative Power of Cloth and Its Creation. In *Textile Traditions of Mesoamerica and the Andes*, edited by Margot Blum Schevill, Janet Catherine Berlo, and Edward B. Dwyer, 3–15. Garland, New York.

Schirmer, Jennifer. 1993. The Seeking of Truth and the Gendering of Consciousness: The *Comadres* of El Salvador and the *CONAVIGUA* Widows of Guatemala. In *"Viva": Women and Popular Protest in Latin America*, edited by Sarah A. Radcliffe and Sallie Westwood, 30–64. Routledge, London.

Schroeder, Susan. 1997. Introduction to *Indian Women of Early Mexico*, edited by Susan Schroeder, Stephanie Wood, and Robert Haskett, 3–22. University of Oklahoma Press, Norman.

———. 1992. The Noblewomen of Chalco. *Estudios de Cultura Náhuatl* 22: 45–86.

Seed, Patricia. 1988. *To Love, Honor, and Obey in Colonial Mexico: Conflicts over Marriage Choice, 1574–1821*. Stanford University Press, Stanford.

Seeger, Anthony. 1981. *Nature and Society in Central Brazil: The Suya Indians of Mato Grosso*. Harvard University Press, Cambridge, Mass.

Seligmann, Linda J. 1993. Between Worlds of Exchange: Ethnicity among Peruvian Market Women. *Cultural Anthropology* 8(2): 187–213.

———. 1989. To Be In Between: The *Cholas* as Market Women. *Comparative Studies in Society and History* 31(3): 694–721.

Sell, Barry. n.d. The Spiritual Mothers of Tula and Other Episodes in the Life of an Indigenous Confraternity. Unpublished essay.

Sempowski, Martha, and Michael Spence. 1994. *Mortuary Practices and Skeletal Remains at Teotihuacan*. University of Utah Press, Salt Lake City.

Serra Puche, Mari Carmen. 2001. The Concept of Feminine Places in Mesoamerica: The Case of Xochitécatl, Tlaxcala, Mexico. In *Gender in Pre-Hispanic America: A Symposium at Dumbarton Oaks*, edited by Cecilia F. Klein, 255–83. Dumbarton Oaks, Washington, D.C.

Service, Elman. 1971. *Spanish-Guaraní Relations in Early Colonial Paraguay*. Greenwood Press, Westport, Conn.

Sesia, Paola M. 1997. "Women Come Here on Their Own When They Need To": Prenatal Care, Authoritative Knowledge, and Maternal Health in Oaxaca. In *Childbirth and Authoritative Knowledge: Cross-Cultural Perspectives*, edited by Robbie E. Davis-Floyd and Carolyn F. Sargent, 397–420. University of California Press, Berkeley.

Sethi, Raj Mohini. 1999. *Globalization, Culture and Women's Development*. Rawat, New Delhi.

Seymour-Smith, Charlotte. 1991. Women Have No Affines and Men No Kin: The Politics of Jivaroan Gender Relation. *Man* (n.s.) 26(4): 629–49.

Shaffer, Brian S., Karen M. Gardner, and Joseph F. Powell. 2000. Prehistoric and Ethnographic Pueblo Gender Roles: Continuity of Lifeways from the Eleventh to the Early Twentieth Century. In *Reading the Body: Representations and Remains in the Archaeological Record*, edited by Alison E. Rautman, 139–49. University of Pennsylvania Press, Philadelphia.

Shapiro, Judith. 1987. Men in Groups: A Reexamination of Patriliny in Lowland South America. In *Gender and Kinship: Essays toward a Unified Analysis*, edited by Jane Fishburne Collier and Sylvia Junko Yanagisako, 301–23. Stanford University Press, Stanford.

———. 1976. Sexual Hierarchy among the Yanomama. In *Sex and Class in Latin America*, edited by June Nash and Helen Icken Safa, 86–101. Praeger, New York.

———. 1971. Review of *Yanoáma: The Narrative of a White Girl Kidnapped by Amazonian Indians*. *American Anthropologist* 73(6): 1331–3.

Sheets, Payson. 1992. *The Ceren Site: A Prehistoric Village Buried by Volcanic Ash in Central America*. Harcourt Brace Jovanovich, Fort Worth, Tex.

Sherman, William L. 1979. *Forced Native Labor in Sixteenth-Century Central America*. University of Nebraska Press, Lincoln.

Sherzer, Dina, and Joel Sherzer. 1976. *Mormaknamaloe*: The Cuna Mola. In *Ritual and Symbol in Native Central America*, edited by Philip Young and James Howe, 21–42. University of Oregon Anthropological Papers no. 9, Department of Anthropology, University of Oregon, Eugene, Ore.

Sherzer, Joel. 1983. *Kuna Ways of Speaking: An Ethnographic Perspective*. University of Texas Press, Austin.

Shoemaker, Nancy, ed. 1995. *Negotiators of Change: Historical Perspectives on Native America Women*. Routledge, New York.

Sigal, Pete. 2000. *From Moon Goddesses to Virgins: The Colonization of Yucatecan Maya Sexual Desire*. University of Texas Press, Austin.

Sikkink, Lynn. 2001. Traditional Medicines in the Marketplace: Identity and Ethnicity among Female Vendors. In *Women Traders in Cross-Cultural Perspective: Mediating Identities, Marketing Wares*, edited by Linda J. Seligmann, 209–25. Stanford University Press, Stanford.

Silverblatt, Irene. 1998. Family Values in Seventeenth-Century Peru. In *Native Traditions in the Postconquest World*, edited by Elizabeth Boone and Tom Cummins, 63–89. Dumbarton Oaks, Washington D.C.

———. 1991. Interpreting Women in States: New Feminist Ethnohistories. In *Gender at the Crossroads of Knowledge: Feminist Anthropology in the Postmodern Era*, edited by Micaela di Leonardo, 140–71. University of California Press, Berkeley.

———. 1988. Women in States. In *Annual Review of Anthropology*, edited by Bernard J. Siegel, Alan R. Beals, and Stephen A. Tyler, 17: 427–60. Annual Reviews, Palo Alto, Calif.

———. 1987. *Moon, Sun and Witches: Gender Ideologies and Class in Inca and Colonial Peru*. Princeton University Press, Princeton.

Siskind, Janet. 1973. *To Hunt in the Morning*. Oxford University Press, New York.

Siverts, Kari. 1993. "I Did Not Marry Properly": The Meaning of Marriage Payments in Southern Mexico. In *Carved Flesh / Cast Selves: Gendered Symbols and Social Practices*, edited by Vigdis Broch-Due, Ingrid Rudie, and Tone Bleie, 225–36. Berg, Oxford.

Skar, Sarah Lund. 1993. Marry the Land, Divorce the Man: Quechua Marriage and the Problem of Individual Autonomy. *Carved Flesh / Cast Selves: Gendered Symbols and Social Practices*, edited by Vigdis Broch-Due, Ingrid Rudie, and Tone Bleie, 129–46. Berg, Oxford.

———. 1981. Andean Women and the Concept of Space/Time. In *Women and Space: Ground Rules and Social Maps*, edited by Shirley Ardener, 35–49. St. Martin's Press, New York.

———. 1979. The Use of the Public/Private Framework in the Analysis of Egalitarian Societies: The Case of a Quechua Community in Highland Peru. *Women's Studies International Quarterly* 2: 449–60.

———. 1978. Men and Women in Matapuquio. *Journal of the Anthropological Society of Oxford* 9(1): 153–60.

Sklair, Leslie. 1995. *Sociology of the Global System*. New ed. Prentice Hall, London [1990].

Slade, Doren L. 1992. *Making the World Safe for Existence: Celebration of the Saints among the Sierra Nahuat of Chignautla, Mexico.* University of Michigan Press, Ann Arbor.

————. 1976. Kinship in a Nahuat-Speaking Community. In *Essays on Mexican Kinship,* edited by Hugo Nutini, Pedro Carrasco, and James M. Taggart, 155–86. University of Pittsburgh Press, Pittsburgh.

————. 1975. Marital Status and Sexual Identity: The Position of Women in a Mexican Peasant Society. In *Women Cross-Culturally: Change and Challenge,* edited by Ruby Rohrlich-Leavitt, 129–48. Mouton, The Hague.

Smith, Carol A. 1995. Race-Class-Gender Ideology in Guatemala: Modern and Anti-Modern Forms. *Comparative Studies in Society and History* 37(4): 723–49.

Smith, Mary Elizabeth. 1983a. The Mixtec Writing System. In *The Cloud People: Divergent Evolution of the Zapotec and Mixtec Civilizations,* edited by Kent V. Flannery and Joyce Marcus, 238–45. Academic Press, New York.

————. 1983b. Regional Points of View in the Mixtec Codices. In *the Cloud People: Divergent Evolution of the Zapotec and Mixtec Civilizations,* edited by Kent V. Flannery and Joyce Marcus, 260–66. Academic Press, New York.

Smith, Michael E. 1996. *The Aztecs.* Blackwell, Oxford.

Smith-Ayala, Emilie. 1991. *The Granddaughters of Ixmucané: Guatemalan Women Speak.* Translated by Emilie Smith-Ayala. Women's Press, Toronto.

Smole, William J. 1976. *The Yanoama Indians: A Cultural Geography.* University of Texas Press, Austin.

Snow, K. Mitchell. 2001. Beliefs of Our Ancestors: Maruch Santiz Gomez Opens a Window into Contemporary Mayan Life. *American Indian* 2(3): 10–11.

Sokoloff, Shoshanna. 1993. The Proud Midwives of Juchitán. In *Zapotec Struggles: Histories, Politics, and Representations from Juchitán, Oaxaca,* edited by Howard Campbell, Leigh Binford, Miguel Bartolomé, and Alicia Barabas, 267–78. Smithsonian Institution Press, Washington, D.C.

Sommer, Doris. 1991. *Foundational Fictions: The National Romances of Latin America.* University of California Press, Berkeley.

Somonte, Mariano G. 1969. *Doña Marina, "La Malinche."* N.p., Mexico.

Sousa, Lisa M. 1997. Women and Crime in Colonial Oaxaca: Evidence of Complementary Gender Roles in Mixtec and Zapotec Societies. In *Indian Women of Early Mexico,* edited by Susan Schroeder, Stephanie Wood, and Robert Haskett, 199–214. University of Oklahoma Press, Norman.

————. 1996. Native Women's Responses to Wife-Beating in Seventeenth-Century Southern Mexico. Paper presented at the Tenth Berkshire Conference on the History of Women, Chapel Hill, N. C., June 7–9.

Sousa, Lisa M., C. M. Stafford Poole,., and James Lockhart. 1998. *The Story of Guadalupe: Luis Laso de la Vega's Huey tlamahuiçoltica of 1649.* Translated and edited by Lisa Sousa, C. M. Stafford Poole, and James Lockhart. Stanford University Press, Stanford.

Spahni, Jean-Christian. 1981. *Los indios de América Central.* Translated by Alyne Blanchard. Editorial Piedra Santa, Guatemala City.

Sparks, Carol Douglas. 1995. The Land Incarnate: Navajo Women and the Dialogue of Colonialism, 1821–1870. In *Negotiators of Change: Historical Perspectives on Native American Women,* edited by Nancy Shoemaker, 135–56. Routledge, New York.

Spedding P., Alison. 1997."Esa mujer no necesita hombre": En contra de la "dualidad andina"—imágenes de género en los Yungas de La Paz. In *Más allá del silencio:*

Las fronteras de género en los Andes, vol. 1, *Parentesco y género en los Andes*, edited by Denise Y. Arnold, 325–43. ILCA, La Paz.

Speed, Shannon. 2003. Actions Speak Louder Than Words: Indigenous Women and Gendered Resistance in the Wake of Acteal. In *Women of Chiapas: Making History in Times of Struggle and Hope*, edited by Christine Eber and Christine Kovic, 47–69. Routledge, London.

Spielmann, Katherine A. 1995. Glimpses of Gender in the Prehistoric Southwest. *Journal of Anthropological Research* 51(2): 91–102.

Spinden, Herbert J. 1935. Indian Manuscripts of Southern Mexico. *Annual Report of the Smithsonian Institution, 1933*, 429–51. Washington, D.C.

Spores, Ronald. 1997. Mixteca Cacicas: Status, Wealth, and the Political Accommodation of Native Elite Women in Early Colonial Oaxaca. In *Indian Women of Early Mexico*, edited by Susan Schroeder, Stephanie Wood, and Robert Haskett, 185–97. University of Oklahoma Press, Norman.

———. 1984. *The Mixtecs in Ancient and Colonial Times*. University of Oklahoma Press, Norman.

———. 1974. Marital Alliance in the Political Integration of Mixtec Kingdoms. *American Anthropologist* 76(2): 297–311.

———. 1967. *The Mixtec Kings and Their People*. University of Oklahoma Press, Norman.

Stark, Louisa. 1985. The Role of Women in Peasant Uprisings in the Ecuadorian Highlands. In *Political Anthropology in Ecuador: Perspectives from Indigenous Cultures*, edited by Jeffrey Ehrenreich, 2–23. Society for Latin American Anthropology, State University of New York, Albany.

———. 1979. Division of Labor and the Control of Economic Resources among Indian Women in the Ecuadorian Highlands. *Andean Perspectives* 3: 1–5.

Stavenhagen, Rodolfo. 1988. *Derecho indígena y derechos humanos en América Latina*. El Colegio de México, Mexico City.

Stavenhagen, Rodolfo, and Diego Iturralde, eds. 1990. *Entre la ley y la costumbre: El derecho consuetudinario indígena en América Latina*. Instituto Indigenista Interamericano, Mexico.

Stavig, Ward. 1999. *The World of Túpac Amaru: Conflict, Community, and Identity in Colonial Peru*. University of Nebraska Press, Lincoln.

———. 1995. "Living in Offense of Our Lord": Indigenous Sexual Values and Marital Life in the Colonial Crucible. *Hispanic American Historical Review* 75(4): 597–622.

Stephen, Lynn. 2002a. *Zapata Lives! Histories and Cultural Politics in Southern Mexico*. University of California Press, Berkeley.

———. 2002b. Sexualities and Genders in Zapotec Oaxaca. *Latin American Perspectives* 29(2): 41–59.

———. 1991. *Zapotec Women*. University of Texas Press, Austin.

Stephenson, Marcia. 1999. *Gender and Modernity in Andean Bolivia*. University of Texas Press, Austin.

Stern, Steve J. 1999. The Changing Face of Gender Complementarity: New Research on Indian Women in Colonial Mexico. *Ethnohistory* 46(3): 607–21.

———. 1995. *The Secret History of Gender: Women, Men, and Power in Late Colonial Mexico*. University of North Carolina Press, Chapel Hill.

———. 1993. *Peru's Indian Peoples and the Challenge of Spanish Conquest: Huamanga to 1640*. 2nd ed. University of Wisconsin Press, Madison [1982].

Steward, Julian H., and Louis C. Faron. 1959. *Native Peoples of South America.* McGraw-Hill, New York.

Stier, Frances. 1982. Domestic Economy: Land, Labor, and Wealth in a San Blas Community. *American Ethnologist* 9(3): 519–37.

Stocks, Kathleen, and Anthony Stocks. 1984. Status de la mujer y cambio por aculturación: Casos del Alto Amazonas. *Amazonia Peruana* 5(10): 65–77.

Stølen, Kristi Anne. 1991. Gender, Sexuality and Violence in Ecuador. In *Gender, Culture and Power in Developing Countries*, edited by Kristi Anne Stølen, 80–105. Centre for Development and the Environment, Oslo.

———. 1987. *A media voz: ser mujer en la sierra ecuatoriana.* CEPLAES, Quito.

Stoler, Ann Laura. 2002. *Carnal Knowledge and Imperial Power: Race and the Intimate in Colonial Rule.* University of California Press, Berkeley.

Stoll, David. 1999. *Rigoberta Menchú and the Story of All Poor Guatemalans.* Westview Press, Boulder, Colo.

———. 1990. *Is Latin America Turning Protestant? The Politics of Evangelical Growth.* University of California Press, Berkeley.

Stoltz Chinchilla, Norma. 1998. *Nuestras utopías: Mujeres guatemaltecas del siglos XX.* Agrupacíon de Mujeres Tierra Viva, Guatemala.

Stothert, Karen E. 2003. Expression of Ideology in the Formative Period of Ecuador. In *Archaeology of Formative Ecuador*, edited by J. Scott Raymond and Richard L. Burger, 337–421. Dumbarton Oaks, Washington, D.C.

Stone, Andrea. 1988. Sacrifices and Sexuality: Some Structural Relationships in Classic Maya Art. In *The Role of Gender in Precolumbian Art and Architecture*, edited by Virginia E. Miller, 75–103. University Press of America, Lanham, Md.

Storey, Rebecca. 1992. *Life and Death in the Ancient City of Teotihuacan: A Modern Paleodemographic Synthesis.* University of Alabama Press, Tuscaloosa.

Stout, D. B. 1948. The Cuna. In *Handbook of South American Indians*, 7 vols., edited by Julian H. Steward, 4:257–68, Bureau of American Ethnology, Bulletin 143, Smithsonian Institution, Washington, D.C.

———. 1947. *San Blas Cuna Acculturation: An Introduction.* Viking Fund Publications in Anthropology no. 9, New York.

Strecker, Mathias. 1987. Representaciones sexuales en el arte rupestre de la region Maya. *Mexicon* 7(2): 34–37.

Stromquist, Nelly P. 1992. *Women and Education in Latin America*, edited by Nelly P. Stromquist. Lynne Rienner, Boulder, Colo.

Suárez Guerra, Mirtha. 1975. La mujer indígena del valle boliviano. *América Indígena* 35(3): 519–27.

Sued-Badillo, Jalil. 1979. *La mujer indígena y su sociedad.* Editorial Antillana, Rio Piedras, Puerto Rico.

Sugiyama, Saburo. 1992. Rulership, Warfare, and Human Sacrifice at the *Ciudadela*: An Iconographic Study of Feathered Serpent Representations. In *Art, Ideology, and the City of Teotihuacan*, edited by Janet Catherine Berlo, 205–30. Dumbarton Oaks, Washington, D.C.

Sullivan, Thelma D. 1982. Tlazolteotl-Ixcuina: The Great Spinner and Weaver. In *The Art and Iconography of Late Post-Classic Central Mexico*, edited by Elizabeth Hill Boone, 7–35. Dumbarton Oaks, Washington, D.C.

Susnik, Branislava. 1965. *El indio colonial del Paraguay.* 2 vols. Museo Etnográfico "Andres Barbero," Asunción, Paraguay.

Swain, Margaret Byrne. 1989. Gender Roles in Indigenous Tourism: Kuna Mola, Kuna Yala, and Cultural Survival. In *Hosts and Guests: The Anthropology of Tourism*, edited by Valene L. Smith, 83–104. University of Pennsylvania Press, Philadelphia.

———. 1982. Being Cuna and Female: Ethnicity Mediating Change in Sex Roles. In *Sex Roles and Social Change in Native Lower Central American Societies*, edited by Christine A. Loveland and Franklin O. Loveland, 103–23. University of Ilinois Press, Urbana.

Sweely, Tracy L. 1999. Gender, Space, People and Power at Cerén. In *Manifesting Power: Gender and the Interpretation of Power*, edited by Tracy L. Sweely, 155–72. Routledge, London.

Sweet, David. 1981. Francisca: Indian Slave. In *Struggle and Survival in Colonial America*, edited by David G. Sweet and Gary B. Nash, 274–91. University of California Press, Berkeley.

Taggart, James M. 1983. *Nahuat Myth and Social Structure*. University of Texas Press, Austin.

———. 1975. *Estructura de los grupos domésticos de una comunidad nahuat de Puebla*. SEP, Mexico City.

Taller de Historia Oral Andina. 1986. *Mujer y resistencia comunaria: Historia y memoria*. HISBOL, La Paz.

Taller de Historia y Participación de la Mujer. 1986. *Polleras libertarias: Federación Obrera Femenina, 1927–1964*. Tahipamu, La Paz.

Tanner, Nancy. 1974. Matrifocality in Indonesia and Africa and Among Black Americans. In *Women, Culture and Society*, edited by Michelle Zimbalist Rosaldo and Louise Lamphere, 129–56. Stanford University Press, Stanford.

Tapia, Mario E, and Ana de la Torre. 1993. *La mujer campesina y las semillas andinas*. UNICEF and FAO, Lima.

Tate, Carolyn E. 1999. Writing on the Face of the Moon: Women's Products, Archetypes, and Power in Ancient Maya Civilization. In *Manifesting Power: Gender and the Interpretation of Power in Archaeology*, edited by Tracy L. Sweely, 81–102. Routledge, London.

Tax, Sol. 1963. *Penny Capitalism: A Guatemalan Indian Economy*. University of Chicago Press, Chicago [1953].

Taylor, Clark L. 1995. Legends, Syncretism, and Continuing Echoes of Homosexuality from Pre-Columbian and Colonial Mexico. In *Latin American Homosexualities*, edited by Stephen O. Murray, 80–99. University of New Mexico Press, Albuquerque.

Taylor, Douglas MacRae. 1951. *The Black Carib of British Honduras*. Viking Fund Publications in Anthropology, no. 17, Wenner-Gren Foundation for Anthropological Research, New York.

Taylor, William B. 1979. *Drinking, Homicide, and Rebellion in Colonial Mexican Villages*. Stanford University Press, Stanford.

Taube, Karl. 1983. The Teotihuacán Spider Woman. *Journal of Latin American Lore* 9(2): 107–89.

Terborg, Roland. 1996. Identidad y impacto cultural. *Dimensión Antropológica* 3(7): 113–45.

Terraciano, Kevin. 2001. *The Mixtecs of Colonial Oaxaca: Ñudzahui History, Sixteenth through Eighteenth Centuries*. Stanford University Press, Stanford.

————. 1998a. Crime and Culture in Colonial Mexico: The Case of the Mixtec Murder Note. *Ethnohistory* 45(4): 709–47.

————. 1998b. Native Expressions of Piety in Mixtec Testaments. In *Dead Giveaways: Indigenous Testaments of Colonial Mesoamerica and the Andes*, edited by Susan Kellogg and Matthew Restall, 115–40. University of Utah Press, Salt Lake City.

Thompson, J. Eric S. 1970. *Maya History and Religion*. University of Oklahoma Press, Norman.

————. 1939. *The Moon Goddess in Middle America with Notes on Related Deities*. Publication 509, contribution 29, Carnegie Institution of Washington, Washington, D.C.

Thurner, Mark. 1997. *From Two Republics to One Divided: Contradictions of Postcolonial Nationmaking in Andean Peru*. Duke University Press, Durham, N.C.

Tice, Karin E. 1995. *Kuna Crafts, Gender, and the Global Economy*. University of Texas Press, Austin.

Tierney, Patrick. 2000. *Darkness in El Dorado: How Scientists and Journalists Devastated the Amazon*. Norton, New York.

Tiffany, Sharon W., and Kathleen J. Adams. 1993. Anthropology's "Fierce" Yanomami: Narratives of Sexual Politics in the Amazon. *NWSA Journal* 6(2): 169–96.

Tinker, Irene. 1990. *Persistent Inequalities: Women and World Development*. Oxford University Press, Oxford.

Tirado, Thomas C. 1991. *Celsa's World: Conversations with a Mexican Peasant Woman*. Center for Latin American Studies, Arizona State University, Tempe.

Tizón, Judy. 1994. Transformaciones en la Amazonía: Estatus, género y cambio entre los Asháninka. *Amazonía Peruana* 12(24): 105–23.

————. 1984. Subordinación de la mujer amazónica: Modernización y desarollo. *Extracta* 4: 7–13.

Todorov, Tzvetan. 1984. *The Conquest of America: The Question of the Other*. Harper and Row, New York.

Torres de Araúz, Reina. 1980. *Panama Indígena*. Instituto Nacional de Cultura Patrimonio Historico, Panama.

Torres de Ianello, Reina. 1957. *La mujer cuna de Panama*. Ediciones Especiales del Instituto Indigenista Interamericano, Mexico City.

Townsend, Janet, Emma Zapata, Jo Rowlands, Pilar Alberti, and Marta Mercado. 1999. *Women and Power: Fighting Patriarchies and Poverty*. Zed Books, London.

Trexler, Richard C. 1995. *Sex and Conquest: Gendered Violence, Political Order and the European Conquest of the Americas*. Cornell University Press, Ithaca, N.Y.

Tschopik, Harry, Jr. 1946. The Aymara. In *Handbook of South American Indians*, 7 vols., edited by Julian H. Steward, 2:501–73. Bureau of American Ethnology, Bulletin 143, Smithsonian Institution, Washington, D.C.

Tsing, Anna. 2001. The Global Situation. In *Schools of Thought: Twenty-Five Years of Interpretive Social Science*, edited by Joan W. Scott and Debra Keates, 104–38. Princeton University Press, Princeton.

Turner, Terence S. 1979. The Gê and Bororo Societies as Dialectical Systems: A General Model. In *Dialectical Societies: The Gê and Bororo of Central Brazil*, edited by David Maybury-Lewis, 147–78. Harvard University Press, Cambridge, Mass.

Ubelaker, D. H. 1984. Prehistoric Human Biology of Ecuador: Possible Temporal Trends and Cultural Correlations. In *Paleopathology at the Origins of Agriculture*, edited by Mark Nathan Cohen and George J. Armelagos, 491–513. Academic Press, Orlando.

Uriebe Iniesta, Rodolfo, and Bartola May May. 1994. La mujer *Yoko Ishik* en la transición a la modernidad y la modernización. *América Indígena* 54(1 and 2): 213–22.

Vail, Gabrielle, and Andrea Stone. 2002. Representations of Women in Postclassic and Colonial Maya Literature and Art. In *Ancient Maya Women*, edited by Traci Arden, 203–28. AltaMira Press, Walnut Creek, Calif.

Valcárcel, Daniel. 1947. *La rebelión de Túpac Amaru*. Fondo de Cultura Económica, Mexico City.

Valcárcel, Gustavo. 1985. La condición de la mujer en el estado incaico. *Socialismo y Participación* 29: 63–70.

Valderrama Fernádez, Ricardo, and Carmen Escalante Gutiérrez, eds. 1996. *Andean Lives: Gregorio Condori Mamani and Asunta Quispe Huamán*. Translated by Paul Gellas and Gabriela Martínez Escobar. University of Texas, Austin.

Valencia Vega, Alipio. 1978. *Bartolina Sisa: La virreina aymara que murió por la libertad de los indios*. Librería Editorial "Juventud," La Paz.

Valero, Helena. 1984. *Yo soy Napëyoma: Relato de una mujer raptada por los indígenas yanomami*. Compiled by Renato Agagliate; edited by Emilio Fuentes. Monografía no. 35, Fundación La Salle de Ciencias Naturales, Caracas.

Van Young, Eric. 2001. *The Other Rebellion: Popular Violence, Ideology, and the Mexican Struggle for Independence, 1810–1821*. Stanford University Press, Stanford.

Van Zantwijk, R.A.M. 1960. *Los indígenas de Milpa Alta, herederos de los aztecas*. Instituto Real de los Tropicaos, Amsterdam.

Varón Gabai, Rafael. 1990. El Taki Onqoy: Las raíces andinas de un fenómeno colonial. In *El retorno de las huacas*, edited by Luis Millones, 331–405. Instituto de Estudios Peruanos and Sociedad Peruana de Psicoanálisis, Lima.

Vázquez García, Verónica. 1997. Mujeres que "respetan su casa": Estatus marital de las mujeres y economía doméstica en una comunidad nahua del sur de Veracruz. In *Familias y mujeres en México*, edited by Soledad González Montes and Julia Tuñón, 163–94. El Colegio de México, Mexico City.

———. 1996. Donde manda el hombre, no manda la mujer: Género y tenencia de la tierra en el México rural. *Cuadernos agrarios* (Chapingo, Mexico) (n.s.) 13 (May–June): 63–83.

Velazquez, Margarita. 1987. Educación para la mujer indígena. In *Las mujeres en el campo: Memoria de la Primera Reunión Nacional de Investigación sobre Mujeres Campesinas en México*, edited by Josefina Aranda B., 311–31. Instituto de Investigaciones de la Universidad Autónoma Benito Juárez de Oaxaca, Oaxaca de Juárez, Oaxaca, Mexico.

Vergara Ormeño, Teresa. 1997. Migración y trabajo femenino a principios del siglo XVII: El caso de las indias en Lima. *Historica* 21(1): 135–57.

Villanueva, Margaret A. 1985. From *Calpixqui* to *Corregidor*: Appropriation of Women's Cotton Textile Production in Early Colonial Mexico. *Latin American Perspectives* 44(1): 17–40.

Villanueva, Zarela. 1999. Legislative and Judicial Reforms Regarding Domestic Violence: Costa Rica. In *Too Close to Home: Domestic Violence in the Americas*, edited by Andrew R. Morrison and María Loreto Biehl, 153–57. Inter-American Development Bank, Washington, D.C.

Villa Rojas, Alfonso. 1969a. The Tzeltal. In *Handbook of Middle American Indians*, vol. 7, *Ethnology*, pt. 1, edited by Evon Z. Vogt, series edited by Robert Wauchope, 195–225. University of Texas Press, Austin.

———. 1969b. The Maya of Yucatan. In *Handbook of Middle American Indians*, vol. 7, *Ethnology*, pt. 1, edited by Evon Z. Vogt, series edited by Robert Wauchope, 244–75. University of Texas Press, Austin.

———. 1945. *The Maya of East Central Quintana Roo*. Publication no. 559, Carnegie Institution of Washington, Washington, D.C.

Villas Boas, Orlando, and Claudio Villas Boas. 1973. *Xingu: The Indians, Their Myths*, edited by Kenneth S. Brecher. Translated by Susan Hertelendy Rudge. Farrar, Straus and Giroux, New York.

Violencia contra la niñez en el contexto de la guerra y la impunidad. 1999. Cuaderno Divulgativo no. 2/99, PRONICE, Guatemala City.

Visweswaran, Kamala. 1997. Histories of Feminist Ethnography. In *Annual Review of Anthropology*, edited by William H. Durham, E. Valentine Daniel, and Bambi B. Schieffelin, 26: 591–621. Annual Reviews, Palo Alto, Calif.

Vogt, Evon Z. 1969. *Zinacantan: A Maya Community in the Highlands of Chiapas*. Harvard University Press, Cambridge, Mass.

Wachtel, Nathan. 1977. *The Vision of the Vanquished: The Spanish Conquest of Peru through Indian Eyes, 1530–1570*. Translated by Ben and Siân Reynolds. Harper and Row, New York.

Wade, Peter. 1997. *Race and Ethnicity in Latin America*. Pluto Press, London.

Wadsworth, Ana Cecelia, and Ineke Dibbits. 1989. *Agitadoras de buen gusto: Historia del Sindicato de Culinarias (1935–1958)*. TAHIPAMU/HISBOL, La Paz.

Wagley, Charles. 1977. *Welcome of Tears: The Tapirapé Indians of Central Brazil*. Oxford University Press, New York.

———. 1941. *Economics of a Guatemalan Village*. Memoirs of the American Anthropological Association, no. 58. American Anthropological Association, Menasha, Wisc.

Wallerstein, Immanual. 1974. *The Modern World System*. Academic Press, New York.

Ward, Kathryn. 1990. *Women Workers and Global Restructuring*. Cornell International Industrial and Labor Relations report no. 17, ILR Press, Ithaca, N.Y.

Warren, Kay B. 1998. *Indigenous Movements and Their Critics: Pan-Maya Activism in Guatemala*. Princeton University Press, Princeton.

Wearne, Phillip. 1996. *Return of the Indian: Conquest and Revival in the Americas*. Temple University Press, Philadelphia.

Weaver, Muriel Porter. 1993. *The Aztecs, Maya, and Their Predecessors: Archaeology of Mesoamerica*. 3rd ed. Academic Press, San Diego [1972].

Webre, Stephen. 2001. The Wet Nurses of Jocotenango: Gender, Science, and Politics in Late-Colonial Guatemala. *Colonial Latin American Historical Review* 10(2): 173–97.

Weinberg, Bill. 2001. Bio-Piracy in Chiapas. *Nation*, August 20/27, 23.

Weismantel, Mary. 2001. *Cholas and Pishtacos: Stories of Race and Sex in the Andes*. University of Chicago Press, Chicago.

———. 1997. Time, Work-Discipline, and Beans: Indigenous Self-Determination in the Northern Andes. In *Women and Economic Change: Andean Perspectives*, edited by Ann Miles and Hans Buechler, 31–54. Society for Latin American Anthropology, Washington, D.C.

————. 1988. *Food, Gender, and Poverty in the Ecuadorian Andes.* University of Pennsylvania Press, Philadelphia.

Werner, Dennis. 1984a. Paid Sex Specialists among the Mekranoti. *Journal of Anthropological Research* 40(3): 394–405.

————. 1984b. *Amazon Journey: An Anthropologist's Year among Brazil's Mekranoti Indians.* Simon and Schuster, New York.

————. 1984c. Child Care and Influence among the Mekranoti of Central Brazil. *Sex Roles* 10(5–6): 395–404.

West, Robert C. 1964a. Surface Configuration and Associated Geology of Middle America. In *Handbook of Middle American Indians*, vol. 1, *Natural Environment and Early Cultures*, edited by Robert C. West, series edited by Robert Wauchope, 33–83. University of Texas Press, Austin.

————. 1964b. The Natural Regions of Middle America. In *Handbook of Middle American Indians*, vol. 1, *Natural Environment and Early Cultures*, edited by Robert C. West, series edited by Robert Wauchope, 363–83. University of Texas Press, Austin.

Whalen, Michael E. 1981. *Excavations at Tomaltepec: Evolution of a Formative Community in the Valley of Oaxaca, Mexico.* Memoir no. 12, Museum of Anthropology, University of Michigan, Ann Arbor.

Whallon, Robert. 1986. A Spatial Analysis of Four Occupation Floors at Guilá Naquitz. In *Guilá Naquitz: Archaic Foraging and Early in Oaxaca, Mexico*, edited by Kent V. Flannery, 369–84. Academic Press, Orlando.

Whitecotton, Joseph W. 1977. *The Zapotecs: Princes, Priests, and Peasants.* University of Oklahoma Press, Norman.

Whitten, Dorothea Scott. 2003. Connections: Creative Expressions of Canelos Quichua Women. In *Crafting Gender: Women and Folk Art in Latin America and the Caribbean*, edited by Eli Bartra, 73–97. Duke University Press, Durham, N.C.

————. 1981. Ancient Tradition in a Contemporary Context: Canelos Quichua Ceramics and Symbolism. In *Cultural Transformations and Ethnicity in Modern Ecuador*, edited by Norman E. Whitten, Jr., 749–75. University of Illinois Press, Urbana.

Whitten, Norman E., Jr. 1976. *Sacha Runa: Ethnicity and Adaptation of Ecuadorian Jungle Quichua.* University of Illinois Press, Urbana.

Wilson, Samuel M. 1990. *Hispaniola: Caribbean Chiefdoms in the Age of Columbus.* University of Alabama Press, Tuscaloosa.

Wood, Stephanie. 1998. Sexual Violation in the Conquest of the Americas. In *Sex and Sexuality in Early America*, edited by Merril D. Smith, 9–34. New York University Press, New York.

————. 1998b. Gender and Community Influence in Mesoamerica: Directions for Future Research. *Journal de la Société des Américanistes* 84(2): 243–76.

————. 1997. Matters of Life at Death: Nahuatl Testaments of Rural Women, 1589–1801. In *Indian Women of Early Mexico*, edited by Susan Schroeder, Stephanie Wood, and Robert Haskett, 165–82. University of Oklahoma Press, Norman.

Wood, Stephanie, and Robert Haskett. 1997. Concluding Remarks. In *Indian Women of Early Mexico*, edited by Susan Schroeder, Stephanie Wood, and Robert Haskett, 313–30. University of Oklahoma Press, Norman.

Woodrick, Anne C. 1995. A Lifetime of Mourning: Grief Work among Yucatec Maya Women. *Ethos* 23(4): 401–23.

Wright, Pamela. 1995. The Timely Significance of Supernatural Mothers or Exemplary Daughters: The Metonymy of Identity in History. In *Articulating Hidden Histories: Exploring the Influence of Eric R. Wolf*, edited by Jane Schneider and Rayna Rapp, 243–61. University of California Press, Berkeley.

Wright, Robin, with the collaboration of Manuela Carneiro De Cunha et al. 1999. Destruction, Resistance and Transformation—Southern, Coastal, and Northern Brazil (1580–1890). In *The Cambridge History of the Native Peoples of the Americas*, vol. 3, pt. 2, edited by Frank Salomon and Stuart B. Schwartz, 287–381. Cambridge University Press, New York.

Young, Kate. 1978. Modes of Appropriation and the Sexual Divison of Labour: A Case Study from Oaxaca, Mexico. In *Feminism and Materialism: Women and Modes of Production*, edited by Annette Kuhn and AnnMarie Wolpe, 124–53. Routledge and Kegan Paul, London.

Young, Philip D. 1971. *Ngawbe: Tradition and Change among the Western Guaymí of Panama*. University of Illinois Press, Urbana.

Zavala, Silvio. 1984. *El servicio personal de los indios en la Nueva España*. 7 vols. El Colegio de México, Mexico City.

Zevallos Quiñones, Jorge. 1989. *Los caciques de Lambayeque*. Gráfica Cuatro, Trujillo, Peru.

Zihlman, Adrienne L. 1981. Women as Shapers of Human Adaptation. In *Woman the Gatherer*, edited by Frances Dahlberg, 75–120. Yale University Press, New Haven.

Zuidema, R. T. 1977. Inca Kinship. In *Andean Kinship and Marriage*, edited by Ralph Bolton and Enrique Mayer, 240–81. Special publication no. 7, American Anthropological Association, Washington, D.C.

Zulawski, Ann. 1995. *They Eat from Their Labor: Work and Social Change in Colonial Bolivia*. University of Pittsburgh Press, Pittsburgh.

———. 1990. Social Differentiation, Gender, and Ethnicity: Urban Indian Women in Colonial Bolivia, 1640–1725. *Latin American Research Review* 25(2): 93–114.

Zuñiga, Madeleine. 1989. La mujer indígena en Perú (Situación educativa de la mujer indígena). In *Mujer indígena y educación en América Latina*, edited by Anna Lucía D'Emilio, 281–313. UNESCO/I. I. I, Santiago.

———. 1988. En busca de una nueva educación para la mujer indígena en el Peru. *Ideología* (Ayacucho) 11 (December): 5–32.

Zur, Judith N. 1998. *Violent Memories: Mayan War Widows in Guatemala*. Westview Press, Boulder, Colo.

INDEX

abduction, of brides
  in lowland cultures, 134, 149–150
  Nahua, 96–97, 208n.22
abortion, 80, 211n.68
abstinence, as birth control, 135
abuse, spousal. *See* domestic violence
Abya Yala, Continental Encuentros of
      Indigenous Women of the First
      Nations of, 173
acculturation, 3–4, 99
  during Conquest era, 58, 197n.11
  religious (*see* missionaries)
activism. *See also* specific type
  current forms of, 170, 173, 177
  defensive nature of, 121–122, 169–170,
    215n.110
  international level, 171–173, 175
  by Mayas
    contemporary, 170, 174–175, 236n.2
    institutionalized, 122–124, 179,
      216n.114, 216n.116, 216n.118
    modern, 100, 116, 120–123, 125,
      215n.110, 216n.114, 216n.116,
      216n.118
    religious, 124–125, 217n.128
    social, 102–121, 123–124, 217n.124
  media's role, 10, 127, 170, 218n.2, 236n.2
  modern Nahuas, 100–103
  national level, 171–173, 176
  organizations of, 179–180
  regional level, 170–171
adultery
  in Andean culture, 50–51, 195n.98
  in modern cultures, 99, 111, 211n.68
advocacy groups, 101
Afro-indigenous peoples, 8, 158, 186n.15,
  232n.88
afterlife, beliefs about, 13–14, 23
agency. *See also* activism
  during colonial era, 53–54, 84, 195n.1,
    204n.116

forms of, 6, 170, 177
globalization impact on, 91–92, 169, 199
labor metaphors for, 6, 91
of modern Nahuas, 91, 99
Agency for International Development
    (USAID), 231n.85
agendas, contemporary
  for development
    rural, 131–132, 140, 171, 223n.35,
      231n.85, 232n.87
    technological, 102, 124
  of indigenous women, 157, 169–177
  nation-building, 91, 157
agriculture
  in Andean culture, 48–50
  contemporary, 129–130, 132, 140
  during colonial era, 65–66, 70, 72
  gender hierarchy in, 12–14, 35, 91
  by lowland cultures, 145–146
  maize-dominant, 25, 29, 35, 40, 48, 50,
    63, 91
  by Mayas, 112–115, 125, 212n.74, 213n.78
  by Nahuas, 92, 94–95, 102, 207n.9
  in prehispanic Mesoamerica, 25, 29, 35,
    40
  by Zapotecs, 107
Aguaruna women, 153
AIDS, in Central America, 162, 234n.105,
    236n.123
alcohol consumption
  by Andeans, 133–134
  by Central Americans, 234n.103
  domestic violence related to, 111, 119,
    133, 227n.63
  as increasing, 9, 120, 122
  resistance toward, 100–101, 125
allies, against domestic violence, 76–77,
    202n.82
Amazonian peoples, 148, 172. *See also* low-
    land cultures
AMMOR, 171, 179

Anacaona, rejection of Spanish, 58–59
Andeans, 129–142
  contemporary
    authority of, 129–131, 133, 140,
      220n.16
    cultural changes for, 141–142
    family life of, 133–135, 220nn.15–16
    inheritance rights, 133, 219n.12,
      220n.16
    labor divisions, 129–133
    migration trends, 132, 140–141,
      223nn.35–36
    political roles, 136–140, 221n.24
    subordination in, 138–140
  exotic sex images of, 127, 129
  female authority roles, 43–44, 47–49
  female deities of, 48–49, 78
  gender complementarity, 8, 11, 17, 42–48
    contemporary, 132, 134–136, 138, 140
  gender hierarchy, 50–51, 195n.98
  gender images
    artistic, 41–44
    contemporary, 127–129, 218n.2
    early vs. late, 18, 41–42, 44, 46, 48
    Mesoamerica vs., 18, 41
    naturalistic, 41–43
  Inka (see Inka Andeans)
  marketing activities of, 65, 129–130
  prior to Inka (see pre-Inka Andes)
  ritual complementarity, 42–44, 46, 49–50
  supernatural images
    early civilizations, 41–43, 46, 48
    later civilizations, 48–49
anetaw, 154
ANFASEP, 138, 179
animal husbandry, 40, 94
  contemporary, 115, 130–132, 156
ANMUCIC, 172, 179
anthropology
  of Central Americans, 158, 232n.88
  of lowland cultures, 143–144, 148,
    224n.43
  of Mayas, 115, 118
  of Nahuas, 92, 101–102
  as research source, 6–7, 9–10, 129,
    186n.16, 218n.2
anti-Mexica sentiment, of Nahua women,
    56, 196n.5
aqlla wasi, 50
Arawak peoples, 158
archaeology
  groups identified by, 20, 188n.2
  as research source, 6–7, 9–11
Archaic period, 12–13
army surveillance, of Mayas, 121–122,
    215n.110
Arpasi, Paulina, 174
artistic images
  of Andean gender, 41–44, 46
  of Maya gender, 35–37, 124

ASOMUGA, 236n.123
authority. See also power
  of Andeans, 129–131, 133, 140, 220n.16
  in Central Americans, 160, 162–167,
    233n.96
  female dominant (see matriarchy)
  of in-laws, 75–76, 96–97, 99, 117
  in lowland cultures, 147, 149, 151–153
    patterns of, 153–155, 229n.74, 229n.76,
      230n.77, 230n.80
  male dominant (see patriarchy)
  of Mayas, 115, 118–120, 125, 217n.128
  of Nahuas, 97–101
  of Zapotecs, 108–111, 210n.59
autonomy
  of Andeans, 137
  of Central Americans, 164, 167
  decline of
    during colonial era, 70–71
    modern, 106–107
  global trends, 9, 171, 175, 186n.16
  of lowland cultures, 148, 153, 155, 157,
    231n.83
  of Mayas, 120–121
  of Nahuas, 99
  of Zapotecs, 106–107
ayllu, 49
Aymara women, 129, 137–138, 141, 174
Aztec empire. See also Mexica
  geographical areas of, 22–23
  term relevancy, 18, 20, 188n.1, 189n.14
Aztlan (Place of the Herons), 23

Barasana peoples, 150
Barrios de Chungara, Domitila, 127–128,
    176, 238n.19
Bartolina Sisa Federation of Peasant
    Women of Bolivia, 137
Bastidas Puyucahua, Micaela, 85
beauty, physical
  of Garifuna women, 236n.120
  of Zapotec, 103–105, 209n.43
Beijing Draft Platform for Action, 172
belief systems, earliest women's role, 13–14
Belize
  ethnogenesis in, 158, 232n.88
  modern Mayas of, 112, 160, 211n.71,
    232n.88
betrothal period, 73–74, 201n.64
bigamy, during colonial era, 72–73, 201n.61
bilingualism, 138, 143, 165, 224n.43
  of Nahuas, 53–56, 124, 195n.2
biological identities, mixed. See ethnic-
    racial identities
biopiracy, 172
birth control. See contraception
birth rituals
  by Central Americans, 163, 235n.107
  in prehispanic Mesoamerica, 23, 39
bisexuality, 29, 191n.37

Black Carib, 8, 186n.15. *See also* Garifuna
Bolivia
  highland cultures of (*see* Andeans)
  peasant activism in, 137
  tropical cultures of (*see* lowland cultures)
Bororo women, 146, 229n.74
Brazil, tropical cultures of. *See* lowland
  cultures
breastfeeding
  labor related to, 64, 71, 199n.41
  malnutrition and, 119–120
bride rituals
  contemporary, 134, 151
  of Mayas, 117
  of Nahuas, 96–97, 208n.22
bride service, 73–74, 201n.64
bridegroom, labor of prospective, 73, 96
burial rituals
  Andean, 42–43, 48
  earliest, 13–14
  in prehispanic Mesoamerica, 22–23,
    37–38, 193n.64
business interests. *See* capital

cacica, of colonial Nahua, 81, 85, 203n.102
Cacuango, Dolores, 136, 173
capital, control of
  by Andeans, 130, 133
  by Central Americans, 166–167,
    236n.121
  investments for development, 171
  by Mayas, 114–117, 213n.88, 214n.95
  by Nahuas, 95–96
  by Zapotecs, 105–106
capitalism, global, 186nn.16–17
capitals, regional, 50
capture, of brides. *See* abduction
capullanas, 49
cargo system, positions held by women, 100
Caribbean
  ethnogenesis in, 8, 19, 158, 186n.15,
    232n.88
  Spanish conquest of, 58–59, 195n.2
cash income. *See* wages
Catholicism
  colonial rebellion against, 81–85,
    204n.112, 204nn.116–117
  gender role beliefs, 72–74, 78
  of lowland cultures, 156, 229n.73
  of modern Mayas, 118, 120, 124
Catinac Xom, Juana, 177
cattle ranching, 94–96, 102, 156
CCP, 174, 179
CEH, 174, 179
CENDOC-Mujer, 179
census. *See* population trends
Central Americans, 157–167
  diversity of, 157–158, 232n.88
  domestic violence and, 160–161,
    234n.97

education of, 165, 167, 236n.123
gender images, 127–128, 218n.2
household authority roles, 160, 162–163,
  233n.96, 235n.104
inheritance rights, 160, 233nn.95–96
labor divisions, 159–160, 164, 233n.95
market economies of, 164–167, 236n.121
media influence, 10, 127, 218n.2
political roles, 163–165, 167
procreation beliefs, 161–163, 234n.103,
  234n.105
sexuality patterns, 161–162, 234n.99
Central Mexico. *See* Mesoamerica
ceramics. *See* pottery
ceremonial authority. *See* rituals
Chaco War (1930s), 137
Chagnon, Napolean, 127, 142–143, 218n.2
chain stores, 210n.50
chastity. *See* virginity
Chiapas
  confraternities and, 79–80, 84–85
  Mayas and, 112–113, 115–116, 119–121,
    124, 211n.71
  political activism and, 100, 121, 170,
    236n.2
Chicomoztoc (Seven Caves), 23
child abandonment, during colonial era, 67,
  199n.41
childbirth. *See* midwifery
childcare
  contemporary, 135, 160
  earliest women's role, 12, 35, 42
  personal services for, 65–66, 199n.41
  resistance to, 71–72
Chile, current activism, 172, 177, 238n.19
Chimalma (Shield Lying), 23
chola, 8, 129, 132, 222n.34
church attendance
  during colonial era, 79–80
  modern, 124–125, 141, 217n.128
Cihuacoatl, 29–31
Circum-Caribbean region. *See* Caribbean
civil society dynamics, 9, 108, 122, 173–174
civil war, in Guatemala, 121–123, 215n.110
class and class differences. *See* social status
Classic Mesoamerica period, 18, 20, 32,
  35–36, 38
clothing pins (tupu pins), 43
clothing styles
  of Andeans, 131, 135, 140, 222n.34
  of Central Americans, 160, 166, 232n.90
  of lowland cultures, 156
  of Mayas, 112–113, 118, 121, 124
  of Nahuas, 102
  of Zapotecs, 103–104
CNMI, 179, 216n.118
CNPA, 110, 179
Coatlicue (Snake Skirt), 29
COCEI, 110–111, 179
COCOPA, 179

coercion
    of modern Nahua brides, 96–97,
        208n.22
    for sex, in conquest era, 57–61, 197n.15,
        197n.19
    for textile production, in colonial era,
        67–69, 199n.45
COFADER, 138, 179
coffee plantations, 212n.74, 213n.87
collective ownership, of land, 176
colonial era. *See also* Conquest era
    family life
        evolutionary, 71–74, 81, 200n.57,
            201n.58, 201n.61
        as violent, 74–78, 202n.74, 202n.82,
            202n.84, 203n.88
    female deities transformation during,
        78–79
    gender impact of, 4–5, 10–11, 23, 26–27
    labor organization changes, 11, 26, 63–71,
        198nn.35–36
        as forced, 65, 67, 69–70, 199n.45,
            200n.46
        property ownership rights, 66, 69–71,
            200n.49, 200n.51
        protest during (*see* resistance)
        religious life, 71–73, 78–81, 200n.57,
            201n.58, 203n.100
        sexual abuse during, 60, 197n.19
        tribute payments impact, 66, 199nn.38–
            39
colonias, modern Maya, 121–122, 215n.110,
    217n.126
Columbia
    current activism, 172
    early female images, 13–14
    tropical cultures of (*see* lowland cultures)
comadre, modern Zapotec as, 108–109
commodities
    conquerors' demand for, 57–58, 63–65,
        196n.11
    female ownership of, 70, 200n.51
    in lowland cultures, 155–156, 230n.83
commodities distribution. *See* market
    economies
commodities production. *See* labor
communications development, Nahua and,
    102
community(ies)
    Andean, 133–136, 140, 220n.15, 221n.24
    Central American, 163–164
    colonial era resettlement of, 72
        uprisings and, 82–85, 204n.112,
            204nn.116–117
    Maya, 112, 115, 118, 120, 122, 213n.78,
        215n.110
    Nahua, 91–93, 99, 101–102, 207n.8
    Zapotec, 105, 107–109
compadrazgo system, of modern Zapotec,
    108–109

compensation, for labor, 65, 67. *See also*
    wages
COMPITCH, 170, 179, 236n.3
complementarity, 7
    activism supporting, 4, 175–176
    activism undermining, 169, 175
    of Andeans, 42–48
        contemporary, 132, 134–136, 138, 140
        colonial era decline of, 86–89, 205n.127
    in lowland cultures, 147, 155
    of Mayas
        modern, 118–120, 125, 214nn.95–96
        prehispanic, 36, 40, 192.50, 192n.59,
            193n.75
    of Nahuas, 92–103, 207n.9
    of Native Americans, 20
    of Ñudzahui, 30, 32–35
    in prehispanic Mesoamerica, 23–24,
        29–30, 32, 36, 190n.25
    of Zapotecs, 103, 106–107
compulsory labor, during colonial era, 65,
    67, 69–70, 199n.45, 200n.46
CONAIE, 136, 180
CONAVIGUA, 123, 174, 179
concubinage, during colonial era, 60, 67,
    196n.11
CONFENAIE, 172, 180
conflict(s)
    family
        labor-related, 75–77, 134
        of Mayas, 119, 125, 214n.95,
            217n.128
        subordination-related, 6–7, 119,
            185n.5, 186n.13
    female-on-female, 119, 220n.15
    marital (*see also* domestic violence)
        in lowland cultures, 153, 229n.71
        of Nahuas, 97, 99
    market economies and, 65, 81–82, 119,
        203n.102
congregacion policy, 72
congresses, national vs. international, 100,
    171–172, 174
Conquest era. *See also* colonial era
    in Andean culture, 48–49, 51
    commodities demand, 57–58, 63–65,
        196n.11
    ethnic-racial identities from, 53–54,
        56–57, 196n.5, 196nn.7–8,
        197n.12
    gender roles during, 55–63, 197n.19
    impact of, 11, 53–54, 86–89, 195n.2
    marital relations of, 57–59, 196n.7,
        196n.11, 197n.12
    sexual relations during
        coercive, 57–61, 197n.15, 197n.19
        consensual, 57–58, 196n.11, 197n.15,
            197n.19
        resistance to, 59–60, 63
        violent, 57, 59–61, 197n.15, 197n.19

constitutional proposals, for autonomy, 171,
    175
contemporary era
    activism, 101, 137–138, 141–142, 170–177,
        223n.35, 236n.2, 238n.19
    agendas
        for development, 131–132, 140,
            223n.35, 231n.85, 232n.87
        of indigenous women, 157, 169–177
        nation-building, 91, 157
    Andean revolution and, 129–141
    Central American empowerment,
        92–103
    gender complementarity, 129–138, 140,
        220n.16
    gender images, 127–129, 218n.2
    globalization impact, 140, 155, 165,
        169–170
    tropical lowland culture struggles,
        142–157, 224nn.45–46, 225n.48
Continental Encuentros of Indigenous
    Women of the First Nations of
    Abya Yala, 173
contraception, 208n.24
    access to, 135, 157, 162, 234n.103
    forced, 100, 120, 156, 173, 210n.60
    for Mayas, 120, 215n.104
contracts, for labor, 65–66
cooperatives
    for domestic violence resistance, 101
    for health care, 170, 179, 236n.3
    for labor access, 107, 146
    for marketing, 101–102, 116–117, 157,
        213n.88
    for mola production, 164–165, 167,
        236n.121, 236n.123
corn. See maize entries
corn meal, preparation of, 91–95
corn mills, 95, 102, 207n.15
Cortés, Hernán
    amorous history of, 56–57, 60, 195n.7
    translator for, 53–56, 69, 195n.2
cosmology, in Inka culture, 48–49
cosponsors, modern Zapotec as, 108–109
Costa Rica
    current activism, 171
    ethnogenesis in, 158, 232n.88
counterinsurgency groups, violence by,
    121–122, 215n.110
court system. See judicial courts
courtship rituals, modern
    of Andeans, 134–135
    of Mayas, 117
    of Nahuas, 96–97, 208n.22
Coyolxauhqui (Bells on Cheek), 29–30, 53
craft production
    by Central Americans, 158–159, 167
    during colonial era, 72
    as housework vs. productive labor, 9, 112,
        115–116, 212n.72

by lowland cultures, 145, 157
by Mayas, 112–113, 115–117, 120, 212n.72,
    213n.88
by Nahuas, 101
in prehispanic Mesoamerica, 22, 25–26,
    30–32, 34
Zapotec transmission of, 107, 210n.52
creator deity, 48
crime(s), domestic violence-related, 77,
    203n.88
cross-gender unity, 186n.13
Cuauhtemoc, 56, 60, 196n.5, 196n.7
CUC, 122, 180
cultural change
    by Andeans, 141–142
    current proposals for, 171, 173, 175
    ethno-racial mixing and, 8, 186nn.14–15
    global, 5, 8–9, 186nn.16–17
    in lowland cultures, 156–157, 232n.87
    by Mayas, 123–125, 217n.128
    periods of, 11–12, 22
    by Zapotecs, 107, 111
cultural diversity
    of lowland cultures, 142–145, 148, 157
    media undermining of, 143, 157, 172,
        232n.87
    of modern Mayas, 112–113, 211n.71
cultural products, woven, by Mayas,
    112–113, 116–117
cultures
    archaeological, 20, 188n.2
    symbolic beliefs of, 118, 169
Cunningham, Myrna, 174
curanderas, 162
curers. See healing and healers

daily life. See family life
dancing, 98, 162–163
"dancing sickness," 83
day sign reading, in prehispanic Mesoamer-
    ica, 27–28, 189n.24
death rituals
    in lowland cultures, 153, 229n.73
    of modern Nahuas, 98
    in prehispanic Mesoamerica, 23, 27
debts, labor-related, 67. See also tribute pay-
    ments
decision-making. See also authority
    earliest women's role, 12
    exclusion from, 170
deities
    female (see goddess/Goddess)
    male (see god/God)
    supreme, in prehispanic Mesoamerica,
        21–22, 29, 188n.4
democratization, support for, 122, 170–172
demographics. See outmigration; popula-
    tion trends
depósito, as labor practice, 69, 73, 199n.45,
    200n.46

development plans
    of indigenous women, 157, 169–177
    rural agendas, 131–132, 140, 157, 171,
        223n.35, 231n.85, 232n.87
    technological, 102, 124
devil, female deities linked to, 79, 84
Díaz, Porfirio, 94
diplomacy, in prehispanic Mesoamerica,
    22, 27
discrimination
    gender shaped by, 137, 185n.5
    personal accounts of, 174–175, 177
disease
    in Central Americans, 161–162, 234n.105,
        236n.123
    during colonial era, 71–72
    in lowland cultures, 152, 156
disobedience, domestic violence and, 75–76,
    82–83
division of labor. See also labor
    among Andeans, 129–133
    among Central Americans, 159–160, 164,
        233n.95
    during colonial era, 65–66, 198n.36
    as complementary, 7, 12–13, 64
    emergence of, 12–13
    in lowland cultures, 143–145, 224nn.45–
        46, 225n.48
    maize-driven, 91
    among Mayas, 39–40, 112, 118, 212n.
        72–73
    among Nahuas, 92–93, 100, 207n.9
domestic service
    by Andeans, 131–132, 137, 141
    during colonial era, 60, 198n.35, 199n.40.
        65
        as abusive, 66–67, 69, 199n.41
        resistance to, 71–72
    by Mayas, 114
    by Nahuas, 92–94, 102
    by Zapotecs, 107
domestic violence
    among Andeans, 131, 133–135, 141,
        220n.15
    among Central Americans, 160–161,
        234n.97
    during colonial era, 74–77, 202n.74,
        202n.82
        consequences of, 76–78, 202n.84,
            203n.88
    current activism, 9, 170, 172, 175–177
    in lowland cultures, 150–151, 154,
        227n.60, 227n.63, 228n.64
    among Mayas, 214n.95
    among Nahuas, 99, 209n.30
    sanctuary vs., 169
    among Zapotecs, 111, 211n.68
domestic work. See housework
domestication, emergence of, 12
domination, gender shaped by, 6–7, 185n.5

drama, modern Maya, 124, 217, n.126
drug wars, 134
dynastic patterns. See succession rights

earth deities
    in Andean culture, 48
    in prehispanic Mesoamerica, 20, 23, 29, 38
economic development
    Andeans and, 129–132, 140, 223n.35
    during colonial era, 75–77, 82–83, 85–86
        as exploitative, 66–71, 199n.45,
            199nn.39–41, 200n.46
    current activism, 171, 173, 176
    emergence of, 12–13, 94
    gender impact of, 4–5, 11, 20
    global (see globalization)
    Nahuas and, 94–96, 101–103, 207n.15
    in prehispanic Mesoamerica, 20, 26–27,
        39
    as undermining reciprocity, 95–96, 157,
        232n.87
    Zapotecs and, 107, 110
economic exploitation
    during colonial era, 66–69, 199n.45,
        199nn.39–41, 200n.46
        indigenous transformations, 87–88,
            205n.127
    of contemporary Andeans, 134–135, 137,
        220n.16
    of females, 9, 169, 187n.31
economic markets. See market economies
economic status
    of Central Americans, 160–161, 164–167,
        233nn.95–96, 236n.121
    domestic violence related to, 75–77,
        82–83, 85
    of lowland cultures, 145–147, 155–157,
        230n.83
    of Mayas, 115–121
economic units
    during colonial era, 70–71, 86
    of Mayans, 114–117, 124, 213n.78,
        213n.88
    of Nahuas, 94–96
    in prehispanic Mesoamerica, 22, 27
eco-tourism, 101
Ecuador
    current activism, 171–172
    early female images, 12–13, 187n.31
    highland cultures of (see Andeans)
    tropical cultures of (see lowland cultures)
education
    activists' demands for, 172, 177
    of Andeans, 50, 141–142
    of Central Americans, 165, 167, 236n.123
    of lowland cultures, 155–157, 231n.84
    of Mayas, 116, 123–124, 217n.124
    of Nahuas, 96, 102
    in prehispanic Mesoamerica, 22–23,
        25–27, 38

embroidered products, 165–167
empire, gender impact of, 20, 23, 188n.1
employers, during colonial era, 65, 199n.40, 200n.51
employment. *See* occupations; wages
enclosure
  colonial era emphasis on, 71, 74, 202n.68
  as gender clustering, 12–13
encomendero, 66–68, 81
encomienda, as forced labor, 65, 67, 69
environmental despoilment, activism against, 172
EPR, 180, 216n.118
erotic art, of Moche culture, of Peru, 41–43, 46
ethnic identities
  activism downplaying, 91, 172, 175
  activism supporting, 172–173, 175–176
  in Andean communities, 49, 129, 220n.15
  indigenous, 5, 7–8, 18, 186nn.14–15, 188n.1
    groups included, 20, 188n.2
  of Mayas, 115, 118–119
ethnic-racial identities
  in Central America, 158, 232n.88
  class differences and, 8, 66, 87, 186nn.14–15, 205n.125
    violence based on, 74–78, 150, 202n.74, 202n.82
  continuation of, 87–88, 140, 156, 205n.125, 222n.34
  as nobility, 57–58, 60, 196nn.7–8
  origin of, 53–54, 56–57, 196n.5, 196nn.7–8, 197n.12
ethnography
  of Andeans, 129, 135
  of Central Americans, 158, 164–165
  of lowland cultures, 143–144, 152, 224n.45
  of Mayas, 112–113, 115, 211n.70, 214n.96
  of Nahuas, 91, 101–102
  as research source, 8, 10, 87, 127, 186nn.14–15, 218n.2, 218n.4
  of Zapotecs, 103–106, 111
evil, female deities linked to, 79
exchange relations
  for ceremonial materials, 108, 132, 154, 163
  during Conquest era, 57–58, 65, 196n.11
exploitation
  economic (*see* economic exploitation; labor)
  social (*see* subordination)
EZLN, 170, 173, 180
  Mayas' role, 122–123, 216n.114, 216n.116

factories, labor roles in
  during colonial era, 65–66, 198n.36
  foreign-owned, 171

by Mayas, 116–117
by Nahuas, 95, 102, 207n.15
family groups. *See* kin and kinship systems
family life
  activism consequences for, 4, 169–171, 175–177
  in Andean culture, 50, 133–135, 220nn.15–16
  during colonial era
    civil codes for, 87–88, 205n.128
    evolutionary, 71–74, 81, 200n.57, 201n.58, 201n.61
    labor demands impact, 69–73, 75–77
    as violent, 74–78, 202n.74, 202n.82, 202n.84, 203n.88
  in prehispanic Mesoamerica, 22, 25, 27, 33–34, 39–40
  rural vs. urban, 77, 87, 205n.125
feasting ritual
  in Andean culture, 43–44, 134
  of Central Americans, 163, 235n.107
  in lowland cultures, 153, 229n.73
  of Zapotecs, 108–109
FEDEFAM, 138, 180
FEI, 136, 180
female deities. *See* goddess/Goddess
female images
  See also women/woman
  earliest images, 13–14, 187n.31
  prehispanic Mesoamerica expressions, 28–29, 36, 38, 190n.35, 192n.60
female life-cycle. *See* life-cycle transitions
female purity. *See* virginity
feminist movement. *See* women's rights
fertility, female
  in Andean culture, 42–43, 48
  earliest images of, 13–14, 187n.31
  Nahua ritual for, 98
  in prehispanic Mesoamerica, 21, 23, 29, 36, 38–39, 192n.60
films, on contemporary women, 127–128, 218n.2
financial control. *See* capital
First Aztec Congress, 100
fishing, cultural roles for, 94, 145–146
FOMMA, 124, 180, 217n.126
food preparation
  in Andean culture, 43–44, 48
  by Central Americans, 159, 233n.95
  commercial
    during colonial era, 64–65, 199n.40
    conflicts involving, 65, 81–82, 203n.102
    modernization of, 94–95, 207n.15
  earliest women's role, 12
  by Nahuas, 92–95, 207n.15
  in prehispanic Mesoamerica, 22, 25, 35, 91
foreign interests
  activism against, 171–172
  activism by, 173

Formative period, 12–13, 187n.31
Fox, Vicente, 171
freedom of movement, for work. *See* outmigration
friars. *See* missionaries
frustration, domestic violence and, 134,
   220nn.15–16
Gálvez, Xóchitl, 174
GAM, 123, 180
gang rape, 150, 154, 162, 227n.60
Garifuna women
   domestic violence and, 160–161, 234n.97
   education of, 167, 236n.123
   ethnogenesis of, 8, 158, 186n.15, 232n.88
   family roles, 160, 162
   sexuality of, 161, 234n.99, 236n.120
Garinagu. *See* Garifuna women
gathering peoples, Paleoindians as, 11–12
gender asymmetry
   emergence of, 13–14
   in prehispanic Mesoamerica, 36, 190n.25,
      191n.36
   status shaped by, 6, 185n.5
gender clustering, emergence of, 12–13, 71,
   74, 202n.68
gender conflict. *See* conflict(s)
gender differentiation
   inequality disguise and, 6–7, 185n.5,
      186n.13
   through names, 35
gender hierarchy
   in Andean culture
      contemporary, 132, 134, 136, 140
      prehispanic, 50–51, 195n.98
   during colonial era, 75–76, 81, 87–88,
      205n.127
   during conquest era, 60–63, 197n.19
   earliest evidence of, 11–17, 187n.40
   influencing factors, 6–7, 185n.5
   in lowland cultures, 142–145, 149–150,
      155, 230n.80
   of Mayas, 118–119, 125, 214n.95, 217n.128
   of Nahuas, 29–30
   in prehispanic Mesoamerica, 22–23,
      27–29, 34, 36, 40, 190n.25
   in workplace, 9, 187n.31
   of Zapotecs, 111
gender identity
   activism impact on, 91, 175–176
   in Andean culture, 49–50, 138
   meaning of, 5–6, 185n.5
   Mesoamerica images of
      Andean vs., 11, 18, 41
      artistic, 35–37, 41–44
      early, 11, 18, 41–42, 44, 46, 48
      later prehispanic, 18–52, 91
      Maya, 35–41
      modern Nahuas, 91–92, 206n.4–5
      Northern and Central Classical,
         18–30

Ñudzahui Postclassical, 30–35
   prehispanic, 23–24, 26, 28–30, 33, 36
   of Nahuas, 97–98
gender relations
   complementary (*see* complementarity)
   earliest, 11–17
   formalized (*see* marriage and marital
      roles)
   sexual (*see* sexual relations)
gender roles
   activism emphasis of, 175, 177
   of Central Americans, 160–161, 234n.99
   during colonial era
      family-related, 71–81
      labor-related, 63–71
      politics-related, 71, 81–86
   conceptual views, 4–6, 11
   during conquest era, 55–64, 197n.19
   earliest, 11–17
   of Mayas, 112, 117–118, 120, 125,
      212n.72–73, 214nn.94–96
   in prehispanic Mesoamerica, 19–30,
      190n.25
      Mexica, 22–30, 191n.36
      Nahua, 26–27
      Teotihuacan, 19–22, 26
   Spanish beliefs about, 72
   supernatural, in Andean culture, 41–49
genealogies
   as dynamic force (*see* kin and kinship
      systems)
genocide, 176
geographical areas
   of Aztec empire, 22–23
   colonial era narrowing of, 87, 205n.125
gifting rituals, 98, 109
global markets, 107, 113, 120, 165
globalization
   activism based on, 170–171, 173, 177
   meaning of, 5, 8–9, 186nn.16–17
   scope of impact
      contemporary, 140, 155, 165,
         169–170
      modern, 92, 107, 113, 120, 126
glossary, of multilinguistic terms, 180
goddess/Goddess
   colonial transformations, 79
   earthly associations, 20, 38
   fertility connection, 21, 29, 38
   Inka Andean, 48–49
   in lowland cultures, 154, 230n.77
   in prehispanic Mesoamerica, 23, 25,
      28–29, 39
      bisexual nature of, 29, 191n.37
      powerful images, 20–22, 32, 38, 78
   pre-Inka Andean, 41–42
   of Teotihuacan, 20–21, 32, 188n.4
god/God
   Inka Andean, 48–49
   in prehispanic Mesoamerica, 20–23

godmothers, modern Zapotec as, 108–109
gold mining, in lowland cultures, 155–157
Good, Kenneth, 148
goods. *See* commodities
governing positions, held by women
   during colonial era, 81–86, 204n.112,
      204nn.116–117
   contemporary, 100, 173–175
   of Zapotecs, 108, 110, 210n.59
governmental organizations, political rela-
     tions with, 92, 100, 120, 157
grinding, of corn, 91–95, 102
grisi siknis, 162
Grupo de Mujeres (Women's Group), 123
Guaraní, relations with Spanish, 57–58, 63,
     197n.11
Guatemala
   activism in
      contemporary, 171, 173–174, 176–177
      modern, 121–122
   Black Caribs of (*see* Garifuna)
   civil war impact, 121–123, 215n.110
   education rates, 123–124, 217n.124
   indigenous identities, 8, 10
   Mayas of, 112–114, 116–117, 120–124,
      211n.71, 213nn.87–88
guerilla groups, of indigenous women,
     122–123, 216n.118
Guyana, 143

haciendas, 70
   labor wages for, 212n.74, 213n.87
healing and healers
   Andeans as, 135–136
   Central Americans as, 162, 234n.105
   in colonial era, 80
   earliest women's roles, 12, 35
   in lowland cultures, 152–153
   Mayas as, 112, 118–119, 212n.72
   modernization of, 88–89, 97, 108, 112
   Nahuas as, 97–98
   pulque role, 64–65
   regional cooperatives for, 170, 179,
     236n.3
   Zapotecs as, 108–109
health care, access to, 172–173, 177
   of Andeans, 135, 140, 223n.35
   discrimination through, 100, 173,
     210n.60
   gynecological (*see* contraception; mid-
     wifery)
   of lowland cultures, 152, 231n.85
   of Mayas, 119–120, 213n.78, 215n.104
   of Nahuas, 100, 103
health care cooperatives, 170, 179, 236n.3
health patterns. *See also* alcohol consump-
     tion
   of Central Americans, 161–162, 234n.103,
     236n.123
   during colonial era, 71–72

   in lowland cultures, 152, 156–157
   of Mayas, 119–120, 215n.104
   reproductive (*see* reproductive rights/
     responsibility)
hechicería, 80
"hegemonic leadership," 11
herbal cures. *See* healing and healers
highland cultures. *See* Andeans
history
   as research source, 6, 9–10, 91
   women's, 4–6, 11
homicide. *See* murder
homosexuality, 161, 191n.35
Honduras, ethnogenesis in, 8, 158,
     232n.88
honor, emphasis on
   colonial era, 71–72, 74, 76, 202n.68
   contemporary, 119, 220n.16
Horcasitas, Fernando, 90
horticulture
   gender hierarchy in, 12–14, 35, 40
   by lowland cultures, 145
   by Mayas, 113–115
house plots, of females, 70, 88, 96, 200n.49,
     205n.128
household units
   in Andean culture, 50
   contemporary, 129–131, 133–134,
     140
   of Central Americans, 160, 165
   during colonial era, 72, 200n.57,
     201n.58
     domestic violence related to, 76–77
   in lowland cultures, 146, 148–149, 153,
     156, 226n.54
   of Mayas, 117–118, 121–122
   of Nahuas, 91, 96
   nuclear family, 72, 91, 201n.58
   postmarital patterns (*see* residence pat-
     terns)
   in prehispanic Mesoamerica, 22, 25, 91
   as sanctuary, 169
   single-parent, 9, 72, 166–167, 200n.57
   of Zapotecs, 106–107
housework
   by Central Americans, 158–159
   craft production vs., 9, 112–113, 115–117,
     120, 212n.72, 213n.88
   by lowland cultures, 145
   by Nahuas, 91–94
   personal services for (*see* domestic ser-
     vice)
   in prehispanic Mesoamerica, 22, 25,
     39–40
   productive labor vs., 9, 12, 63, 91, 140
huasipunguerísmo, 70
Huasteca women, 96, 98. *See also* Nahuas
Huayna Capac, 50–51
Huitzilopochtli (Hummingbird on the
     Left), 23, 29

human resources. *See also* labor
 loss of men as (*see* outmigration)
 shortage of women, 147, 149, 156,
  225n.50
human rights violations, current activism,
  101, 137–138, 172
human sacrifices, in Moche culture, 42–43,
  46
humiliation. *See* subordination
hunting peoples
 in lowland cultures, 145, 152–153,
  225n.46
 Mexica as, 25
 Paleoindians as, 11–12
husband-wife relations. *See* marriage and
 marital roles
hybridity. *See* ethnic-racial identities

Iberian conquerors
 labor demands of, 66, 71
 religious beliefs of, 78–79
 sexual domination by, 54, 59–60, 63, 74
Icha, Juana, 84
identity
 gender (*see* gender identity)
 sexual, 5–6, 173, 185n.5
 symbolic history of, 169
idolatry, during colonial era, 80, 83–84
imprisonment
 protective custody vs., 69, 199n.45,
  200n.46
 for religious deviations, 83
 for tribute payment failure, 66, 199n.39
income. *See* wages
independence. *See* autonomy
Indians, indigenous peoples vs., 7–8, 127,
  129, 206n.5
indigenous women
 archaeology of, 11–17, 187n.31, 187n.40
 autobiographies of, 90, 173–174
 conceptual descriptions, 7–8, 91
 current agendas of, 157, 169–177
 introductory remarks, 4–5, 11
 as traitors, 56, 196n.5
 as transformative agents, 3–4
industrialization, Nahua roles with, 95, 102,
  207n.15
inequality, gender
 disguise of, 7, 186n.13
 questioning of, 170
infanticide, 72, 99
infidelity. *See* adultery
inheritance rights
 of Andeans, 133, 219n.12, 220n.16
 of Central Americans, 160, 233nn.95–96
 during colonial era, 70–71, 200n.51
  bilateral, 201n.57
 of lowland cultures, 147–148
 of Mayas, 117, 213n.91
 of Nahuas, 96

 in prehispanic Mesoamerica, 27, 34,
  200n.56
 of Zapotecs, 108
INI, 116, 180
injuries
 self-inflicted, 153, 229n.71
 workplace, 152
Inka Andeans
 kinship system, 49, 72
 labor patterns, 49–50, 65
 parallelism in, 7, 11, 49
 predecessors of (*see* pre-Inka Andes)
 privatization of land, 69–70
 resistance to Spanish, 60–61, 63, 195n.2
 spiritual cosmology, 48–49
 virginity emphasis, 50–51, 194n.96
in-laws
 authority over husbands, 75–76, 96, 117
 authority over wives, 97, 99
inna ritual, of Central Americans, 163,
  235n.107
Inquisition, 80
INRA, 180
Institutional Revolutionary Party, 125,
  210n.59
intentions, as agency, 6
intercourse. *See* sexual relations
interdependence. *See* complementarity
international level, of activism, 171–173,
  175
International Women's Conference (1995),
  172
Internet, as research source, 10
intimidation, 76, 150, 215n.110, 227n.60
involuntary servitude, during colonial era,
  65, 67, 69, 199n.41
Isthmus of Tehuantepec
 dress styles of, 103–104
 women of (*see* Zapotec)
Itzamná (Lizard House), 38
Ix Mol, 39
Ixchel (Lady Rainbow), 38

jealousy, sexual, 76, 99, 135, 152
Jesuit priests. *See* missionaries
Jiménez, Cándida, 171
Jiménez, Luz, 90, 92
joint titling, of land, 175–176
judicial courts. *See also* lawsuits
 during colonial era
  domestic violence actions, 77,
   203n.88
  female participation, 82–83, 204n.112
  marketplace representatives, 81–82,
   203n.102

Kakchiquel language, 117
Kalapalo women, 154
Karp, Eliane, 139–140
Keyukleayñ Pu Zomo, 172

kin and kinship systems
in Andean culture, 49, 133–134
of Central Americans, 160, 164
colonial era impact, 72, 200n.56
as domestic violence mediators, 76–77,
202n.82
in lowland cultures, 147–148
of Mayas, 117–118
of Nahuas, 98
in prehispanic Mesoamerica, 22, 25–26,
28–29, 34, 37, 40
as sanctuary, 169
Kuna women
education of, 165
ethnogenesis of, 158, 232n.88
family roles, 160, 162, 165, 233n.96
gathering houses of, 163–164
multi-island cooperatives of, 167,
236n.121
photographic images of, 127, 218n.2
sexuality of, 161–163
kupry, 152
kurakas, 49

labor, productive
in Andean culture, 49–50
contemporary, 129–132, 134–135, 137,
140, 220n.16
by Central Americans, 160–161, 164–165,
167, 233nn.95–96, 236n.121
during colonial era, 63–71, 198nn.35–36
family life impact, 69–73
craft production as, 9, 112–113, 115–117,
120, 212n.72
early women's, 12–13, 187n.27, 187n.31
exploitation of, 67, 69, 169, 199n.45,
200n.46
in contemporary Andeans, 134–135,
137, 220n.16
indigenous transformations, 87–88,
205n.127
forced institutions of, 65, 69–70, 199n.45,
200n.46
family conflicts related to, 75–77
foreign control of, 171
gender complementarity for, 7, 12, 64,
107
globalization impact on, 171–173, 177
housework vs., 9, 12, 63, 91, 169
by lowland cultures, 143–145, 224nn.45–
46
by Mayas, 39–40, 112–113, 115–117, 120,
212nn.72–74, 213n.88
by Nahuas, 91–96, 207n.9
in prehispanic Mesoamerica, 22, 24–26,
28, 34–35
seasonal, 94
by Zapotecs, 106–107, 210nn.52–53
labor drafts, rotational, 65
labor unions, 110, 137–138, 236

land ownership
in Andean culture, 50–51
contemporary, 133, 137, 219n.12,
220n.16
by Central Americans, 160, 233nn.95–96
during colonial era, 66, 69–71, 81,
200n.49, 200n.51
increase of collective, 87–88, 205n.128
current activism, 170, 172, 175–176
in lowland cultures, 156
by Mayas, 115, 117, 213n.91
by Nahuas, 96, 100
in prehispanic Mesoamerica, 26–27,
34–35
by Zapotecs, 108
languages. See linguistic groups/patterns
Latin America
conferences held in, 172–173
gender patterns across, 92, 206n.4
indigenous identities, 8, 186n.14
land rights activism, 175–176
leadership positions held in, 174
lowland cultures of (see lowland cultures)
media influence, 10, 127, 218n.2
law enforcement, during colonial era, 71
laws. See legislation
lawsuits, during colonial era
female defense examples, 82–83, 204n.112
marketplace, 65, 81–82, 203n.102
over labor compensation, 67
over landholdings, 70
leadership, parallel lines of, 7
activism for, 173–174
in Andean culture, 48–50
contemporary, 133–134, 136, 138
in Central America, 163–165, 167
during colonial era, 70–71, 81–86,
204n.112, 204nn.116–117
among Mayas, 112, 118–119, 125, 212n.72,
217n.128
among Nahuas, 97–98
in prehispanic Mesoamerica, 20, 24, 26,
28–34, 190n.25
among Zapotecs, 106–107
legal cases. See judicial courts; lawsuits
legal rights
during colonial era, 82
constitutional proposals for, 171, 175–176
legislation, active roles in, 174, 176
lesbians, Zapotec portrayed as, 103, 111,
209n.43
life-cycle transitions
Andean rituals for, 133
of Central Americans, 158, 160, 162–165,
232n.90
earliest images, 13–14, 187n.31
in lowland cultures, 151, 153
Nahua work related to, 94
in prehispanic Mesoamerica, 32
Zapotec rituals for, 108–109

linguistic groups/patterns
  of Andeans, 129, 138, 140
  Aymara, 129, 138
  bilingual, 53–56, 124, 138, 143, 165,
    195n.2, 224n.43
  of Central Americans, 158, 165
  Kakchiquel, 117
  of lowland cultures, 142, 148, 156–157,
    231n.84
  members of, 20, 188n.2
  mestizo, 197n.11
  multilingual glossary, 180
  Nahuatl, 53–56, 92–93, 102, 195n.2,
    207n.8
  Pueblo, 195n.2
  Spanish, 103, 124, 231n.84
  term relevancy, 18, 188n.1
  translators for conquerors, 53–56, 195n.2
literacy movements. See education
literature review, 4–5, 135, 218n.2
loans, small business, 101
local level, of activism, 170–171, 176, 236n.3
López, María, 84–85
love magic, practitioners of, 80–81,
  203n.100
lowland cultures, 142–157
  authority roles, 147, 149, 151–153
    patterns of, 153–155, 229n.74, 229n.76,
      230n.77, 230n.80
  complementarity in, 147, 155
  current activism by, 172
  diversity of, 142–145, 148, 157
  education in, 155–157, 231n.84
  gender hierarchy of, 142–145, 149–150,
    155, 230n.80
  gender images of
    contemporary, 127–128, 143–144,
      218n.2
    prehispanic, 19–20, 188n.2
  kinship patterns, 147–148
  labor divisions, 143–145, 224nn.45–46,
    225n.48
  languages of, 142, 148, 156–157, 231n.84
  marital relations in, 148–150, 226n.56,
    227n.63
    power struggles, 153, 229n.71
    as violent, 151, 227n.63, 228n.64
  misogyny in, 142, 147, 150
  residence patterns, 148–149, 226n.54,
    227n.57
  ritual roles, 151, 153, 229nn.72–73
  spiritual power in, 153–155, 229n.27,
    230n.77
  violence in
    domestic, 150–151, 154, 227n.60,
      227n.63, 228n.64
    political, 150, 156, 173, 231n.84
Loza, Remedios, 174
lunar deities
  of Inka Andeans, 48

of prehispanic Mesoamerica, 38–39,
  191n.37

macharetkit, 161
magic, indigenous practitioners of, 80–81,
  203n.100
Mai Huna women, 153
maize
  grinding of, 91–95
  as modern cash crop, 94, 113
maize beer, 50, 63
maize deity, 29, 48, 118
malaria, 156
Maldonado, Arías, 57
male deities. See god/God
Malinalli (Malintzin), 55–56, 195n.3
Malintzin
  as Cortés' translator, 53–56, 69, 86,
    195n.2
  loyalty to Spanish, 56, 63, 196n.5
  name debate about, 55–56, 195n.3
malnutrition
  among Central Americans, 161–162
  in lowland cultures, 157
  among Mayas, 119–120, 215n.104
Mama Huaco deity, 48–49
Mamaquilla deity, 48
mamaqunas, 50
manioc, 145–147
Mapuche
  current activism, 172, 176–177, 238n.19
  female authority modernization,
    88–89
maquiladoras, 116
Marian devotion, in colonial Catholicism,
  78–79
Marina (Malintzin), 55–56, 195n.3
market economies, 170
  of Andeans
    contemporary, 129–132, 140
    prehispanic, 41–43, 48
  of Central Americans, 160–161, 164–167,
    233nn.95–96, 236n.121
  during colonial era, 64–66, 198n.36
    as exploitative, 67, 69, 71, 88, 199n.45,
      205n.128
  conflicts involving, 65, 81–82, 119,
    203n.102
  of lowland cultures, 145–147, 155–157,
    230n.83
  of Mayas, 112–117, 212n.74, 213nn.
    87–88
  of Nahuas, 100–103
  in prehispanic Mesoamerica, 20, 26–27,
    39–40
  taxation on, 65, 86
  of Zapotecs, 105–107, 210n.50,
    210nn.52–53
marketing cooperatives, 101–102, 116–117,
  157, 213n.88

marriage and marital roles
  activism emphasis of, 175, 177
  in Andean culture, 50–51
    contemporary, 133–135, 140, 220n.16
  during colonial era, 72–73, 201n.58,
    201n.61, 201n.64
  during conquest era, 57–59, 196n.7,
    196n.11, 197n.12
  domestic service exploitation vs., 65–67,
    71–72, 199nn.38–41
  in lowland cultures, 148–150, 226n.56
    power struggles, 153, 229n.71
    as violent, 151, 154, 227n.63, 228n.64
  of Mayas, 117–118, 120, 161, 214nn.94–
    96, 234n.99
  of Nahuas, 96–99, 208n.22, 208n.24
  in prehispanic Mesoamerica, 27, 32–34,
    190n.35
  of Zapotecs, 111
martial society. See militarism
Mary (mother of Jesus), colonial references
    to, 78–79, 88
masculinity. See also men/man
  assertions of, 134, 153, 220n.16, 229n.71
  conquest associations, 54, 60–63, 197n.19
  in prehispanic Mesoamerica, 28, 190n.35
Maseualsiuamej Mosenyolchikahuanij, 101
matchmakers, during colonial era, 73, 80,
    201n.64
matriarchy, 21, 38
  exotic, of Zapotecs, 103, 108–111
matricide, 29
matrifocal cultures, 110–111, 211n.65
matrilineal transmission, of Zapotec craft
    production, 107, 210n.52
matrilocal residence, 75–76, 96, 117
  in lowland cultures, 149, 226n.54
Mayans, 35–41
  activism by
    contemporary, 170, 174–175, 236n.2
    modern, 100, 116, 120–123, 125,
      215n.110, 216n.114, 216n.116,
      216n.118
    religious, 124–125, 217n.128
    social, 102–121, 123–124, 217n.124
  artistic gender images, 35–37
  complementarity of
    elite historical, 36, 40, 192n.59,
      193n.75
    modern, 118–120, 214nn.95–96
  craft production by, 112–113, 115–117,
    120, 212n.72, 213n.88
  cultural diversity of modern, 112–113,
    211n.71
  female deities, 38–39
  female rulers, 37, 193n.61
  kinship systems, 37, 40, 200nn.56–57
    modern, 117–118, 214n.94
  labor divisions, 39–40, 112, 118,
    212nn.72–74

language translators of, 53–56, 195n.2
male dominance, 40–41
market economies of, 112–117, 212n.74,
    213nn.87–88
marriage patterns, 117–118, 120, 161,
    214nn.94–96, 234n.99
noblewomen of, 36–37, 40, 192n.58,
    193n.75
resistance to Spanish, 59–60, 63,
    195n.2
sense of agency, 170
sexuality symbols, 36, 161, 192n.60
women warriors, 37–38, 193n.64
mayordomas, modern Zapotec as, 108
media
  activism through, 170, 236n.2
  as research source, 10, 127, 218n.2
  undermining diversity, 132, 143, 155,
    157, 172
mediators, 154
  of domestic violence, 76–77, 202n.82
medical care. See health care
medical practices. See healing and healers
Mehinaku women, 150, 229n.76
Mekranoti women, 152–153
Menchú, Rigoberta, 90, 122, 126, 173–174,
    212n.74
men/man
  dominant power of (see patriarchy)
  erotic emphasis, 43, 46
  gender identity impact, 5–6, 185n.5
  honor emphasis, 71–72, 74, 76, 119,
    202n.68, 220n.16
  victory associations, 24, 40, 189n.16
menstruation, beliefs about, 119, 151–152,
    162–163
merchants
  distributive (see selling/reselling)
  shipping, Zapotec as, 105–106
Mesoamerica, 11
  burial rituals of, 14–15, 22–23
  gender images
    Andean vs., 18, 41
    later prehispanic, 18–52, 91
    Maya, 35–41
    modern Mayas, 112, 211nn.70–71
    modern Nahuas, 91–92, 206nn.4–5
    Northern and Central Classical,
      18–30
    Ñudzahui Postclassical, 30–35
    prehispanic, 23–24, 26, 28–30, 33, 36
  marketing activities in, 64–65
  psychological patterns, 206n.4
mestizo
  origin of, 53–54, 56–57, 196n.5,
    196nn.7–8, 197n.12
  racial hierarchy of, 8, 141
Mexica
  behavioral norms of, 27–28, 190n.35
  early migration of, 23

Mexica (*continued*)
    female deities of, 28–29, 191n.37
    gender parallelisms, 23–24, 28, 30 26
    government politics of, 26, 28, 190n.25
    household units of, 25
    kinship system of, 25–26
    Malintzin as traitor to, 56, 196n.5
    military values of, 22–24, 189n.14
    productive work of, 24–26
    religious beliefs of, 23, 26, 28, 189n.24
    resistance to Spanish, 59–60, 63
    schooling by, 23–24, 26
Mexican Revolution, 110, 125, 211n.63
Mexico
    burial rituals of, 14–15
    constitutional activism, 171
    early female figurines, 13–14, 19
    indigenous identities, 8, 186n.14
    marketing activities in, 64–65
    media influence, 10
    modern Mayas of, 112, 211n.71
    prehispanic gender images (*see* Meso-
      america)
Mexico City. *See* Tenochtitlan
Micaela Bastidas Community, 137
microbanks, 101
middlewomen, Zapotec as, 105, 210n.50
midwifery, 80
    by Andeans, 135
    in Central America, 162, 234n.105
    cooperatives of, 170
    in lowland cultures, 152–153, 228n.70
    by Mayas, 112, 118
    by Nahuas, 94, 97
    by Zapotecs, 108–109, 210n.60
migration, modern
    of Andeans, 132, 140–141, 223nn.35–36
    in Central America, 159–160, 233n.96
    as labor loss (*see* outmigration)
    of Nahuas, 94, 100, 102
militarism
    of Andeans, 134
    of Aztec empire, 22
    emergence of, 17, 21–22
    environmental impact of, 173
    female participation, 24, 27, 189n.14
      during Spanish conquest, 60, 63
    Great Goddess association, 188n.4
    of Mayas, 40–41
    of Mexica, 22–24, 29, 189n.14
    as power expression, 21, 35
Milpa Alta, 90, 92, 100
milpa community, of Mayas, 112–113, 115,
    213n.78
mines, 50, 137
    gold, in lowland cultures, 155–157
    labor roles in, 65–66, 69, 198n.36
Miskito women
    ethnogenesis of, 8, 158, 232n.88
    family roles, 160, 162, 165, 167

    sexuality of, 161–162
misogyny, in lowland cultures, 142, 147, 150
missionaries. *See also* priests
    in Central America, 161, 235n.107
    as domestic violence mediators, 76,
      202n.82
    household restructuring by, 72, 161,
      200n.57, 201n.58
    labor role of, 66–67, 199n.36
    in lowland cultures, 155–157
    protests against, 83, 124–125
Mixtecs
    rebellion by, 211n.63, 216n.118
    as research focus, 34, 103–104
    term relevancy, 18, 188n.1
mobility, for work. *See* outmigration
Moche culture, of Peru, 41–43
modern era, 90–126
    Andean revolution and, 129–141
    Central American empowerment,
      92–103
    Maya images, 112–125
    Nahua complementarity, 92–103
    Oaxaca matriarchy, 103–111
    overview of, 90–92, 125–126,
      206nn.4–5
    tropical lowland struggles, 142–157
modernization
    of commercial food preparation, 94–95,
      207n.15
    of healing practices, 88–89, 97, 108, 112
    of Mapuche female authority, 88–89
    resistance to, 131
mola production, by Central Americans,
    160–161, 166, 233nn.95–96
    cooperatives for, 164–165, 167, 236n.121,
      236n.123
monogamy, as missionary focus, 72, 161,
    200n.57, 201n.58
montequitl, 73
Moon Goddess. *See* lunar deities
moral authority, 85, 164, 175
moral code, of Garifuna women, 161,
    234n.99
Moravians, in Central America, 161,
    235n.107
mortality rates, of Central Americans, 162
    infant, 162, 234n.105
mortuary goods. *See* burial rituals
Moteuczoma, 57, 195n.7
motherhood. *See* childcare; reproductive
    rights/responsibility
mother's clubs, 157, 167
Mundurucú peoples, 146, 149–150, 153,
    155–156
murder
    domestic-related, 74–78, 202n.74,
      202n.82, 202n.84, 203n.88
    of women, for sexual resistance, 59–60,
      63

Nahuas
   bilingualism of, 53–56, 195n.2
   community variations, 92–93, 102,
      207n.8
   complementarity of
      modern, 92–103, 207n.9
      prehispanic era, 26–27, 30, 33, 190n.25
   family life of, 25
   female deities of, 25, 29, 78
   judicial leaders of, 81, 203n.102
   market economies of, 100–103
   military values of, 24, 28, 30, 189n.14
   religious beliefs of, 26
   submissive images of, 29–31
      modern, 92–100, 208n.24
   term relevancy, 18, 188n.1
Nahuatl
   descendant statistics, 92–93, 102, 207n.8
   translators of, 53–56, 195n.2
naming ceremonies, in lowland cultures,
      153, 229n.73
National Council of Indigenous Women,
      171
National Indigenous Congress(es), 171–172
national level, of activism, 171–173, 176
national markets, 107, 167
nationalization. *See* nation-states
nation-states
   formation of, 11, 91, 157
   indigenous meanings, 8, 142, 157,
      186nn.14–15
   media influence on policies, 10, 132
   political relations and, 92, 150
   resistance to contemporary, 131–132,
      232n.87
Native Americans, contemporary Border-
      lands, 20
nature deities
   in Andean culture, 48–49
   in prehispanic Mesoamerica, 20, 23, 38
neolocal residence pattern, postmarital, 97,
      117, 227n.57
New Laws (1542), 200n.46
New Spain. *See* colonial era
New World, as Spanish sexual paradise,
      58–59, 195n.2
newspapers, as research source, 10, 218n.2
Nicaragua, ethnogenesis in, 158, 232n.88
nobility
   labor exemption for, 65–66
   in prehispanic Mesoamerica, 22, 25, 27,
      32–35
   Maya, 36, 40, 192n.58, 193n.75
   relations with Spanish, 57–58, 60, 66, 69,
      196nn.7–8
   Zapotecs as, 103–111
non-governmental organizations (NGOs)
   activism role, 174, 176
   political relations with, 92, 120, 157,
      231n.85

Northern Mexico, Classical gender images,
      19–30
Novelo Canche, Rosario, 175
nuclear family households, 72, 91, 201n.58
Ñudzahuis
   gender complementarity, 30, 32–35
   kinship systems of, 72
   labor divisions, 34–35
   religious beliefs of, 79
   term relevancy, 18, 188n.1

Oaxaca. *See also* Mixtec
   matriarchy in, 103, 108–111 (*see also*
      Zapotec)
   as research focus, 103–105
Oaxaca summit, 173
occupations, contemporary
   of Andeans, 140, 223n.35
   of Nahuas, 93–96
oil economies, 95
omekit, 161
organizations. *See also* specific acronym
   of activism, 179–180, 216n.116
   of solidarity, 122–124, 216n.114, 216n.118
   unionized, 110, 137–138, 236
Ortega, Isabel, 174
Otavalo, labor divisions, 129–131
outmigration
   in Central America, 159–160, 164,
      233n.95
   family disruption from, 72, 78, 138, 140,
      201n.58
   labor patterns related to
      during colonial era, 64, 198n.26
      contemporary, 138, 140–141,
         232n.87
      modern, 94–95, 102, 107, 122
ownership rights. *See* land ownership
Oxhutzcab, 113

Pacal, 37
Pacari, Nina, 136, 174
Pachamama deity, 48
Paleoindians, 11–12
Palikur women, 144
palm plaiting, 210n.52
Paloma burial sites, 16–17
Panama. *See also* Kuna women
   gender roles in, 160, 171
parallelism, 7
   in Andean culture, 49–50, 138
   of authority, 20, 26, 49, 81
   colonial era, 79–86, 204n.112,
      204nn.116–117
   modern Nahua, 26–27, 30, 33, 97–98
   in prehispanic Mesoamerica, 23–24, 26,
      28, 30, 33, 36
paramilitary groups
   modern Maya, 121–122, 215n.110
   violence by, 121, 173, 176

patriarchy
    in colonial era, 75–76, 81, 87–88,
        205n.127
    of lowland cultures, 142–145, 149–150,
        155, 230n.80
    of Mayas, 118–119, 125, 214n.95,
        217n.128
    of Nahuas, 91–92, 97, 208n.24
patriliny
    in lowland cultures, 147–148
    of Mayas, 37, 40, 200n.56
    of Nahuas, 96
patrilocal residence, postmarital
    of Andeans, 133
    of Nahuas, 96–97, 99
    of Zapotecs, 107
peasant activism, 95, 97, 137–139, 142
Pentecostalism, 141
personal power, as agency, 6
personal service, during colonial era
    as abusive, 66–67, 69, 199n.41
    domestic, 60, 65–66, 198n.35, 199n.40
    resistance to, 71–72
Peru
    burial rituals of, 16–17
    current activism, 172, 174
    highland cultures of (see Andeans)
    Moche culture of, 41–43
    peasant activism in, 138–139
    tropical cultures of (see lowland cultures)
photography
    of contemporary women, 127–128,
        218n.2
    by Mayas, 124
physical abuse/agression
    as punishment, 134, 150–151
    violent (see domestic violence)
piety, during colonial era, 79
Pizarro, Gonzalo, 51, 57, 60, 63, 196nn.7–8
Plan Puebla Panama, 171
plantains, 145–146
plantation labor, wages for, 212n.74, 213n.87
poetry, modern Maya, 124
political activism, 4–5, 11
    by Andeans, 136–140, 221n.24
    defensive nature of, 169–170, 173
        colonial era, 82–86, 204n.112,
            204nn.116–117
        modern era, 121–122, 215n.110
    history of, 7, 13, 169
    international level, 171–173, 175
    local level, 170–171, 176, 236n.3
    by Mayas
        contemporary, 170, 174–175, 236n.2
        modern, 100, 116, 120–123, 125,
            215n.110, 216n.114, 216n.116,
            216n.118
    media role, 170, 236n.2
    of Nahuas, 100–101
    national level, 171–172, 174, 176

regional level, 170–173
    of Zapotecs, 109–110, 211n.63, 211n.65,
        216n.118
political systems/status
    in Andean culture, 49–50
        contemporary, 132, 134, 136, 139–140
    of Central Americans, 163–165, 167
    during colonial era, 70–71, 81–86,
        204n.112, 204nn.116–117
    in lowland cultures, 153–154, 229n.76
    of Mayas, 115
    moral clean up, 175
    of Nahuas, 91–92, 96, 99–100
    in prehispanic Mesoamerica, 22–23,
        26–28, 32–34, 37, 190n.25
    "sacralized vs. martialized," 7, 22
    of Zapotecs, 108, 210n.59
political violence, 150, 156, 173, 231n.84. See
        also rebellions
polygyny
    during colonial era, 72–73, 201n.61
    modern, 94, 118
population trends. See also migration
    during colonial era, 64, 198n.26
        census categories, 88, 205n.127
        family disruption from, 72, 78,
            201n.58
    of contemporary women, 129, 218n.4
    labor patterns related to
        colonial era, 64, 198n.26
        modern Nahuas, 94–95, 100, 102
    of modern Mayas, 112, 211n.71
Postclassic Mesoamerica period, 18–19,
        23–24, 30, 32, 35, 38
post-Nahua communities, 95, 158, 186n.14
pottery
    iconography of, in Moche culture,
        41–44, 47–48
    production of
        during colonial era, 66
        by lowland cultures, 145, 147, 156–157
        by Mayas, 112, 115
poverty
    in Central America, 161–162
    domestic violence related to, 134,
        220nn.15–16
    feminization of, 102–103, 126
    of Nahuas, 102–103
    in prehispanic Mesoamerica, 27
    protests against, 125, 129, 137
power
    in Andean culture, 43–44, 47–49
    authenticated (see authority; rulers)
    during colonial era, 79–86, 204n.112,
        204nn.116–117
    conquest era assertions of, 60–63,
        197n.19
    conquest impact on, 70–71, 75
    earliest women's, 12–14, 17, 187n.31,
        187n.40

modern Nahuas, 97–98
personal perspectives, 6–7, 13
in prehispanic Mesoamerica, 20–22,
24–26, 28–30, 189n.17, 190n.25
Preclassic Mesoamerica period, 13, 20
pregnancy. See reproductive rights/respon-
sibility
prehispanic era, of Mesoamerica, 18–52, 91
Andean power, 41–51
Maya patriarchies, 35–41
Northern and Central peoples, 19–30
overview of, 18–19, 51–52, 91, 188n.1
postclassic Ñudzahui elite, 30–35
pre-Inka Andes
early gender images, 11, 18, 41
female authority images, 43–44, 47–48
human sacrifices of, 42–43, 46
sexuality expressions, 43, 46
supernatural images, 41–44, 48
premarital sexual relations, 134–135, 151–152
PRI, 180
priestesses
in Andean culture, 42, 50, 194n.96
in prehispanic Mesoamerica, 22–23, 26,
39, 189n.17, 189n.24
priests
as domestic violence mediators, 76,
202n.82
household restructuring by, 72–74,
200n.57, 201n.58
labor exploitation by, 67, 69
midwives concern, 80
in prehispanic Mesoamerica, 22–24
transformation of female deities, 78–79
procreation. See reproductive rights/
responsibility
prodemocracy movements. See democratization
profits, occupational. See capital; wages
"Prominent Woman," 43, 47
property rights. See land ownership
prostitution, 176. See also personal service
protective custody, for labor, 69, 199n.45,
200n.46
Protestantism
of Andeans, 141
in lowland cultures, 141, 156
of Mayas, 120, 124–125, 217n.128
protests
community defense-related
during colonial era, 82–85, 204n.112,
204n.117
contemporary, 153, 169–170
of Mayas, 121–122, 215n.110
political (see political activism;
rebellions)
puberty ceremonies
by Central Americans, 158, 162–163,
232n.90
of lowland cultures, 151–152

public roles
of Andeans, 129, 131, 136
of Central Americans, 163–165, 167
in lowland cultures, 154, 229n.76
of Mayas, 112, 118–119, 214n.100
public works projects
contemporary agenda for, 102, 140, 157,
171, 223n.35, 231n.85
in prehispanic Mesoamerica, 23
Puebla women, 98, 101. See also Nahuas
Pueblo language, 195n.2
Pueblo women, 20, 188n.3
pulque trade, 64–65
punishment
for domestic violence, 77–78, 203n.88
physical abuse as, 134, 150–151
for protesting, 83
social, in prehispanic Mesoamerica, 27

Q'eqchi women, 170
Quechua language, 129
Quichua women
activism by, 175
labor divisions, 146–147, 224n.46
visionary power of, 153, 229n.73
Quimseña women, 131, 135
Quito's Hotel Rey, 130, 135
quya, in Andean culture, 49

racial identities
indigenous, 7–8, 186nn.14–15
mixed (see ethnic-racial identities)
racism
activism against, 174
origins of, 8, 66, 186nn.14–15
source of, 87, 205n.125
rainforest groups. See lowland cultures
Rama women, 161
Ramona, Comandante, 122, 216n.114
rape
during conquest era, 59–61, 197n.19
female definition of, 197n.15
gang, 150, 154, 162, 227n.60
modern trends, 119, 134, 176
rapto, as bride abduction, 96–97, 208n.22
rebellions, collective female participation in
colonial era, 83–85, 109, 204n.117
modern, 109–110, 121, 136, 211n.63
reciprocal exchanges, of labor for goods,
108, 132, 154, 163
reciprocity, gender-based, 35, 148
modern undermining of, 95–96, 157,
232n.87
reducción policy, 72
refugee camps, modern Mayan, 121–123,
215n.110, 217n.126
regional level, of activism, 170–171
relationships. See gender relations
religion
in Andean culture, 49, 141

religion (*continued*)
    colonial era practices, 71–73, 78–81,
        200n.57, 201n.58, 203n.100
        resistance demonstrations, 82–85,
            204n.116
    earliest women's role, 13, 17
    of lowland cultures, 229n.73
    of Mayas, 118, 120, 123–124, 217n.126,
        217n.128
    Nahua practices, 92, 98–99
    in prehispanic Mesoamerica, 22–23, 26,
        34, 38–39, 189n.24
    reproductive rights positions, 74, 173
    as undermining diversity, 88, 172
    Zapotec practices, 108–109
religious activism
    during colonial era, 82–85, 204n.116
    by modern Mayas, 120, 124–125,
        217n.128
rental payments, for young women, 67
repartimiento
    family power conflicts related to, 75–76
    as forced labor, 65, 67, 69
reproductive rights/responsibility. *See also*
        contraception
    of Andeans, 135
    Catholic beliefs about, 74
    of Central Americans, 161–163, 234n.103,
        234n.105
    current activism, 173, 176
    earliest women images, 13–14, 39,
        187n.31
    in lowland cultures, 151–152
    of Mayas, 119–120, 215n.104
    of Nahuas, 91–92, 99
resettlement, forced community, 72
    uprisings with, 82–85, 204n.112,
        204nn.116–117
residence patterns, postmarital
    of lowland cultures, 148–149, 226n.54,
        227n.57
    matrilocal, 75–76, 96, 117, 149, 226n.54
    of Mayas, 117–118
    neolocal, 97, 117
    patrilocal, 96–97, 99, 107
resistance, during colonial era
    to domestic violence, 59–60, 63, 101
    to personal service labor, 71–72
    political, 82–86, 204n.112, 204nn.
        116–117
    to sexual relations, 59–60, 63
    to Spanish, 59–61, 63, 195n.2
revolt. *See* rebellions
rituals
    in Andean culture, 42–44, 46, 49–50
    contemporary, 134–136
    by Central Americans, 158, 162–163, 165,
        232n.90, 235n.107
    during colonial era, 80, 83
    earliest women's role, 12–14

    in lowland cultures, 151, 153, 229nn.72–
        73
    of Mayas, 118–119
    of Nahuas, 97–98
    in prehispanic Mesoamerica, 22–23, 26,
        29, 35, 39, 189n.24
    spending authority for, 108–109, 115, 132,
        154, 163
    of Zapotecs, 108–109, 111
robo de la novia, as Nahua marital practice,
        97, 208n.22
rubber production, by lowland cultures, 155
rulers. *See also* nobility
    in Andean culture, 49
    complementary images of, 33–36, 40,
        192n.59, 193n.75
    in Mesoamerica, 22, 37, 193n.61
    religious (*see* priestesses; priests)
rural development
    in Andean cultures, 140, 223n.35
    in lowland cultures, 157, 231n.85

sacred images. *See also* deities
    as power expression, 21–22, 43, 108
sales tax, 65
San Blas region, 158, 232n.88. *See also* Kuna
    women
sanctions. *See* punishment
sanitary facilities, in Central America, 161
Sanumá women, 146–147
schools and schooling. *See* education
science, women patrons of, 38
seasonal laborers, 94
secretarial work, 96
self-defense, community-based
    during colonial era, 82–85, 204n.112,
        204n.117
    contemporary modes of, 153, 169–170
    by Mayas, 121–122, 215n.110
self-esteem, of Mayas, 115, 124
self-help groups, 124, 137, 147, 157, 231n.85
self-sacrifice rituals, 39
selling/reselling. *See also* market economies
    by Andeans, 132
    by Central Americans, 165
    by Mayas, 115, 121
    by Nahuas, 94, 101–102
    by prehispanic Mesoamericans, 27
    by Zapotecs, 105, 210n.50
Sendero Luminoso (Shining Path), 137–138
señoríos (seignorial domains), 49
serfdom, 70
SERNAM, 177, 180
servinacuy, 140
sex objects, exotic
    Andeans women as, 127, 129
    lowland women as, 152
    Quimseña women as, 131, 135
    Zapotec women as, 103–105, 209n.43
sexual harassment, 135

sexual identity, meaning of, 5–6, 173, 185n.5
sexual jealousy, 76, 99, 135, 152
sexual relations
    activism for rights, 173
    during colonial era
        cruel marital, 74–78, 202n.74, 202n.82
        idolatrous, 84
        parental concerns about, 74–75,
            202n.68
    during conquest era
        coercive, 57–61, 197n.15, 197n.19
        consensual, 57–58, 196n.11, 197n.7,
            197n.12
        resistance to, 59–60, 63
        violent, 57, 59–61, 197n.15, 197n.19
    extramarital, 76, 99, 135, 152
    premarital, 134–135, 151–152
    for procreation vs. pleasure, 74, 119
sexual violence. See also rape
    during conquest era, 57, 59–61, 197n.15,
        197n.19
    current activism, 119, 176
    in lowland cultures, 151, 227n.63,
        228n.64
sexuality
    in Andean culture, 43, 46, 48, 50, 195n.98
        contemporary, 129, 135
    of Central Americans, 161, 234n.99
    conquerors, impact on, 53–54
    female (see female images)
    of lowland cultures, 151–152
    male (see masculinity)
    of Mayas, 112, 119, 211n.70, 214n.95,
        215n.104
    of Nahuas, 97, 208n.24
shamans
    in Central America, 162, 165
    in lowland cultures, 153, 229n.27,
        230n.77
    Mapuche, modernization of, 88–89
    Mayas as, 112, 212n.72
    Nahuas as, 97–98
Shipibo women, 157
shipping merchants, Zapotecs as, 105–106
single-parent households, 9, 72, 166–167,
    200n.57
Sinú peoples, 13
Siriono women, 152
sirvanacuy, 73
Sisa, Bartola, 85
Sisa, María, 67
Sisa, Quispe, 51, 57, 63, 195n.8
Sisa, Teresa, 77–78
sky deities
    of Inka Andeans, 48
    of prehispanic Mesoamerica, 23, 38–39,
        191n.37
slash-and-burn agriculture, 146, 213n.78
slavery
    of Central Americans, 158–159

during colonial era, 60, 65, 67–69,
    199n.41
in lowland cultures, 144
protective custody vs., 69, 199n.45,
    200n.46
small business loans, 101
Sna Jolobil (House of the Weaver), 116
social activism, 4–5, 11
    by Andeans, 137–138, 141–142, 223n.35
    earliest women's, 12–13, 129, 187n.31
    by Mayas, 102–121, 123–124, 217n.124
    national movements, 171–172, 175–176
social programs, for Nahuas, 102–103
social sanctions, in prehispanic Mesoamer-
    ica, 27
social status
    as activism focus, 176–177, 238n.19
    Andean, 42, 50–51, 195n.98
        contemporary, 137–138
    domestic violence related to, 76–77
    earliest women's, 12–14, 17, 187n.40
    ethno-racial mixing and, 8, 57, 87, 156,
        186nn.14–15, 205n.125
    gender-related, 5–6, 185n.5
    in lowland cultures, 146, 148, 155,
        232n.87
    of Mayas, 115, 117, 119–121
    multiple defining factors, 6–7
    of Nahuas, 101–103, 107
    in prehispanic Mesoamerica, 22, 25,
        27–28, 33–34, 190n.35
    in Spanish relations, 57–58, 66, 196nn.7–
        8, 197n.11
    of Zapotecs, 105, 108–109
solar deities
    of Andeans, 48
    of prehispanic Mesoamerica, 23, 38
soldiers/warriors, women as
    in Andean culture, 48–49
    in lowland cultures, 153–154
    in Maya culture
        historical, 37–38, 193n.64
        modern, 122–124, 216n.114, 216n.116,
            216n.118
    in prehispanic Mesoamerica, 24, 29, 32,
        38, 189n.14, 191n.37, 193n.64
solidarity
    in lowland cultures, 148–149, 226n.56
    organizations of, 122–124, 179–180,
        216n.114, 216n.118
sorcery, 80, 83–84, 203n.100
South America
    burial rituals of, 14
    cultural periods of, 11, 18, 41
    highland cultures of (see Andeans)
    indigenous identities, 8, 127–128
    leadership positions held in, 174
    marketing activities in, 65
    media influence, 10, 127, 218n.2
    tropical cultures of (see lowland cultures)

Spanish conquerors. *See also* conquest era
  loyalty to, 56, 63, 196n.5
  masculinity associations, 54, 60–63,
    197n.19
  religious beliefs of, 78–79
  translators for, 53–56, 195n.2
Spanish language, 103, 124, 231n.84
spinning. *See* weaving
spirit possession, as stress response, 162,
    234n.104
spiritual beliefs. *See* deities; religion; rituals
sponsorships, of Zapotec women, 108–109
spousal abuse. *See* domestic violence
Staff Goddess, 41–42
state-level societies, rise of, 11
state-sponsored labor, during colonial era,
    60, 65, 198n.35
sterilization, 135
  forced, 100, 120, 156, 173, 210n.60
storekeeping
  conflicts involving, 65, 81–82, 119,
    203n.102
  as Nahua occupation, 94
Storm God, 20–21
strikes, labor, 137
subjugation. *See* subordination
submissiveness
  of Nahua women
    modern, 96–100, 208n.24
    prehispanic, 29–31
  of Zapotec women, 111, 211n.68
subordination, of women
  activism against, 175
  in Andean culture, 50–51, 195n.98
    contemporary, 138–140
  during conquest, resistance to, 59–60,
    63, 66
  denial of, 4, 6–7
  emergence of, 13–14
  gender conflict and, 6–7, 185n.5, 186n.13
    among Mayas, 115
  in prehispanic Mesoamerica, 22, 24,
    29–32, 37, 189n.16
  in workplace, 9, 66–69, 187n.31,
    199nn.39–41
subsistence economy, 116, 159, 165, 212n.74
succession rights, in prehispanic Meso-
    america, 34–35, 37, 40
suicide, in lowland cultures, 153, 229n.71
Summit of Indigenous Women of the
    Americas, 173
sun deity. *See* solar deities
supernatural images
  of Inkas, 48–49
  in lowland cultures, 154, 230n.77
  pre-Inka Andean, 41–43, 46, 48
superstition, 83
Surinam, 143
surveillance, army, of Mayas, 121–122,
    215n.110

sustainability, of agriculture, 95, 102
sustenance deities, 29
syncretized images, of female deities, 79

Taki Onqoy, 83
task sharing. *See* division of labor
taxation
  during colonial era, 65, 86, 200n.57
  religious, 125
teaching. *See* education
technology development, modern, 102, 124
Tecuichpochtzin, 57, 195n.7
Tehuantepec, Isthmus of
  dress styles of, 103–104
  insurrections in, 109–110
  women of (*see* Zapotec)
Tenochcan peoples, 24
Tenochtitlan, conquest of, 22–23, 28–29
  resistance to, 60
Teotihuacan
  archaeology of, 20
  gender hierarchy, 22
  Goddess image, 20–21, 32, 188n.4
  government politics of, 21–22, 26
  household units of, 22
teotitecos, 106
Teotitlán, as weaving community, 106–107
Tepanec peoples, 24
terminology, multilinguistic glossary of, 180
textile production. *See* weaving
theater groups, modern Maya, 124
Tiwanaku civilization, 44, 48
Tlakatelilis ritual, 98
Tlatelolcan peoples, 24, 28
Tlatilco burial sites, 14
Tlaxcala women, 98, 102. *See also* Nahuas
Tlazolteotl (Diety of Filth), 29
tobacco products, labor roles for, 65–66,
    198n.36
Toci (Our Grandmother), 29
Toledo, Alejandro, 139–140
Toltecs, 189n.14
  fall of, 19, 22, 24
tool production
  earliest women's role, 12–13
  in prehispanic Mesoamerica, 22, 25, 35
tortilla production, 91, 93, 95
tourism, 101, 116–117, 160, 165
trade
  during Conquest era
    long-distance, 64–65, 67
    sexual relations for, 57–58, 196n.11
  merchant, 105–106 (*see also* selling/resell-
    ing)
trade economy. *See* market economies
trade goods. *See* commodities
trading teams, Zapotec participation,
    105–106, 210n.50
tradition, women guardians of, 4, 89,
    175–176

traitors, indigenous women as, 56, 196n.5
traje, 116–117
transformations
    of modern Nahuas, 100–103
    in post-1492 Americas, 9, 186n.17
    in pre-1492 Americas, 12
translators, for conquerors, 53–56, 195n.2
transportation development, Nahuas and, 102
trial marriages, 140, 151
tribute payments
    during colonial era, 66, 199nn.38–39
    widows' responsibility for, 67–70, 81, 199n.41
Triple Alliance empire, 23, 188n.1
tropical cultures. See lowland cultures
"truck gardens," 113, 115, 212n.74
Tukano peoples, 150
Tula, decline of, 19–20, 22
Tupac Amaru rebellion (1780–1781), 85
Tuyuc, Rosalina, 174
Tzeltal Revolt (1712), 84–85

umbilical cord, gender rituals for, 23
uncu, 44
Union of Yalálag Women, 110
United Nations, supportive programs of, 123, 176
United Women Working Together, 101
URACCAN, 174, 180
urbanism
    Andean patterns, 129–131, 135, 137, 141
    during colonial era
        abuse associations, 66–67, 69, 199n.41
        cultural impact of, 87, 205n.125
        domestic services, 60, 198n.35, 199n.40. 65
        family life impact of, 71–72, 77, 201n.58
        gender impact of, 20, 40, 125
    Nahua patterns, 100, 102–103
    rise of, 11, 22, 40
    Zapotec patterns, 107
uxorilocal residence, 73
    in lowland cultures, 149, 226n.54, 227n.57

Valero, Helena, 143–144, 149, 151, 224n.43, 226n.56
Valley of Mexico, 22–23
venereal disease, 156, 208n.24
Venezuela, tropical cultures of. see lowland cultures
Venus deities, 38
viajeras, modern Zapotec as, 108
violence
    collective female patterns, 84–85, 204n.117
    counterinsurgency, 121–122, 215n.110
    domestic (see domestic violence)
    institutionalized, 134, 150

political, 150, 156, 173, 231n.84
sexual
    during conquest era, 57, 59–61, 197n.15, 197n.19
    contemporary, 119, 151, 162, 176, 228n.64
    workplace, 77
Virgin Mary, colonial references to, 78–79, 88
Virgin of Guadalupe, 79
virginity
    in Andean culture, 50, 135, 194n.96
    colonial emphasis on, 71–74, 202n.68
    religion references, 78–79, 88
    of Mayas, 59, 85, 119
    of Nahuas, 208n.22
    in prehispanic Mesoamerica, 27, 190n.35
virilocal marriage, 148, 150
voting rights, 100, 214n.100

wages
    for Andeans, 131–133, 140–141
    in Central America, 159–160, 165
    family power conflicts related to, 75–76
    gender inequity of, 93
    hierarchical control of, 9, 95
    for labor, 65, 67, 96
    for lowland cultures, 155–156
    for Mayas, 116–117, 212n.74, 213nn.87–88
    for Nahuas, 93–96, 100, 102
    for plantation labor, 212n.74, 213n.87
    for Zapotecs, 107, 210n.52
wak'as deities, of Inkas, 48
war deity, 29
warfare. See militarism
Wari civilization, 44, 48
warriors. See soldiers/warriors
water deities
    in Andean culture, 48
    in prehispanic Mesoamerica, 20, 29
wealth, gender-related
    of Andeans, 130, 133
    in colonial era, 70–71, 81, 88, 200n.49, 200n.51
    of Mayas, 114–117, 120–121, 213n.88, 214n.95
    of Nahuas, 95–96
    in prehispanic Mesoamerica, 26–28, 34
weaving
    as agency metaphor, 6, 94
    in Andean culture
        contemporary, 129–132
        prehispanic, 41–44, 48–50
    during colonial era, 64–66, 198n.26, 198n.28
    as coercive, 67–69, 199n.45
    by lowland cultures, 145, 156–157
    by Mayas, 112–113, 115–117, 124, 212n.72, 213n.88

weaving (*continued*)
  by Nahuas, 94, 102
  in prehispanic Mesoamerica, 30–32, 40
  by Zapotecs, 105–106
wet nurses, 71, 199n.41
widows and widowhood
  economic responsibilities of, 67–70,
    199n.41
  in post-civil war Guatemala, 122–123
will writers, colonial women as, 70, 82, 88,
    200n.49, 200n.51
Wiracocha deity, 48
witches and witchcraft
  as colonial idea, 79–80, 83, 203n.100
  among modern Nahuas, 98–99
women's rights
  indigenous assertions of, 123, 137–140,
    167
  organizations for, 122–124, 179–180,
    216n.114, 216n.116, 216n.118
women's roles. *See* gender roles
women's studies, 4–5, 11
women/woman
  colonial church roles, 79–80
  defeat associations, 24, 189n.16
  dominant power of (*see* matriarchy)
  hatred of, in lowland cultures, 142, 147,
    150
  meaning of, 5–6, 185n.5
  military (*see* soldiers/warriors)
  supernatural, of pre-Inka Andeans,
    41–43, 46, 48
work organization. *See* division of labor
workplace
  injuries in, 152
  specialization of, 12–13, 17

violence in, 77
workplace activism
  by Andeans, 132, 137
  history of, 169
  institutionalized, 110, 137–138, 236
  suppression of, 9, 187n.31
World Conference against Racism, 174

Xalatlaco, 95
Xerente women, 150
Xochiquetzal (Flowery Feather), 29
Xochitecatl, 32

Yanomami women
  contemporary images of, 127, 142–143,
    218n.2
  labor divisions of, 146–147, 224n.46
  marriage solidarity of, 149–150, 226n.56
  political roles, 154, 229n.76
  violence against, 150, 156, 227n.60
yatiri, 135–136
Yucatec, modern Mayans of, 112–115, 124,
    211n.71

Zapatista Army, 122–123, 216n.114,
    216n.116
Zapotec
  ceremonial authority, 108–109, 111,
    210n.60
  exotic sex images of, 103–105, 209n.43
  gender complementarity, 103, 106–107
  market economies of, 105–108, 210n.50,
    210nn.52–53
  as matriarchy, 103, 108–111
  political activism, 109–110, 211n.63,
    211n.65, 216n.118